The Sorites Paradox

For centuries, the Sorites Paradox has spurred philosophers to think and argue about the problem of vagueness. This volume offers a guide to the paradox. It is both an accessible survey and an exposition of the state of the art, with a chapter-by-chapter presentation of all the main solutions to the paradox and all its main areas of influence. Each chapter offers a gentle introduction to its topic, gradually building up to a final discussion of some open problems. Students will find a comprehensive guide to the fundamentals of the paradox, together with lucid explanations of the challenges it continues to raise. Researchers will find exciting new ideas and debates on the paradox.

Sergi Oms is Lecturer at the Department of Philosophy, University of Barcelona. He has published in a number of journals, including *Disputatio, Notre Dame Journal of Formal Logic* and *Synthese*.

Elia Zardini is FCT Research Fellow at the Centre of Philosophy, University of Lisbon, as well as Chief Researcher at the International Laboratory for Logic, Linguistics and Formal Philosophy, National Research University Higher School of Economics. He has published in a number of journals, including *The Journal of Philosophy* and *The Review of Symbolic Logic*, and he is co-editor of *Scepticism and Perceptual Justification* (2014).

Classic Philosophical Arguments

Over the centuries, a number of individual arguments have formed a crucial part of philosophical enquiry. The volumes in this series examine these arguments, looking at the ramifications and applications which they have come to have, the challenges which they have encountered, and the ways in which they have stood the test of time.

Titles in the series

The Prisoner's Dilemma
Edited by Martin Peterson

The Original Position
Edited by Timothy Hinton

The Brain in a Vat
Edited by Sanford C. Goldberg

Pascal's Wager
Edited by Paul Bartha and Lawrence Pasternack

Ontological Arguments
Edited by Graham Oppy

Newcomb's Problem
Edited by Arif Ahmed

The Gettier Problem
Edited by Stephen Hetherington

The Naturalistic Fallacy
Edited by Neil Sinclair

The Sorites Paradox
Edited by Sergi Oms and Elia Zardini

The Sorites Paradox

Edited by

Sergi Oms
University of Barcelona

Elia Zardini
University of Lisbon
National Research University Higher School of Economics

CAMBRIDGE
UNIVERSITY PRESS

CAMBRIDGE
UNIVERSITY PRESS

University Printing House, Cambridge CB2 8BS, United Kingdom

One Liberty Plaza, 20th Floor, New York, NY 10006, USA

477 Williamstown Road, Port Melbourne, VIC 3207, Australia

314–321, 3rd Floor, Plot 3, Splendor Forum, Jasola District Centre, New Delhi – 110025, India

79 Anson Road, #06–04/06, Singapore 079906

Cambridge University Press is part of the University of Cambridge.

It furthers the University's mission by disseminating knowledge in the pursuit of
education, learning, and research at the highest international levels of excellence.

www.cambridge.org
Information on this title: www.cambridge.org/9781107163997
DOI: 10.1017/9781316683064

First published 2019

Printed in the United Kingdom by TJ International Ltd. Padstow Cornwall

A catalogue record for this publication is available from the British Library.

Library of Congress Cataloging-in-Publication Data
Names: Oms, Sergi, editor. | Zardini, Elia, editor.
Title: The Sorites Paradox / edited by Sergi Oms, Elia Zardini.
Description: Cambridge, United Kingdom ; New York, NY : Cambridge University
    Press, 2019. | Series: Classic philosophical arguments | Includes
    bibliographical references and index.
Identifiers: LCCN 2019008720 | ISBN 9781107163997 (hardback : alk. paper) |
    ISBN 9781316615690 (pbk.: alk. paper)
Subjects: LCSH: Sorites paradox. | Vagueness (Philosophy)
Classification: LCC BC199.V34 S67 2019 | DDC 165–dc23
LC record available at https://lccn.loc.gov/2019008720

ISBN 978-1-107-16399-7 Hardback
ISBN 978-1-316-61569-0 Paperback

Contents

Contributors

Hrafn Asgeirsson is Senior Lecturer at the School of Law, University of Surrey.

Inga Bones is Lecturer at the Department of Philosophy, Karlsruhe Institute of Technology.

Pablo Cobreros is Professor at the Department of Philosophy, University of Navarra.

Paul Égré is Senior Researcher at Institut Jean Nicod, CNRS, and Professor at the Department of Philosophy, ENS, PSL University.

Matti Eklund is Professor at the Department of Philosophy, Uppsala University.

Christopher Kennedy is William H. Colvin Professor at the Department of Linguistics, University of Chicago.

İrem Kurtsal is Visiting Assistant Professor at the Department of Philosophy and Religious Studies, Allegheny College.

Ofra Magidor is Waynflete Professor of Metaphysical Philosophy at the Department of Philosophy, University of Oxford.

Sergi Oms is Lecturer at the Department of Philosophy and Member of the Logos Research Group, University of Barcelona, as well as Member of the Barcelona Institute for Analytic Philosophy.

Francesco Paoli is Professor at the Department of Pedagogy, Psychology and Philosophy, University of Cagliari.

Graham Priest is Distinguished Professor at the Graduate Center, City University of New York, and Boyce Gibson Professor Emeritus, University of Melbourne.

Diana Raffman is Professor at the Department of Philosophy, University of Toronto.

David Ripley is Lecturer at the Department of Philosophy, Monash University.

Ricardo Santos is Assistant Professor at the Department of Philosophy and Member of the LanCog Research Group, University of Lisbon.

Scott Soames is Distinguished Professor at the Department of Philosophy, University of Southern California.

Luca Tranchini is Research Fellow at the Department of Computer Science, Eberhard Karls University of Tübingen.

Steven Verheyen is Research Fellow at the Faculty of Psychology and Educational Sciences, KU Leuven, and at the Department of Cognitive Studies, PSL University.

Crispin Wright is Global Distinguished Professor at the Department of Philosophy, New York University, Professor of Philosophical Research, University of Stirling and Regius Professor of Logic Emeritus, University of Aberdeen.

Elia Zardini is FCT Research Fellow at the Centre of Philosophy and Member of the LanCog Research Group, University of Lisbon, as well as Chief Researcher at the International Laboratory for Logic, Linguistics and Formal Philosophy, National Research University Higher School of Economics.

Acknowledgements

We took the decision to co-edit this book in 2014 on the strength of a *camaiot* in the Raval; we celebrated the completion of the book in 2018 with a *camaiot* in the Raval. These unchanging features aside, editing the book has been a long adventure, variously and generously supported by funds from the Marie Skłodowska-Curie Intra-European Research Fellowship 301493, the FCT Research Fellowship IF/01202/2013, the Russian Academic Excellence Project 5-100, the Spanish Ministry of Economy and Competition Project FFI2012-35026, the Spanish Ministry of Economy, Industry and Competitiveness Project FFI2015-70707-P and the FCT Project PTDC/FER-FIL/28442/2017.

Throughout the adventure, we received the essential help of many fellow travellers. At Cambridge University Press, thanks to Hilary Gaskin for presenting us with the challenge of creating a companion to the Sorites Paradox, as well as for her solid guidance, advice and patience throughout the process; thanks also to an anonymous referee for perceptive feedback at different stages, which has helped to improve the overall quality of the book, and to Marianne Nield and Sophie Taylor for taking care of many details. Heaps of thanks to all the other authors for enthusiastically coming on board and for delivering very fine chapters (with astonishing timeliness!): our philosophical dialogue with each of them has been for us a great intellectual experience. Heartfelt thanks to our families: Cristina, Guillem, Alícia, Laura and Miguel – there's no sharp boundary to their ability to bear with us (and they did bear with us). We suspect no revision of classical logic is needed in this case. Finally, Elia thanks Sergi, without whose work on the book his own work would have been impossible; and Sergi thanks Elia, without whose work on the book his own work would have been impossible.

Prelude

An Introduction to the Sorites Paradox

Sergi Oms and Elia Zardini

Topic, Structure, Features and Aims of the Book

This book is about what is nowadays regarded as one of the most venerable and difficult philosophical paradoxes (Priest 2003, p. 9): the Sorites Paradox (in better English, 'Heaper Paradox', from ancient Greek *sōritēs* i.e. heaper, in turn from *sōros* i.e. heap). According to the historiographical tradition (e.g. Keefe and Smith 1997a, p. 3), the paradox was first formulated by Eubulides of Miletus, an eminent member of the Megarian school, a group of philosophers well known to have been under Eleatic influence (Chapter 15 supplies further historical background). The paradox does in fact target the concepts that we mostly use in describing the world *as it appears to our senses* – that is, those concepts (such as e.g. the concept of a heap) that categorise objects as falling on one side or the other of a *distinction that seems not to depend on small differences* – and does boldly attempt to show that such concepts are *incoherent*.

This introduction provides the tools necessary for understanding the Sorites Paradox itself as well as a first orientation concerning its solutions and influence. Part I offers a systematic survey of the main types of solutions to the paradox. Part II delves into the main areas where the paradox has exerted a profound influence. A coda recapitulates the pre-analytic history of the paradox vis-à-vis the state of the art exposed in the previous parts.

The book intends, on the one hand, to *take stock of the vertiginous developments* in thought about the Sorites Paradox that have taken place in the last half century (fn. 37) and, on the other hand, to *address some of the new challenges* that have arisen in the context of such developments. While a few recent excellent readers and collected volumes on vagueness exist (Keefe and Smith 1997b; Fara and Williamson 2002; Beall 2003; Dietz and Moruzzi 2010; Égré and Klinedinst 2011; Ronzitti 2011), from a more *structural* point of view the book constitutes an absolute novelty in several respects (which suits its inclusion in the series *Classic Philosophical Arguments*). First, the book focuses on the Sorites Paradox in particular rather than on vagueness in general.[1] Second, the book is so organised as to

---

[1] In this, the book reflects what has actually been an interesting tendency in the most recent literature on vagueness – witnessed e.g. by many contextualist works – which, in theorising about vagueness, variously prioritises the phenomenon of

provide a systematic treatment of the paradox, by devoting exactly one chapter to each main type of solution to the paradox and to each area where the paradox has exerted a profound influence. Third, each chapter is so conceived as to be accessible to novices in its topic, by gradually leading them from an introductory presentation of its general subject to a discussion of some open problems at the edge of contemporary research.[2] From a more *thematic* point of view, the book also constitutes a substantial novelty, in that it extensively covers fairly recent solutions (i.e. dialetheism and non-transitivism) and somewhat underrepresented areas (i.e. practical philosophy and psychology). Even for those solutions and areas that in general have already received sustained attention in previous publications, the relevant chapter not only provides the state of the art, but also pushes research further on that front, by putting forth new ideas on some selected issues.

Consisting of chapters written by first-rate experts, we hope that the book will significantly advance the debate on the Sorites Paradox, and will thus become essential reading for every researcher on the topic and, more generally, for many philosophers of logic. Moreover, given the book's overall systematic character and each chapter's gradual approach, we believe that it can constitute an excellent source for graduate courses covering vagueness, and that it should also appeal to members of the general educated public curious to find out what the Sorites Paradox is all about. Furthermore, we think that the deep connections, reflected in many of the chapters, that numerous strands of thought on the paradox have with fundamental issues in philosophy of language, epistemology and metaphysics (e.g. context dependence, indiscriminability and spatiotemporality) should make substantial parts of the book stimulating also for scholars specialising in those areas. We intend some chapters to attract an even wider audience, in that they illustrate the ways in which the paradox has acted as a powerful generator of ideas and insights also in the more remote areas of practical philosophy, linguistics and psychology. All in all, we expect that the book will be both a record of the fecund role played by the paradox in all these areas and a spur to further work for those doing research in them.

Characterisation and Extension of Vagueness

The Sorites Paradox arises in connection with the general phenomenon of vagueness, and so this must antecedently be introduced. Most expressions in natural languages are vague,[3] in the sense that, although they apply in some cases and do not apply in others, *they seem*

Sorites-susceptibility over that of borderline cases (e.g. Zardini 2008b, pp. 11–2). Consequently, this introduction itself offers a novel kind of presentation of the lay of the land, which forgoes use of the notion of a borderline case.

[2] The overall book has been designed to be accessible to new graduate students, and only basic notions of philosophy and logic (as well as familiar terminological and notational conventions) are systematically presupposed, which can easily be recovered from any good introduction to philosophy and logic; given the prominence, in the topic, of philosophy of logic and of alternative, philosophically motivated logical systems, Priest (2008) is a particularly helpful source.

[3] Arguably, vagueness attaches not only to *linguistic* representations, but also to *mental* ones, in particular to concepts (contrast with e.g. ambiguity, which would seem to attach only to expressions: plausibly, while a vague expression such as 'heap' corresponds to a single vague concept of a heap, an ambiguous expression such as 'bank' corresponds to the two non-ambiguous concepts of a river bank and of a money bank). Throughout, to fix ideas, we focus on expressions, sometimes switching to concepts when more natural.

to lack a sharp boundary between the former cases and the latter ones. For example, the noun 'heap' is vague: it applies to collections of many enough, say, grains, it does not apply to collections of too few grains, but it seems to lack a sharp boundary between those two kinds of collections – there seems to be no i[4] such that 'heap' applies to collections of i grains but does not apply to collections of $i - 1$ grains.[5]

Although nouns and adjectives are probably the two most paradigmatic linguistic categories of vague expressions, *virtually every linguistic category is affected by vagueness* (Chapter 13). Verbs can be vague, as witnessed e.g. by 'rain': it applies to precipitations of many enough, say, droplets, it does not apply to precipitations of too few droplets, but it seems to lack a sharp boundary between those two kinds of precipitations – there seems to be no i such that 'rain' applies to precipitations of i droplets but does not apply to precipitations of $i - 1$ droplets. Determiners can be vague, as witnessed e.g. by 'many': it applies to groups of many enough, say, people, it does not apply to groups of too few people, but it seems to lack a sharp boundary between those two kinds of groups – there seems to be no i such that 'many' applies to groups of i people but does not apply to groups of $i - 1$ people. Prepositions can be vague, as witnessed e.g. by 'by': it applies to pairs of, say, buildings that are close enough to each other, it does not apply to pairs of buildings that are too far from each other, but it seems to lack a sharp boundary between those two kinds of pairs – there seems to be no i such that 'by' applies to pairs of buildings that are at i yards from each other but does not apply to pairs of buildings that are at $i + 1$ (i' for short) yards from each other. Having noted all this, for concreteness we'll henceforth take as our leading example of vagueness 'bald', focusing on the construction 'A man with i hairs is bald' (which we'll often formalise as Bi). 'Bald' is also vague: it applies to men with 1 hair, it does not apply to men with 100,000 hairs,[6] but it seems to lack a sharp boundary between those two kinds of men – there seems to be no i such that 'bald' applies to men with i hairs but does not apply to men with i' hairs. The sense of 'vagueness' just introduced (i.e. *seeming lack of sharp boundaries between positive and negative cases*) is the one intended in the contemporary philosophical debate on vagueness. The reader is advised to keep it sharply distinct from other senses of 'vagueness' commonly found in ordinary discourse: 'vagueness' in the sense of ambiguity (i.e. the fact that the same syntactic string is associated with *different meanings*, as when one says that 'bank' is 'vague'), 'vagueness' in the sense of underspecificity (i.e. the fact that an expression as used in a certain context is *too general* for the informative purposes of the context, as when one says that 'Something' is a vague answer to the question 'What are you thinking?'), 'vagueness' in the sense of indeterminacy (i.e. the fact that an expression has *unsettled*

---

[4] Throughout, 'i' and its relatives range over the relevant set of natural numbers.

[5] 'Heap' as well as most expressions in natural languages is also multi-dimensional, in the sense that *there is more than one factor* ('dimension of comparison') relevant for its application: to wit, whether a collection of grains is a heap depends not only on their number, but also on e.g. the shape of their arrangement (a row of 100,000 grains on the floor is not a heap). Throughout, we exclusively focus on one single dimension of comparison presupposing that all the other ones are kept fixed from one case to the other (see Zardini 2018c for some discussion of the relation between seeming lack of sharp boundaries and multi-dimensionality).

[6] Background information: apparently, men with around 100,000 hairs are paradigmatically not bald.

application to certain cases, as when one says that it is vague whether 'Newtonian mass' applies to rest mass or relativistic mass).

The Sorites Paradox

The informal characterisation of vagueness given in 'Characterisation and Extension of Vagueness', in this introduction, is fairly minimal and neutral, thereby constituting the common starting point of theories of vagueness, which basically focus on providing a comprehensive account of the seeming lack of sharp boundaries of vague expressions. Now, a very natural such account consists in maintaining that what underlies the *seeming lack of* sharp boundaries is a *real* lack of sharp boundaries: vague expressions seem to lack sharp boundaries because they do indeed lack sharp boundaries! In turn, as already implicitly done in 'Characterisation and Extension of Vagueness', in this introduction, the informal notion of lack of sharp boundaries is very naturally understood as the *non-existence of a positive case immediately followed by a negative cases*: for example, on this understanding, B lacks sharp boundaries iff, for every i, it is not the case that Bi holds and Bi' does not.

It is this very natural account of the seeming lack of sharp boundaries of vague expressions that is apparently shattered by the Sorites Paradox. Focusing on 'bald', the account, which may be called 'the naive theory of vagueness' (Zardini 2008a, pp. 337–40), has it in effect that:

(N_1^{bald})   A man with 1 hair is bald;
(N_2^{bald})   A man with 100,000 hairs is not bald;
(N_{3LSB}^{bald})   For every i, it is not the case that a man with i hairs is bald and man with i' hairs is not bald

(these and similar principles obviously have analogues for other vague expressions, which we assume to be labelled by replacing superscript 'bald' with the relevant vague expression, so that e.g. (N_1^{heap}) is something like 'A collection of 100,000 grains is a heap'; further, we drop a superscript or subscript to refer to the totality of the corresponding principles got by adding a possible value for that superscript or subscript, so that e.g. (N_1) is the totality of the principles ((N_1^{bald}), (N_1^{heap}), (N_1^{rain}), etc.) that identify a paradigmatically positive case of a vague expression, and, at the limit, (N) is the totality of the principles of the naive theory). A prominent version of the Sorites Paradox consists then in apparently showing that (N_1^{bald}) and (N_{3LSB}^{bald}) entail the contradictory of (N_2^{bald}), so that (N^{bald}) would be inconsistent.[7] In detail, by universal instantiation,[8] (N_{3LSB}^{bald}) entails $\neg(B1 \, \& \, \neg B2)$, which, together with ($N_1^{bald}$), by *modus ponendo tollens*,[9] entails $\neg\neg B2$, which in turn, by double-negation elimination,[10] entails $B2$. We can now repeat this argumentative routine to get to $B3$:

---

[7] Throughout, by 'entailment' and its relatives we mean the converse of the relation of logical consequence (so that a sequence of sentences Γ entails a sentence φ iff φ logically follows from Γ), and by 'equivalence' and its relatives we mean two-way entailment. By 'imply' and its relatives we mean instead an operation expressed by an indicative conditional (so that φ implies ψ iff, if φ holds, so does ψ).

[8] Formally, letting as usual $\vdash$ be the relation of logical consequence and φ_{τ_0/τ_1} the result of replacing in φ all free occurrences of τ_1 with free occurrences of τ_0, the principle that $\forall \xi \varphi \vdash \varphi_{\tau/\xi}$ holds.

[9] Formally, the principle that $\varphi, \neg(\varphi \, \& \, \psi) \vdash \neg\psi$ holds.

[10] Formally, the principle that $\neg\neg\varphi \vdash \varphi$ holds.

by universal instantiation, (N_{3LSB}^{bald}) entails $\neg(B2 \ \& \ \neg B3)$, which, together with the just established conclusion $B2$, by *modus ponendo tollens* entails $\neg\neg B3$, which in turn, by double-negation elimination, entails $B3$. By repeating the same argumentative routine another 99,997 times, we eventually get to $B100{,}000$, i.e. the contradictory of (N_2^{bald}).

A closely related version of the Sorites Paradox comes into view by reflecting on a feature of vagueness closely related to seeming lack of sharp boundaries: namely, on the fact that vague expressions seem tolerant, in the sense that it seems that, *assuming that a vague expression applies to a certain case, it also applies to every case similar to it.* For example, it seems that, assuming that 'heap' applies to a collection of i grains, it also applies to collections of $i-1$, $i+1$, $i-2$, etc. grains. Theories of vagueness typically also include an account of the seeming tolerance of vague expressions. Now, a very natural such account consists in maintaining that what underlies *seeming* tolerance is *real* tolerance: vague expressions seem tolerant because they are indeed tolerant! In turn, the informal notion of tolerance is very naturally understood as *implication from a case's being positive to the immediately following case's being positive*: for example, on this understanding, B is tolerant iff, for every i, if Bi holds, so does Bi'.[11]

Let's thus understand (N) as containing not only (N_{3LSB}^{bald}), but also:

(N_{3T}^{bald}) For every i, if a man with i hairs is bald, so is a man with i' hairs.

Another prominent version of the Sorites Paradox consists then in apparently showing that (N_1^{bald}) and (N_{3T}^{bald}) entail the contradictory of (N_2^{bald}), so that (N^{bald}) would again be inconsistent. In detail (and mimicking closely the (N_{3LSB}^{bald})-based version of the paradox), by universal instantiation, (N_{3T}^{bald}) entails $B1 \rightarrow B2$, which, together with (N_1^{bald}), by *modus ponens*,[12] entails $B2$. We can now repeat this argumentative routine to get to $B3$: by universal instantiation, (N_{3T}^{bald}) entails $B2 \rightarrow B3$, which, together with the just established conclusion $B2$, by *modus ponens*, entails $B3$. By repeating the same argumentative routine another 99,997 times, we eventually get to $B100{,}000$, i.e. the contradictory of (N_2^{bald}).

Solutions to the Sorites Paradox

While there are other natural and interesting versions of the Sorites Paradox, the two ones reviewed in 'The Sorites Paradox', in this introduction, stand out for their theoretical centrality and historical salience. Now, according to philosophical tradition (e.g. Sainsbury 2009, p. 1), a paradox is a situation where *apparently true premises apparently entail an apparently false conclusion*,[13] and both the (N_{3LSB})-based and the (N_{3T})-based version of the paradox would seem paradigmatic instances of such understanding: (N_1) and (N_{3LSB})

---

[11] Notice that, to get to the essentials, in our understanding of tolerance we're focusing on the implication *from Bi to Bi'* rather than its converse (which is also involved in the informal notion of tolerance), since the latter is totally compelling and unproblematic. Notice also that our understanding of tolerance is equivalent with our understanding of lack of sharp boundaries only under the assumption that the implication at work in tolerance is material implication (i.e. such that $\varphi \rightarrow \psi$ is tantamount to $\neg(\varphi \ \& \ \neg\psi)$). But that assumption would seem rather perverse, as there would seem to be a world of difference between saying that *positive cases spread over small differences* and saying that *the difference between a positive case and a negative case is not small*.

[12] Formally, the principle that $\varphi, \varphi \rightarrow \psi \vdash \psi$ holds.

[13] Throughout, we understand falsity as truth of the negation (i.e. φ is false iff $\neg\varphi$ is true).

are apparently true and apparently entail (as per the apparently valid argument in 'The Sorites Paradox', in this introduction) the apparently false contradictory of (N₂); (N₁) and (N₃ₜ) are apparently true and they too apparently entail (as per the apparently valid argument in 'The Sorites Paradox', in this introduction) the apparently false contradictory of (N₂).[14]

Keeping fixed such platitudes as (N₁) and (N₂),[15] and focusing on the (N₃ₗₛʙ)-based version of the Sorites Paradox, we are thus faced with the dilemma of either *rejecting (N₃ₗₛʙ)*[16] or *denying the validity of some of the logical principles employed by soritical reasoning*.[17] It's fair to say that the vast majority of solutions to the paradox take the former option (which is not surprising given how minimal the logical resources employed by soritical reasoning are!). On this option, since the soritical argument is valid, it is accepted that (N) is inconsistent, given which the argument can be extended by inferring, by a version of *reductio ad absurdum*,[18] that the negation of (N^{bald}_{3LSB}) holds, and so, by one of the quantified De Morgan laws,[19] that, for some i, both Bi and $\neg Bi'$ hold – i.e. that there is a number of hairs such that adding just one more hair to the scalp of a man with that number of hairs turns him from bald to non-bald! Thricologists will be thrilled. (Let's call the soritical argument as so extended 'Extended Sorites Paradox'.) Solutions to the Sorites Paradox taking the option of rejecting (N₃ₗₛʙ) are thus faced with the dilemma of either *accepting that there is a sharp boundary* or *denying the validity of some of the further logical principles employed by extended soritical reasoning*. Since all those logical principles are valid in classical logic, solutions to the paradox in general are usefully classified as either *preserving classical logic and accepting that vague expressions have sharp boundaries* or *revising classical logic and [accepting (N₃ₗₛʙ) or rejecting that vague expressions have sharp boundaries]* (see fn. 22 for some subtleties concerning the operative understanding of 'classical logic').

---

[14] López de Sa and Zardini (2007, p. 246) criticise the traditional philosophical understanding of paradox as *too narrow*. Their broad line of attack can be applied also in the case of the Sorites Paradox. For example, consider two soritical arguments diverging from the (N₃ₗₛʙ)-based version of the Sorites Paradox only in that they stop at $B10,000$ and $B50,000$ respectively (rather than going up to $B100,000$): in both cases, despite the apparent validity of the argument, its premises apparently *do not support its conclusion* (it is apparently wrong, assuming the premises, to regard the argument as establishing the conclusion), thus engendering a real paradox – yet, $B10,000$ is *apparently true* (rather than apparently false) and $B50,000$ is *apparently uncertain* (rather than apparently false), thereby indicating that the traditional philosophical understanding of paradox is too narrow.

[15] This being philosophy, actually there is also the nihilist option of giving up (N₁) and the trivialist option of giving up (N₂) (Chapters 4, 9 and 11). Given the extreme unattractiveness of such options, we'll henceforth set them aside (see Chapter 4, Section 4.6 and Chapter 11, Section 11.3 for some discussion of nihilism).

[16] Throughout, by 'reject' and its relatives we mean *non-acceptance for principled reasons*. By 'deny' and its relatives we mean instead *acceptance of the negation* (in particular, we understand denial of the validity of a logical principle to be acceptance that the principle is not valid). The distinction between rejection and denial is crucial in many solutions to the Sorites Paradox, since, for some φ, some such solutions (supervaluationism, intuitionism, rejection of excluded middle, some versions of degree theory) reject both φ and $\neg\varphi$ (and so, while they reject φ, they do not deny it) whereas the other such solutions (subvaluationism, dialetheism, some other versions of degree theory) accept both φ and $\neg\varphi$ (and so, while they deny φ, they do not reject it). Notice that, for essentially the same reason, all such solutions rely on an analogous distinction between *a sentence's failing to hold* and *its negation's holding*.

[17] Without going into details here, we should flag that there are actually more logical principles at work in soritical reasoning than those explicitly mentioned in our presentation in 'The Sorites Paradox', in this introduction (see eleven paragraphs further on for some indications and Chapter 9 for an extended presentation and discussion of such principles).

[18] Formally, letting as usual $\Gamma \vdash \varnothing$ mean that Γ is inconsistent, the principle that, if $\Gamma, \varphi \vdash \varnothing$ holds, $\Gamma \vdash \neg\varphi$ holds.

[19] Formally, the principle that $\neg\forall\xi\neg\varphi \vdash \exists\xi\varphi$ holds.

Let's start then our overview of solutions to the Sorites Paradox with the solutions that preserve classical logic and therefore accept that vague expressions have sharp boundaries. In general, because of their acceptance of classical logic, such solutions have a quick and easy answer to the paradox itself: they simply concede the soundness of the extended soritical argument. But, precisely because conceding such soundness requires conceding that vague expressions have sharp boundaries, such solutions are then faced with the formidable task of *providing a reasonable account of vagueness that coheres with such a concession*.

Epistemicism (Chapter 1)[20] accepts that vague expressions have sharp boundaries *in the most natural sense*: there really is a *particular* i – it could be, say, 50,000 – such that both Bi and $\neg Bi'$ hold, similarly to how, say, there really is a particular i – it could be, say, 50,000 – such that i straws (of a certain weight) do not break a (certain) camel's back (at a certain time) and i' straws do. But, if vague expressions have sharp boundaries, what does their vagueness consist in? According to epistemicism, their vagueness consists in certain distinctive epistemic features, the most prominent of which is *our distinctive inability to identify their sharp boundaries*, and much of epistemicist theorising is devoted to accounting for the nature and source of such an inability.

Supervaluationism (Chapter 2) accepts that vague expressions have sharp boundaries *only in a nominal sense*: while there is a sharp boundary, there really isn't any *particular* i such that both Bi and $\neg Bi'$ hold – it is absurd, say, that both $B50,000$ and $\neg B50,001$ hold – similarly to how, on a natural interpretation of the situation, while there is a 20-day period next year in which you'll be on holidays (so much is settled in your work contract), there really isn't any particular 20-day period next year in which you'll be on holidays (which one it is depends on your choice, which you still have to make). When it comes to baldness, no number is The Special One. But how can the existence of such-and-such float free of particular objects' being such-and-such? According to supervaluationism, the *structure* of baldness is settled: it is settled that the basic valuation scheme is classical,[21] that paradigmatic cases such as $B1$ and $\neg B100,000$ are true, that totally compelling and unproblematic principles such as $\forall i(Bi' \rightarrow Bi)$ are true, etc.[22] Therefore, enough is settled to make the existential claim $\exists i(Bi \,\&\, \neg Bi')$ true. However, for *every* i, it is *not settled* that the witness $Bi \,\&\, \neg Bi'$ to that claim is true, even though, because of what is settled, these

---

[20] Notice that, while the admittedly rather sloganised systematic chapter titles fit well with the taxonomical purposes of a companion, for every chapter the authors' personal take on and development of its topic will naturally sometimes transcend what might narrowly be understood under the chapter's title.

[21] Essentially (and assuming that every object has a name): every sentence is either true or false but not both; $\neg\varphi$ is true iff φ is false; $\varphi \,\&\, \psi$ is true iff both φ and ψ are true; $\varphi \vee \psi$ is true iff either φ or ψ are true; $\forall \xi \varphi$ is true iff, for every τ, $\varphi_{\tau/\xi}$ is true; $\exists \xi \varphi$ is true iff, for some τ, $\varphi_{\tau/\xi}$ is true.

[22] Solutions to the Sorites Paradox are possible where supervaluationist ideas and tools are employed but the classicality assumption is abandoned; still, since the key idea of supervaluationism is quite congenial to preservation of classical logic, we focus in our presentation on classical versions of supervaluationism. Similar comments apply to our presentation of contextualism and incoherentism in the next and second next paragraph respectively. The reader is warned that there is an issue (discussed e.g. by McGee and McLaughlin 2004, pp. 132–6) as to whether supervaluationism preserves all the principles that would fairly naturally be listed under the label 'classical logic' (and that it is indeed a merit of the rise of that issue to have underscored *just how fuzzy the boundaries of 'classical logic' are*). However, for our purposes, a natural understanding of 'classical logic' is one as of a logic that basically ensures, as per the spirit of the Sorites Paradox, that the conjunction of (N$_1$), (N$_2$) and (N$_{3LSB}$) is inconsistent and, as per the spirit of the Extended Sorites Paradox, that from such inconsistency it follows that the conjunction of (N$_1$) and (N$_2$) entails that there is a sharp boundary.

cases of unsettledness somehow *fail to combine* (which would prevent the *existence* of a sharp boundary). The upshot is then that there is *underdetermination* as to which object plays the role of being the sharp boundary in the structure of baldness, and that is why the existence of the sharp boundary comes decoupled from any particular object's being the sharp boundary.[23]

Contextualism (Chapter 3) starts with the idea that vague expressions are essentially context dependent, at least in the sense that which cases they apply to varies with context. For example, when judging whether one could benefit from a hair treatment, 'bald' might apply to a man with 50,000 hairs, but, when judging whether one could need a sunscreen, it might not. Contextualism then postulates a pragmatic mechanism determining that, for every pair of cases *whose similarity is salient in a context*, one case is positive *in the context* iff the other case is, so that the sharp boundary of a vague expression in a context is determined to lie outside the cases whose similarity is salient in the context. Much of contextualist theorising is devoted to accounting for the nature and source of the context dependence of vague expressions and in particular of the hiding mechanism. Contextualism attaches great theoretical significance to the existence of such a mechanism: epistemologically, it is claimed that the fact that the sharp boundary as such (i.e. as including the similarity between the last positive case and the first negative case) is never salient explains our inability to identify it;[24] psychologically, it is claimed that the fact that the sharp boundary as such is never salient explains the empirical fact that we're biased to believe (N_{3LSB}). Thus, contextualism accepts that vague expressions have sharp boundaries *only in a relative and negligible sense*: while, in every context, there is a sharp boundary, in different contexts there are different sharp boundaries; moreover, because of the hiding mechanism, in every context the sharp boundary as such is not where we're looking.

---

[23] Subvaluationism (Chapter 2) agrees with supervaluationism about what the latter says is settled, but disagrees about what the latter says is not settled: according to subvaluationism, for *many i*, it is indeed *settled* that the witness Bi & $\neg Bi'$ to the existential claim $\exists i(Bi$ & $\neg Bi')$ is true, even though, because of what is settled, these cases of settledness somehow *fail to combine* (which would prevent the *uniqueness* of a sharp boundary). The upshot is then that there is *overdetermination* as to which object plays the role of being the sharp boundary in the structure of baldness, and that is why the uniqueness of the sharp boundary comes decoupled from any *singular* object's being the sharp boundary. Thus, subvaluationism too accepts that vague expressions have sharp boundaries *only in a nominal sense*: while there is a sharp boundary, there really isn't this time a *singular i* such that both Bi and $\neg Bi'$ hold – it is valid, say, that both $B50,000$ and $\neg B50,001$ hold, but it is also valid, say, that both $B50,001$ and $\neg B50,002$ hold. Again, but for reasons opposite to those submitted by supervaluationism, when it comes to baldness, no number is The Special One. Supervaluationism sweetens the pill of the existence of a (unique) sharp boundary by denying that any particular object is such (and so in effect *accepts a disjunction* – say, $(B45,000$ & $\neg B45,001) \vee (B45,001$ & $\neg B45,002) \vee (B45,002$ & $\neg B45,003) \ldots \vee (B55,000$ & $\neg B55,001)$ – *while regarding each of its disjuncts as absurd*); subvaluationism sweetens the pill of (the existence of) a unique sharp boundary by denying that any singular object is such (and so in effect *rejects a conjunction* – say, $(B45,000$ & $\neg B45,001)$ & $(B45,001$ & $\neg B45,002)$ & $(B45,002$ & $\neg B45,003) \ldots$ & $(B55,000$ & $\neg B55,001)$ – *while regarding each of its conjuncts as valid*). Notice that, since, for every *i*, *i*'s being the sharp boundary entails that, for every $j \neq i$, *j* is not the sharp boundary, according to subvaluationism, for every *i*, it is also valid that $\neg(Bi$ & $\neg Bi')$ holds, and so subvaluationism is the first solution we meet that accepts *each instance* of (N_{3LSB}) (although it rejects (N_{3LSB}) itself – as we've just seen, subvaluationism gives up the traditional idea that *exceptionless universal quantifications and conjunctions must be true*). But, if subvaluationism accepts each instance of (N_{3LSB}), how does it block sorital reasoning? It does by rejecting the conjunction of the premises of one application of *modus ponendo tollens* in the reasoning: taking the last *i* such that it is settled that Bi & $\neg Bi'$ holds, it is settled that Bi holds only in that it is settled that Bi & $\neg Bi'$ holds, whereas it is settled that $\neg(Bi$ & $\neg Bi')$ holds only in that, for some $j \neq i$, it is settled that Bj & $\neg Bj'$ holds, and so the settledness of Bi fails to combine with the settledness of $\neg(Bi$ & $\neg Bi')$.

[24] Thus, we cannot identify the sharp boundary as such neither for *epistemic* nor for *semantic* reasons (as epistemicism and supervaluationism would have it respectively), but for *pragmatic* ones, similarly to how, in every context where there is a closest object that is not salient in the context, we cannot identify that object.

Incoherentism (Chapter 4) comes closest – among classical solutions to the Sorites Paradox – to vindicating (N). Incoherentism diagnoses the problem with the paradox as arising from a clash between *the requirements made on the world by the meaning of vague expressions* and *which requirements the world can accommodate*. Often enough, no such clash arises: for example, the meaning of 'bachelor' encodes both the principle that male human beings about to get married for the first time are bachelors and the principle that bachelors are unmarried, and the world provides lots of candidate extensions verifying both those principles (for there are lots of sets that both include the set of male human beings about to get married for the first time and are included in the set of unmarried objects). Sometimes, however, the clash does arise: a prime example is given by 'true', whose meaning encodes the correlation principle that '*P*' is true iff *P*, but, as the semantic paradoxes sadly demonstrate, keeping fixed classical logic, no set of sentences can be assigned to 'true' as its extension while verifying all the instances of the correlation principle (see Chapter 10 for a presentation of the semantic paradoxes and a discussion of their relations with the Sorites Paradox). Vague expressions are then another kind of case where the clash arises: for example, the meaning of B encodes (N^{bald}), but, as the Sorites Paradox sadly demonstrates, keeping fixed classical logic, no set of numbers can be assigned to B as its extension while verifying all of (N_1^{bald}), (N_2^{bald}) and (N_{3LSB}^{bald}). Thus, vague expressions *fail to have the extension intended in their meaning*. Different versions of incoherentism draw different conclusions from such failure: according to some versions, vague expressions do not get any extension at all; according to other versions, they do get an extension (presumably, one that comes as close as possible to the one intended in their meaning). Keeping fixed classical logic, a natural version of the latter kind would have it that vague expressions get extensions verifying (N_1) and (N_2) but falsifying (N_{3LSB}). Such a version accepts that vague expressions have sharp boundaries *only faute de mieux*: while there is a sharp boundary, there wasn't really supposed to be one.

Because classical logic forces the existence of sharp boundaries for vague expressions, and because such boundaries are deeply problematic in several philosophical respects, the Sorites Paradox arguably represents *one of the best cases for a philosophically motivated revision of classical logic*. Let's then move on to solutions to the paradox that [accept (N_{3LSB}) or reject that vague expressions have sharp boundaries] and therefore revise classical logic. In general, because of their acceptance of (N_{3LSB}) or rejection of sharp boundaries, such solutions have less of a problem than classical solutions in accommodating for vagueness in the first place. But, precisely because acceptance of (N_{3LSB}) or rejection of sharp boundaries requires denial of the validity of classical logic, such solutions are then faced with the formidable task of *providing a reasonable non-classical logic of vagueness that invalidates some of the steps of extended soritical reasoning*.

Intuitionism (Chapter 5) maintains that *the existence of such-and-such an object can only be shown by exhibiting a particular object that is such-and-such*, thereby disagreeing with classical logic (let alone supervaluationism). This requirement of exhibitability on existence might either be taken as intrinsically plausible or be grounded in more fundamental claims, which could be to the effect that the very interpretation of the relevant sentences should proceed in epistemic rather than alethic terms (so that, keeping in mind the shape of the valuation scheme of fn. 21, all there is to the interpretation of the existential quantifier is that $\exists \xi \varphi$ is, say, knowable iff, for some τ, $\varphi_{\tau/\xi}$ is knowable), or to the effect that the truth of the relevant sentences is anyway epistemically constrained (so that, for every τ, $\varphi_{\tau/\xi}$ is true only if $\varphi_{\tau/\xi}$ is knowable, from which it follows that $\exists \xi \varphi$ is true only if, for some τ, $\varphi_{\tau/\xi}$ is knowable), or to the effect that the relevant objects are in some sense 'mental constructions', etc. Intuitionist logic is designed to guarantee the exhibitability of existence, so that the validity of the non-exhibitive principles of classical logic (which sometimes license existential quantifications and disjunctions even when none of their instances or disjuncts are available) is denied. Thus, intuitionism comes closest – among non-classical solutions to the Sorites Paradox – to accepting the validity of the Extended Sorites Paradox: it accepts all of its steps but for the very last one, the relevant quantified De Morgan law being invalid exactly because, in general, one can be in a position to establish its premise (e.g. by reducing to inconsistency the claim that everything is not F) without being in a position to exhibit an object that is F. As per the Extended Sorites Paradox, qua leading to inconsistency (N_{3LSB}) must be denied, but the paradox does nothing to exhibit an object that is a sharp boundary, and so the paradox does not show that there is a sharp boundary.

Rejection of excluded middle (Chapter 6) agrees with supervaluationism on the fundamental point that there really isn't any *particular* i such that both Bi and $\neg Bi'$ hold – again, it is absurd, say, that both $B50,000$ and $\neg B50,001$ hold.[25] But rejection of excluded middle disagrees with supervaluationism in upholding the ancillary traditional idea that *true existential quantifications and disjunctions must be witnessed* (i.e. existence requires particularity), and so in inferring from that lack of witness to rejection that there is a sharp boundary. Since, as per the Sorites Paradox, qua leading to inconsistency (N_{3LSB}) (i.e. the claim that there is no sharp boundary) must also be rejected, and since true disjunctions must be witnessed, the view under consideration rejects the excluded-middle claim that either there is a sharp boundary or there is no sharp boundary (and so denies the validity of the law of excluded middle).[26] The Extended Sorites Paradox is then blocked at the *reductio ad absurdum* step: in general, if one rejects $\varphi \vee \neg\varphi$, and so rejects both φ and $\neg\varphi$, the fact that φ leads to inconsistency is no longer a good reason for accepting $\neg\varphi$.

Dialetheism (Chapter 7) is the first solution we meet that accepts (N_{3LSB}) itself (over and above accepting each of its instances, as subvaluationism already does, see fn. 23). Dialetheism agrees with subvaluationism on the fundamental point that there really isn't a *singular* i such that both Bi and $\neg Bi'$ hold – again, it is valid, say, that both $B50,000$ and $\neg B50,001$ hold, but it is also valid, say, that both $B50,001$ and $\neg B50,002$ hold. And, since,

[25] For every i, intuitionism too rejects that both Bi and $\neg Bi'$ hold, but it does so on the basis that *we are currently not in a position to show* that they do, not (as supervaluationism and rejection of excluded middle do) on the basis that *it is absurd* that they do (indeed, since, contrary to supervaluationism and rejection of excluded middle, intuitionism upholds the traditional idea that *absurdity entails falsity*, for many i intuitionism rejects that it is absurd that both Bi and $\neg Bi'$ hold). For many i, intuitionism *leaves open* the possibility that both Bi and $\neg Bi'$ hold, whereas supervaluationism and rejection of excluded middle *foreclose* that possibility. In our presentation of rejection of excluded middle, rejection is always understood as based on absurdity.
[26] Formally, letting as usual $\varnothing \vdash \varphi$ mean that φ is a logical truth, the principle that $\varnothing \vdash \varphi \vee \neg\varphi$ holds.

again, for every i, i's being the sharp boundary entails that, for every $j \neq i$, j is not the sharp boundary, according to dialetheism, for every i, it is also valid that $\neg(Bi \,\&\, \neg Bi')$ holds. But dialetheism disagrees with subvaluationism in upholding the ancillary traditional idea that *exceptionless universal quantifications and conjunctions must be true* (i.e. failure of singularity requires failure of uniqueness), and so in inferring from that lack of exception to acceptance that, for many i, the contradictory claim obtains that both $Bi \,\&\, \neg Bi'$ and $\neg(Bi \,\&\, \neg Bi')$ hold. Similarly, since dialetheism accepts that, for many i, $Bi \,\&\, \neg Bi'$ holds, a fortiori it accepts that there is a sharp boundary, but, since it accepts each instance of (N_{3LSB}), and since exceptionless universal quantifications must be true, it also accepts (N_{3LSB}) itself (i.e. the claim that there is no sharp boundary), and so, since exceptionless conjunctions must be true, it accepts the contradictory claim that both there is a sharp boundary and there is no sharp boundary. All these contradictions had better not be absurd, and so dialetheism denies the validity of the law of non-contradiction.[27] But, if dialetheism accepts (N_{3LSB}), how does it block soritical reasoning? It does by denying the validity of *modus ponendo tollens*: taking the last i such that $Bi \,\&\, \neg Bi'$ holds, Bi holds but Bi' fails to hold (fn. 16),[28] and so *modus ponendo tollens* leads from premises that hold to a conclusion that fails to hold, which is sufficient for invalidity even in a dialetheic framework. Notice that, if Bi holds but Bi' fails to hold, dialetheism can still maintain that $\neg(Bi \,\&\, \neg Bi')$ holds on the grounds that $\neg Bi$ *also holds* (the falsity of a conjunct being in general sufficient for the falsity of a conjunction) – that both Bi and $\neg Bi$ hold would simply be yet another contradiction that dialetheism can accept. It is less clear how, if Bi holds but Bi' fails to hold, $Bi \rightarrow Bi'$ can still hold (it being less clear what – if any – sufficient conditions for an *implication*'s holding are still met in such a case); however, a simple strategy is to stick to an interpretation of the implication expressed by $\rightarrow$ as material (fn. 11), in which case the same considerations as above apply.

Degree theory (Chapter 8) has it that the application of vague expressions comes in *degrees*, and in particular that a vague expression applies to similar cases with similar degrees of truth. Thus, for example, for every i, there is *at worst only a small drop* in degree of truth from Bi to Bi'. How this basic degree-theoretic tenet reflects on the interrelated questions of whether (N_3) is acceptable and whether and where the Extended Sorites Paradox breaks down depends on several issues (mentioned also in Chapter 9, fn. 5) of degree-theoretic semantics (how the degree of truth of a compound sentence depends – if it does – on the degree of truth of its components), pragmatics (how acceptance and rejection of a sentence relate to its degree of truth) and logic (what relation between the degrees of truth of the premises and that of the conclusion is guaranteed by the validity of an argument). Generally, we can say that characteristic features of degree theory are that it assigns a high degree of truth to each instance of (N_{3T}) (since an implication where there is at worst a small drop in degree of truth from its antecedent to its consequent has a high degree of

---

[27] Formally, the principle that $\varphi \,\&\, \neg\varphi \vdash \varnothing$ holds.
[28] Reason: given that $\neg Bi'$ holds, $\neg Bi''$ holds too, and so, if Bi' held, $Bi' \,\&\, \neg Bi''$ would hold too, contrary to our assumption about i.

truth) and that it treats the argument from Bi and $Bi \rightarrow Bi'$ to Bi' as involving at worst a small drop in degree of truth from its premises to its conclusion: in these respects, degree theory comes closer to vindicating (N_{3T}) than any of the previous solutions to the Sorites Paradox.

Finally, non-transitivism (Chapter 9) accepts (N_3) in its full glory, including the validity of *modus ponendo tollens* and *modus ponens*. Thus, non-transitivism in effect posits a relation of *equivalence* in terms of, say, baldness that always holds between cases *at a short distance* in a soritical series. Since no such relation holds between cases *at a long distance* (as witnessed in the limit by (N_1) and (N_2)), and since short distances eventually add up to a long distance, it follows that *equivalence is not always preserved if, given equivalence between two cases, one of them is replaced by another one at a short distance from – and so equivalent with – it.*[29] In other words, non-transitivism maintains that *equivalence is a non-transitive relation.*[30] Consequently, non-transitivism blocks soritical reasoning by denying an assumption that has so far remained implicit in our presentation and discussion, namely the assumption that, if certain initial premises (such as (N_1^{bald}) and (N_3^{bald})) entail an intermediate conclusion (such as $B2$), and such a conclusion, possibly together with the same premises, entails a further conclusion (such as $B3$), the initial premises on their own entail the further conclusion (an assumption that amounts in effect to a version of the principle of transitivity of logical consequence).[31] Therefore, the initial premises of soritical reasoning ((N_1^{bald}) and (N_3^{bald})) are true, and each of its argumentative routines (from Bi to Bi') is valid: the problem with soritical reasoning is not a *local* one imputable to any of its argumentative routines – rather, it is a *global* one arising from linking together all such delimited, short-distance routines into an overarching, long-distance argument from the very first premises to the very last conclusion.

The Forced-March Paradox

Following the dominant contemporary understanding, we're taking the Sorites Paradox to be the paradox presented in 'The Sorites Paradox', in this introduction – a certain apparently valid *argument* with apparently true *premises* and an apparently false *conclusion*. There is however a broadly related paradox that apparently *does not involve the logical structure of argument, premises and conclusion* (and which Horgan 1994 has drawn contemporary attention to under the name 'Forced-March Paradox').[32] That paradox runs

---

[29] The acute reader will observe that what in the text is in effect supposed to follow is tantamount to the negation of ($N_{3LSB}^{at\ a\ short\ distance}$), and that in the text it is in effect presupposed to follow by extended soritical reasoning. Such a reader is referred to Zardini (2015a, pp. 244–5, fn. 36).

[30] Formally, a relation R is transitive iff, for every objects x, y and z, if Rxy and Ryz hold, Rxz holds.

[31] Formally, the particular version mentioned in the text is the principle that, if $\Gamma \vdash \psi$ and $\Gamma, \psi \vdash \chi$ hold, $\Gamma \vdash \chi$ holds. The alert reader will notice that, strictly speaking, the second occurrence of 'Γ' prevents this version from being an instance of 'transitivity' as defined in fn. 30, but the connection of this and similar versions with transitivity would seem deep enough to justify extension of the notion of transitivity to them (see Chapter 9 for other versions of transitivity of logical consequence).

[32] If such appearances were veridical, that would point to another hitherto unappreciated kind of shortcoming of the traditional philosophical understanding of paradox mentioned in 'Solutions to the Sorites Paradox', in this introduction (additional to the one indicated in fn. 14).

as follows. Consider a subject, Vicky, who is supposed to go through the series of numbers from 1 to 100,000 and be asked, one number i after the other, whether Bi holds. To each such question, Vicky can give whatever answer(s) she likes: she can answer Bi, $\neg Bi$, 'There is no fact of the matter whether Bi holds', 'I don't know whether Bi holds', etc., and she can even answer in a less articulated way by uttering 'Hem', or twisting her face, or leaving the game in protest, etc. Now, presumably, when asked whether $B1$ holds, Vicky simply answers $B1$ and, when asked whether $B100,000$ holds, she does not simply answer $B100,000$, from which it seems to follow that there is a number i about which she simply answers Bi immediately followed by a number i' about which she answers something different. The problem is then that, while Vicky seems forced to *draw a significant distinction* for some pair of neighbouring numbers in the series, for no i is she in a position to *give a reason* for why she is drawing the distinction between i and i' (rather than, say, between i' and i''). This is puzzling because it seems to show that *a subject can be forced to commit to something she has no reason to commit to, even if she is allowed the widest possible range of answers* (including non-committal ones such as 'I take no view about Bi'!).

There is no denying that the Forced-March Paradox raises important issues about *intellectual integrity* and related topics, but what for our purposes is important to realise is that such issues are actually *rather different* from the issues directly raised by the Sorites Paradox: it is one thing to give an account of which series of committal or non-committal answers concerning particular cases of application of a vague expression a subject can give so as at least to preserve her coherence, quite another thing to give an account settling nothing less than the truth on the general issues of whether vague expressions have sharp boundaries and of how this reflects on what vagueness and its logic are. Therefore, a solution to the Forced-March Paradox is unlikely to constitute in itself also a solution to the Sorites Paradox and, vice versa, a solution to the Sorites Paradox is unlikely to constitute in itself also a solution to the Forced-March Paradox (which is not to deny that it is likely that a solution to one paradox will offer some helpful elements in developing a solution to the other paradox).

The difference between the two paradoxes is confirmed by the observation that *the Forced-March Paradox can be run on non-vague expressions just as well* (Zardini 2008b, pp. 277–81). For example, Vicky might be supposed to go through the series of numbers from 1 to 100,000 and this time be asked, one number i after the other, whether i straws break the camel's back.[33] To each such question, Vicky can again give whatever answer(s) she likes. Now, presumably, when asked whether 1 straw breaks the camel's back, Vicky simply answers that it doesn't and, when asked whether 100,000 straws break the camel's back, she does not simply answer that they don't, from which it seems to follow that there is a number i about which she simply answers that i straws do not break the camel's back immediately followed by a number i' about which she answers something different. Again, the problem is then that, while Vicky seems forced to *draw a significant distinction* for

---

[33] Throughout, we assume that the details about the relevant straws and camel are such that 1 straw does not break the camel's back, 100,000 straws do and, for every i, it is not vague whether i straws break the camel's back.

some pair of neighbouring numbers in the series, for no *i* is she in a position to *give a reason* for why she is drawing the distinction between *i* and *i′* (rather than, say, between *i′* and *i″*). Because the Forced-March Paradox thus variously extends beyond the domain of the Sorites Paradox and of vagueness, it receives in the book a less systematic coverage (Chapter 6, Section 6.2, Chapter 7, Section 7.7, Chapter 9, Section 9.5 and Chapter 14, Section 14.4 in particular offer substantial discussions of the paradox from their own perspectives).

The points in the last two paragraphs also have interesting historiographical repercussions. As mentioned in 'Topic, Structure, Features and Aims of the Book', in this introduction, according to the historiographical tradition the Sorites Paradox was first formulated by Eubulides. However, *the paradox that Eubulides actually raised – and the one that was the focus of the ensuing discussions in ancient philosophy* – would rather seem *the Forced-March Paradox* (cf. Chapter 15). If so, the historical emergence of the Sorites Paradox *proper* – the *apparent demonstration of the impossibility of the apparent platitude that vague expressions lack sharp boundaries* – might (fittingly) become a blurred matter.

Influence and History of the Sorites Paradox

As might already have been gleaned from the multifarious issues raised by the various solutions to the Sorites Paradox, the paradox sits at the crossroads of deep threads in philosophy of logic, philosophy of language, epistemology and metaphysics. Unsurprisingly, then, the influence of the paradox in several areas has been profound. As we saw in 'Solutions to the Sorites Paradox', in this introduction, many (classical or non-classical) solutions to the paradox rely on the idea that vague expressions give rise to some sort of indefiniteness (a status *intermediate between plain truth and plain falsity*). In philosophy of logic (Chapter 10), this broad idea has very influentially been appealed to in several of its versions also in the case of the semantic paradoxes (and possibly other paradoxes of self-reference), thus triggering an extremely fruitful interaction between work on the Sorites Paradox and work on the semantic paradoxes.

Moving on to other areas of philosophy, the Sorites Paradox can be abstractly conceived of as an extreme situation where a prima facie plausible principle (in this case, (N_3)) is stress-tested by seeing how it behaves when repeatedly applied to a long series of cases where the difference between the first and last element is big but the difference between any two neighbouring elements is small. Series instantiating this abstract pattern have been constructed and discussed in several areas, either with the aim of refuting the relevant prima facie plausible principle or with the aim of, keeping fixed the relevant prima facie plausible principle, establishing some controversial consequence thereof (since there typically is disagreement whether, notwithstanding their *similarity* with soritical series, such series are *really* soritical, let's call them 'Sorites-like'). In metaphysics (Chapter 11), Sorites-like series have been used, among other things, to try to establish, keeping fixed the prima facie plausible principle that composition is not vague,[34] the controversial principle of *universal composition*.[35] In practical philosophy (Chapter 12), Sorites-like series have been used, among other things, to try to refute the prima facie plausible principle that *certain value-theoretic relations such as being-better-than are transitive*.[36]

Going beyond philosophy, the main bearers of vagueness – expressions and concepts (fn. 3) – are also of course the objects of more empirically oriented studies. In linguistics (Chapter 13), the Sorites Paradox has mainly, and increasingly, acted as a *further constraint* on the adequacy of formal semantic theories, which have in several ways been refined in order to account for the seeming lack of sharp boundaries of vague expressions, typically by integrating in the theory ideas and tools originally developed by some philosophical solutions to the paradox. In psychology (Chapter 14), beyond higher-level issues in the psychology of reasoning raised by the variety of slippery-slope arguments, Sorites-like series have represented a staple experimental setting for the study of perceptual discrimination and conceptual categorisation since the rise of empirical psychology, thereby providing valuable empirical evidence concerning some of the *cognitive underpinnings* of the seeming lack of sharp boundaries of vague concepts; more recently, some such experiments have directly been inspired by philosophical work on the Sorites Paradox. Both disciplines thus offer a prime example of *how a problem native to distinctively philosophical reflection, together with its accompanying characteristically philosophical solutions, has then set notable agendas in the sciences.*

---

[34] Informally, a non-empty class X of objects composes an object y iff y comprises (i) all the members of X and (ii) nothing more. Formally (in terms of parthood), a non-empty class X of objects composes an object y iff, (i) for every x member of X, x is a part of y and, (ii) for every z part of y, for some x member of X, z has a part in common with x.

[35] Formally, the principle that, for every non-empty class X of objects, there is an object composed by X.

[36] As we already noted in 'Topic, Structure, Features and Aims of the Book', in this introduction, and in the last paragraph, the Sorites Paradox comprises issues not only in philosophy of logic, but also in philosophy of language, epistemology and metaphysics, and these are duly treated at the relevant points in Part I. We think it useful to distinguish between, roughly, issues *comprised* by the paradox (e.g. the issue in philosophy of logic of where soritical arguments fail, the issue in philosophy of language of what feature in the semantics of vague expressions accounts for their seeming lack of sharp boundaries, the issue in epistemology of why we cannot identify sharp boundaries, the issue in metaphysics of whether there are objects without sharp boundaries) and issues *influenced* by it (e.g. the issue in philosophy of logic of where Liar-style arguments fail, the issue in epistemology of whether, whenever one knows a premise and validly derives a conclusion from it, one knows the conclusion, the issue in metaphysics of whether the principle of universal composition holds) – vague as such a distinction may be! Part II is about issues of the latter kind in philosophy (as well as about the general bearing of the paradox on work in the sciences). Now, as for philosophy of language, because of the fact that, in this specific sense, the influence of the paradox in it has been as of yet extremely limited – as opposed to the amount of work in it that is comprised by the paradox – Part II contains no chapter devoted to that topic. As for epistemology, because of reasons of space and of the fact that the influence of the Sorites Paradox in it has been as of yet more limited, Part II contains no chapter devoted to that topic, and the following brief indications will suffice. In epistemology, Sorites-like series have been used to try to refute the following prima facie plausible principles: that, *whenever one knows a premise and validly derives a conclusion from it, one knows the conclusion* (Locke 1690, book IV, chapter II, 6; Hume 1739, volume I, part IV, section I; more recently, DeRose 1999, p. 23, fn. 14; Lasonen-Aarnio 2008, p. 171; Schechter 2013; see Zardini 2018a for some critical discussion); that, *whenever one knows both conjuncts, one is in a position to know their conjunction* (Makinson 1965; see Zardini 2018a for some critical discussion); that, *whenever one knows, one is in a position to know that one knows* (Williamson 1992a; see Zardini 2018g for some critical discussion); that certain conditions are such that, *whenever they obtain, one is in a position to know that they do* (Williamson 1995b, 1996a; see Zardini 2012a, 2013b for some critical discussion); that, *whenever one knows that a coin is fair and does not know that it will not be flipped, one does not know that it will not land tails* (Dorr et al. 2014; see Zardini 2018a for some critical discussion); that *all knowledge is evidence* (Zardini 2017).

The book closes with a survey and discussion of the pre-analytic history of the Sorites Paradox in Western philosophy[37] (Chapter 15).[38] While there is still much to be inspired by in the salient episodes of such a history, we think that it is a fair assessment of the historical development to say that the last 50 years or so have witnessed tremendous advances in understanding what the real problems posed by the paradox are, in elaborating systematic approaches to it and in determining its far-reaching consequences in several areas. Work on the Sorites Paradox is one of the jewels in the crown of contemporary analytic philosophy.[39]

---

[37] The subsequent early analytic history of the Sorites Paradox is probably better understood: some of the most prominent figures at the birth of analytic philosophy were aware of the clash between classical logic and (N₃) and solved the paradox by claiming that *(N₃) fails to hold* because some cases in a soritical series are in some sense indeterminate (Frege 1879, §27, p. 64; Russell 1923, p. 85), which they saw as precipitating *failure of the law of excluded middle* and indeed the *inapplicability of logic as a whole* (Frege 1903, §56, pp. 69–70; Russell 1923, pp. 85–6, 88–9), thereby determining that the ideal language of inquiry cannot contain vague expressions. The late analytic history of the paradox can be taken to get going from around the end of the 1960s, when the attempts at understanding how vague expressions work that developed in the previous three decades (beginning with Black 1937) started to eventuate in the main types of solutions to the paradox: epistemicism (Cargile 1969), degree theory (Goguen 1969, who employs ideas already developed in another context by Łukasiewicz and Tarski 1930 and already applied to vagueness by Black 1937), supervaluationism (Fine 1975, who employs ideas already developed and applied to vagueness by Mehlberg 1958), incoherentism (Dummett 1975), contextualism (Kamp 1981), intuitionism (Putnam 1983, who employs ideas already developed in another context by Brouwer 1908), rejection of excluded middle (Tye 1990, who employs ideas already developed in another context by Łukasiewicz 1920 and already applied to vagueness by Körner 1959), subvaluationism (Hyde 1997, who employs ideas already developed and applied to vagueness by Jaśkowski 1948), dialetheism (Ripley 2005, who employs ideas already developed in another context by Asenjo 1966 and already applied to vagueness by Priest and Routley 1989, pp. 389–90) and non-transitivism (Zardini 2008a, 2008b). Alongside the articulation of these solutions, the burgeoning literature on the paradox in its late analytic history has also been widening its scope, bringing the paradox to exert an influence in such diverse areas as philosophy of logic, metaphysics, practical philosophy and epistemology as well as in neighbouring disciplines such as linguistics and psychology (the individual chapters provide further historiographical information on their own topics). Thanks to Dominic Hyde and Rafał Urbaniak for their help with some of these sources.

[38] To the best of our knowledge, neither the Sorites Paradox proper nor the Forced-March Paradox have received sustained discussions in non-Western philosophical traditions. Thanks to Ricki Bliss, Jonardon Ganeri and Mark Siderits for their expert advice on this matter.

[39] Thanks to Paul Égré, Crispin Wright and an anonymous referee for their helpful comments on earlier versions of the material in this introduction. As for the second author, the study has been funded by the FCT Research Fellowship IF/01202/2013 *Tolerance and Instability: The Substructure of Cognitions, Transitions and Collections*. Additionally, the study has been funded by the Russian Academic Excellence Project *5-100*. The second author has also benefited from support from the FCT project PTDC/FER-FIL/28442/2017 *Companion to Analytic Philosophy 2*, while both authors have benefited from support from the Project FFI2015-70707-P of the Spanish Ministry of Economy, Industry and Competitiveness *Localism and Globalism in Logic and Semantics*.

Part I

Solutions to the Sorites Paradox

1   Epistemicism and the Sorites Paradox

Ofra Magidor

1.1   The Epistemicist Solution to the Sorites Paradox

Consider a typical instance of the Sorites Paradox[1]:

A person who is 1000 millimetres (i.e. one metre) in height is not tall.

$\forall n$(if a person who is n millimetres height is not tall, then a person who is $n + 1$ millimetres in height is not tall).

According to epistemicism, resolving the paradox requires no revision whatsoever of classical logic or semantics. The solution to the paradox is simply that the second premise is outright false.

In some ways, this is the most straightforward response to the paradox. First, it is entirely orthodox with respect to classical logic and semantics. Second, given classical logic and semantics, the argument is valid and on the (practically uncontroversial) assumption that it has a false conclusion, it follows that it must have at least one false premise.[2] And while both premises have intuitive appeal, few would deny that if forced to choose, denying the second looks far more palatable than denying the first.[3]

However, reflection on this apparently straightforward response quickly leads to difficulties. After all, if the second premise is false, then its negation is true. This in turn means that there is some specific number n, such that a person who is n millimetres in height is not tall, and yet a person whose height is just one millimetre greater is tall. Even worse, if we are to fully retain classical mathematics, then there must be a *sharp cut-off point* for 'tall': a precise real number k such that anyone who is less than k metres tall is not tall, and anyone who is over k metres tall is tall.[4] But it seems very hard to believe that words such as 'tall' have such sharp cut-off points.

---

[1] Two complications which I ignore: first, 'tall' is context-sensitive. Second, what a person's height is might also be vague (for example, do we include their hair or not?). These complications can be side-stepped by phrasing the paradox against a particular context and with a precise characterisation of the underlying height facts.

[2] Note that classical logic and semantics play a role mostly in establishing this last inference – most views of vagueness that reject classical logic or semantics nevertheless take the argument to be valid. However, see Magidor (2012) for an exception.

[3] For a dissenting voice, see Enoch (2007).

[4] This follows from the *completeness of the real numbers*, which says that any non-empty set of real numbers that has an upper bound has a least upper bound. Since the set {l: a person who is l millimetres in height is not tall} is non-empty and bounded it has a least upper bound k, which will serve as the cut-off point for 'tall'. Note that this leaves open whether or not a person who is exactly k millimetres in height is tall.

Epistemicists do not deny the existence of such sharp cut-off points. Rather, they add a second component to the view which is intended to make this surprising consequence more palatable. According to epistemicism, even though 'tall' has a sharp cut-off point, we do not and cannot know what this point is.[5] And moreover speakers mistakenly take their principled ignorance regarding the cut-off point as evidence that no such cut-off point exists.

The epistemicist solution to the paradox thus consists of two components. First, vague terms, just as non-vague ones, have ordinary classical semantic-values and do not require any revision of classical logic or semantics. In particular, each person is either tall or not tall, and for each person, it is either true that they are tall or false that they are tall. Second, although words like 'tall' have sharp boundaries, we do not and cannot know what these boundaries are, and this explains why we might be tempted to (falsely) conclude that such boundaries do not exist.

It is easy to see the advantages of epistemicism. It allows us to block the Sorites argument without requiring any revision of classical logic or semantics. Moreover, the view offers a straightforward account of higher-order vagueness, one that is entirely uniform with the treatment of first-order vagueness: the predicate 'definitely tall' also has a sharp cut-off point, although we do not and cannot know where it is. However, the view also faces some significant challenges. Here are what I take to be the four main challenges for the view:

Challenge 1: counter-intuitiveness

The view is highly counter-intuitive – it just seems very hard to believe that there is a specific real number which constitutes the boundary between being tall and not tall.

Challenge 2: the determination of meaning

It is commonly accepted that words have particular meanings by virtue of the way speakers use them. And yet it does not seem that there is anything about the way we use the word 'tall' that is sufficient to determine a particular sharp boundary.

Admittedly, according to semantic externalism it is not *just* the way we use words that determines their meaning: facts about the environment around us, as well as facts about which properties are more natural, can play a role as well.[6] Thus, for example, whether speakers use the word 'water' in an environment where the water-like substance in their vicinity is H_2O or XYZ can determine which of the two substances the word 'water' picks out, and the fact that H_2O is a natural kind can explain why 'is water' in our mouth refers to the property of being H_2O rather than to the less natural property of being a clear tasty

---

[5] When epistemicists say that we *cannot* know the sharp cut-off points of vague terms, they exclude special means of coming to know, such as the testimony of an omniscient being (see Williamson 1997a, p. 926).

[6] See Putnam (1975) and Lewis (1983).

liquid. However, it is hard to see how this point helps with determining sharp boundaries for 'tall': the property of being over 1.781 metres in height exists just as much as the property of being over 1.782 metres in height and both properties seem equally (un)natural. Epistemicism thus faces the challenge of accounting for how vague words get assigned their sharp meaning.

Challenge 3: the explanation of ignorance

According to epistemicism we do not and cannot know the sharp cut-off point for 'tall'. But if 'tall' has a sharp cut-off point, why is it that we cannot discover it?

Challenge 4: the characterisation of vagueness

Vagueness seems to be a distinctiveness phenomenon: the words 'tall', 'bald' and 'intelligent' are vague, while 'even', 'prime' or 'exactly two metres long' are precise. How do we account for this difference? One possibility is to maintain that vague terms have a special kind of semantic-value, for example an incomplete semantic-value which gives rise to truth-value gaps. But this way of characterising vagueness is clearly not available to the epistemicist. Nor can epistemicists merely appeal to the claim that we do not know precisely which people fall under the extension of 'tall'. After all, 'largest twin prime' is a perfectly precise predicate, but we do not (and possibly cannot) know which number, if any, falls under its extension.[7] Epistemicism thus faces the challenge of accounting for this difference.

By far the most comprehensive defence of epistemicism is offered by Timothy Williamson, primarily in his book *Vagueness* (Williamson 1994). In Section 1.2, I summarise Williamson's account and his response to the four challenges raised above. In Section 1.3, I discuss some of the objections that has been raised against Williamson's account and his way of addressing the four challenges. In Section 1.4, I offer concluding remarks.

1.2 Williamson's Epistemicism

In this section I focus on what has been the main defence of epistemicism: Timothy Williamson's. The key feature of Williamson's account consists in how he responds to the third challenge (the explanation of ignorance), but let us start with a brief discussion of Williamson's responses to the first two challenges.

---

[7] A twin prime is a prime number x such that either $x + 2$ or $x - 2$ is also prime (for example, 41 and 43 are twin primes). It is an open mathematical question whether there are infinitely many twin primes, and hence whether there is a largest twin prime and if so which number it is.

Williamson's response to the first challenge (counter-intuitiveness) follows the standard epistemicist strategy: we are tempted to think that vague terms do not have sharp boundaries because, as much as we try, we cannot locate these boundaries or imagine how we might come to find them. However, once we realise that there is a principled reason for why we cannot locate these boundaries, the fact that we cannot find these sharp boundaries no longer provides evidence that they do not exist.[8]

What about the second challenge (the determination of meaning)? Williamson maintains that the meaning of vague words, just like precise ones, supervenes on their use (broadly construed to include facts about one's environment). This means that in any two possible worlds where the word 'tall' is used in precisely the same way, the word has exactly the same sharp cut-off point. However, he stresses that this metaphysical supervenience thesis does not mean that there is any simple recipe that connects the use facts of vague words to their meaning.[9]

Indeed, Williamson maintains that vague words possess a feature that makes the connection between their use facts and meaning especially fragile. Vague words are semantically plastic: their meaning is highly sensitive to the way they are used, so that even slight variations in their use patterns often make for a variation in their meaning. By way of illustration: if in the actual world 'tall' (for a person) picks out the property of being over 1.781 metres in height, then in a close possible world in which the use facts for 'tall' differs from ours only slightly, 'tall' picks out a different property (e.g. the property of being over 1.782 metres). This kind of semantic plasticity sits well with the observation that the property of being over 1.781 metres in height seems just as (un)natural as the property of being over 1.782, because the lack of natural candidates for the meaning of 'tall' can partially explain the semantic plasticity of the term. And it also sits well with Williamson's contention that, while the meaning of vague terms supervenes on their use, the function mapping use patterns to meaning patterns is especially chaotic and intractable. The intractability of the supervenience function is important because it appears that even if we were to be given a very detailed description of all the use facts for 'tall', we still would not be able to say what the sharp boundaries of 'tall' are. It is thus important for Williamson that, even though the meaning of vague terms supervenes on their use, we do not (and cannot) know the precise details of the relevant supervenience function.

---

[8] Of course, this in itself doesn't explain why there are other cases where we are ignorant (possibly principally ignorant) regarding some precise question and yet are not tempted to conclude that there is no fact of the matter. But I take it that Williamson isn't intending to offer here a full prediction of when speakers do or do not make such mistakes. Rather, he is trying to show how the mistake that (according to epistemicism) speakers are making is understandable (even more so given that the rather complex explanation for why we are principally ignorant of sharp-cut off points is unlikely to have occurred to speakers).

[9] Indeed, reflection shows that there isn't a simple recipe even in the case of perfectly precise words. Consider, for example, 'even' (in the mathematical sense). While this term can be defined in a mathematically precise way, it was probably first used without an explicit stipulation of its meaning, which raises difficult questions regarding how many and what kinds of uses were required before the word acquired its meaning. Moreover, the Pythagoreans apparently had a theory of parity according to which the number one was neither 'even' nor 'odd' – whether this means that they had a false theory of parity or that their parity-like terms had slightly different meanings than ours, this case shows that the determination of precise meaning by use facts can be a complicated matter (cf. Williamson 1994, p. 207).

What about Williamson's response to the third challenge (the explanation of ignorance)? One might be tempted to assume that the intractable nature of the supervenience function is sufficient to account for our ignorance: since we do not know precisely how the meanings of vague terms supervene on their use, we cannot calculate their sharp cut-off points from their use facts. However, this explanation is unsatisfactory for two related reasons. First, this would only explain why we cannot know the sharp cut-off points of vague terms by calculating them from the use facts – but it does not explain why we do not know them using other, more direct means. Second, Williamson acknowledges that the mere fact that the supervenience function is highly complex, doesn't entail that it is principally unknowable. After all, there are many highly complex facts of science (including facts relevant to supervenience relations) which we do not necessarily take ourselves to be principally ignorant of. Thus, for example, you might think that the mental supervenes on the physical in very complex ways and still hold hope that science might be able to discover what the relevant correlation between the two domains is.

However, Williamson maintains that there is a crucial disanalogy between the supervenience of the mental on the physical and the supervenience of meaning on use. In the former case, scientific progress begins by amassing some direct observations concerning each of the two realms (e.g. preforming MRIs for the physical realm, and asking subjects whether they are in pain for the mental realm), and then forming scientific theories connecting the two domains. However, he maintains that in the case of vague terms we simply do not have sufficient direct access to facts about meanings. As he puts it: "Everyone with physical measurements *m* is thin' cannot be known *a posteriori* in a parallel way, for no route to independent knowledge of someone with physical measurements *m* that he is thin corresponds to asking someone whether he is in pain' (Williamson 1994, p. 204).[10] The upshot is that our ignorance of the supervenience function is derivative on our ignorance of the sharp cut-off points of vague terms, and thus Williamson wishes to offer a more direct explanation of the latter.

Williamson's direct explanation of our ignorance crucially relies (again) on the claim that vague terms are semantically plastic. An attractive principle in epistemology is that a necessary condition for a belief to count as knowledge is that the belief be *safe*. As a first approximation we can say that X's belief that p is safe just in case there is no close world in which X believes that p, but it is false that p. Suppose for example that you look at a jar full of marbles and form the belief that the jar contains exactly 135 marbles. Suppose that your belief was formed by pure guessing. Even if you happened to guess the correct number of marbles, most people would judge that you do not *know* that the jar contains exactly 135 marbles. One way to explain why your true belief does not constitute knowledge in this case is by pointing out that your belief isn't safe: there are close worlds where you make the same guess (and thus also form the belief that the jar contains 135 marbles), but where the jar contains 136 marbles, rendering your belief false.

---

[10] See also the discussion in Kearns and Magidor (2008, p. 279) and Section 1.3.2 of this chapter.

Now consider the case of 'tall'. Suppose that you form the belief that the sharp cut-off point for 'tall' is precisely 1.781 metres, and let us assume that your belief happens to be true. Nevertheless, claims Williamson, there are close worlds in which 'tall' is used slightly differently, and hence due to the plasticity of 'tall', the word has a slightly different meaning (e.g. it has a cut-off of 1.782). Moreover, since you are not sensitive to such slight variations in use (nor for that matter, to how exactly they affect the meaning of the term), then presumably in some such worlds you nevertheless believe that the cut-off for 'tall' is 1.781. But this latter belief would be false, rendering your actual belief unsafe. The upshot is that, due to semantic plasticity, even if you were to form a true belief concerning the cut-off point for 'tall', that belief would not constitute knowledge.

So far we have focused on our ignorance of *semantic cut-off claims* – claims such as 'The word 'tall' picks out the property of being more than 1.781 metres in height'. However, it is important to observe that we also have a corresponding ignorance which is not directly about the word 'tall' or its semantic-value: we are also ignorant about the boundaries of the property of tallness. Assume for example that the cut-off for 'tall' is 1.781 metres. We do not know claims such as the following: 'A person is tall if and only if they are over 1.781 metres in height' (call this a *non-semantic cut-off claim*). Interestingly, it is such non-semantic claims that appear in typical versions of the Sorites Paradox. The problem, however, is that since these claims are not about the word 'tall', then on the face of it, semantic plasticity seems irrelevant to explaining our ignorance of these. Relatedly, note that if it is true that a person is tall if and only if they are over 1.781 metres in height, then it is *necessarily* true.[11] Of course, in other worlds the sentence expressing this necessary truth might express a different proposition which is false, but that is irrelevant to the necessity of the truth actually expressed. (Compare: it is necessarily true that two plus two equals four, even though in some other possible worlds, the word 'four' denotes the number five, and hence the sentence 'two plus two equals four' expresses a falsehood.) But if the non-semantic cut-off claim is necessarily true, any belief in it trivially satisfies safety: since it is not false in any world, one does not falsely believe it in any close world.

Note, however, that this is an instance of the more general challenge of how to apply the safety principle to necessary truths. Suppose, for example, that you form the belief that $256 \times 31 = 7936$ by simply guessing the result of the multiplication. Just as with the case of the jar of marbles, your belief does not constitute knowledge. However, this time there is no close world in which you falsely believe that $256 \times 31 = 7936$ simply because there is no possible world (close or otherwise) where this proposition is false. In view of such examples, defenders of safety principles usually extend the principle so that it applies more liberally.

---

[11] This is obvious if one thinks that the property of tallness just is the property of being 1.781 in height, but even those who have a fine-grained conception of properties that distinguishes between the two would presumably want to accept that whether or not a person is tall supervenes on their height.

According to *extended safety*, your belief that p is safe just in case there is no close world in which you have a *similar* belief that q, and it is false that q. For example, in the above case there is a close world w in which, when evaluating 256×31, you make a different guess – say 7937. In that world you believe that $256 \times 31 = 7937$, and that belief is false. Although your belief in w has a different content than your actual belief, it is sufficiently similar to your actual belief for the latter to violate extended safety, entailing that it does not constitute knowledge.

Williamson utilises this more liberal conception of safety to argue that semantic plasticity leads to ignorance of non-semantic cut-off claims as well. Suppose you form a true belief in the claim that a person is tall if and only if they are over 1.781 metres in height. On Williamson's account, there is a close world w, one with subtly different use facts, in which you form a very similar belief, one that you would express in w by using exactly the same words ('A person is tall if and only if they are over 1.781 metres in height'). However, due to the semantic plasticity of 'tall', in w, the term picks out a different property (say, the property of being over 1.782 metres) and thus your belief in w is false. Of course, your w-belief has a slightly different content than your actual belief, but Williamson maintains that the close linguistic similarity between the way you phrase these two beliefs (you use the same words, which have nearly identical meanings), is sufficient to render them similar for the purposes of extended safety, thus ensuring that your actual belief does not constitute knowledge.

The explanation of ignorance in terms of semantic plasticity also plays a role in the way Williamson responds to the fourth challenge (the distinctiveness of vagueness): our ignorance in cases of vagueness is ignorance due to a distinct source – namely, semantic plasticity. While we may be ignorant (perhaps irredeemably ignorant) of which number if any fall under the extension of 'largest twin prime', our ignorance in the latter case clearly has nothing to do with plasticity.

In addition to addressing the four challenges, Williamson's account has the following attractive feature: it predicts that while we cannot know truths of the form '"tall" refers to the property of being over k metres in height', we *can* know truths of the form '"tall" refers to the property of tallness'. For consider your belief that 'tall' refers to the property of tallness. Owing to semantic plasticity, there is a close world w in which 'tall' refers to a slightly different property (call it *tallness** – which will be the property of being over k^* metres in height). As above, there is a close world w where you form a belief that you would express by saying '"tall" refers to the property of tallness'. But while this belief has a slightly different content than your actual belief (in w it expresses the content that 'tall' refers to tallness*), this time your w-belief is true in w, and thus does not render your actual belief unsafe. This is an attractive result, not only because it is intuitive that we do know that 'tall' refers to tallness, but also because it shows that there is a sense on which we know what 'tall' means – despite not knowing the sharp cut-off point of the term. (Compare: we may not be able to describe the extension of 'twin prime' in an informative way, but we nevertheless know what the term means).

1.3 Objections to Williamson's Account

Williamson offers a powerful defence of epistemicism, but a range of objections have been raised against his account. For many philosophers, the very idea that words like 'tall' have sharp cut-off points seems too far-fetched to accept – to use Lewis's picturesque language, epistemicism is often met with an 'incredulous stare'. In this section, however, I would like to focus on more concrete objections to the account. I discuss in turn objections to Williamson's response to each of the four challenges.

1.3.1 Counter-Intuitiveness

Recall that Williamson argues that one thing that explains why speakers believe vague predicates do not have sharp boundaries is that they mistakenly infer from their inability to locate these boundaries that no such boundaries exist. Suppose that k is the correct sharp cut-off point for 'tall'. Williamson's account focuses on explaining why speakers do not know that k is the correct cut-off by explaining why, even if we truly believed that it is the cut-off point, that belief would not constitute knowledge. However, Keefe points out that there is a more basic fact that needs to be explained: namely, why speakers do not even believe that k is the sharp cut-off point.[12] Moreover, it seems that it is this latter fact which is relevant to addressing the counter-intuitiveness challenge: when we are trying to explain why speakers find it hard to believe that there are sharp cut-off points, what matters is that they do not *believe* (rather than do not know) of any particular number that it is a sharp cut-off point.

Williamson could respond by saying that speakers do not typically believe that k is the sharp cut-off point because they realise that such a belief would not constitute knowledge. But as Keefe points out, this leaves the question of why speakers think that such beliefs would not constitute knowledge. It obviously will not do to say that it is because speakers accept Williamson's explanation of ignorance – after all, the vast majority of speakers have never even considered this explanation.

Here the dialectic between Keefe and Williamson becomes rather delicate: on the one hand, it is clear that even if Williamson's explanation of ignorance is correct, it does not directly figure in the beliefs of ordinary speakers. On the other hand, even Keefe does not deny that ordinary speakers do not believe that they know (or can know) the sharp boundaries of vague terms.

Perhaps the following analogy can help us to make progress: suppose that most people believe that there is no fountain of youth. I argue that they are wrong: the fountain of youth does exist but it is impossible to find it, which is why everyone else falsely assumes that it doesn't exist. You ask me why the fountain is impossible to find. I respond that it is impossible to find because the Gods keep it hidden: every time someone comes close to

---

[12] Keefe (2000, pp. 71–2). Also relevant is Horwich (1997) who maintains that the very phenomenon of vagueness is characterised by an unwillingness to believe borderline statements rather than in the inability to know them; but see the response in Williamson (1997b, pp. 945–6).

discovering the fountain, the Gods immediately move it to another location. You press me by saying that this only explains why no one *knows* where the fountain of youth is, not why there aren't locations for which speakers *believe* (either falsely or as a luckily true guess) that the fountain is located, especially since other speakers haven't even considered my theory about the Gods moving the fountain. How should I respond to this latter complaint? It is clear that the reason speakers do not believe the fountain is located in any particular location does not involve their accepting my theory about the Gods – speakers don't think the fountain is located at a location *L* simply because they think it does not exist. However, this does not mean that my explanation of their ignorance is irrelevant to accounting for their beliefs. After all, if the Gods hadn't kept the fountain hidden, then perhaps people would have eventually found the fountain and thus altered their belief that it does not exist.[13] Thus at least in so far as the case of hidden sharp cut-off points is analogous to that of the hidden fountain of youth, it seems that Williamson's explanation of ignorance is after all relevant to explaining the lack of belief in sharp cut-off points, even if speakers are not aware of his account.

1.3.2 The Determination of Meaning

Williamson's response to the challenge concerning the determination of meaning is to maintain that the meaning of vague terms supervenes on their use, although the function connecting use facts to meaning facts is chaotic and intractable. Keefe notes that merely asserting that meaning supervenes on use does not help appease the intuition that in cases of vagueness, meaning is underdetermined: it at least *seems* as if nothing determines whether by 'tall' we pick out the property of being over 1.78213 metres rather than over 1.78214 metres in height.[14]

Another worry with the claim that the meaning of vague terms supervenes on their use concerns the question (which I have already discussed briefly above) of why we cannot come to know the relevant supervenience function: we do not (and apparently cannot) know facts of the form 'If speakers were to use language thus and so, the cut-off for 'tall' would be precisely *k*'.[15]

As noted above, the mere fact that the supervenience function is highly complex is insufficient to explain our ignorance, because many other scientific claims – which we do not take ourselves to be principally ignorant of – are highly complex as well. As we have seen, Williamson's explanation for why the meaning-on-use supervenience function is unknowable relies on the claim that we do not have direct access to a sufficient range of meaning facts, and hence cannot come to know how the supervenience function works

---

[13] And note that if they merely formed a true belief that isn't knowledge concerning the claim that the fountain exists, their belief would arguably be less robust (cf. Williamson's discussion of the burglar who merely has a true belief rather than knowledge that there is a diamond in the house in Williamson 2000, pp. 62–4).

[14] Keefe (2000, p. 77).

[15] Note that an explanation in terms of semantic plasticity would not work here, as this sentence expresses a truth in all close worlds.

using standard scientific methods. But it is not clear how satisfying this response is: after all, there are many facts about the meanings of vague terms that we *do* have direct access to (for example that someone who is 1.50 metres in height is not tall or penumbral connections involving vague terms). Just as forming a scientific theory concerning the correlation between the mental and the physical does not require an observation of every single brain in the world, one might maintain that the meaning facts we do have direct access to could provide us with a sufficient basis to gain scientific knowledge of the relevant supervenience function.[16]

In light of both of these challenges, one might propose a different variant of epistemicism, one which shares with Williamson the view that vague terms have sharp cut-off points, but relies on an unorthodox view according to which meaning does not (or at least not fully) supervene on use or other non-semantic facts.[17] Suppose our use facts leave open whether 'tall' picks out the property of being over 1.781 metres or the property of being over 1.782 metres in height. According to this proposal, for each possible world containing the same use facts as ours, there is a primitive semantic fact which states which of the two properties 'tall' picks out. Of course, this proposal might be thought to be even more counter-intuitive and radical than Williamson's: it not only postulates sharp cut-off points, but also primitive semantic facts. However, Kearns and Magidor (2012) argue that there are reasons completely independent of vagueness to accept the view that meaning doesn't supervene on use. For example, they show that similar considerations to those that have driven theorists to reject the supervenience of the mental on the physical (ones involving worlds with purely mental beings or phenomenal zombies) can generalise into arguments against the supervenience of the semantic on the non-semantic.

This proposal is well equipped to address the above objection concerning the determination of meaning: our intuition that the use of vague terms does not fully determine a precise cut-off point is actually correct, and the reason we cannot come to know the relevant supervenience function is that no such function exists. It should be noted, however, that this alternative form of epistemicism faces other challenges. For example, while this view does not take meaning facts to fully supervene on use facts, presumably it will still accept that meaning facts are *constrained* by use facts. But this leaves open the question of how use facts constrain the meaning facts, a question which is also relevant to the issue of how, on this view, to account for higher-order vagueness.

1.3.3 The Explanation of Ignorance

Suppose in the actual world you form a belief that you express by saying 'A person is tall if and only if they are over 1.781 metres in height', and let us suppose that this belief is true. Recall that Williamson argues that this true belief does not constitute knowledge because there is a close world *w* in which the following hold:

[16] See Kearns and Magidor (2008, p. 279, pp. 298–9) for more details.
[17] See Kearns and Magidor (2012) for a defence of this view.

(i) *Semantic Plasticity*: The use facts in *w* differ slightly from ours, entailing that the sharp cut-off for 'tall' in *w* is slightly different.

(ii) *Similar Belief*: In *w*, you nevertheless form a very similar belief to your actual one, a belief that in *w* you would also express by using the same words: 'A person is tall if and only if they are over 1.781 metres in height'. (Of course, given (i) this belief is false in *w*.)

Moreover,

(iii) *Meta-Linguistic Safety*: The linguistically similar false belief you have in (ii) entails that your actual belief is not safe and thus does not constitute knowledge.

Objections have been raised against each of the three components of this explanation.

Let us begin with *Semantic Plasticity*: why should we think that in close worlds where 'tall' is used slightly differently, it has a different meaning? Note for a start that we must accept that in at least some cases, two worlds which differ only slightly in use facts, differ in meaning facts. Indeed this point has nothing to do with vagueness. Consider a precise word such as 'prime'. It is not a necessary truth that this particular combination of graphic symbols or sounds picks out the property of being prime – there is some possible world w_n in which speakers use the word so differently than we do, that it refers to some completely different property (e.g. the property of being a cat). Moreover, we can construct a series of worlds $w_1, \ldots, w_n$ connecting the actual world w_1 to w_n such that in any two adjacent worlds of the series, the use facts differ only slightly. Since in the actual world 'prime' picks-out the property of being prime and in w_n it does not, there must be two adjacent worlds in the series where the meaning of 'prime' shifts, entailing that there are cases where small shift in use makes for a shift in meaning.

However, for precise terms like 'prime' we can assume that such shifts between close worlds are very rare. One plausible hypothesis of why this is so involves Lewis's theory of eligibility.[18] According to this theory, the meaning of a term is determined by a combination of two factors: first, how well it fits with our use facts, and second how natural the property it picks out is. More natural properties serve as 'reference magnets' – properties that are easier to refer to, which means a wider range of uses succeed in latching on to the property (as long as it's a reasonably good fit for use). Since the property of being prime is a natural one, 'prime' is not semantically plastic: many different use patterns for 'prime' pick out the property of being prime. It is only when use facts diverge so significantly from our current use so as to render primeness no longer a reasonable fit for our use facts that the meaning of the term shifts. However, in all close worlds, 'prime' has the same meaning it actually does.

Why not think that 'tall' follows a similar pattern, namely that it picks out the same property in the actual world and in all close worlds? As we have seen, Williamson's response is that this has to do with the lack of natural properties as candidate meanings for

---

[18] See Lewis (1983).

'tall': since the property of being over 1.781 metres in height seems just as natural as the property of being over 1.782 metres, it is hard to see how a range of different use facts would consistently pick out one property over the other.

Although it *seems* plausible that all candidate meanings for 'tall' are equally natural, some authors have argued that perhaps naturalness is less transparent than is usually assumed in these discussions. That is, it might turn out that unbeknownst to us, the property of being over 1.7812 is much more natural than any other properties in the vicinity.[19] More cautiously, Mahtani argues that although it is implausible *tout court* that some such height property is natural, *conditional* on accepting the (in itself arguably implausible) claim that vague predicates have sharp cut-off points, the additional claim that there are such hidden naturalness facts might be quite likely: after all, it would be far less surprising that a word like 'tall' refers to the property of, say, being over 1.7813 metres in height if it turned out that this property serves as a natural reference magnet. If these suggestions are correct, vague terms are not semantically plastic which would undermine Williamson's explanation of ignorance.[20]

This kind of objection to semantic plasticity is weak in the sense it merely questions whether vague terms must be semantically plastic, but it does not give any reason to think that vague terms are not semantically plastic. However, a stronger direct argument against plasticity is suggested by Dorr and Hawthorne.[21] Suppose that George is telling us about his date with Bill, and mentions that his date wasn't tall. In this situation we can truly utter counterfactuals such as the following:

If George had gone out with Paul instead, he would have said his date was tall!

The problem is that if 'tall' is semantically plastic, it is hard for utterances of such counterfactuals to come out as true. For consider the closest possible world *w* in which George goes out on a date with Paul rather than Bill. In *w*, the use facts of 'tall' are presumably slightly different than the actual ones (for example, in *w* but not in the actual world, George utters the sentence 'Wow, you are pretty tall!' when he first sees his date, adding one more use of the word 'tall'). So by semantic plasticity, 'tall' picks out a slightly different property (call this property 'tall*'). But then in *w* George does not say that his date was tall, since in *w* no sentence George utters in the situation expresses the proposition that his date is tall.[22] Of course, in *w* George might well utter the words 'My date was tall!', but remember that in *w* those words amount to George's saying that his date was tall*. Defenders of semantic plasticity thus at the very least face the challenge of explaining how such a counterfactual can be true.[23]

---

[19] See Mahtani (2004) and Cameron (2010).

[20] Note though that in that case one could offer an alternative explanation of our ignorance of sharp cut-off points in terms of our ignorance of naturalness facts (see Cameron 2010).

[21] See Dorr and Hawthorne (2014), and also related remarks concerning temporal plasticity in Kearns and Magidor (2008, pp. 286–7).

[22] Of course if tallness is the property of being over, say, 1.798 metres in height, George could utter the sentence 'My date was over 1.798 metres in height', but we are assuming that in close worlds George does not make such odd reports about his date.

[23] Dorr and Hawthorne discuss several attempts to respond to this challenge, but show they face serious difficulties. On the other hand, they also raise problems for rejecting plasticity altogether.

Next, consider *Similar Belief*, namely the claim that if in the actual world you have a belief that you would phrase by saying 'A person is tall just in case they are over 1.781 metres in height', then in close worlds you have a corresponding belief that you would put using exactly the same words. Why should we think that in close worlds you would still have a belief that you would express using exactly the same words? Suppose in the actual world you formed your belief about the boundaries of tallness by quick reflection or a guess concerning what the cut-off of tallness might be. In that case, it is very plausible that your guess is not sensitive to subtle differences in use facts, and hence in at least some close worlds where use facts differ slightly, you would endorse exactly the same sentence. The problem, however, is that we do not really need Williamson's sophisticated explanation via semantic plasticity to tell us that guessing or crude reflection are not good methods for acquiring knowledge about subtle matters. What if instead you formed your belief via some very reliable careful method for discovering cut-off points? In that case, we can expect that in worlds where the cut-off point for 'tall' is, say, 1.782 (rather than 1.781) you would apply the same careful method and reach a conclusion that you would put using a different sentence ('A person is tall just in case they are over 1.782 metres in height'). Of course, it is hard to imagine what kind of method could play this role. But Williamson's explanation of ignorance was supposed to go beyond merely noting that we cannot imagine a method by which we might discover the sharp cut-off points of vague terms.[24]

Finally, consider *Meta-Linguistic Safety*. Williamson's account relies on a particular version of the safety principle: one according to which your belief that *s* counts as unsafe (and hence does not constitute knowledge), if there is a close world in which you have a corresponding false belief which is *linguistically* similar, namely a belief that you would phrase using the same words. However, Kearns and Magidor (2008), argue that this kind of meta-linguistic safety is not a necessary condition on knowledge. To do so, they provide a series of cases where an agent has a belief that violates meta-linguistic safety, but arguably nevertheless constitutes knowledge.

Consider for example the following case: suppose that Joe and Bill are two identical twins. The use facts of the community determine that the name 'Joe' picks out the first twin Joe, and the name 'Bill' picks out the other twin, Bill. However, suppose that since it is very easy to confuse the two twins, many times when speakers see Bill they refer to him using the name 'Joe' and vice versa. Let us suppose that these confusions are so frequent, that had a few more speakers mixed the names up, this would have simply shifted the semantic-value of these names: thus, there is a close world *w* where the name 'Bill' refers to Joe and the name 'Joe' refers to Bill.

Now, suppose that Joe spends a year in Australia, far away from his twin brother Bill. In Australia, Joe becomes friends with Jill. Jill comes to know Joe by the (correct) name 'Joe', does not know he has a twin brother, and is under no risk of ever encountering

---

[24] Versions of this objection are raised in Keefe (2000, pp. 74–5), Gómez-Torrente (2002, pp. 112–3), and Kearns and Magidor (2008, pp. 283–8). As Keefe points out, part of the problem is that since we do not really actually believe in particular cut-off points, it is hard to conjecture what methods we would have used if we had such beliefs.

his twin brother. After interacting a lot with Joe, Jill forms the belief that Joe is a nice guy. Suppose Jill's belief is true and based on a lot of excellent evidence (Joe has been a good friend to her, volunteers in the community, and so forth). It seems clear that Jill's belief constitutes knowledge. However, Jill's belief violates meta-linguistic safety. This is so, because in *w*, Jill still has a belief that she would phrase using the sentence 'Joe is a nice guy' (simply because she would mistakenly assume that 'Joe' in *w* picks out Joe). However, for reasons entirely unavailable to Jill, the name 'Joe' in her mouth in *w* picks out Bill. And assuming that Bill is not nice, her *w*-belief would be false, rendering her actual belief not meta-linguistically safe. It is hard to see how her unfortunate linguistic mistake in *w*, though, can impact Jill's knowledge about Joe's niceness in the actual world.

In response to this objection, Williamson could respond as follows: Meta linguistic safety isn't, in full generality, a necessary condition on knowledge. Rather, knowledge requires extended safety, but which beliefs count as similar in the sense required for extended safety is a highly delicate matter that might not be susceptible to philosophical analysis (at least not to non-circular analysis, i.e. one that does not appeal to the concept of knowledge). And while in the particular case of vague terms it turns out that meta-linguistically similar beliefs count as similar, this might not generalise to other cases.[25]

Indeed, similar manoeuvres could be made in response to (nearly) all the objections raised above.[26] That is, the epistemicist could address the worries about whether vague terms really are semantically plastic by stipulating that they are, or whether speakers really do form beliefs using the same sentence in close worlds by stipulating that they do. The idea would then be that the various stipulations figuring in the explanation of ignorance are not intended to be motivated independently of their roles in this explanation. The explanation of ignorance can be thought of in the first instance as merely a model for how the ignorance of vague terms could in principle arise, where the reason for accepting this model as realistic being that it successfully explains why we do not know the sharp boundaries of vague terms.[27]

The question then turns on whether this more modest interpretation of the explanation of ignorance is dialectically satisfying. The answer depends in part on what one expects to achieve from such an explanation. If one is already convinced of the existence of sharp boundaries (for example, because it is entailed by classical logic and mathematics), one might find this sort of model for why they are unknowable highly illuminating. On the other hand, if one starts out as very sceptical that vague predicates even have sharp boundaries,

[25] For a general defence of the claim that safety can only be analysed using the concept of knowledge, see Williamson (2000). For a critical discussion of the use of this claim in the context of explaining our ignorance of vague terms, see Kearns and Magidor (2008, p. 297) and Sennet (2012, p. 279).
[26] I say 'nearly' because I don't think this point helps to address Dorr and Hawthorne's worry.
[27] By analogy, consider an interpretation of Lewis's account of counterfactuals which accepts that there is no non-circular understanding of similarity amongst worlds (i.e. that similarity is explained using counterfactuals). Suppose one wanted to explain why, on one's view, counterfactuals are non-transitive: $A \square\rightarrow B$ and $B \square\rightarrow C$ does not entail $A \square\rightarrow C$. The Lewisian account does offer an explanation in the sense that it provides a model for how this can come about (i.e. if the closest A world is a $B\&\neg C$ world, but there is an even closer world where $\neg A$, B, and C). However, it will not provide any independent argument that this structure is in fact realised, and thus would not convince someone who is sceptical that there are any actual counterexamples to the transitivity of counterfactual conditionals.

but finds the existence of sharp boundaries easier to accept if coupled with a compelling independent argument to the extent that if such boundaries exist they must be principally undiscoverable, this more modest interpretation of Williamson's explanation of ignorance might well fall short.

1.3.4 The Distinctiveness of Vagueness

The fourth challenge for epistemicism was to account for what is distinctive about vagueness. Williamson's response is to maintain vagueness is associated with a distinctive kind of ignorance – one arising due to semantic plasticity.

A general challenge to the characterisation of vagueness in terms of semantic plasticity is suggested by Sennet.[28] Imagine a possible world w, where a community of speakers speak a language very much like English, and indeed use 'tall' just as we do. However, in all worlds close to w, there is a daemon who ensures that 'tall' has exactly the same sharp cut-off point as in w, ensuring that the term is not semantically plastic. (One way the daemon can achieve this is by adding more use facts to exactly balance out variations in use among the other speakers in the community.) The problem is that it seems that in w, the community's use of 'tall' is just as vague as ours and they are equally ignorant of its sharp cut-off point, despite the fact that the term is not semantically plastic.

A natural response to this challenge is to maintain that even if in one sense of 'close' the daemon is present in all close worlds, that is not the sense relevant to our assessment of knowledge. On the relevant understanding of closeness, there are some close worlds on which the daemon is not present allowing the term to be plastic after all. Whether we accept this response is related to the issue discussed at the end of Section 1.3.3, as to whether the explanation of ignorance is intended to rely on an independent understanding of closeness.

Let me turn to an entirely different challenge to the characterisation of vagueness in terms of a particular kind of ignorance due to plasticity. To do so, we first need to note that not every sentence containing vagueness involves ignorance. The word 'tall' is vague, but we still know that 'A person who is two metres in height is tall' or that 'If x is taller than y, then if y is tall so is x'. Rather, ignorance only arises in the case of *borderline* statements. Thus to be more precise, the hypothesis is that borderline statements are characterised in terms of the distinctive kind of ignorance, and vagueness is characterised via its susceptibility to borderline cases. The question is then whether Williamson's account offers an adequate characterisation of borderlineness.

Let us suppose that we are generally sympathetic to Williamson's explanation of ignorance of particular borderline cases. Still, it is surprisingly difficult to extract from this explanation a set of necessary and sufficient conditions for a sentence's being borderline. Following Williamson's explanation of ignorance, we might try the following: a true sentence 's' is borderline[29] just in case there is a close possible world w in which:

---

[28] Sennet (2012).
[29] A false sentence 's' can then be said to be borderline if, and only if, its true negation is borderline.

(i) due to semantic plasticity, 's' expresses in *w* a different proposition than it actually does;

(ii) the proposition 's' expresses in *w* is false in *w*;

(iii) if in the actual world speakers have a belief that they would express using 's', they have a similar belief that they express using the same words in *w*.

As Caie (2012) and Magidor (2016) argue, however, this explanation will not work for the following reason. Suppose that in the actual world the sharp cut-off point for 'tall' is 1.781 metres, and Jill is 1.8 metres tall (let us assume this is sufficient to make her definitely tall). Now consider a close world *w* in which, due to the semantic plasticity of 'tall', the sharp cut-off for 'tall' is 1.782. Assume also that in *w*, Jill is a bit shorter than she actually is: in *w* she is only 1.78 metres tall. The problem is that according to the above account 'Jill is tall' would come out as borderline: the sentence expresses a different proposition in *w* (namely, the proposition that Jill is taller than 1.782 metres in height) and that proposition is false in *w* (because Jill's height in *w* is 1.78 metres < 1.782 metres). Finally, we can simply stipulate that the doxastic attitude of speakers are such as to satisfy clause (iii) of the condition. However, as Jill is definitely tall in the scenario, the prediction that the sentence is borderline is incorrect.

It is clear what went wrong. When assessing whether 'Jill is tall' is borderline, we are interested in close worlds that differ only in the meaning of the word 'tall', not in the underlying conditions relative to which the truth of the sentence is assessed, such as Jill's height. However, it is not obvious how to translate this observation into a condition on borderlineness. Magidor (2016) proposes that we can make progress by appealing to the notion of metaphysical ground. The proposal is to require that whatever facts ultimately ground the fact that *s* (in the actual world) would be held fixed in the close world *w*. Thus, in the above example, what actually grounds the fact that Jill is tall is her precise height (i.e. the fact that she is 1.8 metres tall). But then we should only consider close worlds in which Jill's height is also 1.8 metres, and the above problem would not arise. Even if in a close world *w* 'tall' has a slightly different cut-off than it actually has, 1.8 metres would presumably be above that cut-off, and the proposition expressed by 'Jill is tall' in *w* would be *true* rather than false, so the account would predict that the sentence is not borderline, just as we expected.

However, while this addresses the problem with the current example, it may be too restrictive because of examples such as this. Consider the sentence 'The word 'frequent' is used frequently'. Suppose that 'frequent' is used fairly frequently, so that it is borderline whether the word is used frequently or not. The problem is that part of what metaphysically grounds the fact that 'frequently' is used frequently, is precisely the complete use facts for the word 'frequently'. But if we only consider close worlds in which we are holding fixed these use facts, then due to the supervenience of meaning on use, the word would have exactly the same sharp cut-off as it actually does, so clause (i) of the condition (the requirement that due to semantic plasticity the sentence expresses a different proposition in *w*) will not be satisfied, and the sentence would falsely be predicted to be definite rather than borderline. The problem is that we want to hold fixed the underlying conditions relative to which the sentence is assessed, but in doing so, we are also accidently holding fixed the meaning of the relevant vague words. It is thus not clear that there is any systematic way of *only* holding fixed the underlying conditions, and thus get an adequate characterisation of borderlineness in terms of the distinctive kind of plasticity.

1.4 Concluding Remarks

The epistemicist view of vagueness, offers a straightforward response to the Sorites Paradox. As we have seen, though, the view faces several challenges. We have discussed Williamson's attempt to respond to these challenges and some objections to his responses.

Even if one finds these objections compelling, one should not be too quick to dismiss epistemicism in favour of alternative views. For one thing because in discussing these objections one should be careful not to hold epistemicism to higher standards than the competing views. While our discussion focused on the challenges as they apply to epistemicism, many of these challenges can be equally raised against competing views. Consider the determination of meaning: supervaluationists face the challenge of explaining how our use facts manage to pick out one set of admissible precisifications over another. Or consider the explanation of ignorance: fuzzy logicians face the challenge of why we do not (and apparently cannot) know exactly which degree of truth 'Jill is tall' receives.[30] And even concerning the distinctiveness of vagueness, non-classical views arguably have difficulties in giving a criterion that distinguishes vagueness from other apparent cases of truth-value gaps, e.g. ones due to semantic paradoxes such as the Liar.

Moreover, we should not lose sight of the significant advantages that epistemicism offers: both its full retention of classical logic and semantics, as well as its straightforward treatment of higher-order vagueness. These considerations give us strong reasons to keep developing the details of the view, rather than abandoning it altogether.[31]

---

[30] Of course, supervaluationists or fuzzy logicians might ultimately wish to deny that we succeed in picking out a specific set of admissible precisifications or degrees of truth, but these ways of developing the views bring with them other challenges. (See Chapters 2 and 8 in this volume.)

[31] Thanks to the editors of this volume for their helpful comments on this chapter.

2 Supervaluationism, Subvaluationism and the Sorites Paradox

Pablo Cobreros and Luca Tranchini

2.1 S'valuationism

2.1.1 Motivation

The classical principle of bivalence states that every non-ambiguous declarative sentence has a truth value 'true' or 'false' and not both. But this principle turns problematic when we consider vague predicates. For it is part of the phenomenology of vague predicates that speakers tend to hesitate, not giving a firm answer to the question whether the predicate applies in borderline cases. Imagine we collect a group of competent English speakers and run the following experiment. We show a picture of André the Giant and ask whether André is thin. People will answer 'no' to this question (assuming the question is placed in a normal context, where the relevant comparison class is, say, a Caucasian male). We then show a picture of Mahatma Gandhi and place the corresponding question; people will answer 'yes' this time. Now suppose we show a picture of Tim (where Tim is a borderline case of the predicate 'thin') and we ask whether Tim is thin. Whether they will refuse to give an answer, say 'yes' and 'no' or give some sort of qualified answer, we don't know. What is sure is that they won't show the sort of agreement they had for the previous cases, even if (seemingly) all relevant information about Tim in order to address the question is available. In this sense, competent speakers show a certain kind of symmetry towards assertion and denial in borderline cases. Now, given this sort of symmetry in our dispositions, how can one of the sentences 'Tim is thin' and 'Tim is not thin' be true and the other false? That is, how can meaning make a difference where use seems to see none?[1]

The s'valuationist strategy to deal with vague predicates rests on the idea of *reasonable ways of making precise*: different ways in which we could define a classical extension (a set of objects to which the predicate applies) for a vague predicate. The idea is that objects in the borderline area might belong to some of these classical extensions and not to some others. Thus, there are reasonable ways of making precise the predicate 'thin' that will render the sentence 'Tim is thin' false, and there are ways of making 'thin' precise that will

---

[1] Timothy Williamson holds that it is either true or false that he is thin but that no one knows (and perhaps cannot know) whether he is thin (see Chapter 1 in this volume). In a case of perfect symmetry in use, however, he says he is not thin (Williamson 1994, p. 208).

make the sentence true (by contrast, there is no reasonable way of making 'thin' precise that renders 'André is thin' true). Ways of making precise should respect some meaning-based constraints such as comparative relations and analytic connections between different expressions.[2] If, for example, Franca is older than Bianca, a way of making precise 'is a baby' that counts Franca as a baby but not Bianca is not reasonable, so that 'If Franca is a baby, then Bianca is a baby' is true in every reasonable way of making 'is a baby' precise. Similarly, a way of making precise 'is a baby' that counts Franca as a baby should also count Franca as a child, so that 'Franca is a baby but she is not a child' is false in every reasonable way of making precise these predicates. For this last reason, ways of making precise cannot proceed *locally* but should take into account all expressions of the language (we will later talk about 'precisifications' as ways of making precise all expressions of the language).

In order to respect semantic symmetry the s'valuationist holds that each of these ways of making vague expressions precise are on a par. Now, in relation to the truth-value of sentences, ways of making precise can be on a par in two different ways: disjunctively or conjunctively. We can say that a sentence is true just in case it is true *in some* ways of making the vague expression precise, or that it is true just in case it is true *in all* ways of making the vague expression precise. The first can be dubbed as 'subtruth' and the second as 'supertruth'. Subvaluationism and supervaluationism differ on precisely which is the relevant notion of truth.[3]

The disjunctive and conjunctive feature of the truth-definition of subvaluationism and supervaluationism, respectively, makes these theories both very different and very similar. Very different because they instantiate apparently opposite logical and semantic characteristics: paraconsistency versus paracompleteness, overdetermination versus underdetermination. Very similar because each of these opposite properties are a sort of mirror image of the other. We will call this symmetry *duality* and will characterise it as an equivalence at the level of inferences between the subvaluationist and supervaluationist logics: an inference holds in one logic exactly when the contrapositive inference holds in the other logic.

2.1.2 S'valuationism, More Formally

The foregoing ideas can be put in a more formal dress. Before that, though, we should consider two remarks. Firstly, the s'valuationist theory is, primarily, a theory about the meaning of vague expressions and, as such, the perspective of this section will be primarily semantic. We discuss proof theoretic aspects of the theory in the third part of the chapter. Secondly, s'valuationist logics are sensitive to the choice of *framework* and to the choice of language.[4]

---

[2] These are called *penumbral connections* in Fine's classical paper (Fine 1975, p. 270); Fine takes this feature as the main argument for supervaluationism.

[3] The term 'supervaluationism' comes from van Fraassen's work on free logic (van Fraassen 1966). The idea goes back to Mehlberg (1958, pp. 256–9) as pointed out in the introduction fn. 37, but the classical locus is Fine (1975). A more recent defence can be found in Keefe (2000). The classical paper on subvaluationism as applied to vagueness is Hyde (1997). According to Hyde, central ideas of subvaluationism applied to vagueness go back to Jaśkowski (1948).

[4] The terminology is taken from Humberstone (2011, chapter 1.12).

For example, in the classical propositional language, supervaluationist consequence for the multiple-premises/single-conclusion framework is equivalent to classical propositional consequence. But when we allow arguments with multiple conclusions, supervaluationist logic no longer coincides with classical logic, even for the classical propositional language. In this section we will stick to the multiple-premises/multiple-conclusions framework and will introduce s'valuationist logics for the classical propositional language and for the language augmented with a simple modality. We will opportunely point out relevant aspects of the logics for different frameworks.

We will review a number of facts relating the different logics under discussion. In order to avoid verbosity we have decided to give a proof sketch of those that might be not completely obvious or that might give an insight to these relations.

2.1.3 The Classical Propositional Language

Let $\mathcal{L}$ be the classical propositional language with a denumerable set of propositional variables: $p, q, r \ldots$, classical constants: $\wedge, \vee, \supset, \neg$ and parenthesis: (and). As is well known, a classical interpretation for this language is a mapping from variables to the set of truth-values true or false (that is, an interpretation is a function $\mathbb{I} : Var \longrightarrow \{0, 1\}$). An interpretation for propositional variables extends to any other formula of the language according to the following clauses:

- $\mathbb{I}(A \wedge B) = 1$ iff $\mathbb{I}(A) = \mathbb{I}(B) = 1$
- $\mathbb{I}(A \vee B) = 0$ iff $\mathbb{I}(A) = \mathbb{I}(B) = 0$
- $\mathbb{I}(A \supset B) = 0$ iff $\mathbb{I}(A) = 1$ and $\mathbb{I}(B) = 0$
- $\mathbb{I}(\neg A) = 1$ iff $\mathbb{I}(A) = 0$

A way of making precise the vague predicate 'thin' will give us a candidate extension for the predicate and, therefore, a corresponding truth-value for any sentence of the form 't is thin' (where t is any singular term). Since we are dealing with a propositional language, by 'a way of making precise a predicate' we will directly understand a way of assigning a truth-value to those sentences involving the predicate. Further, since ways of making precise cannot proceed locally (as they must respect *penumbral connections*) we will directly talk about *precisifications*. A precisification is, informally, a way of making precise *all* vague predicates of the language. Formally speaking, a precisification is an assignment of truth-values to all (atomic) sentences of the language. That is, a precisification is a classical interpretation.

A s'valuationist interpretation $\mathbb{S}$ is a set of classical interpretations: $\mathbb{I}', \mathbb{I}'' \ldots$. We will say that a formula A is *subtrue* just in case $\mathbb{I}(A) = 1$ for at least one $\mathbb{I} \in \mathbb{S}$ and that A is *supertrue* in $\mathbb{S}$ just in case $\mathbb{I}(A) = 1$ for all $\mathbb{I} \in \mathbb{S}$. The concepts of *supertruth* and *subtruth* are *duals* in much the same way the quantifiers '$\exists$' and '$\forall$' are. In particular, A is subtrue in a s'valuationist interpretation $\mathbb{S}$ just in case $\neg A$ is not supertrue in $\mathbb{S}$.

Since logical consequence is a matter of necessary preservation of truth, it will depend on what is the relevant notion of truth. For subvaluationists logical consequence is the preservation of subtruth in all s'valuationist interpretations:

Δ is a subvaluationist consequence of Γ, written $\Gamma \vDash_{SbV} \Delta$, just in case there is no $\mathbb{S}$ such that

$$\text{for all } A \in \Gamma \text{ there is a } \mathbb{I} \in \mathbb{S}, \mathbb{I}(A) = 1 \text{ and}$$
$$\text{for all } B \in \Delta \text{ and all } \mathbb{I} \in \mathbb{S}, \mathbb{I}(B) = 0^5$$

For supervaluationists, logical consequence is the preservation of supertruth in all s'valuationist interpretations:[6]

Δ is a supervaluationist consequence of Γ, written $\Gamma \vDash_{SpV} \Delta$, just in case there is no $\mathbb{S}$ such that

$$\text{for all } A \in \Gamma \text{ and all } \mathbb{I} \in \mathbb{S}, \mathbb{I}(A) = 1 \text{ and}$$
$$\text{for all } B \in \Delta \text{ there is a } \mathbb{I} \in \mathbb{S}, \mathbb{I}(B) = 0$$

Though the formal definitions might appear a bit intricate, the informal reading is easy: $\Gamma \vDash_{SbV} \Delta$ just in case there is no s'valuationist interpretation where all premises are subtrue and no conclusion is subtrue. Similarly, $\Gamma \vDash_{SpV} \Delta$ just in case there is no s'valuationist interpretation where all premises are supertrue while no conclusion is supertrue.

The concept of *subtruth* fits with the idea that vagueness is a matter of *over*determination of meaning: in borderline cases sentences are both subtrue and subfalse. The concept of *supertruth* fits with the idea that vagueness is a matter of *under*determination of meaning: in borderline cases sentences are neither supertrue nor superfalse. Corresponding to this, subvaluationist consequence is *paraconsistent* in the sense that the set of formulas $\{A, \neg A\}$ is satisfiable. Similarly, supervaluationist consequence is *paracomplete* in the sense that the set of formulas $\{A, \neg A\}$ is not valid. The way in which subvaluationist consequence is paraconsistent and supervaluationist consequence is paracompelete is peculiar, though. We present some results about subvaluationist, supervaluationist consequence and classical logic first and return to that point afterwards.

Duality follows again from the definition of the concepts of *subtruth* and *supertruth*. In particular, subvaluationist and supervaluationist consequence are each other's duals in the sense that

Fact 1 (Duality)

$$\Gamma \vDash_{SbV} \Delta \iff \neg(\Delta) \vDash_{SpV} \neg(\Gamma) \qquad (\text{where: } \neg(\Sigma) = \{\neg A \mid A \in \Sigma\})$$

---

[5] We will write $\vDash \Delta$ for $\emptyset \vDash \Delta$ and $\Gamma \vDash$ for $\Gamma \vDash \emptyset$. In the multiple-premises/multiple-conclusions framework the empty set on the left works as a tautology and on the right as a contradiction, therefore '$\vDash \Delta$' means 'the set Δ is valid' and '$\Gamma \vDash$' means 'the set Γ is not satisfiable'. We also write $\Gamma \vDash A$ instead of $\Gamma \vDash \{A\}$.

[6] Though this is the classical view, some authors claim that supervaluationism is compatible with the understanding of truth as *local truth* and, correspondingly, with logical consequence as *local consequence*. We believe with Williamson (1995a) that this is not true. See Section 2.2.5 for discussion of this.

$\Gamma \nvDash_{SbV} \Delta$ means that there is a s'valuationist interpretation such that for each A in Γ there is at least a point where A is true while all B in Δ are false everywhere. Equivalently, for each B in Δ, $\neg B$ is true everywhere while for each A in Γ there is at least a point where $\neg A$ is false. That is, $\neg(\Delta) \nvDash_{SpV} \neg(\Gamma)$ □

This fact might help the comparison of these logics with classical logic. Both logics share some affinities to classical logic for the classical language.[7] To begin with, all three have the same sets of valid and unsatisfiable formulas (we write $\vDash A$ to mean validity and $A \vDash$ to mean unsatisfiability). There are two key ideas to understand this connection: first, that precisifications are classical interpretations and, second, that within the classical language we cannot rule out s'valuationist interpretations containing a single precisification.

Fact 2 $A \vDash_{CL} \Longleftrightarrow A \vDash_{SpV}$ (cf. Fine 1975, pp. 283–4, Keefe 2000, pp. 175–6)

Suppose A is false in all classical interpretations. Then there is no s'valuationist interpretation where A is supertrue (since these are made out of classical interpretations). Suppose now that A is (classically) true in a classical interpretation $\mathbb{I}$, then it is supertrue in at least one s'valuationist interpretation (to wit: $\mathbb{S} = \{\mathbb{I}\}$).   □

Classical consequence is self-dual in the sense that an inference is classically valid just in case its contrapositive is classically valid. Therefore $\vDash_{CL} A$ iff $\neg A \vDash_{CL}$ iff $\neg A \vDash_{SpV}$ (by the previous fact) iff $\vDash_{SbV} A$ (by the duality between $\vDash_{SpV}$ and $\vDash_{SbV}$). Thus, collecting the iffs, $\vDash_{CL} A$ iff $\vDash_{SbV} A$. Similar arguments show the following

Fact 3 $A \vDash_{SpV} \Longleftrightarrow A \vDash_{CL} \Longleftrightarrow A \vDash_{SbV}$ and $\vDash_{SbV} A \Longleftrightarrow \vDash_{CL} A \Longleftrightarrow \vDash_{SpV} A$

which tells us that the three logics agree on the set of valid formulas and on the set of unsatisfiable formulas. In fact, the agreement with classical logic extends for the supervaluationist case when we allow for more premises (adding more than one thing on the left) and for the subvaluationist case when we allow for more conclusions (adding more things on the right).

Fact 4 $\Gamma \vDash_{SpV} A \Longleftrightarrow \Gamma \vDash_{CL} A$

If $\Gamma \nvDash_{SpV} A$, then there is a s'valuationist interpretation $\mathbb{S}$ where all elements of Γ are supertrue but A is not. But then, any of the $\mathbb{I} \in \mathbb{S}$ where A is not true is a countermodel showing $\Gamma \nvDash_{CL} A$. Suppose now that $\Gamma \nvDash_{CL} A$ and let $\mathbb{I}$ be the corresponding countermodel. Then $\mathbb{S} = \{\mathbb{I}\}$ is a countermodel showing $\Gamma \nvDash_{SpV} A$.   □

Duality yields the corresponding result for $\vDash_{SbV}$:

[7] Cf. the introduction to this volume, fn. 22.

Fact 5 $A \vDash_{SbV} \Gamma \iff A \vDash_{CL} \Gamma$

These facts show that $\vDash_{SpV}$ coincides with classical logic for multiple-premises/single-conclusion arguments and subvaluationism coincides with classical logic for single-premise/multiple-conclusions arguments (in the form of the slogan: $\vDash_{SpV}$'s classicality extends to the left, $\vDash_{SbV}$'s classicality extends to the right).

Fact 6 $\Gamma \vDash_{CL} \Delta \not\Longrightarrow \Gamma \vDash_{SpV} \Delta$

In particular: $\vDash_{CL} A, \neg A$ since in every classical interpretation either $\mathbb{I}(A) = 1$ or $\mathbb{I}(\neg A) = 1$ but $\not\vDash_{SpV} A, \neg A$ since there is a s'valuationist interpretation $\mathbb{S} = \{\mathbb{I}', \mathbb{I}''\}$ where $\mathbb{I}'(A) = 1$ and $\mathbb{I}''(A) = 0$. □

Fact 7 $\Gamma \vDash_{CL} \Delta \not\Longrightarrow \Gamma \vDash_{SbV} \Delta$

In particular: $A, \neg A \vDash_{CL}$ but $A, \neg A \not\vDash_{SbV}$. □

A paraconsistent logic is one in which *Explosion* ($A, \neg A \vDash$) fails. A paracomplete logic is one in which *Implosion* ($\vDash A, \neg A$) fails. $\vDash_{SpV}$ and $\vDash_{SbV}$ are, respectively, paracomplete and paraconsistent logics, but they are paracomplete or paraconsistent in a peculiar way. Recall that $\vDash_{SpV}$ and $\vDash_{SbV}$ agree with classical logic in the set of valid and unsatisfiable formulas and, therefore, $\vDash_{SpV} A \vee \neg A$ and $A \wedge \neg A \vDash_{SbV}$. Thus, these logics are *weakly* paracomplete and *weakly* paraconsistent logics.[8] Another way to look at this peculiarity is noticing that the following fails:

Conjoining premises, disjoining conclusions: $\Gamma \vDash \Delta \iff \Gamma' \vDash \Delta'$
(where Γ' comes from Γ by possibly conjoining some of its members and Δ' from Δ by possibly disjoining some of its members).

In $\vDash_{SbV}$ the comma in the premises and conjunction work in a different way, because though $A, \neg A \not\vDash_{SbV}$ we have that $A \wedge \neg A \vDash_{SbV}$. The same goes for the comma in the conclusions and disjunction for $\vDash_{SpV}$ since we have $\vDash_{SpV} A \vee \neg A$ but $\not\vDash_{SpV} A, \neg A$. This fact is connected to the more general claim that $\vDash_{SpV}$ and $\vDash_{SbV}$ are not *truth-functional* (see Section 2.2.2).

2.1.4 The $\mathbb{D}$-Augmented Language

Within theories motivated by borderline cases, it is natural to consider the language augmented with a *definiteness* operator, so that a is a borderline case of a predicate P just in case neither $\mathbb{D}Pa$ nor $\mathbb{D}\neg Pa$. Though $\mathbb{D}$ is not a classical connective, in the context of theories of vagueness the 'classical logic' for $\mathbb{D}$ corresponds to some normal modal logic.[9] Modal semantics (Kripke models) have a natural s'valuationist interpretation and provide in this way a natural s'valuationist reading of $\mathbb{D}$.

---

[8] See Hyde (2007, pp. 75–6). Hyde credits this terminology to Arruda (1989). For strongly paracomplete and paraconsistent approaches see Chapters 6 and 7 in this volume respectively.

[9] As an example, Williamson, who is committed to classical logic, adopts a normal modal logic for $\mathbb{D}$ (Williamson 1994, chapter 8, Appendix).

Formulas of our augmented language have this aspect: $\mathbb{D}A \supset A$, $\neg\mathbb{D}A \wedge \neg\mathbb{D}\neg A$, $\mathbb{D}(A \supset B) \supset (\mathbb{D}A \supset \mathbb{D}B)$. An interpretation for this language will be a triple $\langle W, R, \mathbb{I} \rangle$ where W is a non-empty set, R a relation in W and $\mathbb{I}$ a function from variables and elements of W to the set of truth-values $\{1, 0\}$.

Informally W is a set of *precisifications* since possible worlds in Kripke models, like precisifications, are classical interpretations. The relation R between precisifications records the idea that whether some precisification is reasonable might vary from precisification to precisification.[10] In Kripke models this relation is used to obtain systems of modal logic weaker than S5. The semantics for S5 does not permit higher-order indeterminacy, so this relation seems to be required if we want to make room for higher order vagueness (see Section 2.2.4).

An interpretation $\langle W, R, \mathbb{I} \rangle$ extends to the formulas of the language in the expected way (we write $\mathbb{I}_w(A) = 1$ to mean that the formula A takes value 1 in precisification w):

- $\mathbb{I}_w(A \wedge B) = 1$ iff $\mathbb{I}_w(A) = \mathbb{I}_w(B) = 1$
- $\mathbb{I}_w(A \vee B) = 0$ iff $\mathbb{I}_w(A) = \mathbb{I}_w(B) = 0$
- $\mathbb{I}_w(A \supset B) = 0$ iff $\mathbb{I}_w(A) = 1$ and $\mathbb{I}_w(B) = 0$
- $\mathbb{I}_w(\neg A) = 1$ iff $\mathbb{I}_w(A) = 0$
- $\mathbb{I}_w(\mathbb{D}A) = 1$ iff   for all $w^{\dagger}$, if $wRw^{\dagger}$ then $\mathbb{I}_{w^{\dagger}}(A) = 1$

The definition of $\mathbb{D}$ captures the idea of *definiteness* in s'valuationist semantics: that something is definite (in a given precisification) means that it is true in all precisifications (relative to that first precisification). The particular behavior of $\mathbb{D}$ will depend on the constraints placed over the relation R. It is generally agreed that the notion of *definiteness* connected to vagueness requires R to be reflexive, but there's not much more consensus than that (see Williamson 1994, p. 159; Varzi 2007b, p. 639).

In normal modal logics, logical consequence is standardly defined as preservation of truth in each world of each interpretation (called 'local consequence' below). This corresponds to the idea that the relevant notion of truth is 'truth in a world'. Supervaluationist and subvaluationist logics depart from standard modal logics in this point. For the supervaluationist, truth is supertruth, that is 'truth in all worlds'; logical consequence should, therefore, preserve this property (this is called 'global consequence' below). Subvaluationists, in turn, are committed to preservation of subtruth, 'truth in some world', called 'subvaluationist consequence' below.

Δ is a local consequence of Γ, written $\Gamma \vDash_{\mathsf{L}} \Delta$, just in case there is no interpretation $\langle W, R, \mathbb{I} \rangle$ and $w \in W$ such that

$$\text{for all } A \in \Gamma \ \mathbb{I}_w(A) = 1 \text{ and for all } B \in \Delta \ \mathbb{I}_w(B) = 0$$

Δ is a global consequence of Γ, written $\Gamma \vDash_{\mathsf{G}} \Delta$, just in case there is no interpretation $\langle W, R, \mathbb{I} \rangle$ such that

---

[10] See Williamson (1994, pp. 159–60) for a more detailed presentation.

for all $A \in \Gamma$ and all $w \in W$ $\mathbb{I}_w(A) = 1$ and
for all $B \in \Delta$ there is a $w \in W$ such that $\mathbb{I}_w(B) = 0$

Δ is a subvaluationist consequence of Γ, written $\Gamma \vDash_S \Delta$, just in case there is no $\langle W, R, \mathbb{I}\rangle$ such that

for all $A \in \Gamma$ there is a $w \in W$ such that $\mathbb{I}_w(A) = 1$ and
for all $B \in \Delta$ and all $w \in W$ $\mathbb{I}_w(B) = 0$

We saw that, for the classical propositional language, subvaluationist and supervaluationist logics contain the same set of valid and unsatisfiable formulas. For the $\mathbb{D}$-augmented language the connection is even weaker. The set of subvaluationist unsatisfiable formulas coincides with the set of locally unsatisfiable formulas and the set of globally valid formulas coincides with the set of locally valid formulas.

Fact 8

(i) $\vDash_G A \Longleftrightarrow \vDash_L A$
(ii) $A \vDash_S \Longleftrightarrow A \vDash_L$

On the other hand, the set of locally valid sentences is strictly included in the set of subvaluationist valid sentences, and the set of locally valid sentences is strictly included in the set of globally unsatisfiable sentences. The first bit of this is given in the following fact:

Fact 9
$\vDash_L A \Longrightarrow \vDash_S A$
$A \vDash_L \Longrightarrow A \vDash_G$

To see that the inclusion is strict, consider the sentence $\neg A \vee \mathbb{D}A$. This sentence is not locally valid (it is equivalent to $A \supset \mathbb{D}A$), but it is subvaluationist valid since, in those interpretations where $\neg A$ is false everywhere (against the first disjunct), $\mathbb{D}A$ is true somewhere (actually, everywhere). Dually, $A \wedge \neg\mathbb{D}A$ is locally, but not globally, satisfiable.

Attending to inferences involving non-empty premises and conclusions, the following pair of inferences are noteworthy,

Fact 10 [$\mathbb{D}$-intro and $\neg\mathbb{D}$-elim]

(a) $A \vDash_G \mathbb{D}A$[11]
(b) $\neg\mathbb{D}A \vDash_S \neg A$

These two inferences are not locally valid. The local validity of inference (a) would easily trivialise the modality: since by *Conditional Proof* we could obtain $\vDash A \supset \mathbb{D}A$, which added to a system as strong as T (the system corresponding to models where accessibility is reflexive) would lead to the Trivial system (the system corresponding to models with a

---

[11] This inference must not be confused with *Necessitation* in normal modal logics: necessitation says that *the validity* of A guarantees *the validity* of $\Box A$, in rule form: $\vDash A \Longrightarrow \vDash \Box A$.

Table 2.1 *Some classical metainferences*

Name	Premises		Conclusion
Conditional Proof	$A \models B$	$\Longrightarrow$	$\models A \supset B$
Contraposition	$A \models B$	$\Longrightarrow$	$\neg B \models \neg A$
Proof by cases	$A \models B$ & $C \models B$	$\Longrightarrow$	$A \vee C \models B$
Contradiction	$A \models B$ & $A \models \neg B$	$\Longrightarrow$	$\models \neg A$

single reflexive world) where modalities play no role in the truth-conditions of formulas (see for more details Hughes and Cresswell 1996, pp. 64–8). This fact calls attention to the failure of *Conditional Proof* in global consequence. Together with *Conditional Proof* some classical metainferences fail for supervaluationist logic for the $\mathbb{D}$ augmented language.[12]

Consider, for example, *Proof by Cases*. We have $A \models_G \mathbb{D}A$ and so we also have $A \models_G \mathbb{D}A \vee \mathbb{D}\neg A$. For identical reasons, $\neg A \models_G \mathbb{D}A \vee \mathbb{D}\neg A$. But, on the other hand, $A \vee \neg A \nvDash_G \mathbb{D}A \vee \mathbb{D}\neg A$. The verification of other cases is left to the reader. We come back to the failure of these metainferences in Section 2.3.

In order to conclude this section we point at two different ways in which we can connect global and local consequence on the one hand and subvaluationist and local consequence on the other. The first makes use of a *universal modality* and shows a straightforward connection between these forms of consequence. The second is more indirect but avoids the use of expressions not already in the language.

Universal modality. $\mathbb{I}_w(\mathbb{D}^u A) = 1$ iff for all $w^\dagger$ $\mathbb{I}_{w^\dagger}(A) = 1$

The difference between the universal modality $\mathbb{D}^u$ and the standard modality $\mathbb{D}$ is that the second is restricted to R-related worlds, while the first quantifies over all worlds in an interpretation without restriction. Let's write $\mathbb{D}^u(\Sigma)$ for the set $\{\mathbb{D}^u A \mid A \in \Sigma\}$ and $\neg\mathbb{D}^u\neg(\Sigma)$ for $\{\neg\mathbb{D}^u\neg A \mid A \in \Sigma\}$.

Fact 11

(a) $\Gamma \models_G \Delta \iff \mathbb{D}^u(\Gamma) \models_L \mathbb{D}^u(\Delta)$

(b) $\Gamma \models_S \Delta \iff \neg\mathbb{D}^u\neg(\Gamma) \models_L \neg\mathbb{D}^u\neg(\Delta)$ (cf. Cobreros 2008)

The second way of connecting global and subvaluationist consequence to local validity proceeds in two steps. We first connect global and local consequence for multiple-premises/

---

[12] Subvaluationist logic for the $\mathbb{D}$-augmented language also fail to validate some classical metainferences, this time resting on the inference $\neg\mathbb{D}A \models_S \neg A$. Consider, for example, the case of *Contradiction* in Table 2.1. We have that $\neg\mathbb{D}A \wedge \neg\mathbb{D}\neg A \models_S \neg A$ and $\neg\mathbb{D}A \wedge \neg\mathbb{D}\neg A \models_S A$, but $\nvDash_S \mathbb{D}A \vee \mathbb{D}\neg A$.

single-conclusion arguments via the *generated submodel theorem*. We then show a connection between global consequence for multiple-premises/single-conclusion arguments and global consequence for multiple-premises/multiple-conclusions arguments. Duality provides the corresponding relations for subvaluationist consequence.

Lemma 1 (Generated submodel)[13] Let Γ be a set of formulas and $\langle W, R, \mathbb{I} \rangle$ an interpretation with a point $w_0 \in W$ such that $\mathbb{I}_{w_0}(A) = 1$ for all $A \in \Gamma$. Then, the interpretation $\langle W^\dagger, R^\dagger, \mathbb{I}^\dagger \rangle$ defined:

- $W^\dagger = \{w \mid w_0 R^n w\}$ $(n \in \omega)$
  ('R^n' means 'n steps along the relation R')
- $R^\dagger$ and $\mathbb{I}^\dagger$ are the restrictions of R and $\mathbb{I}$ to $W^\dagger$,

is such that $\mathbb{I}^\dagger_{w_0}(A) = 1$ for all $A \in \Gamma$

This lemma captures the idea that the value of formulas in a given world w_0 cannot depend on worlds that are not connected to w_0 in any finite number of R-steps.

$\mathbb{D}^\omega$**-set.** $\mathbb{D}^\omega \Gamma = \{\mathbb{D}^n A \mid A \in \Gamma, \ n \in \omega\}.$

That is, $\mathbb{D}^\omega \Gamma$ contains all the elements of Γ plus all the elements of Γ prefixed with $\mathbb{D}$, plus all the elements of Γ prefixed with $\mathbb{DD}$ and so on.

Fact 12 $\Gamma \vDash_G A \iff \mathbb{D}^\omega \Gamma \vDash_L A$

The right to left direction is quite straightforward. Lemma 1 plays a role in the left to right direction. Assume $\mathbb{D}^\omega \Gamma \nvDash_L A$: this means that there is an interpretation with a world w_0 where all elements of $\mathbb{D}^\omega \Gamma$ are true and A is false. This interpretation might still not be an interpretation showing $\Gamma \nvDash_G A$ because it might contain some worlds w^* where some of the elements of Γ are not true. But because all elements of $\mathbb{D}^\omega \Gamma$ are true in w_0 these worlds w^* cannot be reached from w_0 in a finite number of R-steps. By Lemma 1 the generated submodel starting from w_0 shows that $\Gamma \nvDash_G A$. See Cobreros (2013, p. 481). □

Let $\neg \mathbb{D} \neg^\omega \Gamma$ be the set $\{\neg \mathbb{D} \neg^n A \mid A \in \Gamma, \ n \in \omega\}$. The dual of Fact 12 gives us the corresponding connection between subvaluationist and local consequence.

Fact 13 $A \vDash_S \Gamma \iff A \vDash_L \neg \mathbb{D} \neg^\omega \Gamma$

Fact 14 $\Gamma \vDash_G \Delta \iff \exists A \in \Delta : \Gamma \vDash_G A$

The right to left direction is trivial. For the other, suppose that there is no $A \in \Delta$ for which $\Gamma \vDash_G A$. This means that for each $A \in \Delta$ there is a model $\langle W, R, \mathbb{I} \rangle_A$ such that:

$\mathbb{I}_w(B) = 1$ for all $B \in \Gamma$ and all $w \in W$ and $\mathbb{I}_w(A) = 0$ for some $w \in W$

---

[13] See Blackburn et al. (2001, p. 56). Humberstone (2011, p. 285) credits this theorem to Segerberg (1971).

Let all these models be disjoint; that is, if $\mathcal{W}$ is the set containing all the sets of worlds W in any of these models, $\bigcap \mathcal{W} = \emptyset$ (similarly, let's call $\mathcal{R}$ and $\mathcal{I}$ to the set of all R and all $\mathbb{I}$ in these models). Next consider the result of pasting together all these models, $\mathcal{M} = \langle W^\dagger, R^\dagger, \mathbb{I}^\dagger \rangle$ where

- $W^\dagger = \bigcup \mathcal{W}$
- $R^\dagger = \bigcup \mathcal{R}$
- $\mathbb{I}^\dagger = \bigcup \mathcal{I}$

Note that, except for universality, properties of R in all the original models like reflexivity and transitivity are preserved. This means that in the absence of a universal modality, the new model won't change the truth value of any formula. This model shows that $\Gamma \nvDash_G \Delta$ $\square$

Fact 15 $\Gamma \vDash_S \Delta \iff \exists A \in \Gamma : A \vDash_S \Delta$

A proof of this fact is the dual of Fact 14. $\square$

These last facts show that in the case of global validity, the extension to multiple conclusions is somewhat trivial, since the inference from a set of premises to a set of conclusions is valid just in case the premise set entails at least one formula in the conclusion set. Dually, an inference with multiple premises and multiple conclusions is subvaluationist valid just in case the conclusion set is entailed by at least one of the premises.

2.2 Sorites and More

2.2.1 The Sorites Paradox

Imagine we have a long enough series $\langle a_1, a_2 \ldots a_n \rangle$ of patches of colour. The first is red, the last is not red, but the difference in colour of each adjacent patch cannot be judged by the naked eye. Vague predicates seem *tolerant* in the sense that small differences in the relevant properties do not warrant a difference in the applicability of the predicate, although large differences do.[14] For example, since the difference in colour between adjacent patches is so small, it seems that from the fact that a_1 is red, it follows that a_2 is red as well. More generally, tolerance supports the truth of all conditionals in the following list:

$red(a_1) \supset red(a_2)$
$red(a_2) \supset red(a_3)$
$\vdots$
$red(a_{n-1}) \supset red(a_n)$

Now in classical logic, the fact that the first item in the series is red coupled with the conditionals in the list entail (by several applications of *modus ponens*) that the last item in

---

[14] See 'The Sorites Paradox', in the introduction to this volume, and Chapter 5, Section 5.2.

the series is red. So the fact that the last item in the series is not red together with the fact that the first is red classically entails that some conditional in the list is false. Let this false conditional be

$$red(a_k) \supset red(a_{k+1})$$

Classical logic is intolerant since not all conditionals in the list above can be true. Further, classical logic is clearly intolerant, since some conditional in the list above *is false*: its antecedent is true and its consequent false; that is, a_k is the last red item in the series. Tolerance can also be expressed in the form of a single principle:

(Tol) $\forall x \, (red(a_x) \supset red(a_{x+1}))$

For the reasons given above, this principle is classically false, showing once again the intolerant character of classical logic.

Supervaluationism and subvaluationism provide different kind of responses to the Sorites Paradox. *Modus ponens* is valid by supervaluationist standards, and it's also valid joining any number of applications of the rule (that is, the logic is also transitive).[15] Therefore, as in the classical case, the fact that the first item in the series is red together with the conditionals entails that the last item is red. For this reason, not all conditionals in the list can be true (supertrue). But this last claim does not entail that some conditional *is false* (superfalse). In fact, the vagueness of *red* guarantees that no such conditional is false. For suppose that the conditional

$$red(a_k) \supset red(a_{k+1})$$

is false (superfalse). This entails '$red(a_k)$' is true in all precisifications and '$red(a_{k+1})$' is false in all precisifications. But under such a circumstance, no other precisification is admissible. For imagine an alternative precisification that renders, say, $red(a_{k+2})$ true. Given that $red(a_{k+1})$ is false in every precisification, it is false in that alternative precisification and the conditional expressing the penumbral connection $red(a_{k+2}) \supset red(a_{k+1})$ would then be false in that alternative precisification (recall our discussion about *penumbral connections* in Section 2.1). So supervaluationism is intolerant, in the sense that not all conditionals are true, but it is not clearly intolerant, in contrast to classical semantics, since none of them are false.

The situation in the subvaluationist case is different. As we just explained, none of the conditionals above is false in every interpretation; that is, all conditionals are true (subtrue). But the first item of the series is red and the last is not red, not even in the thin sense

---

[15] See Zardini (2008), Cobreros et al. (2012) and Chapter 9 in this volume for tolerant and non-transitive approaches to the Sorites Paradox.

of *subtruth*, since it is red in no precisification. These pieces together show that *modus ponens* does not preserve subtruth.[16] Indeed, consider the case of the pair $\langle a_j, a_{j+1}\rangle$ such that $red(a_j)$ is subtrue but $red(a_{j+1})$ is not. For familiar reasons, $red(a_j)$ must also be *subfalse*: there is at least one precisification where the sentence is false. That precisification shows that the conditional $a_j \supset a_{j+1}$ is subtrue. So the situation is this: subtrue conditional, subtrue antecedent but not subtrue consequent! So in some sense, the subvaluationist response to the Sorites Paradox looks more tolerant than the supervaluationist, since according to the first all conditionals are true. As Zardini (2008, p. 339) points out, however, the failure of *modus ponens* deprives the tolerance principle of its intended force.

The responses to the Sorites Paradox given super- and subvaluationism change when we consider the formulation involving the tolerance principle. According to the s'valuationist semantics, from the list above, some conditionals are true in all precisifications and some are true just in some precisifications, but no conditional is false in all precisifications. One would expect, then, that the universal generalisation (Tol) be not true in all precisifications but not false in all precisifications either. Unexpected as it might be, (Tol) is false in every precisification since in every precisification there is a falsifying instance (though the falsifying instance is not the same in every precisification). Similarly, the negation of (Tol)

$$(\neg\text{Tol}) \quad \exists x\, (red(a_x) \wedge \neg red(a_{x+1}))$$

is true in every precisification, since in every precisification there is a verifying instance (the verifying instance, however, is not the same in every precisification).

This situation is interpreted dually in each s'valuationist theory. For the supervaluationist, the falsity (superfalsity) of a universal generalisation does not entail a falsifying instance (a superfalse instance). Equivalently, the supertruth of an existential generalisation does not entail a verifying instance (a supertrue instance). ($\neg$Tol) is true, the supervaluationist agrees, but the previous feature of supervaluationist semantics prevents the commitment to a sharp boundary (Keefe 2000, pp. 164–5). For the subvaluationist, the truth (subtruth) of all instances of a universal generalisation does not entail the truth of the generalisation itself, and the falsity of all instances of an existential generalisation does not entail the falsity of the generalisation itself.

The tolerance principle (Tol) is equivalent to the conjunction of all tolerant conditionals in the Sorites Paradox above. This leads to the following objection by the defender of supervaluationism. The subvaluationist says that the argument is not valid when taking the conditionals as multiple premises, and says that the argument is valid but unsound when taking the conditionals joined by conjunction into a single premise. This, the supervaluationist continues, looks bad, since the subvaluationist is committed to different responses to what seems to be in essence the same argument (see Keefe 2000, pp. 199–200).

---

[16] Subvaluationist logic, like supervaluationist logic, is transitive.

The previous is certainly an unappealing aspect of subvaluationism. But is not the supervaluationist theory guilty of the same sort of sin? Consider this variation of the Sorites Paradox:

$red(a_1) \wedge \neg red(a_n)$
∴
$(red(a_1) \wedge \neg red(a_2)) \vee (red(a_2) \wedge \neg red(a_3)) \vee \cdots \vee (red(a_{n-1}) \wedge \neg red(a_n))$

Informally the argument says: from the fact that the first item is red and that the last is not, it follows that there is a last red item. This argument is classically valid and, since it has a single conclusion, it is supervaluationist valid as well. The response by the supervaluationist is well known: the validity of this argument does not commit the theory to a sharp boundary since the truth of that disjunction does not entail the truth of some disjunct. In terms of arguments this response amounts to the following claim: although the argument above is supervaluationist valid, the following argument is not:

$red(a_1) \wedge \neg red(a_n)$
∴
$(red(a_1) \wedge \neg red(a_2)), (red(a_2) \wedge \neg red(a_3)), \ldots (red(a_{n-1}) \wedge \neg red(a_n))$

So, in order to address the Sorites Paradox, the supervaluationist is committed to the claim that two arguments that seem to be essentially the same argument are crucially distinct.

The last retort of the supervaluationist seems to be this: although both subvaluationism and supervaluationism fail some very intuitive connections (multiple premises and conjunction in the case of subvaluationism; multiple conclusions and disjunction in the case of supervaluationism) the subvaluationist case is more dramatic. Since this failure appears already in a multiple-premises/single-conclusion framework, which is more natural than the multiple premise/multiple conclusions framework. We leave a more detailed discussion of this point for Section 2.2.3 and turn now to s'valuationism non-truth-functionality.

2.2.2 Truth-Functionality

Classical logic is truth-functional in the sense that the value of a complex sentence can be expressed as a function of the value of its immediate subsentences. So for example, the truth-value of a sentence of the form $A \wedge B$ depends in the usual way on the truth-value of A and the truth-value of B.

Supervaluationism is not truth-functional in the sense that a sentence might be true (supertrue) without any of its immediate subsentences having a (super) truth-value. Suppose, for example, that Tim is borderline thin, so that Tim is thin in some precisifications but not in some others. Despite the fact that 'Tim is thin' is neither (super) true nor (super)

false, the sentence 'If Tim is thin then Tim is thin' is supertrue, since it is true in every
precisification. The way in which subvaluationism is not truth-functional is different, or
more precisely dual to supervaluationism. In subvaluationism a pair of sentences can be
independently satisfiable but not the corresponding conjunction.

S'valuationist non truth-functionality is connected with the aforementioned *penumbral
connections* and, ultimately, to s'valuationist classicality. Notice that supervaluationism
rejects bivalence endorsing truth-gaps but excluded middle is valid and, similarly, subvaluationism rejects bivalence endorsing truth-gluts but contradictions are not satisfiable.
S'valuationist non truth-functionality can, therefore, be expressed by the following pair of
dual invalidities:

(abjunction) $A \vee B \nvDash_{SpV} A, \ B$

(adjunction) $A, \ B \nvDash_{SbV} A \wedge B$ (Hyde 2010, p. 388)

In a first-order language we have the corresponding effects for '∀' and '∃' as we mentioned in the previous section.

There are at least two questions about s'valuationism in relation to the failure of truth-
functionality. The first is what truth-functionality precisely is and whether s'valuationism
fails to be truth-functional. The second is whether non-truth-functionality is a good or bad
feature of s'valuationism (we shall talk about supervaluationism in this section though the
discussion below applies to both theories).

Field discusses one way to give an algebraic, value-functional, presentation of supervaluationism (Field 2008, p. 168). The idea is the following. Suppose we have a s'valuationist
interpretation $\mathbb{S} = \{\mathbb{I}, \mathbb{I}', \dots\}$. The power set of $\mathbb{S}$ forms a boolean algebra, and its elements
can be taken as values in the following way: let a valuation v assign to variable p the set
of interpretations of $\mathbb{S}$ such that $\mathbb{I}(p) = 1$. This valuation extends to complex formulas
interpreting conjunction as intersection, disjunction as union and negation as complemen-
tation.[17] This valuation provides 'the right results' in the sense that for any formula A, A
is supertrue in $\mathbb{S}$ if and only if $v(A) = \mathbb{S}$ and A is superfalse in $\mathbb{S}$ just in case $v(A) = \emptyset$.
As a toy example, consider the language containing only two atomic sentences, p, q and a
supervaluation $\mathbb{S} = \{\mathbb{I}_1, \mathbb{I}_2, \mathbb{I}_3\}$ such that:

$\mathbb{I}_1(p) = 1, \ \mathbb{I}_1(q) = 0$
$\mathbb{I}_2(p) = 0, \ \mathbb{I}_2(q) = 1$
$\mathbb{I}_3(p) = \mathbb{I}_3(q) = 0$

This s'valuationist interpretation models a situation in which neither p or q are supertrue,
but they stand in a relation of contrariety: there is a valuation in $\mathbb{S}$ in which they are both
false, but no valuation in $\mathbb{S}$ in which they are both true. The algebra generated by $\mathbb{S}$ is the
following $\mathbf{2^3}$ boolean algebra:

---

[17] A strategy of this sort is already pointed out in van Fraassen (1970, pp. 65–6).

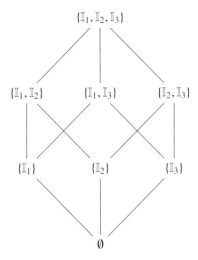

and the corresponding valuation is $v(p) = \{\mathbb{I}_1\}$, $v(q) = \{\mathbb{I}_2\}$. Note that, for example, $v(p \vee \neg p) = \{\mathbb{I}_1\} \cup \{\mathbb{I}_2, \mathbb{I}_3\} = \mathbb{S}$ and that $v(p \wedge q) = \{\mathbb{I}_1\} \cap \{\mathbb{I}_2\} = \emptyset$ as expected.

Field takes this connection as showing that there is no deep difference between s'valuationism approaches and degree theories:

> It's common to distinguish supervaluational approaches to vagueness from degree-theoretic approaches, but this is misleading: supervaluational approaches are in effect degree-theoretic, they use Boolean degrees. The genuine distinction that underlies this way of talking is that standard degree-theoretic approaches use degrees in which the top value 1 can't be reached by joins: $a \sqcup b = 1$ implies $a = 1 \vee b = 1$. (Field 2008, p. 169)

This claim of Field's contrasts with the claim of Fine's according to which no natural truth-value approach can give a semantics allowing for indeterminate sentences and respecting *penumbral connections* (Fine 1975, p. 270). Though Fine's claim is somewhat vague (what is a 'natural' truth-value approach?) we think it correctly points out that understanding supervaluationism as based on any kind of degrees is conceptually mistaken (even if we can give a value-functional presentation of it). The reason is, in a nutshell, that the higher or lower position between values in a boolean algebra does not represent, in their s'valuationist reading, any closeness to truth or to falsity. In the previous example, $v(p) = \{\mathbb{I}_1\}$ and therefore $v(\neg p) = \{\mathbb{I}_2, \mathbb{I}_3\}$. But the fact that the value of $\neg p$ is higher than the value of p does not make the first in any sense 'truer' than the second (see Cobreros and Tranchini 2014).

The second question is whether s'valuationist failure of truth-functionality is an acceptable feature. Defenders of supervaluationism agree that the failure of truth-functionality is not something particularly nice, but it is a cost that other positive features of the theory, penumbral connections, outweighs. Thus Fine:

> I do not wish to deny that LEM is counter-intuitive. It is just that external considerations mitigate against it. In particular, an adequate account of penumbral connections appears to require that the logic be classical. (Fine 1975, p. 286)

and Keefe:

It could be objected that the conservatism about classical logic is inappropriate and unsustainable in the face of vagueness, and, in particular, that the law of excluded middle is a part of classical logic that should be given up because of vagueness. But, first, note that if a theory is to capture the truth of penumbral connections of the form $Fa \lor Ga$, for incompatible F and G, then it will also count as true $Fa \lor \neg Fa$: there is no reasonable way of counting one true but not the other. (Keefe 2000, p. 164)

Critics claim that non-truth-functionality misrepresents the meaning of logical constants. Thus, in relation to the supertruth of $(\neg\text{Tol})$,

$(\neg\text{Tol})$ $\exists x \,(red(a_x) \land \neg red(a_{x+1}))$

Rolf, for example, comments:

does supervaluation give a true description of the truth-conditions of the English phrase "there is"? I think not. We have some grasp of what would make sentences of the form "There is a P" true. Now, if supervaluations were right about the truth-conditions for "there is", we would find it completely acceptable that there was an n'th hair, the loss of which turned Tom bald or, more generally, that all changes are instantaneous. The very fact that we find [$\neg Tol$] unacceptable shows that "there is" does not have the truth-conditions which supervaluationism says it has. (Rolf 1984, p. 232)[18]

At some point, the discussion derives into a battle of intuitions. Keefe (2000) and Edgington (1997) try to provide examples of independent evidence for non-truth-functionality of disjunction; but these are convincingly criticised in Hyde (2010). In this context, Fara (2010) is an interesting attempt to provide an argument against the supervaluationist failure of truth-functionality. The supervaluationist justification for the truth of some disjunctions without any disjunct being true depends on the idea that there is a sense in which each disjunct could have been true. But Fara shows that the supervaluationist is committed, not only to true disjunctions without true disjunct, but to true disjunctions *without satisfiable disjuncts* (not satisfiable, by supervaluationist standards). With the $\mathbb{D}$ operator we can express the notion of borderline case:

$\mathbb{B}A \;=_{df}\; \neg\mathbb{D}A \land \neg\mathbb{D}\neg A$

Now notice that $A \land \mathbb{B}A \vDash_{\mathsf{G}}$ (we cannot have both A and $\mathbb{B}A$ true in every point in a model) so that sentence is not satisfiable by supervaluationist standards. At the same time, $\mathbb{B}A$ *is* satisfiable and $A \lor \neg A$ is true in every point of every model, which means that $\mathbb{B}A \land (A \lor \neg A)$ is true in exactly those points of a model where $\mathbb{B}A$ is. Finally, $\mathbb{B}A \land (A \lor \neg A)$ is classically equivalent to $(\mathbb{B}A \land A) \lor (\mathbb{B}A \land \neg A)$ and therefore this last is true in those points of models where $\mathbb{B}A$ is true. But note that each disjunct is unsatisfiable by supervaluationist standards.

---

[18] See also Sanford (1976), Kamp (1981) and Tappenden (1993).

2.2.3 Logic Naturalness

Super- and subvaluationism are dual logics, as we pointed out above, and therefore, valid inferences of one logic appear in the other in *contrapositive* form (see Fact 1 above). This duality is a reasonable ground for the idea that these theories go together: either both succeed or both fail (see Hyde 1997).

Fine considers briefly the possibility of truth-value gluts, but dismisses the subvaluationist proposal without much argument (Fine 1975, p. 267). By contrast, Keefe devotes some pages to the issue (Keefe 2000, pp. 197–200). Keefe's arguments are basically two. The first is, as we saw at the end of Section 2.1, that the subvaluationist is committed to different responses to what seems to be essentially the same argument. The second is that, despite duality, 'there are very substantial deviations from classical logic on the subvaluationist picture'. Keefe mentions two such cases, the failure of *adjunction* and the failure of *modus ponens*,

(*Adjunction*) $A,\ B \nvDash_{SbV} A \wedge B$
(*Modus Ponens*) $A,\ A \supset B \nvDash_{SbV} B$

We agree with Keefe that the aforementioned failures are not particularly nice, but what about the related failures in supervaluationism? In particular, *adjunction* fails in supervaluationism as critics in the previous section are eager to stress. What makes the failure of one more palatable than the failure of the other? Keefe's answer:

> But we do not use multiple-conclusion arguments in ordinary life and it is reasoning in vague natural language that is in question. Multiple-conclusion logic is not intended as a logic of ordinary arguments (its study primarily has the role of providing a system for elegant analogies with multiple-premise logics) and its theses are questionably included among the body of 'traditional' logic. The contrast with the failure of adjunction is clear. (Keefe 2000, 198)

Hyde provides, we think, a convincing response to Keefe's claim on the naturalness of multiple-premises/single-conclusion arguments over multiple-premises/multiple-conclusions arguments. His argument is, briefly, the following. Given that we should assert what is true and deny what is not true, logical consequence constrains what we are in a position to assert and deny given what we assert and deny. If, for example, $A \vDash B$ then we are not in a position to assert A and deny B. Where denial is equivalent to assertion of the negation, multiple conclusions are not necessary to represent all constraints on assertion and denial since, for example, the validity of abjunction in classical logic might equally well be represented by the non-assertability of the corresponding set:

$A \vee B,\ \neg A,\ \neg B \vDash_{CL}$

When denial is different to the assertion of the negation, the use of multiple conclusions in the representation of constraints is no longer dispensable.[19] Consider the following inference:

[19] Not, at least, without the aid of a non-classical expression.

$A \vee B, \ \neg A, \ \neg B \vDash_{\mathsf{SpV}}$

Indeed, the supervaluationist is not in a position to assert $A \vee B$ together with the negation of A and the negation of B although she can assert $A \vee B$ while denying A and denying B. For this reason the appeal to the naturalness of multiple-premises/single-conclusion arguments is not available: the supervaluationist needs multiple conclusions to provide a complete picture of his own logical theory (Hyde 2010, pp. 394–6). A manifestation of the dependency of supervaluationism on multiple conclusions can be seen in the claim that the ($\neg$Tol) does not commit the theory to the assertion of any instance:

$\exists x \, (red(a_x) \wedge \neg red(a_{x+1}))$

$\nvDash_{\mathsf{SpV}}$

$red(a_1) \wedge \neg red(a_2), \quad red(a_2) \wedge \neg red(a_3), \dots \quad red(a_{n-1}) \wedge \neg red(a_n)$

2.2.4 Higher-Order Vagueness

Vague predicates seem to show no sharp boundaries between the positive and the negative cases of the predicate. Thus, for example, there seems to be no sharp boundary between the red and the non-red items in a suitable Sorites series. Second-order vagueness has to do with the absence of a boundary between the clearly red and the not clearly red, as well as with the absence of a boundary between the not clearly not red and the clearly not red. Third-order vagueness has to do with the absence of a sharp boundary between the clearly clearly red and the not clearly clearly red, as well as... Well, higher-order vagueness has to do with all this seeming absence of sharp boundaries.[20] Consider again our definition of a borderline case in terms of $\mathbb{D}$:

$\mathbb{B}A \ =_{df} \ \neg \mathbb{D}A \wedge \neg \mathbb{D}\neg A$

Then second-order vagueness can be defined as the existence of borderline cases of borderline cases and third-order vagueness as the existence of borderline cases of borderline cases of borderline cases. There is no seemingly reason to stop at any particular finite order, 'even if high orders of vagueness are somehow ruled out by empirical factors, that would not entitle the logician to treat them as impossible' (Williamson 1994, p. 158).

Suppose the logic for $\mathbb{D}$ is as strong as the normal modal logic **S5**. It follows from this assumption that if something is definite, then it is definitely definite and if it is not definite then it is definitely not definite and therefore

(Not 2nd) $\neg \mathbb{D}\mathbb{D}A \wedge \neg \mathbb{D}\neg \mathbb{D}A \vDash_{\mathsf{S5}} \bot$

---

[20] See Williamson (1999) for a precise characterisation of higher-order vagueness.

So S5 does not allow for second (or higher) order vagueness. In order to make room for higher-order vagueness then, the $\mathbb{D}$ operator should obey a logic weaker than S5 (see Williamson 1999, p. 134). Exactly which logic should govern the notion of definiteness is a controversial matter, even among epistemicists (e.g., Williamson 1994, p. 228 argues that S4 should fail while Bobzien 2011 argues it should hold). We turn now to a specific challenge to supervaluationism.

The supervaluationist claims that there is no sharp transition between the red items and the non-red items in a Sorites series because the definitely red items are separated from the definitely not red items by some that are neither definitely red nor definitely not red. That is, no definitely red item is followed by a definitely not red item:

(GP *red*) $\mathbb{D}red(x) \supset \neg\mathbb{D}\neg red(x')$

(where x' is the successor of x in the Sorites series) ('GP *red*' stands for *gap principle* for the predicate *red*.)

There is no sharp transition either from the definitely red to the not definitely red because no definitely definitely red item is followed by a definitely not definitely red item:

(GP $\mathbb{D}red$) $\mathbb{D}\mathbb{D}red(x) \supset \neg\mathbb{D}\neg\mathbb{D}red(x')$

In general, there is no sharp transition from the definitely^n red to the not definitely^n red because no definitely definitely^n red item is followed by a definitely not definitely^n red item:

(GP $\mathbb{D}^n red$) $\mathbb{D}\mathbb{D}^n red(x) \supset \neg\mathbb{D}\neg\mathbb{D}^n red(x')$

Fara (2003) shows that, given the commitment to global consequence, the supervaluationist cannot endorse indefinitely many *gap principles* for any finite Sorites series. That is, the set of all gap principles is globally unsatisfiable for any finite Sorites series.[21] The significance of Fara's result is not free of controversy, but it looks bad anyway that the supervaluationist cannot endorse all gap principles for *any* Sorites series, no matter how long.

Given this, the supervaluationist might consider the possibility of endorsing local consequence instead of global consequence. But this, we believe, is a non-starter (see Section 2.2.5). Yet there is still one, supertruth-friendly, way to resist Fara's argument. We agreed that, in order to accommodate higher-order vagueness, the semantics of $\mathbb{D}$ must be weaker than S5. Notice that, for the supervaluationist, $\mathbb{D}$ is an object-language expression of supertruth – as both provide the way to characterise the notion of *borderline case*. Now, if the semantics for $\mathbb{D}$ is weaker than S5 and logical consequence is global validity, there

---

[21] See Cobreros (2011a) for a formal proof of Fara's argument.

is a mismatch between $\mathbb{D}$ and the notion of truth preserved by logical consequence. The notion of truth preserved by global consequence is that of *true everywhere in a model* and that would correspond, in the object language, to a universal modality (as witnessed by Fact 11). So the supervaluationist can claim that the notion of truth preserved by logical consequence is not that of global truth, but truth at all accessible points in a model or *regional truth*. Gap-principles are regionally satisfiable for finite Sorites series. The strategy is proposed in Cobreros (2008) and Cobreros (2011b), with response in Fara (2011).

The troubles don't stop here, however. By the Fact 12 above, we know that any globally valid argument is also locally valid when premises are assumed to be 'definite enough'. This means that not only regionalists have troubles endorsing the *definitisation* of gap-principles for any finite Sorites series, but also any theory committed to local validity does. Interestingly, subvaluationist logic is weak enough to endorse the definitisation of gap-principles (see Cobreros 2011a; see Zardini 2013a for higher-order Sorites arguments requiring fewer assumptions).

2.2.5 Going Local?

Some authors, Varzi (2007b) and Asher et al. (2009), have advocated the view that the supervaluationist should step back and endorse local consequence instead of global consequence. The arguments are mostly motivated by non-appealing features of supervaluationist logic, including the failure of classical metainferences in the $\mathbb{D}$ augmented language and Fara's paradox of higher-order vagueness. While a discussion of their positions deserve more careful analysis, we would like to raise here just one objection.

That global consequence is, by supervaluationist standards, the relevant notion of logical consequence, follows from the following two statements:

(i) Truth is supertruth.
(ii) Logical consequence is a matter of necessary preservation of truth.

Thus, someone endorsing local consequence cannot endorse both (i) and (ii). Given the central role of supertruth in the explanation of borderline cases and the Sorites Paradox, the rejection of (i) in favour of *local truth* raises the question of what is really left from the original motivation for supervaluationism.[22] The endorsement of (i) and rejection of (ii) seems to be more supervaluationist-friendly (this seems in fact to be the position of Varzi 2007b). Either way, endorsing local validity seems to run into trouble under the following platitude:

(iii) If an argument from Γ to Δ is valid, one is not in a position to assert all its premises and deny all its conclusions.

---

[22] Williamson (1995a) already convincingly argues that a theory of vagueness endorsing classical logic and a disquotational notion of truth is committed to an epistemic reading of definiteness: vague predicates have semantic sharp boundaries and indefiniteness reflects our ignorance about its location.

For consider the inference

$$\exists x \, (red(a_x) \wedge \neg red(a_{x+1}))$$
$$\therefore$$
$$red(a_1) \wedge \neg red(a_2), \quad red(a_2) \wedge \neg red(a_3), \ldots \quad red(a_{n-1}) \wedge \neg red(a_n)$$

The inference is not globally valid; thus, under global consequence, it is possible to assert its premise and deny all its conclusions. This embodies the traditional supervaluationist response to the Sorites Paradox: although $\exists x \, (red(a_x) \wedge \neg red(a_{x+1}))$ is supertrue, no instance is supertrue. Under local consequence and assuming (iii), however, this sort of response is no longer available. The local validity of the argument and the truth (be it either global or local) of the premise precludes denying all its conclusions. But in that case what should then be our attitudes towards the instances of $\exists x \, (red(a_x) \wedge \neg red(a_{x+1}))$? Under local consequence, one should at least be open to the idea that there is a last red item. At this point, it seems to us, the boundary with epistemicism blurs.

2.3 Proof Theory

In this section we provide an abstract completeness result for global consequence for multiple premises and single conclusion. The result is abstract in the sense that we will assume that there is some proof system for local consequence and obtain from this assumption a proof system for global consequence.

Note in the first place that global consequence is strictly stronger than local consequence; since any global counterexample to a given argument is a local counterexample, but not the other way around (think, in particular, of the fact that $A \vDash_G \mathbb{D}A$).

Suppose now that we have a multiple-premises/single-conclusion proof system $\mathscr{L}$, adequate (sound and complete) for $\vDash_L$. Let $\vdash_L$ denote the consequence relation associated to this system. A first guess is that in order to obtain a proof system for $\vDash_G$ we have just to add a rule to $\mathscr{L}$ allowing us to pass from A to $\mathbb{D}A$, something like this:

$\mathbb{D}$**-intro** $\Gamma \vdash A \Longrightarrow \Gamma \vdash \mathbb{D}A$[23]

The resulting system is certainly complete (as we will show in a moment) but its soundness will depend on the rules already in the original system (if this includes any rule corresponding to one of the meta-inferences of Table 2.1 the system will be unsound). We will address the completeness issue first.

Recall that $\Gamma \vDash_G A$ is equivalent to $\mathbb{D}^{\omega}\Gamma \vDash_L A$ (Fact 12). Let $\vdash_G$ denote the consequence relation associated to the system $\mathscr{G}$, which results from the addition of $\mathbb{D}$-intro to $\mathscr{L}$.

---

[23] This rule must not be confused with the *necessitation* rule of normal modal logics, which, in relation to $\mathbb{D}$-intro above can be written $\Gamma \vdash A \Longrightarrow \mathbb{D}\Gamma \vdash \mathbb{D}A$ (note that the more standard formulation without premises: $\vdash A \Longrightarrow \vdash \mathbb{D}A$ is a particular case).

Theorem 2 [⊢$_G$-completeness] $\Gamma \vDash_G A \implies \Gamma \vdash_G A$

Proof

(i) Assume: $\Gamma \vDash_G A$,

⇓

(ii) $\mathbb{D}^\omega \Gamma \vDash_L A$

⇓

(iii) $\mathbb{D}^\omega \Gamma \vdash_L A$

⇓

(iv) $\mathbb{D}^\omega \Gamma \vdash_G A$

⇓

(v) $\Gamma \vdash_G A$

□

Step from (i) to (ii) is based on our previous Theorem 1. Step from (ii) to (iii) is based on the completeness of $\vdash_L$ with respect $\vDash_L$. Step from (iii) to (iv) is based on the fact that $\vdash_G$ is an extension of $\vdash_L$ (anything that is $\mathscr{L}$-provable is $\mathscr{G}$-provable). The last step is shown in the next:

Fact 16 Let $\mathscr{L}$ contain the following rules:

Ref $A \in \Gamma \implies \Gamma \vdash_L A$

Cut $\Gamma \vdash_L A$ & $\Delta \vdash_L B_1, \ldots \Delta \vdash_L B_n$ (for all $B \in \Gamma$) $\implies$ $\Delta \vdash_L A$

then it can be shown, for the resulting proof system $\mathscr{G}$ that

$$\mathbb{D}^\omega \Gamma \vdash_G A \implies \Gamma \vdash_G A$$

(We leave to the reader the verification of this fact. As a hint, note that, since proofs are finite, a proof from $\mathbb{D}^\omega \Gamma$ to A might make use of at most a finite number of formulas in $\mathbb{D}^\omega \Gamma$.)

Theorem 4 shows how to find a proof system complete for $\vDash_G$ for multiple-premises/single-conclusion arguments in the $\mathbb{D}$ augmented language. The task now is finding suitable restrictions on the application of *problematic* rules that do not destroy the previous completeness argument. Stating formally what these restrictions should be depends, of course, on the particular proof system. As an illustration consider the system of *formal proofs* in Hedman (2006, pp. 14–22) plus the rules:[24]

$$\text{KNec} \quad \frac{\Gamma \vdash A}{\mathbb{D}\Gamma \vdash \mathbb{D}A}$$

$$\mathbb{D}\text{-Intro} \quad \frac{\Gamma \vdash A}{\Gamma \vdash \mathbb{D}A}$$

---

[24] We can add further rules to cover different extensions of normal modal logic K; see Beall and van Fraassen (2003, p. 193).

In this system, a proof for a statement of the form $\Gamma \vdash A$ is a finite sequence of statements of the form $\Sigma \vdash B$ each of which is justified by a rule of the system (possibly invoking previous statements in the sequence) and whose last statement is $\Gamma \vdash A$. As an example, consider the proof for normal modal logic axiom (K) (in argument form) $\mathbb{D}(A \supset B) \vdash \mathbb{D}A \supset \mathbb{D}B$:

$$\text{KNec} \cfrac{\supset\text{-elim} \cfrac{A \supset B \vdash A \supset B}{A \supset B, A \vdash B}}{\supset\text{-intro} \cfrac{\mathbb{D}(A \supset B), \mathbb{D}A \vdash \mathbb{D}B}{\mathbb{D}(A \supset B) \vdash \mathbb{D}A \supset \mathbb{D}B}}$$

The last step invokes $\supset$-introduction which we know cannot be unrestrictedly applied in the presence of $\mathbb{D}$-Intro. The restriction on the applicability of $\supset$-introduction should not rule out the proof above and, in general, should not destroy the completeness argument above. The easiest way to do this is, to our knowledge, avoiding the application of any *problematic* rule (or even, any non-structural rule) if $\mathbb{D}$-Intro has been previously applied in the proof. This might look like a drastic condition, but it does not destroy the argument in Theorem 2. Consider the inference from $A \vdash B \supset \mathbb{D}A$ which is globally valid. The following way of constructing a proof seems natural:

$$\supset\text{-intro} \cfrac{\mathbb{D}\text{-intro} \cfrac{A, B \vdash A}{A, B \vdash \mathbb{D}A}}{A \vdash B \supset \mathbb{D}A}$$

This proof, however, is ruled out by the previous restriction on $\supset$-introduction. We can still construct a proof following a different route:

$$\text{Cut} \cfrac{\mathbb{D}\text{-intro} \cfrac{\supset\text{-intro} \cfrac{\mathbb{D}A, B \vdash \mathbb{D}A}{\mathbb{D}A \vdash B \supset \mathbb{D}A}}{A \vdash \mathbb{D}A}}{A \vdash B \supset \mathbb{D}A}$$

The restriction grants that any locally valid proof is globally valid. In turn, $\mathscr{G}$-proofs that are not $\mathscr{L}$-proofs in such a system follow the same pattern of reasoning as in Theorem 4: assume premises are as definite as you need, apply $\mathscr{L}$-reasoning and 'reduce' the $\mathbb{D}$ operators in the premises in the last step via transitivity.

A brief digression about the philosophical significance of this result. There is a discussion on whether the supervaluationist theory can still be considered 'classical' for the $\mathbb{D}$ augmented language, given the counterexamples to classical metainferences in Table 2.1, even for multiple-premises/single-conclusion arguments. Williamson (1994, p. 152) claims that, concerning the classicality of the theory, these failures are disastrous for supervaluationism. Keefe (2000, p. 180) suggests that counterexamples to classical metainferences occur just when the inference $\mathbb{D}$-intro is around and that otherwise the logic is classical. Varzi (2007b, p. 657) complains that Keefe's suggestion is too vague to be convincing. Cobreros (2011c) claims that the above result gives precise content to Keefe's suggestion.

Our proof theory so far extends to multiple-premises/single-conclusion. This would be fine if denial would be expressible in terms of assertion, but we know that in the supervaluationist theory this is not the case (see the final part of Section 2.2). Further, we could extend this proof system to subvaluationism dualising its rules, but we would just cover single-premise/multiple-conclusions arguments. Taking into account Fact 14 we could set a proof theory for multiple-premises/multiple-conclusions this way: in order to check $\Gamma \vdash_G \Delta$, check whether $\Gamma \vdash_G B$ for some $B \in \Delta$. This, however, does not look very efficient since when $\Gamma \nvdash_G \Delta$ it requires checking that for each $B \in \Delta$ no proof can be found. Whether there is a result similar to the one given above, to capture global proofs via a single rule formulated in the language under consideration, we don't know.[25]

---

[25] A proof analysis for global consequence for the $\mathbb{D}$-augmented language in the multiple-premises/multiple-conclusions framework can be given based on Fact 11, with the extra aid of a universal modality $\mathbb{D}^u$. See Cobreros (2008) for an approach of this sort using tableaux. Relatedly, in Tranchini and Cobreros (2017) we show, in a self-contained and accessible manner, how to construct multiple-premises/multiple-conclusions sequent systems for global consequence, using labelled calculi in the style of Negri (2011).

3   Contextualism and the Sorites Paradox

Inga Bones and Diana Raffman

Any adequate treatment of the Sorites Paradox that takes it to be a fallacy must do at least two things. First, it must solve the paradox; in other words, it must expose the flaw in the paradoxical argument and, if necessary, supply an appropriate logic and semantics for vague terms. Most theorists of vagueness find the flaw in the major (universal) premise:[1] it is false, or super-false, or indefinite, or ambiguous, for example. Second, an adequate treatment must diagnose our persistent intuition that the premise is true: if the premise is defective in one or another of these ways, why is it intuitively so appealing?

We make a point of distinguishing between these two tasks – solving the paradox and diagnosing its intuitive appeal – in order to situate contextualism in the theoretical landscape. As will become clear, most contextualist accounts are dynamic in nature;[2] they are framed in terms of episodes of verbal behaviour and psychological or social processes that occur (e.g.) at certain times or in a certain order. As a result, while they deliver substantive, often plausible diagnoses of the intuitive pull of the soritical premise(s) – their appeal derives in one way or another from the context-sensitivity of the central soritical term – contextualist accounts by themselves typically do not offer resolutions of the Sorites Paradox. Rather, they are coupled with non-contextualist solutions – supervaluationist, or degree-theoretic, or epistemic solutions, for example.

The point can be brought out clearly in terms of the distinction between the Sorites Paradox proper and the so-called *forced march* or *dynamic Sorites* (Horgan 1994; Soames 1999).[3] Consider for example a series of 30 coloured patches progressing from a central blue (#1) to a central green (#30), and suppose that each patch differs only incrementally (i.e. is either indiscriminable or just noticeably different in colour) from the next. The Sorites Paradox then goes like this:

1. Patch #1 is blue.
2. For any *n*: if patch #*n* is blue, then patch #($n + 1$) is blue.
3. Therefore, patch #30 is blue.

---

[1] We will use the universally generalised and conditional forms of the paradox as our examples.
[2] Pagin (2010) is an exception; cited by Kamp and Sassoon (2016, p. 415).
[3] See also 'The Forced-March Paradox', in the introduction to this volume.

But #30 was stipulated to be green, hence not blue: contradiction. In contrast, the forced march Sorites is an informal version of the argument (probably best viewed as a thought-experiment or a puzzle) framed in terms of the hypothetical applications of a vague predicate by a competent speaker who proceeds step by step along a Sorites series. On pain of incompetence, the speaker must classify patch #1 as blue. Then since #2 is so similar to #1, it seems he must classify #2 as blue; and then #3 as blue, and so on until finally he must classify #30 as blue. At the same time, and also because he is competent, the speaker must classify #30 as not blue. Thus it seems his very competence with 'blue' forces him to contradict himself.

Our present point is that, owing to their dynamical character, contextualist accounts typically address only the forced march puzzle, not the paradox proper. Notice that the latter contains no reference to verbal behaviour (e.g. applications of 'blue') by a speaker at a time, or to episodes of forced marching, or to revisions of previous classifications, among other things; in general it contains no reference to temporal factors. It refers only to an ordered set of hues (ages, heights, etc.) in the abstract, as it were, independently of any information about actual uses of the terms in question. Hence a treatment couched in terms of actual uses will typically fail to touch the paradox itself (though of course it may help to dismantle the forced march puzzle and diagnose the appeal of the major premise).

Friends and foes of contextualism alike acknowledge that most if not all soritical terms are sensitive to contextual factors. At 45 years of age, Margot Fonteyn was old compared with ballerinas but not compared with choreographers; you may be tall for the purpose of reaching the light switch but not for the purpose of dusting the ceiling fan; a given salary may make a person rich in contrast to middle income but not rich in contrast to upper middle income; Roger may be talented at tennis but at golf not so much. With such examples as these in mind, some opponents of contextualism have argued that although soriticality and context-sensitivity often go together, soriticality persists even given a single fixed context (e.g. Williamson 1994, pp. 214–5; Keefe 2000, p. 10).[4] If this criticism were correct, contextualist accounts would be no help even in treating the forced march (much less the Sorites Paradox proper). However, while the objection is effective with respect to contextual factors of the usual sort – comparison classes, contrastive categories, times, places and so on – it doesn't take account of contextual factors of the kind that contextualists often have in mind. According to at least some contextualists, soritical terms are also sensitive to more fine-grained, 'non-standard' contextual factors,[5] such as variations in speakers' interests (Fara 2000) and order and anchoring effects (e.g. Raffman 1994, 2014). Consequently, the extensions of vague predicates can shift with these fine-grained contextual factors even when all standard contextual factors have been fixed.[6]

---

[4] Furthermore, terms such as 'the highest score', 'older than the average age' and 'tallest' are context-sensitive but not (at least not obviously) soritical.

[5] We borrow the term 'non-standard' from Åkerman (2012, p. 472).

[6] This isn't to say that their fine-grained shifts of extension are unconstrained; among other things, such shifts can occur only in the penumbral area between a vague predicate and its negation, not in the vicinities of clear cases.

In Section 3.1, we distinguish several contextualist diagnoses of the appeal of the soritical (major) premise of the paradox. In Section 3.2 we point out three advantages of contextualist approaches, taking into account some recent experimental findings. We present and evaluate some objections to contextualism in Section 3.3, and then in Section 3.4 we consider the prospects for a recent descendant of contextualism that is meant to solve the paradox proper as well as the forced march puzzle.

3.1 Varieties of Contextualism

Dissatisfied with many-valued and supervaluationist treatments of the paradox, Hans Kamp introduced a contextualist account in his seminal essay *The Paradox of the Heap* (1981, reprinted in Kamp 2013).[7] At the time of its publication, the distinction we noted above, between solving the paradox proper and diagnosing its appeal, had not been recognised and discussed to the extent it currently is. We say this because, unlike the subsequent contextualist accounts his work inspired, Kamp's contextualist views are not always easily classified as lying on one side of this distinction or the other. Semantic and logical aspects of vague words are woven together with the character of their competent use by ordinary speakers. (Indeed, linguists are often sceptical of the very distinction at issue, wanting to bind semantics and use much more tightly together.) Therefore, in what follows we will try to keep our discussion of Kamp's account as neutral as possible with respect to the distinction between solution and diagnosis, as we are putting it.

On Kamp's view, each instantiation of the major premise is true because its antecedent is included among the sentences supposed to be true for the evaluation of its consequent, and the neighbouring values referred to in the two sentences are only incrementally different:[8] $\ulcorner A \rightarrow B \urcorner$ is true in a context C if, and only if, either A is false in C, or B would be true in a distinct context C^* consisting of C together with A (for Kamp, a context just is a set of sentences). In a classical framework we would then expect the major premise, the universal generalisation, also to be true since all of its instances are true; but then the paradox would reawaken. To avoid this result, Kamp defines the universal quantifier non-truth-functionally in such a way that it can be false when all of its instances are true: a sentence of the form $(\alpha)\Phi\alpha$ is true in contexts (i) where its instances are true *and* (ii) that remain coherent when the universal premise itself is added. Since adding that premise would produce an incoherent context that 'assign(s) opposite truth values to one and the same sentence' (Kamp 2013, p. 291), the premise is false despite all of its instances being true. Of course, the negation of the universal premise is classically equivalent to the statement that there is a number n such that patch #n is blue and patch #($n + 1$) is not blue; and that seems intuitively unacceptable where the two patches differ only incrementally. So Kamp rejects

---

[7] See Fara (2000) for helpful discussion of Kamp's view.
[8] Kamp endorses a principle of 'equivalence of observationally indistinguishable entities'.

the classical equivalence and holds that the existential claim is false in the relevant contexts because it has no true instances in those contexts.

Kamp's treatment of the multi-conditional version of the paradox is somewhat less explicit, but as before the definition of the conditional plays a leading role. The argument begins in a context C_1 in which 'B(#1)' (= 'Patch #1 is blue') is stipulated to be true; the definition of the conditional is satisfied by 'B(#1)→B(#2)', and so by *modus ponens* 'B(#2)' is added to C_1, yielding a new context C_2. By the same reasoning, B(#3) is added to C_2 to yield a new context C_3; and so on. Progress continues until we find ourselves in a context that 'forces upon a predicate an extensional inconsistency' (2013, p. 306). This happens when we arrive at a context that is committed to the truth of '~B(#n)' on independent grounds: we can *see* that patch #n is (e.g.) green. Such a context will be incoherent: it will contain 'B(#(n−1))', 'B(#(n−1))→B(#n)' and '~B(#n)'. In this framework, *modus ponens* is not fully valid: 'This is a direct consequence of our semantics, which was designed to allow both $P(k+1)$ and $P(k+1) \rightarrow P(k+2)$ to be true in certain contexts in which $P(k+2)$ is not' (Kamp 2013, p. 304).[9]

Kamp's contextualism is in many respects intuitively appealing, and it has immediately to hand a diagnosis of the seeming truth of the major premise: the premise seems true because all of its instances are true. At the same time, the non-standard semantics of the universal quantifier may be hard to accept. Be that as it may, Kamp's approach has inspired a variety of subsequent contextualist efforts to explain the plausibility of the major premise. These accounts can be understood within the framework of at least three largely orthogonal distinctions: (i) *psychological* versus *pragmatic* versions of contextualism (Åkerman 2012), (ii) *boundary-shifting* versus *extension-shifting* versions (Åkerman and Greenough 2010a), and (iii) *indexical* versus *non-indexical* versions (MacFarlane 2009; Åkerman and Greenough 2010b). Psychological contextualists take contexts to be constituted at least partly by psycholinguistic states of individual speakers, whereas pragmatic contextualists take contexts to include conversationally established standards of application. Boundary-shifting versions of contextualism posit hidden sharp boundaries between the positive and negative extensions of a vague term, explaining that we cannot know where these boundaries lie because they are constantly moving around. In contrast, extension-shifting accounts eschew the idea of sharp boundaries altogether.

The third distinction, between indexical and non-indexical strains of contextualism, requires some elaboration. Following MacFarlane (2009), we take a linguistic expression (type) to be context-sensitive just in case its content and/or extension varies relative to some feature(s) of an operative context; that is, a sentence is context-sensitive just in case it expresses different propositions and/or receives different truth-values relative to different contexts. According to indexical contextualists about vague terms, a vague predicate, like

---

[9] In a postscript to the original (1981) paper, Kamp (2013, p. 318) abandons the irregular definition of the universal quantifier and concludes that *modus ponens* is the true culprit in both the universal and multi-conditional ('multi-sentence') versions of the paradox. He does not fully spell out what he has in mind, however.

an indexical, has different semantic contents, and therefore different extensions, relative to different contexts (e.g. Soames 2002, p. 445, also Chapter 6 in this volume, Section 6.2). Non-indexical contextualists, on the other hand, maintain that contextual shifts affect only the extensions of vague predicates, not their contents (e.g. Raffman 1994; Fara 2000). They will say for example that 'Margot is old' has the same content, 'says the same thing', with respect to different contexts, although the truth-value of the sentence may vary across them.

With this brief sketch of the three distinctions in hand, let's have a closer look at several of the contextualist accounts.

Raffman's (1994, 1996) psychological contextualism takes contexts to include speakers' psycholinguistic states, specifically their verbal dispositions to apply or withhold the soritical term in question. Those dispositions are affected not only by familiar factors such as comparison class and contrastive category, the order in which the values in question are considered, and whether they are considered singly or, for instance, in pairs. Raffman hypothesises that every instance of the major premise of the Sorites Paradox is true with respect to neighbouring values considered pairwise, i.e. two together simultaneously (e.g. 1994, p. 47). For instance, when competent speakers in a forced march consider two incrementally different ages pairwise, they will always classify them in the same way – both old or both not old (or both borderline old). But when neighbouring ages are presented singly or one at a time, there will be, indeed must be, some two neighbours such that the first is classified as old (tall, rich…) and the second is not.

This state of affairs is not as counterintuitive as it seems, Raffman claims, because a speaker's verbal dispositions undergo a distinctive change at the moment of her switch from 'old' to 'not old' or 'borderline' (or conversely) between neighbouring ages, with the result that the two otherwise conflicting classifications are made relative to different contexts. Suppose that on a given occasion a speaker doing a forced march classifies 43 years as old and 42 years as not old for a ballerina. If she is then queried again about 43 immediately after the switch, she will now classify it also as not old. This 'backward spread' of the extension of 'not old' has the effect of smoothing out the category switch so that the speaker can go from 'old' to 'not old' without disrupting the effective continuity of the series, i.e. without crossing any sort of boundary. (Raffman's is said to be an extension-shifting view; cf. Åkerman and Greenough 2010a, p. 276.)

In later work (2014), Raffman reports the results of an experiment performed with psychologists Delwin Lindsey and Angela Brown, which found that ordinary speakers applying 'blue', 'green' and 'borderline' to the hues in a blue/green Sorites series did in fact produce the pattern of classifications just described, in several different conditions.[10] Speakers classified neighbouring patches in the same way whenever the

---

[10] Lindsey and Brown, psychologists at Ohio State University, can be contacted at lindsey.43@osu.edu and brown.112@osu.edu, respectively. Among other philosophers who have done empirical studies of ordinary speakers' uses of vague predicates are Égré et al. (2013), Ripley (2011) and Serchuk et al. (2011). See also Chapter 14 in this volume.

patches were presented pairwise; hence the switch between 'blue' and 'borderline' (or 'blue' and 'green') always occurred *between*, never *within*, pairs. Furthermore the speakers' patterns of classification confirmed the "backward spread" hypothesis (2014, chapter 5). Raffman's view may plausibly be regarded as a form of non-indexical contextualism. She writes: 'The Sorites is solved independently of any particular meaning analysis of the predicate [. . .]. All that is required to solve the puzzle is a claim about the correct application or *extension* – as opposed to the meaning analysis or *intension* – of the predicate at issue' (1994, p. 58).[11]

Soames (1999, 2002 and Chapter 6 in this volume) and Shapiro (2003, 2006) defend pragmatic contextualist diagnoses of the appeal of the major premise, together with three valued and supervaluationist resolutions (respectively) of the paradox. Their contextualism takes contexts to include conversationally established standards of application. Within a certain range of cases, speakers have discretion to alter the standards of application of a soritical predicate and adjust its extension accordingly. Following Lewis (1979), Shapiro models the dynamics of conversational contexts in terms of a 'score' that is continually up-dated as a conversation evolves (2006, pp. 12ff.). For example, a conversational participant may exercise her discretion by classifying a penumbral case x for 'tall' as tall. If her classification goes unchallenged by her interlocutors, 'x is tall' is put on the conversational record or 'scoreboard'. Suppose that x's height was previously too short to qualify as tall. With this revision of the record, a new conversational standard for tallness is established, according to which x's height is now included in the extension of the predicate. (Shapiro's and Soames's accounts too are said to be *extension-shifting*.) At the same time, all sentences that were previously on the record but fail to meet the new standard, in particular 'x is not tall', are erased.

Like Raffman, Soames and Shapiro take it that a competent speaker, or a group of speakers, switch or 'jump' (Shapiro 2006, p. 20) at some point in a forced march; in other words, there is a pair of neighbouring values x and x' such that the former is classified as Φ and the latter as not Φ (or borderline). However, this jump from 'Φ' to 'not Φ' necessarily co-occurs with a shift in conversational standards and, hence, in context. On Shapiro's model of conversational dynamics, a jump from 'x is tall' to 'x' is not tall' is accompanied by an updating of the scoreboard so that as soon as 'x' is not tall' is put on the record, 'x is tall' is removed. This procedure ensures that no differential classification of incrementally different heights ever appears on the scoreboard; as Shapiro (2006, p. 23) puts it, the scoreboard never contains a 'strong counterexample' to the major premise. That is why the major premise seems true. Soames and Shapiro differ as to whether shifts in conversational context affect the *content* of a vague term in addition to its extension: Soames, who defends a version of indexical contextualism, says 'yes', Shapiro 'no'.

---

[11] Of course, one may question the extent to which use of non-observational vague predicates such as 'old' and 'rich' would exhibit the same pattern; see Raffman (2014, chapter 5) for some reasons to be optimistic.

Fara (2000, 2008) advances an *interest-relative* contextualist diagnosis of the appeal of the premise, coupled with an epistemicist solution of the paradox proper.[12] In her view, vague predicates are interest-relative in the sense that their extensions are determined by what is significant for a speaker given her interests or purposes at the time. Just for example, suppose you want to buy a tall cherry tree for the backyard. It would be inefficient for you to measure the heights of two available trees, differing by one millimetre, in order to ascertain which is taller. Given your purpose, it doesn't matter which you choose – 'they are the same for present purposes' (2008, p. 328). On the other hand, if you are investigating the effects of a certain insecticide on tree growth, fine-grained discrimination might be essential.

According to Fara, in a forced march the speaker's interest is in traversing the series as efficiently as possible.[13] Consider a speaker marching along a Sorites series for the predicate 'tall for a cherry tree'. Fara writes:

> Among whatever other interests I may have, I also have a standing interest in efficiency that causes me to avoid making discriminations that are too costly. A discrimination between two cherry trees that are very similar in height will be very costly given my interest in efficiency. But the discrimination will be costlier still when I am actively considering the two trees as live options for my purpose. If the trees are similar enough in height, I'll regard them as 'the same for present purposes'. (2008, pp. 327–8)

In effect, the size of the increment tolerated by a vague predicate is determined at least partly by the speaker's cost/benefit analysis of discriminations between neighbouring values. Whatever its 'width', the tolerance of 'tall for a cherry tree' ensures that whenever two neighbouring heights are 'raised to salience' (i.e. considered pairwise), they are regarded as 'the same for present purposes' and either both are in the predicate's extension or neither is. This is why the major premise in the Sorites Paradox proper seems true even though one of its instances must be false: each instance is in fact true while a speaker is considering it, when the similarity of the values referred to in its antecedent and consequent is salient, but not all instances are true simultaneously.

Which instance(s) are not true? At the moment of the switch from 'tall' to 'not tall' in the forced march, a speaker's interest in efficiency causes the boundary between the two predicates to move elsewhere, *eo ipso* causing their extensions to change. Fara:

> [T]he reason that we are unable to say just which instance or instances of [the major premise] are not true is that when we evaluate any given instance, for any particular x and y that differ in height by just 1 mm, the very act of our evaluation raises the similarity of the pair to salience, which has the effect of rendering true the very instance we are considering. We cannot find the boundary of the extension of a vague predicate in a Sorites series for that predicate, because the boundary can never be where we are looking. It shifts around. (2000, p. 59)

---

[12] Åkerman and Greenough (2009, p. 277), Kamp and Sassoon (2016, p. 403). According to Fara's epistemicist solution of the paradox proper, a sharp boundary in a Sorites series for 'tall for a cherry tree' divides the tall heights from the not tall; and bivalence is preserved.

[13] The basis for this claim is unclear; couldn't one stroll leisurely along a series?

(Fara's contextualist diagnosis of the appeal of the premise is said to be a boundary-shifting approach.) If each instantiation of the major premise is true so long as we are considering it (so long as it is salient), and if, as a result, we never encounter the sharp boundary in a forced march, no wonder the major premise of the paradox seems true.[14]

Fara's account appears to allow that although the speaker in a forced march can never know where the boundary of the predicate is now (because it's never where he is looking), he can know where it was immediately preceding any category switch. Each switching point in a forced march may mark not the present but rather the immediately preceding location of the boundary. After all, if the boundary had not been located at the switching point, there would have been no need for it to move; the boundary needs to move only if it will otherwise lie where the speaker is looking. The following remark by Stanley, characterising Fara's view, is suggestive in this regard: 'When we look for [a] boundary of the extension of ['tall for a cherry tree'] in its penumbra, our very looking has the effect of changing the [extension] of the vague expression so that the boundary is not where we are looking' (2003, p. 269).

3.2 Three Virtues of Contextualism

Contextualism about vagueness and soriticality appears to have at least three appealing features. First, as the preceding discussion suggests, contextualist approaches offer substantive, viable diagnoses of the intuitive plausibility of the major premise of the Sorites Paradox. Raffman hypothesises that we think the major premise is true because it is so similar to the true claim that if value #*n* in a Sorites series is Φ, then #(*n* + 1) is Φ *insofar as #n and #(n + 1) are considered pairwise* (cf. Raffman 1994, p. 47). According to Soames (1999, p. 215),[15] we confuse the major premise with a closely related but true metalinguistic principle that a speaker who characterises #*n* as Φ is thereby committed to a standard of application that counts the predicate as applying to #(*n* + 1) as well.[16] In Fara's view, we think the major premise is true because 'any instance of it we consider is in fact true at the time we consider it' (2000, p. 59). Shapiro (2006, p. 8) urges that we mistake the major premise for the following claim: 'Suppose that two objects *a*, *a'* in the field of *P* differ only marginally in the relevant respect [. . .]. Then if one competently judges *a* to have *P*, then she cannot competently judge *a'* in any other manner.'[17]

---

[14] Appealing to the psychological variety of aggregation-failure phenomena, Sweeney and Zardini (2011) object to contextualist diagnoses which claim that speakers' inclination to accept each considered instance of the major premise as true explains their inclination to accept the major (universal) premise itself as true. Regarding a psychological version of the lottery paradox, for example, 'one might be inclined to accept of each participant of a fair lottery that she will lose, but one is typically not inclined to accept that everyone will lose' (2011, p. 261). However, the lottery case is importantly different from the Sorites Paradox: we believe of each lottery ticket only that it has a high probability of losing, whereas on at least many contextualist accounts of vagueness, each instance of the premise of the paradox is taken to be (unqualifiedly, absolutely) true.

[15] See also Chapter 6 in this volume, Section 6.2, especially pp. 123ff.

[16] This commitment is defeasible, of course; in every forced march, the commitment is superseded by some pair of neighbouring patches.

[17] Of course, all of these contextualist explanations are at least partly empirical, specifically psychological hypotheses, and one might reasonably question what role such sophisticated 'principles' could play in causing speakers to mistakenly believe the major premise. We set this important question aside here.

Second, and equally significant, most contextualist diagnoses of the intuitive appeal of the major premise also have the resources to explain how a speaker is able to switch from one predicate to another, between incrementally different values in a Sorites series, without disrupting its effective continuity. This mystery lies at the heart of the Sorites Paradox, and most non-contextualist theories are not able, or don't try, to address it. Third, insofar as they allow speakers' classifications of penumbral cases to vary with non-standard contextual parameters in addition to standard ones, contextualist approaches square well with the actual use of vague words by competent speakers. Unlike most three-valued, supervaluationist, epistemic, and degree-theoretic approaches, contextualists take the character of actual use – in particular its highly variable character – to be part of the data their accounts should explain; comporting with (accommodating, reflecting) ordinary usage is surely a virtue in any linguistic theory. As an example, Williamson appears to hold that in the vast majority of borderline cases, ordinary speakers' applications of vague words are competent but (unbeknownst to us) mistaken. Keefe (2000, p. 212) concludes that speakers should refuse at the start to be marched down a Sorites series, because going along inevitably leads to classificatory errors (see also Horgan 1994). Ascription of chronic error in the use of our own words can justifiably be seen as ad hoc. On the contrary, rules of good theory construction dictate that, all else being equal, an account that does not have us incurably mistaken is preferable to one that does.

3.3 Some Shortcomings of Contextualism

Perhaps the principal shortcoming of most contextualist views, be they pragmatic, psychological or interest-relative, is that they don't provide a solution to the Sorites Paradox proper. Because they take the categorial status of values in the penumbra to be determined ultimately by speakers' judgments – by either their (tacit) communal agreement or their individual psychological states or interests – most if not all contextualist accounts apply only to the forced march or dynamical paradox. To that extent they provide at most a necessary component of a fully fledged treatment of the paradox, viz. a diagnosis of the intuitive appeal of the major premise. To provide a solution to the paradox proper, the contextualist accounts must be coupled with an account of a different kind (viz. epistemicist, supervaluationist, multi-valued, etc.)

Stanley (2003) criticises species of contextualism that draw on the alleged similarity between vague expressions and indexicals (cf. Soames 1999, 2002). Suppose you are performing a forced march with the vague predicate 'heap', proceeding step by step along a Sorites series of collections of sand grains. The first is clearly a heap, the last is clearly not, and each collection in between differs only incrementally (say by a single grain) from the next. If 'heap' is indexical, Stanley observes, its content is stable across verb phrase (VP) ellipsis. For example, in the sentence 'John lives here, and Jill does too', the content of the indexical 'here' is determined by its initial occurrence and remains constant in its second, elided occurrence. Because VP ellipsis precludes context-shifts, the contents of overt and elided indexicals are identical. By analogy, the extension of 'heap' should be the same in all its occurrences in this elliptical Sorites:

(ES) If [collection #1] is a heap, then [collection #2] is too; and if [#2] is, then [#3] is; and if [#3] is, then [#4] is;... and if [#(n − 1)] is, then [#n] is too.

In assimilating vague predicates to indexicals, Stanley argues, the contextualist forfeits an explanation as to why each conditional in ES appears unassailable. Typically the contextualist would explain the appeal of the conditionals in terms of a (gradual) change in a relevant contextual parameter (e.g. a standard of application) and the corresponding adjustment of the predicate's extension across the series. But that strategy is not available in cases of ellipsis like the one above.

   Raffman (2005a, p. 245) argues that vague predicates are better understood on the model of gradable adjectives, whose extensions, unlike those of indexicals, are not always stable across ellipsis. Consider the gradable adjective 'big' in the following sentence:

   That elephant is big, and that flea is, too.

Here, the operative comparison class changes from the first occurrence of 'big' to its second, tacit occurrence (Ludlow 2010, pp. 519–20). If the context-sensitivity of vague predicates resembles that of gradable adjectives rather than indexicals, their extensions might well shift under VP ellipsis.

   Åkerman (2012, pp. 476–7) points out that Stanley's original argument can be strengthened, however. Even if vague predicates are not indexical, surely they can be combined with indexicals, thereby fixing their extensions under ellipsis. Consider 'big' in the following sentence, for example:

   That elephant is big relative to the current comparison class, and that flea is [big relative to the current comparison class], too.

Here, Åkerman maintains, the second (tacit) occurrence of 'big' inherits its comparison class from the first. We could use a similar device to fix the relevant contextual parameter (e.g. the conversational standard of application) for the vague predicate 'heap':

(ES*) If [collection #1] is a heap relative to the current conversational standards, then [collection #2] is too; and if [#2] is, then [#3] is; and if [#3] is, then [#4] is;... and if [#(n − 1)] is, then [#n] is too.

How could the contextualist respond to this strengthened version of Stanley's original argument? According to Åkerman (2012, p. 477), the contextualist can say that we are unlikely to have reliable pre-theoretic linguistic intuitions about examples like ES*; after all, *conversational standard* is a theoretical notion whose understanding presupposes familiarity with the respective contextualist theories. Or maybe we do have reliable intuitions, but negative ones: is it *intuitively* correct to say that 'heap relative to the current conversational standard' is tolerant across a difference of one sand grain? If not, Stanley cannot help himself to ES*.

Alternatively, perhaps a more effective reply by the contextualist would be that the complex predicate 'heap relative to the current conversational standards' is also vague, so that its extension shifts in the same way as the extension of 'heap'. For example, maybe it's vague as to which conversational standard exactly is in force in a given situation, or whether the current standard is strong enough to classify a given collection of sand grains as a heap.[18] Or, alternatively still, the contextualist might argue that the most plausible reading of the following sentence lets the extension of 'big' vary even in the presence of the indexical:

> That elephant is big relative to the current comparison class, and that flea is too.

The idea would be that the latter sentence is most naturally read this way:

> That elephant is big relative to its current comparison class [*viz.*, elephants], and that flea is big relative to *its* current comparison class [*viz.*, fleas].

(Indeed, presumably the sentence must be read in this way if it's to count as true.) Of course, pragmatic considerations play a role. If the flea in question is known to be enormous, the size of a school bus, then the comparison class might be read as fixed (especially with the emphasis on 'flea'). But that is not always required.[19]

Indexical strains of contextualism have also been criticised for their epistemic implications concerning belief reports and indirect speech (cf. Keefe 2007, pp. 286–7). In the case of paradigmatic indexical expressions such as 'I' and 'today', competent speakers are normally aware of the fact that their contents can vary with the operative context. More to the point, speakers are normally in a position to track relevant changes of context and adjust their utterances accordingly. However, the sensitivity of soritical predicates to non-standard contextual parameters is less obvious and typically goes unnoticed by competent speakers;[20] for example, changes in standards and in speakers' verbal dispositions often go unnoticed or even undetected. If that's right, then unbeknownst to us we are talking past each other much of the time. Such a result seems intuitively implausible.

Keefe (2007) notes also that contextualist accounts seem to render many instances of everyday reasoning problematic. For instance, if Anna says 'Vronsky is tall', using a certain standard of tallness, and Fred responds by saying 'Ginger is tall too', using a different standard of tallness, the conclusion expressed by saying 'Vronsky and Ginger are both tall' is not licensed. But isn't that just how context-sensitivity works in ordinary language? If Anna says 'Margot Fonteyn is old', comparing her to ballerinas, and Fred says 'The Acropolis is old', comparing it to buildings, then 'Margot and the Acropolis are both

---

18 Thanks to the editors of this volume for suggesting this reply.

19 Stanley (2003) also questions the scope of Fara's (non-indexical) interest-relative analysis, observing that it applies only to expressions that admit of comparative analyses (e.g. 'tall' is analysed in terms of 'taller than'). 'Medium' and 'heap' (e.g.) are probably vague but have no comparative forms and are arguably infelicitous in comparative constructions. For example, two flames on a gas stove can be one closer to (being) medium than another, but not 'more medium'; similarly 'very medium', 'too medium'. Fara's interest-relative view is best regarded as (part of) a semantics for gradable adjectives, rather than a theory of vagueness. Fara responds to Stanley in Fara (2008).

20 Soames (1999, p. 213) observes that most shifts in conversational standards are 'subtle, indeed imperceptible'.

old' is not licensed. Furthermore, in borderline cases, competent speakers do in fact issue inconsistent judgments; of a 40-year-old ballerina, you might say on one occasion that she is old, on another that she is not old. But it doesn't follow that she is both old and not old, or even that you think she is.

3.4 A (Non-Contextualist) Descendant of Contextualism

The multiple range theory of vagueness is a non-contextualist descendant of contextualism that seeks both to solve the Sorites Paradox proper and to diagnose its intuitive appeal within a unified theoretical framework. Where contextualist approaches diagnose the intuitive appeal but typically are coupled with other theories (e.g. epistemicism or supervaluationism) to solve the puzzle, the multiple range theorist ties semantics and dynamics (use) more tightly together.

On this view, the vagueness of an expression consists in its having multiple equally permissible, arbitrarily different ways of being applied, relative to a single context (Raffman 2014).[21] In particular, in a Sorites series, the vagueness of a term is reflected in its possession of multiple equally permissible, arbitrarily different stopping places relative to any given context.[22] A permissible stopping place is simply any value in a Sorites series at which a competent speaker can stop applying a given vague predicate 'Φ' and switch to 'not Φ' or some other incompatible term; a stopping place is always in the penumbra. Any adequate theory of vagueness must countenance the existence of permissible stopping places, since a competent speaker must stop applying 'Φ' before the end of the series. For example, in a Sorites series of ages from 90 to 50, relative to, say, the comparison class of western Europeans in 2016 – make the context as fine-grained as you like – speakers can permissibly stop applying 'old' at any of a variety of ages: 70, 65, 63.5, and so on. Different speakers will stop at different ages, and the same speaker will stop at different ages on different occasions.[23]

Crucially, on the multiple range theory, any stopping place in a Sorites series is arbitrary: there can be no reason, in the nature of the case, for stopping at any particular place. Hence stopping places have no legislative force; speakers cannot justifiably charge each other with error when they stop at different places, nor can a given speaker justifiably think he is correcting his past use when his own stopping place changes. Consequently, there can be no genuine argument as between different stopping places. A boundary, on the other hand, would be legislative; speakers who failed to stop applying 'old' at its boundary with (e.g.)

---

[21] The multiple range theory is a semantic theory of vagueness that preserves bivalence primarily by means of an incompatibilist analysis of borderline cases; see Raffman (2005b, 2014, chapter 2).

[22] Contexts are defined by such factors as decisive dimensions, comparison classes and contrastive categories; they may also include purposes, speaker interests and standards of application, among other things. Roughly, on the multiple range theory, the content of a vague predicate in a given use is determined by the term's dictionary definition together with the operative context. Applications of vague predicates have their contents relative to contexts and their truth-values relative to ranges of application; see pp. 74–5, and Raffman (2014, chapter 3).

[23] Support for this claim is extrapolated from experiments by Raffman et al. on the use of colour predicates, reported in Raffman (2014, chapter 5). One could of course question whether use of a non-observational term such as 'old' or 'rich' would yield the same results.

'middle-aged' would be making a mistake, and if we knew where the boundaries were located argument and correction would be possible. A fundamental tenet of the multiple range theory is that vague terms have multiple permissible, arbitrarily different stopping places but no boundaries.

We have noted that the multiple range theorist seeks to solve the paradox and diagnose its intuitive appeal within a single unified theoretical framework. She does this by regarding the multiplicity of permissible ways of applying a vague term as evidence of its semantic structure. Specifically, she proposes that the multiplicity of application is reflected in the term's semantics in the form of multiple ranges of application. A range of application is just an abstract representation, in the semantics, of a permissible way of applying the term. A bit more formally: a range is a set of values (types, properties) to whose instantiations the term can competently be applied. Thus a range of application of 'tall' is a set of heights and a range of application of 'old' is a set of ages. A set of tall buildings or old people (instantiations of tallness or oldness) is one among multiple extensions of 'tall' or 'old', relative to the operative context.

The basic idea is that, relative to a given context, a vague word has multiple ranges of application, and each of those ranges in turn may have different extensions at different possible worlds. For example, in our series of ages 90–50, one range of application of 'old' (e.g. compared with western Europeans in 2016) might contain the ages 90–70, another 90–65, another 90–63 and so on. Some ranges of application of 'old', 'borderline' and 'middle-aged' are pictured in Figure 3.1. Notice that each predicate has some ranges that overlap with some ranges of the other two. According to the theory, a sentence or utterance applying a vague term is true or false at a context, relative to each range of application that includes the value to which the term is being applied. The figure indicates that for a person who is 63 years of age, the sentence '*x* is old' is true relative to the third range of 'old' and to the fourth range and to the fifth, and false otherwise. The sentence '*x* is borderline old' is true relative to each range of 'borderline' except the fourth, and false relative to the latter. Analogously for '*x* is middle-aged'.[24] On the multiple range theory, truth just is truth relative to a range of application.

On the multiple range view, the Sorites Paradox dissolves because, on pain of equivocation, all of its premises must be evaluated relative to the same range of application of 'old'. And since, for any context, each range of 'old' specifies a last age, the major premise of the paradox is false relative to each range of the predicate. Here the multiple range theorist is talking about the Sorites Paradox proper, not the forced march. As explained above, she is able to do this because of the reflective relationship between ranges of application of a predicate and permissible ways of applying it. As far as resolving the paradox is concerned, perhaps the most important idea in the multiple range theory is that the 'last' Φ value in a range of application is just a permissible stopping place, not a boundary. If there are

---

[24] Raffman warns that ranges of application should not be confused with precisifications; see her (2014, pp. 102–3) for details. In particular, ranges contain no boundaries, only permissible stopping places (see note 24); and the multiple range theory contains nothing analogous to supertruth. An application of a vague word is true or false relative to each range of application containing the value in question; period.

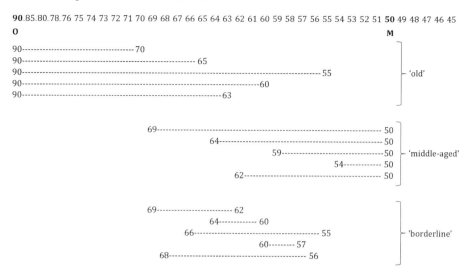

Figure 3.1 Some ranges of application of 'old', 'middle-aged' and 'old [middle-aged] borderline' (adapted from Raffman 2014, p. 98).

competent speakers, a Sorites series has to contain permissible stopping or shifting places; and presumably no one thinks that these are, or even provide evidence of, sharp boundaries. The distinction is crucial.

Like some of the contextualists cited earlier, the multiple range theorist suggests that we find the major premise (and instances of the universal premise) appealing partly because of their similarity to a pragmatic rule that we actually do (unconsciously) follow:

(I) For any vague term 'Φ': If x and x' differ only incrementally on a decisive dimension, then x is Φ if, and only if, x' is Φ *insofar as x and x' are considered pairwise.*

It is essential to appreciate that when we go to evaluate the premise, we have no alternative but to compare (or imagine comparing) *the two values x and x'*; how else could we evaluate it? Such an evaluation is just a comparison of the two values. Therefore, our intuition that the premise is true holds only with respect to the pairwise consideration of neighbouring values.

One might have the impression that, notwithstanding the multiple range theorist's claim to the contrary, the theory is ultimately just a species of contextualism. But although the multiple range theory can be seen as a descendant of certain contextualist views, it is not a contextualist approach. Most important is the role played by ranges of application. Among other things, the introduction of ranges enables the theory to provide a resolution of the Sorites Paradox proper, not just the forced march.[25] Because the theory characterises

---

[25] The notion of a range also makes possible the development of a multiple range semantics of vague terms; unlike at least some contextual accounts, the multiple range framework does not need to be coupled with a semantics of a different type, e.g. multi-valued or supervaluationist (cf. Raffman 2014, chapter 4).

sentences containing vague words as true (false) *relative to ranges*, it may be natural to conceive of ranges as a type of context, but that would be a mistake. A context is a set of factors of a kind that competent speakers can normally select or reject at will, that they can intentionally choose to take into account in their application of a term; for instance, you can choose to relativise your use of 'old' to buildings instead of ballerinas, or your use of 'rich' to a contrast with 'upper middle income' instead of 'middle income'. Speakers are typically aware of, and can say, which context they are relativizing to in a given utterance.[26] To put the point another way, competent speakers normally have a degree of control over the contexts relative to which they apply vague terms; and they choose the contexts they do for reasons – because a certain context is topically relevant to a current conversation, or simply because it is the one currently in use. In contrast, speakers do not normally choose or decide upon the ranges to which they will relativise their applications of vague words, or take those ranges into account. Rather, they simply decide how they will classify a given item, and relativisation to certain ranges comes along automatically, for free, as it were. Moreover, in the variable transitional region between categories, speakers' classifications, a fortiori the sets of ranges to which those classifications are relativised, are determined by brute psychological mechanisms. Thus these classifications are not made for a reason; as we have explained, our classifications of variable items are made arbitrarily, without (non-trivial) justification. For these reasons among others, range-relativity is not plausibly viewed as a species of context relativity.[27]

---

[26] The multiple range theorist will say that the content (intension) of a vague term, relative to a context, is a function of the operative context together with the dictionary definition of the term.

[27] For discussion of the multiple range theory and some objections and replies, see Égré (2015), Raffman (2015), Sainsbury (2015), and Scharp (2015).

4   Incoherentism and the Sorites Paradox

Matti Eklund

4.1 Introduction

Consider the Sorites Paradox, and other philosophical paradoxes such as the Liar Paradox. The standard way of approaching them is by appeal to the *semantic values* – by which I mean something at the level of reference, broadly construed – of the key expressions employed in stating the paradoxes. A central plank in such an approach is often a logic of vagueness or a formal theory of truth. The friend of the approach then tries to explain the phenomena at hand by appeal to these semantic values. Call an approach like this a *reference-based* approach to a paradox. The simplest kind of reference-based approach seeks to resolve the paradox by appeal to the nature of those things that the key expressions represent. For example, one might seek to resolve the Sorites Paradox, which has its source in vagueness, by saying that vague predicates stand for vague properties, and then give a theory of the nature of these vague properties. Call such an approach *metaphysical*. Not all reference-based approaches to paradoxes need be metaphysical. One prominent approach to vagueness and the Sorites Paradox is supervaluationism.[1] The supervaluationist does not hold that the semantic values of vague expressions are in and of themselves vague. Instead she says that vague expressions are semantically indeterminate, and these expressions refer to different things under different possible precisifications. Supervaluationism does not seek to explain the Sorites Paradox by appeal to the nature of the individual referents of vague expressions, so it is not a metaphysical approach. But supervaluationism is still a reference-based approach, seeking to explain vagueness by appeal to facts about the reference of vague expressions; specifically, by appeal to the fact that these expressions have a multitude of candidate referents.

Of course, there are alternatives to reference-based approaches to paradoxes. One could at least in principle simply deny that vague language, or truth talk, is factual, and attempt to use this as the basis for a response.[2] Perhaps the friend of this approach could say that our failure to resolve the Sorites Paradox is somehow due to

---

[1] The classic reference is Fine (1975). See also Keefe (2000) and Chapter 2 in this volume.
[2] See MacFarlane (2016) for a recent approach of this kind.

a mistaken assumption to the effect that the vague language is factual. Or one could say that in addition to their semantic values, the relevant expressions have associated with them rules of use, not relating in any immediate way to contribution to truth-conditions, and the paradox in question is explained by appeal to features of these rules of use.

The *incoherentist* view of the Sorites Paradox, which I favour, is another alternative to reference-based approaches. This view says, roughly, that the paradoxes arise because of an inconsistency in meaning-constitutive rules. These rules do not operate alongside and independently of truth-conditions but also help determine the truth-conditions of sentences containing vague expressions. Since the rules are inconsistent, the truth-conditions cannot be such as to actually validate the rules. This, the thought is, explains why it is so hard to come up with a satisfactory account of the truth-conditions of vague sentences. This incoherentist view does not break as radically with the tradition of explaining paradox by appeal to truth-conditions as the two suggestions previously mentioned do, for the rules she appeals to are held to be relevant to the determination of truth conditions. However, comparing these other alternatives is still helpful when it comes to illustrating the sort of strategy the incoherentist employs.

In what follows I will explain the incoherentist view I favour, present what I see as main arguments for such a view, discuss some purported objections and compare other incoherentist views in the literature.[3] While some of what I say explains and summarises what is in the existing literature, primarily the discussion of objections contains much that is novel.

4.2 Incoherentism

When briefly characterising incoherentism just above, I spoke of meaning-constitutive rules. Perhaps I should have used scare quotes around 'rule' to distance myself from this way of speaking. Lots of things can be, and have been, meant by talk of semantic rules, and I would want to distance myself from most of them. Even so, my own appeal to 'rules' will still be controversial.

What I am supposing – later I will return to this supposition, but for now just bear with me – is that to employ an expression with a given meaning is to take on certain *commitments*, or to have certain kinds of *dispositions* to use the expression in a given way. Some of these commitments or dispositions may fail to be consistent with each other.

---

[3] Dummett (1975) and Horgan (1994) have earlier defended versions of incoherentism. I have myself defended incoherentism in, e.g., my (2002) and (2005). Nihilism, the view according to which vague predicates fail to be true of anything, defended by e.g. Peter Unger (1979a, 1979b, 1979c, 1980a), Wheeler (e.g. 1975, 1979), Heller (1990), Ludwig and Ray (2002) and Braun and Sider (2007) is often mentioned alongside incoherentist views (Williamson 1994, chapter 6, mentions Dummett as a nihilist). But nihilism is importantly different from incoherentism. Saying that an expression is governed by inconsistent rules is one thing; saying that it is empty is another. The former may be held to entail the latter (though that is not my view – see below); it is not in the least plausible that the latter entails the former. I will return to nihilism (as defended by Unger) in Section 4.6.

My favoured version of the view focuses on dispositions instead of commitments, and in what follows I will focus on my favoured version of the view.

We may then say that a given language is inconsistent exactly if competence with all elements of that language involves dispositions to accept things that are inconsistent with each other. Talk of language being inconsistent hardly has a pretheoretically clear meaning. I am using the locution partly stipulatively.

The account of competence just sketched does not by itself say anything about the semantic values of the expressions of an inconsistent language. One perhaps natural suggestion would be that when the rules governing an expression are inconsistent, then the expression simply lacks a semantic value (or it has a trivial semantic value: for example, a predicate would be empty). I see two problems with this. First, this seems implausibly radical: it yields that nothing is old, or red, or a mountain, etc. Anyone who embraces this radical idea is apt to want to draw a distinction between assertible and non-assertible sentences of, for example, the form '___ is old', and so mitigate the problem by saying that those of these sentences we would take to be true are at least assertible. However, deciding under what conditions sentences are assertible presents much the same problems as deciding under what conditions they are true, and supposing one can come up with a satisfactory theory of assertibility, why not simply use that also as a theory of truth? Second, a different problem is that the incoherence is holistic. It is not just the rules for one expression that lead to incoherence. The rules governing vague expressions lead to problems only jointly with assumptions about logic.[4] If the incoherence is holistic, exactly which expressions should then be taken to be empty?

Instead I prefer a view that allows vague expressions to have non-trivial semantic values despite the fact that vague expressions are inconsistent in the way indicated. Here is one way of allowing for this. Consider the theory of reference-determination in the spirit of Lewis.[5] Following Carnap, Lewis held theoretical terms to be somehow implicitly defined by the theories in which they occur. In the simplest case, the referent of a theoretical term is whatever makes true the sentences of the theory wherein the term occurs. But we certainly want to say that theoretical terms occurring in false theories can refer, so we can't always say exactly that. What Lewis does is to allow that the term refers to what comes closest, and close enough, to making true those sentences of the theory. Closeness is here not just a matter of what, quantitatively, makes true the most sentences. Overall best fit is what is at issue; qualitative considerations enter in as well. And if it turned out that a given theory was inconsistent, the same would apply. Inconsistency is not relevantly different from mere falsity. It is presumably obvious where I am going with this: the relationship between the semantic values of vague expressions and the rules, in the sense gestured at, which govern them is, I suggest, like that between the semantic value of a theoretical term introduced by an inconsistent theory and the sentences of that theory.

---

[4] See e.g. Zardini (2008a) (see also Chapter 8 in this volume, Section 8.3.4, and Chapter 9, Section 9.3).
[5] See e.g. Lewis (1970b, 1972, 1997).

It is reasonable to speculate that it is indeterminate just what the semantic values of vague expressions are: it is indeterminate what assignment comes closest to making true the principles that function as meaning-constitutive rules. But vague expressions have non-trivial semantic values; it is only that it is indeterminate what these non-trivial semantic values are.

These general remarks are consistent with many different specific views regarding what the semantic values of the relevant expressions are. The main point for present purposes is that a language being inconsistent need not be bound up with the relevant expressions having trivial semantic values or lacking semantic values altogether. It is possible, of course, to think that what has just been sketched is only one factor in reference-determination, and other considerations enter in as well. One might even hold that the principles it is part of our competence to be disposed to accept do not contribute in any direct way to reference-determination: instead some kind of causal theory of reference is correct.

If languages can be inconsistent in the way characterised, one can attempt to diagnose some philosophical paradoxes as arising from inconsistency of our language. The form of the diagnosis is that among the assumptions that lead to absurdity through the paradoxical reasoning are some that are untrue but underwritten by competence.

In the case of vagueness, the present topic, a natural way to spell out the incoherentist idea would be to say that tolerance principles are meaning-constitutive for vague predicates, where a tolerance principle for a predicate F is:

Tolerance: Some small enough difference in F's parameter of application never matters to F's applicability, even while some large enough difference sometimes does.

It is tolerance principles that underwrite the Sorites Paradox. Take a specific version of the paradox:[6]

(1) Someone who is 1400 mm tall is not tall.
(2) For all n, if someone who is n mm tall is not tall, then someone who is $n + 1$ mm tall is not tall.
(C) So, someone who is 2900 mm tall is not tall.

The 'some small enough difference never matters' part underwrites the major premise, (2); the 'some large enough difference sometimes matters' underwrites both that there will be an intuitively acceptable premise such as (1) and an intuitively unacceptable conclusion such as (C).

My view is that not only is vagueness a source of inconsistency in language of the kind outlined, but also that this is crucial to understanding vagueness and the Sorites Paradox. I will defend this claim in Section 4.3. One could in principle agree that vagueness is a source of inconsistency in the way described, but hold that this is not very interesting – that the key to obtaining a theoretical understanding of vagueness and the Sorites lie elsewhere.

---

[6] See 'The Sorites Paradox', in the introduction to this volume.

Consider in this connection what I said above about semantic values. The dispositions constitutive of competence are dispositions to accept incoherent things, but help determine consistent, non-trivial truth-conditions. This means that the incoherentist view I defend is in principle compatible with any standard view on the truth-conditions of vague sentences found in the literature, and does not immediately provide support for one of these views over others. Philosophers of a certain bent of mind will then ask: what is the point? Doesn't the incoherentist suggestion leave everything as it is? This is a possible and understandable reaction, but it betrays commitment to a reference-based approach to the paradox. For what it amounts to is that suggestions that do not have any immediate implications regarding reference do not have any important implications as far as the paradox is concerned.

4.3 Arguments for Incoherentism

If the incoherentist view is correct, that nicely explains a number of phenomena related to vagueness and the Sorites. In this section I will go through these things.

Recalcitrance. The hypothesis explains the seeming irresolubility of the Sorites Paradox: why every proposed solution seems intuitively unsatisfactory. A natural way to see the literature is this. Proposed semantics for vagueness leave the extensions of vague predicates with unintuitively sharp boundaries; new semantics are proposed, meant to get around this; those semantics are argued not to avoid the problem; and so on. A seeming problem with a fully classical and bivalent theory is that an arbitrarily small difference in the relevant dimension given this theory implausibly makes for a difference between it being true that something is F and false that something is F, for F a vague predicate. If in response to this problem a many-valued or fuzzy theory is proposed, a version of the original problem remains. There are still unwanted boundaries, this time between, e.g., the true and the neither-true-nor-false, or the perfectly true and the less than perfectly true. A seeming lesson of the philosophical discussion of the Sorites Paradox is that this generalises. Any otherwise acceptable assignment of semantic values to expressions of our language yields unwanted boundaries. Incoherentism does not get around this. Nor is it meant to. What it does yield is that no assignment of truth-conditions to vague sentences will fully satisfy the meanings of vague expressions. It then predicts the phenomenon of recalcitrance. The incoherentist can say that one cannot expect there to be an otherwise acceptable assignment of truth-conditions to vague sentences that avoids these unintuitively sharp boundaries. All one can hope for is that some assignments come close enough to respecting the meaning of vague expressions that these expressions have semantic values. Needless to say, friends of specific accounts of vagueness found in the literature will think they have their own ways of getting around the problem, and to properly make an argument from recalcitrance one would need to discuss individual proposals separately.

Flip-flopping. The issue of recalcitrance has to do with what happens when we try to *theorise* about vagueness. Focus now not on theorising about vagueness but on the actual *use* of vague expressions. Arguably, one distinctive feature of what happens in Sorites cases is that speakers are apt to flip-flop. An item that is classified one way at first can be classified a different way later and the speaker never comes to a stable verdict. This phenomenon underlies the appeal of contextualist account of vagueness.[7] But it is also neatly explained by appeal to the idea that vague expressions are governed by inconsistent 'rules'. Consider the following example. You work in a paint shop. You're being told that paradigmatic red paint goes in the left corner and paradigmatic yellow paint goes in the right corner. For any two jars of paint, if the paint in the jars is sufficiently alike they should go in the same corner. If the paint shop is sufficiently well stocked, the jars of paint constitute a Sorites series, and there is no way you can obey these instructions. Assuming you don't notice the inconsistency in the instructions, you will vacillate, in a way familiar from the vagueness literature. Having classified a jar of paint one way and put it in the right corner, you can notice its similarity to jars of paint put in the other corner and so revise your verdict on that; but having done so, you will think other jars of paint put in the right corner should be reclassified. But then…Of course, you will soon realise the futility of your undertaking; but the same applies in the case of vague expressions. Any classification is bound to fail to respect some meaning-constitutive principle governing the expression. That does not mean that vague predicates are empty – any more than the paint store employee succeeds in her task by not dividing up the jars at all.

The nature of vagueness.[8] What is it for an expression, for example a predicate, to be vague? Here is one kind of suggestion found in the literature:

(BORDERLINE) For a predicate to be vague is for it to have possible borderline cases.

But what is a borderline case? Do we have an independent handle on what borderline cases, in the relevant sense, are? To elaborate: if a predicate F has borderline cases if and only if some sentences of the form '___ is F' are neither true nor false, then there are phenomena other than vagueness which give rise to borderline cases. For (BORDERLINE) to provide an acceptable account of the nature of vagueness, 'borderline case' must mean something more specific. But here the worry arises that to elucidate the intended sense of 'borderline case' one must speak of lack of truth-value *due to vagueness*, and then we no longer have a very informative characterisation of vagueness.

A different suggestion is:

(SORITES-SUSCEPTIBILITY) For a predicate to be vague is for it to be *Sorites-susceptible*.

But what is it for a predicate to be Sorites-susceptible? For it to be such as to make some Sorites reasoning sound? No, for the Sorites reasoning is not sound. Is it then for it to make some Sorites reasoning *seductive* – that it be such that we are actually disposed to be taken in by the reasoning? But that proposal yields that vagueness is just a psychological phenomenon. Suppose we stopped having the disposition to be taken in by Sorites

---

[7] See e.g. Fara (2000), Kamp (1981), Raffman (2014), Shapiro (2006), Soames (1999) and Chapter 3 in this volume.
[8] This theme is developed in Eklund (2005).

reasoning using 'old' – perhaps because of there being greater awareness of the problems with such reasoning. The proposal at issue does not immediately have the consequence that 'old' would change its meaning; but it does have the consequence that 'old' would cease to be vague. I think a reasonable proposal regarding vagueness makes vagueness a matter of meaning, in such a way that a vague expression cannot cease to be vague without change in meaning.

However, appeal to (SORITES-SUSCEPTIBILITY) does work if Sorites-susceptibility is written into the meanings of vague predicates in the way outlined in the characterisation of the incoherentist view. Then the vagueness of an expression is not just a matter of whether we happen to be taken in by some associated Sorites reasoning. It is a matter of something that is constitutive of the meaning of the predicate.

Vagueness and semantic indeterminacy. It is generally agreed that vagueness in some way gives rise to or is associated with semantic indeterminacy. Note the *gives rise to* or *is associated with*, rather than *is identical with*. It should be uncontroversial that there are sources of semantic indeterminacy other than vagueness, for example partial definition, and the indeterminacy phenomenon Hartry Field (1973) discusses in connection with Newtonian 'mass'.[9] But even if vagueness is not identical to semantic indeterminacy one can wish for an account of how vagueness is connected to semantic indeterminacy.

Standard models for what the semantic indeterminacy associated with vagueness would be like are unsatisfactory, connected to how theories of the Sorites Paradox generally are unsatisfactory. Saying that a vague predicate carves up the domain into three classes, those entities it is true of, those it is false of and those such that it is indeterminate whether it applies, is unsatisfactory as it gives rise to unintuitive sharp boundaries.

Some theorists, those who appeal to metaphysical vagueness and those inclined to favour epistemicist accounts, may of course deny any connection between vagueness and semantic indeterminacy, and they can appeal to the problems in making good sense of the indeterminacy in question as part of their case for the denial.[10] However, I believe that the incoherentist view can serve as a basis for a nice account of the relation between vagueness and semantic indeterminacy.[11]

Distinguish between first-level indeterminacy and second-level indeterminacy:

A sentence is first-level indeterminate if it (due to indeterminacy) lacks classical truth value under some acceptable assignment of semantic values. A sentence is second-level indeterminate if (due to indeterminacy) it has different truth values under different acceptable assignments of semantic values.[12]

[9] What Field discusses is that given what we know today, there is no quantity that exactly satisfies the conception associated with mass in Newtonian physics. Instead there are two quantities – relativistic mass and rest mass – that are both best candidates. Field thinks 'mass' as used by Newtonians is semantically indeterminate as between relativistic mass and rest mass.

[10] However, arguably the unwanted boundaries problem arises also for the metaphysical indeterminacy theorist.

[11] See especially Eklund (2010b).

[12] The reason for the added 'due to indeterminacy' in the first definition is that there may be other reasons for lack of classical truth value besides indeterminacy, for example presupposition failure. I know of no corresponding need for a similar clause in

An *acceptable assignment* of semantic values is here a best possible account of semantic values. An acceptable assignment in this sense is not the same thing as a precisification, as 'precisification' is used in the discussion of supervaluationism about vagueness.[13] The way traditional supervaluationists think about it, vagueness gives rise to an expression's having a multitude of precisifications, corresponding to the ways of making the expression precise, compatibly with the meaning it is currently endowed with. Each precisification is classical. Moreover, a sentence is true iff it is true under all precisifications, false if, and only if, false under all precisifications, and neither true nor false if, and only if, it has different truth-values under different precisifications. Supervaluationism is only a framework for modelling first-level indeterminacy. The correct assignment of a semantic value to a sentence that receives different truth-values under different precisifications is *neither true nor false*.

Note that there can be second-level indeterminacy without such first-level indeterminacy: it can be that some sentences have different truth-values under different acceptable assignments but under no assignment does a sentence lack a determinate classical truth value.

The concern about standard accounts of the semantic indeterminacy associated with vagueness is that saying that vague expressions carve up their domains into more than two classes fails to get around the problem of unwanted boundaries. This is a strike against postulating that vagueness is bound up with first-level indeterminacy. (An assignment of semantic values to vague expressions given which there is first-level indeterminacy does not do appreciably better in accommodating the intuitive picture associated with vagueness than does an assignment of semantic values to vague expressions given which there is no such indeterminacy.) But it is reasonable to speculate that given an incoherentist view on vagueness, vagueness is regularly associated with second-level indeterminacy: if there is no way to satisfy the constraints imposed on truth-conditions by what is constitutive of meaning, why suppose there will still in general be a unique best assignment of truth conditions?[14] One can then accommodate the sense that vagueness is somehow associated with semantic indeterminacy by saying that it is associated with second-level indeterminacy. If one likes, one can also say that it is also associated with first-level indeterminacy, but there is no longer the same theoretical need to say this. One has accounted for the connection to indeterminacy already by appeal to the tie to second-level indeterminacy.[15] Of course, it is intuitively repugnant also to think that vagueness gives rise to there being a tripartite distinction between what is true under all acceptable assignments, what is true under some but not all acceptable assignments and what is true under no acceptable assignments. But this intuitive repugnancy, although real, is not very pressing; for there is no reason to think

the second definition, but it does not hurt to include it. Because of the occurrences of this clause, the characterisation of first- and second-level indeterminacy is not a reductive characterisation of what indeterminacy amounts to.

[13] See again Fine (1975) and Chapter 2 in this volume.

[14] This is not to say that incoherentism is the only view on vagueness that could have this consequence.

[15] In the literature, there are also general concerns about what semantic indeterminacy is supposed to be – see Merricks (2001b) and Taylor and Burgess (2015). The suggestion mentioned does not immediately help with those concerns.

our competence with vague expressions should be a reliable source regarding the structure of what acceptable assignments there are.

Returning to the question of indeterminacy and the problem of unwanted boundaries, here is the relevant point. Unwanted boundaries are in some way a flaw in a given assignment, since an assignment purports to be a correct representation of the semantic values of the expressions of the language, and the counterintuitiveness is a strike against it succeeding in this. But incoherentism says that we are stuck with unwanted boundaries. Any assignment will be flawed in the sense of not fully respecting the meaning-constitutive principles for vague expressions.

I say that vagueness is associated with second-level indeterminacy, but I would not want to commit to the claim that every vague expression has to be associated with such indeterminacy. Suppose for example that reference magnetism is real: that some things expressions might mean are intrinsically more eligible to be meant (more 'reference-magnetic').[16] Then it can be that for some vague expressions there is a unique best assignment of a semantic value; that is the reference-magnetic semantic value in the vicinity, so to speak. Among what otherwise would have been a multitude of acceptable assignments, there is one that has the expression stand for something reference-magnetic. I would say that in this case the expression is vague but not semantically indeterminate. That seems to me to be the right result. But I wouldn't rest any argumentative weight on it, but regard these cases as spoils to the victor. Alternatively, one could distinguish two different kinds of vagueness, vagueness with respect to sense and vagueness with respect to reference, and say that an expression has the latter feature only if it has different semantic values under different assignments.[17]

4.4 Objections regarding Competence

Turning to objections to the incoherentist view proposed, let me start by, in this section, considering the most obvious one: while incoherentism might be nice if it works, it requires an implausible view of meaning and competence. The underlying view is what I will call an SCR-view, where the SCR stands for *selective conceptual role*. It is a conceptual role view, for it associates an expression with a particular role in a speaker's cognitive economy – that

---

[16] The label reference magnetism is from Hodes (1984). The idea as it has come to be discussed derives from Lewis (1983, 1984), although there is a discussion in the literature regarding what exactly Lewis's views on this were – see e.g. Schwarz (2014).

[17] There is a connection between the themes brought up in the present section and epistemicism. If 'epistemicism' is understood simply as the view that vagueness is compatible with both bivalence and classical logic, then the above suggests a defence of epistemicism different from those prominent in recent discussions. The idea is that each acceptable assignment is fully bivalent (at least as far as vagueness is concerned), and the only way the indeterminacy comes in is through there being different acceptable assignments. Since bivalence holds under each acceptable assignment, bivalence holds *simpliciter*. Already Campbell (1974), an early defence of some sort of epistemicism, brought up a version of this idea, under the label 'semantic uncertainty'. (The label 'uncertainty' is not ideal: it suggests that the phenomenon is merely epistemic.) Compare too Nick Smith (2008) on 'plurivaluationism'. Smith essentially defends a fuzzy view on vagueness but with the twist that he adds that there is (what I call) second-level indeterminacy: different assignments ascribing different (fuzzy) truth-values to sentences are all acceptable (see Chapter 8 in this volume, Section 8.2, especially pp. 158–9).

One main argument for epistemicism is to the effect that there is no avoiding unacceptable sharp boundaries anyway. But despite the undeniable strength of those arguments, it is hard to swallow the consequence that something about our use of expressions determines a unique best assignment of semantic values (see Chapter 1 in this volume, Section 1.3). The current proposal accepts those epistemicist arguments while avoiding this consequence.

characterised by the dispositions vis-à-vis the meaning-constitutive-principles – and says competence with an expression involves associating it with the right role. It is selective, for as opposed to holistic views it says that only some of the representations involving the expression that one accepts or is disposed to accept are constitutive of what meaning one uses the expression with.

There are two different perspectives from which one can attack the underlying view on meaning and competence. One can accept an SCR-view on competence but hold that for general reasons what competence disposes one to accept can never be incoherent in the way that incoherentism postulates, or one can reject an SCR-view in favour of something different entirely, for example the view that to be competent with an expression just amounts to having some capacities or other in virtue of which one uses it with the customary reference. Let me start by considering the view that although an SCR-view is acceptable, languages cannot be inconsistent in the way discussed.

A problem for an SCR-view that aims to leave room for meanings to be inconsistent is that anyone who realises that some sets of principles lead to inconsistency – for example a philosopher studying the Sorites Paradox – will plausibly thereby be disinclined to accept all of these principles. And we don't want to say that this philosopher thereby loses her semantic competence.

However, this problem arises for any SCR-view given which the cognitive relation between a competent thinker and the meaning-constitutive principles is something like belief. But already independent considerations show that such an identification is too simple-minded. If anything has the status of a meaning-constitutive principle, the sentences expressing basic logical laws surely do. But for pretty much any basic logical law, one can find logicians and philosophers rejecting the sentences expressing them; and since these logicians and philosophers are (the argument goes) unquestionably competent, these sentences cannot be meaning-constitutive.[18] Hence, the argument runs, it is somewhat trickier than might have been expected to identify the cognitive relation in question. But then simple-minded suggestions regarding the nature of the cognitive relation anyway do not work.

What might the cognitive relation plausibly be? Any discussion here will have to be brief. But one suggestion is that it is something like *taking it to be the default position that*... (implicitly, of course. The claim is not that speakers actually think of the expressions they use in these terms). Strikingly, counterexamples to taking the cognitive relation to be something like (dispositions to) belief or acceptance always involve someone having a *special reason* to deny the supposed analyticity. Timothy Williamson has prominently called attention to Vann McGee's rejection of *modus ponens* when criticising the notion of epistemic analyticity, and he has also called attention to how speakers can for specific reasons reject instances of the schema 'every F is an F'. But strikingly, the examples involve thinkers armed with specific reasons to reject the epistemic analyticities. If one imagines

---

[18] See Williamson, e.g. (2007), for discussion.

someone rejecting *modus ponens* or instances of 'every *F* is an *F*' without special reason to do so, it becomes considerably more doubtful that this thinker, social externalism aside,[19] uses these terms with their standard meanings.[20] Another suggestion is to turn to normative characterisations, and speak of what speakers are entitled to accept instead of what they actually believe or are disposed to believe.[21]

If the meaning-inconsistency view couldn't be combined with a plausible view on reference-determination – if, say, the meaning-inconsistency view had the consequence that the semantic values of vague expressions are undefined or empty – then there could be reason for a friend of an SCR-view to reject the possibility of a meaning-inconsistency view at least for philosophically significant cases. But I argued above that the Lewisian picture of reference-determination straightforwardly allows that vague predicates have non-empty extensions, even if inconsistent in the way outlined.

Next, turn to Wright's important (1975) discussion of incoherentism about vagueness. (Wright's immediate target was Dummett 1975, which I will get to later.) Wright thinks meaning-consitutive principles cannot be inconsistent. One central point he makes is that meaning-constitutive rules cannot be inconsistent while sufficing, by themselves, to confer meaning upon an expression: since any use of the expression can be made to fit with the meaning-constitutive rules, these rules do not rule out anything.[22] He says for instance that '[t]he rules of [a game supposed to be governed by inconsistent rules] do not provide an account of how the game is played, for it is possible that someone might grasp them yet be unable to participate' (Wright 1975, p. 362).

However, distinguish between the claim that a full account of an expression's meaning (or of how a game is played) can be provided by a mere list of inconsistent rules (or as I would prefer to put it when speaking in my own voice, meaning-constitutive principles) and the claim that some rules governing an expression are individually or jointly inconsistent. What Wright casts doubt on is the former claim, but incoherentism is only committed to the latter. Surely the view that meaning-constitutive principles can be inconsistent does not carry with it a commitment to the view that our competence can be *exhaustively* described by appeal to a *mere list* of these inconsistent rules: matters like how the rules are to be weighted are also relevant.

Some theorists want nothing to do with SCR-views, the possibility of incoherentism aside. Let me turn to this. Prominent among such theorists are those who hold that all there is to the semantics of an expression is its reference, plus aspects that do not directly relate to truth-conditions, such as conventional implicature – they eschew the notion of meaning-constitutive principles entirely. Call these theorists *referentialists*.[23] It would obviously take

---

[19] Social externalism is, roughly, the view that what an expression means as used by a speaker can be determined in part by the speaker's social environment.

[20] See Williamson (2007) and, for discussion, Eklund (2007) and (2010a). Williamson uses these examples to criticise SCR-views; what I hold is that the examples only put pressure on how SCR-views are best construed. Wright (2004, p. 169) gestures toward the sort of idea I am describing here.

[21] See Scharp (2013, chapter 2).

[22] See Wright (1975, pp. 361ff).

[23] The label is from Williamson (2009).

us too far afield to assess fully generally whether a referentialist view or an SCR-view is preferable. But some things specifically pertaining to the case of vagueness are worth bringing up.

One thing I would press against a referentialist is that she will have a hard time accommodating vagueness as genuinely a feature of the meaning of an expression. If the meaning of an expression just consists in its reference, then the only way an expression can be vague is if its referent is vague, or maybe if, along the lines of supervaluationism, it has different candidate referents – but these resources are too meager to capture vagueness, for there can be non-vague expressions that behave referentially in the same way that vague expressions do. Suppose for example that a simple fuzzy theory is the correct theory of vagueness, and suppose that someone is tall* to degree 1 iff that person is at least 1900 mm, tall* to degree 0 iff that person is 1800 mm or less, and tall* to degree d if in between, where d=(the person's height in mm−1800)/100. 'Tall*' is hardly vague, despite having a fuzzy semantics. There is no reason why it would invite a Sorites Paradox; the principle that a tiny difference in height makes no difference to tall*ness lacks plausibility. Or compare a simple version of supervaluationism, where what marks an expression as vague simply is its having different possible precisifications. Compare then a predicate 'nice', stipulated to behave as follows: a number is nice if <13; not nice if >15.[24] One might add that for any *n*, if n is nice then *n*−1 is likewise nice. 'Nice' then has different precisifications, since nothing has been said about the classification of 13, 14 and 15. 'Nice' behaves referentially as vague predicates behave according to this simple version of supervaluationism, but it is not vague. Now, a simple fuzzy theory and simple supervaluationism are, precisely, simple theories. For all I have actually argued, more sophisticated theories could succeed in characterising vagueness referentially. That would have to be judged on a case by case basis. But I believe the strategy illustrated by these simple cases generalises. Importantly, the argument is not to the effect that what the theories say about the referential properties of vague expressions is mistaken but only that it does not suffice to characterise vagueness.

Some theorists believe in metaphysical vagueness. They may think that vague singular terms refer to vague entities, and vague predicates ascribe vague properties; and that the vagueness of the expressions is due to the vagueness in the entities that they refer to and ascribe. If these theorists are right, then of course something about the reference of vague expressions separates them from non-vague expressions: all and only vague expressions refer to vague entities. The referentialist can say that this distinguishes the reference of vague expressions from the reference of other expressions.

Elsewhere, I have given separate arguments against metaphysical vagueness.[25] But there is a point to be made even if metaphysical vagueness does obtain. Let the *truth value-contribution* of an expression be the complete set of facts regarding what it contributes to the truth-values of sentences in which it is used. Using this notion, the point of my above argument is that the truth value-contribution of a vague expression can be the same as the

[24] Compare Fine (1975, p. 266).
[25] See Eklund (2013).

truth value-contribution of a non-vague expression, and this point stands even supposing there is metaphysical vagueness. And this by itself means that theorising about the reference of vague expressions is unlikely to hold the key to the puzzles surrounding vagueness.

What I have been talking about is just an instance of a more general problem for the referentialist way of thinking about meaning. Consider normative language. Some expressions ('right', 'wrong', etc.) seem to be normative as a matter of their meanings. A referentialist would have to say that any such expression would have to classify as such in virtue of what it refers to. But this is problematic: normative and non-normative expressions can corefer. A quick argument to that effect is that one could easily introduce a non-normative expression with the same reference as a normative expression (consider for example 'let 'flurg' refer to whatever the third word uttered by someone over six feet tall in the year 2073 refers to', and suppose that third word is 'right').[26]

One suggestion for a would-be referentialist who happily lives with the consequence that vagueness and evaluativeness cannot be semantic features is that she might take these features to be *metasemantic* rather than semantic: these are not features of the meaning of an expression but have to do with how the reference of the expression is determined. In the case of vagueness, she can say that the vagueness of an expression has to do with how its reference is determined. She can then defend a slimmed down version of what the incoherentist holds: the language users' acceptance of tolerance principles helps determine the reference of vague expressions.

4.5 Further Objections

I have discussed at some length objections to incoherentism that focus on the underlying conception of meaning and competence. Let me now turn to some other objections.

Charity. One possible objection is that even if inconsistent languages such as those described are possible, charity militates against the hypothesis that we speak such an inconsistent language. Even though it is a theoretical possibility that we speak such a language, other interpretive possibilities are vastly preferable. But there's a question of how charity is supposed to come into it. Charity would enter into it most obviously if the incoherentist view but not opposing views ascribed incoherent beliefs to us. But such a claim would be doubly mistaken. First, and most importantly, on any reasonable view, we are prone to incoherent beliefs when it comes to vagueness. That is why the Sorites Paradox arises. Second, a plausible version of incoherentism speaks not of what competence demands that we believe but instead of, for example, what competence disposes us to accept. This means that appeal to charity has even less purchase.

Note too that in principle it can be overall more reasonable for a thinker to employ quick but dirty rules – rules that are easy to employ but which may lead the thinker astray in some special cases – than for her to employ corresponding considerably more complex

---

[26] I discuss this in chapter 4 of Eklund (2017).

rules guaranteed never to lead her astray but considerably less economical to employ.[27] All else equal, an interpreter deciding which of these sets of rules to interpret a thinker as employing may well be led by some charity-like principle positively to prefer to interpret the thinker as employing the quick but dirty rules.

The consideration just presented works best if one understands 'rules' in the context as an algorithm the thinker's cognitive system employs. This goes beyond how 'rules' has been glossed earlier in the discussion and one must hence be careful. There is still a general lesson in the vicinity.

Tolerance without incoherence. The last few years have seen an increase in interest in accepting tolerance principles at face value but making such revisions in logic – specifically in what structural rules are accepted – that this does not lead to absurdity.[28] This is one way in which the theoretical landscape has changed since I first defended the incoherentist view here outlined. Any theorist who can accept tolerance principles at face value can adopt the account of the nature of vagueness that I presented. So the existence of views such as that described shows that the argument concerning the nature of vagueness and the argument from flip-flopping do not favour incoherentism over all possible competitors, even if these arguments are otherwise good as far as they go. I still think incoherentism is to be preferred over these non-incoherentist tolerance views. For one thing, I think incoherentism is uniquely well placed to capture the sense that there can be no fully adequate account of the truth-conditions of vague sentences; and, relatedly, explain the phenomenon of recalcitrance. Of course, to make this point against those who favour non-incoherentist theories that respect tolerance, it would have to be shown that these theories are indeed unsatisfactorily counterintuitive. I will not attempt to do this here.

One way in which the rejection of structural rules differs from other proposed revisions of logic is in that whereas one can see logics that differ over the semantics of individual logical expressions as corresponding to different languages, structural rules are not tied to language in the same way. The reason this is relevant is the following. So long as we are dealing with descriptions of different possible languages, one can say that the question of which possible language we speak is to be decided by a theory of interpretation. But if structural rules are not tied to language in the same way, things may look different. However, although structural rules may not strictly be part of language it can still obviously be that different thinkers, or different groups of thinkers, employ different structural rules. A theory of interpretation for a thinker or group of thinkers will then concern not only what language is employed by also such matters as what rules of reasoning are employed; and when it comes to the question of which interpretation is correct, it is a package deal.

Vagueness without tolerance. Much of the supposed attraction of the view stems from its supposed ability to satisfactorily answer the question of what the nature of vagueness is. In

---

[27] See e.g. Cherniak (1984).
[28] See e.g. Zardini (2008a) and Chapter 9 in this volume.

other words, it is due to the attraction of saying that tolerance principles are meaning-constitutive for vague expressions. But it can be argued that not all vague expressions are plausibly governed by tolerance principles. First, tolerance principles are formulated for predicates, but there are arguably vague expressions of other categories (consider, for example, vague quantifiers). Second, even focusing on the specific case of predicates, what about a predicate such as 'has few children for an academic'? This seems to be a vague predicate, but because the associated Sorites series would be so short, there is no associated compelling version of the Sorites Paradox.[29]

Complexity. By far the most serious objection to incoherentism, as far as I am concerned, is this. Vagueness would seem to be a ubiquitous feature of languages. But if the proposed incoherentist view on vagueness were correct, that would hardly be so. For why would it be a ubiquitous feature of languages to have meaning-constitutive principles of this rather peculiar kind for a large range of predicates? Other theories more readily account for the ubiquity of vagueness. On a theory on which vagueness is at bottom metaphysical, a language is vague simply because it contains expressions referring to the vague things in the world. On a supervaluationist theory, vagueness arises simply because of semantic indecision. Call this objection to incoherentism the objection from complexity.

One incoherentist response to this objection is just to insist upon the arguments in favour of the view, and say that these arguments yield that we must accept the view: maybe it is antecedently unlikely that what the incoherentist postulates is a ubiquitous feature of languages, but somehow or other it must be so. This response can be bolstered by closer consideration of the supposedly simpler theories that would avoid the objection from complexity.

An incoherentist can try to present the supervaluationist with a dilemma. A very simple form of supervaluationism will say that an expression's vagueness consists in the expression having multiple precisifications. This feature is likely to be ubiquitous. There will be vagueness thus conceived in all natural languages. But this simple supervaluationism will not do. Any partially defined expression will be classified as vague. If in response to this the supervaluationist complicates her theory, she will face the same sophistication problem as incoherentism does. Why think this complex phenomenon would be thus ubiquitous? The supervaluationist then faces a version of the problem of complexity.

A similar issue arises when it comes to metaphysical vagueness. On a simple view of metaphysical vagueness, vagueness is plausibly ubiquitous but the simple view is too simple to be satisfactory; given a more complex view the ubiquity is again hard to explain. An example of a simple view would be one where metaphysical vagueness simply gives rise to there being some sentences lacking classical truth-values. A more sophisticated view tries to get around the obvious problems faced by this simple account by adding complexity, but then a version of the problem of complexity arises.

---

[29] See Weatherson (2010) for this kind of challenge; and see Eklund (2006) for some discussion of it. (Despite what the publication dates indicate, Eklund 2006 in part responds to Weatherson 2010.)

4.6 Related Views

In this last section let me consider some views in the literature similar to mine – those of Terence Horgan (1994), Peter Unger (1979a, 1979b, 1979c, 1980a) and Michael Dummett (1975). Horgan and Dummett are plausibly classified as incoherentists, and Unger's view is similar in spirit.[30]

Horgan (1994) presents a kind of thesis–antithesis–synthesis argument where the thesis is that vagueness is impossible (because of leading to contradiction), the antithesis is that vagueness is possible (because clearly actual) and the synthesis is:

Vagueness in THE WORLD is impossible; vagueness in thought and in language is incoherent and yet is actual (and hence possible) anyway. (Horgan 1994, p. 179)

The world itself cannot be vague, but our representations of it can be. It is only that vague language and thought are incoherent. This is of course completely consonant with the incoherentist view that I have stated.

Horgan is rather cavalier about the nature of the supposed incoherence in thought and language. He says:

For purposes of this paper I can leave it open how best to cash the general notion of logical incoherence. Roughly, a concept is logically incoherent if someone who employs it correctly thereby becomes committed, at least implicitly, to accepting statements that jointly entail a contradiction. (Horgan 1994, p. 180)

He does not directly address the question of how the supposed incoherence affects the truth-conditions of vague sentences, but instead spends some time arguing that the incoherence is insulated in such a way that it does not 'propagat[e] itself destructively through our thought and discourse'.[31] That point is actually rather obvious, independently of the specifics of incoherentism; for somehow or other we can have inconsistent beliefs without that having seriously damaging consequences. It is not clear why having inconsistent meaning-constitutive beliefs (or dispositions thereto) would need to be any different in that regard.

Peter Unger (e.g. 1979a) holds that when F is a 'vague discriminative term' the following holds:

There is some relevant dimension of difference D such that (i) if something differs from an F minutely along D, then it also is an F, and (ii) if something is an F, then there is some actual or possible differing substantially along D which is not an F. (Unger 1979a)[32]

This yields via familiar Sorites reasoning that there are no Fs. The assumption that something is F leads to contradiction.[33]

---

[30] As discussed in fn. 3, Unger's view is not strictly an incoherentist view. It is, however, similar enough that comparing Unger's view is useful. Unger's views are also discussed in Chapter 11 in this volume, Section 11.3.

[31] Ibid.

[32] The exact formulation in the text is my own. Unger's own statements are found on p. 181 (rough version) and p. 182 (more careful general version).

[33] Other relatively recent theorists who have held that vagueness implies emptiness or lack of truth include Wheeler (e.g. 1975, 1979), Heller (1990), Ludwig and Ray (2002) and Braun and Sider (2007).

Unger's reasoning leads to many radical conclusions. There are no heaps, no clouds, no persons, no one knows anything, etc. To my mind, Unger simply overlooks the sort of possibility that I explore in what I say about reference-determination. Even if Unger is completely right about what principles in some sense govern vague predicates, the semantic values of vague expressions can fail to render them true.

It is in principle possible, of course, to attend to the possibility I call attention to and still conclude with Unger that vague expressions are empty. One can have a theory of how meaning-constitutive principles constrain or determine semantic values that yields that incoherence always carries emptiness in its wake. Or one can, in principle, allow that expressions governed by incoherent meaning-constitutive principles are non-empty but hold that features specific to the case of vagueness make it the case that vague expressions are empty: for example, one could hold that tolerance is so central to the use of vague predicates that no assignment of semantic values that fails to respect tolerance comes 'close enough'. But let me here again stress what was said earlier about assertibility. If one holds that vague expressions have no, or only trivial, semantic values, then one will want to draw a distinction between vague sentences that are properly assertible and those that are not. But if one succeeds in drawing such a distinction, cannot the theory of assertibility one then can construct function equally well as an account of truth-conditions?

Michael Dummett (1975) says that the use of vague expressions is 'intrinsically in-consistent' and that there can be no 'coherent logic' of vague expressions. This is in an otherwise very careful and clear article, but Dummett does not elaborate much. And the slogans Dummett uses are not very clear. One can easily come up with uncharitable ways of reading this. Start with the talk of 'no coherent logic'. What does this mean? That there is a logic of vague expressions, but it is incoherent? If so, what does this mean? A certain kind of theorist could propose that a paraconsistent logic is appropriate for a vague language, but that can hardly be what Dummett has in mind. Or that there is no logic of vague expressions? But what does that mean, in light of the fact that some arguments involving vague expressions are clearly valid and some are clearly non-valid. As for 'intrinsically inconsistent', what does this mean? Can I not use a vague expres-sion, and with its customary meaning, but apply it only to some paradigm positive cases, disapply it only to some paradigm negative cases and maintain a studious silence when it comes to everything in between? If so, the use I make of the expression is recognisably consistent.

This is not to say that one cannot interpret Dummett more charitably. The talk of the use of vague expressions being intrinsically inconsistent can be interpreted to mean that some-one using a vague expression with its customary meaning takes on incoherent obligations or has incoherent dispositions. The talk of there being no coherent logic of vagueness can be interpreted to mean that there can be no logic of vagueness that respects the meaning-constitutive principles of all the expressions of our language. In other words, Dummett can be interpreted in such a way that what he says is fully consonant with the incoherentist view presented and defended earlier in this chapter.

5   Intuitionism and the Sorites Paradox

Crispin Wright

5.1 Introduction – the Basic Analogy

Mathematical platonism may be characterised as the conviction that in pure mathematics we explore an objective, abstract realm that confers determinate truth-values on the statements of mathematical theory irrespective of human (finite) capacities of proof or refutation. This conviction crystallises in the belief that classical logic, based on the semantic principle of bivalence, is the appropriate logical medium for pure mathematical inference even when, as of course obtains in all areas of significant mathematical interest from number-theory upwards, we have no guarantee of the decidability by proof of every problem. In this respect – the conviction that the truth-values, *true* and *false*, are distributed exhaustively and exclusively across a targeted range of statements irrespective of our cognitive limitations – an epistemicist conception of vagueness[1] bears an analogy to the Platonist philosophy of mathematics. Let us characterise a vague predicate as basic just if it is semantically unstructured and is characteristically applied and denied non-inferentially, on the basis of (casual) observation. The usual suspects in the Sorites literature – *bald*, *yellow*, *tall*, *heap* and so on – are all of this character and will provide our implicit focus in what follows. Epistemicism postulates a realm of distinctions drawn by such basic vague concepts that underwrite absolutely sharp 'cut-offs' in suitable soritical series,[2] irrespective of our capacity to locate them. For the epistemicist, the principle of bivalence remains good for vague languages – or if it does not, it is not vagueness that compromises it – and classical logic remains the appropriate medium of inference among vague statements. An indiscernible difference between two colour patches in a soritical series for *yellow* may thus mark an abrupt transition from yellow to orange; the impression of the *indeterminacy* of that distinction is merely a reflection of our misunderstanding of our ignorance of where the cut-off falls. For the epistemicist, the Sorites Paradox is accordingly easily resolved. It is scotched by the simple reflection that its major premise will always be subject to counterexample in any particular soritical series. If the initial element is yellow and the

---

[1] As supported by, among others, Cargile (1969), Horwich (1998b), Sorensen (1988) and, in its most thoroughgoing development, Williamson (1994). See also Chapter 1 in this volume.

[2] We understand a 'suitable' Sorites series for a predicate F to be *monotonic*, that is, one in which any F-relevant changes involved in the move from one element to its immediate successor are never such that the latter has a stronger claim to be F than the former.

final element is orange, then there must be an adjacent pair of elements, one of which is yellow while the next is orange. It is just that we, in our ignorance, are in no position to identify the critical pair.

On one understanding of it, the *ur*-thought of intuitionism as a philosophy of mathematics is a rejection of the idea of a potentially proof-transcendent mathematical reality as a *superstition*: something that there is, simply, no good reason to believe in. For the intuitionist, the mathematical facts are justifiably regarded as determinate only insofar as they are determinable by proof, and the relevant notion of proof needs accordingly to be disciplined in such a way as to avoid any implicit reliance on the platonist metaphysics. So, in any area of mathematics where we lack any guarantee of decidability, the logic deployed in proof construction cannot rely on the principle of bivalence and hence – according to the intuitionist – cannot justifiably be classical. In particular the validity of the law of excluded middle, which intuitionism understands as depending on the soundness of bivalence, can no longer be taken for granted. There is evident scope for a similar reaction to the epistemicist conception of vagueness. The latter is a commitment to a transcendent semantics for vague expressions, which construes them as somehow glomming onto semantic values – properties in the case of vague predicates – that are possessed of absolutely sharp extensions, potentially beyond our ken. The conception that vague expressions work like that may likewise impress as the merest superstition. Perhaps a little more kindly, it may impress as merely *ad hoc*, for there is not the slightest reason that speaks in favour of it except its convenience in the context of addressing the Sorites.[3] Say that an object, *o*, is *F-surveyable* just in case *o* is available and open to as careful an inspection as is necessary to justify the application of *F* to it whenever it can be justified. For the epistemicist, reality is such that the application of any meaningful basic vague predicate, *F*, to an *F*-surveyable object must result in a statement of determinate truth value, true or false. For an intuitionistic conception of vagueness – one conceived on the model of mathematical intuitionism – a satisfactory semantics and logic for basic vague predicates must eschew commitment to any such claim.

The avoidance of such a commitment is of course common ground with any instance of the long tradition of theories about vagueness that construe borderline cases as examples of *semantic indeterminacy*: as cases where the rules of the language leave us in the lurch, so to speak, by issuing no instruction for any particular verdict. Here, though, the intuitionist credits the epistemicist with a crucial insight: that vagueness is indeed a *cognitive* rather than a semantic phenomenon; that our inability to apply the concepts on either side of a vague distinction with consistent mutual precision is not a *consequence* of some kind of indeterminacy or incompleteness in the semantics of vague expressions, but is constitutive of the phenomenon.

---

[3] I have sometimes encountered in discussion the impression that the motivational shortfall here is addressed by Williamson's argument that knowledge everywhere requires a margin of error. Not so. What that argument establishes, if anything, is that if there is a sharp cut-off in a Sorites series, we will not be able to locate it. The argument provides no reason to suppose that the antecedent of that conditional is true. I'll say a little more about the Williamsonian argument below. See also Chapter 1 in this volume, Sections 1.2 and 1.3.

Consider this example. Suppose we are to review a line of 100 soldiers arranged in order of decreasing height and to judge of each whether he/she is at least 5 ft 10 in tall – but to judge by eye rather than by using any means of exact measurement. Let the soldiers' heights range from 6 ft 6 in to 5 ft 6 in. This provides a toy model of a Sorites series as conceived by the epistemicist. For while there is indeed a sharp cut-off – there must be a first soldier in the line who is less than 5 ft 10 in tall – our judgements about the individual cases will expectably divide between an initial range of confident positive verdicts and a later range of confident negative verdicts between which there will be a region of uncertainty, where we return hesitant, sometimes mutually conflicting verdicts and sometimes struggle to return a verdict at all. Here, of course, we have a conception of canonical grounds for determining whether a hard case has the property expressed by the predicate at issue, so that is a point of contrast with our situation when we face a Sorites series for a vague predicate as conceived by epistemicism. But putting that disanalogy to one side, it remains that in the soldiers scenario, our patterns of judgement will have exactly the physiognomy that the epistemicist regards as the hallmarks of vagueness. Hence, in her view, there is nothing in our practice with vague concepts that distinguishes it from judgements concerning sharply bounded properties about whose specific nature we are ignorant.

The intuitionist agrees with epistemicism that such a physiognomy of practical judgement is characteristic of vagueness. But intuitionism drops both the assumption that the judgements concerned are answerable to the extension of a sharply bounded property *and* the notion that a different kind of explanation of these characteristic judgemental patterns is called for, in terms, roughly, of shortcomings in – our lack of guidance by – the semantic rules that fix the meanings of the expressions concerned. For the intuitionist, the vagueness of a predicate *consists in* these distinctive patterns in our use of it. They are the whole story. The intuitionist conception of vagueness is thus a *deflationary* conception: it holds that there is no more to the phenomenon than meets the eye, so to speak – that it is unnecessary, is indeed a mistake, to look to some underlying feature of the semantics of vague expressions to explain our characteristic patterns of judgement in the borderline area. (That is not to say that one should not look for an explanation of a different kind.) It is the view of the intuitionist that both epistemicism and indeterminism commit versions of this mistake.

The justification for this charge when the canvassed alternative is semantic indeterminism rests on a complex variety of considerations whose details, for reasons of space, I cannot rehearse here.[4] However there is one such consideration – one relevant aspect of our practice with vague concepts – which is particularly important for the grounding of the most distinctive aspect of the intuitionist approach. Semantic indeterminism interprets borderline cases of a distinction as cases where there is no mandate to apply either of the expressions concerned – where the rules for their use prescribe no verdict. That suggestion does a poor job of predicting one salient aspect of our judgemental practices with vague concepts,

---

[4] For some elaboration see Wright (2003a, 2007, 2010); also Williamson (1994).

namely our uncritical attitude to polar – positive or negative – judgements concerning items in their borderline regions. Provided a verdict is suitably qualified and evinces an awareness that the case is a marginal one, it is not treated as a mark of incompetence, or mistake, to have a view, positive or negative, about any single borderline case.[5] Suppose X struggles to have an opinion whether some shade from the mid-region of the yellow-orange Sorites is yellow enough to count as yellow but Y is of the opinion that it is – just about – yellow. Our sense is that such divergences are just what is to be expected, and that each reaction can be as good as the other. X need not be regarded as coming short; Y need not be regarded as overreaching. Each reaction is quite consistent with full mastery of *yellow* and due attention to the hue concerned.

According to semantic indeterminism, this laissez faire attitude should be regarded as cavalier, for X and Y cannot both be operating as the relevant semantic rules require; the rules cannot both be silent on the relevant hue and mandate Y's qualified verdict of 'yellow'.[6] Yet our ordinary practice reflects no sense of that. We are characteristically open to – as I have elsewhere expressed it (Wright 2003a and 2007), *liberal* about – polar verdicts about borderline cases. To be sure, the indeterminist might be tempted to interpret this liberality as reflecting a sense of respect for our ignorance about in just which cases the rules do in fact fall silent – which are the true borderline cases. But since, if so, there is no evident means of remedying that ignorance, that again would be a step in the direction of objectionably transcendentalising the semantics of vagueness. For the intuitionist, in contrast, there really need be no sense in which one who returns a (qualified) polar verdict about a borderline cases does worse than one who fails to reach a verdict.

The point may seem slight, but it is crucial. For respecting this aspect of our practice as in good standing requires that, in contrast to the view of semantic indeterminism, we should not regard borderline cases as presenting *truth-value gaps*.[7] If borderline cases are truth-value gaps, then someone who returns a polar verdict about such a case actually makes a mistake. And that is just what, according to liberalism, we have no right to think. It follows that we have no right to regard borderline cases as *counterexamples* to the principle of bivalence, and hence that vagueness, as now understood, provides no motive to *reject* bivalence. Since, by rejecting epistemicism, and recognising that we cannot in general settle questions in the borderline region either, we have also undercut all motive to *endorse* the

---

[5] For the purposes of this claim, we may take a borderline case to be any that tends to elicit the judgemental physiognomy characterised earlier among a significant number of competent judges.

[6] To be sure, there is another possibility: we might try to think of the rules as, in the borderline area, issuing *permissions*. Then both a tentative verdict and a failure, or unwillingness, to reach a verdict, may be viewed as rule-compliant. But it is very doubtful that any satisfactory proposal lies in this direction. Presumably among the clear cases the rules must *mandate* specific verdicts rather than merely permit them. So we need to ask about the character of the transition from cases where a positive verdict about F is mandated to cases where it is merely permitted. If this is a sharp boundary, then since there is again no possibility of knowing where it falls, the proposal will have 'transcendentalised' the semantics of F in a manner different from but no less inherently objectionable than epistemicism. But if the transition is accomplished by a spread of further borderline cases – cases that are borderline for the distinction between 'mandatorily judged as F' and 'permissibly judged as F' – then the question arises how, in point of mandate or permission, cases in this category are to be described. For argument that contradiction ensues, see Wright (2003a).

[7] Or indeed as having any kind of 'Third Possibility' status inconsistent with each of truth and falsity *simpliciter*. For further discussion, see Wright (2001).

principle, the resulting position is exactly analogous to the attitude of the mathematical intuitionist to bivalence in mathematics: that it is a principle towards which we should take an agnostic stance.

With these preliminaries in place, let us turn to review how an intuitionistic treatment of the Sorites may be developed in more detail.

5.2 The Tolerance and 'No Sharp Boundaries' Paradoxes

The classic deductive[8] Sorites paradoxes vary in two respects: first in the formal character of the major premise involved, and second – where the major premise is shared – in the manner in which that premise is made to seem plausible. And of course different forms of major premise will call for correspondingly different deductive sub-routines in the derivation of the paradox. Perhaps the most familiar form of the deductive Sorites is what we may call the Tolerance Paradox.[9] As normally formulated, it uses a universally quantified conditional major premise:

TP: $(\forall x)(Fx \rightarrow Fx')$

and proceeds on the assumption of one polar premise, $F1$, and $n-1$ successive steps of universal instantiation and *modus ponens* to contradict the other polar premise, $\sim Fn$. As for motivation, the key thought is, as the title I have given to the paradox suggests, that, such is its meaning, the application of F, and/or the justification for applying it, *tolerates* whatever small changes may be involved in the transition from one element of the series to the next: for instance, that if a colour patch is (justifiably described as) red, a pairwise indiscriminable (or even just barely noticeable) change in shade must leave it (justifiably described as) red; that if a man is bald, the addition of a single hair won't relevantly change matters, and so on. For the examples with which we are concerned, claims of this ilk can seem thoroughly intuitive; and they can be supported by a variety of serious-seeming theoretical considerations.[10] In some cases, indeed, the claim of tolerance may seem absolutely unassailable: how could 'looks red', for example, fail to apply to both, if to either, of any pair of items that look exactly the same? Unfortunate, then, that 'looks exactly the same' is not a transitive relation.

The Tolerance Paradox, however, impressive as it may be in particular cases, is not, or at least not obviously, a paradox of vagueness *per se*. Vagueness is not, or at least not obviously, the same thing as tolerance. Precision must imply non-tolerance, of course, but the converse is intuitively less clear. Ought there not somehow to be some distance between a predicate's possession of borderline cases and its being tolerant of some degree of marginal change? While the claim may indeed seem intuitive, it requires – in the presence

---

[8] As distinguished from the so-called *Forced March Sorites*. For reasons of space, I must forgo discussion of that here. See 'The Forced-March Paradox', in the introduction to this volume.

[9] See also 'The Sorites Paradox', in the introduction to this volume.

[10] For elaboration of some such, see Wright (1975).

of paradox – argument to suggest that *yellow, heap, bald*, etc., are tolerant. But no argument is required to suggest that they are vague. That these predicates are vague is a *datum*.

The No Sharp Boundaries Paradox, by contrast, impresses as a paradox of vagueness par excellence. It works with a negative existential major premise,

NSB: $\sim (\exists x)(Fx \& \sim Fx')$

that may very plausibly seem simply to give expression to what it is for F to be vague in the series of objects in question. For vagueness, surely, is just the complement of precision, and the sentence of which that negative existential is the negation, viz. what I have elsewhere (Wright 2007) called the *unpalatable existential*

UE: $(\exists x)(Fx \& \sim Fx')$,

surely just *states* that F is precise in the series in question: that there is a sharp boundary between the Fs and the non-Fs, and so no borderline cases. If, then, F is in fact vague, the negative existential seems imposed just by that fact, indeed to be a statement of exactly that fact. And now contradiction follows by iteration of a different but no less basic and cogent-seeming deductive sub-routine, involving conjunction introduction, existential generalisation, and *reductio ad absurdum* as a negation introduction rule.[11]

With both paradoxes, there is the option of letting the reasoning stand as a *reductio* of the major premise. If we take that option with the Tolerance Paradox, we treat it as a schematic proof that none of the usual suspects *is* genuinely tolerant of the marginal differences characteristic of the transitions in a soritical series for it. Tolerance, in that case, is simply an illusion. And that is a conclusion we might very well essay to live with, provided we can provide a satisfactory explanation of why and how the illusion tends to take us in, and of what is wrong with the 'serious-seeming theoretical considerations' apparently enforcing tolerance that I have already alluded to.

But not so fast: even if those obligations can be discharged, the proposed response, in the presence of classical logic, is not yet stable. For (allowing its ingredient conditional to be material) the negation of TP, now regarded as established by the paradoxical reasoning, is a classical equivalent of the unpalatable existential. So if our logic is classical, non-tolerance does after all collapse into precision, and to the extent that one feels there should, as remarked above, be daylight between them, that should impress as a black mark against classical logic in this context. Moreover that impression is only reinforced when one considers the option of letting the No Sharp Boundaries Paradox stand as a refutation of NSB. For then all that stands between that result and affirmation of the unpalatable existential is a double negation elimination step. And now, once constrained by classical logic to allow the inference to UE, we seem to be on the verge of admitting that *vagueness itself* is an illusion. That, surely, isn't anything we can live with.

---

[11] That is, the intuitionistically valid half of classical *reductio*, where the latter also allows *reductio ad absurdum* inferences that serve to eliminate negations.

Intuitionism, by contrast, aims at winning through to a position where we can accept each of the Tolerance and No Sharp Boundaries Paradox as a *reductio* of its major premise but refuse in a principled way the inference onwards to the unpalatable existential. We also aim to retain the ordinary conception of an existential statement as requiring a determinate witness for its truth, and thus to avoid any form of the implausible semantic story that construes the statement 'There is in this series a last *F* element followed immediately by a first non-*F* one' as neutral on the question of the existence of a sharp cut-off as intuitively understood. Our path will be to explore, in the light of the general, deflationary conception of the nature of vagueness outlined earlier, what motivation it may be possible to give for broadly intuitionist restrictions on the logic of inferences among vagueness-involving statements. In this we follow a suggestion first briefly floated at the end of Hilary Putnam (1983).[12] If, in particular, we can justify a rejection of double negation elimination for molecular vague statements in general, then it may be possible comfortably to acknowledge that both the Tolerance and the No Sharp Boundaries Paradox do indeed disprove their respective major premises without any consequent commitment to the unpalatable existential, nor consequent obligation either (with the epistemicist) to believe it or (with the supervaluationist) to somehow reinterpret it in such a way that it doesn't mean what it seemingly says.

5.3 Constraints on an Intuitionistic Solution

I propose that we set the following three constraints on the project. First (*Constraint 1*) and most obvious, we need to *motivate* the required restrictions on classical logic in general and, in particular, to explain how a valid *reductio* of TP, or NSB, can fail to justify the unpalatable existential.

Second (*Constraint 2*), as with all attempts to solve rather than merely block a paradox, we must offer a convincing explanation of why the premises that spawn aporia impress us as plausible in the first place, of what mistaken assumptions we have implicitly fallen into that give them their spurious credibility. So in the present instances, we must contrive to explain away the continuing powerful temptation to regard the major premises for the Tolerance and No Sharp Boundaries Paradox as true. I have said much elsewhere to attempt to defuse the attractions of tolerance premises.[13] Here we will focus on the challenge to explain why NSB is *not* a satisfactory characterisation of *F*'s vagueness in the series in question. (We have already implicitly shown our hand on this.)

Finally, (*Constraint 3*) I think it reasonable to require, although I grant it is not wholly clear in advance exactly what the requirement comes to, that Constraints 1 and 2 should, so far as we can manage it, be satisfied in a way that draws on an overarching account of

---

[12] Early discussions of Putnam's proposal, besides my own work from (2001) onwards, include Read and Wright (1985), Putnam (1985), Schwartz (1987), Rea (1989), Schwartz and Throop (1991), Putnam (1991), Mott (1994), Williamson (1996b) and Chambers (1998).

[13] Such an attempt must perforce be somewhat ramified, in order to match the diverse sources of such attraction. My own diagnostic forays run from Wright (1975) through Wright (1987) to Wright (2007).

what the relevant kind of vagueness consists in (i.e. of the nature of the relevant kind of borderline cases.) We are proposing restrictions on what, from a classical point of view, are entrenched, tried and tested patterns of inference. If such restrictions are justified, it may be, to be sure, that that justification is global, applying within discourses of every kind. That is the character, for example, of the meta-semantic considerations about acquisition and manifestation of understanding originally offered by Michael Dummett half a century ago in support of a global repudiation of the principle of bivalence except in areas where decidability is guaranteed. Whatever one's estimate of such arguments, what Constraint 3 is seeking is a justification for relevant restrictions on classical logic that is specifically driven by aspects of the nature of vague discourse. In the present context, that will require putting to work the deflationary conception of vagueness sketched in Section 1.

5.4 Addressing Constraint 1: The Basic Revisionary Argument

In the mathematical case, as remarked, the intuitionistic attitude flows from a rejection of the principle of bivalence, based on a repudiation of platonist metaphysics and insistence that truth in pure mathematics can only consist in the availability of proof.[14] In the case of vague statements, many would be pre-theoretically willing to grant that bivalence is generally unacceptable anyway. Certainly, the metaphysics of meaning implicit in epistemicism has none of the intuitive appeal of, say, arithmetical platonism. But even if it is granted that bivalence is *principium non gratum* where vagueness is concerned, repudiating the principle is one thing and motivating revision of classical logic a further thing. Classical logic need not necessarily fail if bivalence is dropped. How should the intuitionist argue specifically that the *logic* of vague discourse should not be classical?

What I once called the 'basic revisionary argument' is designed to accomplish that result. It runs for any range of statements that are not guaranteed to be decidable but are subject to a pair of principles of *evidential constraint* (EC). That is, for each such statement *P*, each of these conditionals is to hold:

EC: $P \rightarrow$ it is feasible to know P

Not $P \rightarrow$ it is feasible to know Not-P

Now, it is plausible – but with caveats, to be considered in a moment – that each of the usual suspects (*yellow, bald, tall, heap,* etc.) generates atomic predications that exhibit this form of evidential constraint; that is, intuitively, if something is, in the sense characterised earlier, surveyable for *yellow* (that is, it is available for inspection in decent conditions, etc.), and it *is* yellow, then we'll be able to tell that it is; and if it *isn't* yellow, we'll be able to tell that. Intuitively, what colour something is *cannot hide* if and when conditions present themselves in which it is possible to have a proper look at it.[15] And analogously for baldness, tallness and 'heaphood'. The basic revisionary argument is then the observation

---

[14] This argument is central in Wright (1992, 2001, 2007).
[15] The claim that EC holds good for these cases is thus not subject to 'killer yellow' issues.

that, if the law of excluded middle is retained for all such predications, P, then reasoning by cases across the EC-conditionals will disclose a commitment to the disjunction:

  D: It is feasible to know $P \lor$ It is feasible to know not-P

In effect, the thesis that P is decidable. But of that, if the relevant predicate is associated with borderline cases, we have no guarantee. Accordingly we have no guarantee of the validity of the law of excluded middle in application to such statements and therefore have no business reckoning it among the logical laws.

Simply expressed, the thrust of the argument is that a range of statements may be such as both to *lack* any general guarantee of decidability in an arbitrary instance and to *have* a guarantee that if any of them is true, it will be recognisable true and, if false, recognisably false. Imposition of the law of excluded middle onto such statements will then enforce the conclusion that each of them is decidably true or false – contrary to hypothesis. It will amount to the pretence of a guarantee that we do not actually have.

Arguably a very large class of statements are in this position, including not merely vague predications but, for instance, evaluations of a wide variety of kinds, including expressions of personal taste, humour and perhaps (some aspects of) morality. And of course the argument will run for any region of discourse where we reject the idea that truth can outrun all possibility of recognition but have to acknowledge that we lack the means to decide an arbitrary question – exactly the combination credited by the intuitionists for number-theory and analysis.

Suppose then that we disdain the law of excluded middle on this (or some or other) basis. The soritical series we are considering involve a *monotonic* direction of change: that is, any F element is preceded only by F elements, and any non-F element is succeeded only by non-F elements. The reader will observe, accordingly, that once the law of excluded middle is rejected, the sought-for distinction between the unpalatable existential and its double negation is enforced. For the latter is surely established by the inconsistency of NSB with the truths expressed by the polar assumptions. But, given monotonicity, the unpalatable existential is equivalent to the law of excluded middle over the range of atomic predications of F on the series of elements in question.

5.5 One Objection to the Basic Revisionary Argument

So far, so good. But now for the caveats. The EC-conditionals are challengeable on a number of serious-looking counts. First, they are in direct tension with the upshot of Timothy Williamson's recently influential 'anti-luminosity' argument.[16] Familiarly, Williamson makes a case that if knowledge generally is to be subject to a certain form of (putatively) plausible safety constraint, then it must be controlled by a margin of error: in particular, if a subject knows that F holds of an object a, it cannot be that F fails to hold of any object

---

[16] Williamson (2000, chapter 4).

that she could not easily distinguish, using the same methods, from a. The effect is thus that, for elements, x, in a soritical series for F, the following conditional is good:

(It is feasible to know that Fx) $\rightarrow Fx'$,

which, paired with the first of the EC-conditionals, immediately provides the means to show that F applies throughout the soritical series.

Here is not the place for a detailed engagement with Williamson's thesis. But there are a couple of fairly immediate misgivings about it that deserve notice. One is whether the notion of safety that it utilises is indeed a well-motivated constraint on knowledge everywhere, whatever the subject matter and methods employed. Williamson's intuitive thought, if I may venture a precis,[17] is that if a subject comes to the judgement that Fa, and a' is pairwise indistinguishable from a, then the subject must be significantly likely also to judge that Fa' – and now, if the latter is false, she is therefore very likely to make a false judgement using the very methods she used in judging Fa. So those methods are not generally reliable, in which case the judgement that Fa, based upon them, ought not to count as knowledgeable in the first place. Yet if that is the intuitive thought, one salient question is why we should require that, in order to count as a reliable means for settling a question about one item, a method must also be reliable about *others* that, however similar, differ from it. Why could not a machine – a speedometer, for example – that issues a varying digital signal in response to a varying stimulus have an absolutely sharp threshold of reliability, so that its responsive signals are reliable up to and including some specific value, k, in its inputs but then go haywire for inputs of any greater value. In that case, its signals may be regarded as 'knowledgeable' for any input value i, less than but as close to k as you like. If it is not a priori ruled out that our judgements, for some particular pairings of subject matter and methods, are like that, then it is not a priori guaranteed that Williamsonian safety is everywhere a necessary condition of knowledge.

One can envisage the likely rejoinder that as a matter of anthropological fact we are not in any area of our cognitive activities comparable to such a machine. Still, even if that is so, it seems incredible that such a contingency could somehow entail that there are yellows, and instances of baldness, etc., that lie beyond our powers of recognition even in the best of circumstances.

But now grant that the general requirement of safety proposed – again, the proposal that in order to know that P in circumstances C my methods must be such that they could not easily lead me astray in circumstances sufficiently similar to C – grant that this is well motivated everywhere. A second misgiving is that in the way that Williamson puts the proposal to work, no account is taken of the possibility of *response-dependence*: the idea that some kinds of judgement – and here the critic is likely to be thinking of exactly the kinds of judgement, about sensations and other aspects of one's occurrent mental state, that Williamson means to target in directing his argument against the traditional idea of our

---

[17] Compare Williamson (2000, p. 97).

'cognitive home' – are not purely discriminatory of matters constituted independently but are such, rather, that the subject's own judgemental dispositions are somehow themselves implicated in the facts being judged. For any area of judgement where this idea has traction, the supposition that in perfectly good conditions of judgement we might easily respond to what is in fact a non-F case in the way we do to an F case that is very similar to it is in jeopardy of incoherence. Simply, if F-ness and non-F-ness are response-dependent matters, then it cannot legitimately be assumed that, purely on the basis of their similarity in a particular case, we will be at risk of responding to a non-F case in the way we do to an F-case.

To be sure, the heyday of the recent discussion of response-dependence has passed, and rigorous but still dialectically useful formulations of it proved hard to come by when the debates were at their height. Still, many may feel that there is an elusive truth in it, with qualities instantiated in one's phenomenal mental life and Lockean secondary qualities of external objects generally providing two examples of domains to which philosophical justice can be done only by keeping a place for the idea of response-dependence on our philosophical agenda.[18]

I do not think, accordingly, that Williamson's argument, in our present state of understanding, comes anywhere near to establishing that the basic revisionary argument is hobbled by its reliance on the EC-conditionals. Rather the argument sets up yet another philosophical paradox: prima facie plausible thoughts about knowledge in general and a putative requirement of the safety/reliability of methods whereby beliefs are formed, prove to conflict with prima facie plausible thoughts about the luminosity of a range of concepts for which, we would probably otherwise be inclined to think, the EC-conditionals look good. Something has to give. But here cannot be the place to further investigate what.

5.6 Two Further Objections

There are, however, two less theoretically loaded reservations about the role of the EC-conditionals in the basic revisionary argument that should be tabled when what is envisaged is its application specifically to vague expressions. First, no connection has actually been explained to link the EC-conditionals with vagueness as such. All that has been offered is the suggestion that the conditionals are plausible for some examples of vague predicates – for the usual suspects. A general theoretical connection is wanted before there can be any firm prospect of a solution by this route to the Sorites Paradox in general. One senses that a development may be possible of a general connection between vague judgement and response-dependent judgement, grounded in the thought that the status of something as a borderline case is a response-dependent matter. That suggestion, though, once again in the present state of our understanding, is merely speculative.

---

[18] Concerns of this character, although he does not mention the notion, response- (or judgement-) dependence by name nor relate his discussion to the literature about it, are nicely elaborated in Berker (2008).

Second, and perhaps more threatening to this particular strategy for underwriting an intuitionistic treatment of the Sorites, is the conflict between the EC-conditionals and a principle I have elsewhere called *Verdict Exclusion* (VE):

VE: Knowledge is not feasible about borderline cases.

EC and VE are pairwise inconsistent (since, as the reader will speedily see, they combine to enforce contradictory descriptions of borderline cases.) So someone who accepts EC must deny VE. But VE may well impress – indeed has impressed a number of expert commentators[19] – as a datum. In any case, the principle may seem to have powerful intuitive support from the very deflationary conception of vagueness which, I have proposed, should be seen as the mainspring of an intuitionistic treatment. On that conception, borderline cases are constitutively cases whereby subjects characteristically fall into weak, inconstant and mutually conflicting opinions. Any opinion a subject holds about such a case is one that she might very easily, using just the same belief-forming methods, not have held. Surely on any reasonable interpretation of a safety, or reliability, constraint on knowledge, that must count as inconsistent with such an opinion's being knowledgeable.

Elsewhere, I have suggested that an endorsement of VE proves, on closer inspection, to be in tension with liberalism.[20] Let me here make a different point. Once it is given that something is a borderline case, I think the line of argument just outlined for VE is likely to prove compelling. But the crucial consideration is that, of any particular element in a Sorites series, it is *not* a given – except as a contingent point about the sociology of a particular group of judges – that it is a borderline case. Being a borderline case is judge-relative: *x* may be such as to induce the characteristic judgemental difficulties and variability in some but not other competent judges. Let the proposition that *x* is yellow elicit those characteristic responses in some of us but suppose that Steady Freddy consistently judges *x* yellow (though acknowledges that it is near the borderline). Must we deny that Freddy's verdict is knowledgeable? After all, it is, we may suppose, the verdict of someone who gives every indication otherwise of a normal competence in the concept, has normal vision and is judging in good conditions – and judging in a way consistent with his judgement of the same shade on other occasions. It is harsh to say he doesn't know.[21] And if it is at least indeterminate whether Freddy knows, then we do not know VE.

On the other hand, if we take it that the EC-conditionals *are* known to hold good for surveyable predications of *F*, must we not also accept the strange claim that VE is known to be false for such cases and hence that each element in a soritical series for *F* allows in principle of a knowledgeable verdict about its *F*-ness? It's not clear. There is a double negation elimination step in the drawing of that conclusion whose legitimacy might be viewed as *sub judice* in the present dialectical context. Rather than take a stand on the

[19] Schiffer (2016), Rosenkranz (2003), Williamson (1996b).
[20] Wright (2003a).
[21] Some will no doubt say that Freddy has a different concept. But that seems merely ad hoc. What does the difference consist in? Why not say instead that he is steadier than we are in his judgements involving a concept we share?

matter, it may seem that prudence dictates, pro tem, that we reserve judgement on both VE and EC, committing to neither.

Prudence, though, comes at a cost. Unfortunately for the would-be intuitionist, that agnostic attitude requires that we must also be agnostic about the basic revisionary argument. If, in our current state of philosophical information, the strongest relevant claim we can justifiably make about the EC-conditionals is that it is epistemically possible that they hold good for surveyable predications of 'yellow', 'bald', etc., then, supposing we accept the validity of the law of excluded middle, we can validly reason only to the epistemic possibility that D above holds good, i.e. that it is *epistemically possible* that, for each P in the relevant class of statements, it is feasible to know P or it is feasible to know not-P. But that double-modalised conclusion doesn't look uncomfortable – or anyway, not uncomfortable enough to put pressure on the acceptance of excluded middle. In particular, if it is epistemically possible that Steady Freddy indeed knows, then for each P in the relevant range, there epistemically possibly could be a steady subject who knowledgeably judges that it is true (or that it is false.)

The revisionary import of the basic revisionary argument requires more than that the EC-conditionals are epistemically possibly correct.

5.7 Addressing Constraint 1: A Different Tack – Knowledge-Theoretic Semantics

So what now? Well, a suspension, perhaps temporary, of confidence in the basic revisionary argument in this context need not surrender all prospect of a strong motivation for an intuitionistic approach to the logic of vague discourse. The basic revisionary argument attempts to garner the desired result without any particular assumptions about semantics. Let us therefore now instead consider directly what might be the most desirable shape for a semantics to take that is to be adequate for a language – a *minimally sufficient soritical language for F* – that has just enough resources to run instances for a particular vague predicate F of both the Tolerance and No Sharp Boundaries Paradox. Such a language thus contains the predicate F, a finite repertoire of names, one for each member of a suitable soritical series, brackets subject to the normal conventions, and the standard connectives and quantifiers of first-order logic.

Let L be such a language. Since we wish to avoid any commitment to the idea that when F is applied to an object that is surveyable for it, the result can take a truth-value beyond our ken, we have no interest in any semantic theory for L that works with an evidentially unconstrained notion of truth. But nor, since we are now (even if temporarily) agnostic about EC (and therefore also about VE), should such a semantics work instead with a verificationist notion of truth. It follows that we should not choose a truth-theoretic semantics at all.[22] But then what? Well, what any competent practitioner of L has to master

---

[22] I am not here assuming that merely to give a truth-theoretic semantics for some region of discourse must involve explicit commitment to one horn or the other of this alternative. But the question may legitimately be pressed, and the point I am making in the text is that we cannot answer unless at the cost of surrender of agnosticism about EC. Better, therefore, not to

are the conditions under which its statements may be regarded as known or not. We may therefore pursue a semantic theory that targets such conditions directly, in a spirit of aiming at a correct description of what we are in a position to regard as knowledgeable linguistic practice. It will be for the critic to make the case, if there is a case to make, that we thereby misdescribe the practice we actually have.

How to make a start? We don't have much to go on. What is solid to begin with is only that there is a range of polar cases where there is no doubt that Fx may be known, a range of polar cases where there is no doubt that $\sim Fx$ may be known and a range of cases that manifest the uncertainty and variability of judgement that our governing deflationism regards as constitutive of vagueness. But consider the following controversial principle (CP):

> All the *knowable* statements in L are knowable by means of knowing the truth-values of atomic predications – (which we are assured of being able to do only in polar cases.)

According to CP, any of the molecular statements of L, can be known, if they can be known at all, by knowing some of L's atomic statements. So the semantic clauses for the connectives and quantifiers by means of which any particular molecular statement is constructed ought – if that statement is to be reckoned knowable – to reflect an upwards path, as it were, whereby the acquisition of such knowledge might proceed. If we accept CP, we will be looking therefore for a semantics that recursively explains conditions of knowledge for the molecular statements of L in terms of those of their constituents.[23]

Presumably, we are not going to want to accept CP. 'Controversial' somewhat flatters the principle. We will surely want to admit a range of exceptions, cases where a molecular statement plausibly holds good even when its constituents are borderline. Some, for instance, will be general statements that are arguably analytic of the specific vague predicate concerned, such as 'Everything red is coloured'; others may be nomologically grounded in the property concerned, such as maybe 'All heaps are broadest in the base'. A more interesting class of exceptions are what Kit Fine once characterised in terms of the notion of *penumbral connection*.[24] They will concern vague predicates in general. Epistemicists will regard some instances of the law of excluded middle as coming into this category. We will not follow them in that, but we should want to allow, for example, that no matter what F may be, all instances of the law of non-contradiction are knowable as, with respect to the kind of series we are concerned with, are all *monotonicity conditionals*, that is, statements of the form

$$Fx' \rightarrow Fx,$$

invite the question. However, there is more to say about the motivation for the style of semantics about to be proposed. I'll return to the matter at the end.

[23] For ease of formulation, I here count the instances of a quantified statement as among its 'constituents'.
[24] Fine (1975).

notwithstanding whether x is borderline for F. The same will hold for the corresponding generalisations:

$$(\forall x) \sim (Fx \mathbin{\&} \sim Fx), (\forall x)(Fx' \rightarrow Fx), (\forall x)(\sim Fx \rightarrow \sim Fx'), \ldots$$

To be sure, that such claims are knowable is not uncontroversial. It is a familiar feature of many-valued treatments of vagueness that such principles as these are sometimes parsed as indeterminate – when, for instance, indeterminacy in a conjunct is treated as depriving a conjunction of determinate truth, or a conditional with an indeterminate antecedent and consequent is regarded as thereby indeterminate. We are not here taking a stand on the question whether such treatments are appropriate when one accepts their governing assumption, viz. that being a borderline case is a kind of *alethic* status, contrasted with both truth and falsity. But we are rejecting the governing assumption. And when instead borderline-case status is viewed as a cognitive status, as on *our* governing assumption, there is no evident reason to demur at the suggestion that principles of penumbral connection can be known. We can know of structural constraints that knowledge, were it but attainable, of the truth-values of a range of statements would have to satisfy without having any guarantee that we can get to know those truth-values.

These considerations suggest we pursue a theory of knowledge for L that has CP as a motivating base but includes a range of permitted exceptions to it. The theory will incorporate a knowledge-conditional semantics for L and a logic based upon it, but may also contain additional, primitive axioms of penumbral connection and perhaps other axioms analytic of or otherwise somehow guaranteed for a particular choice for F. The semantics will comprise recursive clauses that determine, for each of the quantifiers and connectives of L, the conditions that are necessary and sufficient for knowledge of L-statements in which that operator is the principal operator on the basis of the knowledge-conditions of its constituents.

The natural approach will be something in the spirit of the Brouwer-Heyting-Kolmogorov (BHK) interpretation of intuitionist logic,[25] which, as is familiar, proceeds in proof-theoretic rather than truth-theoretic terms. There is, however, an important point about the BHK interpretation that we need to flag before moving to propose specific clauses for the theory for L that we seek. In logic and mathematics, or so one might plausibly hold, all knowledge (other than of axioms) is conferred by, and only by, proof. So it can look as though BHK-style semantics is already nothing other than a local version of knowledge-conditional semantics. So it is, but expressing matters that way may encourage an oversight. While proofs in logic and mathematics confer knowledge of what they prove, that is not all they do. They also vouchsafe knowledge of what is proved *as* knowledge. Someone who comprehendingly works through a mathematical proof that P learns not merely that P is true but also – assuming their grasp of the concept of knowledge, etc. – that P may now be taken to be part of their knowledge. They establish a right to include P

---

[25] See e.g. Troelstra (2011, section 5.2).

as part of what they may legitimately claim to know. Say that knowledge is *certified* when accomplished in a fashion that legitimises that claim: accomplished in such a way that a fully epistemically responsible, sufficiently conceptually savvy epistemic agent will be aware that they have added to their knowledge. The clauses to follow are to be understood in terms of knowledge that is certifiable – *c-knowledge* – in this sense.[26]

Adapting BHK-style clauses in a natural way, we may accordingly propose:

'*A* & *B*' is knowable just if it's knowable that '*A*' is knowable and that '*B*' is knowable.

'*A* ∨ *B*' is knowable just if it's knowable that either '*A*' is knowable or '*B*' is knowable.

'(∀*x*)*Ax*' is knowable just if it's knowable that for any object in the soritical domain and term, '*a*', known to denote that object, '*Aa*' is knowable.[27]

'(∃*x*)*Ax*' is knowable just if it's knowable that, for some object in the soritical domain and term, '*a*', known to denote that object, '*Aa*' is knowable.

(What about the conditional? Actually, we don't strictly need a treatment of the conditional for the present purposes.[28] And this is fortunate, since the natural proposal:

'*A* → *B*' is knowable just if it's knowable that if '*A*' is knowable, '*B*' is knowable,

raises an awkwardness which I will explain below.)[29]

We can now assert the following Thesis (verification is left to the reader):[30]

Where validity is taken as c-knowability-preservation, and c-knowledge is taken to be factive and closed over c-knowable logical consequence, the clauses above justify rules of deduction for the listed operators coinciding with the common ground for those operators – the standard rules for conjunction introduction and elimination, disjunction introduction and elimination, universal generalisation and instantiation, and existential generalisation and instantiation – recognised by both classical and intuitionist first-order logic.

What about negation? An adaptation of the BHK-style clause along the above lines would run:

'~*A*' is knowable just if it is knowable that '*A*' is not knowable.

---

[26] It is a consequence of some kinds of knowledge-externalism that not all knowledge need be c-knowledge. But the externalist will presumably grant that knowledge often is c-knowledge, since it is not supposed to be a consequence of externalism that our claims to knowledge are mostly imponderable without further investigation. The crucial assumption I am making in what follows is that knowledge achieved by canonical means – typically, casual observation – of clear cases of the 'usual suspects' will be c-knowledge.

[27] Recall that *L* will contain a known name for every element of the soritical domain.

[28] When the major premise for the Tolerance Paradox is formulated, as standardly, as a universally quantified conditional (rather than e.g. as involving a binary universal quantifier) then the paradox does of course depend on the unrestricted use of *modus ponens*. But the intuitionist resolution of the paradox to be proposed will pick no quarrel with that, and is thus neutral on the semantics of the conditional to that extent.

[29] See fn. 31.

[30] 'And how', the dear reader may ask, 'am I supposed to do that when you have nominated no specific logic for the meta-language – here English! – in which I am supposed to run through the relevant reflections?' *Touché*. But the meta-reasoning concerned will require, besides the noted properties of c-knowledge, no more than the rules of inference for 'and', 'or', 'any', 'some' and 'if' which constitute common ground between classical and intuitionist first-order logic.

But that, obviously, will introduce calamity into any account that accepts VE. Our official stance at this point is one of agnosticism towards VE, but it would be good to have the resource of a treatment of the paradoxes that would be robust under the finding that VE was after all philosophically mandated. In any case, and perhaps more telling, BHK-style negation has always been open to the intuitive complaint that it provides a licence to convert grounds for thinking we are doomed to ignorance on some matter into grounds for denial and thus distorts negation as intuitively understood.

There is, however, a natural and much more intuitive replacement:

'~*A*' is knowable just if some '*B*' is knowable that is knowably incompatible with '*A*',[31]

or more generally

'~*A*' is knowable just if some one or more propositions are knowable that are conjointly knowably incompatible with '*A*'.

There is no space here to undertake a proper exploration of the philosophical credentials of this proposal. Still, the reader may find it intuitively plausible that mastery of negation, at least at the level of atomic statements, is preceded in the order of understanding by mastery of which of them exclude which others: being not yellow, for example, is, among coloured things, initially understood as the having of some colour that rules out being yellow. The above proposal reflects the thought that we may take incompatibility among atomic statements as epistemically primitive. Matters change, of course, once molecular statements enter the mix. For molecular statements, incompatibility will, conversely, sometimes be recognisable only by recognising that one or more of them entail the negation of something entailed by the other. That is,

---

[31] The reader should note that there is a question, drawn to my attention by Timothy Williamson, whether we may stably combine this proposed knowledge-theoretic clause for negation with the knowledge-theoretic clause for the conditional flagged earlier:

> '*A* → *B*' is knowable just if it's knowable that if *A* is knowable, *B* is knowable.

For suppose VE is accepted and *A* is such that

 (i) It is knowable that *A* is borderline.
 (ii) Then it is knowable that *A* is not knowable (by VE).
 (iii) So it's knowable that if *A* is knowable, then *B* is knowable (by substitution in ~*A* ⇒ (*A* → *B*) (*ex falso quodlibet*) and closure of knowledge across knowable entailment).
 (iv) So it's knowable that if *A*, then [take some arbitrary contradiction for *B*] (from iii, by the knowledge-theoretic clause for the conditional).
 (v) So it's knowable that ~*A* (by the proposed clause for negation, letting *B* be: if *A*, then [contradiction], and presuming that to be knowably incompatible with *A*).

So the proposed clause degrades after all into the BHK-style knowledge-theoretic clause for negation:

> '~*A*' is knowable just if it is knowable that '*A*' is not knowable,

which is what we were trying to improve on. True, the argument as presented depends on VE, which we have not endorsed. But it will run for any '*A*' that is knowably unknowable. Maybe there are no such statements formulable in a minimally sufficient soritical language. Maybe one should look askance at *ex falso quodlibet*. Still, a concern is raised that will need disinfection in a fully satisfactory general treatment. I will not pursue the matter here.

A pair of (sets of) propositions are knowably mutually incompatible if there is some proposition 'A' such that the one knowably entails 'A' and the other knowably entails '$\sim A$'.

If we now, for convenience, avail ourselves of a dedicated constant, '$\perp$', to express the situation when a set of propositions, X, incorporates each of some pair of knowably incompatible propositions, thus:

$$X \Rightarrow \perp,$$

then the first of the displayed clauses above mandates the following negation introduction rule:

$$(\sim\text{Intro}) \quad \frac{X \cup \{A\} \Rightarrow \perp}{X \Rightarrow \sim A}$$

while the second displayed clause mandates the following negation elimination rule:

$$(\sim\text{Elim}) \quad \frac{X \Rightarrow \sim A \qquad Y \Rightarrow A}{X \cup Y \Rightarrow \perp}$$

That is, intuitively, if a set of propositions entails the negation of some proposition, then adding to it any set of propositions that entail that proposition will result in incompatibility.

Whatever deep justification these proposals may be open to, it will be enough for present purposes if they seem plausibly knowability-preservative in the light of the reader's intuitive understanding of negation. Their most immediately significant consequence is that they allow us to justify intuitionist *reductio* as a derived rule.[32] Given the Thesis flagged above, we thus have all the rules (&I, ∃I, *reductio*) needed to run both the No Sharp Boundaries Paradox and – assuming no question is raised about *modus ponens* – the Tolerance Paradox as well. The upshot, in the presence of assumed knowledge of the polar assumptions, is the following important corollary:

Corollary: When the quantifiers and connectives are understood as above, *there is no option* but to regard the negations of the major premises of the No Sharp Boundaries Sorites as known.

---

[32] At least they do so if we may assume the Cut rule. Intuitionist *reductio* may be represented as the pattern:

$$\frac{X \cup A \Rightarrow B \qquad Y \Rightarrow \sim A}{X \cup Y \Rightarrow \sim A}$$

Suppose we have an instance of right-hand premise. From that and $B \Rightarrow B$ we may obtain by ~Elim:

$$Y \cup \{B\} \Rightarrow \perp$$

From that and the left-hand premise we have, by Cut

$$X \cup Y \cup \{A\} \Rightarrow \perp$$

So by ~Intro, we have

$$X \cup Y \Rightarrow \sim A$$

.

5.8 Addressing Constraint 1 (Cont.): The Payoff

Constraint 1 requires that we explain how and why the *reductio* of the major premises accomplished by the paradoxical reasoning fails to justify the unpalatable existential. This is now straightforward. By the clause for '∃', the knowability of the unpalatable existential requires that for some object in the soritical domain and term, '*a*', known to denote that object, '*Fa* & ~*Fa'*' is knowable – requires, in short, the knowability of a witness to a sharp cut-off. We neither have nor have any reason to think we can obtain that knowledge: no '*a*' denoting any clear case furnishes such a knowable witness. And we have absolutely no reason, either given by the Sorites reasoning itself or otherwise, to think that such a witness may be knowledgeably identified in the borderline area. Since, by the Corollary emphasised at the conclusion of the preceding section, we do know the negations of each of NSB and TP, the respective classical inferences from the negations of NSB and TP to the unpalatable existential fail to guarantee knowability and are thus are invalid in the present knowledge-theoretic setting.

So there is the needed daylight. Constraint 1 is met and the discomfort involved in regarding the soritical reasoning simply as a *reductio* of its major premise is thus relieved.

5.9 Addressing Constraint 2

At least, it is relieved if, as required by Constraint 2, we can neutralise the persistent temptation to regard the major premises for the paradoxes as true. The epistemicist – and indeed almost all theorists of this topic[33] – also share this obligation, of course, so here we, most of us, can march in step. There are a number of sources for the temptation. I'll touch on four.

(i) *Projective error*
The core attraction of NSB is, naturally, simply the other face of the unpalatability of the Unpalatable Existential. And that in turn springs from our inclination to accept that NSB is simply a statement of what it is for *F* to be vague in the series in question. On our overarching conception of what vagueness is, this is a tragic mistake. It is, indeed, the pivotal mistake, 'the decisive step in the conjuring trick' that our intuitive thinking plays on us here. For *F* to be vague is for it to have borderline cases, but its possession of borderline cases is, according to the overarching deflationary conception of vagueness here proposed, a matter of our propensity to certain dysfunctional patterns of classification outside the polar regions.[34] *F*'s being vague is thus a fact *about us*, not about the patterns that may or may not be exhibited by the *F*s and the non-*F*s in a Sorites series. Nothing follows from

---

[33] The exceptions are those theorists who prefer to look askance at the underlying logic of the paradox; for instance at the assumption of the transitivity of logical consequence in this setting (Zardini, see Chapter 9 in this volume) or at intuitionist *reductio* (Fine 1975).

[34] This much is common ground with epistemicism as I understand it. The difference is that we reject the further step of postulating a sharply bounded property, our inability to keep track of whose extension explains the dysfunctionality.

its vagueness about thresholds, or the lack of them, in a Sorites series, or indeed about the details of its extension at all.

The diagnosis of projective error chimes nicely with Constraint 3: the overarching conception of borderline case vagueness we are working under is invoked to undergird the proposed means of satisfying Constraint 2.

(ii) *Inflated normativity*

However, there are other kinds of seductive untruth at work in conjuring the attraction that the major premises exert. One such involves an implicit inflation of the legitimate sense in which competent practice with the usual suspects is constrained by *rule*, and is a crucial factor in the allure of tolerance premises. An example is the general thought that the rules for the use of any of the usual suspects that can be justifiably applied or denied purely on the basis of (varying degrees of casual) *observation*, must mandate that elements in the soritical domain between which there is no relevant (casually) observable difference should be described alike. (For how otherwise could mere observation enable us to follow the rules?) In fact, none of the expressions with which we are concerned is governed by rules that mandate any such thing. But the illusion that they are – indeed must be – so governed has deep sources. As announced earlier, I must forbear to go further into these matters here.[35]

(iii) *An operator shift?*

Both the foregoing, though ultimately misguided, are nevertheless respectable reasons for our inclination to accept the major premises, involving subtle philosophical mistakes. I am not completely confident that some of us, over the last four decades of debate of these paradoxes, may not have fallen prey to a less respectable reason. (I am sure no present reader would be guilty of this.) There is a fallacious transition available in this context of a kind that we know it is easy to slip into: an operator shift fallacy. The transition concerned is that from

> Nothing in the meaning of F (the way we understand it) mandates a discrimination between adjacent elements in the soritical series,

to

> The meaning of F (the way we understand it) mandates that there is to be no discrimination between adjacent elements in the soritical series, so that '$Fx \& \sim Fx'$' is everywhere false.

(iv) *Irrelevant truths*

Finally there are a number of truths in the vicinity that may tempt one to accept NSB but which, on the present deflationary conception of vagueness, adjoined with liberalism,

---

[35] Wright (1975) rehearses what is still the best case known to me for thinking otherwise, and points an accusatory finger at the implicit inflation of normative constraint; the inflation is further explained and debunked in Wright (2007).

simply have no bearing on it. It is true, for example, that no clear cases bear witness to the unpalatable existential, that nobody could justify claiming to have identified a witness in the borderline area and that we (normal speakers) have no conception of what it would be like even to have the impression that we had identified a witness. But these all merely reinforce the impression that UE, the unpalatable existential, is nothing we can justify. The mere possibility of a coherent epistemicism should teach us, if nothing else, at least that such considerations do not parlay into good reasons for its *denial*.

The temptation though dies hard. 'Granted', it may be said, 'that if we are epistemicists, considerations like the above provide no good reason for denial. But what if we are not epistemicists? What if our attitude is, as the governing conception of vagueness that you are proposing itself involves, that there are here no facts behind the scenes: that our best practice exhausts the relevant facts – that "nothing is hidden"? If there are no truth-makers for predications of F and not-F save aspects of our best practice, then – given that our best practice determines no sharp cut-off for F in a suitable series, must we not conclude that there is none? And then is not some version – employing some suitably "wide" notion of negation – of NSB going to be forced on us?'

The question is in effect: how can we avoid treating a fact about us and our judgemental limitations as a fact about the properties of the elements of the series unless we are prepared, with the epistemicist, to invoke some form of transcendent fact? I reply that, while our judgemental reactions no doubt are caused by and reflect properties of the elements of the series, it is a further, unwarranted step to draw conclusions from them about the extension of F. The transition from

Our collective best practice doesn't converge on a sharp boundary for F in the series

to

There is no sharp boundary for F in the series

is still a non sequitur even if we do not admit any practice-transcendent truth-makers for the statements in question. What does follow is at most a conclusion about indeterminacy – that something has not been settled by a convergence in our collective practice. But indeterminacy, conceived as proposed by the intuitionist, is not an alethic status, so *not something that excludes truth*.

Is this too much to swallow? Let the critic have another go: 'Suppose it agreed', she may say, 'that there are just two kinds of ways in which an instance of Fx & $\sim Fx'$ can hold true in the series. One is the epistemicist way. The other is as grounded in the linguistic practice of competent judges in good conditions. Suppose we reject epistemicism. Then surely we are forced to accept the conditional:

If, for no element in the series, is there sufficient agreement among competent judges in good conditions on the truth of the relevant instance of Fx & $\sim Fx'$, then no such statement is true?

So then, since there is no foreseeable such agreement, each such statement is untrue; and now it must be possible to run an NSB Sorites in terms of a suitably wide negation.'

What obstructs this train of thought, as the reader may anticipate, is liberalism. If we accept liberalism about verdicts in the borderline area, we must reject the displayed conditional anyway, even without epistemicism as a background assumption. Liberalism requires that we not insist on available convergence about an atomic statement among competent judges as a necessary condition for its truth. Why should it be any different for molecular statements in general and an instance of Fx & $\sim Fx'$ in particular?

'Not so fast', the critic may continue. 'If we are to leave open the possibility of an instance of Fx & $\sim Fx'$ holding true, and if this possibility is not to be understood as the epistemicist understands it – as a matter of a cut-off in the extension of a property that is the semantic value of F but of whose nature we are not fully aware – and if, moreover, the possibility is not to be understood, either, as realised by a convergence in our best practice on each conjunct, then what is it a possibility of? What other kind of state of affairs, if it obtained, could conceivably be a truth-maker for an instance of Fx & $\sim Fx'$?'

The critic is assuming that there can be no truth without a truth-maker. But let us not question that and consider how an intuitionist might answer her question directly. Let 'Fa' be a non-polar statement. Suppose that a is the last element in the Sorites series for which a competent judge in good conditions – Freddy again – returns a steady positive, if suitably nuanced, verdict. Liberalism requires that we not discount Freddy's verdict about a. But suppose also that a' is the first element in the series for which Teddy, Freddy's epistemic peer, returns a steady negative, if suitably nuanced, verdict. Liberalism requires that we not discount Teddy's verdict either. Should we not then be liberal towards their conjunction? The displayed conditional, however, would force us to dismiss the conjunction of Freddy's and Teddy's respective verdicts as untrue, for that conjunction elicits nobody's assent, however competent, however good the conditions.

The critic may be unpersuaded. 'One can perfectly reasonably be liberal about a pair of verdicts individually but illiberal about their conjunction? Change the example. What if Teddy and Freddy were to steadily disagree about whether Fa? Now there is no option of regarding both as right – yet that does not preclude our taking a liberal view of each verdict on its own. So why should liberalism about Freddy's and Teddy's respective verdicts either side of the putative cut-off provide any leverage towards liberalism about them taken together?'

I reply that such leverage is the default: that liberalism about any pair of judgements individually should extend to their conjunction except in cases where there is antecedent reason to recognise tension – for example, flat contradiction! – between the judgements concerned. Unless, therefore, one is *independently* inclined to see the truth of 'Fa' as in tension with the truth of '$\sim Fa'$', there is no reason to look askance at the conjunction of Freddy's and Teddy's respective steady verdicts. If, however, you consider that you do have good reason to be independently so inclined, you will presumably be independently inclined to accept NSB. The resurgent paradox will then be a deserved nemesis.

5.10 Addressing Constraint 3

The third constraint we imposed on an intuitionistic treatment of the Sorites was the requirement that the first two constraints – explaining how and why there can be a deductive gap between the negation of the major premise and the unpalatable existential, and explaining the spurious plausibility of the different forms of major premises – be met in a way that is informed by an overarching conception of what vagueness consists in. Have we done this?

It is arguable that the second constraint is not really motivated in the case of the Tolerance Paradox. To be sure, the vagueness of a predicate, deflationarily conceived, is nothing that should suggest that it be tolerant. However, the principal motivations to regard e.g. the usual suspects as tolerant have, as remarked, little to do with their vagueness per se and need a separate treatment, not embarked on here. On the other hand, the diagnosis of projective error as responsible for the thought that an NSB premise just states what it is for F to be vague in a relevant soritical series draws heavily and specifically on the deflationary conception of vagueness that I have represented as the heartbeat of an intuitionistic approach.

But what about the first constraint – explaining the deductive gap? Assume that the knowledge-theoretic semantics offered performs as advertised. We have to acknowledge that a semantic theory of this kind might be proposed, for certain purposes, for almost any factual discourse. So the question becomes: what, if anything, is it about vagueness as deflationarily conceived that makes such a semantics appropriate for vague discourse specifically?

Recall that it is essential to our deflationism not merely to regard certain judgemental patterns among competent judges as constitutive of an expression's vagueness but to reject the demand for explanation of these patterns in terms of underlying semantic phenomena – for instance, sharply bounded but imperfectly understood semantic values, incomplete (or conflicting) semantic rules or the worldly side of things being such as to confer truth-statuses other than truth and falsity. That precludes any semantic theory that works with a bivalent notion of truth, truth-value gaps or postulates any kind of third truth-status. Admittedly, the possibility is left open of working with a verificationist truth-conditional theory, as would be mandated by EC. However, no reason is evident why the knowledge-theoretic style of semantics proposed could not amount to one way of implementing the semantic import of EC, nor hence why all the crucial parts of the treatment of the paradoxes proposed could not survive were we to quash any reservations about EC. So we have not closed that particular road by going about things the way I have here. But nor have we committed to travelling it.[36]

---

[36] Versions of this material were presented at the Staff Research Seminar at Stirling, the Philosophy of Maths seminar at Oxford, an Arché seminar at St Andrews in the autumn of 2016, and at colloquia at Brown University and the University of Connecticut in the spring of 2017. I am grateful to all who participated in these meetings for useful feedback, and to Ian Rumfitt and Josh Schechter for helpful additional discussion. Special thanks to the editors of this volume for very searching critical comments that have led to many improvements.

6   Rejection of Excluded Middle and the Sorites Paradox

Scott Soames

6.1 Vagueness, Partial Definition and Rejection of Excluded Middle

Proponents of excluded middle, $\ulcorner$S or $\sim$S$\urcorner$, typically assume that rules governing vague predicates such as 'young' and 'red' are totally defined, and so determine for each object that they are true, or false, of it. Since these rules arise from ordinary uses of the predicates, this assumption raises the question of how such uses could result in distinctions, imperceptible to speakers and undiscoverable by anyone, between e.g. the last second of one's youth and the first second at which one's youth is merely a memory. The difficulty answering this question has led some to hold that vague predicates are only partially defined, being true or false of some things and undefined for others. When P is undefined for o, neither the claim that P is true of o, nor the claim it isn't, is sanctioned. We accept that P is (isn't) true of o just in case we accept *that o is (isn't) $\mathcal{P}$ and that the claim that o is $\mathcal{P}$ is (isn't) true*.[1] In such cases, these claims, and the sentences expressing them, are ungrounded; they can't be known, and even knowledge of all linguistic and non-linguistic facts wouldn't justify accepting them.[2]

Suppose that 'is red' is such a predicate involving the natural kind term 'red' standing for the property of object surfaces responsible for the fact that certain things look similar to us and different from other things.[3] On this assumption, it is a *necessary* truth that o is red if o has the physical property that *actually* explains the relevant appearances. Nevertheless 'is red' is partially defined because it is learned by example. Noting that nearly everyone says of things perceived to be of a given colour shade, RE_1 'They are red', while saying of things perceived to be of shade RA_1 'They aren't red', we accept the rule *Red 1*.[4]

Red
For all o, if o is RE_1, then 'is red' applies to o
For all o, if o is RA_1, then 'is red' does not apply to o

---

[1] '$\mathcal{P}$' is a schematic letter replaceable by the vague predicate that is the value of the meta-linguistic variable 'P'. See chapters 6 and 7 of Soames (1999) for this way of relating truth to ungroundedness.

[2] See pp. 364–70 of Soames (2009).

[3] See pp. 265–6 of the reprinting of Soames (2007) in Soames (2014).

[4] I abstract away from the complicating fact that our criteria for calling some things 'red' – e.g. human hair – are different from our criteria for calling other things 'red' – e.g. cherries.

More experience leads us to adopt additional rules involving further shades until we are counted as understanding the predicate.[5] The requirement that nearly everyone follow the same rules ensures that the language-wide rules governing it don't determine verdicts for all possible cases.

The verdictless cases fall into several classes. Some are characterised as 'red' (or not red) by nearly all speakers who understand the term, even though some others withhold judgement and a few disagree. Depending on the audience, subject and time, speakers may be more expansive in what they count as 'red' than they are in other contexts. Sometimes conversationalists reach implicit agreements to *count* something as 'red' (or not) for current purposes, while realising that different standards may justifiably be applied in other contexts. When this occurs there is no imperative that the adopted standard settle, for objects of each possible shade, whether or not 'is red' is true of them; it is enough that it allows all conversationally relevant objects to be classified. Thus 'is red' will be partially defined. If 'N' names an object for which it is undefined, 'N is red' and its negation will be ungrounded; they will express propositions that can't be objects of knowledge, and their truth or falsity won't be determined by all linguistic and non-linguistic facts. Agents will often be indifferent about how they are classified, saying, if presented with one, '*It is and it isn't*', '*There's no saying*' or '*It doesn't matter, call it what you like*'.

The fact that S and $\ulcorner \sim S \urcorner$ may both be ungrounded bears on the law of the excluded middle. If a disjunction is ungrounded whenever both disjuncts are, the 'law' can't be accepted. But must it be ungrounded? It doesn't, in general, follow from the fact that accepting each of two propositions is unjustified that accepting their disjunction is unjustified. Nor does it follow that one who fails to know each of them also fails to know their disjunction. What about determination of truth by linguistic and non-linguistic facts? If the facts don't determine the truth of a disjunction, the disjuncts of which are ungrounded, then the disjunction will be ungrounded, and the law will fail. But that can't be established without deciding whether $\ulcorner$S or $\sim$S$\urcorner$ is necessary, which is the point at issue.

Thus it remains to be seen whether excluded middle can be combined with partial definition. One way of doing so involves a form of supervaluationism in which one starts with a model M in which some sentences are true, some are false and some are ungrounded. One then stipulates (i) that S is true, if S is true in all admissible bivalent extensions of M, (ii) that S is not true, if S is false in all such extensions and (iii) that other sentences are ungrounded. Since $\ulcorner$S or $\sim$S$\urcorner$ is true in all bivalent models, excluded middle is preserved. The difficulty is that this involves denying the apparent truism *that $\ulcorner$S or R$\urcorner$ can't correctly be called true unless either S or R can correctly be so called*.[6] The story is also explanatorily tendentious. To determine whether S is true, one must first determine whether S is true in all admissible bivalent models. This presupposes a notion of *truth in a model* antecedent to supervaluationist truth and an antecedent logic used to calculate which sentences are true in which models. The idea that there is a hidden notion of truth conceptually prior to the

---

[5] A further factor required for mastery is agreement with one's fellows involving comparative judgements – *x is redder than y*.

[6] This problem is briefly discussed in Chapter 2 in this volume, Section 2.2.2, especially pp. 53ff.

notion of truth needed to defend the 'truth' of the law of excluded middle is implausible. Further, since 'classical' laws of logic are simply taken for granted, no justification for them is given.

Is there another way of combining partial definition with excluded middle that allows (1) to be determinately true when (2a) and (2b) are ungrounded?[7]

1. Either N is red or N is not red.
2a. N is red.
2b. N is not red.

Let 'N*' be a new name designating the same object as 'N' and let 'M' designate a qualitative duplicate of it. Supervaluationism aside, (1), (3) and (4) should all be true or all undefined.

3. N is red or N* is not red.
4. N is red or M is not red.

One might appeal to (5), which is reasonable because R1 and R2 are.

5. It is a necessary consequence of the rules of the language plus the underlying facts that substitution of 'M is red' or 'N* is red' for 'N is red' in any truth preserves truth.
R1. The status of a disjunction is entirely dependent on the status of its disjuncts.
R2. We have as much reason for taking 'N* is red' and 'M is red' to be true as we have for taking 'N is red' to be true.

But this reasoning doesn't establish the truth of (1), because R3 is as compelling as R2 when the referent of 'N' is midway between clear cases of objects of which 'is red' is true and clear cases in which it isn't.

R3. We have as much reason for taking 'N is not red' to be true as we have for taking 'N is red' to be true.

In the presence of R1, R3 leads to (6), which precludes taking (1) to be true, since it assimilates (1) to (1*), which is not evidently true, and indeed is ungrounded if 'red' is only partially defined.

6. It is a necessary consequence of the rules of the language, plus the underlying facts, that substitution of 'N is not red' for 'N is red' (or vice versa) in any true disjunction always preserves truth.
1*. Either N is red or N is red.

In short, recognising partially defined predicates plus ungrounded sentences and propositions precludes accepting all instances of excluded middle. Nor should one accept their

---

[7] Here I apply an operator, 'determinately' to the ordinary (partially defined) predicate 'true' to produce the predicate determinately true. The operator is defined in section 4.1 of Soames (2003). Section 4.2 brings out an interesting consequence of it.

negations, which are ungrounded when the instances are. These considerations lead to Kleene truth tables for logical connectives.

A∨B	T	F	U
T	T	T	T
F	T	F	U
U	T	U	U

A&B	T	F	U
T	T	F	U
F	F	F	F
U	U	F	U

A⊃B	T	F	U
T	T	F	U
F	T	T	T
U	T	U	U

A≡B	T	F	U
T	T	F	U
F	F	T	F
U	U	F	U

~A	
T	F
F	T
U	U

6.2 The Role of Context Sensitivity

Next we add the assumption that 'is red' is not only partially defined, but also context sensitive.[8] A predicate of this sort has a default extension and anti-extension, which are the sets of things to which the language-wide rules plus non-linguistic facts determine that it does, or doesn't, apply. Since these sets don't exhaust all cases, one may expand its extension or anti-extension by predicating it (or its negation) of something not in either set. The rule for doing so, which is part of the meaning of the term, is that when one examines and calls such an object o 'red', and one's hearers go along, the extension of 'is red' is expanded to include o, *plus objects discriminately redder than, or perceptually indistinguishable in colour from, o.* Let RE_2 be a shade that applies to precisely this class. *If an object is RE_2, then 'is red' is true of it* is then a provisional rule that may implicitly be adopted. To apply these ideas to the Sorites, we construct a sequence of n coloured patches starting with shades that are definitely red and ending with shades that definitely aren't (but rather are, say, orange). Adjacent patches are perceptually indistinguishable in colour (when presented side by side in isolation) despite differing minutely in the physical properties responsible for colour perception. Thus, they get imperceptibly less red at each step. This generates a Sorites argument.

---

[8] This view is extensively developed in Tappenden (1993), Shapiro (2006) and Soames (1999, 2002, 2003, 2009). For similarities and differences between Tappenden (1993) and Soames (1999) see pp. 225–6 of the latter. Context sensitivity without partial definition is advocated in Fara (2000) (see also Chapter 3 in this volume, Section 3.1).

P1. x_1 is red.
P2. x_1 is red $\supset x_2$ is red.
       $\vdots$

Pn−1. x_{n-1} is red $\supset x_n$ is red.
    C. x_n is red.

Since P1 is true, C is false and the argument is valid, one must reject at least one premise. This is paradoxical because it seems to require saying of something, 'It's red', while saying of its perceptually indiscernible twin, 'It's not red'. This can't be if, as one is inclined to think, one can't affirm an observational predicate of something and, in the same breath, deny it of its perceptually indistinguishable twin.

The proponent of partial definitions will note that one can reject a premise without denying it. If 'is red' is partially defined, then many of the premises are true and some are ungrounded, making it a mistake to accept them or their negations.[9] Recognising this blocks the derivation of C without requiring standards that divide objects of which the predicate is true from indiscernibly different objects of which it definitely isn't. Still, one wonders whether *rejecting* (as opposed to denying) a premise, by accepting its antecedent while rejecting (as opposed to denying) its consequent, is any better. Can one reasonably say of some x_i 'It's red' while saying, in the same breath, 'I reject the claim that it is' of its perceptually indiscernible twin x_{i+1}?

It is helpful to imagine a situation in which an agent A evaluates the argument dynamically,[10] while being presented with the sequence $x_1, \ldots, x_n$ of coloured patches one by one. Initially A sees x_1, calls it 'red', and accepts P1. With x_1 in sight, x_2 is presented. Since it is perceptually indiscriminable from x_1, A calls it 'red', accepting P2. Patch x_1 is then removed while x_2 remains in sight and x_3 is displayed, which A calls 'red', accepting P3. At some point A applies 'red' to the last patch x_i in the *default extension* of 'is red', thereby accepting premise Pi. Although A is justified in so doing – x_i is *determinately red* after all – explicitly predicating 'is red' of it implicitly changes the standard to one that counts the predicate as true of the perceptually indistinguishable x_{i+1}. Recognising the relationship between the two, A affirms 'is red' of x_{i+1}, tacitly changing the standard again, to one that counts 'is red' as true of x_{i+2}. The process may continue, with new standards adopted and more premises accepted. Eventually, however, A will notice that items to which A is applying 'is red' are more similar to x_n, which A's knows not to be red, than they are to x_1, which is red. So, for some x_k, A will either reject or deny the characterisation 'It's red'.

In so doing, A doesn't reject or deny any proposition to which A had *explicitly* been committed. The property redness$_k$ that A refuses to predicate of x_k differs imperceptibly from redness$_{k-1}$, which A had predicated of x_{k-1}, and so *implicitly* committed himself to recognising x_k as having. Although A repudiates the standard adopted a moment earlier, there is no requirement that temporarily adopted standards not be repudiated when they are no longer useful. If A is now asked about x_{k-1}, maintaining his current standard will require treating it on a par with x_k. The stage is then set for A to move, step by step, back toward x_1, rejecting or denying the application of 'red' to items to which A previously applied it – without thereby rejecting or denying propositions previously explicitly accepted or affirmed. Every judgement A makes, from beginning to end, may be true.

Not realising that the standards governing the use of the predicate imperceptibly change while moving through the sequence, A may find the argument paradoxical. The paradox will be resolved when A realises that each premise is evaluated with respect to its own contextual standards, according to which it is true.[11] Since there is no single context in which the standards governing the predicate make all the premises true, the false conclusion C is blocked.

This is easy to miss because the adjustment in standards that occurs as A moves from x_j to x_{j+1} (or conversely) is the minimum possible change that can occur at that stage. All A is asked to do is to explicitly apply 'is red' (or 'isn't red') to something it has already been determined to be true of. Thus, the most conservative response is to apply it to the new item. Although this results in an imperceptible shift in standards, any other response would involve a bigger shift. Confusing the minimal change in standards with no change at all may leave A at a loss about which premise to reject. In fact, it doesn't matter which premise A rejects as long as A doesn't reject predicating 'is red' of an item in its default extension or 'isn't red' of an item in its default anti-extension.

Some will object to the model's requirement that there be a sharp line dividing items of which the predicate is true from perceptually indistinguishable items for which it is undefined. To make the objection stick, one must distinguish the correct claim that such a line can't straightforwardly be displayed from the contentious claim that there can't be such a line. The former is a consequence of the context principle CP underlying the way standards are contextually adjusted.

CP. For any two items x and y that are perceptually indistinguishable to competent observers under normal conditions, a competent agent A who affirms 'is red' of x when presented with it under such conditions is thereby implicitly committed to a standard that counts the predicate as applying to y as well. (Similarly for 'x isn't red'.)

Imagine A trying to display the line separating the last item x_j in the Sorites sequence to which 'is red' applies from the first item x_{j+1} for which it is undefined. Displaying them, A says of x_j 'It's red', while rejecting a similar characterisation of x_{j+1}. CP renders his remark incoherent. In predicating 'is red' of x_j, A implicitly commits himself to a standard that counts it as true of x_{j+1}, hence undermining his rejection. In applying 'is red' to x_j, A unwittingly placed the line between x_{j+1} and x_{j+2}. Nor would it help if A had said, of x_{j+1},

---

[11] A slight complication is needed to deal with the dividing line separating the last undefined item in the series leading up to the first item in the predicates default anti-extension. The complication is explained in fn. 13 of Soames (2002).

'the predicate is undefined for it', which would either have been false or would have moved the line again. Those who don't realise this will wrongly conclude there was no such line.

CP is also important for generalised non-dynamic versions of the Sorites.

P1. x_1 is red.
P2. For all members x_i, x_{i+1} of the sequence $x_1,\ldots,x_n$, x_i is perceptually indistinguishable in colour from x_{i+1} to competent observers in good light under normal conditions. Any two such x and y are the same colour. So one is red if, and only if, the other is red. Hence, for each x_i of the sequence, x_{i+1} is red if x_i is red.
C. Therefore each member of the sequence, including x_n, is red.

Since P1 is true, C is false and the argument is valid, P2 must be rejected. Here, premises and conclusion are evaluated in a context using a single standard governing 'is red'. In most contexts P2 will be ungrounded. Why, then, is it so seductive? In part most speakers don't distinguish 'is red' not being true of o and its being undefined for o, leading them to think that they can't maintain that an item indistinguishable from something red isn't itself red. In addition, a seductive line of reasoning leads them to conflate CP with P2.

(i) If P2 were false then some x_i would be red even though a perceptually indistinguishable item x_{i+1} wasn't red.
(ii) So, if I said 'It's red' of x_i and 'It's not red' of x_{i+1}, I would speak truly.
(iii) But CP doesn't allow this; if my use of 'is red' is true of x_i, then it is true of x_{i+1}, in which case my use of 'is not red' will not be true of x_{i+1}.
(iv) So, given CP, P2 must be true.

Steps (i–iii) derive the non-falsity of P2 from the truth of CP; step (iv) derives the truth of P2 from that. The latter ignores the difference between ungroundedness and falsity. But the former error is more interesting; the truth of CP doesn't establish the non-falsity of P2. Suppose A has seen x_{i-1} and x_{i+2}, barely discernible in colour, without seeing other items $x_1,\ldots,x_n$. When presented with x_{i-1} and x_{i+2}, A says of x_{i-1} 'It's red' while saying of x_{i+2} 'It's not red'. Given CP, A is committed to counting 'is red' as true of x_i and all items preceding it, and 'is not true' as true of x_{i+1} and all items following it. *In such a context*, 'is red' is totally defined, excluded middle holds and P2 is false, even though CP is true. Failing to see this makes the generalised argument seem paradoxical.[12]

CP specifies commitments undertaken by uses of a partially defined, context sensitive predicate. P2 encompasses all applications of the predicate as used in a single context. The tendency to conflate claims of these kinds leads to errors beyond the Sorites. Consider the strong Kleene tables for conjunction and negation. When P is undefined for the object named by n, they determine that $\ulcorner Pn \urcorner$, $\ulcorner \sim Pn \urcorner$, $\ulcorner Pn \ \& \ \sim Pn \urcorner$, $\ulcorner \sim(Pn \ \& \ \sim Pn) \urcorner$ are ungrounded, and so rejectable. Why, then, does rejecting non-contradiction seem worse than rejecting excluded middle? Probably because *ungrounded* instances of non-contradiction are easily confused with *true* meta-linguistic generalisations in ways that ungrounded instances of excluded middle aren't. When P is both partially defined and context sensitive, it is easy to confuse the ungrounded ⌜~(Pn & ~Pn)⌝ and its ungrounded meta-linguistic counterpart expressed by ⌜Pn & ~Pn⌝ *is not true*, with the defensible (7).[13]

7. No contextual standard governing P counts ⌜Pn & ~Pn⌝ as true.

Similarly, confusing ⌜Pn ⊃ Pn⌝ and its meta-linguistic counterpart expressed by *All instances of ⌜Pn ⊃ Pn⌝ are true* with the seemingly obvious truth (8) may make agents reluctant to reject instances of the former.[14]

8. If a contextual standard counts ⌜Pn⌝ as true, it counts ⌜Pn⌝ as true.

This explanation applies to many penumbral truths involving vague predicates. For example, the ungrounded (9a) is easily confused with the truth (9b).[15]

9a. If a man is bald, then he would be bald if he had one less hair.
9b. No matter what standards governing 'is bald' we adopt, if according to those standards *he is bald* applies to a man, then according to those same standards it would apply to him if he had one less hair.

By contrast, there is no similar truth corresponding to the law of the excluded middle that makes us reluctant to reject it.[16] Consequently, the reason it seems easier to reject than other classical laws may be that rejecting it isn't subject to the pragmatic interference we encounter with the others. Logically, the various laws have the same status. Pragmatically, they differ in what they suggest about the effects of context change.

6.3 The Challenge Posed by Recognising Super-Fine Distinctions

These are ways in which some who reject excluded middle deal with challenges that come in the wake of its rejection. They maintain that in most normal contexts there are no sharp lines dividing items of which 'is red' counts as true from perceptibly indiscernible items of which it counts as not true. If there were, agents' assertive commitments would be implausibly opaque, because the properties truth and falsity we use to assess them would be epistemically inaccessible in many cases. It is hard to believe that rules governing our

---

[13] For a sentence S to be counted as true (not true) by a set of contextually adopted rules is for the claim that S is true (not true) to be a necessary consequence of the rules plus the underlying non-linguistic facts. If rules can be partial, some sentences will neither be counted as true nor as not true. In these cases the rules are silent; for some sentences S the rules don't count S as true and they don't count S as not true.

[14] (7) and (8) are obvious truths, provided it is obvious that P is undefined for o. If it is possible for the relation *is undefined* to fail to be defined for P and o, (7) and (8) may be ungrounded. Responses to this complication, raised in Williamson (2002), are given in Soames (2002, 2003).

[15] See Soames (2002, pp. 440–1).

[16] When it is realised that rules governing predicates may be partial, it is apparent that the meta-linguistic counterpart – *Every contextual standard counts ⌜P or ~P⌝ as true* – of ⌜P or ~P⌝ will be also be false. Nor will it do to suggest that the meta-linguistic counterpart of ⌜P or ~P⌝ is *Every contextual standard either counts P as true or doesn't count P as true*. Although this second meta-linguistic counterpart of the original is true, it is not revealing because it obliterates the partiality of the relevant predicates. For related discussion see Soames (2002, pp. 440–4) and also Soames (2003).

use of language make the distribution of such important properties unknowable. The view sketched here avoids the full force of that worry. However, it does face a weakened form of it. Proponents admit there is a sharp line dividing the *default extension* of 'is red' from perceptibly indiscernible items just outside it.[17] They must explain how this line arises from the use of the predicate in the linguistic community.

The default extension and anti-extension of 'is red' is supposed to be determined by the language-wide rule followed by all competent speakers, i.e. by all who understand it. These speakers are presumed to operate within a broad framework of agreement about items that uncontroversially count as 'red' or 'not red'. Within it they are understood to have somewhat different standards for applying it. Each is disposed (i) to confidently and uniformly apply 'is red' ('isn't red') to items in its default extension (anti-extension) and to expect the same of others, (ii) to less confidently and uniformly apply 'is red' ('isn't red') to other items and to expect their fellow speakers to be similarly variable and (iii) to have no consistent dispositions to apply either predicate to some further items.

If all that were true, it would make sense to posit an unknown but potentially knowable sharp line separating the default extension of the predicate from items for which it is undefined. But we can do that only if we can define what it is to be a competent speaker of the language in a way that doesn't presuppose the picture we are trying to establish. What is it to be a competent speaker of language with partially defined, context-sensitive predicates of the sort here described? Since, by hypothesis, the rule for 'is red' expresses the prescribed understanding of the predicate, it would seem that *all competent speakers* – not just a majority – should be uniformly disposed to affirm it of items in its default extension, and to affirm its negation of items in the default anti-extension. We could test this if we had a non-circular way of identifying either the competent speakers or the language they speak without presupposing the other. Given either, we could define the other. If the language were, by definition, one governed by our rule for 'is red', we could *define* a competent speaker – as far as use of 'is red' is concerned – to be one disposed to confidently and uniformly affirm it of all items in its default extension, and to affirm its negation of items in its default anti-extension – while being free, within certain limits, to affirm either one of other items in different contexts.

But this won't do; we aren't given the language of a group prior to knowing the linguistic dispositions of its members. Thus we must decide whose dispositions are determinative. Surely not those learning the language, who may be ignorant of common usage. Nor can we specify some percentage of a community, say 95 per cent. There is no determining which, or how many, users of an expression are genuinely competent with it, apart from antecedent knowledge of what language we are talking about. Hence, we seem to be at an impasse. Unless we can get beyond it, the view that vague predicates such as 'is red' are partially defined may face a weakened version of the same objection that is faced by the view that they are totally defined.

---

[17] These are items of which 'is red' is undefined in some contexts, and of which it is true in others only because speakers have tacitly adopted a standard that applies to them. See Soames (2003).

6.4 Meeting the Challenge: The Case for Micro-Languages

The problem seems to arise from pursuing our investigation at too high a level of abstraction. Many discussions of vagueness presuppose (i) that the investigated language is spoken by a vast but ill-defined linguistic community, (ii) that the rules governing its predicates make precise, extremely fine-grained discriminations, either between items of which they are true and those of which they are not, or between items for which they are defined and those for which they are not and (iii) that the contents of these rules are somehow abstracted from the totality of uses to which the predicates are put by speakers. This combination of views is hard to accept – whether or not excluded middle is rejected.

How would things look if, instead of conceiving of our (initial) object language as just indicated, we focused on the prerequisites for quick, effective and effortless communication among members of a smaller, identifiable group speaking a micro-language the semantic properties of which are extracted from their linguistic behaviour alone? For this approach to work, we would need to spell out *what it is for (non-deferential) agents to speak the same micro-language* – as far as their use of expressions such as 'is red' and 'isn't red' are concerned. Given this, we could take micro-languages to be constructions abstracted from *non-deferential* uses of expressions by groups of identifiable agents – i.e. from uses in which agents employ their internalised criteria for applying 'is red' or 'isn't red', rather than relying on whatever standards may be employed by others. Although deferential uses of expressions may be plentiful, their contents rest on non-deferential uses. Thus the extraction of linguistic content from patterns of use should naturally focus on overlapping agreements in non-deferential dispositions to apply predicates.

Imagine a sequence of coloured patches $x_1, \ldots, x_n$ ordered under *redder than*, starting from the reddest and ending with a patch that isn't red (relative to some relevant colour contrast). Let R_1 be the reddest shade of red, of which x_1 is an instance. R_2, of which x_2 is an instance, is the next reddest shade. Similarly for the rest. For each adjacent pair R_i, R_{i+1} some items of which R_i is true are *perceptually* redder than some of which R_{i+1} is true, some items of which both properties are true are perceptually indistinguishable and no items of which R_{i+1} is true are perceptually redder than any of which R_i is true.[18] We use these to specify properties implicitly associated by agents with 'is red'. Let R^* be a property predication of which represents o as being of some shade in a particular initial segment of the sequence – *being either R_1, R_2,..., or R_i* – and predication of the negation of which represents o as being of some shade in a non-overlapping final segment of the scale – *being either R_j, R_{j+1},... or R_n*. R^* is true of any item of one of the initial shades, not true of any item of one of the final shades and undefined for other items.

It is not required that R^* be totally defined, which it won't be if the initial and final segments used to specify it don't exhaust the sequence. It is also not required that the same property be associated by an agent with the predicate at all contexts and times. The properties associated with the predicate depend on the dispositions of agents to apply it,

---

[18] As always, when speaking of items as perceptually distinguishable or indistinguishable, I am speaking of pairwise discriminability in a situation in which they are presented together to an agent in isolation from any other items.

which may vary over time, owing to the context of use and the purposes of the inquiry in which the predicate plays a role. For any agent A and time t, there will be items of which A is disposed to confidently and consistently affirm 'it's red', others of which A is disposed somewhat confidently and somewhat consistently to affirm 'it's red', still others of which A has no disposition to confidently and consistently affirm, either 'it's red' or 'it isn't red', further items of which A is disposed somewhat confidently and somewhat consistently to affirm 'it isn't red' and finally items of which A is disposed to confidently and consistently affirm 'it isn't red'. Though capable of varying somewhat over time, these categories may be presumed to be reasonably stable.

We might operationalise these distinctions by tracking A's responses – 'Yes, it's red', 'No, it's not red' or 'I can't say' – to queries about items in the Sorites sequence. Imagine an n-round test, each having two parts. In part 1, A runs through an initial segment until reaching the first item at which A says 'No, it's not red', recording any responses of 'I can't say' or 'I can't tell' that may occur along the way. In part 2, A moves backward through a final sequence and continues until reaching the first item at which A says 'Yes, it's red', recording any responses of 'I can't say' or 'I can't tell' that may occur. Let the (partially defined) property R_A^* identified by the test be the one that is true of items for which A gave an affirmative response on every round of the test, false of items for which A always gave a negative response and undefined for the rest. Take that to be the property associated by A with 'is red' at t.

When the same methodology is applied to members of a group G of agents linguistically interacting with one another, R_G^* is the default property expressed by 'is red', which precisely determines its default extension and anti-extension in a common micro-language they share – if there is such a common language. Whether or not they do share a common language depends on the nature of their overlapping dispositions to apply 'is red' and 'isn't red'.

A Necessary Condition for Speaking the Same Micro-Language
(i) *All members of* G are disposed to confidently and consistently affirm 'is red' ('isn't red') of objects of which R_G^* is (isn't) true. (ii) They are disposed to judge items of which R_G^* is true to be 'redder than' than those for which R_G^* is undefined, which the members of G are disposed to judge to be 'redder than' those of which it is not true. (iii) Their dispositions impose a partial linear ordering under 'is redder than' of items of intermediate stages. (iv) Their disposition to affirm 'is red' ('isn't red') of any item x_{i+1} (x_i) in the Sorites series, conditional on having examined x_i (x_{i+1}) and affirmed 'it's red' ('it isn't red') of it, is very high. (Having examined and judged x_i to be 'red' they are temporarily disposed to judge its perceptually indiscernible twin x_{i+1} to be 'red' as well, and similarly for items judged 'not red'.)[19]

---

[19] Consider point (iii). Although adjacent items in the sequence are perceptually indistinguishable from one another when presented side by side, in isolation from other items they can be expected to differ in which other items in the sequence they are pairwise perceptually discriminable from. The partial ordering will, I think, emerge when these dispositions are taken into account.

Satisfaction of this condition provides a basis of the agreement in applying 'is red' needed for effective communication among (non-deferential) agents using it. But further agreement is also required. If the property R_A^* associated with 'is red' ('isn't red') by A is true of only a fraction of the things of which the property R_B^* associated with 'is red' ('isn't red') by B is true, while being false of many other things of which R_B^* is true, then it is reasonable to take R_A^* and R_B^* to be too different for A and B to count as speaking the same micro-language. Thus we add a further condition:

A Further Condition for Sharing a Micro-Language

For all members A and B of G there is nothing of which R_A^* is true (false) and R_B^* is false (true). In short, no member of G takes some things to be paradigmatic cases of which 'is not red' is true that other members of G take to be paradigmatic cases of which 'is red' is true.

With the addition of this condition, our conception of speaking the same micro-language requires there to be some clearly 'red'/clearly 'red' agreements among agents, some clearly 'not-red'/clearly 'not-red' agreements and no clearly 'red'/clearly 'not-red' dis-agreements – though there may be clearly 'red'/borderline differences and clearly 'not-red'/borderline differences.

If x and y *speak the same micro-language*, then x *speaks the same micro-language as* y and y *speaks the same micro-language as* x. But since those who *speak the same micro-language as* x must all agree with x in certain ways and not disagree in others, and similarly for those who *speak the same micro-language as* y, x can *speak the same micro-language as* y and y *speak the same micro-language as* z, even though x *doesn't speak the same micro-language as* z. Speaking the same micro-language is *sharing at least one micro-language*; typically individuals speak many micro-languages differing all but imperceptibly from one another.

Think of it this way. A micro-language allows some variation among its speakers as long as it doesn't get too great. Two people 'speak the same micro-language' if, and only if, there is a common micro-language they speak. (A can share a language with B, and B can share with C, even if A doesn't share with C.) A shared micro-language is an abstract object – with a phonology, syntax and an assignment of semantic contents to expressions. Since the properties that are semantic contents of some predicates are partially defined, there are variations in how the speakers use those predicates, which means we are going to need contextually sensitive rules to determine what is asserted by speakers who address different speakers of the same micro-language.

Next we define, for each individual x and time t, the notion of a *micro-language L_{xt} centred on x at t*. Agents who speak such a language L_{xt} are those who treat *at least some* items that A treats at t as paradigmatically 'red' ('not red') in the same way A does, and who never treat something that A treats in one of those ways in the opposite way.[20] The

---

[20] A stronger condition would require each agent to treat most of the shades that A takes to be paradigmatic examples of 'red' or 'not red' as A does. I leave it open whether the stronger condition is preferable to the weaker one.

rules of this language dictate (a) that 'is red' applies to things that are instances of shades *all these agents* are disposed to confidently and consistently count as 'red' and (b) that 'is red' doesn't apply to things that are instances of shades that *all the agents* are disposed to confidently and consistently count as 'not red'. 'Is red' is undefined for the rest. The dispositions in terms of which these categories are determined can be given operational definitions that specify the relevant cut-off points as precisely as is desired.

Next we use these ideas to illuminate the propositions asserted and beliefs expressed by uses of sentences containing 'red'. Assume that speakers presuppose their conversational partners *speak the same micro-language as they do – i.e. that they share a micro-language with them.* Suppose this presupposition is satisfied in a conversation A is having with B. If B asks, 'What colour is your car?' and A answers 'It's red', there will be four fixed points around which to construct an interpretation of A's remark. Two are the properties $+R_A^*$ and $\sim R_A^*$, the former encompassing colour-shades instances of which are A's paradigmatically 'red' things and the latter encompassing colour-shades instances of which are A's paradigmatic examples of items that are 'not red'. The second pair of interpretive fixed points are properties $+R_B^*$ and $\sim R_B^*$ that bear the same relation to B as $+R_A^*$ and $\sim R_A^*$ do to A. Either $+R_A^*$ or $+R_B^*$ will also be the property $+R_{AB}^*$ encompassing colour-shades instances of which *both A and B* take to be paradigmatically 'red'. Similarly, either $\sim R_A^*$ or $\sim R_B^*$ will be the property $\sim R_{AB}^*$ encompassing colour-shades instances of which *both A and B* take to be paradigmatically 'not red'.

Though neither A nor B can identify them, these fixed points are identifiable, subject to operational precisification. Imagine orderings of subtly different shades, starting with the clearly red and progressing to the clearly not red. During a given time period, it is plausible to suppose that there is a fact of the matter about which shades an agent would characterise as 'red' in each of n trials of some standard paradigm for eliciting responses; similarly for 'not red'. To suppose this is to suppose that there is a property $+R_A^*$ – which, though not identified by A, is precisely identifiable – instances of which are true of A's paradigmatic 'red' examples, plus a similar unidentified but identifiable property $\sim R_A^*$ instances of which are true of A's paradigmatic 'not-red' examples. The same is true of $+R_B^*$, $\sim R_B^*$, $+R_{AB}^*$ and $\sim R_{AB}^*$.

Let $(R_A^* +/\sim)$ be the *partially defined property* predication of which represents an object as bearing $+R_A^*$ and predication of the negation of which represents it as bearing $\sim R_A^*$; similarly for $(R_B^* +/\sim)$. $(R_{AB}^* +/\sim)$ is defined from the other two, and so may be identical with either of the former two properties or distinct from both. What does A assert when, in answer to B's question – *'What colour is your car? It isn't red is it?'* – A says *'Yes, it's red'*? A and B presuppose their understandings of 'red' each contribute to the contents of their remarks containing it. In a give-and-take conversation like this both take what A asserts to be what B asks about, with 'red' contributing the same content to both. In such cases, common assertive or other speech act contents are imposed on their utterances. Thus, the proposition A asserts in answer to B's question is not, or at least not always, simply the proposition that predicates $(R_A^* +/\sim)$ of the car, nor simply the one that predicates $(R_B^* +/\sim)$.

Nor, I suspect, is it (always) the proposition that predicates $(R^*_{AB}+/\sim)$ of the car. Surely, if the car is something paradigmatically red for A, A's assertion should not be rendered untrue merely because it is of a shade that would not be called 'red' in all n of the trials in terms of which we understand B's dispositions. So long as it is one that would be classified as 'red' in most such trials, there should be no objection to accepting A's assertion. We get this result if we take *the property A to have asserted the car to have* to be an extension $E(R^*_{AB}+/\sim)$ of $(R^*_{AB}+/\sim)$ that is true (not true) of every item of which $(R^*_{AB}+/\sim)$ is true (not true), while also being defined for every item for which $(R^*_{AB}+/\sim)$ is undefined, *except those for which A and B, taken together, have no consistent dispositions to classify one way or the other*. When both A and B are positively disposed to classify items of a given shade as 'red' ('not red'), even if they would not do so on every trial, $E(R^*_{AB}+/\sim)$ is true (not true) of those items. In all other cases $E(R^*_{AB}+/\sim)$ is undefined. These include cases about which one or both of A and B have no definite judgement or belief, either because they tend to arbitrarily vacillate between positive and negative judgements, or because they have no such judgements to make and are indifferent about how, if at all, the items are classified. Items, if any, that A mostly, but not always, classifies as red (not red) but B mostly, but not always, classifies as not red (red) also count as undefined.[21]

The idea extends to linguistically communicating groups of any size. One starts with the speaker A and the group, consisting of $x_1, x_2, \ldots, x_n$, that A addresses. Since A presupposes that there is a common micro-language that A shares with the rest of that group, the first step to determining the assertive content of A's remark is to eliminate anyone x_i who doesn't speak the same micro-language as A, as far as 'red' is concerned. Taking the remaining group, $x_1, x_2, \ldots, x_j$, one considers the micro-language centred on A, of which they are all speakers. Interpreted as a predicate of this language, 'is red' will have an extension that is the set of things of which the property $+R^*_{A,x_1,x_2,\ldots,x_j}$ is true; its anti-extension will be the set of things of which $\sim R^*_{A,x_1,x_2,\ldots,x_j}$ is true. These are instances of shades that A plus each of $x_1, x_2, \ldots, x_j$ take, respectively, to be paradigmatic exemplars of 'red' and 'not red'.

The calculation determining the property $E(R^*_{A,x_1,x_2,\ldots,x_j}+/\sim)$ that the car is asserted to have can then be the same as before. If B is also a member of this larger group, then the set of items for which $E(R^*_{A,x_1,x_2,\ldots,x_j}+/\sim)$ is true (not true) will either be identical with, or a proper subset of, the set of items of which $E(R^*_{AB}+/\sim)$ is true (not true). The simplest way to do the calculation is to let $E(R^*_{A,x_1,x_2,\ldots,x_j}+/\sim)$ be a property that is true (not true) of all items that most of the conversational participants A, $x_1, x_2, \ldots, x_j$ are positively disposed to classify as 'red' ('not red') on most trials, even if they would not do so on every trial.

On this conception, the assertive contents of utterances of micro-language sentences containing the partially defined predicate 'is red' are context sensitive even though the semantic content of the predicate in the micro-language does not change from context to

---

[21] When A predicates 'is red' of x in private thought, the property x is judged to have is the extension of $(R^*_{AB}+/\sim)$ that is true (not true) of those items that would be so classified by A on most trials. In the special case in which A is observing an item x for which the predicate is undefined in A's micro-language, and trying to decide how to (temporarily) characterise it we may take A's decision to apply 'red' to x to ensure that the property predicated of x is true of x and all items perceptually indiscriminable from x by A. Similarly for 'not red'. This special case is subject to the complication mentioned in fn. 9.

context. Let C be a context of utterance in which A is addressing a group all of whom share a micro-language M centred on A. The lines separating the extension and anti-extension of the predicate in M from the items for which the predicate is undefined will be sharp and knowable, but almost always unknown. There need be no default extension or anti-extension because the semantic content of the predicate need not change from one context of use to another. What does change is the partially defined property contributed by the use of the predicate to the proposition asserted by the use of the sentence containing it. This may change from context to context, depending on the dispositions governing the use of the predicate by those to whom A is speaking.[22]

If we thought that all properties had to be totally defined and all instances of excluded middle had to be true, we could revise our discussions of A and B, and of A, $x_1, x_2, \ldots,$ x_j, by identifying $E(R^*_{AB}+/\sim)$ and $E(R^*_{A,x_1,x_2,\ldots,x_j} +/\sim)$ with totally defined properties. In the former case, we could divide the interval between that last item of which $(R^*_{AB}+/\sim)$ is true and the first item to which it is false precisely in half, and take $E(R^*_{AB}+/\sim)_{Total}$ to be true of everything preceding the mid-point and false of everything else. The same procedure could be used for $E(R^*_{A,x_1,x_2,\ldots,x_j} +/\sim)_{Total}$. In both cases, the procedure would impose sharp, imperceptible distinctions between items of which these properties are true and those of which they are false, even if no members of the relevant linguistic group have consistent dispositions to affirm or deny the properties of the items in question. In my opinion, however, this is arbitrary and unmotivated. Language users who, as a group, have no dispositions to consistently apply an observational predicate to a range of items to which they have good epistemic access, and who may not care whether or not it is applied to them are, I think, most reasonably interpreted as using the predicate to express a property that is undefined for those items.

This construction is guided by the following ideas: (i) the semantic contents of our words, and the assertive contents of uses of sentences containing them, are determined by how those words and sentences are used by agents communicating with one another; (ii) the most significant content-determining uses of a predicate such as 'is red' are those in which sincere, non-deferential speakers affirm it, or its negation, of objects in circumstances in which they are epistemically well placed to determine the presence or absence of the properties they judge the object to have; (iii) the semantic and assertive contents of such a predicate for a group of communicating speakers are determined by the dispositions of group members to affirm it, and its negation; (iv) effective communication among such a group, of whatever size or duration, doesn't require complete agreement in dispositions to apply such a predicate, but it does require substantial overlapping agreements in these dispositions and (v) because of this, the semantic and assertive contents of the words used by a non-deferential individual may change slightly depending on those with whom the individual interacts.

---

[22] This may change whether or not the underlying micro-language changes, depending on the specifics of the case.

The construction is useful in giving us a rudimentary understanding of how the precise, knowable (though unknown) demarcations between items in the range of a vague predicate may be determined by the linguistic behaviour of participants in a communicative exchange, or of a broader, but precisely identifiable, linguistic community. Although the construction can be used both by defenders of excluded middle who insist that vague predicates are totally defined, and by opponents of the law who maintain that the predicates are only partially defined, the considerations adduced here seem to favour the latter. The construction also provides a new way of thinking about the context sensitivity of (some) vague predicates. Instead of thinking 'is red' as having a constant Kaplanian meaning that determines (slightly) different semantic contents in different contexts, we may think of uses of it in different contexts as having (slightly) different assertive or other illocutionary contents arising from the changing mix of dispositions of speakers and their audiences, as well as, in some (but not all) cases, the slightly different semantic contents encoded by the predicate in the slightly different micro-languages employed.[23]

In applying the new scheme to the Sorites, two points should be noted. First, since partially defined predicates and properties are retained, paradox-generating premises of non-dynamic versions of the Sorites can be rejected without accepting their negations, just as before. Second, the dynamic version sketched in Section 6.2 can be reconstructed by trading the previous context sensitivity of semantic content for the context sensitivity of assertive (or other illocutionary) content. Recall the featured test case in which an agent A accepts, rejects or refuses to classify patches of colour in an ordered sequence from *definitely red* to *definitely not red* in which the slight difference between an item and its successor is perceptually indiscernible to A. The judgements recorded by A's responses 'Yes, that's red' ('No, that's not red'), are those indicated in fn. 21, concerning A's use of language in private thought. When A predicates 'is red' of an item x_i for which the predicate is undefined in A's micro-language, A predicates a property that is true of x_i and all items perceptually indistinguishable from it, which includes the next item in the sequence, x_{i+1}. This is all we need to get the desirable results about the dynamic Sorites mentioned in Section 6.2.

The point is not that micro-languages fully dispose of the objection to analyses of the sort mentioned there. In order to do that, more would have to be said about the details of that construction and about the relationship between my micro-languages and the thing we call 'English'. If there is such a thing, it may not be a language for which any satisfying account of the Sorites can be given. The reason I haven't offered one is that I doubt that English is a well enough defined entity to support effective theorising about the Sorites. We can, of course, talk about English in our respective micro-languages, but that talk is

---

[23] This emphasis on changes in speaker dispositions is in the spirit of Raffman (1994, 1996). Although Raffman doesn't invoke micro-languages defined by speaker dispositions, her use of disposition change to rebut the Stanley (2003) critique of contextualist theories of vagueness can be employed formulated in terms of micro-languages. See also Chapter 3 in this volume, Section 3.3.

vague – which means that the assertive contents of our utterances containing the term 'English' are vague in the way that the assertive contents of our utterances containing the word 'red' are vague. Just as there are many different but very closely related properties that are assertive contents of various of our uses of 'red', so there are many different but very closely related micro-languages that are the assertive contents of various uses of the term 'English'.

7   Dialetheism and the Sorites Paradox

Graham Priest

7.1 Introduction

A Sorites Paradox arises when a predicate, P, is vague in a certain sense. Specifically, it appears to satisfy a certain tolerance condition: for any object, a, if Pa, and b is any object which differs relevantly from a in only a very small amount – maybe an indistinguishable amount – then Pb too. Or, since the amount of difference concerned is symmetric, we could put it this way: if a and b differ relevantly from each other in only a very small way then Pa is true if, and only if, Pb is true. 'Drunk', 'adult', 'tall', 'bald' are paradigms of tolerant predicates.[1] Given such a predicate, we can construct a sequence of objects $a_0, a_1, \dots , a_n$, such that each member of the sequence differs only minimally in the relevant way from its predecessor, and Pa_0 is clearly true whilst Pa_n is clearly not true. Applying tolerance down the chain allows us to establish that Pa_n is true, thus:

$$\frac{Pa_0 \quad Pa_0 \equiv Pa_1}{\frac{Pa_1 \quad Pa_1 \equiv Pa_2}{Pa_2}}$$

$$\ddots$$

$$\frac{Pa_{n-1} \quad Pa_{n-1} \equiv Pa_n}{Pa_n}$$

It is perhaps more normal to formulate the Sorites with a conditional (from left to right), rather than a biconditional. But the conditional in the other direction is not contentious. And it is the biconditional which expresses tolerance. Hence, using the biconditional is more accurate.[2]

Like its more famous cousin, the Liar Paradox, the Sorites Paradox is reputed to have been discovered (or invented) by the Megarian philosopher Eubulides;[3] but though there are occasional references to it in Ancient Greek philosophy, unlike its more famous cousin

---

[1] See also 'The Sorites Paradox', in the introduction to this volume.

[2] For a general overview of the Sorites Paradox, see Hyde (2011), Sorensen (2012), Keefe (2000), Keefe and Smith (1997b) and, of course, this volume.

[3] According to, for example, to Diogenes Laertius. See Diogenes Laertius (1925, ii, 108). See also the discussion in Kneale and Kneale (1962, esp. p. 108). See also Chapter 15 in this volume.

it has had a very low profile historically. There are, as far as I know, no discussions of it in the great Medieval period of logic.[4] Nor, with one or two exceptions,[5] is it an issue in modern logic – until, that is, the 1960s and 1970s, when it suddenly took off.[6] Since then, it has generated an enormous literature. Why it should have shot suddenly from oblivion in this way, I have no idea.

Since then, the literature has provided a large number of suggested solutions. The one that will concern us in this chapter is a dialetheic solution. In Sorites progressions, the things at the beginning are clearly P; the things at the end are clearly $\neg P$. In the middle there appear to be borderline cases, symmetrically poised between the two. In a dialethic account of the matter, these are both P and $\neg P$.[7] The possibility of this approach was certainly mooted before the lift-off of the Sorites in modern logic.[8] But it was first put squarely on the table, as far as I am aware, by Hyde (1997). Since then, it has been sympathetically explored by a number of people, including Ripley (2005), (2013), Hyde and Colyvan (2008), Weber (2010) and myself (2010a).

7.2 Logical Background

Of course, saying that the borderline cases are both true and false is only a first move in the game. To explain how it is applied requires some logical background, especially concerning paraconsistent logic. Paraconsistent logics are logics which can tolerate contradictions, since the principle of inference $A, \neg A \vdash B$ (Explosion) fails.

There are many paraconsistent logics,[9] and most of them can be deployed in a dialethic solution to the Sorites. But by far the simplest, and one that exposes the crucial moves in play in the Sorites, is LP.[10]

We take a standard first-order language with connectives $\vee, \wedge, \neg$ (*or, and, not*), and quantifiers $\forall, \exists$ (*all, some*). We may suppose that there are no function symbols, and that all the predicates are monadic. $A \supset B$ is defined in the familiar way, as $\neg A \vee B$, and $A \equiv B$ as $(A \supset B) \wedge (B \supset A)$.

An interpretation for the language is a structure $\langle D, \theta \rangle$. D is the non-empty domain of quantification. θ is the denotation function. That is, for every constant, c, $\theta(c) \in D$; and for every monadic predicate, P, $\theta(P)$ is a pair $\langle X, Y \rangle$, where $X, Y \subseteq D$ such that $X \cup Y = D$.[11] X and Y are the *extension* and *anti-extension* of P. Intuitively, the objects in X are those that make P true and the objects in Y are those that make P false. I will write X and Y as $\theta^+(P)$ and $\theta^-(P)$, respectively.

---

[4] Or, for that matter, in any Asian texts I know.
[5] Notably Russell (1923).
[6] See, for example, Goguen (1969) and Fine (1975).
[7] There is, of course, another symmetric possibility: that they are neither P nor $\neg P$. I will comment on this possibility briefly at the end of this chapter.
[8] For example, by Plekhanov (1941, pp. 114ff.), McGill and Parry (1948) and Jaśkowski (1948).
[9] See Priest (2002).
[10] See e.g. Priest (2008, chapter 7).
[11] If one drops this restriction, one obtains the logic of First Degree Entailment (FDE). If one adds the constraint that $X \cap Y = \emptyset$, one obtains classical logic. See Priest (2008, chapter 8).

We define what it is for a sentence (that is, a formula with no free variables) to be true, $\Vdash^+$, and false, $\Vdash^-$, in an interpretation, as follows:

- $\Vdash^+ Pc$ iff $\theta(c) \in \theta^+(P)$
- $\Vdash^- Pc$ iff $\theta(c) \in \theta^-(P)$
- $\Vdash^+ \neg A$ iff $\Vdash^- A$
- $\Vdash^- \neg A$ iff $\Vdash^+ A$
- $\Vdash^+ A \wedge B$ iff $\Vdash^+ A$ and $\Vdash^+ B$
- $\Vdash^- A \wedge B$ iff $\Vdash^- A$ or $\Vdash^- B$
- $\Vdash^+ A \vee B$ iff $\Vdash^+ A$ or $\Vdash^+ B$
- $\Vdash^- A \vee B$ iff $\Vdash^- A$ and $\Vdash^- B$

To give the truth/falsity conditions for the quantifiers, we assume that the language has been augmented by a constant, k_d, for each $d \in D$, such that $\theta(k_d) = d$. $A_x(c)$ is A with every free occurrence of the variable x replaced by the constant c.

- $\Vdash^+ \exists x A$ iff for some $d \in D$, $\Vdash^+ A_x(k_d)$
- $\Vdash^- \exists x A$ iff for all $d \in D$, $\Vdash^- A_x(k_d)$
- $\Vdash^+ \forall x A$ iff for all $d \in D$, $\Vdash^+ A_x(k_d)$
- $\Vdash^- \forall x A$ iff for some $d \in D$, $\Vdash^- A_x(k_d)$

An inference is valid if it preserves truth in all interpretations. That is, $\Sigma \models A$ if, and only if, for all interpretations, $\Vdash^+ A$ when, for all $B \in \Sigma$, $\Vdash^+ B$.

7.3 The Material Conditional and Biconditional

For those unfamiliar with paraconsistent logic, and in virtue of what is to come, it is worth reflecting on *LP* a little further. In classical logic, any situation (interpretation) partitions all truth-bearers into two classes, the true ($\mathfrak{T}$) and the false ($\mathfrak{F}$). The two classes are mutually exclusive and exhaustive. A disjunction is in $\mathfrak{T}$ if one or other disjunct is; in $\mathfrak{F}$ if both are; dually for conjunction; and a truth-bearer is in $\mathfrak{T}$ if, and only if, its negation is in $\mathfrak{F}$, thus:

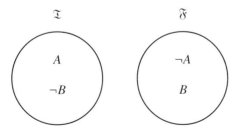

An inference is valid if, and only if, there is no interpretation in which all the premises are in $\mathfrak{T}$, but the conclusion is not. Given this set-up, there is no situation where, for any A,

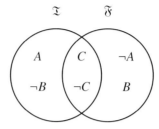

both A and $\neg A$ are in $\mathfrak{T}$. A fortiori, there is no situation where A and $\neg A$ are in $\mathfrak{T}$, and B is not – whatever B chosen. That is, Explosion is valid.

In *LP*, everything works *exactly* the same way, except that in some interpretations the $\mathfrak{T}$ and $\mathfrak{F}$ zones may overlap. Given that negation works in the same way, it follows that if C is in the overlap, so is its negation. Thus we have the following:

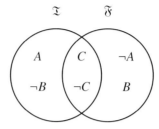

For a situation of this kind, both C and $\neg C$ are in $\mathfrak{T}$ (and in $\mathfrak{F}$ as well; but at least in $\mathfrak{T}$). But B is not in $\mathfrak{T}$. Given exactly the same definition of validity as before, it follows that Explosion is not valid. Note also that the same diagram shows that material detachment for $\supset$ fails, since C and $\neg C \vee B$ are both in the $\mathfrak{T}$ zone whilst B is not.

Turning to the material biconditional: in classical logic if A and B are both in $\mathfrak{T}$ or both in $\mathfrak{F}$, then $A \equiv B$ is in $\mathfrak{T}$. Whereas if one is in $\mathfrak{T}$, and the other is in $\mathfrak{F}$, $A \equiv B$ is in $\mathfrak{F}$, thus:

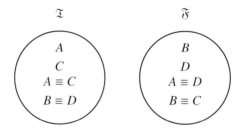

In the paraconsistent case everything is the same, except that the $\mathfrak{T}$ and $\mathfrak{F}$ zones may overlap. Thus we have the following picture:

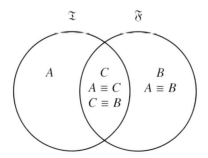

Though a sentence may now be in both zones, it remains the case that if A and B are in the same zone, $A \equiv B$ is in $\mathfrak{T}$; and if one is in $\mathfrak{T}$, and the other is in $\mathfrak{F}$, $A \equiv B$ is in $\mathfrak{F}$. A truth of the form $A \equiv B$ therefore expresses the fact that A and B are in the same zone. Its negation expresses the fact that they are in different zones. In particular, one may check that the following are valid:

- $A, B \vdash A \equiv B$
- $\neg A, \neg B \vdash A \equiv B$
- $A \equiv B \vdash (A \wedge B) \vee (\neg A \wedge \neg B)$
- $A, \neg B \vdash \neg(A \equiv B)$
- $\neg(A \equiv B) \vdash (A \wedge \neg B) \vee (B \wedge \neg A)$

Note that the material biconditional supports detachment no more than does the material conditional. As the above diagram shows, the inference $C, C \equiv B \vdash B$ is not valid.[12]

7.4 The Dialetheic Analysis

Against this background, a dialetheic analysis of the Sorites Paradox can now be explained very simply: all the premises are true, but material detachment is invalid. As we have seen, a standard Sorites argument has premises of the form:

- Pa_0
- $Pa_i \equiv Pa_{i+1}$ (for $0 \leqslant i < n$)

The conclusion is Pa_n.

The state of affairs concerning these statements is given by an interpretation, I, where, for some $j \leqslant k$:

- $\theta(a_i) \in \theta^+(P)$ for $0 \leq i \leq k$
- $\theta(a_i) \in \theta^-(P)$ for for $j \leq i \leq n$

This may be depicted as follows, where + indicates truth, − indicates falsity and ± indicates both:

Pa_0	...	Pa_{j-1}	Pa_j	...	Pa_k	Pa_{k+1}	...	Pa_n
+	...	+	±	...	±	−	...	−

It is easy to check that all the premises are true, and the conclusion is not true. ($Pa_i \equiv Pa_{i+1}$ is both true and false if $j-1 \leqslant i \leqslant k$.) And this is possible because detachment for $\equiv$ fails.[13]

---

[12] I note, also, that if the logic is FDE, and so has truth value gaps, a true material conditional, does not indicate membership of the same zone. Thus, suppose that A is both true and false, and B is neither. Then $(\neg A \vee B) \wedge (\neg B \vee A)$ is true (only).

[13] Hyde himself is more sympathetic to a subvaluationist account of the Sorites (see Chapter 2 in this volume). The basic idea is the same, except that we subvaluate. Given any *LP* interpretation of the above kind, let us call a *sharpening* any classical valuation such that for some $j \leqslant m \leqslant k$, Pa_i is just true up to $i = m$, and just false thereafter. A subvaluation makes a formula *sub-true* if it is true on some sharpening, and *sub-false* if it is false on some sharpening. (Something can be sub-true and sub-false.) Every premise of the argument is now sub-true (and maybe sub-false as well), and its conclusion is just sub-false.

Let us write $A!$ for $A \wedge \neg A$. Then the premises of the Sorites argument do not, note, tell us which i or is are such that $Pa_i!$. That is, they do not entail $Pa_i!$ for any particular i. But the premises and the negation of the conclusion do deliver $\bigvee_{0 \leqslant i \leqslant n} Pa_i!$.[14] That is, they entail that a contradiction occurs *somewhere* in the progression.

I note that one might formulate a version of the Sorites where the major premises are expressed with a detachable biconditional, $\leftrightarrow$ (and LP can certainly be augmented with such a conditional).[15] But the tolerance of a vague predicate is expressed exactly by the thought that successive members of the progression have the same truth value: both true or both false. (Being true *and* false is not a third truth value. It is the possession of two truth values.) So the material biconditional is the correct connective to use to express tolerance. There is no particular reason to suppose that any stronger connection holds. It would be wrong, then, to express tolerance using a non-material conditional, such as a detachable one.

7.5 Identity Sorites

There is another sort of Sorites argument that is worth noting. This uses not a (bi)conditional, but identity.[16] Suppose that our Sorites is a colour Sorites, say between red and blue; and let b_i be the term 'the colour of a_i'. Then if the appropriate tolerance obtains (for example if the colour of each a_i is phenomenologically indistinguishable from the colours of its neighbours), we have each of $b_i = b_{i+1}$, for $0 \leqslant i < n$. By $n - 1$ applications of the transitivity of identity ($a = b, b = c \vdash a = c$), we have $b_0 = b_n$, thus:

$$\frac{\dfrac{b_0 = b_1 \quad b_1 = b_2}{b_0 = b_2} \quad b_2 = b_3}{b_0 = b_3}$$

$$\ddots$$

$$\frac{b_0 = b_{n-1} \quad b_{n-1} = b_n}{b_0 = b_n}$$

But $b_0 = b_n$ is clearly not true: a_0 is not the same colour as a_n.

Sorites arguments are of a piece, and should have the same kind of solution (the Principle of Uniform Solution: same sort of paradox, same sort of solution).[17] The dialetheic solution to the previous kind of Sorites can be extended to this kind very simply. We may define $x = y$ in second-order logic, in the standard Leibnizian way, as $\forall X(Xx \equiv Xy)$, where

---

(So for Hyde, a statement concerning an object in the border area is not, strictly speaking, true and false, but sub-true and sub-false.) Defining validity in terms of the preservation of sub-truth still invalidates material detachment for the conditional and biconditional. However, it also invalidates other things that appear desirable, such as adjunction: $A, B \vdash A \wedge B$.

[14] Pa_0 and $Pa_0 \equiv Pa_1$ entail $Pa_0! \vee Pa_1!$. This, plus $Pa_1 \equiv Pa_2$ entail $Pa_0! \vee Pa_1! \vee Pa_2!$, and so on, till $Pa_0! \vee \ldots \vee Pa_{n-1}! \vee Pa_n$, whence $\neg Pa_n$ delivers the last contradictory disjunct.

[15] See e.g. Priest (2006, chapter 6).

[16] See Priest (2010b).

[17] See Priest (1995, part 3). Cf. Chapter 10 in this volume, Section 10.2.

the second-order variables range over an appropriate set of properties. Note that what the Leibnizian definition requires is that for every property, P, Px and Py have the same truth value.[18] This is exactly what the material biconditional expresses. But if we are in a paraconsistent context, the $\equiv$ is that of a paraconsistent logic. Assuming that second-order quantifiers work as do first-order quantifiers, except with a domain of properties instead of objects, it follows that $=$ is not transitive.[19] That is, $a = b, b = c \nvdash a = c$. Thus suppose, for the sake of illustration, that there is only one property, P, and consider an interpretation where $\theta(a)$ is in the extension of P, but not in its anti-extension; $\theta(c)$ is in the anti-extension of P, but not its extension; and $\theta(b)$ is in both. Then $Pa \equiv Pb$ and $Pb \equiv Pc$ are both true, but $Pa \equiv Pc$ is not. Given that P is the only property, it follows that $a = b$ and $b = c$ are true, but $a = c$ is not.

Since the transitivity of identity fails, the Sorites argument is broken. Thus suppose, to consider the same illustration, that P is 'is a shade of red' (where this is the only predicate). Then the situation is as follows:

$$
\begin{array}{ccccccccc}
Pb_0 & \ldots & Pb_{j-1} & Pb_j & \ldots & Pb_k & Pb_{k+1} & \ldots & P_n \\
+ & \ldots & + & \pm & \ldots & \pm & - & \ldots & -
\end{array}
$$

If $I_{i,j}$ is $b_i = b_j$, we then have:

$$
\begin{array}{ccccccccc}
I_{0,1} & \ldots & I_{j-2,j-1} & I_{j-1,j} & \ldots & I_{k,k+1} & I_{k+1,k+2} & \ldots & I_{n-1,n} \\
+ & \ldots & + & \pm & \ldots & \pm & + & \ldots & +
\end{array}
$$

And the values of $I_{0,i}$ look like this:

$$
\begin{array}{ccccccccc}
I_{0,0} & \ldots & I_{0,j-2} & I_{0,j-1} & \ldots & I_{0,k} & I_{0,k+1} & \ldots & I_{0,n} \\
+ & \ldots & + & \pm & \ldots & \pm & - & \ldots & -
\end{array}
$$

While we are on the topic of other versions of the Sorites Paradox, I note that the present solution deals equally with some prominent versions of these. In one, we do not have a collection of major premises, but a single quantified one: $\forall x(Px \supset Px')$, where the variables range over the a_is and x' is the object next to x. So the argument now is: $Pa_0, \forall x(Px \supset Px') \vdash Pa_n$. Material detachment fails in exactly the same way. This version has a contraposed form: $Pa_0, \neg Pa_n \vdash \exists x(Px \wedge \neg Px')$. The version is valid, but the conclusion does not express the existence of a unique cut-off point. $Pa_i \wedge \neg Pa_{i+1}$ is true for all $j - 1 \leq i \leq k$. More on this matter shortly.

---

[18] I shall speak indifferently of predicates and properties, the use/mention elision circumventing tiresome prolixity (which readers may provide for themselves).

[19] See Priest (2014, chapter 2). The book shows that non-transitive identity has a lot more going for it than what is at issue here.

7.6 Cut-Offs

So much for the basic ideas of a dialetheic account of the Sorites Paradox. We are far from done yet, though. Let us see why by turning to the major objection to the above account.

Come back to our original Sorites. Suppose that one subscribed to classical logic: statements are either true or false, but not both. Then there would be some l such that:

(*) $\forall i \le l \, Pa_i$ and $\forall i > l \, \neg Pa_i$

l is a precise cut-off point. That there should be a cut-off point of this kind seems completely wrong. It appears to be in the very nature of vague progressions that there is no such distinguished point. That is, indeed, what drives the Sorites Paradox.

A dialetheic account of the Sorites has a simple solution to that problem. As just noted, (*) is true for all $j - 1 \le l \le k$. There is, as required, no unique cut-off point.[20]

But, it may fairly be said, the solution has just moved the problem. Before, we had a problem with the cut-off between truth and falsity. Now, we have the same problem with the cut-off between being true (only),[21] and being true and false. This seems just as bad. Indeed, the problem is even worse. We now have *two* cut-off points: there is another between being true and false, and being false (only) as well.[22]

Neither is this simply an artefact of the model of Section 7.4. The very basis of a dialetheic approach to the Sorites is that the objects, a, in a borderline area between those that are P and those that are $\neg P$ are characterised by the conjunction of these extremes, $Pa \wedge \neg Pa$. Now, consider the right-hand borderline in the dialetheic case. (Details with the left-hand one are similar.) If there were objects in a borderline between being P and $\neg P$, and being $\neg P$, they would therefore be characterised by the conjunction $(Pa \wedge \neg Pa) \wedge \neg Pa$. But this is logically equivalent to $Pa \wedge \neg Pa$. (To be borderline between being P and being borderline P is just to be borderline P.) That is, there is no borderline transition between the two categories: the sequence goes straight from one to the other.

One might think that this mislocates the issue. The borderline in question is not that between being P and $\neg P$, and being $\neg P$, but between P being true and P not being true; that is, between those as such that $T \langle Pa \rangle$ and those such that $\neg T \langle Pa \rangle$ (where T is the truth predicate, and angle brackets indicate a name-forming device). If T is a crisp predicate, there will be a precise cut-off point. But if T is a vague predicate, there will be as such that $T \langle Pa \rangle \wedge \neg T \langle Pa \rangle$. Of course, if negation commutes with truth, this is just $T \langle Pa \rangle \wedge T \langle \neg Pa \rangle$. Given the T-schema, this is equivalent to $Pa \wedge \neg Pa$. Hence there is no mislocation: there

---

[20] See Weber (2010) for further discussion.

[21] A frequent objection to a dialetheic solution to the paradoxes of self-reference is that the dialetheist cannot express the claim that something is true only. This is completely incorrect: that A is true and not false is expressed in the obvious way: $T \langle A \rangle \wedge \neg F \langle A \rangle$. What it cannot do is force this claim to be consistent. That is quite another matter; and it is not at all obvious that this is a requirement that should be met. Indeed, it is not even clear that the requirement *can* be met – even by a classical logician. See Priest (2006, section 20.4).

[22] In discussions of the paradoxes of self-reference, there is a phenomenon of the revenge paradox, in which the theoretical machinery of a solution is used to reformulate a new paradox of the same kind – or really just to rephrase the old paradox. The situation we now face with the Sorites Paradox can be thought of as a revenge problem of exactly the same kind. The parity between the two sorts of revenge phenomena is discussed in Priest (2010a). See also Chapter 10 in this volume, Section 10.2.3.

is no separate location. There are good reasons to suppose that negation does not commute with truth.[23] However, even in this case, we are no better off. For there will still be a last a such that $T \langle Pa \rangle$ (even if it is the case that $T \langle Pa \rangle \wedge \neg T \langle Pa \rangle$) and after which it is not.[24] Again, we have a counterintuitive cut-off.

7.7 The Forced March Sorites

Things seem bad. The only way to make them better is to make them worse. The hard fact of the matter is that *whatever solution one endorses*, one is stuck with a precise cut-off point of some kind. One way to see this is to consider the 'forced march Sorites'.[25]

Consider our example Sorites. Let Q_i be the question 'Is it the case that Pa_i?' If asked this question, there is some appropriate range of answers. What these are, exactly, does not matter. They might be 'yes', 'no', 'I don't know', 'yes, probably', 'er...' or anything else. All that we need to assume is that an appropriate answer is justified by the objective state of affairs; specifically, by the nature of Pa_i. (The justification here is semantic, not epistemic. The answerer is personified simply to make the situation graphic.) Now, suppose I ask you the sequence of questions: Q_0, Q_1, ... Given any question, there may be more than one appropriate answer. For example, you might say 'yes'; you might say 'same answer as last time' (having said 'yes' last time). All I insist is that once you answer in a certain way you stick to that until that answer is no longer appropriate. Suppose that in answer to the question Q_0, you answer A. This may also be justified in answer to Q_1, Q_2 and so on. But because of the finitude of the situation, there must come a first i where this is no longer the case, or it would be justified in answer to Q_n, which it is not.[26] Nor is the logic one takes to apply to the situation relevant, be it classical, to have truth value gaps, or to have truth value gluts. How things of the form $\neg Pa_i$ behave does not come into the matter. Thus for some i, Pa_i justifies this answer; Pa_{i+1} does not. The objective situation therefore changes between Pa_i and Pa_{i+1} in such a way. We have a precise cut-off.

Let us consider a couple of replies. Here is one. The existence of a cut-off point seems odd because of the apparently arbitrary nature of its location. Suppose that the correct answer in the forced march Sorites changed at *every* question. The arbitrariness, and so the oddness, would then disappear. But how could it change at every step? One possibility is that to answer the question I simply *show* you the object at issue – which is changing from stage to stage. Another is that an answer is of the form 'It is true to degree r' – as in fuzzy logic – where r is a different real number every time.

[23] See Priest (2006, section 4.7).

[24] There is an important issue here about the logic in which the semantics is given, and so of the sense of 'not' here. However, important as this issue is, it is not relevant here. The claim holds whether the negation is Boolean or paraconsistent.

[25] The term was coined, as far as I know, by Horgan (1994), section 4, though the form of argument is essentially the same as the original Eubulidean version. The version I give here is slightly different from, and, it seems to me, tougher than, the version Horgan gives. For the original formulation of the argument see Williamson (1994, chapter 1) and Keefe and Smith (1997b, chapter 2). What follows in this section comes, essentially, from Priest (2003). See also the 'The Forced-March Paradox', in the introduction to this volume.

[26] There are, in fact, continuous versions of the Sorites, in which there is no such finitude. See Weber and Colyvan (2010). But as that paper makes clear, there are still precise cut-off points: the appropriate least upper bound or greatest lower bound.

The first response raises the question of what, exactly, a language is. If you ask me, for example, what colour something is and I simply show it to you, is this response part of a *language* game? Perhaps so, but even if it is, the point is irrelevant. The Sorites problem is generated by a verbal language, with vague predicates, questions and answers. We need a solution that applies to *that* language.

One response to the second suggestion is similar. Even though, in this, the response to the question is by saying, not showing, a language that can refer to every real number – an uncountable number of entities – is not a language we could speak: we seek a solution for *our* language. But I think that there are greater problems with this response. However one conceptualises degrees of truth, there are Sorites progressions where truth value does not change all the time. Thus, even if you were changed by replacing one molecule of your body with a molecule of scrambled egg, you would still be as you as you could be. You change more than that every morning after breakfast. Similarly, dying takes time, and so is a vague notion. But when your ashes are scattered to the four winds, and thereafter – if not before – you are as dead as dead can be. And if a correct answer to the relevant question does not change at every point, we have a cut-off.

A second reply is to the effect that the answerer may 'refuse to play the game'. Of course, if they do this for subjective reasons, such as the desire to be obstreperous, this is beside the point. They might, however, do so for a principled reason, namely that the rules of the 'game' are impossible to comply with. They lead the answerer, at some point, into a situation where they cannot conform.[27] Now, it would certainly appear that it is possible to comply with the rules at the start: the first few answers present no problem. But then we may simply ask the person to play the game as long as it is possible. If the answer changes before this, the point is made. If, however, they stop at some point before this, it must be because the situation is such as to require them both to give and not give the same answer as before. This was not the case with the question before, so the semantic situation has changed at this point. The only other possibility is for the answerer to say that the game is unplayable right at the start. But this can only be because there is no appropriate answer they can give even in the first case – and presumably, therefore, in all subsequent cases. This is not only implausible; it means that even in the most determinate case there is no answer that can be given. We are led to complete and unacceptable semantic nihilism.

What we see, then, is that any solution to the Sorites will be forced to accept a counterintuitive cut-off of some kind. It cannot disappear it. Of course, how we should theorise this cut-off is another matter. Different theorists do this in different ways. A cut-off may be theorised as a change from truth to falsity; a change from truth to neither truth nor falsity, or to both truth and falsity; a change from being 100 per cent true to less than 100 per cent true; a change from maximal degree of assertibility to less than maximal degree; and so on. Never mind the details. What the forced march Sorites demonstrates is that any solution must face the existence of a cut-off.

---

[27] Arguably, one finds a view of this nature in Dummett (1975).

This is, in fact, the *real* Sorites problem. Anything in a proposed solution before this matter is addressed is just preliminary. A solution to the Sorites must accept the existence of some cut-off point or other, and must explain, given the machinery it endorses, why we find the existence of such a thing counterintuitive. That is all it can do; and it is on the strength of this explanation that it must be judged.

7.8 The Dialetheic Solution

So what is the dialetheic explanation? It is simple. A precise cut-off point is counterintuitive because whatever i we choose, $Pa_{i-1} \equiv Pa_i$ and $Pa_i \equiv Pa_{i+1}$. In other words, Pa_i has the same truth value as each of its neighbours. This is what makes us think that there can be no cut-off. It might be pointed out that, on the present account, some of the negations of the biconditionals are true too; but this is beside the point. Tolerance is the *obvious* feature of vague predicates. We are moved by what is obvious.

We can put the point in another way, by looking at the truth values themselves. Let b_i be 'the (truth) value of Pa_i'. There are only two relevant properties: T and F, being true and being false.[28] What is the value of Tb_i? It is natural to suppose that statements of the form Tb_i are themselves vague. (If the status of 'a is red' is moot, so is that of ' "a is red" is true'.) If truth commutes with negation then $Pa_i \wedge \neg Pa_i$ if, and only if, $T \langle Pa_i \wedge \neg Pa_i \rangle$ if, and only if, $T \langle Pa_i \rangle \wedge T \langle \neg Pa_i \rangle$ if, and only if, $T \langle Pa_i \rangle \wedge \neg T \langle Pa_i \rangle$ if, and only if, $Tb_i \wedge \neg Tb_i$ so the borderline of P lines up with that of T. But even if not, because of the vagueness of T, then between the area where Tb_i is true only and the area where it is false only, there must be a region where Tb_i is both true and false. Thus, for some $0 < x \leqslant y < n$:

$$Tb_0 \quad \ldots \quad Tb_{x-1} \quad Tb_x \quad \ldots \quad Tb_y \quad Tb_{y+1} \quad \ldots \quad Tb_n$$
$$+ \quad \ldots \quad + \quad \pm \quad \ldots \quad \pm \quad - \quad - \quad -$$

If we write E_i for the biconditional $Tb_i \equiv Tb_{i+1}$, we then have:

$$E_0 \quad \ldots \quad E_{x-2} \quad E_{x-1} \quad E_x \quad \ldots \quad E_y \quad E_{y+1} \quad \ldots \quad E_n$$
$$+ \quad \ldots \quad + \quad \pm \quad \pm \quad \ldots \quad \pm \quad + \quad + \quad +$$

Every biconditional is (at least) true. Symmetrically, the same is true for the falsity predicate, $F \langle Pa \rangle$ ($= T \langle \neg Pa \rangle$). Every biconditional of the form $Fb_i \equiv Fb_{i+1}$ is also (at least) true. Since this is so for both the (relevant) properties of the b_i, then $b_i = b_{i+1}$, for all i. That is, the truth value of each statement in the Sorites progression is the same as those of its neighbours. No wonder a cut-off is counterintuitive!

In any given Sorites, there remains the challenge of saying where, exactly, the cut-off between the borderline and non-borderline cases is. To find out, one simply has to take the forced march test. Run down the sequence until you can no longer give the answer

---

[28] Other properties either apply to all truth values, or none, and so need not concern us.

'yes'. That is where it is. Or roughly, anyway: you are not the idealised answerer of Section 7.7 – and neither is anybody else. Individuals have too many subjective factors operating on them. Since meaning is not subjective, but socially embedded, a more accurate guide to the cut-off is to take multiple speakers and circumstances, and aggregate out the answers in some way. This will provide a more robust determination. Note that this is not to say that what is so is what 'an average person' believes: it merely reflects the fact that words are our words, and mean what we use them to mean. Can one find out this meaning by empirical considerations? Of course: this is what empirical linguistics is all about.

7.9 The Epistemic Solution

I have located the heart of the problem with the Sorites Paradox as how to explain why the existence of precise cut-off points seems so counterintuitive, and given a dialetheic explanation. This is not the place to discuss all other possible explanations. However, a major alternative to a dialetheic solution to the Sorites Paradox is an epistemic one, based on classical logic. Let me comment on that.

An epistemic solution to the Sorites Paradox is advocated, among others, by Sorensen and Williamson.[29] This solution takes apparently vague predicates to be precise. (In a sense, then, there are no vague predicates.) In a soritical progression there is a precise cut-off where the sentences turn from true to false or vice versa. The explanation for why one finds the existence of such a cut-off counterintuitive has, then, to be provided in epistemic terms.[30] The most articulated explanation of the matter is given by Williamson, and depends on the fact that we cannot know where the cut-off is. (In particular, then, it cannot be determined by any empirical investigations.) Before we even get to the explanation, let us consider this claim.

Why can we not know where the cut-off point is? This is because of what Williamson calls the 'margin of error principle', which he states as follows: 'A' is true in all cases similar to cases in which 'It is known that A' is true. Why endorse this principle? Because if a and b are effectively the same in terms of the evidence they deliver, but Pa is true and Pb is false, then I cannot know that Pa. My evidential state is not such as to make my belief reliable, so it is not knowledge.[31] Now, suppose that the cut-off point is at Pa_i. That is, Pa_i is true, and Pa_{i+1} is not. Suppose one knows where the cut-off point is. Then one knows that Pa_i is true. But since a_i and a_{i+1} are evidentially indistinguishable, Pa_{i+1} by the margin or error principle – which, *ex hypothesi*, it is not.

A major worry here is that the very phenomenon that explains why we cannot know where the cut-off point is undercuts its very existence. The meanings of vague predicates are not determined by some omniscient being in some logically perfect way. Vague predicates are part of *our* language. As a result, their meaning must answer in the last instance to

[29] See Sorensen (1988, esp. pp. 189–216), Williamson (1994, esp. chapters. 7 and 8) and Chapter 1 in this volume.
[30] I note that, though Williamson endorses classical logic, the possibility of an epistemic explanation of the counterintuitive nature of the cut-off point is, in principle, available for any standard semantics for vagueness.
[31] See Williamson (1994, section 8.3).

the use that *we* make of them. It is therefore difficult to see how there could be a semantic cut-off at a point that is *in principle* inaccessible to agents with our cognitive apparatus. To suppose that such exists would appear to be a form of semantic mysticism.[32]

But set these matters aside. What is Williamson's explanation of the fact that the existence of a cut-off point is counterintuitive? He argues that we find it so because we cannot imagine one; and we cannot imagine one, because we cannot know where it is.[33] Now, 'because' is transitive. If *x* is in the causal chain leading up to *y*, and *y* is in the causal chain leading up to *z*, then *x* is in the causal chain leading up to *z*. (If Johnny cannot go to the movies because his parents refused to give him his pocket money, and they refused to give him the money because he did not clean up his room, then he cannot go to the movies because he failed to clean up his room.) Hence, for Williamson we find the existence of a cut-off counterintuitive because we cannot know where it is. However, the mere unknowability of something does not explain why its existence is counterintuitive. There are many things that we cannot know and whose existence we do not find puzzling at all. For example, there is a well-known model of the physical cosmos according to which the universe goes through alternating periods of expansion and contraction. In particular, the singularity at the Big Bang was just the end of the last period of contraction and the beginning of the current period of expansion. Suppose this is right. Then there must be many facts about what happened in the phase of the universe prior to the Big Bang – for example, whether there was sentient life. Yet all information about this period has been wiped out for us – lost in the epistemic black hole that was the Big Bang. Yet we do not find the existence of determinate facts before the Big Bang counterintuitive. Indeed, we seem to have no problem accepting the thought that there are such things, though they be cognitively inaccessible to us, and ever will be so. That we cannot know the existence of something does not, therefore, explain why we find its existence counterintuitive.[34]

As we saw, Williamson derives his connection between counterintuitiveness and unknowability of the cut-off from two other claims:

- it is counterintuitive because we cannot imagine it;
- we cannot imagine it because we cannot know it.

The preceding considerations do not tell us which of these statements is false. This may depend on what, exactly, Williamson intends in saying that one can imagine something. However, at least prima facie, both of these claims are in trouble.

For the first: I cannot imagine what the suffering of being burnt at the stake feels like. Yet I do not find its existence counterintuitive. Nor can I imagine the experience of what it feels like to drown; but I do not find it counterintuitive to suppose that there is such an experience. For the second, I cannot know whether there are planets outside my light-cone;

[32] As Crispin Wright puts it in his detailed critique of epistemicism (1995). See also Horgan (1994, section 5). See also Chapter 1 in this volume, pp. 22, 29–30.
[33] Williamson (1997c, pp. 218ff.).
[34] Cf. Chapter 1, fn. 8 in this volume.

but I have no problem imagining such. Similarly, I have no way of knowing (this side of death) what an afterlife is like. But I can certainly imagine one.

Williamson's epistemic explanation of why we find the existence of a cut-off point counterintuitive, does not, then, work.

7.10 Inclosure Paradoxes

Before I finish, let me comment on one further, and important, aspect of the Sorites Paradox: its connection with the paradoxes of self-reference, such as the Liar Paradox and Russell's Paradox.

There is a general structure that underlies the paradoxes of self-reference: they all fit the *inclosure schema*.[35] The schema arises when there is an operator, δ, and a totality, Ω (of the form $\{x : \varphi(x)\}$, for some φ), which appear to satisfy the following conditions.[36] Whenever δ is applied to any subset, x, of Ω, of a certain kind – that is, one that satisfies some condition ψ – it delivers an object that is still in Ω (Closure) though not in x (Transcendence). If Ω itself satisfies ψ, a contradiction is forthcoming. For applying δ to Ω itself will then produce an object that is both within and without Ω, so that $\delta(\Omega) \in \Omega$ and $\delta(\Omega) \notin \Omega$. We may depict the situation as follows (× marks the contradictory spot – somewhere that is both within and without Ω):

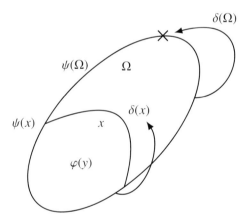

Thus consider Russell's Paradox, for example. Ω is the set of all sets; $\delta(x) = \{y \in x : y \notin y\}$; and $\psi(x)$ is the vacuous condition, $x = x$. Or consider the Liar Paradox. Ω is the set of all truths, $\psi(x)$ is 'x has a name' and $\delta(x)$ is a sentence, σ, of the form $\langle \sigma \rangle \notin \dot{x}$ (where

---

[35] The inclosure schema was first proposed in Priest (1994). Since then, the major controversy over it has been whether Curry's Paradox fits, or ought to fit, the schema. For the most recent round in the controversy, see the appendix of Priest (2017).

[36] I note that the conditions do not *actually* have to be true, just prima facie so (see the second edition of Priest 1995, section 17.2). The inclosure schema is a diagnostic tool, not an argument for dialetheism.

angle brackets are a name-forming operator and $\dot{x}$ is a name of x). In each of these cases it is not difficult to show that the inclosure conditions appear to be satisfied.[37]

Now, the Sorites Paradox is an inclosure paradox too.[38] Given our Sorites sequence, Ω is the set of all a_is such that Pa_i. ψ is the vacuous condition, $x = x$. If $x \subseteq \Omega$ there is a maximum j such that $a_j \in x$. $\delta(x)$ is a_{j+1}. $a_{j+1} \notin x$, by construction (it's the first thing that is not P); and $a_{j+1} \in \Omega$ since Pa_j and a_{j+1} is next to a_j (that's just tolerance). The contradiction is that the first thing that is not P is P.

The fact that the Sorites Paradox is of a piece with the paradoxes of self-reference tells us that they should have the same kind of solution – the Principle of Uniform Solution. This does not mandate a dialetheic solution for Sorites/self-referential paradoxes. However, elsewhere I have argued for a dialetheic solution to the paradoxes of self-reference.[39] And if such be correct, then a dialetheic solution to the Sorites Paradox is exactly what we should expect.

The fact that the Sorites Paradox is an inclosure paradox, together with the Principle of Uniform Solution, provide another argument against an epistemic solution to the Sorites. There is no obvious way in which epistemicism can be deployed to account for the paradoxes of self-reference.[40]

Solutions which invoke truth value gaps, by contrast, are often mooted in the case of both the Sorites Paradox and the paradoxes of self-reference. I find such solutions to the paradoxes of self-reference unconvincing: they cannot happily handle so called 'extended paradoxes'.[41] More to the point here, I see no obvious way of deploying the gap-stratagem to explain why it is that we find the existence of a precise cut-off in a Sorites sequence counterintuitive. In particular, logics with truth value gaps standardly endorse *modus ponens* (and the substitutivity of identicals). They are therefore required to say that some of the major premises of the argument are false, or at least untrue. This does not help an explanation of why we find the existence of a cut-off counterintuitive one iota. It is simply a denial of tolerance (which a dialetheic approach endorses). Any symmetric duality between a gap solution and a glut solution breaks down at this point – if not others.

---

[37] Thus, in the case of Russell's Paradox, suppose that $x \subseteq \Omega$. If $\delta(x) \in \delta(x)$ then $\delta(x) \notin \delta(x)$. So $\delta(x) \notin \delta(x)$. Hence $\delta(x) \notin x$, or it would be the case that $\delta(x) \in \delta(x)$. Hence we have Transcendence. Closure is true by Definition. In the case of the Liar Paradox, suppose that $x \subseteq \Omega$. If $\langle \sigma \rangle \in \dot{x}$, then σ is true, so $\langle \sigma \rangle \notin \dot{x}$. Hence $\langle \sigma \rangle \notin \dot{x}$. So we have Transcendence. But since $\langle \sigma \rangle \notin \dot{x}$, σ is true. So we have Closure. For full details, see Priest (1995, part 3).

[38] See Priest (2010a).

[39] E.g. Priest (2006, part 1).

[40] Horwich (1998, pp. 41–2), attempts an epistemic account of the Liar, claiming that the Liar sentence is either true or false, though one cannot know which. This, however, is not his solution to the paradox, which is to give up certain instances of the T-schema (a completely ad hoc move, given Horwich's views on truth). And, epistemicism provides no explanation of which instances of the T-schema are not true, independent of the fact that they produce contradiction. For a fuller discussion, see Armour-Garb (2004) and Chapter 10 in this volume. And even Horwich has not attempted an epistemic solution to the set-theoretic paradoxes.

[41] For a discussion of such paradoxes, see Beall (2008). It has certainly been argued by some that dialetheic approaches are also subject to the same problem, but I find the arguments unpersuasive – indeed, frequently confused. See Priest (2006, section 20.3).

7.11 Conclusion

In this chapter I have explained some of the core details of a dialetheic account of the Sorites Paradox, together with its attractions. I have not attempted a systematic comparison with other possible solutions, nor a systematic evaluation of the strengths and weaknesses of these. That would take much longer – indeed, in some ways it is what this book is about. Nor do I suppose that what I have said will end any debate. After hundreds of years of hibernation, the genie has finally come out of its bottle – and it is not going to go back in quietly. I think it is fair to say, though, that a dialetheic solution to the Sorites Paradox has so far been given less airplay than most other solutions. No doubt this is because dialetheism itself has been taken to be beyond the pale. That attitude is, I think, slowly changing. Even if few people currently accept dialetheism, it occupies a position in logical space that those not possessing blinkers[42] must engage with. If this chapter generates a greater engagement than has hitherto happened in the context of the Sorites Paradox, it will have served its purpose.[43]

---

[42] That is, blinders, if you speak North American English.
[43] I am grateful to the editors of this volume, Sergi Oms and Elia Zardini, for their comments on the first draft of this chapter, which certainly improved it.

8   Degree Theory and the Sorites Paradox

Francesco Paoli

8.1 Introduction

Degree-theoretical approaches to vagueness and the Sorites variously attempt to flesh out the idea that properties referred to by vague predicates come in degrees, and that sentences containing such predicates can be semantically characterised by means of these degrees. The real or the rational closed unit interval [0, 1] is usually, but not invariably, selected as a universe of degrees, and such a many-valued semantics may – but need not – be wedded to the adoption of some fuzzy logic.

In greater detail, degree theories of vagueness uphold one or more of the following theses, where, for $n < m$, Tm presupposes Tn but is not entailed by it:

T1 *Ontology of degrees.* Whether or not a vague n-ary predicate applies to an n-tuple of individuals in its domain of significance is a matter of degree. Therefore, the truth of atomic sentences that ascribe the properties referred to by these predicates cannot be an all-or-nothing matter. Sentences of this kind are characterised by some semantic value that comes in degrees. Although degrees need not be 'out there in the world' in any metaphysically substantive sense, it is stipulated that they at least form a *set*. The standard choice for such a universe of degrees is the real or the rational[1] closed unit interval [0, 1], but other (finite or infinite) suitably structured sets can be taken to fit the bill. There is also some leeway on how we should interpret degrees: the customary reading is in terms of *degrees of truth*, but it is likewise possible to view the degree assigned to, say, $P(a)$ as a measure of the distance of a from a clear case of a P.

T2 *Truth-functional semantics.* There is no consensus among degree theorists on whether degree assignments to atomic sentences should recursively extend to compound sentences according to some functional pattern that generalises classical valuations into {0, 1}. Authors who follow this route typically embrace valuation clauses for the sentential connectives to the rational interval [0, 1] along the lines of what

---

[1] Since quantifiers are omitted from the present discussion, henceforth we assume that [0, 1] denotes the set of *rational* numbers in between 0 and 1. Whether any such *linearly ordered* set of degrees is adequate for modelling vagueness is a controversial matter, given that vagueness gives rise to apparently incomparable pairs; here, unlike in Paoli (2003), we will not discuss the issue further.

is done in some mainstream fuzzy logic, such as Łukasiewicz infinite-valued logic or product logic.[2]

T3 *Fuzzy consequence relation.* The first obvious benchmark for the adequacy of a degree theory of vagueness is a solution to the Sorites Paradox. Since the Sorites is a seemingly valid argument proceeding from plausible premises, an appropriate account of validity is needed to make sense of what is going on. The natural candidate for this role is some subclassical consequence relation associated with one of the above-mentioned fuzzy logics – which can be defined in various guises in terms of preservation of truth degrees. Still, even truth-functional degree theorists are not unanimous in their readiness to give up the full deductive power of classical logic, and virtually all of them are all too eager to assuage the anxiety of going non-classical by showing that their own suggestions are compatible with some form of 'classical recapture'.

How effective are degree theories in accounting for Sorites phenomena? It is well known that Sorites Paradoxes can present themselves in several different forms, and it is widely held that no proposed solution is worth considering unless it provides a general enough framework where *all* these variants can be dispelled as inconclusive (or where their conclusions can be recommended as acceptable despite their clash with our intuitions). Still, for the purposes of the discussion that follows, it will be expedient to initially select a particular Sorites argument against which we can weigh up the pros and cons of the different degree-theoretical approaches, reserving until later in the chapter an assessment of their applicability to other variants of the paradox.

An intriguing way to look at the Sorites has been suggested by Peacocke (1981). Sorites arguments reveal the mutual incompatibility of two plausible constraints we are tempted to impose on the behaviour of the indicative sufficiency conditional in English:

- from the sentences α and *If α then β*, we should always be in a position to validly infer β (*modus ponens*);
- if the objects named by a and b are similar enough in respects that determine the applicability of the vague predicate P, then the conditional *If $P(a)$ then $P(b)$* is true (*Tolerance*).[3]

Now, let $P(n)$ stand for *A man with n hairs on his head is bald*. $P(0)$ is true by common sense. Each instance of *If $P(n)$ then $P(n+1)$* is true by Tolerance. For all m, $P(m+1)$ validly follows by *modus ponens* from *If $P(m)$ then $P(m+1)$* and $P(m)$. By chaining together all these inferential steps, we eventually end up with the implausible conclusion $P(k)$ (for k as large as you like).

There is a lot of variation in the way degree theorists approach this difficulty, and much of this variation can be traced back to whether they only accept the thesis earlier referred

---

[2] Throughout this chapter, by 'fuzzy logic' we mean what is usually known as Mathematical Fuzzy Logic or fuzzy logic in the narrow sense. Applied researchers, and perhaps the public at large, may be more familiar with the pioneering work by Lofti A. Zadeh (see e.g. Zadeh 1965). However, despite some inroads into philosophy by Zadeh himself (Zadeh 1975), we take the repercussions of this approach on the debate on vagueness to be rather feeble.
[3] See 'The Sorites Paradox', in the introduction to this volume.

to as T1, or whether they go as far as to espouse T2 or even T3. Our next task is to survey some representative proposals in this direction.

8.2 A Survey of Degree Theories

8.2.1 The Standard Fuzzy Account (SFA)

The degree theorist who upholds all of T1–T3 will use a fuzzy logic to solve the Sorites. Although the earliest such proposal, advanced by Goguen (1969), resorts to a relatively esoteric logic in the fuzzy family, which will later become known as *product logic* (Hájek 1998), it is generally agreed (Hájek 1999; Běhounek 2016) that, if any fuzzy logic has to stand reasonable chances to direct us to a way out of this quandary, this is $\mathbf{L}_{\aleph}$, *infinite-valued Łukasiewicz logic* (Hájek 1998; Cignoli et al. 1999). The $\mathbf{L}_{\aleph}$-based solution that we present hereafter, by now in the folklore of the subject, will be labelled the *Standard Fuzzy Account* (SFA). Still, it is not clear (at least to us) whom we should credit with the exact details of it. All the standard references in the area (Lakoff 1973; Machina 1976; Peacocke 1981; Forbes 1983), in fact, distance themselves from this picture under important respects.

To address our chosen version of the Sorites from a fuzzy viewpoint, we need a little extra in addition to the resources of propositional logic: while no quantifiers are involved in the argument, it is none the less desirable to view atomic formulas as carrying some inner predicate structure rather than as unanalysed sentential variables, in order to make clear what it is for a predicate to denote a function of a certain sort. Therefore, we will present $\mathbf{L}_{\aleph}$ in a simplified predicate language $\mathcal{L}_1$ containing an unspecified number of predicates P^n, each one of the appropriate arity n, together with denumerably many individual constants. Atomic formulas have the form $P^n(c_1, \ldots, c_n)$, where P^n is an n-ary predicate and $c_1, \ldots, c_n$ are constants; molecular formulas are those one can form using the connectives $\neg$ (negation), $\sqcap$ (conjunction), $\sqcup$ (disjunction) and $\rightarrow$ (implication, or conditional); the reason why our chosen notation for conjunction and disjunction is at variance with the traditional one will be clear in the sequel.

A *model* is an ordered pair $\mathfrak{M} = (D, i)$, where D is a non-empty set (the domain of *individuals*) and the interpretation function i is such that for any constant c, $i(c) \in D$ and for any n-ary predicate P^n, $i(P^n) \in [0, 1]^{D^n}$. Every interpretation i induces a valuation v as follows:

- if α is the atomic formula $P^n(c_1, \ldots, c_n)$, $v(\alpha) = i(P^n)(i(c_1), \ldots, i(c_n))$;
- if α has the form $\neg\beta, \beta \sqcap \gamma, \beta \sqcup \gamma$ or $\beta \rightarrow \gamma$, $v(\alpha)$ is inductively defined according to the following clauses:

$$v(\neg\beta) = 1 - v(\beta);$$
$$v(\beta \sqcap \gamma) = \min(v(\beta), v(\gamma));$$
$$v(\beta \sqcup \gamma) = \max(v(\beta), v(\gamma));$$
$$v(\beta \rightarrow \gamma) = \min(1, 1 - v(\beta) + v(\gamma)).$$

Observe that $v(\beta \to \gamma) = 1$ just in case $v(\beta) \leq v(\gamma)$. The consequence relation of $\mathbf{L}_{\aleph}$ is so defined:[4] $\Gamma \vDash_{\mathbf{L}_{\aleph}} \alpha$ just in case, for every model $\mathfrak{M} = (D, i)$ with induced valuation v, if $v(\gamma) = 1$ for all $\gamma \in \Gamma$, then $v(\alpha) = 1$.

The above mathematics is elucidated by the following philosophical picture. Members of the interval $[0, 1]$ are interpreted as *truth degrees*. 0 means absolute falsity, 1 absolute truth, while numbers in $(0, 1)$ represent degrees of approximate truth (or of approximate falsity). The closer to 1 a number is, the 'truer' the truth degree it represents. Thus the interpretation of a predicate is a function from n-tuples of individuals to degrees of truth, and $v(P^n(c_1, \ldots, c_n))$ expresses the degree to which the atomic formula $P^n(c_1, \ldots, c_n)$ is true. Given this reading, an $\vDash_{\mathbf{L}_{\aleph}}$-valid argument can be seen as an argument that never leads from absolutely true premises to a less than absolutely true conclusion; we will also say that an $\vDash_{\mathbf{L}_{\aleph}}$-valid argument is $\vDash_{\mathbf{L}_{\aleph}}$-*sound* in case it has absolutely true premises.

Now we can offer a degree-theoretical solution to our Sorites above. For all n, we formalise *If $P(n)$ then $P(n + 1)$* by means of the Łukasiewicz conditional, that is to say, as $P(n) \to P(n + 1)$. The categorical premise and *some* of the conditional premises in our argument are assigned truth degree 1, but the remaining conditional premises are assigned a degree which is slightly less than absolute truth, say $1 - \varepsilon$. This assignment is justified since the value $1 - \varepsilon$ is meant to represent the difference in truth degree between $P(n)$ and $P(n + 1)$, for every n in the borderline area of application of P. From a certain step onwards, the conditional premises begin to 'leak' truth, in such a way that the conclusion of each application of *modus ponens*, computed in a backward manner via the evaluation clause for $\to$, is a tiny bit less true than the categorical or the conditional premise of the same application. In other words, our judgements ascribing P to the successive elements of our Sorites series become little by little ever less accurate, so that, at the end of a very long row of applications of *modus ponens*, we are left with a false conclusion.

Recall that it is commonplace to require of any solution to a logical paradox that it explain both what goes wrong with the argument and why it is that we are taken in by the reasoning. The analysis above lays claim to hitting both marks. The argument is shown to be *unsound* by the previously defined standard, because not all of its premises are absolutely true; yet it is *compelling*, because it is valid and all of its premises are at least very close to being absolutely true.

8.2.2 Objections to the SFA

In so far as such hardcore degree theories as the SFA aim at selling theses T1–T3 as a package deal, they are of course vulnerable to objectors who find fault in *any* of these claims. Although hosts of objections have been levelled against degree-theoretical approaches to

---

[4] Keeping the same language and the same concept of valuation, other choices for the consequence relation are possible. The *Łukasiewicz logic that preserves degrees of truth* $\mathbf{L}_{\aleph}^*$ (Wójcicki 1988; see also Williamson 1994, section 4.10 for a discussion in connection with vagueness) has a consequence relation defined in the following manner for any *finite* set of formulas $\Gamma = \{\gamma_1, \ldots, \gamma_n\}$ and for any formula α: $\Gamma \vDash_{\mathbf{L}_{\aleph}^*} \alpha$ just in case for all valuations v, $v(\gamma_1 \sqcap \ldots \sqcap \gamma_n) \leq v(\alpha)$. Machina (1976) and Forbes (1983) use this consequence relation in place of $\vDash_{\mathbf{L}_{\aleph}}$ in their forays into the Sorites.

vagueness in general, and against the SFA in particular (for a comprehensive review see e.g. Smith 2008), we will select from the literature three representative and amply debated points, respectively directed at T1, T2 and all degree-theoretical approaches that treat the Sorites as a valid but unsound argument. Therefore, the SFA is squarely hit by all of them.

O1) The artificial precision objection. If $P(c)$ is an atomic formula of $\mathcal{L}_1$, the SFA semantics dictates that for any valuation v, $v(P(c))$ is some particular number, say 0.531 if $P(c)$ has to be 'a little more' than half-true. Is it plausible to suppose that there is any fact of the matter that determines whether this particular numerical assignment is more appropriate than any other assignment that comes very close to it? It seems natural to answer this question in the negative, and indeed this objection has been voiced over and over, often in sarcastic tones, by opponents of degree theories, and at times even by their partisans: 'What could determine which is the correct function, settling that my coat is red to degree 0.322 rather than 0.321?' (Keefe 1998, p. 571); 'Vagueness has been replaced by the most refined and incredible precision' (Tye 1994, p. 190). Of course, casting doubts on the assumption that the semantic value of a sentence containing a vague predicate P is a single number in between 0 and 1 calls at least for a revision of the structure of SFA models, to the effect that the semantic value of P can no longer be a single function from individuals to truth degrees. What would be so special about the chosen function? Why not choose another function that has more or less the same range of values?[5]

O2) Objections to truth functionality. If O1 targets all the different variants of the degree-theoretical view, those approaches that rely on a recursive semantics for logical connectives fall prey to a more specific objection. Truth-functional valuations, in fact, predict semantic values for compound sentences about borderline cases that often look at odds with our pre-theoretical intuitions.

For a start, analogues in $\mathcal{L}_1$ of classical tautologies such as the excluded middle or the law of non-contradiction turn out not to be valid on the SFA. If α is an atomic formula such that $v(\alpha) = 0.5$, then $v(\alpha \sqcup \neg\alpha) = v(\alpha \sqcap \neg\alpha) = v(\neg(\alpha \sqcap \neg\alpha)) = 0.5$. However, so it is argued, contradictions should be plain false irrespective of whether the contradictory conjuncts contain vague predicates, and dually for instances of the excluded middle (Kamp 1975; Osherson and Smith 1981; Williamson 1994).

Furthermore, substituting sub-sentences with the same semantic value within a conjunction or a disjunction may get us into trouble. If $v(P(a)) = 0.5$ and $v(P(b)) = 0.4$, then $v(P(a) \sqcap P(b)) = v(\neg P(a) \sqcap P(b)) = 0.4$; however, even if we are prepared to go along with the idea that $P(a) \sqcap P(b)$ is a little less than half-true in this scenario, $\neg P(a) \sqcap P(b)$ should be plain *false*, because if a is P to a greater degree than b, it is impossible that b is P while a is not.[6] It is equally counterintuitive that, under the same assignment, $v(P(a) \sqcap P(a)) = v(\neg P(a) \sqcap P(a)) = 0.5$ (Williamson 1994; Edgington 1997; Keefe 2000). Neither is such a weird result a direct upshot of our choice of the

---

[5]   Various responses given to O1 in the degree-theoretical literature, whose discussion we have to omit in the interests of space, are reviewed in Smith (2008, 2011).

[6]   The fact that in this scenario a is also non-P more than b is P does not detract from the awkwardness of the preceding outcome.

minimum function as a semantic analogue of conjunction. In fact, there can be no binary function $*$ on $[0, 1]$ such that, for $x = 0.5$, $x * (1 - x) = y$ and $x * x \neq y$ for some y (Kamp 1975 points out this fact for $y = 0$). Therefore, unless we introduce even deeper changes in our models, such as modifying our negation clause, no candidate clause for conjunction is better off under this respect.

Finally, similar unwelcome facts affect the conditional. For example, if $v(P(a)) = 0.5$, then $v(P(a) \to P(a)) = v(P(a) \to \neg P(a)) = 1$. We would thus throw into the same lot, and count as absolutely true, instances of the law of identity for conditionals and the contentious sentence 'If John is tall then he isn't tall' (Williamson 1994; Keefe 2000).[7]

O3) The inferential impotency objection. The SFA explanation exposes the Sorites as an unsound but compelling argument, which is deceptive not only because its premises are nearly true, but also because it is *valid*. However, on the $\vDash_{\mathbf{L}_\aleph}$ account, truth degrees strictly less than absolute truth offer no guarantee of being preserved in valid arguments: are then such arguments of much use in inferential practice? And if they are not, doesn't this render the viewpoint less alluring? The fact that less than absolutely true premises are inferentially unsafe in $\mathbf{L}_\aleph$ is a frequent complaint in the literature:

[The SFA] licenses *modus ponens* on clearly true premises, and licenses nothing on not-clearly true premises. It is unable to specify exactly where we should change our inferential habits. And it leaves us inferentially impotent, in the presence of vagueness. (Edgington 1997, p. 303)

With a single designated value the validity of an argument provides no guarantee at all about the value of the conclusion of an argument if any of the premises are less than completely true. So you could take one true and one nearly true premise, follow a valid inference, and end up with a completely false conclusion. Declaring an argument valid may then vindicate its use in a disappointingly narrow range of circumstances. And, to be justified in employing a valid argument, you would have to be justified in thinking the premises were completely true, and that may be a tough demand. (Keefe 2000, p. 105)

8.2.3 Non Truth-Functional Approaches

One possible reaction to O2 is to bite the bullet and dump fuzzy logic together with its truth-functional semantics. The distinctive trait of Dorothy Edgington's theory (1997) consists in reconciling degrees with classical logic via a non-truth-functional approach.

Edgington works in a language $\mathcal{L}_2$ containing a negation $-$, a conjunction $\overline{\wedge}$ and a disjunction $\veebar$. The semantic value of an atomic formula of $\mathcal{L}_2$, say of the form $P(c)$, is a number in $[0, 1]$, called its *verity*. Verities are not to be interpreted as truth degrees,[8] rather, the verity of $P(c)$ reflects how distant c is from a clear case of a P. Verities extend to compound formulas via the familiar rules for probability assignments. In other words, if $v(\beta), v(\gamma)$ denote the verities of β and γ, respectively, then:

---

[7] Again, we cannot dwell on numerous other objections to truth-functionality, which are duly addressed e.g. in Smith (2008, 2015).
[8] For more on the interpretation of verities, see Jones (2015) and Douven and Decock (2017). Note that the recourse to verities leaves Edgington's account vulnerable to O1, which is however brushed off by saying that precise numerical assignments to sentences are simply 'artefacts' of our models.

$$v(-\beta) = 1 - v(\beta);$$

$$v(\beta \overline{\wedge} \gamma) = \begin{cases} v(\beta) \times v(\gamma \text{ given } \beta), \text{ if } v(\beta) > 0 \\ 0, \text{ otherwise;} \end{cases}$$

$$v(\beta \underline{\vee} \gamma) = v(\beta) + v(\gamma) - v(\beta \overline{\wedge} \gamma).$$

Here, $v(\gamma \text{ given } \beta)$ is read as the verity of γ on the hypothetical decision to count β as definitely true. This clause highlights the non truth-functional character of Edgington's semantics, which counters the various objections of the O2 type by providing for the possibility that $\beta \overline{\wedge} \gamma$ and $\beta \overline{\wedge} -\gamma$ may receive different verities even if $v(\gamma) = v(-\gamma)$.[9] Edgington also defines a conditional $\beta \underline{\rightarrow} \gamma$ as $-(\beta \overline{\wedge} -\gamma)$, on the ground that it 'is the weakest conditional, the weakest statement for which *modus ponens* is valid. It is strong enough to generate the Sorites Paradox' (Edgington 1997, p. 307).

The next step in Edgington's agenda is the definition of a notion of validity based on verities. An argument with premises $\alpha_1, \ldots, \alpha_n$ and conclusion β has the *verity-constraining property (VCP)* if, and only if, for all verity assignments v,

$$1 - v(\beta) \le 1 - v(\alpha_1) + \ldots + 1 - v(\alpha_n).$$

Since Edgington explicitly endorses the principle of bivalence and classical logic, she is committed to showing that defining validity in terms of the VCP is consistent with these tenets. Recall that classical logic is normally expressed in a language $\mathcal{L}_0 = \{\sim, \wedge, \vee\}$ (with material implication $\alpha \supset \beta$ defined as $\sim \alpha \vee \beta$), whose valuations are given in terms of a 2-valued (not a $[0, 1]$-valued) semantics. Edgington proves that all and only classically valid arguments have the VCP, at least in the following sense. Given $\Gamma \cup \{\alpha\} \subseteq For(\mathcal{L}_0)$, α follows classically from Γ (in symbols, $\Gamma \vDash_{\mathbf{K}} \alpha$) if, and only if, the argument from Γ' to α' has the VCP, where the formulas in $\Gamma' \cup \{\alpha'\} \subseteq For(\mathcal{L}_2)$ are obtained from the formulas in $\Gamma \cup \{\alpha\}$ by replacing all occurrences of $\sim, \wedge, \vee$ by occurrences of $-, \overline{\wedge}, \underline{\vee}$, respectively.

Finally, the Sorites is explained away as a valid but unsound argument: if a and b denote adjacent elements in the borderline region of a Sorites series for P, then $v(P(b) \text{ given } P(a)) = 1 - \varepsilon$ (for ε suitably close to 0), whence a quick computation shows that

$$1 - \varepsilon \le v(P(a) \underline{\rightarrow} P(b)) = v(-(P(a) \overline{\wedge} -P(b))) = 1 - v(P(a)) \times \epsilon < 1.$$

The very high verities of conditional premises (i.e. their being very close to *clear* truths) account, in Edgington's eyes, for the deceptiveness of the Sorites.[10]

---

[9]   The non-truth-functional character of conjunction reverberates on disjunction as well, given the clause Edgington proposes. This implies that not only the non-contradiction law, but also the excluded middle turns out to have verity 1 come what may.

[10]   Other non truth-functional degree theories are Sanford's fuzzy supervaluationism (Sanford 1975) and MacFarlane's fuzzy epistemicism (MacFarlane 2010).

8.2.4 Fuzzy Plurivaluationism

While Edgington is ready to give up the recursive semantics for the logical connectives in order to salvage classical logic, Smith's proposal in Smith (2008) achieves the same goal while sticking to a Łukasiewicz-style truth-functional semantics. Only, this semantics is divorced by the fuzzy consequence relations that are normally associated to it.[11]

Smith urges that a *fundamental definition* of predicate vagueness is needed to serve as a touchstone against which we can adjudicate debates about vagueness. He proposes to give that definition in terms of *closeness*. A predicate P is vague just in case it satisfies the following condition, for any a and b:[12]

Closeness: If a and b are very close in P-relevant respects, then $P(a)$ and $P(b)$ are very close in respect of truth.

Closeness, for Smith, is the best replacement on offer for Tolerance: it accommodates Tolerance intuitions without leading to inconsistency. A substantial part of Smith (2008) (in particular, the whole of chapter 4) is devoted to arguing that only those theories that countenance degrees of truth can allow for the existence of predicates that satisfy the Closeness definition.

Smith develops his account in the $\rightarrow$-free fragment $\mathcal{L}_3$ of $\mathcal{L}_1$. In this less expressive language an implication connective $\alpha \rightsquigarrow \beta$ can be defined as $\neg\alpha \sqcup \beta$, although we will see that it is not used in the formalisation of the conditional premises of the Sorites. Valuations for $\mathcal{L}_3$ are exactly the same as valuations for $\mathcal{L}_1$, except, of course, that they are restricted to formulas in this fragment. In particular, valuations still map formulas to truth degrees in $[0, 1]$. The semantics favoured by Smith is therefore a full-blooded fuzzy semantics – his chosen consequence relation, though, is slightly more off the wall. For any $\Gamma \cup \{\alpha\} \subseteq For(\mathcal{L}_3)$, α is said to be an *S-consequence* of Γ (written $\Gamma \vDash_S \alpha$) if, and only if, for every valuation v for $\mathcal{L}_3$, if $v(\gamma) > 0.5$ for all $\gamma \in \Gamma$, then $v(\alpha) \geq 0.5$. Observe that this is not a degree-preservational account of consequence: the premises in an argument are required to meet more rigorous standards than its conclusion, for what 'may be safe enough to assert [...] may not be safe enough to serve as the start of the next stage of reasoning'. This is exactly what happens in a Sorites-type argument: 'as we continue to take the output of one stage of the reasoning and feed it back into the inductive premise at the next stage of the slide down the series, our conclusions become progressively shakier' (Smith 2008, p. 223).

S-consequence coincides with classical consequence. To be precise, actually, this claim should be qualified along the lines of our previous discussion of Edgington's VCP: if we are given $\Gamma\cup\{\alpha\} \subseteq For(\mathcal{L}_0)$, we have that $\Gamma \vDash_K \alpha$ if, and only if, $\Gamma' \vDash_S \alpha'$, where the formulas in

---

[11] In more recent work, Smith (2019) partly repudiates this view by veering into the defence of a particular interpretation of the SFA. He makes it clear that retention of classical consequence is not a core component of fuzzy plurivaluationism. A different attempt to reconcile degree-functionality with classical logic has been made by Weatherson (2004), who defends the idea that degrees of truth form a Boolean algebra.

[12] Although this is not the final and complete version of the author's definition (see Smith 2008, p. 156 for the full story), the missing details make no essential difference for our purposes.

$\Gamma' \cup \{\alpha'\} \subseteq For(\mathcal{L}_3)$ are obtained from the formulas in $\Gamma \cup \{\alpha\}$ by replacing all occurrences of $\sim, \wedge, \vee$ by occurrences of $\neg, \sqcap, \sqcup$ respectively. Smith argues that his account has a decisive edge over the SFA, namely, that it preserves two crucial and highly intuitive properties of the classical analysis of conditionality: the equivalence between material implication $\alpha \supset \beta$ and its disjunctive and conjunctive renderings, $\sim \alpha \vee \beta$ and $\sim (\alpha \wedge \sim \beta)$; and the equivalence between $\Gamma, \alpha \vDash_K \beta$ and $\Gamma \vDash_K \alpha \supset \beta$.

One distinctive feature of the solution to the Sorites given in Smith (2008) is that its conditional premises are *not* given their surface conditional reading, but are interpreted as expressions of fundamentally meta-linguistic principles. If they are read as expressions of *Tolerance*, then the argument is *unsound*, because soritical series make situations in which we cannot happily use Tolerance as an approximation of Closeness; but it is *deceptive* in that it is classically valid (hence $\vDash_S$-valid) and all of its premises are at least plausible – because 'Tolerance is a useful approximation of what one believes, in ordinary situations' (Smith 2008, p. 270). If they are read as expressions of *Closeness*, on the other hand, the argument is *invalid*, because the relation of being very similar in respects that determine the applicability of a vague predicate is not transitive. In neither case does the reasoning delineated by the paradox go through.

Having reviewed Smith's solution to the Sorites, let us now assess – proceeding in reverse order – how his approach fares with respect to our representative objections O1–O3. O3, although not considered in its present form, is implicitly parried by Smith in at least two ways. First, as we have seen, the burden of explaining its misleading character does not wholly rest on its being a valid argument; moreover, his system takes into account every case in which the value of the premises is greater than 0.5, which presumably takes some of the sting out of the inferential impotency objection. O2 is countered through a variety of moves: the plausibility of truth-functional verdicts is defended on the strength of empirical data; alternative construals of the faulty sentences are offered in such a way as to dissolve the objections. For O1, Smith advocates an ingenious solution under the label of *fuzzy plurivaluationism*. In a nutshell, many fuzzy valuations of our ordinary vague discourse are equally acceptable, and there is nothing to decide between them. Of course, in order to be acceptable, a candidate correct valuation must meet some constraints: for example, it cannot assign $P(a)$ a lower truth degree than $P(b)$ in case a is P to a higher degree than b is. Other than that, however, there is no fact of the matter as to whether $P(a)$ must receive a particular truth degree. In the plurivaluationist perspective, vagueness results from a combination of *graduality* (vague properties come in degrees) and *indeterminacy* of meaning (semantic states are individuated by valuations, and there are many of them that are equally acceptable).[13]

---

[13] For reasons of space, our survey of degree theories has been very cursory. Let us mention at least a family of broadly fuzzy approaches whose universes of degrees are not limited to the [0, 1] interval, but include possibly *unbounded* algebras. Such approaches typically admit degrees of *absolute* truth and falsity and address a number of problems posed e.g. by natural language comparatives (Peña 1984; Casari 1989; Paoli 2003, 2018).

8.3 An Eclectic Degree Theory

The degree theory we are going to sketch in the sequel tries to combine elements from different suggestions that have been advanced in the literature: we borrow from Smith (2008) the fuzzy plurivaluationist picture; from Běhounek (2014) the idea that indeterminacy of meaning may extend beyond the descriptive component of our language once truth degrees are admitted; from Hájek and Novák (2003) the plea for a more expressive logic than $\mathbf{L}_\aleph$ as an instrument to defuse the Sorites; from Peacocke (1981), finally, the diagnosis of this paradox as, essentially, a fallacy of equivocation.

8.3.1 Classical Logic as an Equivocal Logic

Classical semantics is inappropriate for vagueness because it makes no room for truth degrees – so far, the SFA and an atypical degree theory such as Smith's are on the same page. However, we have seen that Smith intends to abandon the 2-valued semantics but not classical logic, whereas partisans of the SFA argue that we have to settle for the deductively weaker $\mathbf{L}_\aleph$. Our view is somewhere in between: classical logic is not *deductively* faulty but *expressively* inadequate – it makes correct claims in an ambiguous language. Once we include truth degrees in our picture, in fact, we realise that each classical connective splits into an intensional and an extensional incarnation. Let us see what that means.[14]

Paradoxes of material implication have induced several philosophers, from C.I. Lewis's early writings from the 1910s down to the later endeavours of relevant logicians, to lament that classical logic is unable to tell apart two different senses of binary propositional connectives. Let us pick disjunction for the sake of illustration. This connective has an *extensional* sense, under which the truth value of a disjunctive sentence only depends on a separate evaluation of the truth values of the disjuncts; and an *intensional* sense, under which such a truth value essentially depends on the mutual *relevance* between the disjuncts. A similar distinction naturally arises in the context of a discussion of vagueness, once we adopt a degree-theoretical semantics. Take disjunction again as a paradigmatic example. When are we in a position to mark a disjunctive sentence as absolutely true? If we are only interested in a separate evaluation of the truth degrees of the disjuncts, assuming that this happens if and only if at least one of the disjuncts is absolutely true appears as a sensible generalisation of the classical evaluation clause to the more nuanced rational-valued environment. If, however, we believe that a disjunction should somehow express a *comparison* of truth degrees, we could require of an absolutely true disjunction that the amount of falsity in each disjunct (as measured by its closeness to 0) should not exceed the amount of truth in the other (as measured by its closeness to 1). Observe that this is a different, but equally licit, generalisation of the classical truth table clause.

Summing up: in a $[0, 1]$-valued framework, in place of the classical connective $\vee$ we have *two* connectives with different truth conditions (Casari 1989; Paoli 2003):

---

[14] See Paoli (2018) for a more detailed defence of this claim.

- an *extensional disjunction* $\alpha \sqcup \beta$, which is (absolutely) true just in case at least one of α, β is (absolutely) true;
- an *intensional disjunction* $\alpha \oplus \beta$, which is (absolutely) true just in case each one of α, β is at most as false as the other one is true.

$\mathbf{L_{\aleph}}$, as we have seen, evaluates extensional disjunction via the maximum function on the closed unit real interval. And it can express, within $\mathcal{L}_1$, an intensional disjunction $\alpha \oplus \beta$, defined as $\neg \alpha \to \beta$. Upon computing its evaluation clause, we readily see that for any valuation v, $v(\alpha \oplus \beta) = \min(1, v(\alpha) + v(\beta))$. It is now clear why we employed different symbols for classical disjunction and for extensional disjunction in $\mathbf{L_{\aleph}}$. Extensional disjunction is *not* the $\mathcal{L}_1$-match for $\vee$. Rather, classical disjunction is *ambiguous between* an extensional and an intensional meaning; only logics that allow for truth degrees and for non-trivial truth comparisons have the expressive resources to remove this ambiguity by providing different truth conditions for extensional and intensional connectives. Neither $\sqcup$ nor $\oplus$ has, individually, all the properties that characterise classical disjunction: for example, $\oplus$ fails to be idempotent, while the excluded middle in terms of $\sqcup$ is invalid. On the other hand, we argue later that there is a sense in which all the properties of classical disjunction hold of at least one of these connectives.

Although we picked disjunction to make our point, there is nothing special about this connective here. $\mathbf{L_{\aleph}}$ can also distinguish between an extensional conjunction $\sqcap$ and an intensional conjunction $\otimes$ (defined via $\alpha \otimes \beta = \neg(\alpha \to \neg \beta)$), which is (absolutely) false just in case each one of α, β is at most as true as the other one is false; upon computing its evaluation clause, we have that for any valuation v, $v(\alpha \otimes \beta) = \max(0, v(\alpha) + v(\beta) - 1)$. Furthermore, it can distinguish between an extensional conditional $\rightsquigarrow$ (defined via $\alpha \rightsquigarrow \beta = \neg \alpha \sqcup \beta$) and an intensional conditional $\to$ (the Łukasiewicz conditional). $\alpha \rightsquigarrow \beta$ is absolutely true in case either α is absolutely false or β is absolutely true, while $\alpha \to \beta$ is absolutely true if, and only if, α is at most as true as β is. In this perspective, the classical definability of the conditional in terms of negation and disjunction, or of negation and conjunction – whose retention was seen in Smith (2008) as a reason not to adopt $\mathbf{L_{\aleph}}$ even after espousing a $[0, 1]$-valued semantics – is preserved in Łukasiewicz logic: both the intensional and the extensional conditional are definable in terms of negation and the disjunction, or conjunction, in the same (extensional or intensional) family.

This perspective suggests a uniform solution strategy for the different objections we grouped under the O2 label. Virtually all these allegations, indeed, prove unfounded upon acknowledging the intensional–extensional distinction. Observe that the *intensional* excluded middle $\alpha \oplus \neg \alpha$ and non-contradiction law $\neg(\alpha \otimes \neg \alpha)$ come out absolutely true on every valuation. The paradoxical outcomes that may result from substituting by its negation a half-true sub-sentence embedded within a conjunctive or a disjunctive sentence vanish. For example, if $v(P(a)) = 0.5$ and $v(P(b)) = 0.4$, then $v(P(a) \otimes P(b)) = v(\neg P(a) \otimes P(b)) = 0$; so $\neg P(a) \otimes P(b)$ comes out absolutely false, as was to be expected.[15] Finally, while

---

[15] One could still complain that $P(a) \otimes P(b)$ should have a middling value considerably higher than $\neg P(a) \otimes P(b)$. Indeed, it has to be conceded that $\mathbf{L_{\aleph}}$ can tell apart sentences from one another as regards their degrees of truth only within the

it is correct that in a rational-valued semantics there is no binary idempotent connective $*$ satisfying at the same time the non-contradiction principle, we have that the extensional conjunction $\sqcap$ is idempotent while the intensional conjunction $\otimes$ is such that $v(\alpha \otimes \neg\alpha) = 0$ for all valuations v. And this makes perfect sense: two different readings of conjunction are at stake when we require that a contradiction be always absolutely false and when we require that conjunction be idempotent. In the latter case, the conjuncts' truth degrees are evaluated separately, whereas in the former they are compared with each other.[16]

There is, as a matter of fact, one objection of type O2 that sifts through. Recall that weird outcome of the Łukasiewicz semantics according to which, if $v(P(a)) = 0.5$, then $v(P(a) \rightarrow P(a)) - v(P(a) \rightarrow \neg P(a)) = 1$. No appeal to the intensional extensional ambiguity saves the day in this case: $v(P(a) \rightsquigarrow P(a)) = 0.5$ if $v(P(a)) = 0.5$, whence the reading of implication according to which the identity principle is a logical law had better be intensional. Observe, though, that such unwelcome verdicts only arise when the truth degree of some conditional's antecedent[17] is less or equal than 0.5. These many-valued analogues of the material implication paradoxes surely prove that the analysis of natural language conditionality offered by Łukasiewicz logic is far from ideal (Fermüller and Hájek 2011; Novák and Dvořák 2011; Paoli 2003), and that a different logic would be required were we interested in accounting for the relevance features of intensional implication.[18] In so far as we are only concerned with intensional implication as a device for performing truth comparisons, however, the above counterexample and the like lose most of their grimness.

A result essentially due to Grishin and Ono (for the details, see e.g. Troelstra 1992, chapter 5) shows that classical logic can be recaptured within $\mathbf{L}_{\aleph}$ in a sense that is consistent with the view just expounded. Before delving into the technicalities, let us sketch a broad-brush picture of its import. Classical logic works at its best in contexts where truth degrees and truth comparisons play no role. In such circumstances, it does no harm to disregard the linguistic distinctions of which $\mathbf{L}_{\aleph}$ is capable. When vagueness takes the stage, we need to refine our analysis and embrace $\mathbf{L}_{\aleph}$. However, the Grishin-Ono theorem implies that we can still view classical logic as a *correct* logic, provided we disambiguate the logical constants appearing in the entailments it validates, giving each connective occurrence the appropriate (intensional or extensional) reading.

In detail, a *disambiguation* of an $\mathcal{L}_0$-formula α is defined as any $\mathcal{L}_1$-formula obtained from α by replacing: 1) each occurrence of $\sim$ by $\neg$; 2) each occurrence of $\wedge$ by either $\sqcap$ or $\otimes$; 3) each occurrence of $\vee$ by either $\sqcup$ or $\oplus$; 4) each occurrence of $\supset$ by either

---

borderline region of application of the vague predicates they contain; see Paoli (2003, 2018) for more on this shortcoming.

[16] Wright (1975) deplores the fact that the SFA has no convincing story to tell about those versions of the Sorites whose major premises are formulated as negated conjunctions, rather than as implications (*It is not the case that $P(n)$ and not $P(n + 1)$*). Sure, if the 'and' in there is given an extensional reading, it becomes difficult to explain the appeal of premises whose truth degrees can be as low as 0.5. Yet on the intensional reading, $\neg(P(n) \otimes \neg P(n + 1))$ has exactly the same truth degree as $P(n) \rightarrow P(n + 1)$. Therefore, this version of the Sorites does not create further problems of its own for the SFA analysis.

[17] This, of course, also applies to some sentences whose dominant connective is an intensional conjunction or an intensional disjunction – recall that such connectives are *defined* in terms of the Łukasiewicz conditional, whose virtues and vices they inherit.

[18] In Paoli (2007) we defend sub-exponential linear logic as a promising candidate to play that role.

⤳ or →. If an $\mathcal{L}_0$-formula α has more than one occurrence of the same connective, different occurrences can be replaced in different ways within the same disambiguation. According to the Grishin-Ono translation result, whenever $\Gamma \vDash_{\mathbf{K}} \alpha$, it can be shown that there exist appropriate disambiguations $t_\alpha(\alpha)$ of α, and $t_\gamma(\gamma)$ of every $\gamma \in \Gamma$, such that $\{t_\gamma(\gamma) : \gamma \in \Gamma\} \vDash_{\mathbf{L}_\aleph} t_\alpha(\alpha)$. Conversely, if $\{t_\gamma(\gamma) : \gamma \in \Gamma\} \vDash_{\mathbf{L}_\aleph} t_\alpha(\alpha)$, for appropriate disambiguations $t_\alpha(\alpha)$ of α, and $t_\gamma(\gamma)$ of every $\gamma \in \Gamma$, no classically invalid entailment can arise by replacing each connective occurrence in these $\mathcal{L}_1$-formulas by an occurrence of its (unique) 'ambiguous' counterpart. Therefore, $\Gamma \vDash_{\mathbf{K}} \alpha$.

8.3.2 Rational Pavelka Logic

The Grishin-Ono translation theorem suggests that classical logic, though in essence correct, suffers from an expressive inadequacy that renders its claims ambiguous, and that $\mathbf{L}_\aleph$ is a logic where such claims can be disambiguated. Let us now observe that $\mathbf{L}_\aleph$ is subject, in other respects, to different but just as severe expressive limitations. In the language $\mathcal{L}_0$ of classical logic, there are definable propositional constants $\overline{0}, \overline{1}$ that name the *unique* truth values in the classical ontology – the true and the false. In the background of $\mathbf{L}_\aleph$ stands an ontology of truth degrees that is immensely richer, but the language $\mathcal{L}_1$ does not fully keep up with this increase in complexity. In fact, the unique propositional constants that $\mathcal{L}_1$ can define are, again, $\overline{0}$ and $\overline{1}$. Any language that is to step up as a candidate to adequately describe in degree-theoretical terms vagueness-related phenomena should contain names for *all* the truth degrees in its intended ontology. *Rational Pavelka logic* $\mathbf{L}_\aleph^P$ (Hájek 1998, section 3.3) is a linguistic and axiomatic expansion of $\mathbf{L}_\aleph$ aimed at mending this flaw.

The language $\mathcal{L}_4$ of $\mathbf{L}_\aleph^P$ is just $\mathcal{L}_1$ expanded by a denumerable set of propositional constants $\{\overline{r}\}_{r\in\mathbb{Q}\cap[0,1]}$, one for each rational number r in between 0 and 1. It can be axiomatised via the axioms of Łukasiewicz logic plus the following families of axioms, for all rational numbers r, s such that $0 \leq r, s \leq 1$:

$$(\overline{r} \to \overline{s}) \leftrightarrow \overline{\min(1, 1 - r + s)};$$
$$\neg\overline{r} \leftrightarrow \overline{1 - r}.$$

Valuations for $\mathcal{L}_4$ are simply valuations for $\mathcal{L}_1$, with an extra clause to the effect that $v(\overline{r}) = r$, for every rational r in $[0, 1]$. The consequence relation $\vDash_{\mathbf{L}_\aleph^P}$ is defined in terms of preservation of absolute truth, in the same manner as $\vDash_{\mathbf{L}_\aleph}$.

Now, consider a new family of conditionals $\{\to_r\}_{r\in\mathbb{Q}\cap[0,1]}$, defined as

$$\alpha \to_r \beta = (\alpha \to \beta) \oplus \overline{r}.$$

Doing out the relevant valuation clauses, it is immediate to see that $v(\alpha \to_r \beta) = 1$ just in case $v(\alpha \to \beta) \geq 1 - r$. In other words, each $\to_r$ expresses a 'tolerant' conditional that is absolutely true exactly when the Łukasiewicz conditional with the same antecedent and consequent is 'close enough' to being absolutely true – i.e. when its distance from absolute truth is not greater than r.

We will presently see how such tolerant conditionals play a decisive role in our proposed account of the Sorites. In the meantime, let us just observe the following:

Lemma 3 $\rightarrow_r$ *satisfies* modus ponens *if, and only if, r = 0.*

Proof.   From right to left, just observe that $\rightarrow_0 = \rightarrow$. Conversely, let $r > 0$, and let $v(p) = 1$, $v(q) = 1 - r$. Then $v(p) = 1 = v(p \rightarrow_r q)$, while $v(q) < 1$. Thus, $p, p \rightarrow_r q \nvDash_{\mathbf{L}_{\aleph}^p} q$. $\square$

8.3.3 Sorites: The Equivocation Diagnosis

Our new logic $\mathbf{L}_{\aleph}^P$, based on the far more expressive language $\mathcal{L}_4$, permits us to address an unsatisfactory aspect of the SFA. There is reason, indeed, to be bothered by the fact that instances of Tolerance applying to objects in the borderline region of a Sorites series are assigned truth degrees that miss the mark of absolute truth. Although this circumstance is in keeping with the general idea expressed by Smith's Closeness principle, an issue raised e.g. by Zardini (2008b, chapter 2) is left unresolved. Zardini argues that 'we are sometimes willing to stretch the information that we gather about some cases to other cases that are similar but not necessarily identical to them in the relevant respects, and we take such stretching to be *indefeasible*' (Zardini 2008b, p. 39). This seems exactly what happens when we are considering the conditional premise of a Sorites argument: if we are told that John is tall and that Jim's height is very close to John's, we indefeasibly conclude that Jim is tall, too – and it seems as though nothing less than an absolutely true conditional premise can license that much. This worry is of course related to our objection O3: the SFA fails to adequately explain why we are taken in by the Sorites, for even an implicit grasp of the defeasibility of inferences based on 'nearly absolutely true' premises would make speakers refrain from resting their arguments on such a wobbly basis. The deceptiveness of the Sorites deserves to be taken seriously.

In an once influential but by now sadly neglected early reference on the degree-theoretical approach, Peacocke (1981) surmises that the meaning of 'if . . . then' as used in our statements of Tolerance is not the same as the meaning according to which we regard *modus ponens* inferences as licit. When considering a conditional premise in a Sorites argument, we may be willing to stretch the information exactly as described by Zardini in our previous quote, so as to grant the sentence itself nothing short of the status of an *absolute truth*. On the other hand, we would probably hesitate before earmarking *modus ponens* as a reliable inference mode if the 'truth-stretching' meaning of the conditional were at issue. For *modus ponens* to be valid, our conditionals must be watertight sufficiency conditionals that provide for no tolerance margin – indeed, the very presence of Sorites-type paradoxes reveals how dangerous it is to deflect from this reading. An intriguing way out of this dilemma, then, is to regard both *modus ponens* and Tolerance as equally unobjectionable principles holding of *different* conditionals. The Sorites would then be reclassified as a fallacy of equivocation and we would have improved on the SFA by offering a more persuasive explanation of the reasons why we find the argument compelling.

Brushing aside any exegetical issue as to whether this view is in any way faithful to Peacocke's original proposal, we still owe the reader some extra details on how to cash in such an insight in rigorous terms. Rational Pavelka Logic, already advocated by Hájek and Novák (2003) as a formal framework for a solution to the paradox, appears to be the proper tool for accomplishing this goal. The idea we advance is that indicative conditionals of the form *If $P(a)$ then $P(b)$*, when used to reason in vague contexts, indeterminately refer to Pavelka conditionals of the form $P(a) \rightarrow_r P(b)$, for an *unspecified* – but small enough – rational value of r. Intuitively, the value r expresses the extent of our disposition to 'stretch the truth' in evaluating how the information gathered about some cases extends to other cases that are similar but not necessarily identical in the relevant respects. As it often happens in similar situations, bringing some principle (such as *modus ponens* or Tolerance) up for consideration triggers a shift in this disposition that reflects a *charitable* attitude towards the principle itself. Does $P(b)$ invariably follow from $P(a)$ and $P(a) \rightarrow_r P(b)$? Yes – if $r = 0$, that is, if truth is not stretched by an inch. Is a Tolerance conditional $P(a) \rightarrow_r P(b)$ absolutely true? Again, yes – if r is non-zero and large enough to place b in the same lot as a as regards all P-relevant respects. The problem, of course, is that throughout any particular argument, on pain of committing the classical *quaternio terminorum* fallacy, we have to settle on a *single* value of r, and no such number will sink the ball. If $r = 0$, the argument is *unsound*, because some of the conditional premises are not absolutely true. If $r > 0$ the argument is *invalid*, for we are reminded by Lemma 3 that Tolerance conditionals satisfy *modus ponens* for no such strictly positive value. The Sorites is therefore fallacious, while the observation that under some reading its conditional premises are absolutely true offers a better justification of our readiness to endorse them.[19]

It is certainly fair to wonder whether the above account tallies with our general view of Sorites-type paradoxes as generated by a recourse to a logic – classical logic – that, although in a sense correct and thereby compelling, is not expressive enough to accommodate distinctions that arise once we trade the sparse two-valued ontology for the better-stocked setting of truth degrees needed to properly account for vagueness. Actually, given that, here and elsewhere (Paoli 2007; Mares and Paoli 2014), we pointed to the classical logician's confusion between intensional and extensional constants as a source of paradoxes arising in different areas (truth theory, set theory, vagueness, theories of entailment), it might be observed that such a distinction is completely idle in our previous story – although, as we have seen in our discussion of objections to truth-functionality, it plays a role in dealing with penumbral connections, another tough problem of vagueness. More to the point, however, the classical blurring of the intensional–extensional divide is just a *symptom* of an expressive inadequacy that may affect, to a lesser degree, even other fuzzy logics. Pavelka conditionals cannot be expressed in classical logic or in Łukasiewicz logic

---

[19] Although the present treatment shares with Zardini (2008b) a crucial recourse to the speakers' willingness to stretch the information in the analysis of similar cases, there are important differences between our accounts. For Zardini, speakers are willing to *infer* $P(b)$ once they gather the information that $P(a)$, and it is only derivatively on this fundamental inferential disposition that they also accept the conditional *If $P(a)$ then $P(b)$*. Here, on the other hand, the conditional is vindicated while the inference is lost. See, however, later in this section for a variant of the paradox where the latter takes centre stage.

because they both lack *names* for all the truth degrees that are available in a rational-valued framework.

Our view, moreover, is also consistent with fuzzy plurivaluationism, especially in its incarnation recently defended by Libor Běhounek (2014). According to Běhounek, not only there are different, but equally acceptable functions that can act as the semantic values of vague predicates, and there is nothing to decide between them; but such an indeterminacy of meaning (one of the two main ingredients of vagueness, the other one being graduality) also affects our *logical vocabulary*. There is nothing special about the particular truth function on the [0, 1] interval that interprets the Łukasiewicz conditional – other similar truth functions could be put forward as plausible intensional conditionals, and there would be nothing to decide between these different proposals. Actually, the customary approach to T-norm based fuzzy logics (Hájek 1998) simply poses some axiomatic constraints on the behaviour of a putative conditional (or conjunction, or disjunction) in such a way as to weed out awkward operations that may fail obvious desiderata required of such connectives; but all candidates that survive the axiomatic test can lay a claim to function as formal correlates of our sentential logical particles. Pushing this line of thought a little further, exactly as there is no fact of the matter as to whether Keefe's coat is red to degree 0.322 or to degree 0.321, there is no fact of the matter as to whether the parameter r in the conditional premise $P(n) \rightarrow_r P(n+1)$ has value 0.02 or 0.06. Different, equally acceptable models might provide different numerical values for our disposition to 'stretch the truth', and the nature of vagueness is such that it is actually indeterminate which value should be picked as the 'correct' one.

8.3.4 The Validity Sorites

Although we selected an 'implicational' version of the Sorites as the framework for our discussion, we do not really believe that this is a paradox about any particular piece of logical vocabulary. Actually, the recent literature on truth-theoretical and set-theoretical paradoxes suggests that, even in these cases, we should refrain from blaming any principle governing the behaviour of the individual connectives or quantifiers as the source of our contradictions, because there are versions of these antinomies where no logical constant seems to play any role. The moral to be drawn seems that the *structure* of our deductions triggers difficulties that may or may not become visible at the level of sentential connection (Hinnion and Libert 2003; Beall and Murzi 2013; Mares and Paoli 2014; Wansing and Priest 2015).

Indeed, a purely structural version of the Sorites has been suggested to us in conversation by Elia Zardini.[20] It can be argued that the meaning of vague predicates is such that, whenever a and b name adjacent objects in a Sorites series, one can validly (perhaps 'materially') infer $P(b)$ from $P(a)$ with no direct recourse to any conditional or universal

---

[20] See Chapter 9 in this volume, Section 9.3.

premise.[21] This claim sounds consistent with the fuzzy plurivaluationist framework, if we suppose that the meaning of the vague predicate P can constrain the range of our acceptable models so as to validate instances of Tolerance across the board. Then, if we assume $P(0)$ and we assume that for all n, $P(n+1)$ validly follows from $P(n)$, we obtain our paradoxical conclusion $P(k)$ by simply chaining together all these inferential steps.

The challenge posed by this *Validity Sorites* should be clear enough. If the paradox depends, at root, on structural features of our deductions about vague predicates, postulating an ambiguity for implication (or any logical constant, for that matter) is no longer an option. If we are equivocating at all, we are not equivocating over the meaning of connectives. Our suggestion is that in a Validity Sorites we are equivocating over *consequence*. There are two relevant senses of 'validly inferring' that get mixed up in this piece of reasoning. On the one hand, there is plain *logical* consequence with all its structural properties, which are usually taken to include transitivity and some rigorous counterpart of the formality requirement, e.g., substitution-invariance. It is to say the least debatable that, on this understanding of the concept, $P(n+1)$ can be 'validly inferred' from $P(n)$. Perhaps, then, what we have in mind is a weaker (material?) notion of consequence, flexible enough to encompass Tolerance inferences within its scope. But then, one wonders whether this notion can be reasonably considered *transitive*.

This doubt is reinforced by selecting a plausible formal specification of such a notion within $\mathbf{L}_{\aleph}^{P}$. We denote this relation by $\vDash_{\mathbf{L}_{\aleph}^{r}}$ and, for the sake of simplicity, we compare it with $\vDash_{\mathbf{L}_{\aleph}^{P}}$ in the case of inferences with a single premise. While $\alpha \vDash_{\mathbf{L}_{\aleph}^{P}} \beta$ holds whenever any valuation v (determined by an acceptable model of our vague language) such that $v(\alpha) = 1$ is also such that $v(\beta) = 1$, $\alpha \vDash_{\mathbf{L}_{\aleph}^{r}} \beta$ holds whenever any valuation v (determined in the same way) such that $v(\alpha) = 1$ is also such that $v(\beta) \geq 1 - r$. In the latter sense, β validly follows from α if β is within some fixed 'truth-stretching' range of α. Our claim is then that 'validly entails', when used to reason in vague contexts, indeterminately refers to a relation of the $\vDash_{\mathbf{L}_{\aleph}^{r}}$ type, for an *unspecified* – but small enough – rational value of r. The problem, again, is that throughout any particular argument we have to settle on a *single* value of r, and once more no such number will do. If $r = 0$, the argument is *unsound*, because some of the formulas used in its premises do not stand in the $\vDash_{\mathbf{L}_{\aleph}^{r}}$ relation. If $r > 0$ the argument is *invalid*, for the relation $\vDash_{\mathbf{L}_{\aleph}^{r}}$ is not transitive.

These cursory remarks cannot exhaust the issues raised by the Validity Sorites – they are meant to serve as little more than a disclaimer, aimed at dispelling the doubt that we are classifying the Sorites as a paradox of implication. However, for reasons of space, a more extensive discussion of these issues will have to wait for another occasion.[22]

---

[21] There is an undercurrent in the history of logic, from Alexander of Aphrodisias to Bernard Bolzano, which is concerned with the properties of 'material' or 'enthymematic' consequence. In the interests of space, we cannot dwell on the issue. In recent years, Stephen Read has taken up the subject (Read 1994; see also Zardini 2008b).

[22] We gratefully acknowledge the financial support of Regione Autonoma Sardegna within the Project CRP-78705 (L.R. 7/2007), 'Metaphor and argumentation'. Many thanks to Libor Běhounek, to Nick Smith and to the editors of this volume for their precious comments on a first draft of this chapter.

9   Non-Transitivism and the Sorites Paradox

Elia Zardini

9.1   Transitivity and the Sorites Paradox

Non-transitivism is a recent solution to the Sorites Paradox, essentially consisting in *accepting (N)*[1] *and denying the validity of soritical arguments as involving invalid applications of the principle of transitivity (of logical consequence)*.[2] In its simplest and weakest (and most natural) version, the principle of transitivity is:

(T⁻)   If $\varphi \vdash \psi$ and $\psi \vdash \chi$ hold, $\varphi \vdash \chi$ holds.

It is however useful to consider also a more complex and stronger version with initial *multiple premises* and with *side-premises*:

(T)   If $\Gamma_0 \vdash \psi$ and $\Gamma_1, \psi \vdash \chi$ hold, $\Gamma_0, \Gamma_1 \vdash \chi$ holds.

Obviously, (T) entails (T⁻) but not vice versa. There are further variations on the general idea of transitivity, but for most of our purposes these will suffice (we'll see two such variations in fns. 11 and 20).

    It's easy to see that natural versions of the Sorites Paradox do involve applications of (T). Focusing (throughout this chapter and simply for concreteness) on the (N_{3T})-based version of the paradox ('The Sorites Paradox', in the introduction to this volume), essentially by universal instantiation and *modus ponens* (N_1^{bald}) and (N_{3T}^{bald}) entail *B2*, but how does the soritical argument go further to make trouble for (N^{bald})? Well, it first observes that *B2* and (N_{3T}^{bald}) in turn entail *B3*, for then assuming that, *since (N_1^{bald}) and (N_{3T}^{bald}) entail B2, the former entailment suffices for (N_1^{bald}) and (N_{3T}^{bald}) to entail B3 as well*. It is *that* assumption that consists in a questionable application of (T) – without it, the argument gets stuck

---

[1] Throughout, I presuppose the notational and terminological conventions of the 'The Sorites Paradox', in the introduction to this volume.

[2] A non-transitive approach is interesting (and has in fact been explored) also with respect to *other* tough issues in philosophy of logic, such as *relevant validity* (e.g. Lewy 1958), *non-deductive validity* (e.g. Gabbay 1985) and the *semantic paradoxes* (e.g. Ripley 2012). Zardini (2008b, pp. 175–232, 2015a) provides a general overview and discussion of philosophical aspects of non-transitive logics. As for the history of the non-transitive approach to *vagueness*, to the best of my knowledge it's brief. The idea of going non-transitive to solve the Sorites Paradox is briefly mentioned by Weir (1998, pp. 792–4); Béziau (2006), and it was first seriously developed both philosophically and logically by Zardini (2008a, 2008b), whose framework was then adopted by Cobreros et al. (2012) (see fn. 26 for some comparison between these two versions of non-transitivism).

at $B2$.[3] What immediately makes trouble for (N^{bald}) is not the fact that, for every i, $Bi, Bi \rightarrow$ $Bi' \vdash Bi'$ holds (in particular, the fact that $B99{,}999, B99{,}999 \rightarrow B100{,}000 \vdash B100{,}000$ holds does not immediately make trouble for (N^{bald}), as the validity of that argument by no means entails that the negation of (N_2^{bald}) follows from (N_1^{bald}) and (N_{3T}^{bald})); what does immediately make trouble for (N^{bald}) is *chaining together* these '*local*' arguments via repeated applications of (T) into the '*global*' argument $B1, B1 \rightarrow B2, B2 \rightarrow B3, B3 \rightarrow$ $B4\ldots, B99{,}999 \rightarrow B100{,}000 \vdash B100{,}000$ (whose validity does arguably entail that the negation of (N_2^{bald}) follows from (N_1^{bald}) and (N_{3T}^{bald})). Thus, denial of (T) holds promise of affording an until recently ignored solution to the Sorites Paradox.[4] And that promise is indeed kept: it can be shown that, in the non-transitive logics discussed in Zardini (2018b), (N) is consistent (and so, in particular, the negation of (N_2) does not follow from (N_1) and (N_3)).

9.2 The Case for Non-Transitivism

Denial of (T) thus affords a *formally adequate* solution to the Sorites Paradox. But what are the *philosophical reasons* in favour of adopting non-transitivism rather than any other formally adequate solution? A first reason in favour of adopting non-transitivism is fairly straightforward: it just is *intuitively plausible* (at least to many of us) that soritical reasoning is *bad reasoning with good premises* (rather than *good reasoning with bad premises*), and

---

[3] Notice that (T) is also applied in inferring that, since $\forall i(Bi \rightarrow Bi') \vdash B1 \rightarrow B2$ and $B1, B1 \rightarrow B2 \vdash B2$ hold, (N_1^{bald}) and (N_{3T}^{bald}) entail $B2$. However, first, the reasons in favour of non-transitivism (Section 9.2) do not go as far as to call into question *that* – eminently plausible – application of (T). Second, without appealing to that application of (T), the soritical argument still apparently establishes the inconsistency among (N_1), (N_2) *and the instances of (N_3) taken together*, while those instances taken together are just about as plausible as (N_3) is and it is a great virtue of non-transitivism vis-à-vis one of its closest rivals that it allows us to *preserve them taken together over and above preserving (N_3)* (Section 9.3).

[4] Notice that what is needed to block the Sorites Paradox is only denial of *certain instances* of (T). The paradox gives no reason to doubt e.g. that, if $\varphi \& \psi \vdash \varphi$ and $\varphi \vdash \varphi \vee \chi$ hold, $\varphi \& \psi \vdash \varphi \vee \chi$ holds. It is only *certain principles*, such as e.g. *modus ponens*, whose chaining together makes trouble for (N). The instances of (T) involving only other principles, and even those that involve the problematic principles but whose logical form is different from the one of those instances employed in soritical reasoning, can still be nothing less than *formally valid*. Moreover, even some of the instances of (T) with the same logical form as the one of those instances employed in soritical reasoning will still be *acceptable* (although *not formally valid*). Just about the only problematic instances of (T) are those that are, as it were, '*Sorites-critical*' – that is, those that, in a broad sense that is beyond the scope of this chapter to make more precise, employ instances of (N_3) to 'go further' in a soritical series. In fact, on my own view (e.g. Zardini 2008b, pp. 27–9), henceforth setting aside questions of 'empirical paradox', every instance of (T) save for the Sorites-critical ones will still be nothing less than *valid* (although *not formally valid*). For, at least in this area (Zardini 2012b, 2018i), logical consequence is presumably a matter of *necessary truth preservation guaranteed by certain features of the relevant expressions*: sometimes all the relevant expressions are *logical* (as in the argument from 'The glass is not on the table' and 'The glass is on the table or in the cupboard' to 'The glass is in the cupboard', where what does the trick are certain features of 'or' and 'not'), and so the argument is *formally* valid, whereas some other times some of the relevant expressions are *non-logical* (as in the argument from 'There is nothing in the glass' to 'The glass is empty', where what does the trick are certain features of 'nothing', 'in' and 'empty'), and so the argument is *materially* valid (Zardini 2008b, pp. 27–8, 175–6, 2015a, pp. 221–2). Now, non-Sorites-critical instances of (T) can indeed be so understood that *the relevant (non-logical) expressions guarantee that they are non-Sorites-critical and so that they are necessarily truth preserving*, thereby making such instances (materially) valid. Notice that, by the same token, it is in the spirit of (N) to take also '*tolerant arguments*' (such as e.g. the argument from $B50{,}000$ to $B50{,}001$) to be (materially) valid. Attention to the fact that, at least in this area, logical consequence is a matter of a certain kind of *preservation*, and so a matter of a certain kind of *implication*, also makes non-transitivism prima facie more plausible than otherwise: for many kinds of implications, especially those typically employed in ordinary thought, are indeed non-transitive ('If Zé is elected President of Portugal, he will move to Belém' and 'If Zé moves to Belém, he will need to use either tram or bus' are true in a context where Zé is a poor person with no car and no interest in politics, whereas 'If Zé is elected President of Portugal, he will need to use either tram or bus' is not), so that it becomes prima facie more plausible to expect that the kind of implication logical consequence is a matter of is also non-transitive (cf. Zardini 2015a, p. 233, fn. 21). Thanks to Sergi Oms for discussion of non-transitive implications.

that it is bad because of the *iteration* of a certain kind of inference rather than because of any *single* inference of that kind ('It's perfectly fine to infer Bi' from Bi – only, you shouldn't push that too far'). These judgements at the *intuitive* level pretty much force non-transitivism at the *theoretical* level (cf. Section 9.3).

A second reason in favour of adopting non-transitivism begins with the observation that non-transitivism is virtually the only solution to the Sorites Paradox that *preserves the spirit of (N)*, and in particular *the spirit of (N_3)*. On most solutions (epistemicism, supervaluationism, subvaluationism, contextualism, incoherentism, intuitionism, rejection of excluded middle, dialetheism in certain respects, degree theory in certain respects), (N_3) is not accepted (indeed denied, save for rejection of excluded middle and degree theory). On some other solutions (dialetheism in other respects, degree theory in other respects),[5] (N_3) is accepted but at the cost of denying the validity of *modus ponendo tollens* and *modus ponens*, so that one can no longer deductively validly use (N_{3LSB}) to reject, given Bi, the sharp boundary that would then be constituted by $\neg Bi'$ and one can no longer deductively validly use (N_{3T}) to infer tolerantly Bi' from the assumption Bi (cf. Oms and Zardini 2017), which, as will become apparent in the next two paragraphs, robs (N_3) of much of its point. On one solution (nihilism, see Chapter 4 in this volume, Section 4.6 and Chapter 11, Section 11.3), (N_3) is accepted but at the unaffordable cost of denying (N_1).[6]

This observation leads then to the sadly very poorly investigated question of, in addition to the *intuition* in favour of the spirit of (N_3), what the *reasons* are for preserving such spirit. I think that this question has a *plural* answer: there are several independent such reasons, which, in this chapter, I can only all too briefly mention (see Zardini 2008b, pp. 21–71, 2018c for details). First, some properties draw a *coarse-grained* distinction between objects that exemplify them and objects that do not – a distinction that, for some deeper level of reality, requires *non-minimal differences* at that level. For example, if x is a dog and y is not, x and y must differ by more than a nanometrical difference of one atom's location. By contraposition on implication and universal generalisation, (N_{3LSB}^{dog}) follows. Second, some properties have *flexible* application – their application to one case can be *stretched* to similar cases. For example, if x is a time one nanosecond earlier than y, *given the information* that arriving at x is arriving roughly on time one can *conclusively infer* that arriving at y is arriving roughly on time. Since, if arriving at x is arriving roughly on time, *one can be given that information* some way or other (or since one way information can be given is as an *assumption*), by conditional proof and universal generalisation ($N_{3T}^{roughly\ on\ time}$) follows.

---

[5] Explanation concerning dialetheism: (N_{3LSB}) is accepted; (N_{3T}) is accepted for *material* implication but denied for *detachable* implications. Explanation concerning degree theory: if conjunction is '*extensional*' (Chapter 8 in this volume, Section 8.3), (N_{3LSB}) is not accepted; if it is '*intensional*', the situation with (N_{3LSB}) is the same as the one with (N_{3T}), which in turn is as follows. Presumably, the idea is that, for some degree of truth δ that is both smaller than or equal to the degree of truth of (N_1) and greater than the degree of truth of the negation of (N_2), *one can only accept sentences that have degree of truth $\geq \delta$*; if so, presumably, *logical consequence should preserve the property of having degree of truth $\geq \delta$*, and hence, given the existence of a series of *modus ponens* arguments leading from (N_1) to the negation of (N_2), either *modus ponens* is invalid or not every instance of (N_{3T}) has degree of truth $\geq \delta$, in which case not every instance of (N_{3T}) can be accepted.

[6] There is also in principle a solution to the Sorites Paradox opposite to nihilism which we may call '*trivialism*' and which also accepts (N_3) but at the unaffordable cost of denying (N_2) instead. While according to nihilism *nothing* in a soritical series exemplifies a basic vague property, according to trivialism *everything* in a soritical series exemplifies a basic vague property.

Third, some properties are *observational* – for *every* possible positive or negative case (of a certain kind) of any such property, were it to occur, it would be possible to decide it *just by looking*. For example, for every (visible) object, it is possible to know by looking whether that object is close. Since, assuming that x is one nanometre closer than y, because of observationality it is the case that, if x is close and y is not, it is possible to know by looking that x is close and it is possible to know by looking that y is not close, and, since, because of our *limited powers of discrimination*, the consequent of that implication is not the case, by *modus tollens* and universal generalisation (N_{3LSB}^{close}) follows. Fourth, some properties allow for *seamless change* – acquisition or loss of the property that *take time*, and so are accomplished only *throughout an extended time interval* rather than *instantaneously*. For example, when an object seamlessly changes from red to orange, it acquires the property of being orange only throughout the whole temporal stretch of the change, with no instant in that stretch being privileged against all the other ones as the one at which the acquisition really happens. (N_{3LSB}^{red}) follows. Fifth, some objects are *abstracted from non-transitive relations* – their *identity conditions* are fixed by relations *always* holding between *similar enough* objects and *never* holding between *dissimilar enough* objects. For example, the *colours* that x and y look to have (to a subject at a time) are identical iff x and y *would look coloured alike if presented pairwise* (to that subject at that time). Since objects can be so arranged as to form a series where every two neighbouring objects would look coloured alike if presented pairwise even though the first and the last objects would not, letting © be the colour that, say, the first object looks to have, by transitivity of identity and universal generalisation ($N_{3T}^{identical\ with\ ©}$) follows.

A proper appreciation of how far-reaching the reasons for preserving the spirit of (N_3) are is also useful in that it sheds new light on the frequent objection to non-classical solutions (to the Sorites Paradox or anything else) to the effect that *they would 'cripple' our reasoning hinging on the relevant concepts* (e.g. Williamson 1992b, p. 162). Focusing on non-transitivism, as per fn. 4 the objection should immediately be dramatically downsized to the effect that non-transitivism would cripple our reasoning *in Sorites-critical situations* (that is, situations ultimately involving an application of a Sorites-critical instance of (T) – no one is proposing to do mathematics in a non-transitive logic!). Given that in Sorites-critical situations, as I observed three paragraphs back, we actually do intuitively refrain from iterating the relevant kind of inference, it then becomes fairly unclear in what respects non-transitivism is supposed to cripple our reasoning, and fairly clear that a transitive logic, rather than avoiding crippling our reasoning, actually railroads it into unnatural directions. What is now important to realise is that solutions alternative to non-transitivism also cripple our reasoning – admittedly, not the one hinging on (non-vague) *logical* concepts (at least in the case of classical solutions, see the next paragraph), but the one hinging on *vague* concepts.[7] When reasoning with vague concepts, we not only draw inferences hinging on logical concepts, but also inferences hinging *on the vague concepts themselves* – in

---

[7] In fact, *logicality and vagueness arguably overlap*: for example, there arguably are soritical series where it is vague what implies what. Therefore, solutions to the Sorites Paradox alternative to non-transitivism actually also cripple some of our reasoning hinging on (vague) *logical* concepts (insofar as this relies on (N_3), as I'm about to explain in the text).

particular, *on (N₃) – and the latter kind of inference would seem no less crucial in our reasoning than the former kind.* For example, it is vital to the concept of being a good way to cook a risotto that, given the information that a certain way is a good way to cook a risotto, we can infer that every similar way of cooking (for example, by adding one more teaspoon of butter) is also a good way to cook a risotto;[8] indeed, that useful inference is arguably more crucial in our reasoning than the useless inference with the same premise to the conclusion, say, that some way is a good way to cook a risotto, or, more generally, than any set of classically valid inferences that a reasonable version of non-transitivism might deny – even more so if we restrict to reasoning in Sorites-critical situations. When all this is realised, it would rather seem that, on balance, *our reasoning is more crippled by rejecting (N₃) than by denying classical logic.*[9]

A third reason in favour of adopting non-transitivism stems from reflection on the fact that *vagueness would seem to give us little reason to deviate from most of the characteristic principles of classical logic.* For example, despite the recent flurry of approaches to vagueness that either deny the *law of excluded middle* or deny the *law of non-contradiction*, even supposing that my salary is borderline between average and higher than average (so that [it is not average iff it is higher than average]) there is every reason to accept that my salary is either average or higher than average (and so every reason to accept the corresponding instance of the law of excluded middle, see Zardini 2018h for further discussion) and little reason to accept that my salary is both average and higher than average (and so little reason to deny the corresponding instance of the law of non-contradiction). Both claims are not only *intuitively utterly compelling*; they would also seem *inescapable in virtue of fundamental facts about 'salary space'*: salary space is *composed* by an average region plus a lower region plus a higher region – because of such composition, these regions are *exhaustive* and *exclusive* over salary space, so that, since my salary *is* in salary space, it must be in *exactly one* of them.[10] Similarly for many other characteristic principles of classical logic – indeed, *for all the principles encoded in a standard sequent-calculus presentation of classical logic (Gentzen 1934) once they are modified into a pure form in which they are finally freed from the trappings of transitivity that usually encumber them.*[11] Such principles have a good claim to capture *the classical logical essence of the*

---

[8] This is a good instance of the kind of stretching inference mentioned in the last paragraph. I hope it's clear that, while the *particular* instance chosen might appear as *neither very important nor very widespread* in our reasoning, the *kind* of inference in question is indeed *both extremely important and extremely widespread* in our reasoning.

[9] I think that a related dialectic concerning who's crippling whom is available in the case of non-classical solutions to the *semantic paradoxes* (Zardini 2014b, pp. 176–8).

[10] Thanks to Sergi Oms for pushing me to develop these considerations.

[11] For example, the principle of *modus ponens* is encoded in a standard sequent-calculus presentation of classical logic as, say, the principle that, if $\Gamma_0 \vdash \Delta_0, \varphi$ and $\Gamma_1, \psi \vdash \Delta_1$ hold, $\Gamma_0, \Gamma_1, \varphi \to \psi \vdash \Delta_0, \Delta_1$ holds. But that principle is clearly a mishmash resulting from adding the principle of transitivity with *side-conclusions* and with final *multiple conclusions*:

(T^+) If $\Gamma_0 \vdash \Delta_0, \psi$ and $\Gamma_1, \psi \vdash \Delta_1$ hold, $\Gamma_0, \Gamma_1 \vdash \Delta_0, \Delta_1$ holds

to the pure principle of *modus ponens* $\varphi, \varphi \to \psi \vdash \psi$. Some other times, things are a bit more surprising. For example, the principle of *abjunction* is encoded in a standard sequent-calculus presentation of classical logic as, say, the principle that, if $\Gamma_0, \varphi \vdash \Delta_0$ and $\Gamma_1, \psi \vdash \Delta_1$ hold, $\Gamma_0, \Gamma_1, \varphi \lor \psi \vdash \Delta_0, \Delta_1$ holds. But that principle is clearly a mishmash resulting from adding (T^+) to the pure principle of *abjunction* $\varphi \lor \psi \vdash \varphi, \psi$.

traditional logical operations, as, for each such operation, they specify *both how logically strong and how logically weak it is* (for example, *modus ponens* specifies how logically strong implication is and *conditional proof* specifies how logically weak it is). Crucially, the aim of preserving all these principles (and so of preserving the classical logical essence of the traditional logical operations) is by no means in conflict with the aim of developing a non-classical solution to the Sorites Paradox: for classical logic only arises as the result of adding to such *operational* principles (i.e. principles, such as e.g. *modus ponens*, that concern *particular logical operations*) certain *structural* principles (i.e. principles, such as e.g. reflexivity, that concern *the relation of logical consequence itself*). Therefore, it is in principle open to deny classical logic by denying some of its structural principles rather than any of its pure operational principles, and in principle open that to do this would afford a formally adequate solution to the target paradox, thereby providing a *substructural solution* to that paradox. Non-transitivism is precisely a *substructural solution to the Sorites Paradox*.[12]

9.3 Substructural Alternatives?

This naturally raises the question whether there are substructural solutions to the Sorites Paradox that are alternative to non-transitivism but enjoy the same broad three reasons we saw in Section 9.2 be in its favour. Let's focus on what is probably the best candidate. *Non-contractivism* (e.g. Slaney 2011) denies the principle of *contraction*:

(C) If $\Gamma, \varphi, \varphi \vdash \psi$ holds, $\Gamma, \varphi \vdash \psi$ holds

on the grounds that *entailment is destroyed if premises are not repeated at least as many times as they are in fact used to derive the conclusion*. As a consequence of its denial of (C), non-contractivism distinguishes between *combined truth* (of a series of sentences) and *arbitrary truth*, holding that, while the Sorites Paradox shows that the instances of (N_3) are not combinedly true, they still are arbitrarily true (thus accepting (N_3) itself iff understood to the effect that its instances are arbitrarily true). To appreciate better the difference between combined and arbitrary truth, consider, for the special case of two sentences, the two pairs of principles specifying the logical strength and weakness of the two conjunctive operators $\otimes$ and $\wedge$ respectively:

($\otimes$S) If $\Gamma, \varphi, \psi \vdash \chi$ holds, $\Gamma, \varphi \otimes \psi \vdash \chi$ holds;
($\otimes$W) If $\Gamma_0 \vdash \varphi$ and $\Gamma_1 \vdash \psi$ hold, $\Gamma_0, \Gamma_1 \vdash \varphi \otimes \psi$ holds;
($\wedge$S) If $\Gamma, \varphi \vdash \chi$ holds, $\Gamma, \varphi \wedge \psi \vdash \chi$ and $\Gamma, \psi \wedge \varphi \vdash \chi$ hold;
($\wedge$W) If $\Gamma \vdash \varphi$ and $\Gamma \vdash \psi$ hold, $\Gamma \vdash \varphi \wedge \psi$ holds.

---

[12] A further, *more indirect* reason in favour of adopting non-transitivism flows from the fact that, even if one tries to reject it because (N_3) is subject to the Sorites Paradox, in order to account for seeming lack of sharp boundaries one would typically replace (N_3) with the claim that *there are borderline cases*. Unfortunately, given *higher-order vagueness*, it can be shown (Zardini 2006a, 2006b, 2008b, pp. 73–91, 2013a) that such a claim *too* is subject to (*higher-order* versions of) the Sorites Paradox, so that one might just as well stick to (N_3) and face the truth.

These principles reflect the fact that, given failure of (C), $\varphi \otimes \psi$ corresponds to the claim that φ and ψ are combinedly true (for example, given failure of (C), $\varphi \vdash \varphi \otimes \varphi$ does not hold), whereas $\varphi \wedge \psi$ corresponds to the claim that φ and ψ are arbitrarily true (for example, given failure of (C), $\varphi \wedge \neg \varphi \vdash \varnothing$ does not hold). (Clearly, non-contractivism takes it that, in an argument, premises are assumed to be combinedly true.)

On a plausible way of developing it, non-contractivism blocks the Sorites Paradox by – letting the universal quantifier in (N_3) correspond to the claim that its instances are *arbitrarily* true – denying that $B1, \forall i(Bi \rightarrow Bi') \vdash B3$ holds, on the grounds that, because of failure of (C), that does not follow from $B1, \forall i(Bi \rightarrow Bi'), \forall i(Bi \rightarrow Bi') \vdash B3$ holding (which is what is yielded by applying (T) to $B1, \forall i(Bi \rightarrow Bi') \vdash B2$ and $B2, \forall i(Bi \rightarrow Bi') \vdash B3$). According to non-contractivism, it therefore cannot be shown that $B1, \forall i(Bi \rightarrow Bi') \vdash B3$ holds, let alone that $B1, \forall i(Bi \rightarrow Bi') \vdash B100,000$ holds, and so the instances of (N_3) can be arbitrarily true, although they cannot be combinedly true.[13]

Non-contractivism *diverges from the intuitive diagnosis* of what goes wrong in soritical reasoning: it identifies the problem as one of *repetition* (of a premise that is true if taken once),[14] whereas, intuitively, it is rather one of *iteration* (of arguments that are singly valid, see also fn. 19). Moreover, non-contractivism *does not offer a recognisable vindication of the spirit of (N_3)*. For non-contractivism does accept that it is *not* the case that the instances of (N_3) are *combinedly* true (fn. 13), and so, in a natural sense, that *some instance or other* of (N_3) is not true[15] (it also accepts, though, that, *arbitrarily taking any instance*, that instance is true).[16] This commitment and indeed even the weaker commitment to rejecting that the instances of (N_3) are combinedly true are not only repulsive to the *intuition* in favour of the spirit of (N_3); they are also in straightforward conflict with almost all the *reasons* for preserving such spirit given in Section 9.2, as, most naturally understood, almost all of those work by *considering principles that cover the combination of their instances*.[17] The only reason with which these commitments are not in straightforward

---

[13] Reason for the latter: by non-contractivist lights (contrary to non-transitivist ones), soritical reasoning does show that the combined truth of [(N_1^{bald}) and the instances of (N_3^{bald})] entails the truth of $B100,000$. Since the latter sentence is not true, it follows, by contraposition on logical consequence, that the former series of sentences are not combinedly true, which in turn entails, together with the truth of (N_1^{bald}) by *modus ponendo tollens*, that the instances of (N_3^{bald}) are not combinedly true.

[14] A cheap shot at non-contractivism – on which I won't insist too much – is that it rejects, say, that (N_3^{bald}) holds *together with something equivalent with it* such as e.g. ($N_3^{non-bald}$) (intuitively, *both* baldness and non-baldness lack sharp boundaries).

[15] One good way of spelling out the relevant sense is to say that non-contractivism accepts e.g. $(B1 \rightarrow B2) \rightarrow ((B2 \rightarrow B3) \rightarrow ((B3 \rightarrow B4) \ldots \rightarrow ((B99,998 \rightarrow B99,999) \rightarrow \neg(B99,999 \rightarrow B100,000))) \ldots)$ and all its equivalent variants got by swapping in that sentence the last instance of (N_{3T}^{bald}) with any of the previous ones. For, in general, if $\varphi \rightarrow \neg \psi$ and its equivalent variant $\psi \rightarrow \neg \varphi$ hold, that is tantamount to its being the case that, *if one* of φ or ψ holds, *the other* doesn't, which is in turn tantamount to its being the case that, *even if one* of φ or ψ holds, *the other* doesn't, which is yet in turn tantamount to its being the case that, *no matter which one – if either –* of φ or ψ holds, *the other* doesn't, which is finally in turn tantamount to, in a natural sense, its being the case that *one or the other* of φ or ψ does not hold. Thanks to Sergi Oms for pressing me on this point.

[16] Therefore, in this sense, there is indeed a sharp boundary – it's just that it's never where we're looking! Non-contractivism thus achieves by *purely logical* means the same effect that *contextualism* secures instead by *broadly pragmatic* ones (cf. Zardini 2015b, p. 498, fn. 15, 2018f).

[17] To wit, although, for simplicity's sake (with a view at applying to the relevant principle such logical principles as contraposition on implication, *modus tollens* and transitivity of identity), the first, third and fifth such reasons do proceed in terms of taking *an arbitrary instance* with x and y, they could equally compellingly have proceeded in terms of taking *the combination of all instances* with $a_0, a_1, a_2 \ldots$ and $b_0, b_1, b_2 \ldots$: for example, the coarseness of grain of the distinction drawn by certain properties requires that the fact e.g. that, if a_0 is a dog and b_0 is not, a_0 and b_0 must differ by more than a nanometrical difference of one atom's location holds *in combination with* the fact that, if a_1 is a dog and b_1 is not, a_1 and b_1

conflict is the one concerning stretching inferences, as, most naturally understood, that works by *focusing on an arbitrary instance of a stretching inference*. But a little reflection shows that *non-contractivism cannot even account for the whole range of stretching inferences*.[18] For example, stretching inferences are also such that, given the information that 'If the results of future investigations turn out to be as Ann expects, $B50,000$ holds' and 'If the results of future investigations turn out to be as Bill expects, $B50,001$ holds' are combinedly true, one can conclusively infer that 'If the results of future investigations turn out to be as Ann expects, $B50,001$ holds' and 'If the results of future investigations turn out to be as Bill expects, $B50,002$ holds' are combinedly true. But, according to non-contractivism, one can't do that (as, assuming that the implication in question is non-material, one would need the combined truth of two instances of (N_3^{bald})). Or, for another example, stretching inferences are also such that, given the information that $B50,000$ is true, one can conclusively infer that $B50,001$ and $\neg(B50,001 \,\&\, \neg B50,002)$ are combinedly true. But, according to non-contractivism, one can't do that[19] (as, again, one would need the combined truth of two instances of (N_3^{bald})).[20]

must differ by more than a nanometrical difference of one atom's location, and that these hold *in combination with* the fact that, if a_2 is a dog and b_2 is not, a_2 and b_2 must differ by more than a nanometrical difference of one atom's location ...; similarly for the observationality and indiscriminability of certain properties as well as for the identity of certain objects. Notice that the fourth reason works with a principle – seamless change of certain properties – that, in addition to its covering the combination of its instances, delivers (N_{3LSB}) *immediately*, and so without detours through instances, arbitrary or otherwise (since no applications of logical principles of any kind are then needed in the first place).

18 The risotto example in Section 9.2 arguably already proves the point, since it is naturally understood as relying on a *single general* $(N_3^{good\ way\ to\ cook\ a\ risotto})$ *multiple times* (one time for each similar way). One might try to understand the example differently as relying on *multiple specific* $(N_3^{good\ way\ to\ cook\ a\ risotto})$s $((N_3^{good\ way\ to\ cook\ a\ risotto\ butter\text{-}wise})$, $(N_3^{good\ way\ to\ cook\ a\ risotto\ cheese\text{-}wise})$, $(N_3^{good\ way\ to\ cook\ a\ risotto\ wine\text{-}wise}) \dots)$ *one time each* (one $(N_3^{good\ way\ to\ cook\ a\ risotto\ x\text{-}wise})$ for each similar way). But, clearly, each such $(N_3^{good\ way\ to\ cook\ a\ risotto\ x\text{-}wise})$ *relies on* and, given ordinary culinary assumptions, *implies the general idea* that a small difference on a standard dimension of comparison does not make a difference to a risotto: given the balance of flavours in a risotto, if e.g. one more teaspoon of butter does not spoil it, one more teaspoon of cheese (or wine, or stock, or rice ...) does not spoil it. Therefore, if one can use i specific $(N_3^{good\ way\ to\ cook\ a\ risotto\ x\text{-}wise})$s one time each, by exploiting such connections among them one can, pace non-contractivism, use instead a specific $(N_3^{good\ way\ to\ cook\ a\ risotto\ x\text{-}wise})$ i times.

19 On a maybe more plausible but also definitely more hand-waving version of non-contractivism, one can use (N_3) not only *once*, but *a few number of times i*. All the problems raised essentially apply also to such a version of non-contractivism. In particular, the conflict with stretching inferences can be made to emerge by considering, in addition to the former kind of example in the text (taking the case where the given implicational pieces of information are i'), the case where, given the information that the i' sentences 'Number a_j is easily memorisable for Sol' $[j : j \leq i]$ are combinedly true, one can conclusively infer that the i' sentences 'Number a'_j is easily memorisable for Sol' are combinedly true (yet another kind of example that obviously applies also to the version of non-contractivism discussed in the text). A somewhat converse problem (which obviously does not apply to the version of non-contractivism discussed in the text) is that, according to the version of non-contractivism in question, a soritical reasoning with i steps is sound, contrary to the fact that, for $i \geq 2$, such an argument is intuitively unsound. The problem with reasoning by (N_3^{bald}) from Bi to Bi' is not *how many times* (N_3^{bald}) *has been used*, but *whether Bi has in turn been got by applying* (N_3^{bald}) *to Bi − 1*. In other words, the problem with reasoning by (N_3) is not its *repetition* (multiple applications of the same operation), but its *iteration* (application of an operation taking as input the output of another application of the same operation). In yet other words, the problem with reasoning by (N_3) is not (C), but (T).

20 One might think that another substructural solution to the Sorites Paradox alternative to non-transitivism could be *non-monotonicism*, which denies the principle of *monotonicity*:

(M) If $\Gamma_0 \vdash \varphi$ holds, $\Gamma_0, \Gamma_1 \vdash \varphi$ holds.

There are indeed versions of non-monotonicism (e.g. Misiuna 2010), but, to the best of my knowledge, they all account for failure of (M) by treating the operative consequence relation as *non-deductive* (i.e. such that *the truth of the premises supports but need not guarantee the truth of the conclusion*). Such versions are irrelevant for our purposes, as, by falling short of vindicating the idea that the truth of e.g. Bi guarantees the truth of Bi', they do not provide any minimally interesting sense in which *(N_3) is true* (as opposed to *each of its instances being defeasibly acceptable*; but then even a steadfast epistemicist could agree that the truth of Bi typically comes together with – and so supports – the truth of Bi'!). One might think that there

More generally, not only *non-contractivism*, but virtually every *transitive* approach to vagueness that may have the resources to invalidate the *(N₃)-based* versions of the Sorites Paradox is subject to a *substructural* version of the paradox.[21] For, as I noted in fn. 4, it is in the spirit of (N) to take, for every *i*, the tolerant argument $Bi \vdash Bi'$ to be materially valid. The paradox can then be run by employing only these arguments and (T⁻). Stripped of distracting clothing such as *modus ponens* and universal instantiation, the essence of soritical reasoning is nothing but transitivity. When push comes to shove, transitivity just has to go. And, if transitivity has to go for material validity, it is natural to let it go for formal validity too, which suffices for providing a formally adequate solution to the Sorites Paradox without need to abandon further transitivity-free structural or operational principles.

9.4 Tolerant Logics

Let's see how non-transitive logics can be so developed as to satisfy *the formal requirements* of the non-transitivist solution to the Sorites Paradox and do so *in a philosophically illuminating way*. The only family of non-transitive logics I know of that does all this is the family of *tolerant logics* I first introduced in Zardini (2008a, 2008b). The logics are defined *semantically*, in particular *lattice-theoretically*. Say that a $\mathcal{T}$-*structure* $\mathfrak{S}$ is a 6ple $\langle U_{\mathfrak{S}}, V_{\mathfrak{S}}, \leq_{\mathfrak{S}}, D_{\mathfrak{S}}, \mathsf{tol}_{\mathfrak{S}}, O_{\mathfrak{S}} \rangle$, where:

- $U_{\mathfrak{S}}$ is a non-empty set of objects (the *universe of discourse*);
- $V_{\mathfrak{S}}$ is a non-empty set of objects (the *values*);
- $\leq_{\mathfrak{S}}$ is a partial ordering on $V_{\mathfrak{S}}$ such that, for every $X \subseteq V_{\mathfrak{S}}$, the greatest lower bound glb of X and the least upper bound lub of X exist ($\leq_{\mathfrak{S}}$ corresponds to a *complete* lattice);
- $D_{\mathfrak{S}}$ is a non-empty subset of $V_{\mathfrak{S}}$ (the *designated* values);

could be a version of non-monotonicism that treats the operative consequence relation as *deductive*, accounting for failure of (M) on the grounds that *entailment is destroyed if premises are added that are in fact irrelevant for deriving the conclusion*. As a consequence of its denial of (M), such a version of non-monotonicism would distinguish between *joint truth* (of a series of sentences) and *individual truth*. To appreciate better the difference between joint and individual truth, consider, for the special case of two sentences, that, given failure of (M), $\varphi \otimes \psi$ corresponds to the claim that φ and ψ are jointly true (for example, given failure of (M), $\varphi \otimes \psi \vdash \varphi$ does not hold), whereas $\varphi \wedge \psi$ corresponds to the claim that φ and ψ are individually true (for example, given failure of (M), $\varphi, \psi \vdash \varphi \wedge \psi$ does not hold). (Clearly, non-monotonicism takes it that, in an argument, premises are assumed to be jointly true.) By (C), individual truth entails joint truth (but not vice versa); still, since the joint truth of the instances of (N₃) does not entail the truth of any instance of (N₃), the version of non-monotonicism in question is only up to current standard if it holds that the instances of (N₃) are not only jointly true, but also individually true. Yet, even if (T) is replaced by the principle of *cumulative* transitivity:

(T^C)   If $\Gamma \vdash \psi$ and $\Gamma, \psi \vdash \chi$ hold, $\Gamma \vdash \chi$ holds

(a replacement that makes a lot of sense for *non-deductive* non-monotonic consequence relations, much less so for *deductive* ones), it's easy to see that soritical reasoning still shows that the joint truth of [(N$_1^{bald}$) and (N$_3^{bald}$) (understood to the effect that its instances are individually true)] entails that *B1*, *B2*, *B3* … and *B100,000* are jointly true, which is not the case (for it is characteristic of a soritical series that *not all its elements have the same status*).

[21] Thanks to Francesco Paoli for once asking me whether I thought there could be such a version (see also his Chapter 8 in this volume, Section 8.3).

- $\mathsf{tol}_{\mathfrak{S}}$ is a function from $V_{\mathfrak{S}}$ into the powerset pow of $V_{\mathfrak{S}}$ (the *tolerance* function);
- $O_{\mathfrak{S}}$ is a non-empty set of operations on $V_{\mathfrak{S}}$ with, in particular, $\{\mathsf{neg}_{\mathfrak{S}}, \mathsf{imp}_{\mathfrak{S}}\} \subseteq O_{\mathfrak{S}}$.

Without going into details, we assume a *standard first-order language* so that $\mathcal{T}$-structures can be used to evaluate its sentences via a *model*- and *assignment*-relative *valuation* function val (where conjunction and universal generalisation are interpreted as glb, disjunction and particular generalisation are interpreted as lub, negation as neg and implication as imp).

Now, given the richness of $\mathcal{T}$-structures, and in particular given tol, we can use D to generate another set T of interesting values (the *tolerated* values), by setting, for every $\mathcal{T}$-structure $\mathfrak{S}$, $T_{\mathfrak{S}} = \bigcup_{d \in D_{\mathfrak{S}}} \mathsf{tol}_{\mathfrak{S}}(d)$. Following in particular Zardini (2008a, pp. 344–9, 2008b, pp. 102–7, pp. 212–3, 2015a, pp. 256–7), we can interpret designated values to be those values that, when possessed by a sentence, model the fact that *that sentence can safely be used as a premise in further reasoning*, while we can interpret tolerated values to be those values that, when possessed by a sentence, model the fact that, *although that sentence can safely be accepted (possibly as a conclusion of previous reasoning), it might not be the case that it can safely be used as a premise in further reasoning*. In a slogan, while designated values are '*very good*' values, tolerated values are '*good enough*' values.[22] With designated and tolerated values in place, and given the interpretation just sketched of what they amount to, it is very natural to extract from $\mathcal{T}$-structures of kind **X** the corresponding, typically non-transitive, consequence relation:

$(\mathrm{TC}^{\mathbf{X}})$ Δ is an **X**-consequence of Γ ($\Gamma \vdash_{\mathbf{X}} \Delta$) iff, for every $\mathcal{T}$-structure $\mathfrak{S}$ of kind **X**, for every model $\mathfrak{M}$ and assignment ass on $\mathfrak{S}$, if, for every $\varphi \in \Gamma$, $\mathsf{val}_{\mathfrak{M},\mathsf{ass}}(\varphi) \in D_{\mathfrak{S}}$, then, for some $\psi \in \Delta$, $\mathsf{val}_{\mathfrak{M},\mathsf{ass}}(\psi) \in T_{\mathfrak{S}}$.

Obviously, given the extreme liberality of $\mathcal{T}$-structures, we need to restrict to fairly specific kinds in order for $(\mathrm{TC}^{\mathbf{X}})$ to deliver interesting enough logics. Here is a particularly nice restriction. Let a $\mathcal{T}$-structure $\mathfrak{S}$ be of kind **C** iff:

- $V_{\mathfrak{S}}$ is representable as: $\{X : X \in \mathsf{pow}(\{i : i \leq 7\})$ and, if $X \neq \{i : i \leq 7\}$, either, [[for every $i \in X$, i is even] and, [for every i and j, if $i \in X$ and ≤ 4, and j is even and $< i$, $j \in X$] and, [for every i and $j \in X$, $|i - j| < 6$]] or, [[for every $i \in X$, i is odd] and, [for every i and j, if $i \in X$ and ≤ 5, and j is odd and $< i$, $j \in X$] and, [for every i and $j \in X$, $|i - j| < 6$]]\};
- $\leq_{\mathfrak{S}}$ is representable as: $\{\langle X, Y \rangle : X \subseteq Y\}$. Thus, $V_{\mathfrak{S}}$ and $\leq_{\mathfrak{S}}$ jointly constitute the lattice depicted by the following Hasse diagram:

---

[22] The *informal* idea that the kind of value relevant for the premises is *better* than the kind of value relevant for the conclusions can already be found in Ajdukiewicz (1965), who unfortunately associates it with the idea that the resulting consequence relation is *non-deductive*. The idea is *formally* developed by Frankowski (2004) (who is indebted to the formal framework of Malinowski 1990, where, conversely, the kind of value relevant for the premises is *worse* than the kind of value relevant for the conclusions), with the same unfortunate association as Ajdukiewicz'. Neither author applies the idea specifically to the case of vagueness.

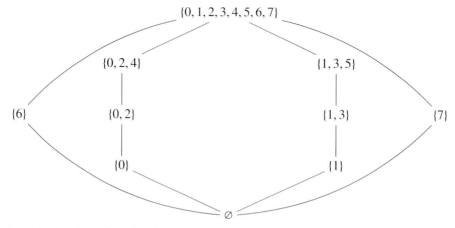

- $D_{\tilde{e}}$ and $\mathsf{tol}_{\tilde{e}}$ determine that, indicating designated values with doubly circular nodes, tolerated but not designated values with simply circular nodes and not tolerated values with square nodes, such values can be depicted as:

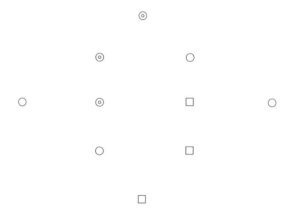

- $\mathsf{neg}_{\tilde{e}}$ is such that, indicating it with pointed edges, it can be depicted as:

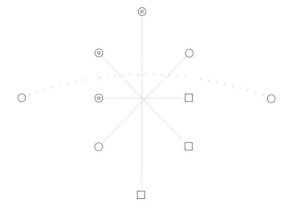

- $\text{imp}_{\tilde{\ni}}$ is such that, for every v and $w \in V_{\tilde{\ni}}$, $\text{imp}_{\tilde{\ni}}(v,w) = \text{neg}_{\tilde{\ni}}(\text{glb}(v, \text{neg}_{\tilde{\ni}}(w)))$.[23]

It's easy to check that (T) does not hold in the tolerant logic **C** resulting from (TC$^{\mathbf{C}}$) (for example, $\varphi, \varphi \to \psi \vdash_{\mathbf{C}} \psi$ – and so $\psi, \psi \to \chi \vdash_{\mathbf{C}} \chi$ – holds, but $\varphi, \varphi \to \psi, \psi \to \chi \vdash_{\mathbf{C}} \chi$ does not) and that, indeed, e.g. (N^{bald}) is consistent in **C** (i.e. (N^{bald}) $\vdash_{\mathbf{C}} \varnothing$ does not hold: for example, consider a **C**-model $\mathfrak{M}$ such that, for every i [$i : 1 \leq i \leq 35{,}000$], $\text{val}_{\mathfrak{M}}(Bi) = \{0,1,2,3,4,5,6,7\}$; for every i [$i : 35{,}001 \leq i \leq 45{,}000$], $\text{val}_{\mathfrak{M}}(Bi) = \{0,2,4\}$; for every i [$i : 45{,}001 \leq i \leq 55{,}000$], $\text{val}_{\mathfrak{M}}(Bi) = \{6\}$; for every i [$i : 55{,}001 \leq i \leq 65{,}000$], $\text{val}_{\mathfrak{M}}(Bi) = \{1\}$; for every i [$i : 65{,}001 \leq i \leq 100{,}000$], $\text{val}_{\mathfrak{M}}(Bi) = \varnothing$). It's also easy to check that **C** validates all the characteristic principles of classical logic of the kind mentioned in Section 9.2: for negation, the *law of non-contradiction* ($\varphi, \neg\varphi \vdash_{\mathbf{C}} \varnothing$ holds) and the *law of excluded middle* ($\varnothing \vdash_{\mathbf{C}} \varphi, \neg\varphi$ holds), so that the fact that $\neg\varphi$ holds consists in the fact that φ fails to hold in some way or other; for conjunction, *simplification* ($\varphi \& \psi \vdash_{\mathbf{C}} \varphi$ and $\varphi \& \psi \vdash_{\mathbf{C}} \psi$ hold) and *adjunction* ($\varphi, \psi \vdash_{\mathbf{C}} \varphi \& \psi$ holds), so that the fact that $\varphi \& \psi$ holds consists in the fact that both φ and ψ hold (analogous points apply to universal quantification); for disjunction, *abjunction* ($\varphi \vee \psi \vdash_{\mathbf{C}} \varphi, \psi$ holds) and *addition* ($\varphi \vdash_{\mathbf{C}} \varphi \vee \psi$ and $\psi \vdash_{\mathbf{C}} \varphi \vee \psi$ holds), so that the fact that $\varphi \vee \psi$ holds consists in the fact that either φ or ψ holds (analogous points apply to particular quantification); for implication, *modus ponens* ($\varphi, \varphi \to \psi \vdash_{\mathbf{C}} \psi$ holds) and *conditional proof* (if $\Gamma, \varphi \vdash_{\mathbf{C}} \Delta, \psi$ holds, $\Gamma \vdash_{\mathbf{C}} \Delta, \varphi \to \psi$ holds), so that, assuming Γ and excluding Δ, the fact that $\varphi \to \psi$ holds consists in the fact that φ does not hold without ψ's holding.

C can interestingly be thought of as getting as close to classical logic as is compatible with the failures of (T) required by (N) *by revising conjunction* (or, what is the same given the *full De Morgan behaviour* of conjunction and disjunction in **C**, *disjunction*) *rather than negation* (contrary to what is done by the vast majority of non-classical solutions to the Sorites Paradox, which critically consider the classical behaviour of negation and uncritically assume the classical behaviour of conjunction). For it can be argued that, in **C**, what fails to be transitive is conjunction rather than negation. For example, while adjunction holds in **C**, contrary to e.g. the law of non-contradiction some instances of (T) involving it as second argument do not (as a consequence, for example, the principle of *metadjunction* (if $\Gamma \vdash_{\mathbf{C}} \varphi$ and $\Delta \vdash \psi$ hold, $\Gamma, \Delta \vdash \varphi \& \psi$ holds) does not hold in **C**,[24] see Zardini 2015b, pp. 520–5 for an in-depth discussion of

---

[23] That makes $\varphi \to \psi$ fully intersubstitutable with $\neg(\varphi \& \neg\psi)$, and so guarantees that a solution to the Sorites Paradox that preserves (N$_{3T}$) will eo ipso also preserve (N$_{3LSB}$) and vice versa, which is not typically the case for non-classical solutions (fn. 5).

[24] Notice that this is no undesirable weakness of **C**: *if we want (N$_3$) together with classical negation, metadjunction just has to fail.* For $B1, B1 \to B2, B2 \to B3, \neg B3 \vdash_{\mathbf{C}} B2$ and $B1, B1 \to B2, B2 \to B3, \neg B3 \vdash_{\mathbf{C}} \neg B3$ hold, and so, if metadjunction held, $B1, B1 \to B2, B2 \to B3, \neg B3 \vdash_{\mathbf{C}} B2 \& \neg B3$ would hold, and hence, by principles of classical negation that are close kin of the law of non-contradiction and the law of excluded middle and that are also valid in **C**, $B1, B1 \to B2, B2 \to B3 \vdash_{\mathbf{C}} B3$ would hold. That would be a catastrophic result, as it would in effect amount to a recipe that, given the validity of the argument from (N$_1^{bald}$) and (N$_3^{bald}$) to Bi, would also validate the argument from (N$_1^{bald}$) and (N$_3^{bald}$) to Bi', thereby surrendering (N^{bald}) to the Sorites Paradox.

metadjunction).[25] As with the other substructural logics of Section 9.3, the finer distinctions drawn by **C** are at the level of operations of *composition* (such as conjunction and disjunction) rather than *negation* (see Zardini 2018d for a specific sustained development of this line of thought).[26]

9.5 Non-Transitivism Forced-Marched

A paradox that is usually associated with the Sorites Paradox is the *Forced-March Paradox* ('The Forced-March Paradox', in the introduction to this volume), and, since that is a paradox that is supposed *to make no assumptions about logic* whereas *a crucial move* of non-transitivism *consists in the adoption of a certain logic*, it is natural to wonder how non-transitivism could deal with it, even more so given that the paradox *apparently forces Vicky to draw an apparently problematic sharp boundary* whereas, as we saw in Section 9.2, non-transitivism is one of the very few solutions to the Sorites Paradox that, by accepting (N_{3LSB}), *denies the existence of such boundaries* (over and above rejecting their existence, which most non-classical solutions do).[27] To wit, henceforth supposing Vicky to be *herself a non-transitivist* and shifting from the *dialogical* level of *answers* to the more crucial *psychological* level of *beliefs*, cutting to the chase it might appear that both:

(FM_1^{bald}) For some i, Vicky believes that Bi holds and does not believe that Bi' holds;
(FM_2^{bald}) The doxastic behaviour described in (FM_1^{bald}) corresponds to a vagueness-related sharp boundary

hold, which would contradict (N_3^{bald}) (or some related ($N_3^{x\text{-}ly\ bald}$)) and thereby condemn her to inconsistency.

---

[25] Notice that a related principle involving negation also fails: it is not the case that, if $\Gamma \vdash_C \varphi$ and $\Delta \vdash_C \neg\varphi$ hold, $\Gamma, \Delta \vdash_C \varnothing$ holds. But I'm inclined to interpret the failure of this principle as essentially again a failure of metadjunction: for, presumably, the law of non-contradiction would be relevant for Γ, Δ only if it entailed *both φ and $\neg\varphi$*, but, presumably, that would in turn be the case only if Γ, Δ entailed $\varphi \& \neg\varphi$ (over and above entailing φ and entailing $\neg\varphi$).

[26] There are of course other interesting restrictions on $\mathcal{T}$-structures that deliver tolerant logics substantially different in some of the respects I've been emphasising. Particularly simple $\mathcal{T}$-structures are those where $V_{\exists}$ is representable as $\{1, 1/2, 0\}$, $\leq_{\exists}$ is representable as $\leq$, $D_{\exists}$ and $tol_{\exists}$ determine that $D_{\exists}$ is representable as $\{1\}$ and $T_{\exists}$ as $\{1, 1/2\}$, $neg_{\exists}(v)$ is representable as $|v-1|$ and $imp_{\exists}(v, w) = neg_{\exists}(glb(v, neg_{\exists}(w)))$. Such $\mathcal{T}$-structures can aptly be said to be of kind $\mathbf{K_3LP}$, since they treat *premises* as the *Kleene logic* $\mathbf{K_3}$ (Kleene 1938) does and *conclusions* as the *logic of paradox* $\mathbf{LP}$ does (Asenjo 1966), and, in the wake of my general application of $\mathcal{T}$-structures to vagueness, have been explored in detail by e.g. Cobreros et al. (2012). $\mathbf{K_3LP}$ can be thought of as getting as close to classical logic as is compatible with the failures of (T) required by (N) *by revising negation rather than conjunction*. Indeed, $\mathbf{K_3LP}$ validates all the principles encoded in a standard sequent-calculus presentation of classical logic even, for better or worse, before they are modified into a pure form in which they are finally freed from the trappings of transitivity that usually encumber them. I much prefer $\mathbf{C}$ over $\mathbf{K_3LP}$, among other reasons, for the simple one that $\mathbf{K_3LP}$ *says a few bad things about (N_3)*. To give two examples, $\mathbf{K_3LP}$ says that (N_1) and (N_2) entail the negation of (N_3) to the effect that, after all, there is a sharp boundary, and that, being inconsistent with (N_3), (N_1) and (N_2) entail that (N_3) implies, say, that there are witches. Meanwhile, both things are not only repulsive to the *intuition* in favour of the spirit of (N_3); they are also in straightforward conflict with most of the *reasons* for preserving such spirit given in Section 9.2, as, very naturally understood, most of those (in particular, the first, third and fourth ones) are reasons not just for *accepting (N_3)*, but also for *rejecting its negation* and *rejecting that it implies that there are witches*. (It does not help to suppose that, for some reason or other, that implication should not be taken seriously. For then also the implication at work in tolerance should not be taken seriously.) The issue is not simply to get to *maintain that there are no sharp boundaries* – we also want to get to *avoid them* and get to *avoid that what we accept implies that there are witches*.

[27] In this section, I substantially draw on Zardini (2008b, pp. 233–305) but recant from his pessimism.

Appearances notwithstanding, I'll argue on independent grounds that there is actually no way of understanding the situation of the Forced-March Paradox so that both (FM$_1$) and (FM$_2$) hold. For (FM$_2^{bald}$) holds *iff Vicky's doxastic behaviour has some tight connection with baldness*, in the sense that something along the lines of 'For every i, Bi holds iff Vicky believes that Bi holds' holds (possibly modified by prefixing the biconditional with something like 'it is likely that' or by prefixing its left-hand side with something like 'it is determinate that'; what follows holds even under such modifications). But, since it is vague up to which i Bi holds, *such a connection plausibly makes it equally vague* up to which i Vicky believes that Bi holds: by non-transitivist lights, that means that (N$_3^{believed\ by\ Vicky\ to\ be\ bald}$) holds, and so (FM$_1^{bald}$) actually does not hold. Therefore, understanding the situation of the Forced-March Paradox so that (FM$_2$) holds, (FM$_1$) doesn't. Similarly, it is extremely plausible that, for every i, if Bi holds, it is *knowable* (by a competent subject such as Vicky) that it does (none of such facts about baldness is beyond our ken),[28] so that, given that Vicky is forced to attend to every number in the soritical series, it can be the case that, *for every i, Bi holds iff she knows that it does*, *which plausibly makes it equally vague* up to which i she knows that Bi holds: by non-transitivist lights, that means that (N$_3^{known\ by\ Vicky\ to\ be\ bald}$) holds. If our knowledge is without boundaries, baldness can lie within it.

So far so good, but what if we now impose the interesting constraint that *Vicky's doxastic behaviour be precise*, thereby enforcing (FM$_1$)? Then, naturally, for some p_0, for every $i \leq p_0$, Vicky believes that Bi holds; for some $n_0 > p_0$, for every i [$i : p_0 < i < n_0$], she does not believe that Bi holds and does not believe that $\neg Bi$ holds; for every $i \geq n_0$, she believes that $\neg Bi$ holds. Since, as per the last paragraph, because of precision there is no longer any tight connection between Vicky's doxastic behaviour and baldness, *such behaviour no longer corresponds to a vagueness-related sharp boundary*: p_0 is not a sharp boundary of any vague property such as baldness (or determinate baldness, or knowable baldness, or comfortable baldness, etc.), it is simply the sharp boundary of her enforcedly precise belief in baldness.[29]

---

[28] Essentially this kind of thesis has been influentially attacked by Williamson (1995b) and defended by Zardini (2012a) (introduction to this volume, fn. 36), in a context, however, where *the core dialectic is neutral* as to whether the subject matter is vague (see Zardini 2012a, pp. 399–400, fn. 34 for a non-transitivist lift of that neutrality).

[29] Notice that Vicky does believe that, if Bp_0 (determinately, knowably, comfortably, etc.) holds, Bp_0' (determinately, knowably, comfortably, etc.) holds, and so she does believe that *there is no vagueness-related difference* between p_0 and p_0' (indeed, since she believes that Bp_0 entails Bp_0', she believes that there is no such difference in a *much more genuine* way than is done by the solutions to the Sorites Paradox mentioned in Section 9.2 on which the entailment does not hold). Such a belief is perfectly coherent with the fact that Vicky believes that Bp_0 holds and does not believe that Bp_0' holds, for there are *very general reasons* for thinking that belief is subject to norms (e.g. of epistemic likelihood, see fn. 30) that determine that *it is not always the case that one should believe what one knows is a logical consequence of what one believes*, reasons that are but amplified on a non-transitive approach (Zardini 2008b, pp. 201–23, 2015a, pp. 245–65). In a sense, then, *in theory* Vicky does not distinguish at all between p_0 and p_0' by *thinking that* they *share* every relevant vague property and so – plausibly assuming that every relevant normatively significant status is vague – *every relevant normatively significant status*; she only distinguishes them *in practice* by *behaving differently with respect to* each of them. Such practice is thereby *deprived of any normative basis and import* – it is *brute*. By enforcing precision in Vicky's doxastic behaviour, we've enforced a setting where ((FM$_1$) holds and) *the choice of which particular number is p_0 is not subject to any norm*, and so we've enforced a setting *requiring* – and hence *licensing* – arbitrariness in her doxastic behaviour (we'll see seven paragraphs further on that non-transitivism is also conducive to further and deeper elements of arbitrariness).

So far so good, but an interesting problem now arises as to how Vicky's doxastic behaviour, in particular her *confidence* (which is also now enforcedly precise), develops in more detail. Plausibly, Vicky would be fairly daft if, [for every $i \leq p_0$, she were *fully* confident that *Bi* holds and, for every $i > p_0$, *not in the least* confident that *Bi* holds], or if, [for every $i \geq n_0$, she were *fully* confident that ¬*Bi* holds and, for every $i < n_0$, *not in the least* confident that ¬*Bi* holds]; it would rather seem that her confidence in baldness should *smoothly decrease* until some $p_1 \geq p_0$ and that her confidence in nonbaldness should *smoothly increase* from some $n_1 \leq n_0$. That would all seem plausible, but the problem arises when we try to model this doxastic behaviour in the framework of *classical probability* (interpreting a *probability measure* pro as a *measure of confidence* or as a *measure of epistemic likelihood*[30] that should be tracked by such confidence). For the classical principle of *differentiality*:

(D) $\mathsf{pro}(\neg\varphi) = 1 - \mathsf{pro}(\varphi)$

will imply that, for some b, on the one hand, Vicky is more confident in *Bb* than she is in ¬*Bb* whereas, on the other hand, while she is similarly confident in *Bb′*, she is at least equally confident in ¬*Bb′* (for concreteness, it is initially natural and helpful to suppose that $\mathsf{pro}(Bb) > 0.5$ whereas $\mathsf{pro}(Bb') = \mathsf{pro}(\neg Bb') = 0.5$). It would then seem that Vicky's confidence in *Bb* and her confidence in ¬*Bb′* are *jointly misplaced*: in general, for every i, if she is more confident in *Bi* than she is in ¬*Bi*, she should not be at least as confident in ¬*Bi′* as she is in *Bi′* (any confidence she may have in ¬*Bi′* should be trumped by a greater confidence in *Bi′*) – otherwise, she will in effect have *relatively strong contrasting expectations* in terms of baldness about i and i' that clash with her belief in (N_3^{bald}).

The problem with classical probability has several ramifications. For one thing, for every i, Vicky thinks that *Bi* and ¬*Bi′* are *incompatible*, but, for many i [$i : 0 < \mathsf{pro}(Bi) < 1$], given the amount of confidence that she has in *Bi*, the amount of confidence that, in classical probability, she has in ¬*Bi′* *exceeds* the amount of confidence that she has rationally left available to place on anything incompatible with *Bi*: in general, *if one thinks that φ and ψ are incompatible, one should not be confident in ψ to an extent greater than the extent to which one is not fully confident in φ.* This becomes particularly vivid in the case of b, since Vicky thinks that *Bb* and ¬*Bb′* are *incompatible* and yet she is more than fifty-fifty confident in *Bb* and at least fifty-fifty confident in ¬*Bb′*! For another thing, for many i [$i : 0 < \mathsf{pro}(Bi) < 1$], in classical probability, Vicky's confidence increases from ¬*Bi* to ¬*Bi′*, which implies that she thinks that it is more likely that ¬*Bi′* holds than that ¬*Bi* holds – i.e. that she thinks that the *risk* of *Bi′*'s not being true *outruns* the risk of *Bi*'s not being true – which is at odds with her thinking that the truth of *Bi* guarantees the truth of *Bi′*, and so with her thinking that the tolerant argument from *Bi* to *Bi′* is *deductively valid* (fn. 4) rather than simply *non-deductively valid* (fn. 20): *in general, if one thinks that φ entails ψ and that it is to some extent likely that φ holds, one should not think that it is more likely that ψ does not hold than that φ does not hold.* This becomes particularly vivid in the case of *b*, since Vicky thinks that *Bb* entails *Bb'* and that *Bb* is more than fifty-fifty likely to hold, and yet she thinks that [*Bb* is less than fifty-fifty likely not to hold while *Bb'* is at least fifty-fifty likely not to hold]! For yet another thing, revising the concrete supposition of the last paragraph, it is actually *psychologically quite unrealistic* to suppose that Vicky will *typically* be able to calibrate her confidence so as to reach at *b'* a *point of perfect equilibrium* between her confidence in *Bb'* and her confidence in ¬*Bb'*. It is *psychologically much more realistic* to suppose that Vicky will *often enough* go from being more confident in *Bb* than she is in ¬*Bb* to being more confident in ¬*Bb'* than she is in *Bb'*. And that even more blatantly clashes with her belief in (N_3^{bald}).

In essence, the problem with classical probability is this. It is in the nature of a soritical series that, for many $i \leq p_1$, *Vicky's confidence decreases slightly from Bi to Bi'*, since, being *i'* further down the series, *Bi'* is slightly less likely than *Bi*. (On my view, so much is acceptable also for the non-transitivist: tolerant arguments are both *deductively valid* (in the sense that the truth of the premises guarantees the truth of the conclusion) and *deeply ampliative* (in the sense that their conclusion can be less likely than the conjunction of their premises), see Zardini 2015a, pp. 262–4 for further discussion.) Unfortunately, in classical probability, such decrease very oddly entails that *Vicky's confidence increases from ¬Bi to ¬Bi'* (up to the point where a relatively great confidence in *Bb* is followed by a similarly great confidence in ¬*Bb'* that is at best only matched, but not trumped, by a similarly great confidence in *Bb'*). What non-transitivism needs is *decrease in positive confidence without increase in negative confidence*. Now, there is a well-known generalisation of classical probability that allows exactly for that: the theory of *belief functions* of Dempster (1967); Shafer (1976). Basically, the idea is to replace the classical principle of *additivity*:

(A) If φ and ψ are incompatible, $\mathsf{pro}(\varphi \vee \psi) = \mathsf{pro}(\varphi) + \mathsf{pro}(\psi)$,

which implies (D), with the weaker principle of *super-additivity*:

($A^{\geq}$) If φ and ψ are incompatible, $\mathsf{pro}(\varphi \vee \psi) \geq \mathsf{pro}(\varphi) + \mathsf{pro}(\psi)$,

which only implies the weaker principle of *sub-differentiality*:

($D^{\leq}$) $\mathsf{pro}(\neg\varphi) \leq 1 - \mathsf{pro}(\varphi)$,

which in turn allows for one to place no confidence whatsoever on ¬φ no matter how much confidence one places on φ.[31]

---

[31] In discussion of certain Sorites-like series (fn. 28), Zardini (2012a) distinguishes between *degrees of belief* and *degrees of confidence* and assumes that the former have super-additive structure. What I'm arguing here is that *even degrees of confidence* (about a *vague* subject matter) have super-additive structure. Besides, on very different grounds arising within a specific version of *dogmatism about perceptual justification*, Zardini (2014a) too argues that *likelihood* has super-additive structure.

Replacing (A) with ($A^\geq$), we can model Vicky's doxastic behaviour so that, for every $i \leq p_1$, her confidence either stays constant or (for many such i) slightly decreases from Bi to Bi', with no confidence whatsoever in $\neg Bi$ and in $\neg Bi'$; for every i [$i : p_1 < i < n_1$], she has no confidence whatsoever in Bi or in $\neg Bi$; for every $i \geq n_1 - 1$, her confidence either stays constant or (for many such i) slightly increases from $\neg Bi$ to $\neg Bi'$, with no confidence whatsoever in Bi and in Bi'. In this super-additive framework, the problem with classical probability totally dissolves with all its ramifications, as it's easy to see from the fact that, in such a framework, *for no i, does Vicky have both some confidence in Bi and some confidence in ¬Bi'* (this straightforwardly takes care of the main problem and its first two ramifications; as for the third one, notice that it is indeed psychologically realistic to suppose that she will typically be able to calibrate her confidence so as to reach at p_1' a point at which she has no confidence whatsoever in Bp_1' and no confidence whatsoever in $\neg Bp_1'$).

If the logic governing φ and ψ is classical logic (but not if it is **C**, see Zardini 2018d), ($A^\geq$) implies the principle of *monotonicity*:

(MON) If φ entails ψ, $\mathsf{pro}(\varphi) \leq \mathsf{pro}(\psi)$.

However, (MON) is untenable by non-transitivist lights: for, by such lights, presumably, $\mathsf{pro}(\forall j(Bj \to Bj')) = 1$, and so, presumably, for every i, $\mathsf{pro}(Bi) = \mathsf{pro}(Bi \,\&\, \forall j(Bj \to Bj'))$, but, as we saw two paragraphs back, for many $i \leq p_1$, $\mathsf{pro}(Bi)$ is slightly greater than $\mathsf{pro}(Bi')$ despite the fact that $Bi \,\&\, \forall j(Bj \to Bj') \vdash_{\mathbf{C}} Bi'$ holds. Therefore, (MON) should be replaced by the weaker principle of *bounded non-monotonicity*:

(BNMON^δ) If φ entails ψ, $\mathsf{pro}(\varphi) \leq \mathsf{pro}(\psi) + \delta$

(where the value of δ is determined by the application in question), which allows for its being the case that, for many $i \leq p_1$, $\mathsf{pro}(Bi) = \mathsf{pro}(Bi') + \delta$ despite the fact that $Bi \,\&\, \forall j(Bj \to Bj') \vdash_{\mathbf{C}} Bi'$ holds. Notice how snugly ($A^\geq$) fits with (BNMON^δ): *($BNMON^\delta$) allows for a drop of δ-probability from the premise to the conclusion of a deductively valid argument, while ($A^\geq$) prevents such a drop to entail any converse rise of probability from the negation of the premise to the negation of the conclusion.* The interaction between ($A^\geq$) and (BNMON^δ) makes it thus possible for some deeply ampliative arguments to be deductively valid.

So far so good, but, for some of us, a little bit of dissatisfaction still remains. For, on the current model, for every i [$i : p_1 < i < n_1$], Vicky has no confidence whatsoever in Bi or in $\neg Bi$ – she is completely *agnostic* about them. However, non-transitivism accepts the law of excluded middle, and so accepts that, even in those cases, *there is a fact of the matter* as to whether Bi holds or not. And, despite Vicky's agnosticism, as we saw seven paragraphs back (whose considerations about knowledge that Bi holds are obviously extendable to knowledge that Bi does not hold), *all* such facts can be known by a subject whose doxastic behaviour is *vague* in the Forced March. But it would seem that *any* such fact can also be known by a subject whose doxastic behaviour is *precise* in the Forced March: taking any such fact, say, Bi, if the slice of the overall epistemic position of the former kind of subject that specifically concerns Bi is good enough to afford knowledge that Bi holds, it would seem that a duplicate of that slice that only differs by being part of an overall precise doxastic behaviour is also good enough to afford knowledge that Bi holds (if anything, the fact that, for some $j \geq i$, one believes that Bj holds *but does not believe that Bj' holds* is a reason for thinking that one's belief that Bi holds is the output of a method that *could less easily have formed a false belief* – and, in this sense, *is more reliable* – than a method such that, for every $j \geq i$, if one believes that Bj holds, one *also believes that Bj' holds*!). It would therefore seem that it should be possible for Vicky to *go through the Forced March without recourse to either vagueness or agnosticism.* But just how?

Since Vicky is now abandoning every agnosticism, it is natural to assume that, for some $p_2 \geq p_1$, for every $i \leq p_2$, she believes for *non-tolerant* reasons (i.e. reasons other than inference by tolerance) that Bi holds, and, assuming that baldness is tolerant of a difference of at most t hairs, that, letting $n_2 = (p_2 + t)'$, for every $i \geq n_2$, she believes for non-tolerant reasons that $\neg Bi$ holds. Given this, what should Vicky believe about p_2'? By construction, Vicky does not have non-tolerant reasons either for believing that Bp_2' holds or for believing that $\neg Bp_2'$ holds, and so she should come to a view by employing instead *inference by tolerance* and the *information* that $B1, B2, B3 \ldots, Bp_2, \neg Bn_2, \neg Bn_2', \neg Bn_2'' \ldots$ and $\neg B100{,}000$ hold (let the tolerance principle $\forall i \forall j\, [j : j \leq t]\, (Bi \rightarrow Bi + j)$ plus that information be Γ). A first crucial logical fact is now that both $\Gamma \vdash_{\mathbf{C}} Bp_2'$ and $\Gamma \vdash_{\mathbf{C}} \neg Bp_2'$ hold (but, given failure of metadjunction, $\Gamma \vdash_{\mathbf{C}} Bp_2' \& \neg Bp_2'$ does not). Therefore, Vicky has *conclusive reasons* (the availability of a sound deductive argument) *either* for believing that Bp_2' holds *or* for believing that $\neg Bp_2'$ holds (but not for *both*). Vicky thus has *two alternative doxastic options* – she has a *doxastic choice* (Zardini 2015b, p. 524).[32]

Suppose then, without loss of generality (fn. 35), that Vicky chooses to infer $\neg Bp_2'$. A second crucial logical fact is now that, while $\Gamma \vdash_{\mathbf{C}} \neg Bp_2'$ holds, for every $i\, [i : p_2' - t \leq i \leq p_2]\, \Gamma \vdash_{\mathbf{C}} \neg Bp_2' \& Bi$ does not[33] (in general, what does not hold in **C** is the principle of *persistence* that, if $\Delta, \varphi \vdash \psi$ holds, $\Delta, \varphi \vdash \psi \& \varphi$ holds).[34] Therefore, while the inference to $\neg Bp_2'$ is correct, for every $i\, [i : p_2' - t \leq i \leq p_2]$ the one to $\neg Bp_2' \& Bi$ is not, and so, if Vicky does choose to infer $\neg Bp_2'$, she should *give up Bi – by inferring the conclusion from the premises, she frees herself from her commitment to some of the premises* (Zardini 2015b, pp. 524–5). But that is exactly what is needed here: Vicky goes from believing that, for every $i\, [i : p_2' - t \leq i \leq p_2]$, Bi holds to believing that $\neg Bp_2'$ holds, but in doing so she is not *expanding* her view that Bi holds to the *more comprehensive* and *untenable* view that Bi and $\neg Bp_2'$ hold; she is rather *changing* her view from the view that Bi holds to the *alternative* and *tenable* view that $\neg Bp_2'$ holds. By accepting $\neg Bp_2'$, for every $i\, [i : p_2' - t \leq i \leq p_2]$

---

[32] Since also expressions such as e.g. 'alive' and 'morally permissible' are vague, in a few cases, far from being simply a matter of labelling, such a choice will have *momentous theoretical and practical significance.*

[33] For every $i < p_2' - t$, the relevant models can instead be so constrained that $\Gamma \vdash \neg Bp_2' \& Bi$ does hold.

[34] Interestingly, failure of persistence is also pivotal in my preferred *non-contractive* approach to the *semantic paradoxes* (e.g. Zardini 2018e).

Vicky abandons Bi, and so she is not drawing any sharp boundary:[35] she verifies (FM_1) and falsifies (FM_2).[36] She manages to jump unscathed.[37]

---

[35] After choosing what to infer, plausibly, Vicky can still access whatever information she had before the choice *that she gave up in the inference but that is consistent with the choice made* (as per the supposition in the text, this would be the information that, for every i [$i : n_2 \leq i \leq (n_2 - 1) + t$], $\neg Bi$ holds; for $i > (n_2 - 1) + t$, see fn. 33). Therefore, if Vicky chooses to infer Bp'_2 instead, she can still access the information that, for every i [$i : p'_2 - t \leq i \leq p_2$], Bi holds, whereas she definitively frees herself from her commitment to $\neg Bn_2$ (since Bp'_2 and $\neg Bn_2$ are inconsistent with $\forall i \forall j$ [$j : j \leq t$] ($Bi \rightarrow Bi + j$)), so that her information is reduced to the information that $B1, B2, B3 \ldots, Bp_2, \neg Bn'_2, \neg Bn''_2, \neg Bn'''_2 \ldots$ and $\neg B100{,}000$ hold. An analogous choice will then present itself for p''_2, etc.; eventually, for some p_3 [$p_3 : p_2 < p_3 < n_2$], Vicky will believe that Bp_3 holds but then infer $\neg Bp'_3$ from the information that $B1, B2, B3 \ldots, Bp_2, \neg B(p_3 + t)', \neg B(p_3 + t)'', \neg B(p_3 + t)''' \ldots$ and $\neg B100{,}000$ hold, thereby, for every i [$i : p'_3 - t \leq i \leq p_2$], definitively freeing herself from her commitment to Bi, and also, for the same reason, for every j [$j : p_2 < j \leq p_3$], from her commitment to Bj. A nice feature of this account is that it makes Vicky's switch *irreversible*: since, for every i [$i : p'_3 - t \leq i \leq p_2$], she definitively frees herself from her commitment to Bi, for every $j \geq p'_3$ she is only left with conclusive reasons for believing that $\neg Bj$ holds but not for believing that Bj holds.

[36] As was mentioned in 'The Forced-March Paradox', in the introduction to this volume, there are versions of the Forced-March Paradox concerning *precise* expressions (which are presumably governed by classical logic rather than **C**). Typically, in those versions, contrary to those concerning vague expressions, *Vicky should be agnostic about a range of cases* – for example, for some i, there is no telling whether i straws break the camel's back. In such versions, the problem is not e.g. that the doxastic behaviour described in ($FM_1^{break\ the\ camel's\ back}$) corresponds to a sharp boundary *for how many straws break the camel's back*, not so much because, by everyone's lights, there is indeed such a boundary, but because, given that Vicky's doxastic behaviour has no tight connection with how many straws break the camel's back, for a few i there is no reason to think that, if she does not believe that i straws break the camel's back, i straws do not break the camel's back. The problem is rather that it is natural to assume that Vicky's doxastic behaviour does have some tight connection with how many straws *she has justification for believing* break the camel's back, so that the doxastic behaviour described in ($FM_1^{break\ the\ camel's\ back}$) would correspond to a sharp boundary *for how many straws she has justification for believing break the camel's back*: because of the vagueness of such justification, that would be a vagueness-related sharp boundary, which would contradict ($N_3^{Vicky\ has\ justification\ for\ believing\ break\ the\ camel's\ back}$) and thereby condemn her to inconsistency. Essentially the same dialectic of the second and third paragraphs of this section then applies. Sorites-like series of the kind just discussed do clearly raise further challenging issues, which, pertaining more to epistemology rather than the philosophy of vagueness (let alone the Sorites Paradox), are however better left for another occasion (Zardini 2018g).

[37] Earlier versions of the material in this chapter have been presented in 2014 in the mini-course 'Philosophical Paradoxes' at Maltepe University; in 2016, in the compact course 'Vagueness and Logic' at the Georg-August University of Göttingen; in 2017, at the sixth *Entia et Nomina* Workshop in Patnem (Ghent University/University of Gdańsk) and at the LanCog Metaphysics, Epistemology, Logic and Language Seminar (University of Lisbon); in 2018, in the course 'Philosophy of Language, Logic and Mind' (University of Lisbon) and in the mini-course 'Vagueness' (Higher School of Economics). I'd like to thank all these audiences for very stimulating comments and discussions. Special thanks go to Laura Delgado, Vitalij Dolgorukov, Zekiye Kutlusoy, Sergi Oms, Güncel Önkal, Francesco Paoli, Dolf Rami, Hili Razinsky, Ricardo Santos and Rafał Urbaniak. At different stages, the study has been funded by the Marie Curie Intra-European Research Fellowship 301493 *A Non-contractive Theory of Naive Semantic Properties: Logical Developments and Metaphysical Foundations* (NTNSP) and by the FCT Research Fellowship IF/01202/2013 *Tolerance and Instability: The Substructure of Cognitions, Transitions and Collections*. Additionally, the study has been funded by the Russian Academic Excellence Project *5-100*. I've also benefited from support from the Project FFI2015-70707-P of the Spanish Ministry of Economy, Industry and Competitiveness *Localism and Globalism in Logic and Semantics* and from the FCT project PTDC/FER-FIL/28442/2017 *Companion to Analytic Philosophy 2*.

Part II

The Influence of the Sorites Paradox

10   The Sorites Paradox in Philosophy of Logic

Sergi Oms

10.1 The Semantic Paradoxes

The Sorites Paradox is one of the most venerable and complex paradoxes in the territory of the philosophy of logic and language. Its influence is present in many other areas of the philosophy of logic; notably, the development of non-classical logics such as many-valued logics (e.g. Tye 1994 or Machina 1976) and substructural logics (e.g. Zardini 2008a; Slaney 2010a);[1] the discussion on logical pluralism (Shapiro 2014) and the research on the notion of truth and its semantics (e.g. Williamson 1994, chapter 7; Keefe 2000, chapter 8), which is closely related to the main topic of this chapter: the relation between the Sorites Paradox and the best known of the semantic paradoxes, the Liar Paradox.

Together with the Sorites, the semantic paradoxes also occupy a very prominent place in research in the philosophy of logic. All these paradoxes crucially involve semantic notions such as, for instance, *truth*, *denotation* or *satisfaction*. Let us begin by introducing some of the main members of the family of the semantic paradoxes.

Berry's Paradox (Russell 1908). Any language that, like English, has a finite vocabulary (that is, a finite number of words) has, in consequence, a finite number of expressions containing fewer than, say, 100 occurrences of words. From this fact it follows that there is a finite amount of natural numbers that can be denoted by an English expression containing fewer than 100 occurrences of words. This means that there are some natural numbers that cannot be referred to by any expression containing fewer than 100 occurrences of words and, by the least number principle (which states that every non-empty set of natural numbers has a least element), it follows that there is a least number, k, that cannot be denoted by any expression containing fewer than 100 occurrences of words. But

> the least natural number not denoted by an expression containing fewer than 100 occurrences of words

contains fewer than 100 occurrences of words and, apparently, it refers to k. Therefore, k is denoted and it is not denoted by an expression containing fewer than 100 occurrences of words. Contradiction.

---

[1] See Chapter 9 in this volume.

Curry's Paradox (Curry 1942). Let γ be a sentence, called a 'Curry sentence', which asserts that if itself is true then ϕ, where ϕ is any sentence whatsoever:

(γ) If γ is true, then ϕ.

Suppose that γ is true. Then, under this supposition, what γ says is the case (is not that what truth is about?); that is, if γ is true, then ϕ. We can now apply *modus ponens* and conclude, under the assumption that γ is true, ϕ. Since we have achieved ϕ under the supposition that γ is true we can now conclude that *if* γ is true, *then* ϕ. We then realise that we just proved γ itself. But if γ is the case – as we have just proven – then γ is true. This means that we have the following two claims: first, that if γ is true, then ϕ and, second, that γ is true. From these, then, applying *modus ponens* again, we conclude ϕ. But ϕ was any sentence, in particular, it could be a contradiction or a false sentence (of course, it could also be a true sentence).

The Liar Paradox. Suppose we have a sentence λ that asserts its own untruth (and let us call such a sentence 'the Liar sentence' or, also, just 'the Liar'):

(λ) λ is not true.

Suppose, now, that λ is true. Then, if λ is true what λ says is the case; but what λ says is precisely that λ is not true, which contradicts our initial supposition that λ is true. Hence we conclude, by *reductio*, that λ is not true. Unfortunately, if λ is not true, then what λ says (that is, that λ is not true) is the case and thus λ is true after all, which contradicts our previous conclusion.

Historically, the Liar Paradox is credited to Eubulides of Miletus (fourth century BC), a contemporary of Aristotle, and famous for his logical puzzles, among which we find the Liar and the Heap (Diogenes Laertius 1925, II, §108).[2,3] In Antiquity, the Liar Paradox was not much discussed. One important exception, though, was the Stoic philosopher Chrysippus who, as far as we know, wrote six books about the Liar and many replies to those who claimed to have solved it (Laertius 1925, VII, §196–7).[4] The paradox was seriously discussed again in the Medieval period, especially in the fourteenth century. One important example of this period is the work of the French philosopher John Buridan (see Read 2002). The Liar remained forgotten until the birth of modern logic and since the twentieth century it has been widely discussed. Among the works devoted to it, it is important to mention the seminal papers by Tarski (1983) and later by Kripke (1975), which contributed to laying the foundations for the research to come.

Traditionally, the Liar and the Sorites have been considered to be unrelated. Nevertheless, there have been several attempts to show that there are important similarities between these two paradoxes and some authors have offered proposals to uniformly cope with both

---

[2] See also Chapter 15 in this volume, Section 15.1.
[3] The Liar Paradox is also known as 'Epimenides' Paradox', named so after the Cretan wise man Epimenides (sixth century BC) who, according to St Paul's Epistle to Titus, said that all Cretans were liars (*Titus*, 1:12).
[4] See Chapter 15 in this volume.

the Liar and the Sorites. Notably, McGee (1991)[5] defended the view that the truth predicate as used in natural languages is inconsistent and that, accordingly, it should be replaced by a new, consistent and scientifically precise notion. Such a new notion of truth, defends McGee, should be treated as a vague predicate (see, for example, McGee 1991, p. 7), which, in turn, implies that the new truth predicate should be understood as a partial predicate. Another seminal paper defending a unified treatment for the Liar and the Sorites is Tappenden (1993).[6] According to him, vague predicates and the truth predicate are similar enough to support a special speech act that Tappenden calls 'articulation'. More recently, Hartry Field has defended in a number of places (see Field 2003a, 2003b, 2008) that the Liar and the Sorites might be connected in the sense that the former is due to 'something akin to vagueness or indeterminacy in semantic concepts like "true" (Field 2003b, p. 262). Field then proposes to treat both phenomena with a logic that rejects the law of excluded middle. Some authors in the paraconsistent tradition have also proposed that the Liar and the Sorites have a common underlying structure (see, especially, Colyvan 2009 and Priest 2010a) and that, as a consequence of this fact, they should be treated uniformly.[7]

In this chapter we will examine when and why, in general, a uniform solution to more than one paradox should be expected and, in particular, why a uniform solution to the Liar and the Sorites should be expected. In order to do this we will need a sufficiently precise idea of what a uniform or common solution to some collection of paradoxes should be. Later, we will focus on the work of Paul Horwich, who has used (broadly epistemicist) ideas that were first applied to solve the Sorites in order to attempt to give a solution to the Liar. We will see in some detail, as a particular example of the influence that the Sorites has had over the treatment of some of the semantic paradoxes, whether the epistemicist approach Horwich presents in order to face the Sorites can be successfully applied to his theory of truth.

10.2 The Liar and the Sorites

10.2.1 Common Solutions

Let us begin by asking ourselves what we would expect from a common solution to a given collection of paradoxes. Think of a screwdriver; it can be used to fix, say, an electrical problem and a plumbing problem or, in case of need, it can even be used to hammer a nail. Would we say, though, that the screwdriver is a common solution to these problems? To my mind, such a claim would hardly be illuminating. It is not this sense of 'common solution' that we have in mind when we think of common solutions to some collection of paradoxes; rather, we want to be able to see that the paradoxes can be solved by a common solution because the phenomena underlying them have something relevant in common that eventually causes the paradoxes. And it is this something in common that

---

[5] See also McGee (1989) and Yablo (1989).
[6] See also Fara (2000), Keefe (2000) and Oms (2010, 2017).
[7] Cf. Chapter 7 in this volume, Section 7.10.

the solution should point at. This is akin to what Chihara (1979) called 'the diagnosis of a paradox'. At least since Tarski,[8] philosophers have considered paradoxes to be analogous to illnesses. Along this line of thought, Chihara proposes to understand the diagnosis of a paradox as the solution to 'the problem of pinpointing that which is deceiving us and, if possible, explaining how and why the deception was produced' (Chihara 1979, p. 590). The diagnosis of a paradox should help us identify the feature (or features) of the concept (or concepts) involved in the paradox that are responsible for its paradoxical nature. But, as Chihara himself notes, we also need to be able to devise, when necessary, safe paradox-free environments for the concepts involved in the paradoxes. Following Chihara (1979, p. 616) and the illness analogy again, we can call such logico-semantic frames we need to adopt in order to block the paradox 'the treatment of a paradox'. Typically, any treatment to a paradox will involve the necessity of rejecting some well entrenched and strong intuitions governing some of the concepts involved (either explicitly or implicitly) in the paradox.

The diagnosis of a paradox and its treatment are, up to a point, independent, in the sense that having found one does not imply having solved the other. Nevertheless, both the diagnosis and the treatment (when the former is needed) are typically intertwined with each other. For example, if we adopt a supervaluational approach to the Sorites, the treatment, which is, roughly, the supervaluational semantics, is used in the diagnosis when the supervaluationist[9] needs to explain why some premises in the Sorites are not true, and why they are nonetheless so compelling.[10]

A common (or uniform) solution to a given collection of paradoxes must point, at the level of the diagnosis, at whatever is causing the paradoxes, which, in turn, must be something common to all of them.[11] This means that a common solution to some collection of paradoxes does not have to necessarily offer a common treatment. For example, there can be common solutions that offer a common diagnosis without offering a common treatment (we will see an example of this in Section 10.3).

Let us turn next to seeing why, given a certain collection of paradoxes, a uniform solution to all of them should be expected.

10.2.2 Why Uniformity?

There are at least two different groups of reasons that can be taken into account in favour of the idea that some paradoxes might have a common solution. First, there is one group

---

[8] In Tarski's own words: 'The appearance of a [paradox] is for me a symptom of disease' (Tarski 1969, p. 66).

[9] See Chapter 2 in this volume.

[10] As I see it, only the diagnosis is a necessary condition for having a solution to a paradox. Notice that a solution to a paradox might not prompt the necessity of a treatment. For example, epistemicist solutions to the Sorites typically endorse classical logic to deal with vague predicates and do not need any change in the language or in the logic (see Chapter 1 in this volume). In this sense, the treatment is not needed. This means that, in general, having a treatment is not necessary in order to be able to offer a solution to a paradox. Nevertheless, in a particular case, it might be that if the diagnosis of a solution implies the necessity of a treatment and the solution does not offer it, then the solution will be incomplete. I am leaving the characterisations of the diagnosis and the treatment of a paradox somewhat vague. I do not think they can be made much more precise; in any case, I hope that the examples we will see throughout this chapter will help to shed light on them.

[11] This idea can be found, for example, in Colyvan (2009, p. 2) or Cook (2013, p. 187).

of reasons related to methodological issues such as simplicity and uniformity. It might be argued that it is worth seeking a uniform treatment for some group of paradoxes because this would be a way to deal with all of them with a minimum of resources. This is especially pressing when we are dealing with paradoxes for the fact that paradoxes involve very plausible but incompatible claims implies that a high price will have to be paid in order to treat them; we might have to eventually abandon some of the core intuitions with respect to some of the concepts involved (explicitly or implicitly) in the paradox. Hence, if we offer a single solution for some different paradoxes, we might have to pay the toll just once. In Dominic Hyde's words:

[H]aving paid the price thought necessary to accommodate the one paradox we achieve the virtue of having to pay no additional price to accommodate the other. (Hyde 2013)

Notice, though, that, in order to gain simplicity when dealing with several paradoxes and, hence, to reduce the amount of resources we need to live with them, we just need a single safe logico-semantic environment in which the paradoxes cannot arise (that is, a common treatment). But as we have seen, in principle, having a common solution (that is, having a common diagnosis) does not guarantee having a common treatment. Nevertheless, it might be thought that methodological points such as uniformity and simplicity still constitute a good reason for beginning the investigation into the search for a common solution.

In the second place, a certain group of paradoxes are sometimes taken to be *of the same kind* and, hence, they should be treated, it is claimed, in the same way. Graham Priest has put this idea in the form of a principle:[12]

Principle of Uniform Solution (PUS)

If a given collection of paradoxes are of the same kind, they should all have the same kind of solution.

Priest defends that PUS is a true principle and, as we will see, that the Liar and the Sorites are of the same kind. Both claims imply, then, that both paradoxes should have the same kind of solution.

Nicholas J.J. Smith (2000) has criticised PUS on the grounds that when some paradoxes are claimed to be of the same kind, what is really claimed is that they are of the same kind at a given level of abstraction: 'two objects can be of the same kind at some level of abstraction and of different kinds at another level of abstraction' (Smith 2000, p. 118). Consider the following sentences:[13]

(i) Bill loves Ben.
(ii) Bob loves Maisy.
(iii) Nancy is standing next to Susan.
(iv) The Earth orbits the Sun.

---

[12] See, for example, Priest (1994, p. 32) or Priest (1995, p. 166) (see also Chapter 7 in this volume, Section 7.10).
[13] The example is adapted from Smith (2000).

Are the facts described by them of the same type? It depends on the level of abstraction. At a low level of abstraction, all facts (i)–(iv) are of different type; they just involve different objects. At a further level of abstraction, though, (i) and (ii) are of the same type; that is, they are facts consisting of a person loving another person. At an even further level of abstraction, (i), (ii) and (iii) are facts of the same kind; they consist of pairs of persons instantiating a relation. Finally, at a high level of abstraction, all facts (i)–(iv) are of the same kind; they are all facts that consist of two objects instantiating a relation. Smith proposes to reformulate PUS so that '[p]aradoxes that share a characterisation at a certain level of abstraction should indeed have solutions which likewise share a characterisation at that level of abstraction' (Smith 2000, p. 119).

According to Priest, though, not all the levels of abstraction are equally important; PUS must be applied to the level of abstraction that takes into account 'the essence of the phenomenon' (Priest 2000, p. 124) and 'locates the underlying causes' (Priest 2000, p. 125) of their paradoxicality. Understood in this way, claims Priest, PUS seems a natural and reasonable principle; as a matter of fact, he claims, it is 'little more than a truism' (Priest 1995, p. 287). To my mind, PUS is indeed a truism if, understood at the level of abstraction intended by Priest, we interpret 'common solution' as 'common diagnosis'; for, then, PUS is just claiming that if two paradoxes share the same paradoxical nature (that is, they share the characterisation at the level of abstraction that captures their underlying paradoxical nature), they should be solved by pointing at this nature, that is, by the same diagnosis. Nevertheless, Priest interprets 'common solution' as 'common treatment' and, so understood, it is not clear at all that PUS is a truism any more. Indeed, in Section 10.3 we are going to explore Horwich's solution to the Sorites and the Liar which I claim can reasonably taken to be a common solution to both paradoxes that offers a common diagnosis but different treatments.[14]

In the next section we will see which are the main reasons we have in the literature for defending that the Sorites and the Liar are of the same kind.

10.2.3 The Liar and the Sorites

Several similarities between the Liar and the Sorites have been raised in the literature in order to support the claim that they are two paradoxes of the same kind (that is, they share the reason behind their paradoxical nature) and that, hence, they should be solved uniformly. Let us examine what I take to be the most important of these similarities.

First, Tappenden (1993) calls attention to the fact that one can decide somewhat arbitrarily the extension of both vague predicates and the truth predicate. One of the features of vague predicates is that their extensions can vary according to circumstances: we can increase in precision a vague predicate if it is necessary in a specific context. These increases in precision are, on the one hand, arbitrary; usually, when a certain context demands sharper

---

[14] Cf. Chapter 7 in this volume, fn. 40. Thanks to Elia Zardini for providing very helpful comments on this issue.

boundaries, we can choose them among a certain set of possibilities. But, on the other hand, not all increases in precision are equally valid. Tappenden proposes an example that will serve as an illustration of that. Suppose we introduce into English the predicate 'tung' whose use is governed only by these rules:

(i) 'tung' applies to anything of mass greater than 200 Kg.
(ii) 'tung' does not apply to anything of mass less than 100 Kg.

If we compare this predicate with 'heavy' we can see, first, that both behave in certain respects in the same way but, second, that they differ in one crucial respect; the idea is that, provided that all our understanding of 'tung' is given by (i) and (ii), we can increase its precision in such a way that, given two objects *a* and *b*, *b* heavier than *a* and both unsettled with respect to the predicate, *b* counts as non-tung while *a* counts as tung. We cannot increase the precision of 'heavy' in this way; if *b* is heavier than *a*, then our understanding of the predicate implies that if *a* is heavy so is *b*. We can say, then, as supervaluationists do, that a precisification (a way of precisifying a predicate) is admissible if the sharper boundaries drawn are acceptable according to the meaning of the predicate. As Tappenden proposes, these constraints on increases in precisions can be seen as assignments of truth values to sentences and the latter example suggests that one of the collections of constraints on precision is one whose members can be formulated thus:

(*) Never make 'heavy' more precise in such a way that the sentence 'If *a* is heavy, so is *b*' become false.[15]

Now, Tappenden's point is that something similar happens in the case of truth. Tappenden claims that the same kind of arbitrariness that can be found in vagueness can also be found when we try to determine the extension of the truth predicate. Specifically, Tappenden mentions the Truth-teller, the sentence τ which is identical to its own truth ascription:

(τ) τ is true.

Notice that we can equally consistently assign τ and its negation to the extension of truth. This shows, according to Tappenden, that the extension of the truth predicate, as in the case of the vague predicates, can, in some cases, be arbitrarily decided. Again, only some of these ways of making truth precise will be admissible according to some constraints that, as in the case of vagueness, can be formulated as assignments of truth values to sentences similar to (*), for instance:

(**) Never make 'true' more precise in such a way that the sentence "'snow is white' is true if, and only if, snow is white' becomes false.

In the second place, another important similarity between vagueness and truth that has been stressed in the literature is the fact that in both cases some or other kind

---

[15] Cf. the notion of *penumbral connection* in Fine (1975).

of indeterminacy is involved. This idea can be found in many places, for example McGee (1991), Tappenden (1993), Field (2003b, 2008), Priest (2010a) and Hyde (2013). The indeterminacy present in both vagueness and truth can have a semantic nature (e.g. in the case of Tappenden and Field), an epistemic nature (e.g. in Paul Horwich) or it can even be, in fact, overdetermination, as in the case of approaches to the paradoxes that defend the existence of truth value gluts; that is, sentences, such as the Liar and the borderline ascriptions of vague predicates, which are both true and false.[16]

In order to defend the claim that the Liar and the Sorites are of the same kind we can follow Graham Priest, and take the apparent instantiation of the same internal structure as a sufficient condition for being the same kind of paradox. Priest has defended that many paradoxes that involve self-reference (the Liar among them) have an apparent common underlying structure that is captured by what he calls 'the inclosure schema' (see, especially, Priest 1994, 1995). More recently, Priest (2010a) has defended that the Sorites also fits this schema. Let us present, first, the inclosure schema and then show how Priest defends that the Liar and the Sorites apparently satisfy it.

Inclosure Schema. There are two monadic predicates $\phi(x)$ and $\psi(x)$ and a one-place function $\delta(x)$ such that:

1. There exists a set Ω such that $\Omega = \{x : \phi(x)\}$ and $\psi(\Omega)$ (*Existence*);
2. If $X \subseteq \Omega$ and $\psi(X)$, then:

   (a) $\delta(X) \notin X$ (*Transcendence*);
   (b) $\delta(X) \in \Omega$ (*Closure*).

The first thing to notice is that if there are ϕ, ψ and δ satisfying 1 and 2, then the limit case where $X = \Omega$ produces a contradiction, for then, by Transcendence, $\delta(\Omega) \notin \Omega$ and, by Closure, $\delta(\Omega) \in \Omega$.

Next, we need to check whether both the Liar and the Sorites satisfy the inclosure schema. Consider the following interpretations for ϕ, ψ and δ:

- ϕ is the property of being true,
- ψ is the property of being definable (where x is definable if, and only if, x is referred to by a non-indexical noun-phrase),
- δ is the function that, given a definable set of sentences X, assigns to X a sentence $\delta(X)$ identical to $\delta(X) \notin X$.

With these interpretations, Ω is the set of all the true sentences, which is definable when there is a truth predicate in the language, so that Existence is satisfied. In order to check whether the clauses in 2 hold, suppose we have a definable set of sentences X such that $X \subseteq \Omega$. Then, $\delta(X)$ will be the sentence σ identical to $\sigma \notin X$.

---

[16] See Chapter 7 in this volume.

Now, what is essentially the Liar reasoning shows that Transcendence and Closure are satisfied. First, since $X \subseteq \Omega$ and Ω is the set of true sentences, all sentences in X must be true. But if σ were in X it would not be true, for σ says, precisely, that it is not in X. Hence, by *reductio*, $\sigma \notin X$, which shows that Transcendence holds. But if $\sigma \notin X$, this means that σ is true and, hence, that $\sigma \in \Omega$, which shows that Closure holds. The contradiction we obtain in the limit case, then, is $\delta(\Omega) \in \Omega \wedge \delta(\Omega) \notin \Omega$. Notice that since Ω is the set of all true sentences, σ is just claiming of itself that is not a member of the true sentences. Hence σ is just the Liar sentence and the contradiction we obtain from the inclosure schema is the conclusion of the Liar Paradox: the Liar sentence is true and not true. We conclude that the Liar Paradox is an inclosure paradox.

Let us turn now to the Sorites Paradox. In order to show that it is also an inclosure paradox, suppose $P(x)$ is a monadic vague predicate and $A = \{a_0, a_1, \ldots, a_n\}$ is a *Sorites series* for P; that is, Pa_0, $\neg Pa_n$ and, apparently, tolerance holds: for any x, $0 \le x < n$, if Pa_x then Pa_{x+1}.

Consider now the following interpretation of the inclosure schema:

- ϕ is the property P (restricted to A),
- ψ is a trivial property, say, self-identity,
- δ is the function that, given a set $X \subset \Omega$, assigns to X the first object $\delta(X)$ in A that is not in X.

Interpreting the inclosure schema that way, Ω is the collection of the objects in A that are P. Notice that $\Omega \ne \emptyset$, for at least $a_0 \in \Omega$ and, besides, $\Omega \subset A$, for $a_n \notin \Omega$. Ω clearly exists and, hence, Existence is satisfied. Take now any set $X \subset \Omega$. By definition of δ, $\delta(X) \notin X$, so that Transcendence is also satisfied. It just remains to show that $\delta(X) \in \Omega$. We have two options, if $X = \emptyset$, then $\delta(X) = a_0$ and, hence, $\delta(X) \in \Omega$ by definition of a_0. Second, if $X \ne \emptyset$, then $\delta(X) = a_{j+1}$, where $0 \le j < n$, such that $P(a_j)$. Then, by tolerance of P, we conclude that $a_{j+1} = \delta(X) \in \Omega$, so that Closure is also satisfied. In this case, the contradiction we obtain at the limit when $X = \Omega$ is, as before, $\delta(\Omega) \in \Omega \wedge \delta(\Omega) \notin \Omega$. Since Ω is the set of objects that are P, the contradiction we reach is that the first object in the sequence A that is not P (which is $\delta(\Omega)$) is P. According to Priest, therefore, both the Liar and the Sorites are inclosure paradoxes. That means, he claims, that they are of the same kind.[17]

We can also try to defend that the Liar and the Sorites are of the same kind by offering less direct reasons. Thus, following Colyvan (2009), we can say that the fact that some paradoxes behave similarly when attempts are made to solve them by either successful or unsuccessful treatments gives us a reason to think that they are of the same kind.

To see how this can be applied to the Liar and the Sorites, Colyvan (2009) proposes to consider the following example. Suppose we advance a solution to the Liar that uses truth value gaps. We do not need to know the details; it suffices to say that the solution claims that the Liar sentence is neither true nor false. Then we are in a situation where we have three semantic statuses for sentences: true, false and neither true nor false. Most

---

[17] For more discussion on this topic see Weber et al. (2014), Oms and Zardini (2017) and Chapter 7 in this volume, Section 7.10.

if not all the solutions to the Liar suffer from what are called 'revenge problems'. In this case, the revenge can be seen to come in the form of a certain sentence, usually called 'the strengthened Liar', whose construction will depend on the details of the theory used to cope with the original Liar. Even in the framework of a given theory, there might be several ways to construct such a sentence; when the theory posits truth value gaps as in our example, we can construct the strengthened Liar by defining a new predicate, 'determinately true', which collapses two of the semantic categories the solution is using. Consequently, the true sentences will be determinately true, but the false and the neither true nor false sentences will not be determinately true. Now, using a sentence that says of itself that it is not determinately true, we get into trouble again. Therefore, in the presence of solutions that use truth value gaps, the Liar behaves in such a way that new problems arise that stem from the definition of a new predicate that turns the tripartite division of the semantic statuses into a bipartite one.

Now, something analogous happens with the Sorites Paradox when the treatment used to solve it uses truth value gaps. Suppose we accommodate the borderline ascriptions of vague predicates by claiming that such ascriptions are neither true nor false. This implies, as in the case of the Liar, a tripartite division of semantic statuses: sentences can be true – the clear cases of application of the vague predicate in question, false – the clear countercases–, or neither true nor false – the borderline cases. The problem that emerges now, and that can be seen as analogous to the strengthened Liar, is higher-order vagueness; vague predicates apparently lack sharp boundaries not only between the clear cases and the clear countercases, but also between the clear cases and the borderline cases, and between the clear cases and the borderline cases of the borderline cases, and so on. At the first level (that is, the seeming lack of sharp boundaries between the clear cases and the borderline cases), given a certain vague predicate P we can produce a strengthened paradox by introducing a new predicate, 'determinately P', so that this new predicate, as in the case of truth, collapses two of the semantic categories the solution is using: clear cases of P will be determinately P but clear counter-cases and borderline cases of being P will not be determinately P. Then, although the use of truth value gaps avoided the sharp boundary between the objects that are P and the objects that are not P, we can now see that a new sharp boundary emerges between the objects that are determinately P and the objects that are not determinately P. The analogy thus established between the Liar and the Sorites, which shows that they behave similarly when treated by a solution that uses truth value gaps, can be taken as evidence for the conclusion that both paradoxes share the roots of their paradoxical nature. For when we reflect on the fact that they respond in a similar way to similar treatments, it might seem natural to suppose that the similar behaviour of the paradoxes in the presence of the treatments is rooted in one and the same cause. Hence, we might conclude that both paradoxes are of the same kind and, consequently, that they should receive a uniform solution.

So far we have seen some reasons to believe that the Liar and the Sorites are of the same kind, in the sense that the reason for their paradoxical nature is the same. We are going to see next one example of such a uniform solution, from Paul Horwich, which can be understood as offering a common diagnosis but different treatments.

10.3 Horwich on the Sorites and the Liar

10.3.1 Vagueness

Horwich defends an epistemic account of vagueness according to which vague predicates have sharp boundaries that we are not capable of knowing. Furthermore, he wants to preserve the law of excluded middle (LEM, which states that any claim of the form ϕ *or not* ϕ is true), which is seen as a basic law of thought, and, consequently, he claims, the principle of bivalence (which claims that every sentence is either true or false and not both) (see, for example, Horwich 1997, 2005). He needs, therefore, a theory of vagueness capable of accommodating all these features and of explaining the phenomenology of vagueness; that is, according to him, our tendency to be unwilling to apply both the predicate and its negation to certain objects while being aware of the fact that no further investigation could be of any usefulness.[18]

Horwich admits that the following claim is counterintuitive:

(*) vague predicates have sharp boundaries, that is, they divide the world into two sharp groups of things; the ones that have the property expressed by the predicate and the ones that haven't.

He claims, though, that in the presence of the Sorites Paradox only two reasonable responses are possible: abandon classical logic or accept (*). Since the former strategy is seen by Horwich as desperate, he proposes to follow the latter. Horwich's proposal for the Sorites, therefore, consists of denying the truth of the main inductive premise (N_{3T}):[19] since we must accept that vague predicates have sharp boundaries, we must accept, given a vague predicate P, that there is a first object a_i in the Sorites series used to construct the paradox such that $\neg Pa_i$; then we cannot but conclude that it is false that if Pa_{i-1} then Pa_i.[20]

But the intuition that vagueness is at odds with sharp boundaries is very strong and, if we try to solve the Sorites Paradox by positing sharp boundaries on vague predicates, we still need to explain why we have such a strong intuition. One of the main roots of our reluctance to accept sharp boundaries for vague predicates is the fact that it seems impossible to find them. But the fact that we are not able to find the sharp boundaries of vague predicates can be best explained, according to Horwich, by the fact that there are no such sharp boundaries. Horwich's response to this line of thought consists of an explanation of why we can't know where the sharp boundaries of our vague predicates are and, consequently, why we can't know the extensions of such predicates. Let us see how this account is articulated.

Horwich proposes to look at the fundamental regularities implicit in our linguistic practice that underlie our use of vague predicates. His proposal is to understand this fundamental regularity as 'approximated by a partial function [...] which specifies

---

[18] See Horwich (1997, p. 930).

[19] See 'The Sorites Paradox', in the introduction to this volume.

[20] Horwich (2005, pp. 85ff.) presents the Sorites Paradox so that the conclusion is the claim that vague predicates have sharp boundaries; that is, the negation of (N_{3LSB}). In this case then, he defends that we must accept the conclusion, even if it seems false.

the subjective probability of [the predicate's] applying as a function of the underlying parameter n (i.e. 'number of grains' for 'heap', 'number of dollars' for 'rich',...)' (Horwich 1997, p. 933). Such regularities, claims Horwich, explain all our uses of vague predicates; they are complete in the sense that any 'decision' (Horwich 1997, p. 934) about the borderline cases of a given vague predicate P has to be a consequence of the underlying partial function. Such a function is partial, according to Horwich, in the sense that no one who has a full grasp of the meaning of a given vague expression will 'confidently apply it to things that are identified as being in the middle range' (Horwich 2005, p. 94).[21] In any case, Horwich further claims that such functions have been implicitly acquired by exposure to sentences reflecting clear instances of P, of not-P, and of not so clear cases close enough to the clear ones.

The fact that these fundamental facts are functions that remain silent with respect to the application of the predicates to certain objects explains why we also must remain silent with respect to such applications; moreover, the fact that these fundamental facts are complete (they explain all our uses of vague expressions) explains why we are confident that acquiring new information will not solve the matter, which is, according to Horwich, the basic phenomenology underlying vagueness (see Horwich 1997, p. 930).

These considerations also explain why we cannot know whether borderline cases are in the extensions of vague predicates; the only way we can be justified in applying a given vague predicate to an object is via the fundamental facts underlying the vague predicate and that, as we have seen, is not possible. Hence, believing an ascription of a vague predicate to a borderline case will never be able to constitute knowledge.

We will not focus here on the virtues or defects of Horwich's account of vagueness; rather, we will investigate whether this approach can be applied to truth and the Liar, as Horwich himself seems to defend.[22]

10.3.2 Minimalism and the Liar

Horwich is a deflationist about truth, which means that, according to him, truth is not a genuine property; the truth predicate is not used to describe anything; true truth-bearers do not share any common property. Horwich's theory of truth, called 'Minimalism', follows the Wittgensteinian rule against overdrawing linguistic analogies; although for some predicates ('table', 'dog', etc.) it makes sense to inquire into the shared characteristics of the things to which they apply, for some others, such as the truth predicate, it does not. If it makes sense to seek some kind of underlying nature in the case of the former kind of predicates, it is because they are used to categorise reality; we cannot presuppose, though, that this is the function of the truth predicate. As a matter of fact, deflationists think that the truth predicate is just a semantic, or logical, device of disquotation, which gives us the resources to affirm infinite lots of sentences and which is in no need of metaphysical or epistemological

---

[21] See also Horwich (1997, pp. 933ff., 2005, p. 94, pp. 98ff.).

[22] For some discussion on Horwich's approach to vagueness see, for instance, Williamson (1997b) and Field (2010).

analysis.[23] In one way or another, deflationists think that asserting that something is true is equivalent to asserting this something itself. This idea about the closeness between a sentence and its truth ascription is usually captured by the T-schema which, in the case of Horwich, is applied to propositions:[24]

(T-schema) $< p >$ is true iff p.

Horwich has defended Minimalism in a number of places (see, especially, Horwich 1998b, 2001, 2010b). One of its main theses is that the instances of the T-schema are conceptually, explanatorily and epistemologically fundamental. In the first place, they are conceptually fundamental because they fix the meaning and implicitly define the truth predicate (Horwich 1998b, p. 145); this is so because the basic and fundamental regularity of use that determines the meaning of 'truth' (which is the concept of truth, for meanings are concepts, according to Horwich) is our disposition to accept all instances of the T-schema. In the second place, the instances of the T-schema are all we need in order to explain all our uses of 'true'; that is why they are explanatorily fundamental.[25] And, finally, the instances of the T-schema are epistemologically fundamental because they are 'immediately known' (Horwich 2010b, p. 36); they cannot be deduced from anything more basic. In other words, according to Horwich, the role of the T-schema with respect to the truth predicate is the same as the partial functions of Section 10.3.1 with respect to vague predicates.

In view of all this, it is not surprising that Horwich's theory of truth, Minimalism, contains as axioms all instances of the T-schema applied to propositions, and nothing else.[26]

Now, as we have shown, the proposition that asserts its own untruth (that is, the propositional version of the Liar) makes the theory consisting of just all instances of the T-schema

---

[23] According to Dummett (1959) this view originated with the work of the German philosopher Gottlob Frege (see, for instance, his 1918). A *locus classicus* for the view is Quine (1986). According to deflationists about truth I would typically be in need of affirming an infinite lot of sentences in situations where I want to express *blind agreement*: suppose I, for some reason, want to express my agreement with everything you said yesterday, even if I do not know exactly what you said. I can express this belief using the following infinite conjunction, where each ϕ_n is replaced by a sentence in the language:

> (If you said yesterday: 'ϕ_1', then ϕ_1) and (If you said yesterday: 'ϕ_2', then ϕ_2) and...

The truth predicate allows you to express this infinite conjunction with a single sentence:

> For every x, if you said yesterday: x, then x is true.

Or, plainly

> Everything you said yesterday is true.

For more details on deflationism about truth see, for instance, Armour-Garb and Beall (1996), Beall and Armour-Garb (2005a) and Burgess and Burgess (2011, chapter 3).

[24] The symbols '$<$' and '$>$' surrounding a given expression e produce an expression referring to the propositional constituent expressed by e. Thus, when e is a sentence, '$< e >$' means *the proposition that e*.

[25] This is an exaggeration; strictly speaking, we will need other theories besides the truth theory to explain all facts about truth, because some of these facts will involve other phenomena. As Horwich says, Minimalism 'provides a theory of truth that is a theory of nothing else, but which is sufficient, in combination with theories of other phenomena, to explain all the facts about truth' (Horwich 1998b, pp. 24–5).

[26] This characterisation is not completely accurate; first, not all instances of the T-schema will be in the theory because of Horwich's views on the Liar Paradox, as we will see; second, as Horwich admits, the theory should also have an axiom claiming that only propositions are bearers of truth (see Horwich 1998b, p. 23, fn. 7, p. 43).

inconsistent in classical logic. Until recently, Horwich's response to this problem had been very succinct. In Horwich (1998) he claims that the lesson the Liar teaches us is that not all the instances of the T-schema are to be included as axioms in the theory (Horwich 1998b, p. 42). Then, the minimalist theory of truth consists of a restricted collection of instances of the T-schema; only those that do not engender Liar-like paradoxes. Which of the instances of the T-schema should be removed, though, was left undetermined.

A proposal of a solution to the Liar based on the previous considerations has been made explicit by Armour-Garb (2004), Beall and Armour-Garb (2005b), Restall (2005) and, though succinctly, by Horwich himself (2010b). Beall, Armour-Garb and Restall have called it 'Semantic Epistemicism'. Horwich claims:

> [W]e can and should preserve the full generality of the law of excluded middle and the principle of bivalence: [The Liar] is either true or false. Of course we cannot come to know which of these truth values it has. For confidence one way or the other is precluded by the meaning of the word 'true' – more specifically, by the fact that its use is governed by the [T-schema] (subject to the above restrictions). Thus, just as it is indeterminate whether a certain vague predicate applies, or does not apply, to a certain borderline case (although certainly it does or doesn't), so (*and for the same reason*) it is indeterminate whether [The Liar] is true or whether it is false. (The emphasis is mine.) (Horwich 2010b, p. 91, fn. 11)

We can now state the two tenets of Semantic Epistemicism, the minimalist stance in the presence of The Liar:

1. The Liar is true or The Liar is false.
2. It is conceptually impossible to know whether The Liar is true or false.

Let us see the rationales for these two points.

First, 1 is an instance of the principle of bivalence. Horwich (1998b, p. 71) justifies this principle applied to all propositions in the following way. Define, first, falsity in terms of absence of truth:

$$< p > \text{ is false iff it is not the case that } < p > \text{ is true.}$$

Then, LEM gives us the desired result. For given a proposition p we have that p or not-p (LEM) and, hence, in particular when p is of the form q *is true*, we obtain that either q is true or it is not the case that q is true; that is, either q is true or q is false.[27]

The reasons for accepting 2 are closely related to our previous discussion of vagueness; as Horwich says in the quote above, the reasons why the truth value of the Liar is indeterminate are the same as in the case of vagueness. So, these reasons are rooted in the fact that the instances of the T-schema in the minimalist theory of truth are explanatorily fundamental with respect to the truth predicate in the same sense as the partial functions mentioned in the case of vagueness are explanatorily fundamental with respect to the vague predicates. In order to know the truth value of the Liar, we would need to be justified in ascribing

---

[27] Whether bivalence is available to Horwich is a contentious matter (see, especially, Beall and Armour-Garb 2005b, section 5, and Schindler 2018, section 4). For the sake of simplicity, in this chapter I will suppose that Horwich can overcome this difficulty.

the truth value in question to the Liar; and such justification can only stem from the Liar instance of the T-schema. However, since that instance is not within the minimalist theory, we cannot know its truth value. The impossibility of knowing the truth value of the Liar is caused, according to Horwich, by the meaning of 'true', which is the concept of truth, which is determined by its use; and that, in turn, is governed by the T-schema. That is why Horwich claims that the impossibility is conceptual.

At this point, it is natural to take Horwich's proposal as offering a common diagnosis for both the Liar and the Sorites: the meanings (concepts) of vague predicates and of the truth predicate are defective (in the first case, the relevant function governing the use of each vague predicate is partial and, in the second case, the collection of instances of the T-schema is restricted) and, given Horwich's theory of meaning, this defectiveness in the concepts in question causes a sort of epistemic indeterminacy when applied to certain objects. The paradoxes arise because we do not take this indeterminacy into account, together with the fact that, given LEM, either the predicates or their negation must apply to these objects. This explains why, in the case of the Liar, the relevant instance of the T-schema is false and, in the case of the Sorites, (N_{3T}) and (N_{3LSB}) are also false.

Notice that there is no treatment required in the case of the Sorites Paradox, for we just accept that vague predicates have sharp boundaries and classical logic is fully preserved. On the other hand, the treatment for the Liar is more complex; according to Horwich, it requires a transfinite fixed-point construction which we are going to briefly present in the next section.

10.3.3 The Liar

As we have seen, Horwich's strategy for the Liar consists of restricting the instances of the T-schema that constitute the minimalist theory of truth so that no paradox can be formulated; what I called above 'the paradoxical instances of the T-schema' must be ruled out of the truth theory. Then, though, a natural question arises: which instances of the T-schema are to count as paradoxical? Horwich (1998b, p. 42) proposes two conditions that this restriction should meet:

Maximality Instances of the T-schema cannot be excluded unnecessarily; the minimal theory of truth should be, if possible, a maximal consistent collection of instances of the T-schema.

Specification There must be a constructive specification of the instances of the T-schema excluded from the minimal theory of truth. Such specification should be as simple as possible.

Unfortunately, though, McGee (1992) showed that Maximality is not enough to determine which instances of the T-schema should be included in the minimalist theory; given any consistent set Δ of sentences, there is a maximal consistent set Γ of instances of the T-schema which entails each one of the sentences in Δ.

Hence, given two incompatible consistent sets of sentences Δ_1 and Δ_2 we can find two maximal consistent sets of instances of the T-schema Γ_1 and Γ_2 such that the former entails every member of Δ_1 and the latter entails every member of Δ_2. Hence, if we are just looking for maximal consistent sets of instances of the T-schema we have no way of choosing between Γ_1 and Γ_2, although they are incompatible.[28] What this means is that 'the mere desire to preserve as many instances of [the T-schema] as possible will give us too little to go on in constructing' (McGee 1992, p. 237) the minimalist theory of truth.

As Gauker (1999) claims, it is not difficult to devise a particular case of McGee's result that might be intuitively easier to grasp. Consider these two sentences:

(λ_1) λ_2 is true.
(λ_2) λ_1 is not true.

They can easily be shown to be paradoxical as follows:

1.	λ_1 is true	Supposition
2.	'λ_2 is true' is true	Identity
3.	λ_2 is true	λ_1-instance of the T-schema
4.	'λ_1 is not true' is true	Identity
5.	λ_1 is not true	λ_2-instance of the T-schema
6.	λ_1 is not true	*Reductio* 1 and 5
7.	'λ_1 is not true' is true	λ_2-instance of the T-schema
8.	λ_2 is true	Identity
9.	'λ_2 is true' is true	λ_1-instance of the T-schema
10.	λ_1 is true	Identity
11.	Contradiction	6 and 9

The instances of the T-schema we used in this argument are the λ_1-instance (steps 3 and 9) and the λ_2-instance (steps 5 and 7). Clearly it is enough to remove one of them in order to avoid the paradox generated by λ_1 and λ_2. But the Maximality principle above does not tell us which one we are supposed to remove; so, supposing for a moment that λ_1 and λ_2 are the only sentences in our language that can generate a paradox, we would have two equally good maximal consistent sets of instances of the T-schema and no way of deciding which one constitutes our truth theory.

Future contingents and Curry's Paradox give us another example of a situation in which maximality alone fails to determine a unique set of instances of the T-schema.[29] Take the sentences

(s_1) Tomorrow there will be a sea battle
(s_2) Tomorrow there will not be a sea battle

---

[28] See McGee (1992) and Weir (1996) for more details on McGee's proof.
[29] Thanks to Elia Zardini for suggesting this example.

which are incompatible in the sense that they cannot be true at the same time. Now consider Curry's Paradox (see Section 10.1) for each one of them; with the aid of Curry's reasoning we will be able to conclude (s_1) and (s_2), which would allow us to conclude a contradiction. But one of (s_1) or (s_2) will be the case and hence, it could be argued, it would be safe to conclude it. This means that we should remove the instance of the T-schema of the (s_i) that will not be the case; clearly, then, maximality is not enough to determine which instance is to be kept.

Hence, we are led to the second condition above: we need to be able to specify, with the use of a constructive specification, a particular consistent set of instances of the T-schema (which might or might not be maximal).

Horwich has tried to overcome the difficulties posed by the Liar Paradox to his theory of truth by offering (2010a) a construction that, although not maximal, would follow a constructive specification. Let us quote the full text:

> We might say that our language L is the limit of the expanding sub-languages L_0, L_1, L_2,... where L_0 lacks the truth predicate; L_1 (which contains L_0) applies it, via the equivalence schema, to the grounded propositions of L_0; similarly, L_2 applies it to the grounded propositions of L_1; L_3 applies it to the grounded propositions of L_2; and so on. Thus an instance of the equivalence schema will be acceptable, even if it governs a proposition concerning truth (e.g. <What John said is true>), as long as the proposition is grounded.

> But which propositions of L_0, L_1, L_2, etc. are the grounded ones? They are those that are rooted, as follows, in the *non*-truth-theoretic *facts*. Within L_0, a proposition is grounded just in case the non-truth-theoretic facts either entail that proposition or entail its negation; thus *all* the propositions of L_0 are grounded. Within L_1, a proposition is grounded just in case it, or its negation, is entailed by a combination of those L_0-grounded facts and the (truth-theoretic) facts of L_1 that are 'immediately' entailed by them via the just legitimised instances of the equivalence schema (which are its applications to the grounded propositions of L_0). Similarly, within L_2, a proposition is grounded just in case it, or its negation, is entailed by a combination of those L_1-grounded facts and the facts of L_2 that are 'immediately' entailed by them via the just legitimised instances of the equivalence schema (which are its applications to the grounded propositions of L_1). And so on. (Horwich 2010a, p. 90)

Horwich thus describes a construction similar to the one proposed in Kripke (1975) and takes the grounded sentences to be the ones whose instances of the T-schema constitute the minimalist theory of truth.[30] The construction can be formalised as in Schindler (2015) in the following way. We begin with the set of true sentences in the language without the truth predicate; let us call this set H_0. Then we take all the sentences that logically follow from H_0 together with the instances of the T-schema of each sentence ϕ such that either ϕ or $\neg\phi$ are in H_0; let us call this set of instances of the T-schema T_{H_0} and the resulting set of sentences H_1. The step from H_0 to H_1 can be generalised to any ordinal σ, so that $H_{\sigma+1} = \{\phi : H_\sigma \cup T_{H_\sigma} \models \phi\}$. Finally, we define the construction on the limit ordinals so that, given a limit ordinal λ, we just collect all the sentences in the previous stages of the construction: $H_\lambda = \bigcup_{\alpha<\lambda} H_\alpha$.

---

[30] This already raises some doubts about whether a deflationist can use the notion of groundedness in order to specify its theory of truth. We may think of this construction, though, as a mere technicality. See Oms (2018b, section 6) for some discussion on this point.

The construction thus defined can be shown to have a fixed point; that is, it can be shown that there is an ordinal ρ where the series stabilises: $H_\rho = H_{\rho+1}$.[31] Let us call this fixed point $\boldsymbol{H}$. Then, according to Horwich, we can take as the minimalist theory of truth $T_{\boldsymbol{H}}$; that is, all the instances of the T-schema of all the sentences such that they or their negation are in the fixed point $\boldsymbol{H}$.

There are several problems, though, with $\boldsymbol{H}$ as it stands. The main one is that it can be shown that this fixed point is reached at the first limit ordinal; that is, $\boldsymbol{H} = H_\omega$,[32] which means that it will not contain any non trivial truth-theoretic generalisation such as, for example, 'any sentence of the form $\phi \rightarrow \phi$ is true', in spite of the fact that it may contain all its particular instances.[33] It remains to be seen whether the construction can be strengthened in order to obtain a richer fixed point and also whether this stronger construction can be justified from a deflationist point of view.[34],[35]

---

[31] This is a direct consequence of set-theoretical considerations together with the fact that the construction is monotonic, that is, for any ordinals τ and ρ, if $\tau \leq \rho$, then $H_\tau \subseteq H_\rho$.

[32] See *Proposition 1* in Schindler (2018).

[33] This is so because in general the instances of a universal statement do not imply the universal statement itself. As a matter of fact, this is a variant of a more general problem for Minimalism: since the minimalist theory is just a collection of instances of the T-schema, it cannot account, at least in principle, for general facts about truth. For more details, responses and rejoinders on this issue see Tarski (1983, p. 257), Gupta (1993a,b), Soames (1997, 1999), Armour-Garb (2004, 2010), Raatikainen (2005), Horwich (1998, p. 137), Horwich (2010b, pp. 43–5, 92–6) and Oms (2018a).

[34] For more details see Schindler (2018) and Oms (2018b).

[35] Thanks to Dan López de Sa and José Martínez Fernández for all their help, extremely valuable comments and suggestions. And, especially, to Elia Zardini, for all his extremely helpful comments and support. During the writing of this chapter, I have benefited from the Project FFI2015-70707P of the Spanish Ministry of Economy, Industry and Competitiveness on *Localism and Globalism in Logic and Semantics*.

11   The Sorites Paradox in Metaphysics

İrem Kurtsal

11.1 Introduction

Sorites-style arguments have appeared in influential discussions about ordinary objects, personal identity, modality, composition and parthood, and persistence through time, as well as in discussions about modality, phenomenal colours, looking the same and the nature of species.[1] In this chapter, I focus on the former group of issues, and present a picture of some of the strategies available for those who find it compelling to affirm the existence of ordinary objects and people, composed of material parts. Two main lines of argument influenced by or based on the Sorites Puzzle have been widely discussed in metaphysics; the first is Peter Unger and Mark Heller's arguments against the existence of ordinary objects and persons, and the second is David Lewis and Ted Sider's arguments for Unrestricted Composition and Diachronic Plenitude. After I present those arguments, first I show how a certain compelling type of response to Unger and Heller's soritical critiques of the standard ontology comes with surprising metaphysical commitments. Second, I argue that contrary to what is often stated, embracing Lewis and Sider's conclusions does not guarantee the existence of ordinary objects and persons; I show what more needs to be established for there to be ordinary objects and persons. Thirdly, I lay out what difference it makes when soritical reasoning is used critically about ordinary object categories, as opposed to more generic categories such as composite object; the upshot is that what I call 'the attributive strategy' is available in responding to the Sorites in the domain of a specific category (e.g. chair) but not in the domain of a generic category (e.g. composite object). If being a composite object is construed as a specification of a more generic entity (such as spacetime regions) then the attributive strategy can be invoked in response to Lewis' and Sider's arguments as well as Unger's and Heller's. My survey ends with brief discussions of views on which composition and persistence facts are autonomous from base level facts, and views that invoke ontic vagueness to block the Sorites.

---

[1] Ordinary objects: Unger (1979b); personal identity: Unger (1979a; 1979c), Parfit (1984); composition and parthood: Lewis (1986), van Inwagen (1990), Sider (2001); persistence!through time: Heller (1990), Sider (2001); modality: Chisholm (1967, 1973), Forbes (1983, 1984, 1986), Heller (1990, pp. 72–4), Leslie (2011), Salmon (1986), Wallace (2014), Williamson (1990); phenomenal colours: Hardin (1998); looking the same: Fara (2001); species: Simons (2013). Vagueness in causation (Torrago 2000) also seems Sorites-susceptible.

11.2 The Value of Sorites Arguments in Metaphysics

When the ground of a vague category admits of minute changes, we can get a Sorites argument going. Therefore, it shouldn't be surprising to find them in virtually every domain of philosophy. Since there are several solutions to the Sorites Paradox on offer, it might be thought that Sorites-related metaphysical disputes are not about distinctively metaphysical puzzles. But there are at least four reasons why this expectation is naïve. First, a standard solution can have different ramifications in different domains of philosophy, and so have distinctively metaphysical ramifications in metaphysics. Secondly, as we will see, a standard solution applied to different Sorites-related arguments about different ontological categories can yield wildly different outcomes (you can get a feel for this difference by reflecting on the difference between the ideas 'a borderline instance of chair' and 'a borderline instance of persistence'). Thirdly, some standard solutions are metaphysical by nature, most notably the view that aspects of the world can be ontically indeterminate. Fourthly, some standard solutions imply that certain surprising metaphysical facts obtain. E.g. Timothy Williamson's epistemicist solution[2] would work for analysing the vagueness of 'bicycle' only if there are things that are almost-bicycles – a kind of object that we would not find listed in a conservative ontological inventory. Fifthly, applications of Sorites in metaphysics are not paradoxes, but (alleged) proofs. They demand acceptance of various conclusions, such as eliminativism about a category, or a revolutionary metaphysics of it.

11.3 Ordinary Objects, Persons and the Sorites Puzzle

Peter Unger (1979b), whose work is also discussed in Chapter 4 of this volume, Section 4.6, has argued that there are no 'such things as pieces of furniture, rocks and stones, planets and ordinary stars, and even lakes and mountains'; in other words, there are no ordinary things:

Finitude: For anything there may be, if it is a stone, then it consists of finitely many atoms

and

Tolerance: For anything there may be, if it is a stone, then the net removal of one atom, or only a few, will not mean the difference as to whether there is a stone in the situation.[3]

Therefore, nothing is a stone.

For if something were a stone, then we could remove atoms from it one by one, and by *Tolerance* every resulting situation would have to contain a stone. But by *Finitude* the situation where there are no atoms left cannot contain a stone. Since it would be a

---

[2] See Chapter 1 in this volume, Section 1.2.
[3] Cf. 'The Sorites Paradox', in the introduction to this volume.

contradiction for that situation to both contain a stone and not contain a stone, we must reject the assumption that led us to it. So, nothing is a stone. Of course, the argument generalises to all ordinary objects (Unger 1979b, pp. 120–1).

Now, if matter is gunky (containing no simples as parts),[4] then *Finitude* is false. Note, however, that in that case the argument can be restated by replacing references to *atoms* in *Finitude* and *Tolerance* with talk of some tiny units (let's say specks) such that our would-be stone is divisible into a finite number of them.[5]

There are situations with so few atoms or specks in them that they contain no stone. But if the relevant version of *Finitude* is true, then we can get to those situations because of *Tolerance*. These ideas regulate our ordinary object concepts. Yet, when taken jointly, they are inconsistent with the existence of those ordinary objects.

Unger's attack is not against the diachronic identity of ordinary objects. It is not that *that stone with which we started out* is no longer present at the situation where there are no atoms (though that's surely also the case), but rather that without some atoms there isn't a stone at all. Mark Heller argues against the existence of ordinary objects in 'our standard ontology', including 'tables, mountains, trees, or people' (1988, p. 112) both in the way Unger does, but also by giving a Sorites argument featuring a particular individual object and its identity over time (1990, p. 72). We begin with a table named Charlie. We remove a chip from Charlie, where a 'chip' is defined as a one cubic millimetre hunk of matter. Standard ontology would have us accept 'Charlie will survive the loss of a single chip' (*Tolerance*). Clearly, though, when we have only one chip, or no chips left, Charlie is no longer there. Heller's diagnosis is that our standard ontology demands that Charlie go out of existence in a gradual, vague way, but that is impossible.

It would be naïve to think that the argument applies only to sticks and stones but doesn't harm us. As both Unger and Heller are keen to point out, it also works against a most cherished kind of ordinary object, *person*. Heller counts people among the members of the standard ontology he renounces, and Unger (1979a, 1979c) develops Sorites arguments explicitly against persons. It is easy to see why the problem easily generalises: person-versions of *Tolerance* and *Finitude* are readily acceptable. And even if persons are not made out of atoms, (or specks, or chips), then as long as whatever matters for personhood (either for *being a person* or for *being the same person as x*) admits of minute gradations and can be found to be present to an insufficient degree, the Sorites can be generated against persons. Consider a Sorites series of pairs where the degree to which members of pairs are continuous (in respect of psychology, physical make up or a mixture of both) starts out very high and dwindles to nothing at the end of the series. Because of *Tolerance* regarding personal identity, there cannot be a diving line where one pair are identical and the next pair are distinct persons (Parfit 1984, chapter 11, parts 84–6).

---

[4] Matter is 'gunky' if, and only if, everything has proper parts, ad infinitum. While everything trivially counts as a part of itself, '*proper* part' means 'part that isn't identical to the whole'.

[5] The only other way for *Finitude* to be false is if there is a stone that is infinitely large. If we weaken the conclusion to allow for this possibility, we still get something very close to eliminativism about stones: the only stones there are, if any, are infinitely large ones.

The general tract of these Sorites applications is to show that Sorites-susceptible concepts are necessarily empty (Unger 1979a, p. 210).[6] However, not only sortal or kind concepts (*chair*, *mountain* or *person*) are in this predicament, but also attributive concepts such as *tall* or *bald*. This should be obvious since, as Unger rightly notes, we cannot rescue ordinary objects from the Sorites by maintaining that they are not substances but phases of other things, the way childhood is a phase of a human being.[7] Suppose that predicates such as 'stone' are disguised phase sortals like 'child'. If the concept *stone* has incoherent application conditions, it hardly matters if it is a substance concept or a phase sortal (Unger 1979b, p. 137). By the same token, Sorites-susceptible attributive concepts should also be necessarily empty! Then there cannot be bald things or thin things. It might be thought that if Unger's argument is sound, then the substances in which baldness or thinness are to inhere wouldn't exist anyway. However, Unger's argument doesn't eliminate all objects: sums, hunks, quantities of matter or particles with precise conditions of identity abound. With a consistent application of eliminativism for all that would fall under Sorites-susceptible concepts, it should follow that none of these physical objects have the properties of being near the North Pole, large, voluminous, fast, etc.[8] This opens the path to charge Heller and Unger with having offered self-defeating arguments. Virtually all of the non-logical predicates in their works are vague! 'The **reasoning here** is **simple**. **Consider** a **stone**, **consisting** of a certain finite number of atoms. If **we** or some **physical process** should **remove**, one atom, without **replacement**, then . . .' (1979b, p. 120). If none of the bold words have application, then no reasoning was given at all. If the argument were sound, it couldn't have existed as *stated* (Williamson 1994, chapter 6.2). Since we did understand the argument, we should be encouraged to think that vague terms *can* do at least part of their job.

There are various solutions on offer for the Sorites Paradox, and in one way or another they all purport to deliver at least the following result: vague concepts can apply in some cases while failing to apply in others. Every account of vagueness will be more in tune with common sense than that there are no ordinary objects or persons. Take Roy Sorensen's version of epistemicism, which comes closest to Heller and Unger in acknowledging how messed up our situation is vis-à-vis vague concepts. Sorensen '*tollenses*' Unger's *modus ponens*: since we know that applications of *Tolerance* would clash with *Finitude*, we must infer that *Tolerance* has to have one false instance.[9] Hence the universal closure of the schema, *Tolerance* (for stones), is false. However, competent users of the concept *stone* are bound to believe and accept every single particular instance of the schema, including

---

[6] Of course, when an ordinary object concept is necessarily empty, this is not just a conceptual matter (whatever that might mean) but also an ontological one. Thus, Heller is careful to emphasise that his arguments primarily concern not the words or concepts of ordinary objects but the would-be objects themselves (1988, pp. 110–1.)

[7] Nothing goes out of existence when a child becomes an adolescent is the thought.

[8] All these concepts have similarly incoherent application conditions. E.g. *Tolerance* for 'large': If something is large, the removal of one atom doesn't result in something that is not large. *Intolerance* for 'large': largeness is not had by those things that have too few non-overlapping atoms.

[9] This is to say that, for a certain value of n, 'If a stone has n-many atoms and one of those atoms is removed, then the resulting situation doesn't contain a stone' must be false.

the false one. Understanding the concept requires this. So, our predicament is a priori (Sorensen 2001, pp. 57–67). But, given the 'tollensing' argument we just saw, even if vague concepts are incoherent we don't have to accept conclusions of Sorites arguments. Here we have a Moorean response to Unger's and Heller's arguments.

Unger's and Heller's arguments are straightforward applications of the Sorites Puzzle with *stone* for *heap*, which is why it is reasonable to expect that a standard solution to the puzzle should be sufficient to address it. However, as I stated earlier and will explain below, even semantic solutions have ontological ramifications. But first, we should examine another major Sorites-type reasoning in metaphysics, the case for Unrestricted Composition that was first articulated by David Lewis and brought to its fullest form and extended to the philosophy of persistence by Ted Sider.

11.4 The Argument from Vagueness for Universal Composition

Suppose we have some material objects (precisely individuated particles, if you prefer). Peter van Inwagen (1990, chapter 2) asked the 'Special Composition Question' (SCQ), *Given some material objects, what does it take for them to compose something?* Commonsensically, it seems things make up a composite whole only when they fulfil certain conditions: perhaps they must be conjoined and be disposed to move together. But this criterion is a vague one; some bits are sort of conjoined but sort of aren't, or they are sort of moving together but sort of aren't. Moreover, being conjoined and moving together isn't sufficient for composing a whole; a random subdivision of a sofa, for example, is hardly thought to be a composite object in its own right. David Lewis observed that our intuitive criteria of composition are vague, so there is no precise criterion of composition which is also appealing to common sense (Lewis 1986, pp. 211–2). The only reasonable way for a criterion of composition to be precise is for it to be maximally permissive, so that composition is not restricted by the criterion at all. According to this proposal, it takes nothing special for two or more things to compose something; the members of any collection, regardless of how they are related (or unrelated), compose something. E.g. there is something composed of the apple on my desk and the last book you read. This is known as Unrestricted Composition (UC). Against the charge that UC goes against common sense, Lewis makes the case that common sense judgments feature implicit restrictions of our quantifiers (pp. 212–3). If I say 'Everything in this store is larger than the trunk of my car', it is understood that I mean to exclude the cash register.[10] So I don't mean everything in this store, but 'everything in this store *normally for sale*'. If UC is true, many more composite objects lie in the difference set of everything and everything normally for sale; for example, the sum of the legs of all the chairs. If I declare, 'Nothing in this store is large enough to cover me,' it is understood that the wall-to-wall carpet does not falsify my claim, because my quantifier is implicitly restricted with 'single piece of clothing.' Similarly, the sum of

---

[10] In this example and the next, there is also an *explicit* restriction on the quantifier, namely, 'in this store'.

the bandanas does not falsify my claim, even though UC entails that it too exists. UC is consistent with our day-to-day claims about what there is or isn't, because the unusual sums it countenances typically lie outside our restricted day-to-day quantifiers.

But couldn't the right answer to the SCQ leave matters vague? Why is the vagueness of the intuitive criteria a deciding factor for finding those criteria unacceptable? The idea is, vague intuitive desiderata for being composite cannot be satisfied unless there is a vague restriction on composition.[11] But a vague restriction on composition is not tenable since there cannot be borderline cases of composition. This is because, says Lewis, it cannot be that for some objects, it sort of is the case and sort of not the case that they have a sum (pp. 212–13).

So composition itself cannot be vague. And 'the only intelligible account of vagueness' (p. 212), the semantic account, cannot be invoked to make sense of 'composite' being vague. According to this view, supervaluationism,[12] vagueness consists in our semantic indecision about which of a multiplicity of precise candidate meanings, which have been called 'precisifications', is the referent or extension of a given term. Sentences that are true (false) on every precisification are determinately true (false), while sentences that are true on some but not all precisifications are indeterminate (Fine 1975; Williamson 1994, pp. 142–64). It follows that only terms with multiple precisifications can be vague. But for a putatively vague case of composition, that composition occurs (or that it doesn't) can be expressed with a sentence which doesn't feature any words that can have multiple precisifications. Lewis indicates that in addition to the connectives, quantifiers and 'is part of' lack multiple precisifications. In the absence of any room for semantic vagueness, such a sentence has to have a determinate truth-value (Lewis 1986, p. 212).

While Lewis's argument doesn't explicitly feature a Sorites series, Ted Sider presents a variation on this argument which does. By a 'case of composition' let us mean a possible situation containing a class of objects under consideration as to whether they compose a sum. Let Φ be a complex determinable property combining the factors intuitively salient for composition to occur; 'all respects that might be relevant to whether composition occurs: qualitative homogeneity, spatial proximity, unity of action, comprehensiveness of causal relations, etc.' (Sider 2001, p. 123). A 'continuous series of cases' will be a finite Sorites spectrum, gathered from any possible worlds, ordered under the relation '___ is less Φ than ___'. The argument then goes:

[11] Nolan (2006) shows a way to reject this premise. It is possible for there to be a precise restriction on composition (and so it is possible for 'composite' to be precise) without any violation of our vague desiderata. Our desiderata are necessary conditions and sufficient conditions that do not amount to a full analysis with individually necessary and jointly sufficient conditions. While composition is always a determinate matter and occurs in some but not all candidate cases, it is possible that each intuitive necessary condition as well as each intuitive sufficient condition of composition is upheld. I am not convinced that this point is enough to justify rejecting Lewis's premise. Some of the intuitive necessary (or sufficient) conditions seem to me to *demand indeterminacy of composition* and cannot be fully upheld without it. For example, intuitively, being stuck together is sufficient for composing something. It is not clear to me that in a situation where this sufficient condition is borderline met but composition that occurs, that intuition is satisfied the same way it would be if the composition occurred in that situation were (somehow) indeterminate.

[12] See Chapter 2 in this volume.

P1: If not every class has a sum, then there must be a pair of cases connected by a continuous series such that in one composition occurs, but in the other composition does not occur.

P2: In no continuous series is there a sharp cut off in whether composition occurs.

P3: In any case of composition, either composition definitely occurs or composition definitely does not occur.

Therefore, every class has a sum (Sider 2001, pp. 123–5).

P1 is true only if composition occurs in at least some cases. That is to say, nihilism about composition (eliminativism about composites) is rejected from the outset. Sider has a separate case against nihilism; it is inconsistent with the empirical possibility that all matter is divisible into parts ad infinitum (pp. 179–80). If there are any cases where composition doesn't occur, then we can form a series of Φ-wise similar cases starting with a positive case of composition and ending with a negative one.

P2 is about what happens somewhere in the middle of our series; what is the transition from positive to negative like? P2 says that if two cases are only minutely different with respect to how Φ they are, then they cannot be different with respect to composition. Sider's defence of P2 goes like this. A minute difference in Φ-ness cannot matter for composition, because if it did, then the difference between a case of composition and a case of non-composition would be 'autonomous' from the difference in the Φ properties. Granted, composition facts would still supervene on those properties, but there would not be sufficient difference between two potential cut-offs to *explain* why the difference in composition facts occur where they did. 'Why is the cut-off here, rather than there?' Sider asks. Even if there is a restriction on composition but it doesn't have a finite or informative statement – and is, to that extent, brute – it is still implausible for extremely similar cases to differ in this respect (p. 124). P2 precludes an abrupt transition in composition facts from one case in the series to the next.

It could be thought that epistemicists following Williamson can maintain a sharp cut-off from a definite positive case of composition to a definite negative one in our series, but this is not accurate. If adopted, this would amount to giving the following explanation for why the sudden difference in composition facts occurs at *that* point of minutest difference in the base facts: 1) There is a multiplicity of cut-off candidates on our series any of which might, for all we know, match the exact semantic value (referent or extension) of 'composite',[13] 2) none of them is naturally more eligible to be the content of 'composite' than any of the others, 3) exactly one of them is really the cut-off, in virtue of our (occurrent and dispositional) use of 'composite' and its cognates, and 4) slight shifts in this use, which would have resulted in a corresponding shift in semantic value (about the cut-off is), are not detectable by us. 1–4, together with some plausible epistemic principles, yield the consequence that truths regarding a cut-off point and its vicinity are

---

[13] These candidate semantic values can usefully be thought of as akin to the supervaluationist's precisifications.

not knowable by us (Williamson 1994, chapters 7–8 and Chapter 1 in this volume, Section 1.2.).[14]

Here is the problem with invoking this explanation. Suppose that on Sider's Sorites spectrum for composition there are a couple of cases flanking a sharp cut-off that differ; to the right of the cut-off is a composite object, z, but to the left of it we have a case of failing to compose anything. Could z have been left out of the extension of 'composite', or could the case to the left have been in its extension as well as z? Not really: (except in its limiting cases) composition takes a multiplicity of objects a, b, c,... and makes an individual object o that is distinct from each of them. Thus, if existence facts cannot differ based on our linguistic behaviour, composition facts cannot either (Sider 2001, pp. 131–2). If Williamsonian epistemicism were used to maintain the sharp cut-off, this would amount to a sort of linguistic idealism.

While P2 precludes an abrupt transition, P3 is the premise that addresses and vitiates any other possibility for the transition: there are no borderline cases or gradations of composition. To support it, Sider argues, after Lewis, that there are no vague cases of composition, because if there were, then a sentence which doesn't feature any words with multiple precisifications would have to be neither true nor false. Unlike Lewis, what Sider has in mind here isn't a sentence stating that there is something composed of two (or more) other things, but a different sentence, one whose truth depends on the outcome of the case of composition. Suppose there are two atoms and it is indeterminate whether they compose something. Then the 'numerical' sentence N, 'There are exactly two concrete things' will be neither true nor false. This sentence can be expressed using nothing other than logical terms and a predicate 'C' for concreteness:

$$N \quad (\exists x)(\exists y)(Cx \ \& \ Cy \ \& \sim x = y) \ \& \ (\forall z)(z = x \text{ or } z = y)$$

None of the parts of N can be vague, argues Sider (p. 127).[15]

If an unrestricted quantifier could be vague, it would have to have multiple precisifications, which is impossible, argues Sider. If there were multiple precisifications of the unrestricted quantifiers, they would have to differ in respect of the members of their domains. But then the quantifier whose domain lacks a member the other quantifier has cannot be an *un*restricted quantifier.[16] This argument is a bit quick (Koslicki 2003), so Sider pulls out heavier equipment against vague existence in Sider (2003).

---

[14] This is an application of Williamson's account of vagueness to 'composite'. Not to say that Williamson defends 1.4 for 'composite'.

[15] Since abstracta are presumably infinitely many, a numerical sentence expressing that there are exactly two things would be guaranteed to be false, which is why the focus is on concrete things and why we need that predicate 'C'. Even if 'concrete' is vague, presumably it isn't so in a way we cannot artificially bracket. E.g. if it is vague whether propositions are abstract or concrete, this would not make a difference to whether N is true or false (or indeterminate). Though, see Korman (2010, p. 893) for a possible way to exploit the vagueness of 'C'. Furthermore, if gunk is not only possible but necessary, then the likes of N are always false, making this sub-argument unsound.

[16] Barnes (2013) argues that the unrestricted quantifiers could be vague in this way: of two putative unrestricted quantifiers, one could be indeterminately a quantifier (but determinately unrestricted if a quantifier) while the other is indeterminately *un*restricted. This provides a way to defend metaphysically indeterminate existence from the objection that unrestricted quantifiers cannot be vague.

11.5 The Argument from Vagueness for Diachronic Plenitude

Perhaps the most groundbreaking development in recent philosophy of persistence was Sider's use of this model of argument to defend Diachronic Plenitude, on which he went on to build a case for the doctrine of temporal parts.[17]

In the entirety of our universe, throughout all time, which spacetime regions are home to the career of a single object? We can ask a version of this question in terms of the concept of composition. But we have to be careful here. We have considered the Special Composition Question. The diachronic version of the question could be thought of as querying the circumstances for some things to *diachronically* compose a further thing. It's natural to then think that composing diachronically should be a multigrade atemporal relation among things which exist at different times.[18] However, three-dimensionalists reject that objects can be in that relation, so they wouldn't even accept that there are some diachronically composite objects.

According to three-dimensionalism, objects relate to their temporal locations differently from how they relate to their spatial locations; they are not spread out in time the way they are spread out in space. They are wholly present at any moment they exist, as opposed to having distinct and disjoint parts at each of those moments. Diachronic composition can obtain only if the diachronically composite entity is appropriately stretched out across time; a three-dimensionalist might (have to) allow spacetime regions, events or processes to be such diachronic composites, but she does not accept that any *objects* are diachronic composites, having any *objects* as diachronic proper parts.[19]

For this reason, Sider takes care to formulate the temporal question and his proposed answer in terms of the notion of composition that is acceptable to both sides of that debate, namely, composition-at-a-time. Using this notion, let us define 'successive composition' as follows (Kurtsal Steen 2010, p. 80):

The Xs, the Ys, the Zs,...*successively compose* O $=_{df}$

(i) The Xs exist at t_1, the Ys exist at t_2, the Zs exist at t_3,..., and

(ii) t_1, t_2, t_3 are distinct, and

(iii) At t_1 O is composed of the Xs, at t_2 O is composed of the Ys, at t_3 O is composed of the Zs,..., and

(iv) O exists only at t_1, t_2, t_3,...

---

[17] According to Koslicki (2003, p. 111) the dialectic between three- and four-dimensionalism is at a stalemate, and the argument from vagueness 'seems to bear the burden of resolving the relative standoff between the two sides of the dispute over the nature of persistence'. According to Ned Markosian (2008, p. 665), it is 'the most important and powerful argument in [*Four-Dimensionalism*]'. Hudson (2002): 'an ingenious argument from vagueness which mirrors (after first improving upon) David Lewis's famous argument from vagueness for a principle of unrestricted composition (this particular defence, I should note, is really quite powerful and well presented – a genuine highlight of the book)'.

[18] UC would by itself provide the answer – since all classes of objects have sums, all classes whose members include objects from different times would have diachronic sums.

[19] Sometimes diachronic composition/parthood are called atemporal composition/parthood. This use comes from being able to drop the time index altogether. Wednesday is in the middle of the week; this relation between Wednesday and the week can be said to obtain atemporally, or *simpliciter*. Unmarriedness is part of bachelorhood. Presumably this is also an atemporal relation, but not one apt to be called diachronic. Three-dimensionalists as such do not have commitments about whether objects (especially abstract objects) can have atemporal parts in that last sense.

The things that successively compose an object are all that make it up throughout the times it persists. Now we can ask, *Given some objects located at various different times, what does it take for them to successively compose a persisting thing?* Let us call this the Temporal Composition Question (TCQ). To defend his answer to this question, Sider applies the same argument pattern as the one he uses for UC.

(P1') If not every filled spacetime region contains an object that persists exactly through that region, then there must be a pair of putative cases of successive composition connected by a continuous series such that in one, successive composition occurs (there is a persisting thing) and in the other successive composition doesn't occur (there isn't a persisting thing).

(P2') In no continuous series is there a sharp cut-off in whether successive composition occurs.

(P3') In any putative case of successive composition, either the objects definitely successively compose a persisting thing or the objects definitely fail to successively compose a persisting thing.

Therefore,

Every filled spacetime region contains an object that persists exactly[20] through that region (adapted from Sider 2001, p. 135).

We will call the conclusion Diachronic Plenitude (DP); a more thorough statement of it goes like this:

(DP) For any non-empty set S_t of times $t_1, \ldots, t_n$ and any non-empty sets of objects $S_1, \ldots, S_n$ such that the members of S_1 exist at $t_1 \ldots$ and the members of S_n exist at t_n, some x is such that: (a) x exists at each of the times in S_t (b) x overlaps at t_1 every member of S_1 and every part at t_1 of x overlaps at t_1 at least one member of $S_1, \ldots, x$ overlaps at t_n every member of S_n and every part at t_n of x overlaps at t_n at least one member of S_n, and (c) x exists only at the times in S_t.

Before we go on to examine the case for DP, let us examine its alleged significance for persistence through time. Sider argues that DP entails that every object has a temporal part at every moment it exists. Consider some times $t_1 \ldots t_3$. Take an object O_1 that exists at and only at those times, and has certain parts at those times. Now consider another, O_2, which exists only at t_2 and has exactly the same parts as O_1 has then.[21] Is O_2 a part of O_1 at t_2? Sider argues that it is, but his proof requires accepting the following (supplementation) principle (Sider 2001, p. 58):

---

[20] By 'exactly' fitting a region or persisting through a region R I mean the following: the object occupies every part of R and any time or place the object occupies is included in R. This is different from one of the uses of 'exact occupation/location' in the literature, where it has been used synonymously with 'wholly present' (e.g. Gilmore 2006; Donnelly 2011; Donnelly 2011, 30 fn. 11 has a summary of different uses of 'exact location' in the literature.) On my usage, the time when I am is exactly located is my entire lifetime. The spacetime region where I am exactly located is the sum of all my spacetime locations during my entire lifetime. On the other usage, any time I am wholly present (e.g. today at noon) is a time I am said to be 'exactly located', and each instantaneous human-shaped region I ever occupy is a region I 'exactly occupy'.

[21] O_1 could be a piece of clay and O_2 a statue it is formed into for an instant.

(PO) If x and y exist at t but x is not part of y at t then x has some part at t that doesn't overlap y at t.

It is open to the three-dimensionalist to reject (PO) and maintain that O_2 is not a part of O_1 at t_2, that O_1 and O_2 are distinct objects that coincide during t_2 (Koslicki 2003; Varzi 2005; Varzi 2007a; Miller 2008). This means accepting a whole lot of coincidence, but coincidence always and everywhere is actually better than coincidence that happens only between recognisable ordinary objects such as lumps and statues (Bennett 2004; Kurtsal Steen 2010). Three-dimensionalism is actually stronger paired with DP than it is in a classical ontology.

Let us see why. Suppose we have a lump of clay that exists for a year, and an artist shapes it into the likeness of a person's head, in which shape it stays for a week. Suppose that at the end of the week, the artist steps on the bust and crushes it, causing its demise. If we reject that this bust is a temporal part of the clay, and instead accept that during that week the bust and the clay are two coincident objects, an explanation can be demanded with the following speech. *Every time they both exist, the bust and the clay have just the same physical properties. Furthermore, when the crushing happens, nothing happens to the bust that doesn't also happen to the lump. Yet it is said that the crushing, which is just another shape change for the lump, is destructive for the bust. But what is the ground of this claim? There is a contrast between continuing to exist and going out of existence. What explains this contrast when there is no matching contrast between what happened to the lump and the change that would have taken place in the bust if it were to continue existing?*

Now if DP is true, then we don't have to have a contrastive explanation for the events that befell the two objects, because something's going out of existence does not have to be explained in terms of a change that happens to it. Change or no change, at every moment of the lump's existence, something that coincides with it goes out of existence. Thousands of things qualitatively identical to the bust went out of existence at the thousands of moments preceding the crushing. Bust identity and individuation conditions determine (and explain) which of the various coinciding objects is the bust. Since every non-empty region's boundary is the boundary of something or other, generation and substantial change are maximally ubiquitous; therefore no contrastive explanation is necessary. By making co-incidence ubiquitous, DP lightens the three-dimensionalist's explanatory burden regarding coincidence.

This is even more pronounced for the version of DP I prefer, which is not only three-dimensionalist but also modally primitivist. Two objects can be made up of the same parts for the whole duration of their existence. E.g. a candle shaped so as to make a statue of a wood log: the candle and the statue are created by setting the wax in a mold and are destroyed simultaneously by an unfortunate accident involving an absent-minded person and a fireplace. The difference between them is in their 'modal profiles' (Bennett 2004; Leslie 2011; Koslicki 2014, p. 211). A modal profile specifies, for a filled spacetime region, for every determinable, every non-modal property instantiated in the region; and for every property, whether it is had essentially or accidentally. The candle could have tolerated a loss of shape, but not the statue. The modally primitivist version of DP has it that for every modal profile satisfied by the matter in any region of spacetime, there is a distinct object with that modal profile (similar to Bennett 2004). This version of DP lifts yet another explanatory burden from the three-dimensionalist's shoulders. *What explains why the statue has the persistence conditions it has; why, for instance it cannot tolerate loss of shape?* Our answer is analogous to the one we gave before. The matter in the relevant region satisfies two (really, bazillions more) modal profiles. The log-shape is essential on one but not on the other of these. Every modal profile satisfied by the matter in the region is the profile of an object, so there is nothing unexplained.

Now that we have explained that DP is consistent with three-dimensionalism, we return to the argument for DP. Our continuous series is made of putative cases of successive composition that are ordered according to how Ψ they are, and Ψ comprises 'spatial adjacency, qualitative similarity, and causal relations at the various times' (Sider 2001, p. 134), the factors that intuitively would seem to determine whether some things that exist at some times form a persisting individual (that might exist intermittently). Like P1, P1' is made true only if these factors are gradational, and successive composition occurs at least sometimes.

Opponents of this argument have a way of rejecting P2' that doesn't have an analogue for P2. Mereological essentialism is the doctrine that objects are either simples or mereological sums, any part they have they have essentially, and they exist exactly as long as and where all their parts do. Furthermore, mereological essentialism can be combined with the thesis that at any instant, for every set of objects that exists at that instant, those objects have a sum.[22] This combination of views provides a sharp cut-off limiting which persisting things there are, and isn't untoward just on account of being sharp. Unfortunately, if all persisting composites conform to mereological essentialism, then ordinary objects (which clearly change parts over time) don't exist. Nihilists can reject P1' just as P1 – they could maintain that the only persisting things are simples. As we saw, this is at odds with an empirical possibility.

What is not an option, according to Sider, is a view in which the only persisting things are the ordinary objects like trees or planets. There is no precise criterion for persistence through time that allows a motivated, sharp cut-off in the Sorites series of candidates. If we allow a motivated but vague criterion, then we would usher in 'count indeterminacy'; the number of concrete objects would be indeterminate in a way that cannot be ascribed to semantic vagueness. For example, if we say that there is a composite object composed of some bits if, and only if, the bits are *F* (and when they are *F*), and there are possible cases where bits are indeterminately *F*, three different kinds of indeterminacy emerge: (1) indeterminacy as to whether some objects have a sum at a given time, (2) indeterminacy as to whether an object at a certain time is identical with an object at another time and (3) indeterminacy as to when an object begins or ceases to exist. In each case, in some non-gunky possible world, 'There are *n* concrete objects' would be neither true nor false for

---

[22] This composition thesis is not the same as UC because, unlike this thesis, UC's domain is not restricted to objects that exist at the same instant.

some value of *n*. Here is why. The first kind of indeterminacy would entail that there is a possible world where for some objects it is indeterminate whether they ever have a fusion. The second kind of indeterminacy would straightforwardly bring about an indeterminacy in how many things there are. The third kind of indeterminacy would entail that in some world it is indeterminate whether an object comes into existence at all (Sider 2001, pp. 136–7).

11.6 Chair- and Person-Sorites versus Composition- and Persistence-Sorites: What Is the Difference?

Sider notes that the argument from vagueness is not 'just another Sorites' (p. 125); and suggests that we can resist Unger's Sorites against ordinary objects in whichever way we find it fit to dissolve the Sorites Paradox (p. 188). In this section I unpack the crucial difference between these two metaphysical uses of Sorites reasoning.[23] This will enable us to appreciate a rather penetrating novel response to the arguments from vagueness, namely the supersubstantivalist response.

If Unger's argument is 'just another Sorites', and if we can dissolve Unger's argument in some standard fashion, it could be thought that we can rely on that standard solution and respond to the SCQ and the TCQ with 'only when the would-be composites are tables, chairs, stones, etc.'? This would involve insisting that there is no such thing as composition *simpliciter*, but rather chair-composition, stone-composition, etc. If the occurrences of 'composition' in the arguments from vagueness are read univocally in this object-specific manner, then a restrictive response to the SCQ or the TCQ should be able to piggy-back on the fact that in a Sorites series of cases of (say) chair-composition, in some sense or other, there is a sharp cut-off,[24] making chair-versions of P2 and P2' is false.

Unfortunately, proponents of restricted composition or successive composition cannot maintain the restrictions they desire using this strategy. The proposal has enormous metaphysical implications. Suppose, for example, that we analyse the vagueness of 'chair' using the semantic or epistemic strategy. Either there is something in the extension of some but not all precisifications of 'chair' (supervaluationism) or there is something which is a member of a set that would have been the extension of 'chair' if our behaviour were slightly different (epistemicism). Now this idea that a borderline-chair lies in some precisifications of 'chair', or that a non-chair could have ended up in the extension of 'chair', had we used that term a little differently, requires the actual *existence* of that individual borderline-chair or non-chair. Thus, the semantic and Williamsonian epistemic accounts of the vagueness of ordinary object sortals require the existence of individuals that are not ordinary objects such as chairs but somewhat exotic composites such as almost-chairs (Kurtsal Steen 2014; also see López de Sa 2006). An almost-chair as a kind of object is no small addition to our metaphysical inventory. It is not something the friend of restricted composition would

---

[23] Korman (2010) explains their difference in terms of the numerous additional premises that are parts of the complete argument from vagueness.

[24] On supervaluationism, it is true on every admissible precisification that there is a sharp cut-off (see Chapter 2 in this volume, Section 2.2.1). On epistemicism, there is simply a sharp cut-off (see Chapter 1 in this volume, Section 1.1).

have pre-theoretically accepted. Furthermore, given higher-order vagueness, the vagueness of 'almost-chair' can lead to almost-almost-chairs, and so on. The inventory expands if we have vagueness along another dimension: which sortals count as ordinary object sortals to begin with? This is still a long way from UC or DP, but proponents of supervaluationism and epistemicism cannot constrain composition with ordinary objecthood and must accept highly permissive answers to the SCQ and TCQ. Therefore, we cannot use the sharp cut-offs of ordinary object sortals to motivate sharp cut-offs for composition or successive composition because the former require that highly permissive (if not all-out permissive) responses to the SCQ or TCQ be true.[25]

Back to our question of this section, namely what is the crucial difference between the Sorites against chairs and the Sorites that leads to UC and DP? One obvious (but not that significant) difference is the difference in their directions. Let us call it 'omning' when a Sorites argument corners us into the direction where 'they all do', and let us call it 'nihiling' when it corners us into the direction where 'none do'.[26] While Unger and Heller offer a nihiling Sorites reasoning to show that nothing can be an ordinary object, Sider uses an omning Sorites reasoning to show that every class of objects has a sum, (and that every class of objects from different times successively compose an object – I'll omit repeating this in what follows). Given Sider's argument, were it not for the empirical possibility of gunk, we would have as much reason for nihiling composites as we do for omning them. Similarly, van Inwagen nihils artefacts, after explaining that the only alternative to nihiling them is omning them.

[I]f you can make a statue on purpose by kneading clay, then you can make a gollyswoggle [something which essentially has a certain random shape] by accident by kneading clay. But if you can make a gollyswoggle by accident by kneading clay, then you must, as you idly work the clay in your fingers, be causing the generation and corruption of the members of a compact series of objects of infinitesimal duration. That is what seems to me to be incredible (van Inwagen 1990, p. 126).

There is a deeper difference between the Unger/Heller arguments about things like stones or chairs as such, and the Lewis/Sider arguments about composites, or persisting things as such, and it has a direct bearing on which responses are available against them. The categories problematised by these arguments differ in how generic and how specific they are. A stone (*specific*) is a composite object (*generic*). The first consequence of this difference I want to underline is the following. The notion of a borderline instance has different ramifications for these categories. Both epistemically borderline chairs (chairs/non-chairs we cannot know to be chairs/non-chairs) and semantically borderline chairs (things that fall under some but not all admissible precisifications of 'chair') exist on a par with, or have as much being as, chairs. But if there were a borderline case of composition or persistence then its very being would be borderline (which is arguably impossible to grasp).

---

[25] I have focused only on the standard solutions offered by epistemicism and supervaluationism. I haven't explored if another type of standard solution can be combined with the thought that there is no composition except ordinary object composition. Dan Korman's approach, which I lay out later in under the title Ontic Vagueness, can be seen as an application of this type of strategy.

[26] My friend Carla Chelotti has helped me coin 'omning'.

The number of things in a finite world hinges on the generic categories composition and successive composition because these are relations that make one (additional being) out of many, rather than being additional attributes or specifications of an already accounted for thing or things. Because of that, sometimes (though not always) borderline composition and borderline successive composition would lead us to borderline being. Not always, since sometimes borderline composition would pertain to whether a bona fide composite has this further part, as well as all the uncontested parts. In those cases, that the composite exists is determinate, although some of *its* composition profile is indeterminate (Hawley 2002, 2004). Whenever it is indeterminate whether two or more bits have any sum at all, this would imply borderline being for the would-be composite. Lewis said, 'What is this thing such that it sort of is so and sort of isn't, that there is any such thing?' (1986, p. 212–3). As we will see below, even philosophers who believe that there can be ontic vagueness don't endorse a 'thing such that it sort of is so and sort of isn't, that there is any such thing'. The latter is fairly universally thought of as absurd.

The second consequence of the fact that the arguments by Unger and Heller on the one hand and Lewis and Sider on the other problematise categories that differ in how generic/specific they are is this. Even if Sider's arguments establish UC and DP, they do not guarantee the existence of any of the composites and persisting things which are ordinary things. Thus, a common way of introducing UC, as 'the thesis according to which there are not only tables and cats but also sums of tables and cats', is actually not quite accurate.[27] We can prove this as follows: it isn't inconsistent or unprincipled to accept UC and DP on the basis of the argument from vagueness while eschewing ordinary objects on the basis of the Sorites.[28] In fact, we can repeat Unger's argument *against the backdrop of UC*: consider a supposed chair. Take a sum which is a strong candidate to be that chair. Now consider Sum-minus, which is the first sum minus a small bit, maybe a drop of dried paint on the chair. Sum-minus has everything to be the chair (or a chair) too. And so does Sum-minus-minus, and so on, until we reach just a single chip. If the single chip is not a/the chair, then neither can the first sum be a/the chair. This is an instantaneous version of the Sorites, not based on removal of parts. A very closely related problem is the 'problem of the many' (Unger 1980b), arising from the existence of too many overlapping objects, each of which qualifies to be the very same kind of thing, wherever common sense would find just one (Unger's solution is, once again, to do away with ordinary objects).

Here is the third consequence we should take away from our comparison of the two lines of Sorites arguments. Recall how ordinary objects can be saved from the Unger/Heller Sorites using accounts of vagueness explained above; supervaluationism or epistemicism. On both views, a vague term such as 'chair' or 'cat' has multiple precisifications. By and large what makes a precisification admissible, on both views, is the use of the term,

---

[27] I thank Dan Korman for putting the point this way in conversation. See chapter 9.4 in Korman (2015) for a similar manoeuvre that enables invoking an ontic solution; the postulating of a DEO, 'a definitely existing object that the borderline composers are a borderline case of composing' (p. 166).

[28] Van Cleve (2008) accepts Sider's argument for UC but denounces ordinary objects on pain of too many kinds of coincident objects.

including its utterances and how it appears in inferences, and speakers' dispositions as well as actual linguistic behaviour. If supervaluationism is true, then this leaves us with many admissible precisifications. If Williamson's epistemicism is true, then the use of the term determines a single precisification as the only admissible one. On both accounts, it is in virtue of the use of a term (or concept, if you like) that a sum does or doesn't fall under a given precisification of the term.[29] Let us call it *the attributive strategy* when we respond to a Sorites-type argument about a specific category in the following way: (i) we invoke either the epistemic or the semantic account of vagueness to explicate the vagueness of the category, (ii) we limit members of the specific category in tune with common sense or rational intuition (e.g. some but not all stone candidates are stones), (iii) we affirm that there is a generic kind K of being which underlies the specific vague category, that membership in the specific category is an attribute some but not all Ks have, (iv) we cannot allow the specific kind K to have borderline cases on pain of ushering an arguably absurd notion of borderline being, (v) the generic kind K is either plenitudinous or at any rate Ks far exceed the members of the vague category. In our discussions so far, the categories 'composite' and 'persisting thing' were always in the place of K. But if they could be construed not as generic, count-increasing categories, but as specific, attributive concepts somewhat akin to 'chair' or 'cat', it would be viable to invoke the attributive strategy to explicate how these categories can be vague the same way ordinary object concepts are. Indeed, supersubstantivalists can achieve exactly this feat. They can place spacetime regions in the K slot and move 'composite object' to the specific slot.

The supersubstantivalists I have in mind hold that there is a plenitude of spacetime regions, that some but not all spacetime regions are composite objects, and that there are spacetime regions that are borderline cases of being a composite object (Wake 2011; Nolan 2014).[30] Maybe other ontologies can be offered that replace K with other types of 'underlying' entities. Such non-orthodox ontologies can draw power from being able to restrict composition in tune with common sense, make sense of borderline cases of composition, and do so while maintaining an epistemic or semantic account of vagueness. They will be able to treat the arguments from vagueness in a fashion analogous to how we can treat the Unger/Heller Sorites arguments against chairs.

By reflecting on what crucial difference there is between the two main lines of Sorites reasoning in metaphysics, we were able to make three observations: 1) DP or UC by themselves do not guarantee the existence of ordinary objects, 2) something like the attributive strategy is necessary to save ordinary objects from the Sorites puzzle in tune with common sense (so that, for example, some but not all chair candidates are chairs), 3) the attributive strategy cannot be invoked on a generic category but can be invoked on a specific category, therefore if 'composite object' is construed as a specification of some other entity, e.g. a

---

[29] Exceptions to this are sortals expressing natural kinds. If a precisification draws a more natural joint than its rivals, it can trump all use.

[30] I am thankful to Dan Korman for (among other things) pointing out the supersubstantivalist way of achieving this feat.

spacetime region, then it can be maintained that some but not all composition candidates are composites.

11.7 The Sorites Puzzle and Origin Essentialism

Another apparent instance of the Sorites Puzzle is known as 'the Modal Paradox', 'Chandler's Puzzle' or 'Chisholm's Puzzle'. There are at least two different versions of this, but owing to space constraints I will limit my discussion to one of them. Consider an artefact or a natural object; it could not have started out composed of parts all of which are distinct from the parts it was in fact composed of. However, it *could* have started out composed of almost all of the same parts, except for some chip a (where a 'chip' is, as before, a word for a one cubic millimetre hunk of matter), in the place of which is located a distinct chip, a^* (perhaps with the same functionality). As we accept this last thought, we are assenting to a modal, as opposed to temporal, version of our Tolerance principle. So, in possible world W^*, a^* and not a is a part of the object as it starts to exist. By the same token, though, in another possible world, W^{**}, the same object differs from how it is in W^* in respect of one chip; it has a^* for a and b^* for b. So it differs from the actual world in respect of two chips. If n is the number of chips our object is discretely divisible into, it seems that by n-many iterations of these alternating chips we would be considering a possible world where the same object is made out of completely different matter than it actually originally had. But that contradicts our statement that an object couldn't have had totally distinct original parts than the ones it has in fact had.

Whether soriticality plays a crucial role in this puzzle is a matter of some controversy. It seems not, since we can artificially generate a version of the puzzle that does not rely at all on vagueness. Leslie (2011), for example, discusses an axe made of three parts, a blade, a shaft and a handle. We can stipulate that the same axe would have existed if instead of one of these three parts an alternate was attached, but that it had to have at least two of the same parts. Our puzzle arises just the same, despite the precise essence, since 'two worlds over' there is an axe that by transfer of identity is identical to our axe but by the precise essence rule should not be identical to our axe.

So, arguably, vagueness or soriticality is not essential to the puzzle. It should be noted, however, that our stipulation did not make axe identity entirely determinate. Had we said that our axe could not have had another blade, but that it could have been made with another handle and another shaft, we would not have ended up with the contradictory consequences. It could be said that to fully remove soriticality from our scenarios we are required to introduce such complete determinacy (Forbes 1983, fn. 11).

There are presuppositions by rejecting which we can block the paradox. By rejecting the axiom of S4 that $\Diamond\Diamond A \to \Diamond A$, we can put a limit to this essence drift at W^* (Salmon 1986). However, since there is something fundamentally similar between this modal puzzle and the diachronic identity issues we examined above, where chips are removed over time, it might seem untoward to reject the S4 axiom but retain the principle that 'if it is at some time the case that it is at some time the case that A then it is at some time the case that

A' (Williamson 1990, p. 142). Forbes (1983) introduces a degree-theoretical logic (a type of solution to the Sorites Puzzle discussed in Chapter 8 of this volume), coupled with the rejection of transworld identity in favour of counterpart theory.

Whether or not soriticality is essential to the paradox, the availability of a modal Sorites series of cases, and the analogies between time and modality generally, can be considered motivation enough to explore analogous approaches to both puzzles. In this vein, Meg Wallace argues that if Sider's argument for temporal parts succeeds, then an analogous argument from vagueness shows that objects have modal parts (Wallace 2014). An entailment of this view is the rejection of transworld identity, which is the modal analogue of three-dimensionalism.

Recall that the immediate conclusion of Sider's argument from vagueness, DP, which is his permissive response to the TCQ, is actually consistent with three-dimensionalism. If we ask the question, *Across all the possible worlds, which modal profiles are those of objects whose essences are indicated by those modal profiles?*[31] the modally full version of DP I explained above answers it in an analogously permissive (omning) way: all of them. DP was consistent with three-dimensionalism, and similarly Modally Full Plenitude (MFP) is consistent with transworld identity. Leslie (2011) shows how MFP would provide a solution to the modal paradoxes we have been considering. Suppose that an object o starts out made of n^*-many chips. For every natural number n between 1 and n^*-1 (inclusive), there is a different modal profile specifying 'could have been originally composed of maximum n of its chips being different than the ones it had'. MFP entails that there are at least n^*-1 coincident objects where o is, each one with a differently tolerant essence.[32] Suppose that Axo is a three-part (handle, shaft, blade) axe-like thing and has the modal profile 'could have been originally composed of maximum one of its components being different than the ones it had'. Then there are possible worlds where it has the original blade, shaft and handle, and there are different-handle worlds where it has the same blade and shaft and a different handle, but there are no worlds where it has a different handle and a different shaft. In new-handle-and-new-shaft worlds there are things of the same sort as Axo, but Axo is not identical with them.

11.8 Groundedness and Autonomy

In this section I will present a type of response to the argument from vagueness that allows a sharp cut-off in composition or successive composition without invoking the standard solutions of supervaluationism or epistemicism. These responses depend on severing the tie between the composition or persistence facts and the base level facts according to which the Sorites series is ordered. The first suggestion we will examine is from John Hawthorne. Let us begin by noting that a sharp cut-off in a continuous series of cases could

---

[31] Cf. Wallace's 'Dia-Cosmic Composition Question' (2014, p. 361).
[32] By excluding 0 we are in keeping with Tolerance, and by excluding n^* as an acceptable number we disallow complete laxity of original parts. These are not restrictions that are entailed by MFP, but in light of arguments for tolerance or origin essentialism, MFP can be amended in such respects to yield the most feasibly permissivist essentialism we can come up with.

be indiscriminable by us in a way that has nothing to do with vagueness. For example, we might be looking at a series of pairs of things that are close in height. Suppose that the pairs of things Pair 1 $\langle o_1, o_2 \rangle$ and Pair 2 $\langle o_3, o_4 \rangle$ are next to each other, ordered according to how indiscriminable the pairs are from each other by us. It could be that while o_1 and o_2 are identical in height, o_3 and o_4 are not. Looking at them with our naked eye, we may not be able to draw a line between Pair 1 and Pair 2 not because 'identical in height' is vague, but because our powers of discrimination are not good enough to successfully ascertain its precise application conditions (Hawthorne 2008, pp. 106–9).

In some areas, notably in the philosophy of consciousness, a similar indiscriminability without vagueness could be ascribed to states of consciousness. Maybe the 'macroscopic' is autonomous from the microscopic supervenience base. On a continuous series of microscopically similar cases, there might be a sharp cut-off in consciousness. Under the microscope, the difference between case n and case $n + 1$ appears no different from the difference between case $n + 1$ and case $n + 2$. But at the macro level, $n + 2$ is the first in the series where there is a conscious being, whereas all the ones before it are not. It is not impossible to imagine circumstances where this would be the most apt description. One alternative is to countenance Panpsychism on the basis of a Sorites argument based on this series (thus, omning). This move, Hawthorne says, would be exactly analogous to the above argument for UC; we are to agree with UC (and DP) because (given other constraints) the alternative is for composition or successive composition facts to be autonomous from micro-level facts (Hawthorne 2008, p. 108). Consider how nutty it would be to accept Panpsychism because of this argument. We might want to be similarly wary of the arguments for UC and DP.

Like P2, P2' can be resisted if we embrace that successive composition facts are not vague but are nevertheless unknown because we cannot discern when their precise conditions are met. As Hawthorne suggests, somewhere along the series (or perhaps in multiple places along the series) there could be adjacent cases that differ insignificantly from the point of view of microphysical Ψ-facts, but differ in that one marks the entire compositional profile of a persisting individual through exactly all of its career, while the other does not. This would mean that 'successive composition' or 'the entire career of a single object' are not vague expressions.

We don't have a general rule for when we can tolerate a supervenient phenomenon to have a sharp metaphysical cut-off even though its supervenience base is gradational. What is it about consciousness that makes it not untoward to maintain an autonomous sharp cut-off (if indeed it is not untoward), and how can we know if it obtains in composition or persistence through time?

One option is to postulate a conceptual link between consciousness and composition (e.g. 'the only composites are those that are conscious') and then the autonomous sharp cut-off in composition piggy-backs on that of consciousness. For example, take Trenton Merricks' understanding of composition: some objects collectively compose a further object if and only if they have 'non-redundant causal powers' – they are collectively engaged in an activity that cannot be reduced to the sum of their individual activities (Merricks 2001a, 2005). While Merricks does not address the TCQ separately, we can reasonably extrapolate these individuation principles from his answer to the SCQ: a composite keeps on persisting just as long as its having of non-redundant causal powers continues. Suppose that none of the following is vague, and necessarily so: (a) for any multiplicity of things, whether all of them collectively have non-redundant causal powers and (b) when the collective non-redundant causal powers of a certain multiplicity of things begin, when they end. Then we can have sharp metaphysical cut-offs in our series of (successive) composition. It is not enough for (a) and (b) to be determinate in the actual world, because when it comes to count indeterminacy a merely possible case is as deadly as an actual one. For this view to succeed, it must be that in no possible world there could be borderline cases of whether some particle is or is not among a class of things that collectively have certain non-redundant causal powers. But whether there are such borderline cases strikes me as an empirical and non-metaphysical question. I am drawn to concluding that Merricks' is not an apt solution.[33]

Even if it is true that facts about whether a given collection has non-redundant causal powers cannot be vague, there is another Sorites worry. As we saw, Parfit's Sorites spectra for *person* problematise not 'being a person' but 'being the same person as *x*' and more notably, 'being the same person as *I*'. An instance of 'having non-redundant causal powers' is an event or process – what does its identity consist in so that *this* having of non-redundant causal powers here now is the same having of non-redundant causal powers as that certain one in 1975? A non-circular answer is going to mention relations between stages of processes, likely a Sorites-susceptible one.

Another way to maintain the autonomy of composition facts is to defend that there is no ground at all for composition – some classes of objects have sums, some don't, but not in virtue of their Φ-relatedness. Occurrences of composition (whatever they are) don't stem from Φ-relatedness; they are brute. This would mean that P2 is false; our series contains a sharp cut-off, but this shouldn't be surprising since there is no correlation between Φ-relatedness and composition anyway (Markosian 1998, 2008). Of course, if there is no correlation we should expect many haphazardly distributed cut-offs, rather than exactly one somewhere roughly in the middle. In fact, there is no reason to expect the one end of our spectrum to contain a positive case of composition and the other a negative case. If composition facts float free from Φ-facts, as the brute composition thesis has it, then P1 is also false; we may not be able to line up candidates on a Sorites spectrum at all. For my part I do not understand why the brute composition thesis is considered less revolutionary than UC. It seems to me that brute composition is consistent with it being the case that of two living cats, one is a composite of its cells and 'the other' is not, or that a rickety old chair is a composite of chips of wood but 'a' brand new table is not. I would find these harder to believe than UC. But any assurances I might be offered as to why these would not be the case would tie composition facts back to the base level facts, thereby undermining the bruteness thesis.

---

[33] See Barnes (2005) for an excellent discussion of Merricks (2005).

11.9 Ontic Vagueness

Perhaps the most radical response to Sorites-related worries about composition, persistence or the identity conditions of ordinary objects is ontological: the views according to which there are cases where composition and parthood, identity or existence is indeterminate. It must be noted that philosophers who endorse these theories maintain not that there are things with borderline existence, but that it is indeterminate whether there is a composite composed of certain cells, or whether the number of things in a situation is two or three, whether something at t_1 and something at t_2 are identical and so on (van Inwagen 1990; Hawley 2002, 2004; Barnes 2013, 2014; Korman 2015). Ontic vagueness accounts help reject P3 and P3'.

Solutions that postulate a defensible and reasonable ground of restricted composition or persistence through time tend to be at peace with ontic vagueness. E.g. van Inwagen (1990) maintains that simples compose something if, and only if, their activity constitutes a life, which he allows to neither definitely obtain nor definitely fail to obtain. He uses fuzzy sets (sets membership to which is a matter of degree) to analyse the ontic vagueness of a cell's being caught up in a life. And, he appeals to a three-valued logic to allow indeterminacy of identity.[34]

Korman's composite inventory is more expansive than van Inwagen's, including not just living things but kites, umbrellas and carousels. He maintains it by invoking a constitution relation, a relation not reducible to identity or composition. Objects are not identical to sums but are 'constituted' by them. The only sums there are the object-constituters, so composition is restricted (thanks to ordinary objecthood being restricted). Sometimes an object is constituted by a sum which is such that it is indeterminate whether it has a certain particle p as a part. Korman's account would allow us to reject P3 since the p-inclusive case would be one where composition neither definitely occurs nor definitely does not occur. More specifically, Korman holds that a numerical sentence can lack a determinate truth value, and explains this in terms of the quantifiers having indeterminate domains (2015, sections 5.3–5.5 and 12.3).

To my mind, the biggest obstacle to indeterminate identity or existence is first-personal. Even if it provides a common-sense way to recover and restrict ordinary objects, it fails to do right by our selves:

Most of us believe that we are not like heaps, because our identity must be determinate. We believe that, even in such 'borderline cases', the question 'Am I about to die?' must have an answer. [...] If someone will be alive, and will be suffering agony, this person either will or will not be me. One of these must be true. And we cannot make sense of any third alternative, such as that the person in agony will be partly me. I can imagine being only partly in agony, because I am drifting in and out of consciousness. But if someone will be fully conscious of the agony, this person cannot be partly me (Parfit 1984, p. 233).

---

[34] In addition to T and F, a third truth-value is ½. ½ is the truth-value that P would have if, and only if, 'Indef P' is true. 'Indef' stands for 'indefinitely'.

Maybe I can imagine becoming borderline alive, but I cannot imagine being borderline identical to something that is (definitely or borderline) alive. I also cannot imagine it being indeterminate whether I came into existence at all. I should confess that these and other denials of indeterminacy of existence, identity, or composition can be impressionistic.

In general, Sorites arguments do not come packed with conclusive reasons against ontic vagueness, leaving much room for ingenious developments. I cannot do justice here to all of the many ways ontic vagueness can be invoked to analyse vague composition and vague persistence.[35]

11.10 Conclusion

Arguments that feature Sorites series challenge some of our most well-entrenched common sense beliefs about what there is by taking us to eliminativism, UC, DP or to the more plenitudinous (three-dimensionalist or modally primitivist) versions of these. There are ways of resisting their conclusions, but doing so requires maintaining astounding theories such as the constitution view, brute composition, that the only composites are living/conscious beings, that there can be ontological indeterminacy, that logic is not two-valued...E. J. Lowe said, 'arguments appealing to vagueness almost never convince an opponent – they almost always lack persuasive power – because opponents always suspect them, generally rightly, of involving some sort of sleight of hand. In any case, there almost always turn out to be ways, whose ingenuity matches that of the arguments in question, of challenging those arguments, so that at best we are left with a standoff' (Lowe 2013, p. 266). Exactly because it takes ingenious theories to resist these arguments, they continue to advance metaphysics; hence their glorious place.[36]

---

[35] Another intriguing conception is by Jessica Wilson (2013): ontic vagueness occurs when something has a determinable property (e.g., having a boundary) without having any specific determinate of that determinable (e.g., a determinate boundary). Invoking this account in our context would seem to require identifying a determinable property that a class of things can have, determinates of which would be 'have a sum' and 'not have a sum'.

[36] Thanks to my colleagues at Bogazici University who approved my leave and had to work harder in my absence, to Peter van Inwagen and Lisette Bolduc for providing refuge in their NC home, to Laurie Paul and her UNC colleagues, especially the Transformative Experience reading group, who included me and kept me going, to Kelly James Clark who sought and found means of financial support. To Eric Boynton and Provost Cole who supplied an office, a home, an income and the most welcoming atmosphere possible, to Allegheny College faculty for open arms, to the students who accepted me in their theatre and healed me with art, to my therapist whose skills are uncanny, to Dan Korman who lovingly talked me through the issues raised in this chapter when I thought I couldn't even form complete thoughts, and to Ruth Groff who kept her light on and checked on my progress, and of course to my most patient editors Elia Zardini and Sergi Oms. And thanks to Mark, whose love is determinate and essential.

12   The Sorites Paradox in Practical Philosophy

Hrafn Asgeirsson

In this chapter, I discuss some of the main ways in which the Sorites Paradox is relevant to practical philosophy.[1] I begin by distinguishing between two types of roles that Sorites arguments play in the recent literature – one indirect and one direct. The most prominent indirect role that such arguments play is a demonstrative one; Sorites arguments are used to show that a particular predicate has borderline cases, from which something of philosophical interest is supposed to follow. It has been argued, for example, that if moral predicates have borderline cases, then most – if not all – forms of moral realism must be false. It has also been argued that the fact that legislation is riddled with vague predicates shows that we need to revise the standard notion of the Rule of Law.

When Sorites arguments are employed in a more direct way, they are typically used to show either that the first item in the Sorites series is practically problematic or that tolerance is – i.e. the paradox is seen as a motivation to deny one or more premises in the reasoning, rather than, say, deny the validity of the argument or bite the bullet vis-à-vis its conclusion.[2] The paradox has been used, for example, as the basis for a slippery slope argument against abortion at any time, arguing soritically from its permissibility at some time t_0 after conception to a seemingly absurd conclusion of its permissibility at some time t_n – say, just prior to birth. Here, the 'solution' is to reject the first step in the reasoning. The paradox has also been used as a basis for criticism of several important arguments that in one way or another involve the transitivity of value – including, for example, an argument against the adequacy of orthodox decision theory. In these cases, the 'solution' is to reject the inductive step, i.e. to reject tolerance.

The first part of the chapter surveys some of the ways in which the Sorites Paradox has figured in arguments in practical philosophy in recent decades, with special attention to arguments in which the paradox plays a more direct role. Given the limitations of space, some significant work – much of it recent – cannot be covered here, but hopefully the illustrative discussion will still be informative, if not complete. To highlight what is at stake, I will outline some of the most prominent arguments in the literature, all of which

---

[1] Note that I will assume a (very) basic familiarity with the paradox in the following discussion. For an overview of the basic notions involved, see the introduction to this volume, especially 'The Sorites Paradox'.

[2] For an overview of the main solutions to the paradox, see 'Solutions to the Sorites Paradox', in the introduction to this volume.

involve the transitivity of value in some way: Ruth Chang's 'chaining' argument for the novel value-relation *parity*, Warren Quinn's 'self-torturer' argument against the adequacy of orthodox decision theory and Larry Temkin's 'continuum' argument (later 'spectrum' argument) against the transitivity of *better-than*.[3]

The second part is slightly more probative, focusing on two main themes. First, I further address the relationship between the Sorites Paradox and the three arguments mentioned above, by elucidating in what sense they rely on (something like) tolerance principles. Secondly, I briefly discuss the prospect of rejecting the respective principles, aiming to show that we cannot do so for Quinn's and Temkin's arguments, since – unlike in genuine Sorites scenarios – the principles do not function as independent premises in the reasoning but, rather, follow from certain fundamental features of the relevant scenarios. I also try to further distinguish between these two arguments and Chang's chaining argument by showing that not even adopting what is arguably the most radical way to block the Sorites Paradox – that of weakening the consequence relation – suffices to invalidate the former two arguments. They may of course be problematic in other respects, but if such a radical solution to the paradox does not block them, then at least we have very strong reason to believe that they are not genuinely soritical.

Weakening the consequence relation invalidates Chang's argument, however. It doesn't immediately follow that the argument is soritical, but it does mean that – on the account under consideration – it fails for the same reasons as the Sorites Paradox. In both cases, logic has been 'pushed too far', so to speak; chaining together simple, 'locally' valid, argument forms ends up producing an invalid, complex argument form.

12.1 The Sorites Paradox and Practical Philosophy: Some Examples

The following overview of the influence of the Sorites Paradox in practical philosophy is by necessity both selective and fairly brief. As I mentioned, I want to try to impose a bit of structure on the discussion by distinguishing between two types of roles that Sorites reasoning plays in the literature. One is indirect, in the sense that Sorites reasoning plays a part in establishing that a particular predicate has borderline cases, which in turn has certain purportedly important implications for the domain in question. The other role of the paradox is more direct, in that certain important arguments in practical philosophy are charged with being soritical, and fault is found with the respective tolerance principles.

Although this twofold categorisation is a useful starting point, we should not attach too much importance to it. As we will see even from this selective overview, the variation within each category is so great that the distinction between indirect and more direct applications of Sorites reasoning is ultimately not all that informative. And, as is to be expected, many of the interesting bits tend to be related to the particular domains of application. Nevertheless, the discussion here should still provide clear indication of how developments

---

[3] See Chang (2002), Quinn (1990) and Temkin (1996), respectively.

in philosophy of language and philosophical logic, generated specifically in response to the Sorites Paradox, may have significant implications for several important arguments in practical philosophy.

12.1.1 Indirect Uses of Sorites Reasoning

The Debate about Moral Realism

One of the areas of practical philosophy in which the Sorites Paradox has been most influential is the recent debate about moral realism.[4] Here, the paradox is typically used demonstratively to show that moral predicates have borderline cases, the existence of which presents a large prima facie problem for the idea that the truth of moral judgements is independent of the attitudes associated with them – i.e. that such judgements report facts.

As Shafer-Landau (1995) points out, it is easy enough to see why moral realism might be thought to be at odds with vagueness. Moral realism may seem to naturally favour *epistemicism* – i.e. the view that in each borderline case there is a fact of the matter whether the relevant predicate applies, albeit an unknowable one.[5] Such irremediable ignorance can also – on this view – account for our lingering disagreements about moral matters and our doubts about what to do in moral dilemmas: these phenomena are persistent because the ignorance in question cannot even in principle be resolved.

However, Shafer-Landau says, if epistemicism about moral vagueness is true, we end up with implausibly many unknowable moral truths, given the prevalence both of seemingly irresolvable disagreement about moral matters and of cases in which competing values appear to fail to resolve the issue at hand. Irrespective of the plausibility of epistemicism in other domains, he thinks, moral realism carries with it some commitment to significant epistemic access to the relevant facts (if they exist).[6]

Now, on a simplistic view of the available options, this could easily seem to motivate a rejection of moral realism. If it seems implausible that morality is fully determinate yet ubiquitously unknowable (as epistemicism about moral vagueness may seem to entail), then one may wish to try to explain moral disagreement without reference to moral properties. Just as some have argued that the lesson to be learned from the Sorites Paradox is that there are no heaps, bald men or clouds, so too a non-cognitivist can claim that the paradox shows that there is no generosity, bravery or goodness. In short, the response here to the implausibility of epistemicism – either wholesale or specifically in the domain of morality – is to embrace *nihilism* (again, either wholesale or specifically with respect to moral properties): if there are no precise moral properties, then there are no moral properties at all.[7] Or so this line of reasoning goes.

---

[4] For a general overview of moral realism, see e.g. Sayre-McCord (2017).
[5] For what has become the classic exposition and defence of epistemicism, see Williamson (1994). See also Chapter 1 in this volume.
[6] See also Schoenfield (2015) for further arguments against epistemicist explanations of the vagueness of moral predicates.
[7] Or such properties are necessarily uninstantiated. Thanks to Elia Zardini for helpful comments on this point. For a wholesale approach to nihilism, see Unger (1979b); see also Chapter 4 in this volume, Section 4.6, and Chapter 11, Section 11.3.

As Shafer-Landau correctly points out, however, such a move is unnecessary. We can reject both epistemicism and nihilism and retain moral realism even in the face of widespread
irresolvable disagreement and conflict of values. Shafer-Landau's preferred view is one on
which we can make sense of *vague properties* – i.e. real properties that have 'indeterminate
extensions', as he calls it.[8] A property P has an indeterminate extension, on this view, if,
for some object o (or set thereof), there is no fact of the matter (and so no truth about)
whether o instantiates P. In the moral domain, for example, there may be no fact of the
matter whether a person, or an action, instantiates generosity.

At least prima facie, there are certainly other accounts of vagueness available to the
moral realist – in particular, so-called *semantic* accounts, such as *contextualism* and *supervaluationism*. Many authors argue, however, that purely semantic explanations of moral
vagueness are problematic.[9] The reason is that such accounts generally posit what has
come to be known as a *shifty* semantics for vague predicates, which doesn't sit well with
what we tend to consider as acceptable ways to resolve moral borderline cases. Put very
briefly, the worry is that – in some significant sense – purely semantic views allow for
borderline cases to be resolved by linguistic considerations alone. If that is correct, then
such accounts have – at least from a moral realist perspective – counterintuitive implications
for how we can resolve vagueness-related moral quandaries. Intuitively, a *real* solution to
such quandaries requires some reference to reasons, rather than merely choosing to use
our words differently.[10] Consequently, these authors think that moral predicates require
a *rigid* semantics, on which semantic vagueness is grounded in ontic vagueness. Taking
moral vagueness seriously, then, arguably requires locating the vagueness 'in the world'.
Or so this line of reasoning goes. The properties 'in the world' that Shafer-Landau –
specifically – has in mind are non-natural, non-reducible moral properties, constituted by
natural properties.[11]

Constantinescu (2013), however, argues that the moral realist has fewer options than
one might think, insofar as we want to be able to take moral vagueness seriously. In
particular, he argues that ontic moral vagueness is not compatible with non-naturalist moral
realism such as Shafer-Landau's. The reason, he says, is that it is plausible to suppose
that vague moral properties are generally multiply realisable by a very wide range of
underlying properties, which entails – on his view – that such properties are essentially
disjunctive. Insofar as we are supposed to take non-natural moral properties to be constituted by natural properties, as Shafer-Landau suggests, this gets non-naturalism into
trouble, Constantinescu argues. The root of the problem, he thinks, is that there just doesn't
seem to be anything that sufficiently unites the (open-ended) set of natural disjuncts in
such a way to justify the claim that moral properties are real (insofar as the existence of

---

[8] Shafer-Landau (1995, pp. 84 and 93).
[9] See e.g. Shafer-Landau (1994), Constantinescu (2013) and Schoenfield (2015).
[10] Arguably, moral realists are also committed to a view on which moral propositions are – if true – true independently of our
attitudes towards them (or towards the associated facts), which may seem to conflict with the conversational discretion
afforded by shifty semantics. I think there are ways around this worry, but it is easy enough to see why this is likely to make
moral realists uneasy with explanations that rely on such semantics.
[11] See e.g. Shafer-Landau (2003). For a more general overview of moral non-naturalism, see e.g. Ridge (2014).

disjunctive properties turns on similarities between disjuncts). Constantinescu's concern, then, is that due to the vagueness of moral properties there is – on the non-reductive view – no underlying natural property, or set thereof, that is capable of constituting any moral property.[12]

This is a general problem for moral realism, of course, but one that the naturalist is able to get around by appealing to other considerations to justify the claim that moral properties exist, such as causal efficacy. Since non-natural properties are generally taken to be causally inert, such considerations are not available to the moral non-naturalist, however.[13] Or so Constantinescu argues. If that is correct, then it seems that taking moral vagueness seriously within a realist framework favours moral naturalism.

Arbitrariness and the Rule of Law

In philosophy of law, Sorites-susceptibility has also been used indirectly to argue that we need to revise the standard notion of the Rule of Law. Unlike in the debate about moral realism, which centres on the vagueness of moral predicates, nothing here hangs on the vagueness of legal predicates, as such. Rather, the mere fact that legislation is riddled with predicates that admit of borderline cases shows that some legal cases cannot be resolved in a principled way, which introduces arbitrariness into the law – a known adversary of the Rule of Law.

Endicott (2000) has us imagine a set of identical defendants, for example, all of whom must – by law – be prosecuted 'within a reasonable time' (Endicott 2000, p. 188). Now, a single day is not going to make a difference to whether or not someone is or isn't prosecuted within a reasonable time, but for some pair of identical defendants within the borderline region the law cannot but prosecute one yet dismiss the charges against the other (insofar as the law wishes to avoid prosecutions that clearly violate procedural rules).[14] As a result, Endicott says, the law (i) fails to treat like cases alike, (ii) promotes discretion on behalf of legal officials and (iii) lacks predictability, all of which Endicott takes to be inconsistent with what is traditionally considered fundamental Rule of Law qualities.[15]

Since vagueness is – on Endicott's account – not only in fact pervasive in law but also a *necessary* feature of it, he takes this to present a very significant challenge to the standard notion of the Rule of Law. The ideal, therefore, must be reconstructed.[16] It is of course possible to regard vagueness in the law as a necessary evil, and to hold that the ideal state of affairs is one in which vagueness in the law is limited as much as possible. However,

---

[12] My own response to Constantinescu's concern is that vagueness is not really doing any specific work here. If moral properties are multiply realisable in the way he suggests, then they are so not in virtue of being vague but – rather – in virtue of being (incommensurately) multidimensional. For a discussion of the relationship between these two semantic phenomena, see e.g. Asgeirsson (2015). Broad multiple realisability remains a challenge for non-reductive non-naturalist views, but this is a general metaphysical problem, not specifically related to moral vagueness.

[13] For a discussion, see e.g. Enoch (2017).

[14] Note that Endicott's argument relies on a tolerance principle for the term 'within a reasonable time'. Since most theorists of vagueness reject tolerance principles, this is problematic. However, Endicott's main point could (more or less) be made by appeal to borderline cases instead of tolerance. Thanks to Elia Zardini for helpful comments here.

[15] See Endicott (2000, pp. 188–9).

[16] See Endicott (2000, pp. 189ff.).

Endicott points out that minimising vague law may very well take us further away from the Rule of Law ideal, as precision may also introduce arbitrariness by failing to reflect 'the reasons on which a law ought to be based' (Endicott 2000, p. 192). Abandoning the 'reason of the law', Endicott thinks, is certainly inconsistent with the Rule of Law, properly understood, but vagueness does not necessarily entail this; it may involve doing so, of course, but so may precise regulation. And sometimes, he concludes, the ability of legal officials to treat like cases in different ways, based on the underlying justification of the relevant law(s), significantly outweighs the costs associated with (i)–(iii) above.

Having given these two examples of indirect uses of Sorites reasoning, I want to now move on to more direct applications. Slippery slope arguments sometimes make positive use of Sorites reasoning, but the paradox is mainly used critically, to undermine potentially significant arguments of various sorts, each of which involves the transitivity of value in some way. These critical applications will be the focus here. First, however, the Sorites series as a slippery slope.

12.1.2 Direct Uses of Sorites Reasoning

Slippery Slopes

The classical example of Sorites reasoning used in slippery slope arguments involves arguing from the permissibility of abortion at some time t_0 after conception to a seemingly absurd conclusion of its permissibility at some time t_n – say, just prior to birth. Here, the 'solution' is to reject the first step in the reasoning: abortion at time t_0 after conception is impermissible.

The 'solution' crucially depends on treating the argument as valid but unsound – hence the strategy to reject the initial premise (and, importantly, to maintain tolerance). This strategy, however, tends not to be considered a viable general strategy for dealing with the paradox. And even if it were, it doesn't work for individual claims alone – rather, rejecting for example the initial premise in the argument above would really amount to embracing the nihilist conclusion that *nothing* is permissible.[17] That's definitely not what proponents of slippery slope arguments are after.

The main problem for slippery slope applications of Sorites reasoning, then, is that any feasible response to the paradox will either (i) reject tolerance (i.e. some step in the reasoning other than the initial premise), (ii) reject the validity of the argument or (iii) bite the bullet and accept the paradoxical conclusion(s). So whichever way we go, any slippery

---

[17] That is, this 'solution' really amounts to holding that – like other vague predicates – the predicate 'is permissible' is empty; see e.g. Keefe and Smith (1997a, pp. 12–3) and Chapters 4, Section 4.6 and Chapter 11, Section 11.3 in this volume. Note that the nihilist strategy applies to all moral predicates, including 'is obligatory'. This may seem – by way of standard duality – to entail that everything is permissible. Space is too limited for me to go into this matter more substantially, but the best way to explain these seemingly contrary commitments of the nihilist strategy – I believe – lies in the distinction between strong and weak permission, where the latter is defined simply as the absence of obligation and the former as something above and beyond that. What the moral nihilist is committed to, then, is, on the one hand, that nothing is strongly permissible and, on the other, that everything is weakly permissible, which is entirely consistent. For a discussion of strong versus weak permission, see e.g. von Wright (1963, pp. 86–7), Alchourrón and Bulygin (1971, chapter 7), and Navarro and Rodríguez (2014, pp. 78–80).

slope argument relying on a Sorites series in any robust sense will end up being problematic in some fundamental way. It doesn't follow, however, that there are no respectable versions of slippery slope arguments involving something like a Sorites series, but what will be doing most of the work in such arguments are empirical considerations about the likely consequences of accepting certain morally relevant judgements or rules.[18] As a result, these arguments are not genuinely soritical.

Critical Arguments

As I mentioned, the main direct application of the Sorites Paradox is – perhaps unsurprisingly – critical. And in fact, several important arguments in the recent literature in practical philosophy depend on being able to resist the charge that they ultimately depend on soritical reasoning. I cannot discuss all of them here, but will outline some of the most prominent ones to highlight what is at stake.

Chang's chaining argument for parity Chang (2002) argues that in addition to the relations of *better-than*, *worse-than* and *equally-good-as* there is a fourth value-relation: *on-a-par-with*, or *parity*. Consider Mozart and Michelangelo.[19] We start by assuming that we cannot find a common scale on which we can measure the degrees to which the two artists are creative, although we can count both as very creative. We therefore think that it is false that 'either one is better than the other or they are of equal value', with respect to creativity.[20] Chang's motivating idea for the parity relation is that we would presumably still accept the claim that the imaginary painter Talentlessi – who happens to be very bad, and so is at the opposite end of the spectrum relative to Michelangelo – is less creative than Mozart. This generalises, in the sense that, for any relata r and r', r and r' can be compared with respect to a feature F if r is a 'nominal' instance of F and r' is a 'notable' instance of F, or vice versa, even if there exists no natural common metric with which we can measure the Fness of r and r'. If this is right, absence of a natural common metric does not entail incomparability. And since we can compare Mozart and Talentlessi with respect to creativity, we can do the same for Mozart and Michelangelo, on the assumption that comparability is preserved through successive, small enough differences in the relevant quality underlying our judgements of creativity.[21] But since we have already accepted that none of the three standard comparative relations applies to the pair, we need the relation of parity to account for such cases.[22] Or so the argument goes.

---

[18] See e.g. Williams (1995).

[19] See Chang (2002, pp. 673–5).

[20] See Raz (1986, p. 324).

[21] Chang (2002, p. 674); Chang calls this the Small Unidimensional Difference Principle. The justification for the principle, she says, is its 'deep intuitive appeal'; see ibid., p. 675. I discuss this principle below.

[22] In Chang's view, parity may explain a wide range of cases – in addition to Mozart/Michelangelo, she mentions a number of other relevant pairs: a career in accounting versus a career in skydiving, an afternoon at the museum versus hiking in the woods, and a duty to keep promises versus a requirement to avoid unnecessary pain; see Chang (2002, p. 659). Note that we might of course – contra Chang – take the upshot of the argument to be that such pairs are (after all) equally F, perhaps on the basis that intuition strongly suggests that comparative relations are limited to the standard three. This is often referred to as the Trichotomy Thesis. Do we have reason to think that the Small Unidimensional Difference Principle is *more* intuitive that

Quinn, and Tenenbaum and Raffman, on the Puzzle of the Self-Torturer Quinn (1990) presents us with the *puzzle of the self-torturer*, in order to put pressure on one of the fundamental ideas of orthodox decision theory – that the perfectly rational agent should 'see every moment as a possible new beginning in their practical lives', as he puts it.[23]

Consider a person who is fitted with a device that can deliver a continuous range of electric shock. The device has 1,001 settings, from 0 to 1,000, and the difference between each pair of adjacent settings is so small as to be imperceptible. It is first set to 0, accompanied with the offer to increase the setting by 1 and receive $10,000. If the person chooses to increase the setting, she is then presented with the same offer. The puzzle is that for each offer accepting it maximises expected utility, yet at 1,000 the person would gladly pay the money she has gained for the setting to be returned to 0.[24]

Quinn identifies the above-mentioned prescription to maximise expected utility at each choice point as the culprit; we should instead pre-select a stopping point and stick to it. As a more general practical matter, he thinks, such a strategy will help us draw the line, for example, between one more bite and too many bites, between puffs of pleasant smoking and lung cancer, or between pleasurable moments of idleness and wasted lives.[25] What this means, Quinn thinks, is that we have to supplement the orthodox view of rational decision-making with what he calls a 'quasi-deontological' element – that of being *bound* in our future choices.[26] This will allow agents with non-transitive preferences to act rationally by pre-selecting a stopping point, thereby avoiding the self-torturer's predicament. But in doing so, we give up what he calls the *Principle of Strategic Readjustment*: once the agent has picked a stopping point, it is – contra orthodoxy – not rational for her to change her mind even if that would better serve her preferences.[27]

Tenenbaum and Raffman (2012) draw similar conclusions about the shortcomings of orthodox decision theory from the puzzle, but propose a different solution from Quinn's pre-selection strategy (and similar plan-based strategies). The agent, they say, doesn't just care about money and freedom from pain, she cares about making *enough* money and – crucially – about living a *relatively* pain-free life. These attitudes are importantly different from momentary preferences and constitute what Tenenbaum and Raffman call 'vague projects'.[28] In particular, in relation to the puzzle, the latter project – on grounds of instrumental necessity – permits the agent to stop turning the dial at some non-specific point within a certain (fuzzy) range (since the competing projects are vague, there is no optimal trade-off point between pain and money). Or else the agent's vague project is not realised. But this requires the agent not to maximise expected utility based on her

---

the Trichotomy Thesis? The point I'm getting at here is well captured by the adage that one person's *modus ponens* may be another's *modus tollens*. Thanks to Elia Zardini for helpful comments on this point.

[23] Quinn (1990, p. 90).
[24] Ibid., p. 79.
[25] Ibid.
[26] Ibid., p. 89.
[27] Ibid., p. 88.
[28] Tenenbaum and Raffman (2012, pp. 99–106).

preferences for available actions 'considered in isolation', as they put it.[29] Thus, despite the difference in the proposed solution from Quinn's (there is no pre-selected/planned stopping point), they identify as the culprit the same aspect of the orthodox view: it requires all the practically relevant aspects of the agent's make-up to figure directly in her momentary choices. Vague projects, however, are just not like that, Tenenbaum and Raffman say. The extent to which such projects are accomplished can only be assessed, they claim, 'in light of the entire period during which they were, or ought to have been, executed' (Tenenbaum and Raffman 2012, p. 102).

Quinn, and Tenenbaum and Raffman, then, take the self-torturer to show that *rationally-preferable-to* is not a transitive relation, and think that any complete theory of rationality must adequately address and accommodate this. And while Tenenbaum and Raffman are silent on this, Quinn takes *better-than* to be transitive; plausibly, on Quinn's view, the puzzle is generated in part by this structural difference between these two key relations. For each adjacent pair of settings, there is a significant difference between them in terms of monetary pay-off but no perceivable difference in terms of pain, so it is always rational to prefer the higher setting to the lower (current) one. But, since *rationally-preferable-to* is not transitive there is no inconsistency involved in the self-torturer's preference to, say, prefer setting 0 to setting 1,000. The same is not true of *better-than*, Quinn thinks. If a further increase in the setting were always *better*, then setting 1,000 would – via transitivity – be better than setting 0. Since action should – in Quinn's view – track goodness rather than merely preference-satisfaction, a complete theory of rational action must (among other things) make up the shortfall when the latter does not align with the former.

Temkin's continuum argument against the transitivity of better-than I hope to have made clear how much work the assumption that *better-than* is transitive does in Quinn's overall argument. Fortunately for Quinn, this is a pretty standard assumption in value theory. Temkin (1996), however, provides what he calls a 'continuum' argument (later 'spectrum' argument) for the controversial thesis that *better-than*, in the 'all things considered' sense, is – or at least *may* be – non-transitive. The argument is ultimately supposed to motivate us to 'rethink our understanding of the good, moral ideals, and the nature of practical reasoning' (Temkin 1996, p. 210).

Put very roughly, the dilemma Temkin intends to expose is that – due to arguments like the one below – we will have to either give up some of our most robust ideas about how to evaluate lives or else reject transitivity, which would fundamentally upset what is commonly taken to be our best understanding of practical rationality. The former more or less carries its significance on its sleeve. The latter, among other things, would affect not only many of our commonsensical choice strategies (such as choice by elimination) but also many of our most accomplished models in game theory, decision theory and economics.[30] A lot is at stake, then.

[29] Tenenbaum and Raffman (2012, p. 102).
[30] See e.g. Temkin (2014).

Temkin's continuum argument against the transitivity of *better-than* rests on three fundamental claims, the first and third of which he thinks are deeply entrenched in the way we think about the goodness of outcomes (the second is taken to be a straightforward truism):[31]

Claim 1: For any unpleasant or 'negative' experience ... it would be better to have that experience than one that was only a little less intense but twice as long.[32]
Claim 2: There is a continuum of unpleasant or 'negative' experiences ranging in intensity, for example from extreme forms of torture to the mild discomfort of a hangnail.
Claim 3: A mild discomfort for the duration of one's life would be preferable to two years of excruciating torture, no matter the length of one's life.[33]

Temkin's idea is that, starting with excruciating torture for a limited amount of time, decreasing the intensity slightly but increasing the duration significantly will make for a worse state of affairs (Claim 1). However, repeating this pattern of reasoning (Claim 2) will also – assuming that the 'all things considered better than' relation is transitive – yield the conclusion that excruciating torture for a limited amount of time is better than very mild discomfort for a vast amount of time (contra Claim 3). The conclusion is that the *all-things-considered-better-than* relation is not transitive, unless – of course – we are willing to give up at least one of the three fundamental claims. Either way, we are required to give up certain fundamental ideas about the nature of goodness and/or practical rationality.

Historically, Temkin has been in favour of rejecting transitivity. One of the more significant upshots of doing so is that it allows us to block certain arguments for what is known as the *Repugnant Conclusion* – roughly, that for any world full of happy people there is another world full of unhappy people which is better simply in virtue of being significantly more populated.[34] In recent work, however, Temkin says that rather than counting equivocally in favour of non-transitivity, continuum arguments instead expose

---

[31] Temkin (1996, p. 179). Temkin's argument develops a line of argument first introduced in Rachels (1993); see also Rachels (1998). For Temkin's reason to think that Claims 1–3 are – and should be – claims to which most people are deeply committed, see Temkin (2012, pp. 26–44).

[32] This is an instance of what Temkin calls the *First Standard View: Trade-Offs between Quality and Number Are Sometimes Desirable*; see Temkin (2014, p. 65). See also Temkin (2012, p. 30).

[33] This is an instance of what Temkin calls the *Second Standard View: Trade-Offs between Quality and Number are Sometimes Undesirable Even When Vast Numbers Are at Stake*; see Temkin (2014, p. 65). See also Temkin (2012, p. 32).

[34] See Parfit (1984, pp. 388 and – generally – 381ff.). See also Arrhenius and Tännsjö (2017). Rejecting transitivity of course only blocks those arguments that rely on a piecemeal transition from a world, A, with n happy people to a world, Z, with n + m unhappy people, such that – repugnantly – Z is better, or at least no worse, than A (assuming transitivity).

Total utilitarians are stuck with the Repugnant Conclusion irrespective of any such argument, simply in virtue of the pairwise comparison between A and Z (because the latter contains more total happiness than the former). Average utilitarians, on the other hand, are not affected simply by pairwise comparison, but are – according to Parfit – able to get around the incremental arguments only because the average principle violates what he calls the principle of mere addition: roughly, that adding worthwhile lives to A will not make the resulting world, A+ worse (and may in fact make it better); see Parfit (1984, p. 420). But, and here is the rub, if we accept this principle (and make certain other plausible assumptions), as we arguably should if we accept that welfare affects goodness in a significant way, then we can – assuming transitivity – incrementally rearrange the quality and distribution of happiness such that we eventually conclude that Z is better (or at least no worse) than A; see Parfit (1984, pp. 419ff.).

Temkin's (1996) suggestion is that rejecting transitivity allows us both to block such incremental arguments and to explain why we can accept that, for any (ordered) pair of adjacent worlds in the series from A to Z, the latter is better than then former, while also accepting that Z is not better than A. Temkin's fundamental idea is that the factors relevant to evaluating the relative goodness of adjacent worlds may be different from the factors relevant to evaluating non-adjacent worlds; see e.g. Temkin (2014, p. 539). Thanks to the editors for prompting me to clarify this.

us to a difficult dilemma in theorising about morality and action. '[T]he question of which of the premises should be given up', he says, 'is a difficult one about which people are deeply divided, and about which there is unlikely to be a consensus for years to come';[35] the way forward, he thinks, is 'murky, at best'.[36]

The Sorites charge All three arguments naturally invite the idea that they might be soritical, and thereby fallacious. Temkin, for example, spends a great deal of effort to resist this charge. His main argument is that unlike his continuum argument, Sorites reasoning can be rejected once we get clear about how to interpret the relevant tolerance principle. The paradox, on his view, trades on treating insignificant differences as no differences at all. In the case of 'bald', for example, we can either take the relevant principle to be that adding or subtracting one hair will not make a significant difference with respect to someone's being bald. But then the tolerance principle – although true – is no longer apt to fuel the paradox. Or we can take the principle to be that adding or subtracting one hair will not make any difference whatsoever to someone's being bald, in which case the principle is false. Either way, the Sorites reasoning is blocked, Temkin argues. But no such revisionary strategy is available with respect to his continuum argument, he thinks – morality, unlike language, is not a matter of convention. The only way to avoid the conclusion of his argument is to 'revise substantially our understanding of the world', he says.[37]

As for Quinn's self-torturer, Elson (2016) argues that the reasoning involved in the puzzle is an instance of Sorites reasoning. Tenenbaum and Raffman think that it isn't, but provide fairly limited argument to that effect. Primarily, they rely on the fact that the series involved in the self-torturer case is not unidimensional or monadic – the agent isn't faced with a series of indiscriminable steps from bearable to unbearable pain, but with deciding whether each step is compensatable by $10,000.

Elson argues – contra Tenenbaum and Raffman – that fallacious Sorites reasoning is not limited to monadic predicates, and invokes what he calls 'essentially comparative desires', the function of which is to ground a 'practical Sorites' directly in the comparative task itself, rather than in any vague monadic predicate occurring in the description of the relevant desire.[38]

An essentially comparative desire with respect to some feature F is a desire for things that are more F rather than less F, or vice versa.[39] The self-torturer, for example, has a desire for less pain rather than for more pain, and a desire for more money rather than for less money. Given that these generate vague utility functions for the self-torturer, it will be vague at what setting she rationally prefers less pain to more money. This, Elson says, means that we get a Sorites on 'maximises expected utility': counting upwards from

---

[35] See Temkin (2014, pp. 64–5).
[36] Ibid., p. 58.
[37] Temkin (1996, p. 201). A number of people have responded to Temkin's claim that his argument is not soritical, some of whom he has replied to in Temkin (2012); see especially chapter 9 and Appendices C and D.
[38] Elson (2016, pp. 478–82).
[39] Ibid., p. 482.

setting 0, there will be a non-definite number of settings that determinately maximise expected utility, counting downwards from setting 1,000 a non-definite number of settings that determinately do not maximise expected utility, and somewhere in between those two sets a non-definite number of settings for which it is vague whether they maximise expected utility.[40] Elson thus agrees with Tenenbaum and Raffman that the self-torturer is not trying to discern at what step the pain has gone from bearable to unbearable, but concludes that she *is indeed* 'proceeding along a Sorites series of dial-turns from those with clearly positive marginal utility to those with clearly negative marginal utility, attempting to decide where the positive/required ones end and the negative/impermissible begin' (Elson 2016, p. 486). It seems, then, that we can represent the puzzle of the self-torturer as a Sorites on something like 'step *n* is compensatable by $10,000', at least once we get clear about the two essentially comparative desires involved in the application of the predicate. Or so Elson argues.

Elson (2014) also argues that – despite Chang's argument to the contrary – her chaining argument depends on the Sorites-susceptibility of the predicate 'is (in)comparable with'. Chang's defence against the Sorites charge is that not all arguments that have a Sorites-like structure are unsound (she ask us to consider, for example, mathematical induction). Rather, it's the *vagueness* of the relevant predicate that is doing the paradoxical work. But in the chaining argument, she says, vagueness is doing no such work. If it were, she continues, then it would be true of such cases as the one involving Mozart and Michelangelo that one artist is better than the other or they are equally good, although indeterminate which of the three standard relations holds.[41] But since she finds this analysis implausible, and provides several arguments in support of that view,[42] she rejects the idea that the chaining argument is soritical.

Elson, however, argues that although Chang provides good reasons to think that the above analysis of Mozart and Michelangelo type cases is implausible, her chaining argument could still be trading on vagueness in the relevant predicate, in particular if – contra Chang – we adopt a view on which the two artists are determinately incomparable (i.e. none of the standard comparative predicates applies).[43] On the suggested view, there are three basic regions in relation to Mozart, separated by fuzzy boundaries: *worseness*, *incomparability* and *betterness* – inhabited, respectively, by Talentlessi, Michelangelo and the (hypothetical) SuperMichelangelo. As Elson points out, since Chang's arguments do not rule out such an analysis, and the analysis involves elements that ground typical instances

---

[40] Elson's analysis has the counterintuitive implication that it is not rational for the self-torturer to prefer setting 1,000 to setting 999, despite the imperceivable difference in pain between them and the added $10,000. The explanation, on Elson's analysis, is that – at this point – the disutility of pain will have significantly outweighed the utility of money. As we will see below, I think that – ultimately – this analysis is not available.

[41] Chang (2002, p. 665).

[42] Ibid., pp. 682ff.

[43] While structurally similar, this is different from the suggestion in fn. 23 – i.e. that Michelangelo and Mozart are *equally good*. My guess is that Elson's reluctance to embrace that analysis comes from a motivation to preserve some of Chang's intuitions about the pair, while still providing a diagnosis on which the argument is soritical.

of the paradox, we do seem to have a plausible view on which the chaining argument is fallacious. The Sorites charge sticks, Elson thinks.[44]

12.2 Tolerance and Transitivity

In order to make the Sorites charges stick, much hangs on showing that we can construct a plausible tolerance principle for each case. Let me address them in the same order as the arguments were initially presented, starting with Chang's argument for the parity relation.[45]

Chang's argument crucially relies on what she calls the *Small Unidimensional Difference Principle: If Talentlessi is comparable with Mozart, then Talentlessi+ is also comparable with Mozart.*[46] Talentlessi+, here, is just what we get by minimally improving Talentlessi along a single dimension of creativity. And so on for Talentlessi++, etc. Apply this principle to the relevant series and we eventually get comparability between Michelangelo and Mozart.

In Quinn's case, and Tenenbaum and Raffman's, the relevant principle can be formulated in the following way: *If step* n *is compensatable by $10,000 (or: maximises expected utility), then step* n+1 *is compensatable by $10,000 (or: maximises expected utility).* Apply this principle to the relevant series and we eventually get to an outcome that leaves the agent worse off than she initially was (i.e. setting 0 is better than setting 1,000, even taking into account the financial gain).

Finally, in Temkin's case, the tolerance principle – if there is any – is arguably the following, motivated in large part by Claim 1: *If it would be better to have experience e_1 than e_2, which is only a little less intense but twice as long than e_1, then it would be better to have e_2 than e_3, which is only a little less intense but twice as long as e_2.* Apply this principle to the relevant series and we eventually conclude that excruciating torture for a limited amount of time is better than very mild discomfort for a vast amount of time.

12.2.1 Can We Reject the Tolerance Principles?

The most popular strategy for blocking the Sorites Paradox is to reject one of the conditional premises, in which case the respective tolerance principle is false. This is indeed the strategy that Elson opts for in his critique of Tenenbaum and Raffman's argument (which would carry over to Quinn's as well); and although Elson is not explicit about whether the same holds for his critique of Chang's argument, I will assume that he favours the same strategy across different cases. In addition, I will further assume that many would prefer this strategy for Temkin's argument as well, at least insofar as the aim is to show it to be soritical.[47]

---

[44] See Elson (2014, pp. 564–7).
[45] In what follows, I take the tolerance principles to be material conditionals.
[46] Chang (2002, p. 674).
[47] For related recent discussions of Temkin's argument, see Nebel (2017) and Pummer (2017). And for suggestions for further reading, see Nebel (2017, fn. 30), and Pummer (2017, fn. 21).

There is a wide variety of accounts on which tolerance principles are false. For our purposes here, however, the details do not matter – the main task is to evaluate whether it is plausible to reject the ones identified above. I will argue that – although not strictly necessary – it *may* make sense to do so in the case of Chang's argument for parity, but not in the case of the other arguments. The reason is that in the former case the tolerance principle figures as an independent premise in the reasoning, while in the latter two cases the relevant principles in fact *follow from* certain features of the scenarios on which the arguments rely.

Consider the self-torturer's predicament. On both Quinn's and Tenenbaum and Raffman's diagnosis, the main features driving the puzzle are, first, the assumption that the rational agent ought to maximise expected utility at each choice point and, second, the fact that at each point the agent does so by taking the money and upping the setting one increment. Thus, it follows from the inherent features of the example that for each antecedent/consequent in (any instance of) the tolerance principle, we can independently verify that it is true. In genuine Sorites scenarios, this is not the case, which opens up the possibility of rejecting the relevant principle. But since the tolerance principle here follows from features inherent in the scenario, we cannot reject it without rejecting some of the underlying features as well. Then the argument succeeds, however.[48]

A similar analysis applies to Temkin's example. On any theory of the good on which – other things being equal – welfare affects goodness, we have independent grounds for thinking that each antecedent/consequent is true. Consequently, the tolerance principle here also follows from the example itself, unlike the Sorites case. If that is correct, then the Sorites charge does not stick and we have to reject either that welfare affects goodness in the way exemplified by Claims 1 and/or 3 or that *better-than* is transitive.

Things are different in the case of Chang's Small Unidimensional Difference Principle, since the principle does not follow from the example itself; rather, it is grounded more or less in the same kinds of concerns that generally motivate tolerance principles involved in straightforward instances of the Sorites Paradox.

It is indeed intuitively plausible that comparability is preserved between each adjacent pair of points in a relevant series, but we have independent reasons to accept the sentences involved *only* in the case of the initial premise – i.e. the first antecedent in the chain. The rest of our rational commitments are then supposed to follow from the application of basic logical operations, namely of successive applications of *modus ponens*. This indeed opens up the possibility of rejecting the relevant principle, as Elson suggests we do, although – as we will see below – this is not necessary for showing that the argument fails.

---

[48] Since I take the tolerance principles to be material conditionals, the truth of each antecedent/consequent pair suffices for the truth of the relevant principle. Note that this does not entail that there are no borderline cases for the relevant predicate. It just means that it is not soritical relative to the series on which the argument relies. Thanks to Sergi Oms for prompting me to clarify this.

12.2.2 Validity and the Normativity of Consequence

In this final section, I want to try to make it as transparent as possible how the differences above affect the plausibility of analysing the respective arguments as based on fallacious Sorites reasoning. The strategy is to show that even adopting what is arguably the most radical way to block the Sorites Paradox – that of weakening the consequence relation – will not suffice to show that Quinn's self-torturer puzzle and Temkin's continuum argument are invalid. The framework – developed in Zardini (2015a) and outlined below – invalidates Chang's argument, however. This, though, does not necessarily mean that it is really a Sorites argument, as such – but it does mean that it fails for the same reasons as the paradox. The problem with the argument is, as I have indicated, that – unlike Quinn's and Temkin's arguments – we do not have independent reasons to think that each link in the relevant chain is true.

Non-transitive consequence Zardini (2015a) presents a model on which the consequence relation is *non-transitive*.[49] The model validates a number of important classically valid argument forms – such as *modus ponens* – but invalidates certain forms that are notoriously problematic – such as the Sorites Paradox. One of the fundamental ideas in this framework is that consequence is not analysable in terms of truth preservation,[50] or indeed the preservation of any designated value – rather, it is a relation between a set of values assigned to the premises and a (possibly different) set of values assigned to the conclusion(s).[51] Once we are free of the preservation metaphor, Zardini thinks, space opens up for a non-transitive consequence relation (given that the metaphor in effect forces transitivity on us, at least prima facie). Further – and more positive – considerations in favour of non-transitivity come from inference scenarios in which the cogniser has insufficient reason to accept the conclusion(s) of an argument she recognises as classically valid, or perhaps even reasons against doing so, despite having reasons to accept the premises.[52] Since our logical models ought – on Zardini's account – to track the normative relation between an argument's premises and conclusion(s), and since these scenarios are hard to explain away as 'deviant', non-transitivist logics are indeed well motivated, he thinks.

As Zardini points out, we can have either non-inferential or inferential reasons to accept a sentence (or both). In the former case, one is rationally required to treat the relevant sentence as an 'initial point for further reasoning', as he puts it, while in the latter one is rationally required to treat the sentence as a 'terminal point of acceptance'.[53] Thus, if one has non-inferential reasons to accept a set of premises, then one has inferential reasons to accept the sentences that follow from it. However, if consequence is non-transitive, one does not by the same token have inferential reasons to accept the consequences of

---

[49] See also Zardini (2008a, 2008b, 2018b). For an introductory overview, see Chapter 9 in this volume.
[50] Consequence does guarantee truth preservation in an informal sense, however; see Zardini (2015a, pp. 237–44).
[51] Ibid., p. 240.
[52] Zardini (2015a, pp. 251–5).
[53] Ibid., p. 256. See also Smith (2004, pp. 196–9) (cited by Zardini).

these consequences: inferential reasons to accept a set of sentences do not give rise to inferential reasons to accept other sentences. That is, since the relevant normative relation holds only between non-inferential and inferential reasons, and since coupling two valid argument forms together will not necessarily produce a valid argument form, as it does in transitive logics, one will not have inferential reasons to accept the consequences of what one (merely) has inferential reasons to accept.

We see now how this framework blocks the Sorites Paradox. The paradox is generated by iterated instances of *modus ponens*, each of which is valid, yet chained together they produce an invalid argument. We have non-inferential reasons to accept the first sentence in the series – canonically, 'o_1 is F' – and thereby have inferential reasons to accept the next – canonically, 'o_2 is F'. And so long as we are in the determinate extension of 'F', we additionally have (independent, albeit related) non-inferential reasons to accept each successive sentence in the series. But as the series moves on, our non-inferential reasons become weaker and eventually give out. That is, in the series there will – assuming, for ease of exposition, a classical meta-language – be some last o_i, such that (1) we have non-inferential reasons to accept 'o_i is F', (2) we only have inferential reasons to accept 'o_{i+1} is F', and (3) we have no reason at all to accept 'o_{i+2} is F' – despite the fact we accept that 'o_{i+2} is F' follows from 'o_{i+1} is F'.[54] Thus, we have – on this framework – no reason to accept the paradoxical 'conclusion' (since it is in fact not a consequence of the set of Sorites premises). Paradox avoided.

Which arguments does non-transitivity block? As we have seen, it is crucial to the above treatment of the Sorites Paradox that our non-inferential reasons to accept a given sentence in the relevant series give out, and eventually terminate, as the series progresses. This also marks an important difference with respect to the arguments we have been considering. As we will see, even on a logical framework on which the consequence relation is weakened in this way (so as to be non-transitive), Quinn's and Temkin's arguments remain valid, whereas Chang's does not. The former two arguments may of course still be problematic in some respects, but I take this to at least show that the arguments are not fallacious in virtue of being soritical.

First, Quinn's and Temkin's arguments. As we saw, it is a feature of the relevant examples that, at each point in the relevant series, we have non-inferential reasons to accept that the next step maximises expected utility or increases welfare, respectively. Thus, unlike in a genuine Sorites scenario, *the non-inferential reasons do not give out as the series progresses*. The arguments may thus *look* like chaining arguments, but in fact they are not. Using Zardini's terminology, we can say that Quinn's and Temkin's arguments do not involve 'soritical reasons' to accept the progressing series – that is, we do not proceed down

---

[54] At o_{i+2}, we have – on this simplified model – reached the borderline region of 'F'. Note that this model assumes an agnostic attitude towards borderline cases. If we abandon this assumption, we may – in borderline cases – have inferential reasons either for accepting 'o_{i+2} is F' or for accepting 'o_{i+2} is not-F' (rather than no reason either way). On such models, we must – on pain of irrationality – accept one or the other (but not both), rather than remain agnostic. See Chapter 9 in this volume for further discussion.

the slippery slope *due* to having non-inferential reason to accept a tolerance principle. In fact, it is the other way around – we have inferential reasons to accept the respective tolerance principles because we have non-inferential reasons to accept the antecedent and consequent of each of its instances.

In the case of Chang's argument, things are different. Here, we arguably – contra Elson's suggestion – have non-inferential reasons to accept the tolerance principle (given its intuitive appeal), but lack inferential reasons to accept the (classically valid) conclusion that Michelangelo is comparable with Mozart. On a non-transitive framework, the fact that we have non-inferential reasons to accept that comparability is tolerant with respect to small unidimensional differences gives us inferential reason to accept that Talentlessi+ is comparable with Mozart if we have non-inferential reason to accept that Talentlessi is. But as the series progresses, our non-inferential reasons to accept the relevant consequent/antecedent give out – this much is agreed upon, although it is not part of the scenario in question that our reasons fully terminate, which in turn makes it unclear whether we are dealing with a genuine Sorites series. Still, as we get closer in the series to Michelangelo, the weight of our non-inferential reasons to accept the relevant sentences decreases to a point at which we are no longer rationally required to accept the sentence in question. At this point, all that remains are inferential reasons to accept it. And one step further, there is no reason at all to accept the relevant sentence. On this account, then, Chang's chaining argument is invalid and therefore does not succeed in establishing the case for parity.

13   The Sorites Paradox in Linguistics

Christopher Kennedy

13.1 Introduction

Statements of the Sorites Paradox often take the form in (1).

(1)   If x is α and there is a y such that x is just a bit more α than y, then y is α.

More often than not, α is a gradable adjective such as *long, tall, short, young, happy, healthy, tasty* or *bald*, which can be substituted directly for α in (1) without changing anything else about the sentence. But with slight modifications to the surrounding syntax, α can take the form of other grammatical categories as well: it can be a noun or noun phrase (*if x is a heap of sand and there is a y such that x is just a bit more of a heap of sand than y, then y is a heap of sand*), a verb or verb phrase (*if x likes broccoli and there is a y such that x likes broccoli just a bit more than y, then y likes broccoli*), a prepositional phrase (*if x is near the ocean and there is a y such that x is just a bit nearer the ocean than y, then y is near the ocean*) and so forth.

These kinds of examples illustrate the feature of vague predicates that has been of primary interest to linguists: independent of grammatical category, vague predicates generally have both an unmarked 'positive' form – the bare version of α that appears both in the initial premise of the argument and in the apparently paradoxical conclusion – and a comparative form that is used as the basis for the inductive step. In fact, vague predicates – and in particular GRADABLE ADJECTIVES such as *tall, big, fast* and *heavy* – generally have more than just positive and comparative forms; they appear in a host of complex constructions that are used to express different 'degrees' to which the predicate applies to its argument, some of which are illustrated in (2).

(2)   a.   Kim is very/really/rather/quite tall.

b.   Kim is 2 metres tall.

c.   Kim is less tall than Lee.

d.   Kim is tall compared with Lee.

e.   Kim is as tall as we expected her to be.

f.   Kim is too tall to fit in this seat.

g.   Kim is tall enough to reach the ceiling.

h.   Kim is so tall that she has to buy special clothes.

The challenge presented by these examples for semantic theory is to come up with an analysis of the meanings of words and phrases such as *tall*, *heap of sand*, *likes broccoli* and *near the ocean* that simultaneously explains their semantic and pragmatic properties in the unmarked, positive form and provides the basis for a compositional account of comparatives and the other complex constructions in (2). Central to this challenge is an explanation of the fact – already evident from a close examination of (1) – that the positive form is vague (in the sense of being incompatible with sharp distinctions) but the comparative form is not, at least for mono-dimensional predicates such as *tall(er)*.[1] In setting up the scenario in which we discover that we are unwilling to judge some x and y differently for α when they are minimally distinct with respect to α – that α is necessarily tolerant,[2] to use Wright's (1975) terminology – we crucially rely on the fact that we are willing to judge them differently for *more α than*.

The story of the Sorites Paradox in linguistics – and the story of vagueness in linguistics more generally – is intertwined with the story of the semantic analysis of constructions such as those in (2), in particular comparatives, and of the analysis of the grammar of gradability more generally, especially the grammar of gradable adjectives. This work can be (somewhat coarsely) divided into two traditions, which differ, essentially, in whether vagueness or comparison is taken to be basic. In the first approach, which emerges out of work on the Sorites Paradox in philosophy of language, vagueness is basic, and a semantics for gradability is built on top of a logic for vagueness. In the second approach, which is more rooted in syntax and linguistic analysis, gradability is taken to be basic and vagueness is derived. In Sections 13.2 and 13.3, I describe these analytical traditions in more detail, with close attention to the empirical arguments that both motivate and challenge them, and to the ways that they inform, and are informed by, theorising about the Sorites Paradox. Section 13.4 discusses a second class of gradable adjectives that present a challenge for existing analyses of the relation between gradability and vagueness, because they have positive forms that do not give rise to the Sorites Paradox, and Section 13.5 concludes with a discussion of recent work in linguistics that is specifically geared towards understanding the Sorites in terms of communication in the presence of semantic uncertainty.

13.2 From Vagueness to Comparison

The first attempts within linguistics to provide a compositional analysis of the semantics of comparative constructions built directly on work in the philosophical literature geared towards understanding vagueness and the Sorites Paradox. These attempts are similar in

---

[1] It is less clear that the same distinction holds between multi-dimensional predicates such as *clever* and *good*. To keep the discussion focused, I will limit my attention to mono-dimensional gradable predicates for most of this chapter, but I will say a bit more about multi-dimensional gradable predicates in Section 13.5.

[2] See 'The Sorites Paradox', in the introduction to this volume, and Chapter 5, Section 5.2.

treating comparatives as expressions that manipulate or constrain parameters relevant for fixing the extension of the positive form, but differ in the details of what this parameter is.

The first kind of analysis is briefly gestured at by Lewis (1970a) and then worked out in substantive detail, alongside a comprehensive syntactic analysis of comparatives, by McConnell-Ginet (1973). Following Lewis, McConnell-Ginet assumes that the extension of a vague predicate is determined by an element of the index of evaluation (an array of parameters relative to which extensions are fixed) called a DELINEATION COORDINATE, which is a value in an ordering appropriate to the type of concept the predicate describes (height, weight, temperature, etc.) that represents the boundary between the things the predicate is true and false of. The denotation of *tall* on this view, for example, is as stated in (3). (Here and throughout, $[\![\alpha]\!]^{\pi}$ means 'the extension of α (an expression of the object language) relative to parameter π'.)

(3) $[\![tall]\!]^{d} = \{x \mid x's \text{ height is at least as great as } d\}$

The comparative can then be analysed as an expression that quantifies over delineations: *taller than* expresses a relation between individuals such that there is a delineation that makes *tall* true of the first and false of the second.[3] More generally, for any gradable adjective α:

(4) $[\![more\ \alpha]\!]^{d} = \{\langle x, y \rangle \mid \exists d'[[\![\alpha]\!]^{d'}(x) \wedge \neg[\![\alpha]\!]^{d'}(y)]\}$

Kamp (1975) develops an analysis of comparatives that is conceptually identical to the Lewis/McConnell-Ginet analysis, but is formalised in terms of a supervaluationist approach to vagueness (cf. Fine 1975 and Chapter 2 in this volume). (The key difference between the two approaches is that the former is partial, allowing for extension gaps, but the latter is not.) In Kamp's analysis, rather than quantifying over delineations, comparatives quantify over the (possibly partial) models relative to which vague predicates are assigned extensions. Given a general 'consistency constraint', which ensures that for any objects x, y, if x is in the positive extension of α relative to some model M and y is not (see Klein 1980; van Benthem 1982), there is no M' such that y is in the extension of α and x is not, the semantics of the comparative can be stated as in (5).

(5) $[\![more\ \alpha]\!]^{M} = \{\langle x, y \rangle \mid \{M' \mid [\![\alpha]\!]^{M'}(x)\} \supset \{M' \mid [\![\alpha]\!]^{M'}(y)\}\}$

Taller than, on this view, expresses a relation between individuals x, y in a model M such that the models that make *tall* true of x are a proper superset of the models that make *tall* true of y. Note that it need not be the case that *tall* is true of x or y in M: *tall* could be false or undefined for one or both of them (the latter for borderline cases). Given the consistency constraint, the truth conditions of *taller than* effectively require just that there

---

[3] Note that this analysis says nothing about whether a delineation is or is not usable in the positive form. For example, it may be the case that there is no context in which the two smallest things in the universe would ever be appropriately described as tall. But the analysis is committed to the position that if they differ in height, there is a delineation that makes *tall* true of one of them and false of the other.

be some model in which *tall* is true of *x* and false of *y*, similar to what we saw with the Lewis/McConnell-Ginet analysis.

A hybrid of these two approaches is developed by Klein (1980) (see also Wheeler 1972; van Benthem 1982; van Rooij 2011a, 2011b; Burnett 2016), who analyses gradable predicates as expressions whose extensions are determined relative to subsets of the domain of discourse called COMPARISON CLASSES. Comparison classes provide the domain of the predicate and are fixed by the context, like the delineation coordinate. They also provide the basis for fixing the extension of the predicate, as a function of the way that objects in the comparison class distribute relative to the gradable concept the predicate is used to describe (height, weight, etc.), in a way that allows for partiality, like the partial models in a supervaluationist analysis. Finally, interpretations of gradable predicates are also subject to a variant of the consistency constraint, such that for any *x*, *y*, if *x* is in the positive extension of α relative to some comparison class *C* and *y* is not, there is no *C'* such that *y* is in the extension of α and *x* is not, and also to a general informativity principle that stipulates that for any *C*, the positive and negative extensions of α relative to *C* must both be non-empty. Since the comparison class provides the domain of the predicate, this latter constraint rules out singleton comparison classes, and together with consistency allows for the two ways of defining the semantics of comparatives shown in (6a–b), owing to Klein (1980) and Wheeler (1972) respectively.

(6)   a. $[\![more\ \alpha]\!]^{C} = \{\langle x, y\rangle \mid \exists C'[[\![\alpha]\!]^{C'}(x) \wedge \neg[\![\alpha]\!]^{C'}(y)]\}$
      b. $[\![more\ \alpha]\!]^{C} = \{\langle x, y\rangle \mid [\![\alpha]\!]^{\{x,y\}}(x) \wedge \neg[\![\alpha]\!]^{\{x,y\}}(y)\}$

These different approaches to comparatives are similar in that each of them derives the meaning of the complex form *more* α in terms of the meaning of α, and in particular each makes crucial use of the theoretical machinery brought to bear in the analysis of the vagueness of α to do so. Kamp's approach is most directly tied to a particular account of the Sorites Paradox, since it is committed to a supervaluationist semantics; the other two accounts are compatible with supervaluationism but are equally compatible with e.g. contextualist or epistemicist approaches to the Sorites.

These analyses are also similar in their responses to the challenge of explaining why the comparative form is not vague, even though the positive form from which it is derived is vague. In each account, vagueness in the positive form is ultimately tied to indeterminacy or uncertainty about the parameter relative to which its extension is determined in a context of utterance: the delineation coordinate, the model or the comparison class. In the case of comparatives, however, these parameters are fixed in a fully determinate and compositional way.

Note, however, that it follows from the fact that the meaning of the comparative is stated in terms of the meaning of the positive that each of these analyses must be committed to the position that the positive form, contrary to normal appearance and use, is in fact compatible with a precise meaning (as noted by both Kamp 1975 and Klein 1980). To see why, consider the different interpretations assigned by these analyses to the sentence in (7), which are spelled out in (8).

(7) Kim is taller than Lee.

(8)   a. $\exists d'[[\![tall]\!]^{d'}(\mathbf{k}) \wedge \neg[\![tall]\!]^{d'}(\mathbf{l})]$ McConnell-Ginet

    b. $\{M' \mid [\![tall]\!]^{M'}(\mathbf{k})\} \supset \{M' \mid [\![tall]\!]^{M'}(\mathbf{l})\}$ Kamp

    c. $\exists C'[[\![tall]\!]^{C'}(\mathbf{k}) \wedge \neg[\![tall]\!]^{C'}(\mathbf{l})]$ Klein

    d. $[\![tall]\!]^{\langle\mathbf{k},\mathbf{l}\rangle}(\mathbf{k}) \wedge \neg[\![tall]\!]^{\langle\mathbf{k},\mathbf{l}\rangle}(\mathbf{l})$ Wheeler

In a context in which Kim's height is greater than Lee's height by a very small amount – say 5 millimetres – (7) is both true and felicitous, regardless of how tall either of them actually is, which in turn means that there must be delineations/precisifications/comparison classes relative to which Kim is in the extension of *tall* and Lee is not. It follows that on all of these views, the tolerance of the positive form cannot be 'hardwired' into the lexical semantics of gradable predicates, since the positive form is, by hypothesis, the lexical entry.

But this in turn leads to apparently paradoxical results when we look beyond 'explicit' comparison constructions involving morphologically marked adjectives, such as (7), to instances of 'implicit' comparison constructions involving the positive form, such as (9) (Sapir 1944; Kennedy 2007a, 2011; van Rooij 2011a).

(9) Kim is tall compared with Lee.

(9) entails that Kim's height exceeds Lee's height, just like (7), a result that is most plausibly obtained by assuming that the semantic function of *compared with* is to cause the denotation of *tall* to be fixed in such a way as to make it true of Kim and false of Lee, just like the comparative. But (9) differs from (7) in that it is infelicitous in the context described above, in which Kim and Lee differ in height by a very small amount, and indeed in any context which reproduce the 'minimal distinctions' property of soritical reasoning. ((9) is also different from (7) in implicating that Kim is not tall, as pointed out by Sawada 2009.)

Positive adjectives used as modifiers in definite descriptions show similar behaviour. In a context in which I am asked to identify two individuals standing next to each other in front of a wall which indicates that their heights are 1.75 metres and 1.5 metres respectively (like a police line-up), either of the utterances in (10) would be felicitous ways for me to say who is who.

(10)   a. The tall one is Kim; the short one is Lee.

    b. The taller one is Kim; the shorter one is Lee.

Note that (10a) is acceptable regardless of whether a height of 1.75 metres would otherwise be sufficient to justify characterising Kim as tall (e.g. if the comparison class is adult American males). This is because, as we have seen, positive *tall* is context dependent, and in a context involving just two individuals its meaning can be fixed in a way that makes it true of one individual and false of the other – in this case as a way of satisfying the uniqueness presuppositions of the definite determiner. However, if the context is one in which the heights of the two individuals are very similar – e.g., if one is 1.75 metres tall and the other is 1.745 metres tall, as in the scenario described above – only the utterance involving the morphologically comparative form in (10b) is acceptable.

In sum, the problem of implicit comparison is that the very same assumptions that enable a compositional analysis of the comparative form of an adjective in terms of the meaning of the positive form lead to a paradox. The truth and felicity of (7) and (10b) in the minimal distinctions context means that there must be delineations, precisifications or comparison classes that make *tall* true of Kim and false of Lee; yet the infelicity of (9) and (10a) means that these delineations, precisifications and comparison classes cannot be used to fix the extension of *tall* in a minimal distinctions context. Evidently, the relevant valuations are compositionally manipulable by the comparative morphology, but otherwise inaccessible to the positive form, even when other features of the utterance, such as the meaning of *compared with* or the presuppositions of the definite article, should promote their use. The challenge for proponents of the semantic analyses of positive and comparative adjectives described in this section is to derive these results in a principled way. (See van Rooij 2011a for one attempt to do so, and Kennedy 2011 for a response.)

The explicit/implicit distinction also helps further define the evaluation criteria for accounts of the Sorites Paradox. If it is assumed that one of the analyses outlined here (or the equivalent) correctly characterises the semantics of vague predicates, then tolerance – whatever is responsible for judgements about the inductive premise – cannot be a matter of lexical semantics, since the lexical semantics of vague predicates (or at least positive form gradable adjectives such as *tall* and *bald*) is compatible with precise interpretations. It must instead have something to do with constraints on how a vague predicate can be interpreted or justifiably used in contexts of utterance, or with properties of contexts, or perhaps with the interaction between contexts and the semantics of generalising statements such as the inductive premise – as in e.g. epistemicist and contextualist accounts of vagueness. But whatever the account is, it should also say something about why tolerance obtains not only in generalising statements such as the inductive premise, but also in implicit comparison constructions, in which we might otherwise expect the semantic and pragmatic properties of the rest of the utterance ought to make such 'inaccessible' contexts or interpretations accessible.

13.3 From Comparison to Vagueness

The analyses of comparatives described in Section 13.2 all share the feature of defining the meanings of complex degree constructions in terms of the meanings of the positive form, and in particular in terms of the analytical assumptions that are involved in accounting for the vagueness of the positive form. In this sense, these analyses are directly connected to work in philosophy of language on the Sorites Paradox. Alongside these analyses we find a second set of approaches that are not connected to work on vagueness or the Sorites, but are instead more closely connected to work in semantic theory on the compositional analysis of other linguistic phenomena. This line of work effectively takes the complex constructions illustrated in (2) as the starting point, and asks what kind of lexical meaning for a bare gradable adjective such as *tall* best captures the full range of meanings of the complex forms, without any special concern for the vagueness of the positive form or the proper account of the Sorites Paradox.

The answer that this line of work provides is that the various complex forms are not derived directly from the positive form, but instead both the positive and comparative (and other complex) forms are derived from a more basic lexeme that denotes a relation between individuals and some other value – typically some kind of measurement value, or DEGREE – as in (11). (See e.g. Bartsch and Vennemann 1972; Seuren 1973; Cresswell 1976; von Stechow 1984; see Klein 1991 and Bale 2009 for detailed discussions of how degrees can be modelled in terms of equivalence classes of individuals, rather than as independent model-theoretic objects.)

(11) $[[tall]] = \{\langle x, d \rangle \mid x's$ height is at least as great as $d\}$

On this view, to be a gradable predicate is just to denote a relation between individuals and degrees. The function of the complex constituents that combine with the adjective in such examples as (2) is to fix the value of the degree argument, thereby providing a standard of comparison, and turning the relation into a property that holds of an object just in case it has a degree of the relevant property that is at least as great as that standard. The predicate in (2b), for example, denotes the property of having a height that is at least as great as the degree denoted by *2 metres*; the comparative of inferiority in (2c) denotes the property of having a height that is exceeded the degree of Lee's height; the comparative of superiority simply switches the ordering relation; and so on.

The similarity between (11) and the delination-based semantics for gradable predicates in (3) is not accidental. In effect, degree-based (and other relational) analyses take the lexical meanings of gradable predicates to be de-contextualised variants of the meanings assumed by the vagueness-based approaches discussed in the previous section, where the interpretive parameter used to fix the extension of a vague predicate is reanalysed as one of the arguments of the relation. The fact that comparatives are not vague, on this view, is unremarkable, since their meanings are derived from forms with fixed meanings such as (11), which are also not vague. In short, whether a predicate built out of a gradable adjective is vague or not does not depend on the denotation of the adjective, but rather on the meaning introduced by the degree morphology with which it composes.

For this very reason, it is the vague positive form that, somewhat paradoxically, presents the trickiest analytical challenge, for two reasons. The first is a compositional one. The denotation of *tall* in (11) expects two arguments: a degree-denoting one and an individual-denoting one. But there is no constituent in the surface form of a sentence containing positive *tall* to saturate the degree argument and thereby convert it from a relation between degrees and individuals to a property of individuals, which is the semantic type it must have when it is used as a modifier or predicate. The usual response to this problem is to hypothesise a phonologically null, 'positive degree' morpheme which does this job, or to assume default saturation by a free variable over degrees, or default existential binding of the degree argument. These are all analytical options that are independently motivated for other cases of 'implicit argument' saturation, but appeal to such operations in one language are typically motivated by pointing to another language in which the hypothesised argument slot is obligatorily realised by overt morphosyntax. The same cannot be said for the positive form of a gradable adjective: there is no language in the world that we know of in which a gradable adjective must compose with some overt morphosyntax to create a predicate with positive form meaning (Klein 1980; Francez and Koontz-Garboden 2015; Grano and Davis 2017). This is deeply mysterious if gradable adjectives denote relations rather than properties of individuals – if they are basically two-place rather than one-place – and it is a mystery that so far has not been satisfactorily resolved by proponents of relational analyses of gradable adjectives.

Alongside the compositional challenge is the question of how exactly to characterise the semantics of the positive form, once a particular assumption about how composition actually works has been adopted, and the further question of whether the semantic analysis adopted provides insights on vagueness or the Sorites Paradox. The latter question is particularly salient in the relational analysis, given the fact that the lexical meaning of a gradable predicate such as (11) is not itself vague, but it is a question that, until fairly recently, has not received a great deal of attention from scholars in linguistics, for understandable reasons. As noted above, the relational approach emerged out of a research programme aimed at understanding and giving compositional analyses of complex degree constructions, which manifest a great deal of grammatical complexity and variation both within and across languages (see e.g. Stassen 1985; Beck et al. 2009; Bochnak 2013). The semantics of the grammatically simple positive form is usually presented as an afterthought – if it is addressed at all – and discussion of the implications of a particular semantic analysis for vagueness and the Sorites Paradox is rare.

The simplest analytical option is simply to assume that composition of the relational meaning in (11) with a null positive morpheme reproduces one of the lexical semantic analyses described above, such that the degree argument of the adjective is constrained to exceed a threshold degree whose value is fixed by a contextual parameter, as in delineation analyses (see e.g. Barker, 2002; Kennedy and McNally, 2005), possibly in a partial way, as in supervaluationist analyses (see e.g. Sassoon 2009, 2013).[4] These analyses do not provide new options for analysing the Sorites Paradox that are not already present in corresponding approaches that treat the positive form as basic, but they do provide the basis for a more explanatory account of implicit comparison, if not a fully satisfactory one.

Recall from earlier that in a context in which Kim and Lee differ minimally in height, (12a) is infelicitous but (12b) is fine.

(12)   CONTEXT: Kim is 90 cm tall; Lee is 89.5 cm tall.

    a.   # Kim is tall compared with Lee.

    b.   Kim is taller than Lee.

---

[4] Actually, neither Barker nor Sassoon introduce degrees into the object language, but both make use of degrees in the model theory in ways that reproduce the relational analysis in the meta-language.

As we have already seen, if the comparative is derived from the positive, this difference between explicit and implicit comparison is puzzling. The infelicity of (12a) indicates that there is no way of fixing the meaning of *tall* that makes it true of Kim and false of Lee when they differ minimally in height, as would expected if *tall* were necessarily tolerant. But the felicity of (12b) requires that there be such a way of fixing the meaning of *tall* in such a context, since this is what is required by the meaning of the comparative, which means that *tall* is not necessarily tolerant.

If, however, the comparative is not derived from the positive, and instead both positive and comparative are separately derived from a more basic relational meaning like (11), this paradox disappears. The meaning of the adjectival predicate in (12a) is a function of (11) and a phonologically null positive morpheme, so we may assume from the infelicity of (12a) that, whatever the semantic contribution of the positive morphology is, the result of composition with (11) is indeed a meaning that is necessarily tolerant – regardless of whether it is used in an implicit comparison construction such as (12a) or in the inductive premise of the Sorites Paradox. But this assumption makes no additional predictions about (12b), since the meaning of the adjectival predicate in this example is a function of (11) and the comparative morpheme. As long as the comparative morpheme derives a meaning that is not subject to tolerance – e.g. if it simply entails that the degree to which Kim is tall exceeds the degree to which Lee is tall – we can accommodate the difference between (12a) and (12b). Of course, these assumptions do not yet provide an explanation of why the positive is subject to tolerance, but they draw a compositional distinction between implicit and explicit comparisons that cannot be drawn in non-relational analyses. Moreover, our compositional semantic assumptions do not commit us to a particular analysis of tolerance: since we need not assume that the positive form ever has a precise interpretation, we open the door to an analysis of tolerance that is rooted in its semantics – or more precisely, in the semantics of the positive morpheme. Specifically, since the positive form is compositionally derived in a relational analysis, it is possible to introduce explicit semantic content into the truth conditions of the positive form that is not shared by comparative and other degree-modified forms, via the semantic content of the positive morphology; this is an option that is unavailable in lexicalist analyses, though as we will see, not all compositional analyses take advantage of it.

For example, one common approach along these lines, geared towards encoding the intuition that the positive is true only of objects that fall above some threshold in a distribution, assigns a denotation to the positive morpheme that restricts the degree argument of the adjective to degrees that exceed an average, norm or some other value that is a function of the distribution of objects in an explicit or implicit comparison class on an adjective-appropriate scale (see Bartsch and Vennemann 1972, 1973; von Stechow 1984; Bierwisch 1989; Kennedy 1999 for variants of this idea). Another strategy is to analyse the positive morpheme in such a way that it constrains the degree argument of the adjective to exceed a contextually determined 'neutral zone' on a scale (see e.g. Heim 2006; von Stechow 2009). When combined with a theory of antonymy that characterises pairs like *tall* and *short* as encoding inverse ordering relations, this kind of analysis semantically encodes the intuition that there are regions on e.g. the height scale in which objects count as neither tall nor short.

Like their 'content light' cousins, which merely reproduce lexicalist denotations for the positive via semantic composition, these 'content heavy' analyses of the positive form do not provide new options for analysing the Sorites Paradox, and arguably fare worse than the former in helping us understand the appeal of the inductive premise – and answering what Fara (2000) calls the 'psychological question' about the Sorites – since the denotations they provide for the positive form are less indeterminate than denotations that reproduce lexicalist analyses. The truth conditions of (13a) on a 'greater than average' semantics for the positive, for example, are as in (13b). But the latter is easily rejected, while the former is not.

(13)   a. If x is tall and there is a y such that x is just a bit taller than y, then y is tall.

    b. If x's height is at least as great as the average height for class X, and there is a y such that x's height is just a little bit greater than y's height, then y's height is at least as great as the average height for class X.

Likewise, these analyses have a hard time accounting for constraints on implicit comparison. A very natural way of thinking of the function of the *compared with* phrase in (12a), for example, is that it restricts the comparison class to the set consisting of just Kim and Lee. But if that is the case, then even if Kim's height is only slightly greater than Lee's it will still be the case that it exceeds the average height for the class {Kim, Lee}.

The problem with these approaches, in a nutshell, is that they make the semantic content of the positive too similar to that of the comparative, and so too determinate, leaving very little room for vagueness (Bogusławski 1975). The alternative is to assume that the positive introduces semantic content that results in vague truth conditions. Cresswell (1976), for example, characterises the positive as requiring the degree argument of the adjective to be 'towards the top of the scale'; Fara (2000) argues that it should 'significantly exceed an average' (cf. Solt 2009); Bogusławski (1975) says it should be 'noteworthy'; and Kennedy (2007b) says that it should represent a degree that 'stands out' relative to the kind of scale the adjective uses. Of all the semantic analyses of the positive within the relational tradition, these approaches are most sensitive to the Sorites Paradox, and to providing an account of tolerance more generally. Fara (2000), for example, argues that the 'significantly greater than' relation is interest relative in a way that derives tolerance, and Kennedy (2007b) provides a pragmatic account of why it can never be the case that for two objects that differ minimally along a scalar dimension, one object can be judged to have a degree of the relevant property that 'stands out' while the other does not (with two key exceptions, which I will return to in the next section). In these kinds of analyses, the explanation of intuitions about the inductive premise of the Sorites and the explanation of the infelicity of implicit comparisons in minimal differences contexts are the same: both emerge from the semantic content of the positive form, which gives rise to tolerance.

However, these kinds of accounts face a challenge of undergeneration when we look beyond the core cases of soritical adjectives to a wider range of data. As I pointed out in Section 13.1, soritical arguments can be constructed using expressions from a range of different grammatical categories, not just from gradable adjectives. An account of tolerance that is based on the details of the compositional analysis of gradable adjectives, via the semantics of the positive form morphology, says nothing about these other cases.[5] Such an analysis is bound to be incomplete as a full explanation of vagueness, then, no matter how well it explains the particular case of gradable adjectives.

That said, an analysis in which tolerance emerges from the semantics of the positive form is of course consistent with the possibility that it can also arise in other ways, from other features of meaning or use. The argument for the relevance of semantic content is rooted in linguistic facts, namely the difference in acceptability between explicit and implicit comparison constructions in minimal difference contexts, which is difficult to explain on accounts that do not tie tolerance to the content of the positive form. If this argument is correct, then the fact that tolerance is also observed in constructions that do not involve positive form gradable adjectives means that the origins of tolerance are heterogeneous, and our best theory will be one that can explain what unifies the different semantic, pragmatic or other factors that bring it about.

13.4 Absolute Adjectives

The discussion so far has focused on different attempts to capture a key linguistic property of vague predicates that is evident in the Sorites Paradox: the fact that such predicates are obligatorily tolerant, but have compositionally derived comparative forms that are not. And as we have seen, in the case of gradable adjectives, the analysis of comparison – and gradability more generally – is closely tied to the analysis of tolerance. Approaches such as the ones discussed in Section 13.2 take the positive form of a gradable adjective to be basic, assume an essentially tolerant meaning for it, and derive gradability from this meaning (in terms of the partitioning of the domain relative to different valuations of the predicate allowed by the consistency constraints). Approaches such as those discussed in Section 13.3, on the other hand, assume an essentially gradable, relational meaning as the lexical content of the adjective, and derive the tolerance of the positive form compositionally, in the mapping of the underlying relational meaning to a property. In both types of analysis, then, the expectation is that if a predicate is gradable – if it can appear in comparatives and other degree constructions such as the ones illustrated in (2) – then it should display tolerance in its positive form, and should give rise to the Sorites Paradox.

As it turns out, there is a class of gradable adjectives that, like other members of this class, combine readily with comparative and other degree morphology, but which need

---

[5] With a couple of interesting exceptions (such as certain kinds of verbs describing changes of state; see Kennedy and Levin 2008; Bobaljik 2012), there is no empirical evidence in support of generalising the (de-)compositional analysis of the positive form of gradable adjectives to all vague expressions, regardless of grammatical categories.

not display the kind of tolerance in their positive forms that all of the analyses discussed so far would lead us to expect (Rusiecki 1985; Cruse 1986; Rotstein and Winter 2004; Kennedy and McNally 2005; Kennedy 2007b). Adopting terminology from Unger (1975), Kennedy and McNally (2005) refer to such adjectives as ABSOLUTE gradable adjectives, and distinguish two kinds. Maximum standard absolute adjectives such as *straight, empty, dry* and *flat* require their arguments to have a maximal degree of the relevant property, and minimum standard absolute adjectives such as *bent, wet, scratched* and *bumpy* merely require their arguments to have some degree of the relevant property.

These properties of absolute adjectives are evident in entailment relations between comparatives and positives (Kennedy2007b). As shown by (14), ordinary gradable adjectives such as *tall* and *short* – which are also referred to as RELATIVE gradable adjectives when it is important to distinguish them from their absolute cousins – lack entailments from comparative to positive:

(14)   a. x is taller than $y \Rightarrow x/y$ is (not) tall

       b. x is shorter than $y \Rightarrow x/y$ is (not) short

Absolute adjectives, however, display a different pattern. A comparative involving a maximum standard adjective such as *straight* entails the negation of the positive for its second argument, and a comparative involving a minimum standard adjective like *bent* entails the corresponding positive for its first argument:

(15)   a. x is straighter than $y \Rightarrow y$ is not straight

       b. x is more bent than $y \Rightarrow x$ is bent

The pattern in (14) is what we expect from any of the theories of the positive form discussed in Sections 13.2 and 13.3: the comparative effectively requires its arguments to differ in height, such that the first has more/less than the second, but says nothing about whether their heights are significant, stand out, exceed an average or anything else (relative to the different orderings that the antonyms impose). The pattern in (15), on the other hand, is not expected from any of the views we have discussed so far, and instead indicates that positive *straight* requires its argument to be maximally straight (and so is false of y in (15a), since y must be less straight than x), and that positive *bent* requires its argument to merely have some degree of bend (and so is true of x, which has some bend if it is more bent than y).

This has consequences for the Sorites Paradox: as pointed out by Kennedy (2007b), absolute gradable adjectives do not lead to paradox in the same way as relative gradable adjectives. More precisely, although we might be inclined to accept (16a) and (16b) in most contexts, we may also reject these claims in a way that is impossible in soritical arguments involving relative adjectives such as *tall* and *short*.

(16)   a.   For any x, if x is straight, and there is a y such that x is just a bit straighter than y, then y is also straight.

       b.   For any x, if x is bent, and there is a y such that x is just a bit more bent than y, then y is also bent.

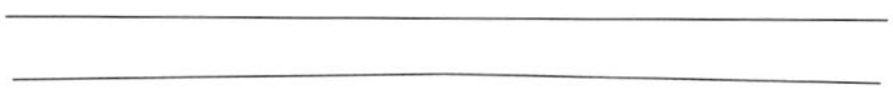

Figure 13.1

Put another way, while relative adjectives are inherently tolerant, absolute adjectives allow for what Pinkal (1995) calls NATURAL PRECISIFICATIONS: (16a) can be rejected because *straight* can be used to mean (something like) 'perfectly straight', and (16b) can be rejected because *bent* can be used to mean (something like) 'minimally bent'.[6] This is also shown by the contrast between absolute and relative adjectives in implicit comparison contexts. The two lines in Figure 13.1 differ minimally along two dimensions: degree of bend and degree of length. (17a) is infelicitous, as we have seen, because *long* and *short* cannot be used to distinguish between objects that differ minimally in length (as is required, in this case, by the presuppositions of the definite description). In contrast, (17b) is felicitous because *straight* and *bent* can be used to distinguish between two objects that differ minimally in degree of bend.

(17)   a.   # The long line is straighter than the short line.
       b.   The straight line is longer than the bent line.

If facts such as those above are interpreted as indicating that the lexical meanings of absolute adjectives are essentially fixed, then the challenge they present for approaches that derive gradability from a semantics for tolerance is to explain where gradability comes from. The most articulated response to this challenge is provided by Burnett (2016), who bites the bullet and assigns absolute adjectives precise meanings – *straight*, for example, denotes the property of being perfectly straight – but provides a means of deriving tolerant meanings pragmatically in a way that can then support comparative formation.

The challenge of absolute adjectives for approaches that derive tolerance from gradability is to explain why their positive forms have precise interpretations based on maximal or minimal thresholds rather than the tolerant, 'norm-based' denotations that are assigned to positive form relative adjectives. Responses to this challenge have made key use of a lexical semantic difference between classes of adjectives that relational analyses are particularly well equipped to model: gradable adjectives differ in whether they encode scalar concepts that are based on open or closed scales. This distinction can be diagnosed

---

[6] Philosophers might object at this point that nothing (with the relevant physical properties) is perfectly straight, and correspondingly that everything (again with the relevant properties) has minimal bend, rendering such meanings unusable. And indeed, actual uses of *straight* and *bent* communicate something more like 'relatively close to straight' or 'relatively bent'. But this makes it all the more remarkable that absolute adjectives can be used to make sharp distinctions in ways that relative adjectives cannot. Whether 'imprecise' uses of absolute adjectives are a function of semantic content or pragmatic reasoning is a question of current debate, relevant not just for gradable adjectives but also numerals, measure terms, temporal phrases, place names and so forth. See Lasersohn (1999), Krifka (2007), Syrett et al. (2010), Lassiter and Goodman (2014), Burnett (2016), Leffel et al. (2016) and Klecha (2018) for discussion and analyses.

by looking at acceptability with certain types of modifiers (Rotstein and Winter 2004; Kennedy and McNally 2005; Kennedy 2007b; Syrett 2007). The modifier *completely*, for example, introduces the entailment that an object has a maximal degree of a gradable property, and so combines only with adjectives that use scales with maximum values, while the adjective *slightly* entails that an object exceeds a minimum degree, and so selects for adjectives that use scales with minimum values. As the following examples show, there is a correlation between the relative/absolute distinction and scale structure: absolute adjectives have closed scales; relative adjectives have open scales.[7]

(18)	a.	completely straight/empty/flat	ABSOLUTE MAX.
	b.	#completely long/heavy/big	RELATIVE
(19)	a.	slightly bent/open/striped	ABSOLUTE MIN.
	b.	#slightly long/heavy/big	RELATIVE

Two different kinds of explanations for this correlation have been proposed in the literature. In the first approach, scale structure plays a direct role in the determination of thresholds of application and the relative/absolute distinction. The maximum and minimum degrees on closed scales provide salient values for coordination on thresholds, and threshold interpretation is optimised to select such values whenever possible (Kennedy 2007b; Potts 2008; Toledo and Sassoon 2011; Qing and Franke 2014a, 2014b). Open scales, in contrast, lack any 'natural transitions' (to use Williamson's 1992b term) that could provide coordination points for thresholds, and so have highly context dependent and uncertain interpretations. In the second kind of approach, the role of scale structure is more indirect. Decisions about thresholds are based not on formal semantic properties of gradable adjectives, but rather emerge from Bayesian reasoning that takes into account probabilisitic prior knowledge about the distribution of objects in a gradable adjective's domain relative to its scale (Lassiter and Goodman 2014, 2017; the basic mechanisms of this approach are described in more detail in the next section). The domains of open scale adjectives tend to have normal distributions (our experience with nails, for example, tells us that there are relatively few very short and very long ones, but lots in between), which give rise to similarly shaped curves for threshold probabilities and relative interpretations. The domains of closed scale adjectives have non-trivial probability mass at the scalar endpoints (there are lots of straight or nearly straight nails), which give rise to threshold probabilities that are much narrower and skewed towards the endpoints, giving rise to absolute interpretations – albeit ones that are 'less absolute' than in the first kind of approach.

---

[7] The examples in (19b) are crucially unacceptable on interpretations that are parallel to the most prominent interpretations of the examples in (19a), which would be paraphrased as 'a slight amount of length/weight/size'. These examples can have a different kind of interpretation, paraphrasable as 'slightly *too* long/heavy/big', i.e. as expressions of slight excess. But in such cases the semantics of excess provides a minimum standard for the modifier to interact with, namely the minimum degree that counts as excessive for the relevant purpose.

13.5 Recent Developments

The two approaches to the relative/absolute distinction discussed in Section 13.4 differ in the role that scalar distinctions play in determining meaning, but they share the core intuition that this distinction – which is, at its core, the question of whether a predicate is necessarily tolerant or not – emerges from the mechanisms involved in determining the communicative content of utterances that introduce semantic uncertainty. In the case of positive form gradable adjectives, the uncertainty is about the threshold that an object must reach in order to count as having the property in question. Absolute interpretations show that the principles involved in fixing thresholds are optimised to minimise uncertainty (based on scalar representation, domain distribution or perhaps a combination of both); relative interpretations, and tolerance, result when threshold uncertainty cannot be minimised.

Threshold uncertainty clearly does not present a problem to communication, however, and one of the important contributions of Lassiter and Goodman's (2014, 2017) work is to provide a model for how communication with vague predicates actually works, and in so doing provide new insights on the Sorites Paradox. The core idea of Lassiter and Goodman's model is that a 'pragmatic listener' computes a probability distribution for the value of an uncertain variable in an utterance as a function of a relevant set of prior values and the assumption that speakers choose particular utterances (over relevant alternatives) with (at least) a goal of optimizing informativity. In the case of gradable adjective interpretations, the model uses prior knowledge of the distribution of the degrees to which the objects in the adjective's comparison class possess the scalar concept associated with the adjective to derive a probability distribution on thresholds, and a corresponding posterior probability about the scale position of an object that is described as having the property expressed by the adjective.

As illustration, suppose that (20) is uttered in a context in which the comparison class consists of the sorts of nails that are encountered in typical household carpentry contexts, the lengths of which are approximately normally distributed.

(20)   That nail is long.

The further below the mean that a particular length is, the more likely it is that an arbitrary nail has at least that much length, and the further above the mean that a particular length is, the less likely it is that an arbitrary nail has that length. Given the speaker's preference for informativity, a low value for the adjective's threshold of application (e.g. one that makes *long* true of 75 per cent of the comparison class) will be assigned low probability, because the resulting meaning would be too weak, while a high value for the threshold (e.g. one that makes *long* true of only 1 per cent of the comparison class) will also be assigned a low probability, because the resulting meaning would be too strong. The output of the model in a simple case such as this is a posterior probability distribution over thresholds that is shifted upwards from the prior distribution over the comparison class, and a posterior probability for the length of the target of predication that is shifted still further up the scale.

Put another way, the model predicts that (20) will be heard to communicate something roughly equivalent to 'the length of this nail is significantly greater than the average length of nails in the comparison class', which, as we have seen, is an accurate paraphrase of its truth conditions. But more than that, Lassiter and Goodman (2017) show that the model also makes specific quantitative predictions about the plausibility of the inductive premise of the Sorites Paradox, and the extent to which it should be heard as compelling, which vary as a function of different semantic parameters, such as the granularity of the scale and different ways of modeling the semantics of the inductive premise of the Sorites (in particular involving different approaches to the semantics of the conditional). This work not only provides a fully explicit account of communication with, and intuitions about, vague language; it also opens up the possibility of subjecting different accounts of the Sorites to experimental investigation.

Lassiter and Goodman's model is rooted in the idea that tolerance reflects uncertainty about threshold values; recent work by Grinsell (2017) develops the hypothesis that tolerance emerges from uncertainty about the factors that are involved in making decisions about thresholds in the first place. Focusing on MULTI-DIMENSIONAL adjectives such as *healthy* and *talented*, Grinsell observes that such expressions have meanings that are formally comparable to multi-dimensional decision problems of the sort studied by Arrow (1950, 1959) in his work on social choice. Just as the decisions of a legislature involve an aggregation of the individual choices of multiple agents with distinct and possibly conflicting preferences, the extension of a predicate such as *healthy* involves an aggregation of choices along multiple, independent dimensions of measurement, such as blood pressure, body temperature, weight and so forth. Arrow proved that given a certain reasonable set of constraints on the decision-making process, the aggregation of set of individual choices into a single multi-dimensional choice function is guaranteed to fail transitivity – it will allow for rankings of A over B, B over C, and C over A – even if the rankings produced by the individual dimensions are linear. Grinsell argues that the same set of Arrowian principles constrain the denotations of multi-dimensional predicates, with the same result. For example, if we know that Kim has better blood pressure than Lee and Lee is less overweight than Pat, we may judge (21a) and (21b) to be true, but it does not guarantee that (21c) is true.

(21)   a.   Kim is healthier than Lee.

     b.   Lee is healthier than Pat.

     c.   Kim is healthier than Pat.

According to Grinsell, the Sorites Paradox emerges as a concrete manifestation of the Arrowian constraints on multi-dimensional meanings. On the one hand, these constraints entail that the tolerance relation expressed in the comparative form of a multi-dimensional predicate is not transitive, in which case the inductive premise of the Sorites is not guaranteed to be true, and the paradoxical conclusion does not follow. At the same time, the Arrowian constraints (in particular the one known as Independence of Irrelevant Alternatives) requires the aggregation procedure to respect pairwise judgments in a way that gives rise to our intuitions that the inductive premise is true (cf. Fara's 2000 Similarity Constraint).[8]

An obvious challenge for this kind of analysis is the fact that vagueness is not limited to multi-dimensional predicates, as we have seen throughout this chapter. (Likewise, vagueness does not disappear if we hold fixed all the dimensions of a multi-dimensional predicates except for one.) The denotation of *tall* is (arguably, at least) based on a single factor, height, and replacing *healthier* with *taller* in (21) leads to very different judgements: if Kim is taller than Lee, and Lee is taller than Pat, then it absolutely follows that Kim is taller than Pat. Adopting a degree-theoretic approach to gradable adjective meaning of the sort discussed in Section 13.3, Grinsell suggests that the locus of multi-dimensionality in uni-dimensional adjectives is not the adjective denotation itself, but rather in the 'significantly greater than the norm' semantics associated with the positive form of relative adjectives in particular. However, this response relies on a very specific solution to the compositional challenge discussed in Section 13.3 – one in which there is a phonologically null morpheme that introduces the relevant multi-dimensional meaning – which is motivated mainly by theoretical considerations and not linguistic ones. An intriguing alternative to Grinsell's solution would be to put the 'social' back in social choice, and attempt to explain vagueness and the Sorites Paradox not in terms of Arrowian constraints on the denotations of the predicates involved, but rather in terms of Arrowian constraints on the social problem of coordination on uncertain denotations by a community of language users.[9]

---

[8] See Chapter 14 in this volume, Section 14.3.2.

[9] Many thanks to Sergi Oms and Elia Zardini for their very helpful comments on the first draft of this chapter. I also wish to express a special debt of gratitude to my friend Delia Graff Fara, who first challenged me to look beyond the traditional role that philosophical work on vagueness and the Sorites Paradox has played in providing tools for semantic analysis, and see as well the role it could play in evaluating semantic and pragmatic theories, and in achieving a more sophisticated and empirically rich understanding of patterns of linguistic behaviour. This chapter is dedicated to her memory.

14   The Sorites Paradox in Psychology

Paul Égré, David Ripley and Steven Verheyen

This chapter examines some areas of theoretical and experimental psychology in which the Sorites Paradox has had an influence or has been an object of study. Our goal is to show not only different manifestations of the Sorites in psychology, but also how psychological modelling and behavioural data can cast light on the puzzle raised by the paradox.

The first aspect we consider concerns the *psychology of reasoning and argumentation*. Sorites arguments are often conflated with 'slippery slope arguments', typically used *a contrario* to argue that a line should be drawn at a specific location of a vague domain, on pain of reaching an undesirable or absurd outcome, or alternatively that no line can be drawn at all. In Section 14.1 we start out with a brief history and overview of work done on slippery slope arguments, to highlight that such arguments are not intrinsically wrong: fundamentally they are inductive arguments, whose acceptability depends on the strength of the relation between the antecedent and the consequent of their conditional premises, and on the utility attached to specific outcomes. As such, slippery slope arguments tend to be handled in a probabilistic framework.

The second and more significant area of influence we consider concerns the study of similarity in *psychophysics* and in the *psychology of concepts*. The main premise of a Sorites argument involves the notion of sufficient similarity between objects, and states that if two objects are sufficiently similar they must produce identical judgements as to whether some property applies or not. Section 14.2 presents some influential accounts of the relation between discrimination and categorisation in psychophysics, and underscores the centrality of probabilistic modelling to deal with Sorites-susceptible predicates quite generally.

We distinguish, following Raffman (1994) and Dzhafarov and Dzhafarov (2012), two versions of the main premise of the Sorites, one pertaining to discrimination (same versus different comparison task) and one pertaining to categorisation (assignment under a common lexical category). We look first at the psychology of discrimination, and at how the notion of just noticeable difference introduced by Fechner can be related to the tolerance principle, namely the idea that some differences can be so small as to make no difference in terms of discrimination.[1] We then look at the psychology of categorisation proper, and

---

[1] See 'The Sorites Paradox', in the introduction to this volume.

review how small differences in terms of similarity to a prototype affect decisions of membership to a category.

In the remaining sections we survey various lines of experimental work based on transition series between distinct prototypes. Such series, omnipresent in several domains of experimental psychology, involve so-called morphs, namely gradual alterations of a prototype connecting it to another prototype. Section 14.3 looks at two paradigms involving unordered presentations of stimuli drawn from such morphing series: the first concerns studies on *categorical perception*, the second concerns studies of the effect of *simultaneous presentation* of stimuli on categorisation. Finally, Section 14.4 surveys work on *dynamic Sorites*, that is on ordered transitions between prototypes.

To highlight the importance of such transition series in psychology, we deliberately reproduce several examples of stimuli in this chapter. One message of this chapter is that the manner in which such stimuli are presented (whether isolated, in pairs, in random order or in a specific order) is essential to the way in which similarity between stimuli influences their assignment to a common category.

14.1 Slippery Slopes and the Psychology of Reasoning

Traditional definitions of a Sorites argument distinguish a narrow sense and a broad sense of the term. In the entry 'Sorites' of Peirce and Baldwin's *Dictionary of Philosophy and Psychology*, two senses are distinguished in that way (Peirce 1902). On a specific and marked sense, it is a particular fallacy, namely the sophism of the heap of wheat usually credited to Eubulides of Miletus. On a generic and neutral sense, a Sorites is merely a 'chain of syllogisms'.

The two meanings are obviously related, because the sophism of the heap can be presented as such a chain of syllogisms. Le Chevalier de Jaucourt, in the earlier *Encyclopédie* of Diderot and d'Alembert, writes about the argument of the heap: 'that argument is composed of several propositions, differing little from one another, and chained in such a way that, after beginning with a manifest and incontrovertible truth, one moves, little by little, to an obviously false conclusion' (cited in Cayrol 2016). However, not all chains of arguments need be faulty according to the broad definition of a Sorites. Le Chevalier de Jaucourt, in the same entry, mentions a number of precautions that one may take in order for a chain of arguments, that is a Sorites in the generic sense, to preserve the truth of its first premise down to its final conclusion.[2]

---

[2] He writes:

To avoid surprise, one needs to ensure that everything that is said of the attribute be also said of the subject. That there be no ambiguity in the terms, nor in the propositions. That one insert no negative propositions among affirmative ones. That the proposition that immediately precedes the conclusion not be negative, unless the conclusion might also be negative. That the link and gradation that must be between the propositions be right. Finally, that there be in the Sorites no particular proposition, except maybe for the first. Such are, in brief, the wise rules that Facciolati has detailed in a discourse on insoluble arguments; one can consult it.

One area of particular interest in relation to the previous definitions concerns the psychology of reasoning, and the analysis of so-called slippery slope arguments (SSAs). Different forms of SSAs have been distinguished in the literature, two of which are sometimes called *horrible result SSA* and *arbitrary result SSA* (see Williams 1995; Lode 1999; Volokh 2003), which we may present as follows:

(1) If A_0 then A_1; if A_1 then A_2;...; if A_{n-1} then A_n; but A_n is bad; therefore A_0 is bad. (horrible result SSA)

(2) If A_0 then A_1; if A_1 then A_2;...; if A_{n-1} then A_n; therefore there is no $i < n$ for which it is rational to have that A_i and not A_{i+1}. (arbitrary result SSA)

Both argument forms are soritical in that they rely on the existence of a 'series of gradual intervening steps' (Hahn and Oaksford 2006) between the antecedent and the consequent of each conditional. However, the two arguments are not interchangeable. They do not yield identical conclusions and they are used for different purposes. The first one is used to prescribe drawing a line (at the origin of the Sorites sequence), whereas the second type indicates that a line cannot be drawn and bolsters scepticism.

An early illustration of a slippery slope argument can be found in Bossuet's treatise of logic addressed to the Dauphin (Bossuet 1677; see Cayrol 2016, to whom we are indebted). Bossuet uses the following example to illustrate the definition of a Sorites as a 'heap of propositions':

Whoever authorises violent enterprises ruins justice; whoever ruins justice breaks the link that unites the citizens; whoever breaks the society link generates divisions within a state; whoever generates divisions within a state exposes it to an obvious danger; therefore, whoever authorises violent enterprises exposes the State to an obvious danger.

Bossuet's example is best cast in the form of a horrible result SSA (by adding the premise 'but exposing the State to an obvious danger is bad', and then by adding a further conclusion of the form 'therefore authorising violent enterprises is bad'). A case that more easily lends itself to either type is the following:

(3) a. If abortion may be legal at 1 week of pregnancy, then it may as well be legal at 2 weeks; but if it may be legal at 2 weeks, it may as well be legal at 3 weeks;...; but if it may be legal at 31 weeks, then it may be legal at 32 weeks; but making abortion legal at 32 weeks is bad. Therefore, that abortion may be legal at 1 week of pregnancy is bad.

  b. If abortion may be legal at 1 week of pregnancy, then it may as well be legal at 2 weeks; but if it may be legal at 2 weeks, it may as well be legal at 3 weeks;...; but if it may be legal at 31 weeks, then it may be legal at 32 weeks; therefore, there is no week such that it is rational that abortion may be legal that week and not the next.

SSAs are generally presented as fallacies or sophisms. The general thought that SSAs, like soritical arguments more generally, are incorrect arguments, is epitomised in the following passage from Blackburn (2002):

Slippery slope reasoning needs to be resisted, not just here but everywhere. It is exemplified in the paradox of the bald man, known as the Sorites Paradox. [...] Consider the imposition of a speed limit, say 30 miles per hour, and make it the law. We do not really believe that 29 miles per hour is always safe, and 31 is always not. But we would not listen to someone saying, 'There is no principled place to draw a line, so we can't have a limit'. Nor would we listen to Sorites reasoning forcing the limit forever upwards, or forever downwards to zero. So, if we think the abortion issue does need moralising and politicising, nothing stops us from fixing a particular term of pregnancy beyond which abortion is generally prohibited. (Blackburn 2002, p. 64)

In this passage, Blackburn argues primarily against arbitrary result SSAs, suggesting that they are always fallacies. On the other hand, as pointed out by Lode (1999) and Hahn and Oaksford (2006), horrible result SSAs need not be fallacies. They may be seen as instances of a broader class of 'empirical' or 'rational grounds' SSAs, which can be used to rationally argue in favour of drawing the line at the origin. Bossuet's example, clearly, is not intended as a fallacious argument, but rather as a compelling argument leading from sound conditional premises to a sound conditional conclusion. In principle therefore, SSAs ought to fall under the generic-neutral definition of a Sorites: like other chains of propositions, they can have sound instances and unsound instances, although the unsound instances will create more trouble, and will generally be seen as more emblematic of the notion.

Hahn and Oaksford (2006)'s main point is that the acceptability of 'empirical' or 'rational grounds' horrible result SSAs varies as a function of the strength of the probabilistic connection between the consequent and the antecedent in the conditional, and as a function of the negative utility of the outcome (how bad or 'horrible' the outcome is supposed to be). This was experimentally confirmed by Corner, Hahn and Oaksford (2011) for horrible result SSAs of length 1, by having participants rate the acceptability of argument strength as a function of the utility and probability of outcomes.[3]

The results of Corner et al. (2011) can be brought to bear on the discussion of arbitrary result SSAs more broadly. That is, the consideration of the probability of conditional premises can serve to determine where the line should be drawn. Consider legal dispositions on abortion. Depending on the place, the line is effectively drawn between antecedent and consequent at values (in terms of age of embryo) for which, despite equal steps in weeks, the developmental differences appear larger. To put it otherwise, the conditional statement 'if you allow abortion at one week, you may allow it also at two weeks' appears to have higher validity than the conditional statement 'if you allow abortion at five weeks, you may allow it also at six weeks', if it is felt that the strength of the association between 5 and 6 is smaller than the strength of the association between 1 and 2, and possibly even weaker than at other places. An example is Ohio's 'heartbeat bill', drawing the line between five and six weeks on account of the emergence of a noticeable heartbeat in embryos during that step.

More generally, the strength of an SSA ought to depend on the inductive strength of each conditional premise and on the length of the chain, since intuitively the longer the

---

[3] Corner et al. (2011) do not use explicit conditional sentences to test those predictions, but they use related constructions (e.g. 'We should oppose the legalisation of euthanasia in the UK, as it will lead to an increase in the number of instances of medical murder', Corner et al. 2011, p. 148).

chain the weaker the probabilistic connection between the last consequent A_n and the first antecedent A_0.[4]

On Hahn and Oaksford's account, SSAs thus fall under a broader Bayesian account of inference and argumentation. Such an account can explain the sensitivity of other kinds of arguments to context. From our perspective, there are two virtues of the account of slippery slopes outlined by Hahn and colleagues using the notion of conditional probability: one is the fact that such an account avoids rejecting soritical reasoning as always flawed. The other is that it highlights a connection between soritical reasoning and probabilistic reasoning, which we will see to be of importance in other areas of the psychology of the Sorites Paradox.[5]

14.2 Discrimination and Categorization

Viewed abstractly, the Sorites Paradox can be presented as a puzzle concerning the impact of similarity on judgement. The main premise of a Sorites argument says that if two objects are sufficiently similar, then they will be judged alike. To say that they will be judged alike can mean two different things: that similar objects will be treated alike in terms of discrimination (same versus different recognition), or that similar objects will be treated alike in terms of categorisation (assignment under a lexical category).[6] In this section we consider how both principles are approached in psychophysics. The focus in this section is mostly foundational, and concerned with the centrality of probabilistic modelling for an adequate representation of both discrimination and categorisation.

14.2.1 Similarity in Discrimination

Whether and in what sense two very similar objects will be judged alike is in a way part of the initial project of psychophysics (Fechner, 1860). Fechner was interested in measuring the effect of variations of physical magnitudes on perceived magnitudes. For example, he was interested in *the extent* to which a weight physically heavier than another would be perceived as heavier. Importantly, Fechner did not concern himself exclusively with the effect of small variations of physical magnitude on perceived magnitude, but with the general problem of the relation between the two kinds of magnitude. As a limiting case, however, Fechner was interested in the problem of the minimal difference in physical magnitude that it would take for a difference in sensation to be perceived (what he called

---

[4] In logic, this feature may be characterised in at least two ways: either in terms of a conditional connective showing failures of transitivity; or in terms of a consequence relation failing transitivity. On the former kind of approach, see for instance Adams (1998); on the latter see for example Cobreros et al. (2012) and Chapter 9 in this volume.

[5] See in particular Lassiter and Goodman (2017) for a more recent Bayesian account of soritical reasoning with vague adjectives. Their account compares various ways of formalising the main conditional premise of the Sorites in probabilistic terms. On their account too the size of the step is crucial in determining the probability of the main conditional premise of the Sorites, which is typically less than 1.

[6] Terminology varies in psychology: studies on categorical perception oppose discrimination tasks and identification tasks. In this chapter we preferably use the term 'categorisation' instead of 'identification' to refer to the assignment of an item under a higher-type category.

a Just Noticeable Difference or JND). On the assumption that such a difference exists, we may state the relation between physical difference and perceived similarity as follows:

(4) $|w(x) - w(y)| \leq \varepsilon \rightarrow x \sim_W y$.

This says that if the difference in weight between x and y is less than some positive value ε, then x and y will be qualitatively perceived as having the same weight. Whether there is a positive value ε of physical difference along some relevant dimension, such that *absolutely* no difference will be perceived is a difficult problem that quickly aroused discussion among Fechner's contemporaries. This problem obviously bears a connection with what Wright (1976) has called the *tolerance principle*, the idea that there might be some positive degree of change of some property 'insufficient ever' to make a judgemental difference.[7]

The way this problem was solved, already by Fechner, is by appeal to statistical methods. The observation of psychophysicists is that even when two stimuli are successfully discriminated along some sensory continuum on one or several occasions, there remains a probability of confusing them. That probability would materialise in terms of the number of failures to discriminate the stimuli over sufficiently many trials. Conversely, even when two stimuli are very hard to discriminate, one may find evidence that they are not perceived as entirely alike by running sufficiently many trials and by looking at the proportion of success at discrimination.[8] Because of that, the common wisdom in contemporary psychophysics is to think of what counts as a 'just noticeable difference' as being relative to a probabilistic threshold, whose choice is not unique but is set conventionally. Luce (1959, p. 34) presents the idea of JND as follows:

The essential idea is to pick a probability cutoff π, $\frac{1}{2} < \pi < 1$, and to say that alternatives discriminated more than 100π per cent of the time are more than one JND apart; those discriminated less often are one JND or less apart. [...] That is to say, it is meaningless to speak of JNDs without specifying the probability cutoff that was used to define them – a point unfortunately all too often ignored in the experimental literature.

On that approach, $x \sim_W y$ is thus definable in terms of the probability of confusing x and y relative to a statistical threshold, and the value of the constant ε is in fact relative to that threshold. That is, $x \sim_W y$ if, and only if, $1 - \pi \leq Pr(x, y) \leq \pi$, where $Pr(x, y)$ is the probability of selecting x within the set $\{x, y\}$ (see Luce 1956, Definition 3).[9] For illustration, suppose that $\pi = 0.79$, then x will be declared noticeable from y if x is selected more than 79 per cent of the time, or if y is selected more than 79 per cent of the time.

In psychophysics various paradigms exist for the measurement of that probability, such as the two-alternative forced choice task (2AFC), in which for example two color patches x and y are presented on a screen, and in which participants must decide whether a third patch z is identical to x or y. The patch z is always one of x or y: typically, when x and

---

[7] See 'The Sorites Paradox', in the introduction to this volume, and Chapter 5, Section 5.2.
[8] See Borel (1950), Hardin (1988) and Raffman (2011) for discussions of that issue.
[9] Luce also defines the relation $xL_W y$ as $P(x, y) > \pi$. Intuitively, it means 'at least one π-jnd larger', and $x \sim_W y$ thus means 'no more than one π-jnd apart', the latter being a reflexive, symmetric, but typically non-transitive relation.

y are physically similar, it will be hard to have accurate matching judgements, and the proportion of correct answers will allow the experimenter to decide whether x and y are more or less than one JND apart. Note that on that approach of the definition of a JND, the highest degree of confusion is when the confusion probability between x and y is close to 0.5, meaning the capacity to discriminate between x and y is at chance level.

According to Dzhafarov and Dzhafarov (2012) a *comparative* Sorites sequence is a sequence of stimuli $(x_1, \ldots, x_n)$, such that adjacent stimuli in the sequence are pairwise indiscriminable in the sense of being in the relation $x_i \sim_W x_{i+1}$, but such that x_1 and x_n are not in that relation. Luce (1956) points out that we find an abundance of such comparative sequences in which one is indifferent between adjacent members of the sequence, but not indifferent between more distant members (Luce's topical example involves a series of 401 cups of coffee with increasing amounts of sugar, such that we can't distinguish the sweetness of adjacent cups of coffee, but we can definitely taste the difference between the cups with the smallest and largest amounts of sugar). This implies that indifferences are not transitive, a point central to Luce's account of indifference, and captured by his approach via probability cut-offs: it is easy to find triples x, y, z of stimuli such that $Pr(x, y)$ and $Pr(y, z)$ are both below π but $Pr(x, z)$ is not. This means that two or more members of a sequence can be less than one JND apart, while the ends of the sequence are more than one JND apart.[10]

14.2.2 Similarity in Categorisation

The conditional sentence (4) states that if the physical difference between two objects is small enough, then the perceived difference between them will be small. This should be compared with the standard premise of the Sorites Paradox, which may be put as follows:

(5) $x \sim_W y \to (P_W x \leftrightarrow P_W y)$.

Whereas (4) says that a small *physical difference* produces no difference in *discrimination*, (5) states that a small difference in discrimination makes *no* difference in the assignment under an abstract category. For example, if the difference in perceived weight (W) between two objects is small enough, then both should be declared 'heavy' (P_W), or both should be declared 'not heavy'.

Dzhafarov and Dzhafarov (2012) relate the latter premise to what they call *categorical* Sorites sequences: a categorical Sorites sequence is a sequence of stimuli $(x_1, \ldots, x_n)$ such that adjacent members are in the $\sim_W$ relation, and yet such that x_1 satisfies P_W but x_n does not. Such sequences undeniably exist, but they cannot exist consistently with the admission of (5) assuming the logic and the conditional to be classical.[11] The existence

---

[10] Luce (1956) contains an algebraic account of the notion of intransitive preference, and of its relation to the corresponding of preference, in what is known as the theory of semi-order relations. See van Rooij (2011b) for a presentation of Luce's account.

[11] We have deliberately modified the exact definition of a categorical Sorites sequence given by Dhzafarov and Dhzfarov. On their definition, it directly follows that such sequences cannot exist. We prefer to say that sequences whose adjacent members

of such sequences is in fact the reason why the literal interpretation of (5) is rejected by so many accounts of the Sorites (viz. Borel 1907, 1950; Williamson 1994; Dzhafarov and Dzhafarov 2012; Raffman 2014).

What is the situation in psychophysics? The dominant view is that in the same way in which the relation $x \sim_W y$ expresses a probabilistic dependence in the discrimination between x and y, the biconditional in (5) should be weakened to a relation expressing a probabilistic dependence in the identification of x and y under a common category. In other words, (5) should be weakened to:

(6) $x \sim_W y \rightarrow (P_W x \approx P_W y)$, where $P_W x \approx P_W y$ if, and only if, the probability of judging $P_W x$ is close to the probability of judging $P_W y$

In the case of weight, this says that if two objects have almost identical weights, then the probability of categorising each of them as heavy will be almost identical (see Égré, 2011a). Note that this principle is weaker than (5) because it does not prevent small differences along the dimension of similarity from making a difference along the dimension of categorisation. When we combine (6) and (4), we see that if two objects are sufficiently similar to be indiscriminable, then the probabilities of subsuming them under the same category will be relatively close, but that is not to say that the objects will invariably be assigned to the same category (Borel 1907). One way of summarising this is to say that psychophysical models of categorisation do not endorse the tolerance principle (5), but they nevertheless support a probabilistic version of what Smith (2008) has called the *closeness* principle.[12] Smith's closeness principle says that if two items x and y are very close in terms of their *P*-relevant properties, then the truth values attached to Px and Py should be close. Assuming only two truth values are available to begin with, a different way of cashing out that idea is in terms of probabilities (instead of degrees of truth).[13]

The upshot is that items that are highly similar *may* but *need not* be categorised in the same way in all circumstances. When imagining two very similar colour patches that would be indiscriminable, one is strongly pulled to the view that either both of them will necessarily be perceived and categorised as red, or that neither of them will be. Raffman (1994) tempers that intuition by stressing that discrimination and categorisation obey distinct constraints:

If we are mystified by our ability to draw categorial distinctions between patches we can't tell apart, that is partly because we are setting things, as it were, from the discriminator's point of view. The discriminator has no memory to speak of, and certainly no memory of the sort required for categorial distinctions. Hence he fails to notice the progressive change in the appearance of the patches as he moves along the series. The categoriser, on the other hand, has a rather good memory [   ] We might

---

are hard to tell apart exist, but to highlight that the tolerance principle, classically interpreted, is problematic in combination with such sequences.

[12] See Chapter 8 in this volume, Section 8.2.

[13] See Égré (2011b) for an interpretation of closeness along those lines, and Lassiter and Goodman (2017) on various ways of articulating the tolerance principle probabilistically in a Bayesian setting. This is consistent with the idea of representing the tolerance principle more qualitatively than quantitatively. See Cobreros et al. (2012) for a qualitative version of the tolerance principle, and Égré (2011a) and Égré (2016) for some bridges between qualitative and probabilistic representations.

capture the idea by envisioning the category as a mental elastic band anchored at one end to the stored prototype. (Raffman 1994, pp. 48–9)

Raffman's view here is faithful to the idea that categorisation of an item is a function of the similarity of that item to a prototype stored in memory. Discrimination, on the other hand, is fundamentally a local process of comparison.[14]

14.2.3 Threshold Models

Various probabilistic models of categorisation exist in psychology that satisfy the constraint stated under (6). In this section we consider two examples belonging to the family of *threshold* models (Borel 1907; Hampton 2007; Verheyen, Hampton and Storms 2010; Égré 2016; Verheyen, Dewil and Égré 2018), introduced explicitly to handle vague predicates. Such models view the subsumption of a stimulus under a category as relative to an inner threshold value lying on a continuum. Category membership is fixed by whether the stimulus is perceived as above or below the relevant threshold along the relevant dimension, but interstimulus differences are handled probabilistically.

The first example we consider is a pioneering model outlined in Borel (1907) in relation to the Sorites Paradox. Borel's model is a Gaussian model of categorisation as a function of imperfect discrimination. When discrimination is perfect, observation will be exempt from noise, and category membership will be represented by a step function (Figure 14.1, left): any item above the threshold will be a category member, and any item below a non-member. When discrimination is imperfect, on the other hand, category membership is represented by a smooth function as a result of noise: the typical form of such a function is a sigmoid function derivable as a cumulative normal distribution function (see Figure 14.1, right) with the inflection point centred on the threshold, and whose slope at that point depends on the amount of noise in discrimination.[15] As Figure 14.1 exemplifies, small variations in the physical properties of the stimulus (such as height in cm) are matched by small variations in the probability of categorising an item under a given category (such as 'tall'), in agreement with (6). However, the relation between physical similarity and categorisation is not linear, since identical differences along the physical axis can be matched by more or less difference in the probability of categorising an item under a given label.

The second example we consider is Hampton's (2007) threshold model of the relation between membership and typicality. In Hampton's approach, as in Raffman's picture of categorisation, similarity is relative to a prototype for the category. The decision whether to categorise an item as *P* or not *P* is therefore a function of the similarity of that item to the representation of the prototype in memory. When the similarity exceeds a certain inner threshold, the model predicts a verdict of membership. As shown by Hampton (1998), actual data collected by McCloskey and Glucksberg (1978) concerning the relation between

---

[14] See also Chapter 3 for a discussion of Raffman's view in terms of contextualism.
[15] See Égré and Barberousse (2014) and Égré (2017) for details on the derivation of the function from first principles.

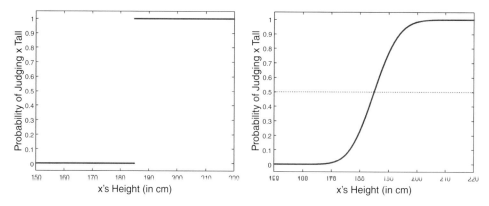

Figure 14.1 Hypothetical categorisation curves for 'Tall' as a function of physical height. On the left, a step function, with a threshold at 185 cm; on the right, a smooth function, based on the cumulative normal distribution relative to the same threshold.

binary membership judgements and typicality ratings are adequately fitted by a cumulative normal distribution. McCloskey and Glucksberg collected binary membership judgements of 30 participants and typicality judgements from a distinct group of 24 participants about 492 items taken from 18 distinct categories. Hampton (1998) represented average judgements of membership across participants as a function of the typicality ratings obtained for the other group (Figure 14.2, left). What they found is that items most typical of a category (viz. a car relative to the category vehicle, or a diamond relative to the category of precious stones) and items entirely atypical for a category (such as shoes for vehicles, or granite for precious stones) have a very high probability of being respectively included in or excluded from the category. For items of intermediate typicality (say a parachute for the category vehicle or zircon relative to precious stones), the degree of membership is itself intermediate.[16]

Figure 14.2 shows the distribution of average membership judgements as a function of typicality for the separate categories 'Vehicle' and 'Precious Stone'. In each case, membership is indeed a sigmoid function (represented by the best fitting logistic function). As those data confirm, small differences in typicality again make small but non-null differences in membership judgements. This pattern, importantly, is not just operative at the group level. When binary membership judgements are collected within-subject, and the same item is presented multiple times to a participant, the average degree of membership of each item can be calculated in the same way, and individual psychometric functions present the same characteristic shape (see for example Égré, de Gardelle, and Ripley 2013, for individual data pertaining to colour terms).

---

[16] See Verheyen et al. (2010) for a replication and probabilistic account of the McCloskey and Glucksberg findings, and Verheyen et al. (2011) for an extension that includes (dis)similarity to prototypes of two competing categories.

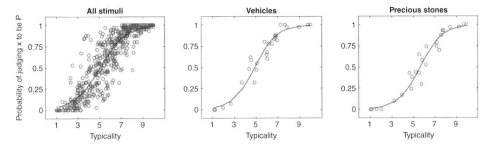

Figure 14.2 Scatterplots of the percentage of participants in McCloskey and Glucksberg (1978) providing a positive categorisation versus average item typicality for all stimuli (left), the category of vehicles (middle) and the category of precious stones (right) along with the best fitting logistic function.

14.2.4 Typicality and Family Resemblance

To conclude this section, we may highlight further aspects of the influence of the Sorites Paradox concerning the centrality of the notion of prototype in categorisation. One point of contact worth mentioning between philosophy and psychology around the Sorites can be found in Wittgenstein (1953)'s remarks in §65 to 78 of the *Philosophical Investigations* on the limits of criterial definitions, and in the subsequent work of Rosch and Mervis on the notion of family resemblance (Rosch and Mervis 1975).

Wittgenstein in this passage argues for the impossibility of defining a concept such as 'game' by the possession of necessary and sufficient criteria of application. Instead, Wittgenstein argues, card games, ball games, and other kinds of games form a family in which 'we see a complicated network of similarities overlapping and criss-crossing' (§66). Various games can therefore be ordered depending on how many features they have that overlap. As Rosch and Mervis (1975, p. 575) summarise,

a family resemblance consists of a set of items of the form AB, BC, CD, DE. That is, each item has at least one, and probably several, elements in common with one or more other items, but no or few elements are in common to all items.

Basically, therefore, a family resemblance is a set of items with soritical structure, in the sense that each such set can be ordered with adjacent items having one or more features in common, but such that the first and last item in the sequence may have no features in common. What Wittgenstein's remarks suggest is that the limits of a concept such as 'game' could be hard to find precisely in virtue of that soritical structure, namely in virtue of the fact that items pairwise are highly similar. Rosch and Mervis appear to agree with that, but what they point out, and what McCloskey and Glucksberg's data confirm, is that in cases in which a concept appears to have no clear boundary in relation to that family resemblance structure, the degree as well as the ease to which membership is decided is a function of the centrality of the item in the category. There is more, in other words, to the notion of family resemblance than the existence of local similarities: there is the idea that among a set of items with a family resemblance, some items are more stable than others relative to the assignment to that common category. Rosch and Mervis operationalise this in terms of what they call a *family resemblance score*. For example, 'chair, sofa, table… lamp, telephone' all have various features that may justify assigning them to the category 'furniture', but in that list the more typical items are in fact also those that share the most features with other items in the family (i.e. those that have a higher family resemblance score).

On the one hand, therefore, local similarities in a set of items with family resemblance structure might explain why it is so difficult to draw non-arbitrary boundaries for the corresponding category. On the other hand, this difficulty seems helped, in practice, by the fact that some items are much more central than others in the set, and can serve as reference points to decide category membership. Rosch and Mervis's notion of family resemblance is particularly relevant for nominal or multidimensional categories, for which several features can be distinguished, even if the notion of typicality is applicable to a wider range of Sorites-susceptible cases, including adjectival categories (see, for instance, Verheyen and Égré 2018). Another aspect worth stressing is the fact that in their studies on nominal categories, items are all in general pairwise discriminable (viz. an apple versus an avocado relative to the category 'fruit') unlike stimuli generally examined in relation to adjectival categories (viz. two adjacent shades in relation to the category 'yellow', or two close heights relative to 'tall'), but categorisation can nevertheless give rise to inconsistent verdicts both between- and within-subjects (considering both an apple and an avocado to be a fruit on one occasion, but denying that avocado is a fruit on another; see McCloskey and Glucksberg 1978 and Verheyen et al. 2010).

14.3 Unordered Transitions Between Categories

In this section we examine the relation between discrimination and categorisation in experimental paradigms in which intermediate stimuli drawn from gradual transition series between two prototypes are presented in a random order. We highlight that aspect since randomness is generally a way of blocking specific order effects, which we will discuss in Section 14.4. We look at two sets of phenomena that suggest that the relation between discrimination and categorisation is more complex than what is assumed in the main premise of the Sorites Paradox. We first discuss the phenomenon of categorical perception. We then refine the discussion in the previous section by reporting on the effect of presenting pairs of more or less distant stimuli on the ascription under a common category.

14.3.1 Categorical Perception

The main premise of a (categorical) Sorites (5) asserts that if two colour patches, say, are indiscriminable, then they will be assigned to the same abstract category. As Raffman's earlier quote warns us, that view presupposes that discrimination is mostly what drives categorisation. One phenomenon of particular interest in that regard is categorical perception.

The phenomenon concerns the converse influence that categorisation (assignment under a linguistic label) appears to exert on discrimination. Harnad (1987, p. 3) describes it as follows: 'The effect is best described as a qualitative difference in how similar things look depending on whether or not they are co-classified in the same category'.

More specifically, categorical perception involves two components. The first is the fact that, over a variety of sensory continua, subjects are able to maintain a reliable category boundary within each continuum. The second is the observation that for stimuli that are *physically* equally spaced along the relevant continuum, discrimination across categories appears to increase over discrimination within each category ('category boundary' effect). The effect was first observed in the perception of phonemes (see Repp 1984, for a review), but has been documented since in a number of other domains, in particular in the perception of colours and facial expressions (Calder et al. 1996).

The first experiments in the case of phonemes concerned the perception of syllables with distinct onset consonants. Liberman et al. (1957) were able to construct a series of syllables interpolated between syllables unambiguously identified as /be/ or /ge/. They tested both participants' discrimination and categorisation performances. They measured discrimination using an ABX paradigm: participants were presented with triads of sequential phonemes, first A, then B and then a third phoneme X, which was one of A and B, and which they had to judge as being identical either to A or to B.[17] In the second part of the experiment, participants had to identify each phoneme along the continuum as either /be/ or /ge/. Both in the discrimination task and in the categorisation task, stimuli were presented in random order along the continuum.

The notion of category boundary in the categorisation task is defined as the position of the point of subjective equality (50 per cent of trials categorised as /be/) along the continuum. Discrimination performance is measured as the percentage of correct responses over consecutive pairs along the stimulus set. The main observation was an increase in discrimination performance for stimulus pairs that straddle the category boundary, compared with stimulus pairs on either side of the boundary, despite equal physical distance. Figure 14.3 presents data collected by Calder et al. (1996) based on a stimulus set involving 11 pictures, with two prototypes of either a sad or a happy face (see Figure 14.3) with 9 morphs interpolated between them. As the figure shows, discrimination increases over pairs nearer the point of subjective equality for categorisation, and decreases on either side of that threshold.

The phenomenon of categorical perception raises several questions that we can only briefly mention in this chapter. The first is how much the phenomenon is sensitive to the discrimination task used. Repp (1984) reports variability depending on the structure of the task (considering various alternatives to the ABX task), but concludes that the phenomenon is overall robust. The second is whether the same phenomenon occurs for all kinds of sensory continua and for all subjects. The answer to that question appears to be

---

[17]   The ABX paradigm can therefore be viewed as a sequential 2AFC paradigm (see Section 14.2).

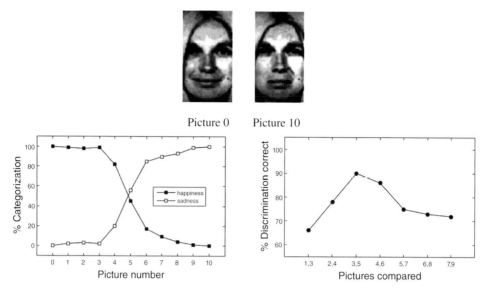

Picture 0   Picture 10

Figure 14.3 Categorisation and discrimination data for pictures of faces ranging from happy (0) to sad (10), based on Calder et al. (1996)'s data, Fig. 2 (reprinted by permission of Taylor & Francis, www.tandfonline.com). Discrimination shows a peak toward the point of subjective equality for categorisation.

negative, since discrimination does not always show a peak depending on the stimulus and the perceiver (Repp 1984). A third question is whether it is adequate to describe categorical perception as an effect of categorisation on discrimination, rather than the other way around.[18] It is widely considered to be the case, for classical psychophysics assumes discrimination to be monotonically decreasing for stimuli with a fixed physical difference (on account of Weber's law, which states that perceived changes are proportional to the initial stimulus), but the question is widely debated (Macmillan 1987). A related question one may ask is whether categorical perception might be an artefact of the assumption that stimuli are one-dimensional (Macmillan 1987). As Figure 14.3 shows, discrimination performance for facial expressions can reach 90 per cent at the category boundary, which might exceed the relevant threshold used to define a JND. If that is so, however, one may think of a different way of constructing the stimulus set, where the steps along the continuum are not just physically equal, but perceptually equal (each leaving performance at the same level). Doing so, however, would involve densifying the region of intermediate stimuli along the salient physical dimension in order to leave discrimination approximately constant.

While the phenomenon invites much more discussion than we can go into here, it is important to acknowledge that the findings related to categorical perception have spurred the

---

[18] See also Quine (1970) and Verheyen and Storms (2011).

development of probabilistic accounts of categorisation (see for instance Macmillan 1987 for a survey). A more substantive perspective is that the assignment under a category may not be solely a function of discrimination relative to a threshold, but may actually obey separate constraints.

14.3.2 Categorisation of Pairs of Stimuli

Classic studies of categorical perception generally investigate the categorisation of stimuli sequentially. What happens, however, when a stimulus is presented simultaneously with a similar one? That question is of particular interest, for some philosophers of vagueness have argued that in a context in which two items are 'saliently similar', they should be categorised alike. Fara (2000) calls this principle the *similarity constraint*. This is a weakening of the standard tolerance principle, for it restricts it to the simultaneous presentation of two objects. We may represent it as follows:

(7) If $x \sim_w y$ *and* x, y are presented side by side, then *in the context of that presentation* $P_W x \leftrightarrow P_W y$.

This says that two objects that are hard to tell apart, *when presented side by side*, should be assigned the same category in that specific context.[19] Prima facie the effect of a joint presentation should be to enhance similarity, and therefore to encourage the assignment of two adjacent stimuli in a Sorites sequence under a common category, but one may wonder if that is really so, in particular for borderline cases showing less stability over successive trials.

We do not know of any study that addresses exactly that question, but two papers by Hampton and colleagues are of relevance to that issue (Hampton et al. 2005; Hampton et al. 2012). Hampton and associates investigated the influence of the presentation of a stimulus of varying similarity on the categorisation of a borderline stimulus, both within and across the category boundary. In their leading experiment, Hampton et al. (2005) first presented participants with nine colour patches spanning the region between a blue prototype and a purple prototype, in a random order. For each participant, they determined the borderline patch b closest to the participant's point of subjective equality, taken to represent the underlying participant's category boundary. In a second phase, participants were shown pairs drawn from seven out of those nine patches (the prototypes were excluded), at varying distance from each other in the series. Participants had to decide whether only the right patch, only the left, both or neither was blue (respectively purple).

The responses of main interest concerned the categorisation of the borderline patch b relative to context patches $b+1, b+2$ and $b+3$ (toward the purple end) and similarly relative to context patches $b-1, b-2$ and $b-3$ (toward the blue end). When the context patch was more than one step away, what was found was a robust contrast effect: the probability of judging

---

[19] See Égré (2011a, p. 86) for a more explicit formalisation of this constraint. The effect of the relativisation is that in the context $\{a, b\}$, a and b may both be judged P_W, but in the context $\{b, c\}$, b and c may both be judged $\neg P_W$.

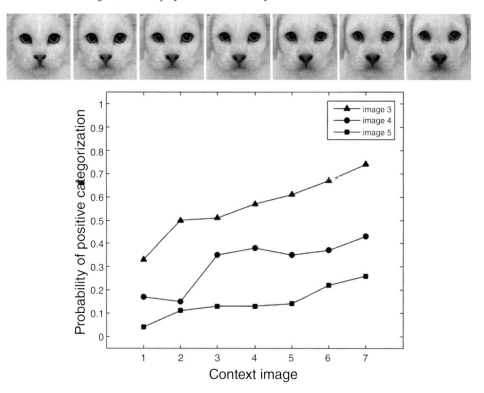

Figure 14.4 Hampton, Estes and Simmons (2005)'s cat–dog morphing series and mean probabilities of categorisation of target image as *cat* as a function of context image (based on Hampton et al. 2005, fig. 6).

b as of the same category as the context hue was decreased in both directions. Only when the context hue was one step away was a tendency toward assimilation observed, and that assimilation effect amplified when participants were given the choice between only 'both' and 'either' answers (Hampton et al. 2012). The contrast effect was replicated with different choices of colours and also with morphs presenting ambiguous stimuli between a typical dog face and a typical cat face (see Figure 14.4). Figure 14.4 presents the mean probabilities of categorising the middle pictures of that stimulus set as a function of other context pictures. For example, when the target image is compared with the most cat-like picture (1), we see that participants will tend to categorise it less as a cat, whereas when the target image is compared with the most dog-like picture (7), they tend to categorise it more as a cat.

Regarding the constraint of salient similarity, Hampton et al.'s data nevertheless suggest that for adjacent items from a series of morphed images presented together, there will be a tendency toward assimilation, namely toward assignment in the same category. This effect is fragile, however, for as soon as the step increases, the context picture will tend to push the borderline stimulus outside the category to which the context picture belongs. We note also that Hampton et al. do not report the mere proportion of '(only) left' and '(only) right' responses when target is picture x_i and context is x_{i-1} or x_{i+1}. It would be interesting to check if that proportion stays approximately constant across the range or increases toward the category boundary (that is, with participants assenting less to 'both' or 'neither' judge- ments than they do toward the prototypes). If it stays constant, this would be a more direct confirmation of the constraint of salient similarity. Otherwise, coherently with categorical perception effects, we may have to conclude that the constraint of salient similarity itself is modulated by how distant the items compared are to the prototype of the category.

14.4 Ordered Transitions between Categories

In Section 14.2 we considered the problem of how similarity to a prototype impacts upon categorisation when stimuli drawn from a Sorites sequence are presented in no specific order. In Section 14.3 we looked at the more specific problem of how salient similarity can favour assimilation under a common category in borderline cases in similarly un- ordered conditions. In this section we consider actual experiments done on so-called *dy- namic Sorites* or *forced-march Sorites* (Horgan 1994), namely ordered transitions between two prototypes by small steps.[20] Ordered transitions of that kind are of particular interest, because they pose the problem of how and when a category switch occurs along a Sorites sequence. We first consider dynamic transitions and their effect on discrimination, and then continue with the effect they have on categorisation.

14.4.1 Slow Motions and Change Detection

Some case studies exist in psychology that involve what we may call *dynamic compara- tive Sorites*, namely ordered sequences of stimuli in which the task is for participants to report whether there is a change or not. The task, in those cases, is concerned purely with discrimination.

The best example we can think of is in the field of change detection. An abundant literature concerns the phenomenon of change blindness in the visual domain (Simons and and Levin 1997; O'Regan, Rensink and Clark 1999). One influential paradigm involves the comparison between two pictures shown in alternation, with a brief flicker or disruption between them, sometimes with the inclusion of some distractors (see O'Regan 2001 for a review). A more or less extended portion of the original picture scene is altered between consecutive pictures (an object is added or removed), and often participants are unable to detect the change or they take time and effort to correctly report it.

While flickering pictures appear to bear no relation to the Sorites, one class of stimuli used to evidence change blindness is of particular interest in relation to dynamic Sorites, and concerns the phenomenon of blindness to slow changes. A demonstration available on O'Regan's website (http://nivea.psycho.univ-paris5.fr/ECS/sol_Mil_cinepack.avi) and

---

[20] See 'The Forced-March Paradox', in the introduction to this volume.

Figure 14.5 Three images from Chabrier's slow change movie (at 0 sec., 2 sec. and 44 sec.). The original images are colored: at 0′ and 2″, the carousel's floor looks red, it looks purple at 44″.

programmed by Renaud Chabrier is a 44 sec. long animation based on the gradual alteration of a still image depicting a carousel. The animation involves a very progressive alteration of the luminosity and then colour of the platform of the carousel. The animation provides a striking example in which the image appears not to change at all from one picture to the next, even a few seconds apart (compare at 0 sec. and 2 sec. in Figure 14.5). By the end of the animation, one may easily fail to have noticed any change, or fail to accurately report where the change took place. When the movie is rewound straight to its first picture, however, the contrast in luminosity and colour with the last picture is sufficiently marked to be immediately noticeable (see Figure 14.5, compare between 0 sec. and 44 sec.).

Slow changes not only confirm that comparative Sorites sequences exist, but their main interest lies also in the fact that it is easy when the rate of change is low enough to not even detect a change between the first and the last image. This indicates that dynamically the similarity between adjacent pictures can supersede the memory of more distant pictures, thereby maintaining an illusion of identity between the first and the last picture. O'Regan does not report specific measurements based on this paradigm, but such examples may be used to vindicate the idea that short of a vivid memory of the first stimulus seen, or short of the right attentional guidance, there is a soritical adaptation effect in such sequences: the similarity between consecutive pictures can dynamically override the dissimilarity between more distant pictures.

14.4.2 Ordered Transitions between Prototypes

We now consider some studies of dynamic categorical Sorites, namely ordered transitions between stimuli in which the main task is to subsume each stimulus seen under one or more categories. We highlight three studies in that domain, whose results are remarkably consistent with each other, and which evidence a robust order effect in dynamic Sorites.

Three Studies Based on Morphing Series

A first influential study in that area originates in work conducted by Raffman on colour categorisation, conducted with psychologists Lindsey and Brown (Raffman 2011, 2014). Raffman and colleagues presented participants with a set of 37 colour patches interpolated between a typical blue and a typical green patch. They presented the stimuli in five distinct orders: random, from green to blue, from blue to green, and then in two 'reversal' conditions, in which participants, as soon as they switched category along a given order, were marched backward to the preceding stimuli they had just categorised in opposite order. Participants had the option to categorise each stimulus either as 'blue' or 'green', or they could opt out by using a third '?' response.

Raffman reports two main findings from that study. The first is that, in the standard ordered conditions, participants tended to switch category earlier from blue to green, and earlier from green to blue, rather than later, compared with the reverse order and the random order. This phenomenon, sometimes called *negative hysteresis*, or *enhanced contrast* between categories, was found earlier by Kalmus (1979) and has been replicated since in Égré et al. (2013) and Stöttinger, Sepahvand, Danckert and Anderson (2016) (see below). The second main finding is that participants in the reversal condition continued to apply to the preceding patch the category to which they had just switched. For example, a participant who categorised stimulus 18 as blue and stimulus 19 as green would continue to categorise stimulus 18 as green when marched backwards after the switching. To Raffman and colleagues, this phenomenon is indicative of a local form of (positive) hysteresis: participants carry on with the category they just switched to without seeing a discrepancy with their earlier categorisation. In line with the earlier analyses of Raffman, this indicates that borderline stimuli in a Sorites sequence can receive inconsistent verdicts without contradiction, meaning that the same items can be judged *P* and not *P* but on separate occasions (see also Section 14.2 on within-subject inconsistency).

In a related study, Égré et al. (2013) ran a similar task, except that they did not include the reversal conditions, and they included fewer items within each sequence (15 items). Instead, they measured participants' responses along two colour sets (green–blue and yellow–orange, see Figure 14.6), and they ran two different tasks with different groups of participants: a perceptual matching task in which participants were shown triads of colour patches and had to decide whether the target was more similar to either of the two typical end shades of the colour set to which it belonged, and a linguistic categorisation task in which those end shades were replaced by the names of the categories of which they were typical ('yellow' versus 'orange', 'blue' versus 'green'). What they found was a striking contrast in the results of the two tasks. In the perceptual task, participants showed no order effect: that is, the participants' points of subjective equality (point of 50 per cent application of a given category) were situated at about the same location along the stimulus set, irrespective of the order in which the stimuli were presented. In the linguistic task, by contrast, the participants showed the same order effect reported by Kalmus and Raffman, namely negative hysteresis: participants switched category earlier along the continuum when going from green to blue (orange to yellow), and similarly when going from blue to green (yellow to orange). Figure 14.6 shows Égré et al.'s data concerning the average selection of the category 'orange' depending on the order in which the fifteen shades were presented. Irrespective of the order in which the stimuli were presented, the psychometric curves show the usual sigmoid shape, but in the linguistic task we see that the point of subjective equality is shifted to an earlier position along the stimulus set when going from yellow to orange, as opposed to from orange to yellow. The point of subjective equality in the random condition

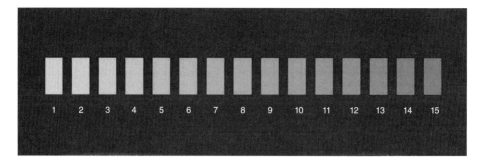

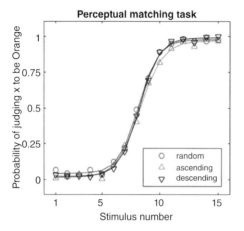

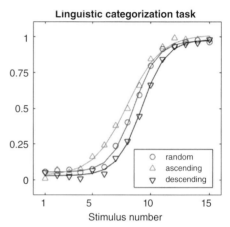

Figure 14.6 Average percentage of 'orange' responses for the fifteen color stimuli from Égré et al. (2013)'s yellow–orange colour set (top, in shades of grey: stimulus 1 is actually Yellow, stimulus 15 actually Orange), in the random, ascending, and descending order conditions of the perceptual matching task (bottom left) and the linguistic categorisation task (bottom right), along with the best fitting logistic functions (reprinted by permission of Springer Nature, *Journal of Logic, Language and Information*, 'Vagueness and Order Effects in Color Categorization', P. Égré, V. de Gardelle, D. Ripley, 2013).

is located between those of the ordered conditions. In the perceptual matching task, on the other hand, the psychometric curves basically overlap for all three orders.

More recently, Stöttinger et al. (2016) have designed a class of 40 picture sets each consisting of 15 pictures gradually morphing the silhouette of an object into the silhouette of another object (see Figure 14.7 for an example). The series were divided into four sets, either morphing an animate object to an animate object (such as a cat into a rabbit), an inanimate to an inanimate (such as a pear to a violin), an animate to an inanimate, or the other way around (viz. a bodybuilder to a pair of scissors, or conversely).[21] This time

---

[21] See Fisher (1967) for early examples of similar stimuli, much less controlled, however, than Stöttinger et al. (2016)'s. See Égré (2009, 2011a) and Pelofi et al. (2017) for philosophical perspectives on such examples concerning the relation between vagueness and perceptual ambiguity.

Figure 14.7 One of Stöttinger et al. (2016)'s forty picture sets, morphing a pear into a violin (reprinted by permission of Springer Nature, *Behavior Research Methods*, 'Assessing Perceptual Change with an Ambiguous Figures Task', E. Stöttinger et al., 2016).

the authors used a naming task: participants had to freely type in the name of the object they saw, instead of being given a forced-choice between two names (Kalmus 1979 used a similar naming task with colours). Instead of administering the three orders within subjects, the authors assigned one group of participants to the two ordered conditions, and assigned another group of participants to the random order condition. A comparison of the results across categories confirms that participants switch category earlier rather than later in the ordered conditions, although the underlying data is complex.[22] Unlike Égré et al. (2013), Stöttinger et al. did not run a separate perceptual matching task to see if the order effect was specific to linguistic categorisation.

14.4.3 Interpreting Negative Hysteresis

Across the studies reviewed, we see that the phenomenon of negative hysteresis appears to be robust in cases of linguistic categorisation. The phenomenon deserves emphasis, for part of the philosophical literature based on introspection had predicted positive instead of negative hysteresis in such ordered transitions (see Égré et al. 2013, for a review). How can the finding be explained?

Égré et al. (2013) review two possible explanations. One possible explanation would be to suppose, in agreement with the epistemic model of vagueness discussed in Bonini et al. (1999), that participants switch categories when they become uncertain of the membership of the stimulus, basically when they are within the margin of error needed to apply a category with confidence. The epistemic account presupposes that vague categories have a sharp but unknowable boundary, however, an assumption that is widely controversial. Égré et al. (2013) point out that the finding of negative hysteresis is compatible with a distinct model, in which categories are allowed to have multiple boundaries, but in which participants would basically switch category as soon as they step into the borderline area of competition between distinct verdicts.

A relevant model of the permissibility of multiple boundaries is proposed in Douven et al. (2013). In this model, which bears some affinity with supervaluationism (see Douven

---

[22] In particular, although the overall data shows a tendency to switch early, more individual series show participants switching later than show them switching earlier, and most individual series do not show a significant difference in either direction. Moreover, the series showing the largest effect in either direction is one in which participants switch early, but there are some reasons to worry about this series. First, the size of the order effect this series shows is out of step with the other 39 series, coming in almost twice as large as the second-largest difference in either direction. Secondly, participants clearly struggled to decipher one of the endpoint images in this series, with 34 per cent of participants unable to identify it (p. 205).

et al. 2016), the vagueness of concepts is explained by the admission of multiple proto-types for a given category. Borderline cases of a category correspond to cases that can be categorised in opposite ways, depending on which typical values have been selected to decide category membership. If we apply that model to the finding (something not done in Égré et al. 2013), the removal of an order effect in the perceptual condition could possibly be explained by the salience in perception, and thus in working memory, of *exactly two* specific prototypes for distinct categories. When such anchoring values are replaced by names of categories, participants behave as if they were sampling those anchoring values from a wider set, including more typical values than the two anchors of the perceptual task.

Note that this model by itself does not explain the direction of the effect (negative as opposed to positive hysteresis). However, Égré et al. (2013) point out that when participants are marched from a clear yellow to a clear orange, they start applying a category based on a strict membership criterion. Rationally, they should wish to signal a change as soon as they enter the borderline area, instead of continuing to apply the same name and change their criterion without notice. If the borderline area is spread around the middle stimulus in each series, then one would therefore expect them to switch earlier rather than later.

14.4.4 Borderline Cases: Either, Neither or Both?

Dynamic transitions involving morphed stimuli are also interesting to get a sense of whether stimuli in the middle range are likely to be perceived as belonging to *either* or even *both* of the end categories or whether they are more likely to be perceived as belonging to *neither*.

An interesting finding in Stöttinger et al. (2016) in this regard is that participants almost always correctly and unambiguously identified the first and last picture of each series under the expected name. For the middle objects in each series, there is an increase in the use of third names, but the use of a third name is generally marginal over the use of the names of the end stimuli (it peaks around 10 per cent on average across the 40 sets). Closer inspection of their data reveals some variance across picture sets, however. In the series morphing a butterfly into a bowtie, for example, middle objects are hardly ever classified under a third category. In the series mapping a broom to a gun, the middle objects are more often seen as being a third kind of object (such as a paddle or a stick). Overall, however, what appears is that depending on the order of the transition, participants have no difficulty assigning the same stimulus to either of the opposing categories rather than to neither, as also demonstrated in Raffman's reversal cases.

In Égré et al. (2013), following work done by Ripley (2011) and Alxatib and Pel-letier (2011), it was investigated whether and to what extent participants would agree to conjunctive descriptions of the form 'both yellow and orange' and 'both yellow and not yellow' to categorise middling stimuli in the colour sets. Overall, what Égré et al. (2013) found was that ascriptions of the form 'both P and Q' and 'both P and not P' steadily increased and reached their maximum for the middle stimuli in each series, where they were used significantly more than either of their conjuncts. The finding confirms that participants have no difficulty recognising that a borderline case can be assigned to either of the categories in those cases, but moreover that participants do not view the categories as exclusive of each other, but as admitting some overlap instead. Stöttinger et al.'s study could make us think that it is an artefact, for it is not the same thing to categorise an object under *either* of two categories P and Q alternatively depending on the context and to categorise it as being under a conjunctive category of the form 'both P and Q'. However, Stöttinger et al.'s study does not concern the ascription of adjectival categories, but of noun categories. A fair amount of general knowledge may block the inference from the observation that an object has two distinct features to the conclusion that it has both features at the same time. For example, a real-world object may not easily be categorised as 'both a pair of scissors and a bodybuilder', even as its silhouette is likely to be perceived as sharing features of either kind of object, because we tend to envisage animate and inanimate objects as two exclusive categories in the first place, and no human bodybuilder could be thought of as a pair of scissors. Malt (1990) has established that animate categories in particular are mutually exclusive, while inanimate categories admit overlap. She asked participants to judge whether objects described as 'halfway between' two animate or two inanimate categories (1) were probably one or the other category, (2) could be called either one or (3) could not be part of either category, and found that participants predominantly chose the first response option for animate objects, but tended to choose the second response option for inanimate objects. For a more elaborate discussion regarding the use of conjunctions of (colour) adjectives and their negation ('borderline contradictions', in the terminology of Ripley 2011) we refer to Ripley (2011), Alxatib and Pelletier (2011), Serchuk et al. (2011) and Égré and Zehr (2018). For broader considerations on the relation between vagueness and multistability in perception, see Égré (2009), Égré (2011a) and Pelofi et al. (2017).

14.5 Conclusions

We may draw two main conclusions from our review of the incidence of the Sorites Paradox in psychology. The first and maybe the most obvious one is that the Sorites Paradox can be operationalised and studied empirically. We have seen various ways in which Sorites sequences have been created and studied, whether in a static or in a more dynamic setting. A second conclusion is that whenever this has been done, results are almost always accounted for in a probabilistic manner. Regarding that aspect, we can highlight four more specific points.

The first point, based on the discussion we gave of slippery slope arguments, is that soritical reasoning may be best viewed as a chain of propositions, the overall strength of which is dependent on the inductive strength of each conditional premise. The consideration of the probability of these individual conditional premises can serve to determine where in the argument a line should be drawn. A second and more specific lesson we can draw from the studies we reviewed is that the relation between discrimination and categorisation is not as simple as the main premise of the Sorites would suggest. Generally speaking, pairwise indiscriminability between two items does not guarantee that the items in question will always be placed under the same category, even as it makes that co-assignment highly probable.

Our third point is that small differences between items are always likely to make a difference, whether for discrimination or for categorisation, even if those differences may not easily be detectable. In terms of discrimination, a small difference can nevertheless be such as to fall under the threshold picked to define what counts as a just noticeable difference or be such as to go unnoticed altogether (as experiments on change blindness show us). In terms of categorisation, a small difference generally increases or decreases the probability of assigning an item to a category, simply because the item ends up being a little more or a little less distant from the category prototype or anchoring values.

Finally, the tolerance principle is a risky principle, and the best way to represent the dependence of category membership on small differences is in terms of a principle of probabilistic closeness. This does not mean that the literal, non-probabilistic interpretation of the tolerance principle is worthless or not operative in how we judge and categorise. As this chapter has showed us, we do see assimilation and adaptation effects as a result of similarity. More generally, we see that context effects are numerous and subtle, and that the way in which items from a Sorites series are presented has important consequences on either category maintenance or category switching.[23],[24]

---

[23] As we tried to convey in this chapter, Sorites structures are in a sense omnipresent in psychophysics, a discipline created by G. Fechner in 1860. Most of the time, however, psychophysicists are not interested in the Sorites Paradox per se, but they are interested in the effect that small variations of some sensory variable create over some other variable connected to behaviour. Égré and Barberousse (2014) give a historical overview of the way in which Fechner's work seems to have awakened Poincaré's interest for the problem of intransitivities in discrimination, and how Poincaré's reflections in turn may have prompted Borel (1907) to think about the connection between the Sorites and statistics. Some of Borel's pioneering ideas were reinvented and taken much further independently by Duncan Luce in the 1950s (see Luce 1956). Luce's work on semi-orders, though not explicitly on the Sorites, was brought to the attention of linguists and philosophers of vagueness by R. van Rooij in around 2010. Black (1937) is another influential link between the philosophy, the logic, and the psychology of vagueness, with ramifications in fuzzy logic in the 1960s and 1970s in particular. In the psychology of concepts, Rosch and Mervis's highly influential paper (1975) on family resemblance nowhere directly mentions the Sorites, but their ideas relate to work done independently by J. Hampton in the same period. Some of Hampton's posterior work has addressed problems of vagueness very explicitly; see Hampton (2007) for an influential paper.

[24] The authors thank Elia Zardini and Sergi Oms for detailed and helpful comments, as well as Jérôme Dokic and James Hampton for fruitful exchanges on some aspects of this chapter. PE and SV thank the ANR Program TriLogMean ANR-14-CE30-0010-01 for funding, as well as grant ANR-17-EURE-0017 for research carried out at the Department of Cognitive Studies of ENS. SV also thanks the European Research Council under the European Union's Seventh Framework Programme (FP/2007-2013) / ERC Grant Agreement n. 313610.

Coda

15   The Pre-Analytic History of the Sorites Paradox

Ricardo Santos

The Sorites Paradox has a long and interesting history. In the first section of this chapter, I will present a brief and general overview of the pre-analytic history of the Sorites Paradox, from the Ancient Greeks to Kant and Hegel. Then in the first of two case studies I will focus on Chrysippus (a Stoic from the third century BC), the ancient philosopher who worked most on the Sorites: Chrysippus held an epistemic view of vagueness and proposed a strategy to respond to the paradox in the context of a dialectical questioning (similar to what is now commonly called the Forced March)[1] that deserves to be thoroughly examined. In my second case study I will focus on Leibniz, who in my view produced the most interesting work on the Paradox in modern pre-analytic times. Leibniz started by accepting that vague notions have sharp boundaries, but then changed his mind and moved to something like a semantic view of vagueness.

15.1 The Pre-Analytic History of the Paradox

Most probably, we owe the discovery of the Sorites Paradox to Eubulides of Miletus. Eubulides was a philosopher of the Megarian school and a contemporary of Aristotle, who distinguished himself by his outstanding argumentative capacities. Unfortunately, we know very little about him. But Diogenes Laertius[2] attributes to him the formulation of seven arguments 'with interrogative form', among which we find the Liar (*pseudomenon*), the Heaper (*sôritês*) and the Bald Man (*phalakron*). Sextus Empiricus[3] says that logic was the only part of philosophy to which Eubulides dedicated himself and, according to Philodemus, he despised every argument that did not contain syllogisms,[4] thus reinforcing his image of a 'rigorous dialectician'. But Eubulides was also a polemist, frequently accused of using eristic arguments.[5] He was notorious for his great animosity against Aristotle, against whom he wrote a whole book.

---

[1] See 'The Forced-March Paradox', in the introduction to this volume.
[2] In II 108.
[3] *Adv. math.* VII 13.
[4] Cf. Muller (1985, frag. 88 ad fine, p. 36).
[5] An eristic argument, as Plato and Aristotle characterised it, is a bad argument, based upon some tricky fallacy, used for purely competitive purposes, i.e. aiming at victory rather than knowledge.

What did Eubulides' Sorites Paradox look like? Diogenes, as mentioned, tells us that the argument had 'interrogative form'. According to Cicero and Galen, the name given to the argument derives from the example used in it: it was originally an argument about a heap (*sôros*), although it could easily be applied to other similar objects. The closest version to the original is probably the one given by Galen, in his *On Medical Experience*.[6] There the argument is presented, in the context of a dialectical dispute, as a series of questions of the form 'Are *n* grains of wheat a heap?', to which the respondent can only answer 'yes' or 'no'. Starting with *n* = 1 and progressing by successive additions of just one grain, the answer to the first group of questions is indeed easy, since 'no' is the only option that remains faithful to the intuitive notion of a heap. But sooner or later there comes a stage where *n* is sufficiently great and doubt comes in. Faced with a particular question, e.g. 'Are 421 grains of wheat a heap?', and consulting his notion of a heap, the respondent may no longer know which answer is the right one. Here a second consideration enters and starts to play a decisive role: if the respondent is in doubt about a certain question, but he has answered 'no' to the previous one, he then has a very strong reason to answer 'no' to the present question as well, because if he were to answer 'yes' now, he would be admitting that the addition of a single grain was enough to turn what was not a heap into a heap. And that seems to be unacceptable. As Galen says, 'I know of nothing worse or more absurd than that the being or not-being of a heap is determined by a [single] grain of wheat'.[7] To avoid this absurdity, he has to keep answering 'no' as long as the argument goes on. By doing that, he finds himself accepting that not even a million grains is a heap and, in fact, that nothing is a heap – and that is no less absurd.

Thus presented, the paradox of the heap forms an ascending version of the Sorites, i.e. one that proceeds by addition. But the Bald Man Paradox, also described by Galen, proceeds by subtraction: starting with someone whose hair is luxuriant, one is asked what would happen if he were to lose one single hair – would he be bald? And if he were to lose two hairs, would he then be bald? And if he were to lose three hairs? Galen very clearly says that the respondent has only two available options ('You will [...] inevitably have to make one of two answers' (*Med. Exp.* xx 124)): *either* he goes on always answering 'no', eventually admitting that even when no hair at all remains on his head the man is still not bald, *or* there is a moment when he answers 'yes' for the first time, thereby admitting that he has turned bald by the loss of one single hair. Another thing that Galen makes very clear is that the argument has a general structure which, applied to many different things, makes it possible to conclude that, just as there are no heaps nor bald men, there are also no adolescents, no adults or old people, no waves or seas or strong winds, or crowds or cities or nations.[8] The method used to reach all these conclusions was the same, and it was because of it that the Sorites was also known as 'the argument of little by little'. In fact, it

<hr>

[6] XVII 1–3.

[7] In the contemporary discussion of vagueness, this feature of vague predicates is usually called, following Wright (1975, pp. 333–4), their *tolerance*: some changes are just too small to make any difference to the applicability of the predicate (see 'The Sorites Paradox', in the introduction to this volume, and Chapter 5, Section 5.2).

[8] Cf. *Med. Exp.* xvi, 114–5.

is crucial for the argument that the difference between two successive questions be small or even minuscule, since the smaller it is, the stronger will the principle seem that it cannot be right to give them different answers (i.e. to say 'no' to one of them and 'yes' to the other). However, by a very long accumulation, or 'heaping', of very small differences one arrives at a notorious difference, one that justifies a change of category (from hairy to bald, from boy to adolescent, from non-heap to heap, etc.). And there lies the enigma: how can a transition happen in this series, if there is no point in the series at which it does happen?

Unfortunately, we know nothing about Eubulides' understanding of the argument or what lesson he derived from it. We don't even know in what context he came across the problem, or what his aim was when he presented it. Martha Kneale has written: 'it is incredible that Eubulides produced [his paradoxical arguments] in an entirely pointless way [...]. He must surely have been trying to illustrate some theses of Megarian philosophy' (Kneale and Kneale 1962, pp. 114–5). But, if it was so, then we cannot know what those theses were.[9]

In an effort to find a purpose for the invention of the paradoxes, some people have proposed (among other hypotheses) that Eubulides was targeting Aristotle, and that the Sorites was intended to be used in attacking some aspect of Aristotle's philosophy. Maybe it was his theory of the potential infinite (as Beth 1954 has proposed), or his ethical doctrine of the mean (as Moline 1969 has argued, using as evidence the commentaries on the *Nicomachean Ethics* by Aspasius and the anonymous commentator). Some scholars have searched through Aristotle's texts to find possible signs of a reaction to Eubulides' argument, but an examination of the texts does not confirm any of these hypotheses. No text that we know of indicates that Aristotle saw the Sorites as a criticism and that he tried to reply to it. Although scholars understandably find attractive the idea that there was a controversy between Eubulides and Aristotle concerning the Sorites, in fact we have no evidence that Aristotle ever had any interest in the Sorites or was even aware of the argument – though it is natural to assume that he was.[10]

In the Hellenistic period, there are two schools in which we know that the Sorites was well known and discussed: the Stoics and the Academic Sceptics. Diodorus Cronus, student of Apollonius Cronus (himself a student of Eubulides), and inventor of the famous Master Argument, had a mind that was naturally attracted by logical puzzles and paradoxes. It was probably through him that knowledge of the Sorites was transmitted both to Zeno of Citium (*c*. 334–262) and to Arcesilaus (*c*. 316–*c*. 241). For it is known that Zeno studied for some time under Diodorus,[11] and Arcesilaus is said to have 'used Diodorus' logic'.[12] Zeno founded the Stoa, and from the very beginning the study of paradoxes, as a chapter

---

[9] An interesting exercise of speculative reconstruction can be found in Wheeler (1983), showing how Eubulides' arguments could have been used (very much like Zeno's paradoxes) to support the views of Parmenides. Unfortunately, no textual evidence is offered to support the speculation.

[10] Commenting on the passage *Top.* 158ᵃ25–30, Smith (1997, p. 122) attributes to Aristotle the belief that, in dialectic, any 'very lengthy' questioning is bad, because 'no [good] argument has a large number of premisses'. Could this be a sign that Aristotle was not aware of the Sorites or that he was but thought it was a bad argument?

[11] Cf. Diogenes Laertius, vii 5.

[12] Cf. Sextus, PH i 234.

of logic, was part of Stoic teaching. Arcesilaus was the one who, as leader of the Academy, converted the Platonists to scepticism, and he took as his main object of criticism Stoic philosophy, especially their positions regarding the nature and the possibility of knowledge. In that epistemological debate between Sceptics and Stoics, soritical arguments were used and they played an important role.

At the centre of the dispute was the Stoic notion of a cognitive impression. For Zeno, and for the Stoics in general, the kind of knowledge that Socrates did not find in any of his interlocutors is attainable by human beings on the basis of a special class of perceptions or appearances with propositional content, which they called 'cognitive impressions'. It is to these, and to these only, that a wise man will give his assent — thus keeping himself immune from the possibility of error. According to the definition given of it,[13] a cognitive impression, besides being true, also has a maximal clarity and distinction grounded in the very object, or state of affairs, that causes it. According to the Stoic understanding of this clarity, no clear impression could be false: if something is not actually F, then, in the intended sense, it could not be clearly perceived as F. But the Sceptics denied that some special class of impressions are infallible. Arcesilaus, in particular, thought that this could be shown by an argument with soritical form. With any cognitive impression (for example the impression that *this object is red*), it is possible to have another impression which is for us indistinguishable from the first, hence it has the same clarity, but it is caused by an object that is only very slightly different from the first one. One could thus build a series of impressions, each one indistinguishable from the next, but ending with an impression that is obviously false. Since no false impression is cognitive and, if two impressions are indistinguishable, it could not be the case that one is cognitive but not the other,[14] the Sceptic concludes that no impression (even if true) is cognitive after all.

Zeno's successor in the Stoa was Cleanthes of Assos, and after him came Chrysippus of Soli (*c.* 280–206 BC). Chrysippus wrote prolifically on many different subjects, and he tried to systematise Stoic philosophy. Stoic logic was to a great extent his own creation. Unfortunately, none of his treatises has survived in complete form. All we know of them are fragments, which were quoted by authors including Plutarch and Galen. According to the catalogue of his works preserved by Diogenes Laertius, he wrote at least six works on the Liar Paradox (filling a total of 14 books) and at least two works on the Sorites (covering a total of 5 books), all of them lost. In the case of the Sorites, the few things we know of what he thought about it are transmitted in short passages of Cicero and Sextus. Perhaps as a consequence of his defence of the principle of bivalence, Chrysippus seems to have accepted that, in an appropriate Sorites series, there is a sharp boundary between the positive cases and the negative cases (although that has been disputed by some scholars, as we will see later), which is however undetectable. Chrysippus recommended keeping silent – as an expression of an inner suspension of judgement – as the adequate response to the cases in the intermediate zone of the series, around the cut-off point. According to

---

[13] Cf. Diogenes Laertius, vii 46.
[14] This principle is stated in Cicero, *Luc* xiii 40. I will claim that Chrysippus implicitly rejects it in his reply.

this advice, in a Forced March along a Sorites series, the Stoic wise man would start by giving positive answers, until he reaches a point where he shuts his mouth and keeps silent as a sign that he no longer gives his assent to any answer; most probably, if the questioning goes on long enough, there will come a point where the wise man starts answering again, this time negatively.

Chrysippus' solution did not satisfy the Academic Sceptics. Carneades (214–128 BC), one of Arcesilaus' successors, criticised it, casting doubt mainly on the choice, by the Stoic wise man, of the point at which he falls silent. If the first case to which the Stoic does not answer is a case in which the impression is not clear (and, therefore, not cognitive), then the immediately previous case was also not clear (for the difference between them is minuscule and the respective impressions are indistinguishable), and yet the Stoic has given his assent to it. If, on the contrary, the impressions are both clear and cognitive, then the Stoic is refusing to give his assent to a cognitive impression, thereby showing that he himself admits that cognitive impressions are not a safe basis for knowledge – exactly what the Sceptics claim. Carneades concludes, addressing Chrysippus: 'So your art doesn't help you at all against the Sorites.'

After the dispute between Stoics and Sceptics, the Sorites reappears in the first centuries of our era, in the discussion between followers of the main medical schools of the relation between theory and practice. The Empiricists claimed that medicine is an essentially practical discipline, where knowledge increases gradually by the observation of patients and their symptoms; and they criticised harshly those who wanted to base medical knowledge on theoretical and philosophical foundations, describing them as 'Dogmatic'. These others fought back, pointing to a problem at the centre of the empiricist view. If medical knowledge is acquired by experience, but many observations of the same phenomenon are needed to generate empirical knowledge of it, one should ask: How many observations make a piece of empirical knowledge? One single observation is not enough. And two? And three? Etc. The argument tries to force the empiricist to choose between two absurdities: either one single observation turns what is not empirical knowledge into empirical knowledge or there is never any empirical knowledge. The empiricists' reply, which we know from the report of the 'rationalist' Galen (129–*c.* 200 AD), essentially consists in saying that we know from experience that this argument is mistaken, even if we do not know where the mistake lies. That is a quite sensible position to take, even if one would prefer to see a stronger effort to engage with the paradox.

After the end of antiquity, the Sorites fell into oblivion, and for many centuries we hardly see any trace of it. Even in the richest period of medieval logic, the Sorites is absent from the discussions (it does not appear on the list of the 'insolubles'), most probably because of its absence from Aristotle's texts. It reappears in the Renaissance, owing to the influence of Cicero's works. An opponent of the Scholastic (and traditional logic) and defender of the humanist rhetoric, Lorenzo Valla (1407–57) knew it and tried to refute it, insisting that in order to make a heap, every single grain makes some difference. At around this time, there was a shift in the meaning of the word 'Sorites', and it started to be used mainly to refer to a syllogism with more than two premises. It is thus, as 'a syllogism composed of more than three propositions', that a Sorites is defined in the *Logic of Port-Royal* (by Arnauld and Nicole 1992[1662]), and that usage became widespread and quite common in logic textbooks. The connection with Eubulides' original puzzle was lost.

In modern philosophy, it is in the work of Leibniz that we once again find the Sorites Paradox in its original sense. In his *New Essays on Human Understanding* (1704), the old problem of the Bald Man is mentioned twice. Locke had claimed that nature is divided according to nominal essences (not real essences) and that the limits of species are drawn by the mind and by human language, as witnessed by the existence of 'monsters' in the borderline between different species.[15] Leibniz rejects this anti-realist view of species, but he concedes that 'vague notions' such as baldness work in the way indicated by Locke: if they were determined by nature they would have exact limits; but since they are human creations, with limits imperfectly drawn, they give rise to doubtful cases, where there is indeterminacy and variability of opinions, none of which is wrong. It is a way of thinking similar to the one that, in the twentieth century, would be called the semantic view of vagueness, according to which there are borderline cases because vague predicates have a deficient and incomplete meaning. But Leibniz's view was not always like this. In an important study, Samuel Levey (2002) has called attention to two earlier texts where Leibniz discussed the Sorites. Reading those texts, we can see how was it that Leibniz first accepted and later denied that vague notions determine sharp boundaries.

After Leibniz, both Kant and Hegel were acquainted with the Sorites in its ancient version, though they assessed its philosophical significance in very different ways.

In his *Lectures on Logic*, Kant attributes to the ancient Megarians the invention of several 'sophisms', among which he includes the Sorites, the Liar and the Veiled Man. Kant thinks that there are two kinds of fallacies: paralogisms, where one inadvertently makes a formal mistake of reasoning; and sophisms, where the mistake is consciously used in order to embarrass and delude other people. Kant is disparaging about the paradoxes: 'Most of the business of the Megarian school was with sophistries, and most of the tricks were applied by them for miserable purposes, for the tying of knots in order to give others the trouble of resolving them' (Kant 1992, p. 411). Regarding soritical arguments, Kant's diagnosis is that they are fallacious because they rely on 'indeterminate definitions' (Kant 1992, p. 412); that is, definitions of a concept that are not exhaustive, for they do not expose all the distinguishing marks or characteristics of the things falling under the concept being defined. In the *Critique of Pure Reason*, however, Kant acknowledges that at least in the case of empirical concepts, complete definition is never possible. The marks included in a concept such as that of gold or water differ from one person to another, and they change with our experience: 'One makes use of certain marks only as long as they are sufficient for making distinctions; new observations, however, take some away and add some, and therefore the concept never remains within secure boundaries' (Kant 1998,

---

[15] Cf. Locke (1690, III.iii.12–5 and vi.27, 36–7).

A728/B756, p. 638). Kant did not come to see that, if this instability and incompleteness is inevitable, then the embarrassment caused by soritical arguments is more serious than it seemed.

Hegel is more receptive to the Sorites and, in general, to the paradoxes of the ancient Megarians. In his *Lectures on the History of Philosophy*, he includes an entire section on Eubulides, in which he presents and briefly discusses each particular paradox and reflects on its philosophical value. Hegel distances himself from the 'German seriousness' that looks at paradoxes as mere plays with words or malicious tricks, and critically remarks that 'it is in fact easier to set them aside than to refute them' (Hegel 1892, vol. 1, p. 457). Paradoxes are valuable, in his view, because they reveal limitations in the 'ordinary consciousness', which does not recognise that truth consists in the unity of opposites. Truth is not simple, hence 'the mistake is to desire an answer of yes or no'. When discussing the Liar, Hegel states that the right answer is a two-sided answer, of yes *and* no: 'he speaks the truth and lies at the same time, and the truth is this contradiction' (Hegel 1892, vol. 1, p. 461).[16] In the Sorites, Hegel also finds a certain kind of contradiction, between, on one side, the tolerance principle that one grain does not make a heap and, on the other, the undeniable fact that adding one repeatedly 'brings about the change into the opposite' (Hegel 1892, vol. 1, p. 463). How can that be? Hegel stresses the role played by the repetition: it is by repeating, many times over, the operation of adding one grain that the non-heap eventually becomes a heap. The unity of opposites in this case is manifested in the circumstance of a purely quantitative progression resulting in a qualitative difference.

In *The Science of Logic*, Hegel again mentions the Sorites, as evidence that the ancients had already understood the possibility of a dialectical passage from quantity to quality. According to his analysis, the subject who is led on a Forced March along a Sorites series and, at each step, concedes that adding (or subtracting) only one grain cannot make a difference, just to find himself embarrassedly facing something obviously different at the end, is both right and wrong: he is right in a trivial sense because each single addition was, in fact, in itself insignificant and unproblematic; but, more importantly, he is wrong because he didn't give due weight to the fact that the process was being repeated over and over. As Hegel puts it, 'it was not only the repetition that was each time forgotten, but also that the individually insignificant quantities [...] add up, and the sum constitutes the qualitative whole' (Hegel 2010, 21.332, p. 290). This remark is insightful and it can be seen as an anticipation of the view that what is wrong in a typical soritical argument is neither its premises nor any one of its single inferential steps, but the repetition of a certain kind of inference.[17]

---

[16] In the contemporary discussion of the Liar and other semantic paradoxes, this kind of view has been developed, under the name of *dialetheism*, by Priest (2006) and Beall (2009), among others. See Chapter 7 in this volume.

[17] For the development of such a view, under the name of *non-transitivism*, see Zardini (2008a) and Chapter 9 in this volume.

15.2 Case Study 1: Chrysippus' Silence

In antiquity, the Sorites Paradox was generally thought about and discussed in a dialectical context. In the times of Eubulides, Diodorus and Chrysippus, dialectic was much more than simple free rational discussion of questions of common interest. In fact, it was a rather codified practice, a kind of game with conventions and well-defined rules. It took place orally, between two participants, who before starting decided on the distribution of the roles of questioner and answerer, and thereafter these roles remained fixed. The answerer's role was to defend a certain thesis, which the questioner tried to refute by deducing its contradictory from the answers he got from his partner. Once the roles were distributed and the problem and the thesis were chosen, the debate could start. One fundamental rule was that only yes or no questions were admitted,[18] and to each such question (which should also not be long) the answerer should simply say 'yes' or 'no', according to what seemed right to him, no other kind of answer being allowed. Although it was sometimes allowable for the answerer to add a comment, in no case could this comment be made *in place of* the answer. In that kind of dialectical practice, there is a notorious inequality between the two participants. The questioner plays the most active role,[19] since he is the one who mainly leads the discussion or, to put it in a better way, the one who develops the argument – in fact, that was how the debate was understood, as the development of an argument, whose elements were the propositions to which the answerer gives assent. So it is in this context that we should try to understand Chrysippus' recommendation that, when subject to soritical questioning, one should at a certain point stop answering and fall silent. This recommendation is described both by Cicero (106–43 BC) and by Sextus Empiricus (second and third centuries AD):

Chrysippus holds that when you are being questioned step by step, e.g. as to whether three are few or many, you should fall quiet a little while before you come to many (that is what they call *hêsuchazein*). (Cicero *Luc*, xxviii 92)

Chrysippus and his fellow dogmatists say that when the Sorites is being propounded one should, while the argument is proceeding, stop and suspend judgement in order not to fall into absurdity. (Sextus *PH*, ii 253)

Would this reaction be permitted by the rules of the dialectical game? Bobzien[20] rightly criticises Williamson, and indirectly Barnes,[21] for suggesting that instead of keeping silent, the answerer could say, for example, 'I don't know'. In fact, to answer that way would be a violation of the rules. In *The Attic Nights*, Aulus Gellius (second century AD) presents the rule of dialectic according to which one should answer each question with a simple 'yes' or 'no', and he underlines its limitations. The advocates of the rule say that 'those who do

---

[18] Cf. Aristotle, *Top.* 158a15–7.
[19] One can thus understand that a handbook of dialectic such as Aristotle's *Topics* should be mainly addressed to the questioner. Curiously enough, in 159a36–7, Aristotle remarks that, before himself, the answerer's role – his ends and the principles by which he should guide his choice of answers – was never made an object of analysis.
[20] Bobzien (2002, p. 229 and fn. 43).
[21] Cf. Barnes (1982, p. 569, fn. 78).

not observe that rule, but answer more than they were asked, or differently, are thought to be both uneducated and unobservant of the customs and laws of debate' (Gellius, xvi 2). Plato's dialogues contain many examples of this kind of criticism of those who break the rule. But it also had its critics. Menedemus, for example, when Alexino asked him 'Have you ceased to beat your father?', realised that it would be misleading to answer 'no'; and, upon Alexino's insistence that he should just say 'yes' or 'no', Menedemus retorted that 'It would be ridiculous for me to follow your rules, when I can stop you on the threshold.'[22] Gellius thinks that the rule is generally appropriate, but he offers a proviso, saying that 'captious questions do not have to be answered'. Bobzien relies on this text by Gellius and on another one by Simplicius (sixth century AD),[23] and says that 'falling silent is a strategy that in antiquity was used in the 'game' of dialectical questioning' (Bobzien 2002, p. 229). However, one can doubt whether it had been like that since the beginning and that Chrysippus was exploring one possibility offered by the rules that were already in place. There is evidence that in its original version the dialectical game did not allow the option of not answering: in fact, in *Topics* viii 2 Aristotle says that the questioner who goes on asking questions when the other does not answer is blameworthy, because, instead of going on asking, he should stop and criticise his partner, or he should abandon the discussion. We can thus suppose, or at least offer the hypothesis, that Chrysippus was innovating when he advised falling silent as an appropriate strategy to respond to a soritical questioning. He might have reached the conclusion that one of the lessons of the Sorites is exactly that the rules of dialectic had to be expanded, because there are yes or no questions that cannot be given yes or no answers.

Chrysippus' strategy has the immediate advantage of avoiding refutation, that is, of preventing the opponent from claiming victory. We should not forget the competitive dimension that dialectical debates had in antiquity. In general, each debate had a winner and a loser. Eubulides and Diodorus were highly skilled dialecticians and hardly ever lost a debate – although they were frequently accused of unethical behaviour in their practice. The Sorites had a bad reputation (of being a 'fallacious argument') because it was known as an almost infallible recipe for defeating any opponent. The established rules of the dialectical art made it very difficult, perhaps impossible, to escape refutation. 'Sorites are vicious', Cicero writes. It was imperative to be able to 'destroy' Sorites arguments, to block their apparently unstoppable strength. But if someone agreed that n hairs are few, how could he refuse to give his assent to the next proposition, that $n + 1$ are few? Brunschwig rightly remarks that, from the point of view of dialectical practice, what mattered more than the truth of propositions was 'the degree of freedom that they leave to the assent of any interlocutor' (Brunschwig 2009, vol. 1, p. 37). In the Sorites, that freedom seemed to be null. Hence, Chrysippus adopts a radical strategy: by falling silent, we prevent the questioner from deducing the conclusion with *our* premises. It is essentially a defensive strategy. But

---

[22] This story is told by Diogenes Laertius, II 135.
[23] Simplicius (2003, pp. 38–9).

is it successful? Or does it expose the Stoic to well-founded criticism? Carneades criticised it harshly:

'As far as I'm concerned,' says Carneades, 'you can snore as well as fall quiet. But what good does that do? Someone will come along and wake you from your sleep and question you in the same way: 'Take the number you fell silent at – if I add one to that number, will they be many?'' – and you will go on again for as long as you think good. Why say more? You confess that you can tell us neither which is last of the few nor which is first of the many. And that sort of error spreads so widely that I do not see where it may not get to.' 'That doesn't hurt me', he says; 'for, like a clever charioteer, I shall pull up my horses before I get to the end, and all the more so if the place where the horses are coming to is steep. Thus', he says, 'I pull myself up in time, and I don't go on answering your captious questions' If you've got hold of something clear but won't answer, you're acting arrogantly; if you haven't, then not even you see through the matter. If that is because it is obscure, I agree; but you say that you don't go as far as what is obscure – so you stop at cases that are clear. If you do that simply in order to be silent, you gain nothing; for what does it matter to the man who's after you whether he catches you silent or talking? But if up to nine, say, you answer without hesitation that they are few, and then stop at the tenth, you are withholding assent from what is certain and perfectly plain – and you don't let me do that in cases that are obscure. So your art doesn't help you at all against the Sorites, since it does not tell you what is first or last in the increasing and the decreasing sequence. (Cicero *Luc*, xxix 93–4)

Carneades' criticism raises two main questions: one regarding the moment chosen by the Stoic to fall silent; the other regarding the meaning that silence is supposed to have in this context. For Carneades, the two questions are connected, since if Chrysippus were to stop answering when the case is obscure, his silence would mean lack of knowledge and corresponding suspension of judgement – something the Sceptic understands and approves of. But since Chrysippus stops when the case is still clear, what does his silence mean? If his silence is an intentional action, how should it be interpreted?

Bobzien suggests that, as a response to a question such as 'Are 51 few?', silence can mean that there is no fact of the matter.[24] The standard reading (defended by Barnes, Burnyeat and Williamson, among others) sees Chrysippus as an epistemicist – that is, as someone who thinks that there is a sharp boundary between positive and negative cases, but that to locate it is beyond our reach.[25] Bobzien claims, however, that he is rather a gap theorist: in the intermediate zone of the Sorites questioning, sentences would express no proposition and hence would be neither true nor false; bivalence would still hold, but only for propositions. Bobzien thinks that epistemicism is a very counterintuitive view and she resists attributing it to the Stoics, arguing that there is no evidence that Chrysippus thought that 'there is a sharp true/false divide in Sorites-series' (Bobzien 2002, p. 228). Her arguments, though, overlook the fact that there is, in Cicero's text, clear evidence that Chrysippus accepted a sharp and unknowable boundary between *true* and *untrue* cases in a soritical series: 'You confess that you can tell us neither which is last of the few nor which is first of the many. [...] your art [...] does not tell you what is first or last in the increasing and the decreasing sequence'. So according to Chrysippus, in a Sorites series

---

[24] Cf. Bobzien (2002, p. 222 and fn. 45 on p. 229).
[25] See Chapter 1 in this volume.

from F to non-F there is an object which is the last F, but we cannot know which one it is. Surely, after the last F, the next object in the series *fails* to be F – and it is the first one that does. Admitting this much is very counterintuitive – going as it does against the plausible principle that 'one (grain, hair, etc.) cannot make a difference' – and hardly less so than epistemicism itself. Now, in what sense of *failing* to be does the next object fail to be F? In comparison with the acceptance of an undetectable last F, this seems a rather secondary question. The simplest hypothesis, though, is that it is in the normal sense of *not being F*, i.e. the sense that makes the corresponding affirmation false. The suggestion that the next sentence after the last F, e.g. '51 are few', does not express any proposition is indeed very implausible and completely ad hoc. So I will assume that Chrysippus thought that every case is either true or false. But, for present purposes, what matters most is that, even if there were indeterminate cases in the middle of the Sorites series, Chrysippus stops answering before reaching them, before the last F and even before the cases that are obscurely F, in cases still clearly F – therefore, it is certain that his silence does not mean that there is no fact of the matter about the case in question.

If there is an unknowable cut-off point between positive and negative cases, there should also be an intermediate zone in the series with several cases regarding which we cannot know on what side of the cut-off point they lie. Presumably, those are the obscure cases. At first sight, nothing would be more natural than to suppose that it is with respect to these cases that the Stoic falls silent and does not answer. Carneades, however, criticises Chrysippus for falling silent *before that*: 'you say that you don't go as far as what is obscure – so you stop at cases that are clear'; 'you are withholding assent from what is certain and perfectly plain'. In order to understand Chrysippus' reason for stopping before the end of the clear cases, one should consider that his aim is not only to avoid saying 'yes' with respect to negative cases, but also to avoid saying it with respect to cases that are obscure, even if positive. In general, the Stoics thought that one should say and believe only what one knows; that is, one should only give assent to cognitive impressions.[26] If Chrysippus is to follow this principle, he will answer 'yes' to 'Are n few?' only when n are clearly few. But if the boundary between the positive and the negative cases is undetectable, then the boundary between the clear positive cases and the non-clear positive cases will not be less so. We cannot assume that all non-clear cases are clearly non-clear. Just as we cannot know which one is the last positive case, we also cannot know which one is the last clear case. Hence, if we try to hit it we take two risks: it can happen that we stop too early (not saying 'yes' to cases that are clear) or it can happen that we stop too late (saying 'yes' to cases that are not clear). Chrysippus took the second possibility to be a serious failure. Hence his advice to stop before it is too late; that is, to stop reasonably before the last clear case, at a comfortable and safe distance. As Williamson puts it, 'one [should stop] answering 'yes' before it has ceased to be the clearly correct answer' (Williamson 1994, p. 20).

---

[26] It is worth noting that this principle alone would give them good reason to be unhappy with the fundamental rule of dialectic.

By stopping answering, Chrysippus prevents the interlocutor from moving forward to the absurd conclusion with his consent. But that cannot be just a trick: he should be able to say that his reaction is intellectually honest, and not a way of cheating. It matters that the silence be both external and internal: the lack of answer corresponds not to an occultation, but to a genuine suspension of judgement. However, suspension of judgement in face of a clear case is an attitude of doubtful legitimacy.[27] Any attempted defence of Chrysippus is dependent on a specific interpretation of his silence. Carneades equates silence with falling asleep, something with no relevance to or connection with the problem under discussion; but Chrysippus disagrees and compares himself rather to a 'clever charioteer', who makes the most prudent decision. Falling silent is thus an intentional action, resulting from a considered decision. So it has to mean something – and something relevant to the question that was asked. But what? Williamson shows that keeping silent cannot be synonymous with saying 'I don't know' or 'It is unclear', but he does not put forward any alternative. He assures us, however, that he can understand it: 'Silence remains intelligible' (Williamson 1994, p. 20). Is there any proposition such that keeping silent is equivalent to giving assent to it (and that does not evade the question, as would happen were one to say 'I'm bored')? It does not seem that there can be one. Every proposition that we can think of as a reasonable candidate, such as 'This is a good place to stop answering "yes"',[28] entails that the case is a positive one. And this entailment is so obvious that it is implausible that the answerer can fail to see it. Therefore, if he knows that proposition, he also knows that the case is positive, and so he cannot suspend judgement. I conclude that Carneades was basically right in his criticism: keeping silent does not mean anything relevant to the question that was asked and is more like inadvertently falling asleep.

There is, however, an important insight implicit in Chrysippus' strategy. If he stops answering and does not say 'yes' in a case k with respect to which that answer would be clearly correct, he makes a choice: he can say 'yes' or he can say nothing, and, although the quality of the impression he receives from k is enough to justify the stronger reaction, he chooses the weaker one. Besides, his choice is to a certain extent arbitrary, since, although he has reasons to stop answering in the vicinity of k, he does not have reasons to stop specifically at k rather than at $k - 1$ or $k + 1$. In terms of F-ness, there is barely anything noticeable in that case that differentiates it from the previous one, where he knowledgeably answered 'yes'. The reason for deciding to suspend judgement at k is global in nature, not local: it transcends the intrinsic properties of k and it involves considerations about its place in the series, such as its being relatively close to the last clearly positive cases. This fact has an interesting consequence. If we stop answering at k, then there is something we do not

---

[27] Why is that so? Clearness is here taken to be epistemic and I am equating it with the Stoics' notion of cognitiveness (of impressions). When an impression is cognitive it has all that is needed for it to become a piece of knowledge and that is why cognitive impressions tend to cause our assent. Frede (1983, pp. 167–9) argues that the distinctive feature of cognitive impressions is not some phenomenal character that we have to be aware of in order to recognise the impression as cognitive, but rather a causal feature, akin to a power to produce genuine cognitions in our minds. This is compatible with the possibility that in special circumstances, such as those present in the Sorites, we have from other sources compelling reasons to refuse assenting to what is cognitive and clear. Thanks to Elia Zardini for pressing this question.

[28] Thanks to Elia Zardini for providing the example and for helpful discussion of the question.

know about *k* (since we don't even judge) that we could easily have known, if only we had decided to stop one step ahead, at *k* + 1. It may surprise many philosophers that knowledge about an object may depend, not on the evidence available to us regarding that object, but simply on an arbitrary decision of ours to judge or not to judge.

15.3 Case Study 2: Leibniz's Phenomenalism

In his *New Essays on Human Understanding* (1704), Leibniz mentions the Sorites Paradox in the context of a reaction to Locke's anti-realism about essences and species. He starts by stating that 'Ordinarily, [the] boundaries of species are fixed by the nature of things, for instance the line between man and beast' (Leibniz 1982, book III, chapter v, §9). But then he admits that there are also 'vague and imperfect essences, where opinion comes in', and he gives baldness as an example – an all but accidental example, as he himself quickly underlines by recalling that the problem of the boundaries of baldness was 'one of the sophisms of the Ancients'. To that ancient problem,

the true answer is that nature has not determined that notion, and that opinion plays there its role; that there are people about whom one can doubt whether they are bald or not; and that there are ambiguous cases whom some would regard as bald and other would not, just as you have remarked that a horse thought to be small in Holland would be regarded as big in Wales. (Leibniz 1982, book III, chapter v, §9)

We can rightly criticise Leibniz for not distinguishing sufficiently here between vagueness on the one hand and relativity to a standard of assessment given by context on the other; and for not realizing that, even relatively to a single standard, the uncertainty about borderline cases still remains. But what we should particularly notice in his reply is the statement that vague notions are undetermined and have borderline cases for which there is not one objectively correct verdict. A little further on,[29] Leibniz restates this position, when he says that the question of 'how many hairs one should leave on a man's head for him not to be bald' is undecidable, having no determined answer. It seems certain that when he wrote the *New Essays*, Leibniz thought that vague notions do not have exact limits of application, or do not determine sharp boundaries, and that is why they are 'imperfect'.

Leibniz did not always think this way, though. In the dialogue *Pacidius to Philalethes*, written in 1676, he gives a fairly complete presentation of the Sorites Paradox, regarding it as a *surprising* proof that vague notions must have sharp boundaries. As examples he uses poverty, as measured by the number of pennies in one's possession, and nearness, as measured by the number of inches between two objects. Questioned by Pacidius (Leibniz's spokesman), the character Charinus starts by accepting that being poor is a property tolerant to small differences. It seems obvious to him that, if the wealth of two people differs by only one penny, one of them could not be regarded as poor without the same judgement being made about the other. Pacidius then shows him that, if that is so, a poor man can never

---

[29] Leibniz (1982, book III, chapter vi, §27).

cease to be poor, regardless of how many pennies are given to him. At the end, Charinus is forced to admit that 'either nobody ever becomes rich or poor, or one can become so by the gain or loss of one penny' (Leibniz 2001, pp. 153–5) – although he confesses his surprise for having been deluded about it.

In this work, Leibniz's interest in the Sorites is merely instrumental. The dialogue is essentially a reflection on the problem of the continuum, understood as a general metaphysical problem (not just mathematical) about the composition of anything continuous – matter, space, time, movement and so on. In the section where the Sorites is introduced, Leibniz is mainly focused on the difficulties involved in trying to conceive the instant of change. Is there such an instant? Is there, for instance, after the last instant in which someone is alive and before the first instant is which she is not alive, one intermediate instant in which the person dies? If the excluded middle always holds, she would have to be either alive or not alive in that instant – but apparently she could be neither. On the other hand, *as Leibniz understands it in this work*, the Sorites seems to show that there must always be an instant of change – for example the instant when, by the gaining of one penny (or whatever small amount is responsible for the change), someone ceases to be poor or, more precisely, the instant when, by the gaining of one inch (or rather by the completion of a minimum of space in a minimum of time), one object gets near to another. And the question he wants to raise in that section concerns the state of the object in that decisive instant: is the person poor or not poor the instant she changes? Is the object near or not near the instant it changes?

I will not enter here into the complexities of Leibniz's thought about change and the continuum. Suffice it to say that, obviously, between the *Pacidius*, where he accepted that the change from being poor to not being poor must happen 'by the gaining of one penny', and the *New Essays*, where he thought that vague notions like poverty do not have exact limits of application, Leibniz changed his mind on the Sorites. Fortunately, we can locate that change. It happened in March of 1678, when Leibniz wrote a short note to which he gave the title 'Acervus Chrysippi' (Chrysippus' Heap). There he says that vague notions are notions that we do not understand well:

all those notions to which the heap or Sorites of the Stoics applies, such as *wealth*, *poverty*, *baldness*, *heat*, *cold*, *tepidness*, *white* and *black*, *big* and *small*, taken absolutely,[30] are vague imaginary notions, indeed false ones, that is, ones having no corresponding idea. Precisely those notions to which the Stoics' objection cannot be made are understood purely and transparently by us. That is to say, the above notions indicate something with respect to our opinion, which varies. For example, what is cold to one person seems hot to another, truly in each case, and this is even so for the same person at different times. It is the same with poverty. For someone we call poor in a certain respect, we deny to be so in some other respect. (Leibniz 2001, pp. 229–31, A VI, 4, 69)

---

[30] Why 'taken absolutely'? Most probably, Leibniz adds this condition in order to respect the distinction between absolute judgements of the kind '*x* is rich' and comparative judgements of the kind '*x* is richer than *y*'. For a little further on in the note, he remarks: 'Concerning imaginary notions, comparative propositions, at any rate, remain true, and to these the Sorites cannot be raised as an objection' (A VI, 4, 70, p. 231).

As we can see, Leibniz began here to make a close association between vagueness and variability of opinions. If we once again set aside the likely confusion with contextual dependence, his main idea seems to be that, regarding borderline cases, there is not a unique objectively correct answer, and that the different opinions are equally good. This is enough to indicate that Leibniz has now abandoned the acceptance of sharp boundaries. But why? Did he come to the conclusion that the Sorites is not a valid argument after all? Or did he resign himself to accepting that no one ever becomes rich by the accumulation of pennies?

The last option has been defended by Samuel Levey. In his opinion, Leibniz's change of mind led him to a nihilist view, according to which 'vague notions do not truly apply to anything' (Levey 2002, p. 34). In the note, we read that vague notions have no corresponding idea; and Levey interprets this in the light of section 25 of the *Discourse on Metaphysics* (1686), where Leibniz writes that 'we have no idea of a notion when it is impossible', and he says that very frequently we wrongly believe that we understand some notion 'although in fact the notion is impossible'. From this Levey infers that, on Leibniz's new view, vague notions 'involve hidden impossibilities that are revealed by the Sorites Paradox' (Levey 2002, p. 34). And, if they are impossible, then they are true of nothing, as the nihilist claim.

Leibniz has a very specific and elaborate way of understanding what an idea is, and we do not have space to go into its details here. For present purposes, we should simply take into account that, in Leibniz's opinion, it frequently happens that we think about things of which we don't really have an idea. His discussion of the Ontological Argument may provide a helpful illustration: he thinks that the argument establishes only that 'if God is possible, then it follows that he exists' ('Meditations on Knowledge, Truth, and Ideas', in Leibniz 1989, p. 25); and though he accepts that conceivability implies possibility, he believes that God's conceivability is yet to be proved, since 'the fact that we think about a most perfect being is not sufficient for us to assert that we have an idea of it' (Leibniz 1989, pp. 25–6). *Grosso modo*, a notion without a corresponding idea is a notion represented by some word that we understand, i.e. of which we know the meaning, and which we may even define ('nominally'), but that is a notion of something that we cannot really conceive. For instance, we can define the greatest number of all, or the fastest motion, but these notions correspond to something really inconceivable, since it is something impossible, which involves a contradiction. Based on these examples, Leibniz writes that 'there are true and false ideas, depending upon whether the thing in question is possible or not' (Leibniz, *Discourse on Metaphysics*, §23).[31] According to Levey, by saying that richness, baldness and heat are false notions, with no corresponding idea, Leibniz wants to indicate that they are intrinsically incoherent concepts, which include a contradiction and which, therefore, apply to nothing at all. The proof of their impossibility would be provided by the Sorites.

There are good reasons to doubt this interpretation (independent from the extreme implausibility of the nihilist view).[32] Instead of a claim to the effect that there could not be

---

[31] See also Leibniz (1989, p. 26).
[32] See Chapter 4, Section 4.6, and Chapter 11, Section 11.3 in this volume.

bald men or hot things, what we read in the note is that, sometimes, 'what is cold to one person seems hot to another, *truly in each case*' (emphasis added). Just as he accepts that some things are colder than others ('*comparative propositions [. . .] remain true*'), Leibniz does not seem seriously to doubt that there are cold things and hot things, poor people and rich people. However, the main objection to the nihilist interpretation comes in the following lines of the note:

If *poverty*, taken absolutely, were a true notion, it ought to be defined by a certain number of pennies, because it is necessary for someone who is not poor to become poor on the removal of one penny; or he will never become poor at all. Hence the laws come to the aid of this defect, and define a pauper as someone who does not possess some particular number of shillings; and a major as someone who has reached the age of twenty-five. (Leibniz 2001, p. 231, A VI, 4, 69–70)

Leibniz repeats here, almost exactly, the disjunction that in the *Pacidius* he thought was established by the Sorites. But now he adds that one would have to accept that disjunction, *if poverty were a true notion*.[33] On this conditional, Leibniz performs a *modus tollens*, that is to say, he reasons that, since the disjunction is unacceptable (for both disjuncts are obviously false), we should rather conclude that poverty *is not* a true notion. With their stipulation, the laws in fact create a notion of poverty (and of adulthood) that we can easily understand and that is not subject to the objection of the Sorites – but that notion is not the ordinary one. Leibniz now thinks that the ordinary notion of poverty is not a true notion, and that is why it is not right to say that either it has an exact boundary or it does not apply to anything.

  Leibniz intends to explore a third option (beyond the alternative of accepting nihilism or sharp boundaries), on the basis of the *phenomenal* character of vague notions. The last part of the note develops this aspect:

I call those notions imaginary which are not in the things outside us, but whose essence it is to appear to us. Hence whenever we begin to be in doubt, as on the removal of one penny, there ceases to be a problem, and the person in question is neither poor nor rich to me. [. . .] When we are in doubt whether a thing is hot or cold, we call it tepid, therefore tepid is not a definite idea outside of us, but consists in our doubt. (Leibniz 2001, p. 231, A VI, 4, 70)

It could seem that, by calling these notions 'imaginary' and saying that they 'are not in the things outside us' , Leibniz was denying them any objective reality and making them mere 'secondary qualities' that exist only in the mind. That impression is weakened, however, if we take into account that it is generally in these terms that Leibniz describes everything that is material or physical. Bodies are not substances for him, because they have no true unity. Being infinitely divisible, all bodies are just 'beings by aggregation'. Leibniz frequently compares the body to a heap of stones: it is an aggregate of many things, and not a unique being. Curiously, when he denies substantial reality to bodies, and in general to everything having extension, the examples he uses are typically connected with the Sorites, such as 'a flock of sheep', 'a community', 'a people', 'an army', 'a society', 'a

---

[33] He does *not* say 'poverty is not a true notion, because (the Sorites shows that) no one ever becomes poor'.

college'.[34] Just as 'these are moral beings, beings in which there is something imaginary and dependent on the fabrication of our mind' ('Letter to Arnauld', in Leibniz 1989, p. 79), also 'bodies would doubtless be only imaginary and apparent, if there were only matter and its modification' (Leibniz 1989, p. 80). Not being substances, however, these aggregates are not unreal, or mere creations of the mind, since there certainly are substances (indivisible and indestructible) that underlie them: 'every being by aggregation presupposes beings endowed with real unity, because every being derives its reality only from the reality of those beings of which it is composed' (Leibniz 1989, p. 85). While we are incapable of penetrating the profound reality of the things around us, what we have is their appearance, or the way that multiplicity 'appears to us' – as a body, as something blue, hot, etc.

In the case of vague notions, specifically, that phenomenal character typically gives rise to borderline cases, and at the end of the note Leibniz focuses his attention on these cases. He considers what happens when we move forward in the soritical argument and enter the critical zone. He talked previously of variability of opinions and now he talks of doubt: we remove one penny, and we don't know whether what results is someone poor or not. On my reading of the text, Leibniz is being relaxed with his examples: he gives contraries (hot or cold, poor or rich), when he is thinking of contradictories (hot or not hot, poor or not poor).[35] When doubt comes in, Leibniz says, 'there ceases to be a problem, and the person in question is neither poor nor rich [i.e. not poor] to me'. My uncertainty does not correspond to a real cognitive problem, since, given that the notion is essentially phenomenal, if it does not seem poor to me and it also does not seem not poor, then there is nothing further to be examined or to be known. There is not one right answer to my doubt. The principle of the excluded middle does not apply here. Given the phenomenality of the notion, there is no space left for a gap between reality and appearance. If we give a new name to those cases – for example, calling them 'tepid' – that will be just a name we give to the absence of an answer, and not a more fine-grained description of the appearances. As Leibniz puts it, 'tepid consists in our doubt'.

How Leibniz changed his mind from the *Pacidius* to the short note is now quite clear: he abandoned the acceptance of sharp boundaries and he moved on to think that, between the positive cases ('hot') and the negative cases ('not hot'), there is a zone of indeterminacy ('tepid') where, since there is no appearance – and since in this respect 'to be is to appear' – the excluded middle does not hold. Clearly, with this move, Leibniz did not solve every problem of vagueness – as we currently know very well. At least one obvious difficulty that he did not consider is the following. When, at the end of the note, Leibniz mentions the moment 'when we *begin* to be in doubt' and he says that, at that moment, the problem vanishes, one naturally wonders whether he ever realised how problematic it can be to

---

[34] See Galen's examples at the beginning of chapter XVI of *On Medical Experience* (p. 74).

[35] In the *Pacidius*, Leibniz is generally more careful with his use of contradictories as examples, but even there he sometimes slips into giving contraries, as in this case: 'Therefore no one can ever become rich from being poor, nor become poor from being rich, however many pennies are given to or taken from him' (p. 153). Moreover, in the envisaged situation, the more relevant doubt, the one that creates greater difficulties, concerns which of the contradictories applies. See also Leibniz's remark about doubting in the first displayed quotation of this section. Thanks to Elia Zardini for pointing out the need for this justification of my reading.

suppose that there is a precise moment in which doubt begins. If the question previously was whether one penny less is enough to make someone poor, now the pressing question becomes whether one penny less is enough for one to start doubting someone's poverty.

For Descartes, the antidote for doubt was clear and distinct ideas. Leibniz had great esteem for this Cartesian principle, but he thought it was not sufficient. Besides noting that what is clear is often not distinct (but rather confused), he said that we need criteria for the clear and distinct,[36] since it is possible to be fooled and to believe to be clear what in fact is obscure. Strictly, this is compatible with the boundary between the clear and the obscure being sharp but unknowable – and we have found exactly that idea implicit in Chrysippus' advice. But probably Leibniz thought otherwise, preferring to see the clear gradually shading out into the obscure. There is a surprising feature of Leibniz's short note on the Sorites that easily escapes notice, which is the fact that he included *tepidness* in his examples of vague notions. If 'tepid' is for Leibniz, as I have suggested, a kind of metaphor for borderline cases as he conceives of them – in terms of indeterminacy – then by calling attention to the vagueness of tepidness itself, he could be flagging what we now call the phenomenon of *higher-order vagueness*:[37] that the borderline cases are themselves not sharply bounded, and there are possibly borderline borderline cases. If he saw this, though, Leibniz unfortunately did not develop the idea.[38]

[36] Leibniz (1989, pp. 26–7).
[37] See Chapter 2 in this volume, pp. 56–8.
[38] An earlier version of this chapter was presented in April 2017 at the MELL research seminar (LanCog Group, University of Lisbon). I would like to thank the participants, especially David Yates, Diogo Santos, Domingos Faria, Elia Zardini, Elton Marques, Fernando Furtado, Hili Razinsky, José Mestre, Laura Delgado, Luís Veríssimo and Pedro Dinis, for their stimulating questions, comments and discussions. A talk I gave at the Federal University of Rio de Janeiro in September 2017 on the Forced March gave me the opportunity to deepen my understanding of Chrysippus' strategy and its merits. Thanks to all the participants in that seminar and, in particular, for their great questions and discussions, to Guido Imaguire, Célia Teixeira and Roberto Pereira. The editors of this volume, Elia Zardini and Sergi Oms, both gave me numerous comments and raised several questions that led to important improvements, and I am grateful for their help.

References

Adams, E. W. 1998. *A Primer of Probability Logic*. Stanford: CSLI Publications.

Ajdukiewicz, K. 1965. *Logika pragmatyczna*. Warsaw: Państwowe Wydawnictwo Naukowe.

Åkerman, J. 2012. 'Contextualist Theories of Vagueness', *Philosophy Compass* 7: 470–80.

Åkerman, J. and Greenough, P. 2010a. 'Hold the Context Fixed – Vagueness Still Remains', in R. Dietz and S. Moruzzi (eds.), *Cuts and Clouds: Essays on the Nature and Logic of Vagueness*. Oxford: Oxford University Press, pp. 275–88.

2010b. 'Vagueness and Non-Indexical Contextualism', in S. Sawyer (ed.), *New Waves in Philosophy of Language*. Basingstoke: Palgrave Macmillan, pp. 8–23.

Alchourrón, C. and Bulygin, E. 1971. *Normative Systems*. Vienna: Springer.

Alxatib, S. and Pelletier, F. 2011. 'The Psychology of Vagueness: Borderline Cases and Contradictions', *Mind and Language* 26: 287–326.

Armour-Garb, B. 2004. 'Minimalism, the Generalization Problem and the Liar', *Synthese* 139: 491–512.

2010. 'Horwichian Minimalism and the Generalization Problem', *Analysis* 70: 693–703.

Armour-Garb, B. and Beall, JC (eds.) 1996. *Deflationary Truth*. Chicago: Open Court.

Arnauld, A. and Nicole, P. 1992. *La logique ou l'art de penser*. Paris: Éditions Gallimard.

Arrhenius, G., Ryberg, J. and Tännsjö, T. 2017. 'The Repugnant Conclusion', in E. Zalta (ed.), *The Stanford Encyclopedia of Philosophy* (https://plato.stanford.edu/archives/spr2017/entries/repugnant-conclusion).

Arrow, K. J. 1950. 'A Difficulty in the Concept of Social Welfare', *Journal of Political Economy* 58: 328–46.

1959. 'Rational Choice Functions and Orderings', *Economica* 26: 121–7.

Arruda, A. I. 1989. 'Aspects of the Historical Development of Paraconsistent Logic', in G. Priest, R. Routley and J. Norman (eds.), *Paraconsistent Logic: Essays on the Inconsistent*. Munich: Philosophia Verlag, pp. 99–130.

Asenjo, F. 1966. 'A Calculus of Antinomies', *Notre Dame Journal of Formal Logic* 7: 103–5.

Asgeirsson, H. 2015. 'On the Instrumental Value of Vagueness in the Law', *Ethics* 125: 425–48.

Asher, N., Dever, J. and Pappas, C. 2009. 'Supervaluations Debugged', *Mind* 118: 901–33.

Aulus Gellius 1927. *The Attic Nights*. With an English translation by J. C. Rolfe. Cambridge, MA: Harvard University Press.

Bale, A. 2009. 'A Universal Scale of Comparison', *Linguistics and Philosophy* 31: 1–55.

Barker, C. 2002. 'The Dynamics of Vagueness', *Linguistics and Philosophy* 25: 1–36.

Barnes, E. 2005. 'Vagueness and Arbitrariness: Merricks on Composition', *Mind* 116: 105–13.

2013. 'Metaphysically Indeterminate Existence', *Philosophical Studies* 166: 495–510.

2014. 'Fundamental Indeterminacy', *Analytic Philosophy* 55: 339–62.

Barnes, J. 1982. 'Medicine, Experience, and Logic', in J. Barnes, J. Brunschwig, M. F. Burnyeat and M. Schofield (eds.), *Science and Speculation*. Cambridge: Cambridge University Press, pp. 24–68. (Reprinted in J. Barnes (2012), pp. 538–81. Page references are to the reprint.)

2012. *Logical Matters: Essays in Ancient Philosophy II*. Edited by M. Bonelli. Oxford: Clarendon Press.

Bartsch, R. and Vennemann, T. 1972. 'The Grammar of Relative Adjectives and Comparison', *Linguistische Berichte* 20: 19–32.

1973. *Semantic Structures: A Study in the Relation between Syntax and Semantics*. Frankfurt: Athenäum Verlag.

Beall, JC (ed.) 2003. *Liars and Heaps: New Essays on Paradox*. Oxford: Oxford University Press.

(ed.) 2008. *Revenge of the Liar: New Essays on the Paradox*. Oxford: Oxford University Press.

2009. *Spandrels of Truth*. Oxford: Clarendon Press.

Beall, JC and Armour-Garb, B. (eds.) 2005a. *Deflationism and Paradox*. Oxford: Oxford University Press.

2005b. 'Minimalism, Epistemicism and Paradox', in JC Beall and B. Armour-Garb (eds.), *Deflationism and Paradox*. Oxford: Oxford University Press, pp. 85–96.

Beall, JC and Murzi J. 2013. 'Two Flavors of Curry Paradox', *The Journal of Philosophy* 110: 143–65.

Beall, JC and van Fraassen, B. C. 2003. *Possibilities and Paradox*. Oxford: Oxford University Press.

Beck, S., Krasikova, S., Fleischer, D., Gergel, R., Hofstetter, S., Savelsberg, C., Vanderelst, J. and Villalta, E. 2009. 'Crosslinguistic Variation in Comparative Constructions', *Linguistic Variation Yearbook* 9: 1–66.

Běhounek, L. 2014. 'In Which Sense Is Fuzzy Logic a Logic for Vagueness', in T. Lukasiewicz, R. Peñaloza and A. Y. Turhan (eds.), *Logics for Reasoning about Preferences, Uncertainty, and Vagueness*. Oxford: CEUR, pp. 26–38.

2016. 'Determinate Truth in Fuzzy Plurivaluationism', in P. Arazim, T. Lavicka (eds.), *The Logica Yearbook 2016*. London: College, 2017, pp. 1–15.

Bennett, K. 2004. 'Spatiotemporal Coincidence and the Grounding Problem', *Philosophical Studies* 118: 339–71.

Berker, S. 2008. 'Luminosity Regained', *Philosophers' Imprint* 8: 1–22.

Beth, E. W. 1954. 'Le paradoxe du "sorite" d'Eubulide de Mégare', in *La vie, la pensée: Actes du VIIe Congrés des sociétés de philosophie de langue française*. Paris: Presses Universitaires de France, pp. 237–41.

Béziau, J. Y. 2006. 'Transitivity and Paradoxes', *The Baltic International Yearbook of Cognition, Logic and Communication* 1: 87–92.

Bierwisch, M. 1989. 'The Semantics of Gradation', in M. Bierwisch and E. Lang (eds.), *Dimensional Adjectives*. Berlin: Springer, pp. 71–262.

Black, M. 1937. 'Vagueness: An Exercise in Logical Analysis', *Philosophy of Science* 4: 427–55.

Blackburn, P., Rijke, M. and Venema, Y. 2001. *Modal Logic*. Cambridge: Cambridge University Press.

Blackburn, S. 2002. *Being Good: A Short Introduction to Ethics*. Oxford: Oxford University Press.

Bobaljik, J. 2012. *Universals in Comparative Morphology: Suppletion, Superlatives, and the Structure of Words*. Cambridge, MA: MIT Press.

Bobzien, S. 2002. 'Chrysippus and the Epistemic Theory of Vagueness', *Proceedings of the Aristotelian Society* 102: 217–38.

2011. 'If It's Clear, then It's Clear that It's Clear, or Is It? Higher-Order Vagueness and the S4 Axiom', in B. Morison and K. Ierodiakonou (eds.), *Episteme, etc.: Essays in Honour of Jonathan Barnes*. Oxford: Oxford University Press, pp. 189–239.

Bochnak, M. R. 2013. 'Cross-Linguistic Variation in the Semantics of Comparatives'. PhD thesis, University of Chicago.

Bogusławski, A. 1975. 'Measures Are Measures: In Defence of the Diversity of Comparatives and Positives', *Linguistische Berichte* 36: 1–9.

Bonini, N., Osherson, D., Viale, R. and Williamson, T. 1999. 'On the Psychology of Vague Predicates', *Mind and Language* 14: 377–93.

Borel, É. 1907. 'Un paradoxe économique: le sophisme du tas de blé et les vérités statistiques', *La revue du mois* 4: 688–99. (English translation by P. Égré and E. Gray 2014. 'An Economic Paradox: The Sophism of the Heap of Wheat and Statistical Truths', *Erkenntnis* 79: 1081–8.)

1950. *Probability and Certainty*. New York: Walker and Company.

Bossuet, J. B. 1677. *Logique du Dauphin*. Edited by F. Laupiès. Paris: Éditions Universitaires, 1990.

Braun, D. and Sider, T. 2007. 'Vague, So Untrue', *Noûs* 41: 133–56.

Brouwer, L. E. J. 1908. 'De onbetrouwbaarheid der logische principes', *Tijdschrift voor wijsbegeerte* 2: 152–8.

Brunschwig, J. 2009. *Aristote: Topiques*. Paris: Les Belles Lettres.

Burgess, A. G. and Burgess, J. P. 2011. *Truth*. Princeton: Princeton University Press.

Burnett, H. 2016. *Gradability in Natural Language: Logical and Grammatical Foundations*. Oxford: Oxford University Press.

Burnyeat, M. F. 1982. 'Gods and Heaps', in M. Schofield and M. C. Nussbaum (eds.), *Language and Logos*. Cambridge: Cambridge University Press, pp. 315–38.

Caie, M. 2012. 'Vagueness and Semantic Indiscernibility', *Philosophical Studies* 160: 365–77.

Calder, A. J., Young, A. W., Perrett, D. I., Etcoff, N. L. and Rowland, D. 1996. 'Categorical Perception of Morphed Facial Expressions', *Visual Cognition* 3: 81–118.

Cameron, R. P. 2010. 'Vagueness and Naturalness', *Erkenntnis* 72: 281–93.

Campbell, R. 1974. 'The Sorites Paradox', *Philosophical Studies* 26: 175–91.

Cargile, J. 1969. 'The Sorites Paradox', *The British Journal for the Philosophy of Science* 20: 193–202.

Casari, E. 1989. 'Comparative logics and Abelian ℓ-groups', in R. Ferro, C. Bonotto, S. Valentini and A. Zanardo (eds.), *Logic Colloquium '88*. Amsterdam: North Holland, pp. 161–90.

Cayrol, N. 2016. 'Qu'est-ce qu'un sorite?', in J. Pascal, P. Mouzet and V. Tellier-Cayrol (eds.), *Mélanges en l'honneur du Professeur Jean Rossetto*. Issy-les-Moulineaux: LGDJ, pp. 241–64.

Chambers, T. 1998. 'On Vagueness, Sorites, and Putnam's Intuitionistic Strategy', *The Monist* 81: 343–8.

Chang, R. 2002. 'The Possibility of Parity', *Ethics* 112: 659–88.

Cherniak, C. 1984. 'Computational Complexity and the Universal Acceptance of Logic', *The Journal of Philosophy* 81: 739–58.

Chihara, C. S. 1979. 'The Semantic Paradoxes: A Diagnostic Investigation', *The Philosophical Review* 88: 590–618.

Chisholm, R. M. 1967. 'Identity through Possible Worlds: Some Questions', *Noûs* 1: 1–8.
  1973. 'Parts as Essential to Their Wholes', *Review of Metaphysics* 26: 581–603.

Cicero 2006. *On Academic Scepticism.* Translated, with introduction and notes, by C. Brittain. Indianapolis: Hackett Publishing Company.

Cignoli, R., D'Ottaviano, I. M. L. and Mundici, D. 1999. *Algebraic Foundations of Many-Valued Reasoning.* Dordrecht: Kluwer.

Cobreros, P. 2008. 'Supervaluationism and Logical Consequence: A Third Way', *Studia Logica* 90: 291–312.
  2011a. 'Paraconsistent Vagueness: A Positive Argument', *Synthese* 183: 211–27.
  2011b. 'Supervaluationism and Fara's Argument Concerning Higher-Order Vagueness', in P. Égré and N. Klinedinst (eds.), *Vagueness and Language Use.* Basingstoke: Palgrave Macmillan, pp. 207–21.
  2011c. 'Varzi on Supervaluationism and Logical Consequence', *Mind* 120: 833–43.
  2013. 'Vagueness: Subvaluationism', *Philosophy Compass* 8: 472–85.

Cobreros, P., Égré, P., Ripley, D. and van Rooij, R. 2012. 'Tolerant, Classical, Strict', *Journal of Philosophical Logic* 41: 347–85.

Cobreros, P. and Tranchini, L. 2014. 'Supervaluationism: Truth, Value and Degree Functionality', *Thought* 3: 133–44.

Colyvan, M. 2009. 'Vagueness and Truth', in H. Dyke (ed.), *From Truth to Reality: New Essays in Logic and Metaphysics.* London: Routledge, pp. 29–40.

Constantinescu, C. 2014. 'Moral Vagueness: A Dilemma for Non-Naturalism', *Oxford Studies in Metaethics* 9: 152–85.

Cook, R. T. 2013. *Paradoxes.* Cambridge: Polity Press.

Corner, A., Hahn, U. and Oaksford, M. 2011. 'The Psychological Mechanism of the Slippery Slope Argument', *Journal of Memory and Language* 64: 133–52.

Cresswell, M. J. 1976. 'The Semantics of Degree', in B. Partee (ed.), *Montague Grammar.* New York: Academic Press, pp. 261–92.

Cruse, D. A. 1986. *Lexical Semantics.* Cambridge: Cambridge University Press.

Curry, H. B. 1942. 'The Inconsistency of Certain Formal Logics', *The Journal of Symbolic Logic* 7: 115–7.

Dempster, A. 1967. 'Upper and Lower Probabilities Induced by a Multivalued Mapping', *Annals of Mathematical Statistics* 38: 325–39.

DeRose, K. 1999. 'Introduction: Responding to Skepticism'. In K. DeRose and T. Warfield (eds.), *Skepticism: A Contemporary Reader.* Oxford: Oxford University Press, pp. 1–24.

Dietz, R. and Moruzzi, S. (eds.) 2010. *Cuts and Clouds: Essays on the Nature and Logic of Vagueness.* Oxford: Oxford University Press.

Diogenes Laertius 1925. *Lives of Eminent Philosophers.* Edited with an English translation by R. D. Hicks. London: William Heinemann.

Donnelly, M. 2011. 'Endurantist and Perdurantist Accounts of Persistence', *Philosophical Studies* 154: 27–51.

Dorr, C., Goodman, J. and Hawthorne, J. 2014. 'Knowing against the Odds', *Philosophical Studies* 170: 277–87.

Dorr, C. and Hawthorne, J. 2014. 'Semantic Plasticity and Speech Reports', *The Philosophical Review* 123: 281–338.

Douven, I. and Decock, L. 2017. 'What Verities May Be', *Mind* 126: 386–428.

Douven, I., Decock, L., Dietz, R. and Égré, P. 2013. 'Vagueness: A Conceptual Spaces Approach', *Journal of Philosophical Logic* 42: 137–60.

Douven, I., Wenmackers, S., Jraissati, Y. and Decock, L. 2016. 'Measuring Graded Membership: The Case of Color', *Cognitive Science* 41: 686–722.

Dummett, M. A. E. 1959. 'Truth', *Proceedings of the Aristotelian Society* 59: 141–62.

　1975. 'Wang's Paradox', *Synthese* 30: 301–24.

Dzhafarov, E. N. and Dzhafarov, D. D. 2012. 'The Sorites Paradox: A Behavioral Approach', in L. Rudolph (ed.), *Qualitative Mathematics for the Social Sciences: Mathematical Models for Research on Cultural Dynamics*. London: Routledge, pp. 105–36.

Edgington, D. 1997. 'Vagueness by Degrees', in R. Keefe and P. Smith (eds.), *Vagueness: A Reader*. Cambridge, MA: MIT Press, pp. 294–316.

Égré, P. 2009. 'Soritical Series and Fisher Series', in A. Hieke and H. Leitgeb (eds.), *Reduction: Between the Mind and the Brain*. Frankfurt: Ontos Verlag, pp. 91–115.

　2011a. 'Perceptual Ambiguity and the Sorites', in R. Nouwen, R. van Rooij, U. Sauerland and H. Schmitz (eds.), *Vagueness in Communication*. Berlin: Springer, pp. 64–90.

　2011b. 'Review of Nicholas JJ Smith, Vagueness and Degrees of Truth', *Australasian Journal of Philosophy* 89: 177–80.

　2015. 'Borderline Cases, Incompatibilism and Plurivaluationism', *Philosophy and Phenomenological Research* 90: 457–66.

　2016. 'Vague Judgment: A Probabilistic Account', *Synthese* 194: 3837–65.

Égré, P. and Barberousse, A. 2014. 'Borel on the Heap', *Erkenntnis* 79: 1043–79.

Égré, P., de Gardelle, V. and Ripley, D. 2013. 'Vagueness and Order Effects in Color Categorization', *Journal of Logic, Language and Information* 22: 391–420.

Égré, P. and Klinedinst, N. (eds.) 2011. *Vagueness and Language Use*. Basingstoke: Palgrave Macmillan.

Égré, P. and Zehr, J. 2016. 'Are Gaps Preferred to Gluts? A Closer Look at Borderline Contradictions', in E. Castroviejo, G. W. Sassoon and L. McNally (eds.), *The Semantics of Gradability, Vagueness, and Scale Structure. Experimental Perspectives*. Berlin: Springer, pp. 25–58.

Eklund, M. 2002. 'Inconsistent Languages', *Philosophy and Phenomenological Research* 64: 251–75.

　2005. 'What Vagueness Consists in', *Philosophical Studies* 125: 27–60.

　2007. 'Meaning-Constitutivity', *Inquiry* 50: 559–74.

　2010a. 'Review of Timothy Williamson, The Philosophy of Philosophy', *Australasian Journal of Philosophy* 88: 752–4.

　2010b. 'Vagueness and Second-Level Indeterminacy', in R. Dietz and S. Moruzzi (eds.), *Cuts and Clouds: Essays on the Nature and Logic of Vagueness*. Oxford: Oxford University Press, pp. 63–76.

　2013. 'Metaphysical Vagueness and Metaphysical Indeterminacy', *Metaphysica* 14: 165–79.

　2017. *Choosing Normative Concepts*. Oxford: Oxford University Press.

Elson, L. 2014. 'Heaps and Chains: Is the Chaining Argument for Parity a Sorites?', *Ethics* 124: 557–71.

　2016. 'Tenenbaum and Raffman on Vague Projects, the Self-Torturer, and the Sorites', *Ethics* 126: 474–88.

Endicott, T. 2001. *Vagueness in Law*. Oxford: Oxford University Press.

Enoch, D. 2007. 'Epistemicism and Nihilism about Vagueness: What Is the Difference?', *Philosophical Studies* 133: 285–311.

2017. 'Non-Naturalistic Realism in Metaethics' in T. McPherson and D. Plunkett (eds.), *The Routledge Handbook of Metaethics*. New York: Routledge, pp. 29–42.

Fara, D. G. 2000. 'Shifting Sands: An Interest-Relative Theory of Vagueness', *Philosophical Topics* 28: 45–81.

2001. 'Phenomenal Continua and the Sorites', *Mind* 110: 905–35.

2003. 'Gap Principles, Penumbral Consequence and Infinitely Higher-Order Vagueness', in JC Beall (ed.), *Liars and Heaps: New Essays on Paradox*. Oxford: Oxford University Press, pp. 195–221.

2008. 'Profiling Interest Relativity', *Analysis* 68: 326–35.

2010. 'Scope Confusions and Unsatisfiable Disjuncts: Two Problems for Supervaluationism', in R. Dietz and S. Moruzzi (eds.), *Cuts and Clouds: Essays on the Nature and Logic of Vagueness*. Oxford: Oxford University Press, pp. 373–82.

2011. 'Truth in a Region', in P. Égré and N. Klinedinst (eds.), *Vagueness and Language Use*. Basingstoke: Palgrave Macmillan, pp. 222–48.

Fara, D. G. and Williamson, T. (eds.) 2002. *Vagueness*. Aldershot: Ashgate.

Fechner, G. T. 1860. *Elemente der Psychophysik*. Leipzig: Breitkopf und Härtel.

Fermüller, C. G. and Hájek, P. 2011. 'A Conversation about Fuzzy Logic and Vagueness', in P. Cintula, C. G. Fermüller and L. Godo (eds.), *Understanding Vagueness. Logical, Philosophical and Linguistic Perspectives*. London: College Publications, pp. 395–406.

Field, H. 1973. 'Theory Change and the Indeterminacy of Reference', *The Journal of Philosophy* 70: 462–81.

2003a. 'No Fact of the Matter', *Australasian Journal of Philosophy* 81: 457–80.

2003b. 'The Semantic Paradoxes and the Paradoxes of Vagueness', in JC Beall (ed.), *Liars and Heaps: New Essays on Paradox*. Oxford: Oxford University Press, pp. 262–311.

2008. *Saving Truth from Paradox*. Oxford: Oxford University Press.

2010. 'This Magic Moment: Horwich on the Boundaries of Vague Terms', in R. Dietz and S. Moruzzi (eds.), *Cuts and Clouds: Essays on the Nature and Logic of Vagueness*. Oxford: Oxford University Press, pp. 200–8.

Fine, K. 1975. 'Vagueness, Truth and Logic', *Synthese* 30: 265–300.

Fisher, G. 1967. 'Measuring Ambiguity', *The American Journal of Psychology* 80: 541–57.

Forbes, G. A. 1983. 'Thisness and Vagueness', *Synthese* 54: 235–59.

1984. 'Two Solutions to Chisholm's Paradox', *Philosophical Studies* 46: 171–87.

1986. 'In Defense of Absolute Essentialism', *Midwest Studies in Philosophy* 11: 3–31.

Francez, I. and Koontz-Garboden, A. 2015. 'Semantic Variation and the Grammar of Property Concepts', *Language* 91: 533–63.

Frankowski, S. 2004. 'Formalization of Plausible Inference', *Bulletin of the Section of Logic* 33: 41–52.

Frede, M. 1983. 'Stoics and Skeptics on Clear and Distinct Impressions', in M. F. Burnyeat (ed.), *The Skeptical Tradition*. Chicago: University of Chicago Press, pp. 65–93. (Reprinted in M. Frede (1987), pp. 151–76. Page references are to the reprint.)

1987. *Essays in Ancient Philosophy*. Minneapolis: University of Minnesota Press.

Frege, G. 1879. *Begriffsschrift, eine der arithmetischen nachgebildete Formelsprache des reinen Denkens*. Halle: Nebert.

1903. *Grundgesetze der Arithmetik*. Vol. 2. Jena: Pohle.

1918. 'Der Gedanke: Eine logische Untersuchung', *Beiträge zur Philosophie des deutschen Idealismus* 1: 58–77.

Gabbay, D. 1985. 'Theoretical Foundations for Non-Monotonic Reasoning in Expert Systems', in K. Apt (ed.), *Logics and Models of Concurrent Systems*. Berlin: Springer, pp. 439–57.

Galen 1985. *Three Treatises on the Nature of Science*. Translated by R. Walzer and M. Frede. Indianapolis: Hackett Publishing Company.

Gallois, A. 2004. 'Comments on Ted Sider: Four Dimensionalism', *Philosophy and Phenomenological Research* 68: 648–57.

Gauker, C. 1999. 'Deflationism and Logic', *Facta Philosophica* 1: 167–99.

Gentzen, G. 1934. 'Untersuchungen über das logische Schließen I', *Mathematische Zeitschrift* 39: 176–210.

Gilmore, C. 2006. 'Where in the Relativistic World Are We?', *Philosophical Perspectives* 20: 199–236.

Goguen, J. A. 1969. 'The Logic of Inexact Concepts', *Synthese* 19: 325–73.

Gómez-Torrente, M. 2002. 'Vagueness and Margin for Error Principles', *Philosophy and Phenomenological Research* 64: 107–25.

Grano, T. and Davis, S. 2018. 'Universal Markedness in Gradable Adjectives Revisited: The Morpho-Semantics of the Positive Form in Arabic', *Natural Language and Linguistic Theory* 36: 131–47.

Grinsell, T. W. 2017. 'Semantic Indecision'. PhD thesis, University of Chicago.

Gupta, A. 1993a. 'A Critique of Deflationism', *Philosophical Topics* 21: 57–81.

1993b. 'Minimalism', *Philosophical Perspectives* 7: 459–69.

Hahn, U. and Oaksford, M. 2006. 'A Bayesian Approach to Informal Argument Fallacies', *Synthese* 152: 207–36.

Hájek, P. 1998. *Metamathematics of Fuzzy Logic*. Dordrecht: Kluwer.

1999. 'Ten Questions and One Problem on Fuzzy Logic', *Annals of Pure and Applied Logic* 98: 157–65.

Hájek, P. and Novák, V. 2003. 'The Sorites Paradox and Fuzzy Logic', *International Journal of General Systems* 32: 373–83.

Hampton, J. A. 1998. 'Similarity-Based Categorization and Fuzziness of Natural Categories', *Cognition* 65: 137–65.

2007. 'Typicality, Graded Membership, and Vagueness', *Cognitive Science* 31: 355–84.

Hampton, J. A., Estes, Z., Botbol, J. and Jaunbocus, Y. 2012. 'Contrast and Assimilation in Simultaneous Categorization', ms.

Hampton, J. A., Estes, Z. and Simmons, C. L. 2005. 'Comparison and Contrast in Perceptual Categorization', *Journal of Experimental Psychology: Learning, Memory, and Cognition* 31: 1459–76.

Hardin, L. 1988. 'Phenomenal Colors and Sorites', *Noûs* 22: 213–34.

Harnad, S. 1987. 'Psychophysical and Cognitive Aspects of Categorical Perception: A Critical Overview', in S. Harnad (ed.), *Categorical Perception: The Groundwork of Cognition*. Cambridge: Cambridge University Press, pp. 1–25.

Hawley, K. 2002. 'Vagueness and Existence', *Proceedings of the Aristotelian Society* 102: 125–40.

2004. 'Borderline Simple or Extremely Simple', *The Monist* 87: 385–404.

Hawthorne, J. 2008. 'Three-Dimensionalism', in J. Hawthorne, *Metaphysical Essays*. Oxford: Oxford University Press, pp. 85–110.

Hedman, S. 2004. *A First Course in Logic*. Oxford: Oxford University Press.

Hegel, G. W. F. 1892. *Lectures on the History of Philosophy*. Translated by E. S. Haldane and F. H. Simson. London: Kegan Paul, Trench, Trübner & Co.

2010. *The Science of Logic*. Translated and edited by G. di Giovanni. Cambridge: Cambridge University Press.

Heim, I. 2006. ' "Little" ', *Proceedings of Semantics and Linguistic Theory* 16: 17–34.

Heller, M. 1988. 'Vagueness and the Standard Ontology', *Noûs* 22: 109–31.

1990. *The Ontology of Physical Objects*. Cambridge: Cambridge University Press.

Hinnion, R. and Libert, T. 2003. 'Positive Abstraction and Extensionality', *The Journal of Symbolic Logic* 68: 828–36.

Hodes, H. 1984. 'Logicism and the Ontological Commitments of Arithmetic', *The Journal of Philosophy* 81: 123–49.

Horgan, T. 1994. 'Robust Vagueness and the Forced-March Sorites Paradox', *Philosophical Perspectives* 8: 159–88.

Horwich, P. 1997. 'The Nature of Vagueness', *Philosophy and Phenomenological Research* 57: 929–36.

1998a. *Meaning*. Oxford: Oxford University Press.

1998b. *Truth*. 2nd edn. Oxford: Oxford University Press.

2001. 'A Defense of Minimalism', *Synthese* 126: 149–65.

2005. *Reflections on Meaning*. Oxford: Oxford University Press.

2010a. 'A Minimalist Critique of Tarski', in P. Horwich, *Truth-Meaning-Reality*. Oxford: Oxford University Press, pp. 79–97.

2010b. *Truth-Meaning-Reality*. Oxford: Oxford University Press.

Hudson, H. 2002. 'Review of Four-Dimensionalism', *Notre Dame Philosophical Reviews* (http://ndpr.nd.edu/review.cfm?id=1135).

Hughes, G. E. and Cresswell, M. J. 1996. *A New Introduction to Modal Logic*. London: Routledge.

Humberstone, L. 2011. *The Connectives*. Cambridge, MA: MIT Press.

Hume, D. 1739. *A Treatise of Human Nature*. London: John Noon.

Hyde, D. 1997. 'From Heaps and Gaps to Heaps of Gluts', *Mind* 106: 641–60.

2007. *Vagueness, Logic and Ontology*. London: Routledge.

2010. 'The Prospects of a Paraconsistent Response to Vagueness', in R. Dietz and S. Moruzzi (eds.), *Cuts and Clouds: Essays on the Nature and Logic of Vagueness*. Oxford: Oxford University Press, pp. 385–405.

2011. 'Sorites Paradox', in E. Zalta (ed.), *Stanford Encyclopedia of Philosophy* (https://plato.stanford.edu/archives/win2011/entries/sorites-paradox/).

2013. 'Are the Sorites and Liar Paradox of a Kind?', in F. Berto, E. Mares and K. Tanaka (eds.), *Paraconsistency: Logic and Applications*. Dordrecht: Springer, pp. 349–66.

Hyde, D. and Colyvan, M. 2008. 'Paraconsistent Vagueness: Why Not?', *The Australasian Journal of Logic* 6: 107–21.

Jaśkowski, S. 1948. 'Rachunek zdań dla systemów dedukcyjnych sprzecznych', *Studia Societatis Scientiarum Torunensis* 1: 55–77.

Jones, N. 2015. 'Verities and Truth-Values', forthcoming in L. Walters and J. Hawthorne (eds.), *Conditionals, Probability, and Paradox. Themes from the Philosophy of Dorothy Edgington*. Oxford: Oxford University Press.

Kalmus, H. 1979. 'Dependence of Colour Naming and Monochromator Setting on the Direction of Preceding Changes in Wavelength', *British Journal of Physiological Optics* 32: 1–9.

Kamp, H. 1975. 'Two Theories about Adjectives', in E. Keenan (ed.), *Formal Semantics of Natural Language*. Cambridge: Cambridge University Press, pp. 123–55.

1981. 'The Paradox of the Heap', in U. Mönnich (ed.), *Aspects of Philosophical Logic*. Dordrecht: Reidel, pp. 225–77.

2013. *Meaning and the Dynamics of Interpretation: Selected Papers of Hans Kamp*. Edited by K. von Heusinger and A. ter Meulen. Leiden: Brill.

Kamp, H. and Sassoon, G. W. 2016. 'Vagueness', in M. Aloni and P. Dekker (eds.), *The Cambridge Handbook of Formal Semantics*. Cambridge: Cambridge University Press, pp. 389–441.

Kant, I. 1992. *Lectures on Logic*. Translated and edited by J. M. Young. Cambridge: Cambridge University Press.

1998. *Critique of Pure Reason*. Translated and edited by P. Guyer and A. W. Wood. Cambridge: Cambridge University Press.

Kearns, S. and Magidor, O. 2008. 'Epistemicism about Vagueness and Meta-Linguistic Safety', *Philosophical Perspectives* 22: 277–304.

2012. 'Semantic Sovereignty', *Philosophy and Phenomenological Research* 58: 322–50.

Keefe, R. 1998. 'Vagueness by Numbers', *Mind* 107: 427–41.

2000. *Theories of Vagueness*. Cambridge: Cambridge University Press.

2007. 'Vagueness without Context Change', *Mind* 116: 275–92.

Keefe, R. and Smith, P. 1997a. 'Introduction', in R. Keefe and P. Smith (eds.), *Vagueness: A Reader*. Cambridge, MA: MIT Press, pp. 1–57.

(eds.) 1997b. *Vagueness: A Reader*. Cambridge, MA: MIT Press.

Kennedy, C. 1999. *Projecting the Adjective: The Syntax and Semantics of Gradability and Comparison*. New York: Garland.

2007a. 'Modes of Comparison', in M. Elliott, J. Kirby, O. Sawada, E. Staraki and S. Yoon (eds.), *Papers from the 43rd Annual Meeting of the Chicago Linguistic Society Volume 1: The Main Session*. Chicago: Chicago Linguistic Society, pp. 139–63.

2007b. 'Vagueness and Grammar: The Semantics of Relative and Absolute Gradable Adjectives', *Linguistics and Philosophy* 30: 1–45.

2011. 'Vagueness and Comparison', in P. Égré and N. Klinedinst (eds.), *Vagueness and Language Use*. Basingstoke: Palgrave Macmillan, pp. 73–97.

Kennedy, C. and Levin, B. 2008. 'Measure of Change: The Adjectival Core of Degree Achievements', in L. McNally and C. Kennedy (eds.), *Adjectives and Adverbs: Syntax, Semantics and Discourse*. Oxford: Oxford University Press, pp. 156–82.

Kennedy, C. and McNally, L. 2005. 'Scale Structure and the Semantic Typology of Gradable Predicates', *Language* 81: 345–81.

Klecha, P. 2018. 'On Unidirectionality in Precisification', *Linguistics and Philosophy* 41: 87–124.

Kleene, S. C. 1938. 'On a Notation for Ordinal Numbers', *The Journal of Symbolic Logic* 3: 150–5.

Klein, E. 1980. 'A Semantics for Positive and Comparative Adjectives', *Linguistics and Philosophy* 4: 1–45.

1991. 'Comparatives', in A. von Stechow and D. Wunderlich (eds.), *Semantik: Ein internationales Handbuch der zeitgenössischen Forschung (Semantics: An International Handbook of Contemporary Research)*. Berlin: W. de Gruyter, pp. 673–91.

Kneale, W. and Kneale, M. 1962. *The Development of Logic*. Oxford: Clarendon Press.

Korman, D. Z. 2010. 'The Argument from Vagueness', *Philosophy Compass* 5: 891–901.

2015. *Objects: Nothing Out of the Ordinary*. Oxford: Oxford University Press.

Körner, S. 1959. 'On Determinables and Resemblance', *Proceedings of the Aristotelian Society Supplementary Volume* 33: 125–40.

Koslicki, K. 2003. 'The Crooked Path from Vagueness to Four Dimensionalism', *Philosophical Studies* 114: 107–34.

2014. 'Mereological Sums and Singular Terms', in S. Kleinschmidt (ed.), *Mereology and Location*. Oxford: Oxford University Press, pp. 209–35.

Krifka, M. 2007. 'Approximate Interpretation of Number Words: A Case for Strategic Interpretation', in G. Bouma, I. Krämer and J. Zwarts (eds.), *Cognitive Foundations of Interpretation*. Amsterdam: Koninklijke Nederlandse Akademie van Wetenschappen, pp. 111–26.

Kripke, S. A. 1975. 'Outline of a Theory of Truth', *The Journal of Philosophy* 72: 690–716.

Kurtsal Steen, İ. 2010. 'Three-Dimensionalist's Semantic Solution to Diachronic Vagueness', *Philosophical Studies* 115: 79–96.

2014. 'Almost-Ontology: Why Epistemicism Cannot Help Us Avoid Unrestricted Composition or Diachronic Plenitude', *Pacific Philosophical Quarterly* 95: 130–9.

Lakoff, G. 1973. 'Hedges: A Study on Meaning Criteria and the Logic of Fuzzy Concepts', *Journal of Philosophical Logic* 2: 458–508.

Lasersohn, P. 1999. 'Pragmatic Halos', *Language* 75: 522–51.

Lasonen-Aarnio, M. 2008. 'Single Premise Deduction and Risk', *Philosophical Studies* 141: 157–73.

Lassiter, D. and Goodman, N. D. 2014. 'Context, Scale Structure, and Statistics in the Interpretation of Positive-Form Adjectives', *Proceedings of Semantics and Linguistic Theory* 23: 587–610.

2017. 'Adjectival Vagueness in a Bayesian Model of Interpretation', *Synthese* 194: 3801–36.

Leffel, T., Kennedy, C. and Xiang, M. 2016. 'Imprecision Is Pragmatic: Evidence from Referential Processing', *Proceedings of Semantics and Linguistic Theory* 26: 836–54.

Leibniz, G. W. 1982. *New Essays on Human Understanding*. Translated and edited by P. Remnant and J. Bennett. Cambridge: Cambridge University Press.

1989. *Philosophical Essays*. Translated by R. Ariew and D. Garber. Indianapolis: Hackett Publishing Company.

2001. *The Labyrinth of the Continuum: Writings on the Continuum Problem, 1672–1686*. Translated, edited and with an introduction by R. T. W. Arthur. New Haven: Yale University Press.

Leslie, S. J. 2011. 'Essence, Plenitude and Paradox', *Philosophical Perspectives* 25: 277–96.

Levey, S. 2002. 'Leibniz and the Sorites', *The Leibniz Review* 12: 25–49.

Lewis, D. K. 1970a. 'General Semantics', *Synthese* 22: 18–67.

1970b. 'How to Define Theoretical Terms', *The Journal of Philosophy* 67: 427–46.

1972. 'Psychophysical and Theoretical Identifications', *Australasian Journal of Philosophy* 50: 249–58.

1979. 'Scorekeeping in a Language Game', *Journal of Philosophical Logic* 8: 339–59.

1983. 'New Work for a Theory of Universals', *Australasian Journal of Philosophy* 61: 343–77.

1984. 'Putnam's Paradox', *Australasian Journal of Philosophy* 62: 221–36.

1986. *On the Plurality of Worlds*. Oxford: Blackwell.

1997. 'Naming the Colours', *Australasian Journal of Philosophy* 75: 325–42.

Lewy, C. 1958. 'Entailment', *Proceedings of the Aristotelian Society Supplementary Volume* 32: 123–42.

Liberman, A. M., Harris, K. S., Hoffman, H. S., and Griffith, B. C. 1957. 'The discrimination of speech sounds within and across phoneme boundaries', *Journal of Experimental Psychology* 54: 358–68.

Locke, J. 1690. *An Essay Concerning Humane Understanding*. London: Thomas Basset.

Lode, E. 1999. 'Slippery Slope Arguments and Legal Reasoning', *California Law Review* 87: 1469–543.

López de Sa, D. 2006. 'Is "Everything" Precise?', *Dialectica* 60: 397–409.

López de Sa, D. and Zardini, E. 2007. 'Truthmakers, Knowledge and Paradox', *Analysis* 67: 242–50.

Lowe, E. J. 2013. 'Ontological Vagueness, Existence Monism and Metaphysical Realism', *Metaphysica* 14: 265–74.

Luce, R. D. 1956. 'Semiorders and a Theory of Utility Discrimination', *Econometrica, Journal of the Econometric Society* 24: 178–91.

 1959. *Individual Choice Behavior: A Theoretical Analysis*. New York: John Wiley & Sons.

Ludlow, P. 1989. 'Implicit Comparison Classes', *Linguistics and Philosophy* 12: 519–33.

Ludwig, K. and Ray, G. 2002. 'Vagueness and the Sorites Paradox', *Philosophical Perspectives* 16: 419–61.

Łukasiewicz, J. 1920. 'O logice trójwartościowej', *Ruch Filozoficzny* 5: 170–1.

Łukasiewicz, J. and Tarski, A. 1930. 'Untersuchungen über den Aussagenkalkül', *Comptes rendus des séances de la Société des Sciences et des Lettres de Varsovie* 23: 30–50.

MacFarlane, J. 2009. 'Nonindexical Contextualism', *Synthese* 166: 231–50.

 2010. 'Fuzzy Epistemicism', in R. Dietz and S. Moruzzi (eds.), *Cuts and Clouds: Essays on the Nature and Logic of Vagueness*. Oxford: Oxford University Press, pp. 438–63.

 2016. 'Vagueness as Indecision', *Proceedings of the Aristotelian Society Supplementary Volume* 90: 255–83.

Machina, K. F. 1976. 'Truth, Belief, and Vagueness', *Journal of Philosophical Logic* 5: 47–78.

Macmillan, N. A. 1987. 'Beyond the Categorical/Continuous Distinction: A Psychophysical Approach to Processing Modes', in S. Harnad (ed.), *Categorical Perception: The Groundwork of Cognition*. Cambridge: Cambridge University Press, pp. 53–85.

Magidor, O. 2012. 'Strict Finitism and the Happy Sorites', *Journal of Philosophical Logic* 41: 471–91.

 2016. 'Epistemicism, Distribution, and the Argument from Vagueness', *Noûs* 52: 144–70.

Mahtani, A. 2004. 'The Instability of Vague Terms', *The Philosophical Quarterly* 54: 570–6.

Makinson, D. 1965. 'The Paradox of the Preface', *Analysis* 25: 205–7.

Malinowski, G. 1990. 'Q-Consequence Operation', *Reports on Mathematical Logic* 24: 49–59.

Malt, B. C. 1990. 'Features and Beliefs in the Mental Representation of Categories', *Journal of Memory and Language* 29: 289–315.

Mares, E. and Paoli, F. 2014. 'Logical Consequence and the Paradoxes', *Journal of Philosophical Logic* 43: 439–69.

Markosian, N. 1998. 'Brutal Composition', *Philosophical Studies* 92: 211–49.

 2008. 'Restricted Composition', in T. Sider, J. Hawthorne and D. W. Zimmerman (eds.), *Contemporary Debates in Metaphysics*. Malden: Blackwell, pp. 341–62.

McCloskey, M. E. and Glucksberg, S. 1978. 'Natural Categories: Well Defined or Fuzzy Sets?', *Memory & Cognition* 6: 462–72.

McConnell-Ginet, S. 1973. 'Comparative Constructions in English: A Syntactic and Semantic Analysis'. PhD thesis, University of Rochester.

McGee, V. 1989. 'Applying Kripke's Theory of Truth', *The Journal of Philosophy* 86: 530–9.

1991. *Truth, Vagueness, and Paradox*. Indianapolis: Hackett Publishing Company.

1992. 'Maximal Consistent Sets of Instances of Tarski's Schema (T)', *Journal of Philosophical Logic* 21: 235–41.

McGee, V. and McLaughlin, B. 2004. 'Logical Commitment and Semantic Indeterminacy: A Reply to Williamson', *Linguistics and Philosophy* 27: 123–36.

McGill, V. J. and Parry, W. T. 1948. 'The Unity of Opposites: A Dialectical Principle', *Science and Society* 12: 418–44.

Mehlberg, H. 1958. *The Reach of Science*. Toronto: University of Toronto Press.

Merricks, T. 2001a. *Objects and Persons*. Oxford: Oxford University Press.

2001b. 'Varieties of Vagueness', *Philosophy and Phenomenological Research* 62: 145–57.

2005. 'Composition and Vagueness', *Mind* 114: 615–67.

Miller, K. 2008. 'Endurantism, Diachronic Vagueness, and the Problem of the Many', *Pacific Philosophical Quarterly* 89: 242–53.

Misiuna, K. 2010. 'A Certain Consequence Relation for Solving Paradoxes of Vagueness', *Logique et Analyse* 53: 25–50.

Moline, J. 1969. 'Aristotle, Eubulides and the Sorites', *Mind* 78: 393–407.

Mott, P. 1994. 'On the Intuitionistic Solution of the Sorites Paradox', *Pacific Philosophical Quarterly* 75:133–50.

Muller, R. 1985. *Les Mégariques: Fragments et témoignages. Traduits et commentés*. Paris: Librairie Philosophique J. Vrin.

Navarro, P. and Rodríguez, J. 2014. *Deontic Logic and Legal Systems*. Cambridge: Cambridge University Press.

Nebel, J. 2017. 'The Good, the Bad, and the Transitivity of Better than', forthcoming in *Noûs*.

Negri, S. 2011. 'Proof Theory for Modal Logic', *Philosophy Compass* 6: 523–38.

Nolan, D. 2006. 'Vagueness, Multiplicity and Parts', *Noûs* 40: 716–37.

2014. 'Balls and All', in S. Kleinschmidt (ed.), *Mereology and Location*. Oxford: Oxford University Press, pp. 91–116.

Novák, V. and Dvořák, A. 2011. 'Fuzzy Logic: A Powerful Tool for Modelling Vagueness', ms.

Oms, S. 2010. 'Truth-Functional and Penumbral Intuitions', *Theoria: An International Journal for Theory, History and Foundations of Science* 25: 137–47.

2017. 'Articulation and Liars', *Disputatio* 9: 383–99.

2018a. 'Conceivability, Minimalism and the Generalization Problem', forthcoming in *Dialogue*.

2018b. 'Minimalism, Supervaluations and Fixed Points', forthcoming in *Synthese*.

Oms, S. and Zardini, E. 2017. 'Inclosure and Intolerance', ms.

O'Regan, J. K. 2001. 'Thoughts on Change Blindness', in M. Jenkin and L. Harris (eds.), *Vision and Attention*. Berlin: Springer, pp. 281–301.

O'Regan, J. K., Rensink, R. A. and Clark, J. J. 1999. 'Change-Blindness as a Result of "Mudsplashes"', *Nature* 398: 34.

Osherson, D. N. and Smith, E. E. 1981. 'On the Adequacy of Prototype Theory as a Theory of Concepts', *Cognition* 9: 35–58.

Pagin, P. 2010. 'Vagueness and Domain Restriction', in P. Égré and N. Klinedinst (eds.), *Vagueness and Language Use*. Basingstoke: Palgrave Macmillan, pp. 283–307.

Paoli, F. 2003. 'A Really Fuzzy Approach to the Sorites Paradox', *Synthese* 134: 363–87.

2007. 'Implicational Paradoxes and the Meaning of Logical Constants', *Australasian Journal of Philosophy* 85: 553–79.

2018. 'Truth Degrees, Closeness, and the Sorites', forthcoming in O. Bueno and A. Abasnezhad (eds.), *On the Sorites Paradox*. Dordrecht: Springer.

Parfit, D. A. 1984. *Reasons and Persons*. Oxford: Oxford University Press.

Peacocke, C. A. B. 1981. 'Are Vague Predicates Incoherent?', *Synthese* 46: 121–41.

Peirce, C. S. 1902. 'Sorites', in J. M. Baldwin (ed.), *Dictionary of Philosophy and Psychology*. New York: Macmillan.

Pelofi, C., de Gardelle, V., Égré, P. and Pressnitzer, D. 2017. 'Interindividual Variability in Auditory Scene Analysis Revealed by Confidence Judgments', *Philosophical Transactions of the Royal Society B* 372: 1–12.

Peña, L. 1984. 'Identity, Fuzziness and Noncontradiction', *Noûs* 18: 227–59.

Pinkal, M. 1995. *Logic and Lexicon*. Dordrecht: Kluwer.

Plekhanov, G. 1941. *Fundamental Problems of Marxism*. Edited by D. Ryazanov. London: Lawrence and Wishart.

Potts, C. 2008. 'Interpretive Economy, Schelling Points, and Evolutionary Stability', ms.

Priest, G. 1994. 'The Structure of the Paradoxes of Self-Reference', *Mind* 103: 25–34.

1995. *Beyond the Limits of Thought*. Cambridge: Cambridge University Press. (2002. 2nd edn. Oxford: Oxford University Press.)

2000. 'On the Principle of Uniform Solution: A Reply to Smith', *Mind* 109: 123–6.

2002. 'Paraconsistent Logic', in D. Gabbay and F. Guenthner (eds.), *Handbook of Philosophical Logic*. Vol. 6. 2nd edn. Dordrecht: Kluwer, pp. 287–393.

2003. 'A Site for Sorites', in JC Beall (ed.), *Liars and Heaps: New Essays on Paradox*. Oxford: Oxford University Press, pp. 9–23.

2006. *In Contradiction*. 2nd edn. Oxford: Oxford University Press.

2008. *An Introduction to Non-Classical Logic*. 2nd edn. Cambridge: Cambridge University Press.

2010a. 'Inclosures, Vagueness, and Self-Reference', *Notre Dame Journal of Formal Logic* 51: 69–84.

2010b. 'Non-Transitive Identity', in R. Dietz and S. Moruzzi (eds.), *Cuts and Clouds: Essays on the Nature and Logic of Vagueness*. Oxford: Oxford University Press, pp. 406–16.

2014. *One*. Oxford: Oxford University Press.

2017. 'What *If*: The Exploration of an Idea', *The Australasian Journal of Logic* 14: 54–127.

Priest, G. and Routley, R. 1989. 'Applications of Paraconsistent Logic', in G. Priest, R. Routley and J. Norman (eds.), *Paraconsistent Logic: Essays on the Inconsistent*. Munich: Philosophia Verlag, pp. 367–93.

Pummer, T. 2017. 'Spectrum Arguments and Hypersensitivity', *Philosophical Studies* 7: 1729–44.

Putnam, H. 1975. 'The Meaning of "Meaning"', *Minnesota Studies in the Philosophy of Science* 7: 131–93.

1983. 'Vagueness and Alternative Logic', *Erkenntnis* 19: 297–314.

1985. 'A Quick Read Is a Wrong Wright', *Analysis* 45: 203.

1991. 'Replies and Comments', *Erkenntnis* 34: 401–24.

Qing, C. and Franke, M. 2014a. 'Gradable Adjectives, Vagueness, and Optimal Language Use: A Speaker-Oriented Model', *Proceedings of Semantics and Linguistic Theory* 24: 23–41.

2014b. 'Meaning and Use of Gradable Adjectives: Formal Modeling Meets Empirical Data', *Proceedings of the Annual Meeting of the Cognitive Science Society* 36: 1204–9.

Quine, W. V. O. 1970. 'Natural Kinds', in N. Rescher (ed.), *Essays in Honor of Carl G. Hempel*. Dordrecht: Reidel, pp. 5–23.

1986. *Philosophy of Logic*. 2nd edn. Cambridge, MA: Harvard University Press.

Quinn, W. 1990. 'The Puzzle of the Self-Torturer', *Philosophical Studies* 59: 79–90.

Raatikainen, P. 2005. 'On Horwich's Way Out', *Analysis* 65: 175–7.

Rachels, S. 1993. 'A Theory of Beneficence'. BA thesis, University of Oxford.

1998. 'Counterexamples to the Transitivity of Better than', *Australasian Journal of Philosophy* 76: 71–83.

Raffman, D. 1994. 'Vagueness without Paradox', *The Philosophical Review* 103: 41–74.

1996. 'Vagueness and Context-Relativity', *Philosophical Studies* 81: 175–92.

2005a. 'How to Understand Contextualism about Vagueness: Reply to Stanley', *Analysis* 65: 244–8.

2005b. 'Borderline Cases and Bivalence', *The Philosophical Review* 114: 1–31.

2011. 'Vagueness and Observationality', in G. Ronzitti (ed.), *Vagueness: A Guide*. Dordrecht: Springer, pp. 107–21.

2014. *Unruly Words: A Study of Vague Language*. Oxford: Oxford University Press.

2015. 'Responses to Discussants', *Philosophy and Phenomenological Research* 90: 483–501.

Raz, J. 1986. *The Morality of Freedom*. Oxford: Clarendon Press.

Rea, G. 1989. 'Degrees of Truth versus Intuitionism', *Analysis* 49: 31–2.

Read, S. L. 1994. 'Formal and Material Consequence', *Journal of Philosophical Logic* 23: 247–65.

2002. 'The Liar Paradox from John Buridan Back to Thomas Bradwardine', *Vivarium* 40: 189–218.

Read, S. L. and Wright, C. 1985. 'Hairier than Putnam Thought', *Analysis* 45: 56–8.

Repp, B. H. 1984. 'Categorical Perception: Issues, Methods, Findings', *Speech and Language: Advances in Basic Research and Practice* 10: 243–335.

Restall, G. 2005. 'Minimalists about Truth Can (and Should) Be Epistemicists, and It Helps if They Are Revision Theorists Too', in JC Beall and B. Armour-Garb (eds.), *Deflationism and Paradox*. Oxford: Oxford University Press, pp. 97–106.

Ridge, M. 2014. 'Moral Non-Naturalism', in E. Zalta (ed.), *The Stanford Encyclopedia of Philosophy* (https://plato.stanford.edu/archives/fall2014/entries/moral-non-naturalism).

Ripley, D. 2005. 'Sorting Out the Sorites'. MA thesis, University of North Carolina at Chapel Hill.

2011. 'Contradictions at the Borders', in R. Nouwen, R. van Rooij, H. C. Schmitz and U. Sauerland (eds.), *Vagueness and Communication*. Berlin: Springer, pp. 169–88.

2012. 'Conservatively Extending Classical Logic with Transparent Truth', *The Review of Symbolic Logic* 5: 354–78.

2013. 'Sorting Out the Sorites', in F. Berto, E. Mares and K. Tanaka (eds.), *Paraconsistency: Logic and Applications*. Dordrecht: Springer, pp. 329–48.

Rolf, B. 1984. 'Sorites', *Synthese* 58: 219–50.

Ronzitti, G. (ed.) 2011. *Vagueness: A Guide*. Dordrecht: Springer.

Rosch, E. and Mervis, C. B. 1975. 'Family Resemblances: Studies in the Internal Structure of Categories', *Cognitive Psychology* 7: 573–605.

Rosenkranz, S. 2003. 'Wright on Vagueness and Agnosticism', *Mind* 112: 449–63.

Rotstein, C. and Winter, Y. 2004. 'Total Adjectives vs. Partial Adjectives: Scale Structure and Higher-Order Modifiers', *Natural Language Semantics* 12: 259–88.

Rusiecki, J. 1985. *On Adjectives and Comparison in English*. New York: Longman Linguistics Library.

Russell, B. 1908. 'Mathematical Logic as Based on the Theory of Types', *American Journal of Mathematics* 30: 222–62.

 1923. 'Vagueness', *Australasian Journal of Psychology and Philosophy* 1: 84–92.

Sainsbury, M. 2009. *Paradoxes*. 3rd edn. Cambridge: Cambridge University Press.

 2015. 'Vagueness and Semantic Methodology', *Philosophy and Phenomenological Research* 90: 475–82.

Salmon, N. 1986. 'Modal Paradox: Parts and Counterparts, Points and Counterpoints', *Midwest Studies in Philosophy* 11: 75–120.

Sanford, D. H. 1975. 'Borderline Logic', *American Philosophical Quarterly* 12: 29–39.

 1976. 'Competing Semantics of Vagueness: Many Values versus Super-Truth', *Synthese* 33: 195–210.

Sapir, E. 1944. 'Grading: A Study in Semantics', *Philosophy of Science* 11: 93–116.

Sassoon, G. W. 2009. 'Restricted Quantification over Tastes', in M. Aloni, H. Bastiaanse, T. de Jager and K. Schulz (eds.), *Proceedings of the Amsterdam Colloquium*. Berlin: Springer, pp. 163–72.

 2013. *Vagueness, Gradability and Typicality: The Interpretation of Adjectives and Nouns*. Leiden: Brill.

Sawada, O. 2009. 'Pragmatic Aspects of Implicit Comparison: An Economy Based Approach', *Journal of Pragmatics* 41: 1079–103.

Sayre-McCord, G. 2017. 'Moral Realism', in E. Zalta (ed.), *The Stanford Encyclopedia of Philosophy* (https://plato.stanford.edu/archives/fall2017/entries/moral-realism).

Scharp, K. 2013. *Replacing Truth*. Oxford: Oxford University Press.

 2015. 'Tolerance and the Multi-Range View of Vagueness', *Philosophy and Phenomenological Research* 90: 467–74.

Schechter, J. 2013. 'Rational Self-Doubt and the Failure of Closure', *Philosophical Studies* 163: 429–52.

Schiffer, S. 2016. 'Vagueness and Indeterminacy: Responses to Dorothy Edgington, Hartry Field and Crispin Wright' in G. Ostertag (ed.), *Meanings and Other Things*. Oxford: Oxford University Press, pp. 458–81.

Schindler, T. 2015. 'A Disquotational Theory of Truth as Strong as Z_2^{--}', *Journal of Philosophical Logic* 44: 395–410.

 2019. 'A Note on Horwich's Notion of Grounding', forthcoming in *Synthese*.

Schoenfield, M. 2015. 'Moral Vagueness Is Ontic Vagueness', *Ethics* 126: 257–82.

Schwartz, S. 1987. 'Intuitionism and Sorites', *Analysis* 47: 179–83.

Schwartz, S. and Throop, W. 1991. 'Intuitionism and Vagueness', *Erkenntnis* 34: 347–56.

Schwarz, W. 2014. 'Against Magnetism', *Australasian Journal of Philosophy* 92: 17–36.

Segerberg, K. 1971. *An Essay in Classical Modal Logic*. Uppsala: Filosofiska Föreningen och Filosofiska Institutionen vid Uppsala Universitet.

Sennet, A. M. 2012. 'Semantic Plasticity and Epistemicism', *Philosophical Studies* 161: 273–85.

Serchuk, P., Hargreaves, I. and Zach, R. 2011. 'Vagueness, Logic and Use: Four Experimental Studies on Vagueness', *Mind and Language* 26: 540–73.

Seuren, P. A. 1973. 'The Comparative', in F. Kiefer and N. Ruwet (eds.), *Generative Grammar in Europe*. Dordrecht: Reidel, pp. 528–64.

Sextus Empiricus 1933. *Opera*. Edited with an English translation by R. G. Bury. London: William Heinemann.

Shafer, G. 1976. *A Mathematical Theory of Evidence*. Princeton: Princeton University Press.

Shafer-Landau, R. 1994. 'Ethical Disagreement, Ethical Objectivism, and Moral Indeterminacy', *Philosophy and Phenomenological Research* 54: 331–44.

    1995. 'Vagueness, Borderline Cases and Moral Realism', *American Philosophical Quarterly* 32: 83–96.

    2003. *Moral Realism: A Defence*. Oxford: Oxford University Press.

Shapiro, S. 2003. 'Vagueness and Conversation', in JC Beall (ed.), *Liars and Heaps: New Essays on Paradox*. Oxford: Oxford University Press, pp. 39–72.

    2006. *Vagueness in Context*. Oxford: Oxford University Press.

    2014. *Varieties of Logic*. Oxford: Oxford University Press.

Sider, T. 2001. *Four Dimensionalism*. Oxford: Oxford University Press.

    2003. 'Against Vague Existence', *Philosophical Studies* 114: 135–46.

Simons, P. 2013. 'Vague Kinds and Biological Nominalism', *Metaphysica* 14: 275–82.

Simons, D. J. and Levin, D. T. 1997. 'Change Blindness', *Trends in Cognitive Sciences* 1: 261–7.

Simplicius 2003. *On Aristotle's Categories 1–4*. Translated by M. Chase. Ithaca, NY: Cornell University Press.

Slaney, J. 2011. 'A Logic for Vagueness', *The Australasian Journal of Logic* 8: 100–34.

Smith, N. J. J. 2000. 'The Principle of Uniform Solution (of the Paradoxes of Self-Reference)', *Mind* 109: 117–22.

    2004. 'Vagueness and Blurry Sets', *Journal of Philosophical Logic* 33: 165–235.

    2008. *Vagueness and Degrees of Truth*. Oxford: Oxford University Press.

    2011. 'Fuzzy Logic and Higher-Order Vagueness', in P. Cintula, C. G. Fermüller and L. Godo (eds.), *Understanding Vagueness. Logical, Philosophical and Linguistic Perspectives*. London: College Publications, pp. 1–19.

    2015. 'Undead Argument: The Truth-Functionality Objection to Fuzzy Theories of Vagueness', *Synthese* 194: 3761–87.

    2019. 'Consonance and Dissonance in Solutions to the Sorites', forthcoming in O. Bueno and A. Abasnezhad (eds.), *On the Sorites Paradox*. Dordrecht: Springer.

Smith, R. 1997. *Aristotle, Topics I, VIII, and Selections*. Oxford: Oxford University Press.

Soames, S. 1997. 'The Truth about Deflationism', *Philosophical Issues* 8: 1–44.

    1999. *Understanding Truth*. Oxford: Oxford University Press.

    2002. 'Replies', *Philosophy and Phenomenological Research* 65: 429–52.

    2003. 'Higher-Order Vagueness for Partially Defined Predicates' in JC Beall (ed.), *Liars and Heaps: New Essays on Paradox*. Oxford: Oxford University Press, pp. 128–50.

    2007. 'What Are Natural Kinds?', *Philosophical Topics* 35: 329–42. (Reprinted in S. Soames (2014), pp. 265–80. Page references are to the reprint.)

    2009. 'The Possibility of Partial Definition', in S. Soames, *Philosophical Essays*. Vol. 2. Princeton: Princeton University Press. pp. 362–81.

    2014. *Analytic Philosophy in America. And Other Historical and Contemporary Essays*. Princeton: Princeton University Press.

Solt, S. 2009. 'The Semantics of Adjectives of Quantity'. PhD thesis, The City University of New York.

Sorensen, R. A. 1988. *Blindspots*. Oxford: Oxford University Press.

    2001. *Vagueness and Contradiction*. Oxford: Oxford University Press.

2012. 'Vagueness', in E. Zalta (ed.), *Stanford Encyclopedia of Philosophy* (https://plato
.stanford.edu/archives/spr2012/entries/vagueness/).

Stanley, J. 2003. 'Context, Interest Relativity and the Sorites', *Analysis* 63: 269–80.

2005. *Knowledge and Practical Interests*. Oxford: Oxford University Press.

Stassen, L. 1985. *Comparison and Universal Grammar*. Oxford: Blackwell.

Stöttinger, E., Sepahvand, N. M., Danckert, J. and Anderson, B. 2016. 'Assessing Perceptual Change with an Ambiguous Figures Task: Normative Data for 40 Standard Picture
Sets', *Behavior Research Methods* 48: 201–22.

Sweeney, P. and Zardini, E. 2011. 'Vagueness and Practical Interest', in P. Égré and N.
Klinedinst (eds.), *Vagueness and Language Use*. Basingstoke: Palgrave Macmillan,
pp. 249–82.

Syrett, K. 2007. 'Learning about the Structure of Scales: Adverbial Modification and
the Acquisition of the Semantics of Gradable Adjectives'. PhD thesis, Northwestern
University.

Syrett, K., Kennedy, C. and Lidz, J. 2010. 'Meaning and Context in Children's Understanding of Gradable Adjectives', *Journal of Semantics* 27: 1–35.

Tappenden, J. 1993. 'The Liar and Sorites Paradoxes. Toward a Unified Treatment', *The
Journal of Philosophy* 90: 551–77.

Tarski, A. 1969. 'Truth and Proof', *Scientific American* 220: 63–77.

1983. 'The Concept of Truth in Formalized Languages', in A. Tarski, *Logic, Semantics, Metamathematics*. Translated by J. H. Woodger. Edited, with introduction
and index, by J. Corcoran. 2nd edn. Indianapolis: Hackett Publishing Company,
pp. 152–278.

Taylor, D. and Burgess, A. 2015. 'What in the World Is Semantic Indeterminacy?', *Analytic
Philosophy* 56: 298–317.

Temkin, L. 1996. 'A Continuum Argument for Intransitivity', *Philosophy and Public
Affairs* 25: 175–210.

2012. *Rethinking the Good: Moral Ideals and the Nature of Practical Reasoning*.
Oxford: Oxford University Press.

Tenenbaum, S. and Raffman, D. 2012. 'Vague Projects and the Puzzle of the Self-Torturer',
Ethics 123: 86–112.

Toledo, A. and Sassoon, G. W. 2011. 'Absolute vs. Relative Adjectives – Variance within
vs. between Individuals', *Proceedings of Semantics and Linguistic Theory* 21: 135–54.

Torrago, L. 2000. 'Vague Causation', *Noûs* 34: 313–47.

Tranchini, L. and Cobreros, P. 2017. 'Proof Analysis of Global Consequence', *Logique et
Analyse* 60: 355–73.

Troelstra, A. S. 1992. *Lectures on Linear Logic*. Stanford: CSLI Publications.

2011. 'History of Constructivism in the Twentieth Century', in J. Kennedy and R. Kossak
(eds.) 2011. *Set Theory, Arithmetic and Foundations of Mathematics. Theorems,
Philosophies*. Cambridge: Cambridge University Press, pp. 150–79.

Tye, M. 1990. 'Vague Objects', *Mind* 99: 535–57.

1994. 'Sorites Paradoxes and the Semantics of Vagueness', *Philosophical Perspectives*
8: 189–206.

Unger, P. 1975. *Ignorance*. Oxford: Clarendon Press.

1979a. 'Why There Are No People', *Midwest Studies in Philosophy* 5: 177–222.

1979b. 'There Are No Ordinary Things', *Synthese* 4: 117–54.

1979c. 'I Do Not Exist', in G. F. Macdonald (ed.), *Perception and Identity*. Ithaca, NY:
Cornell University Press, pp. 235–51.

1980a. 'Scepticism and Nihilism', *Noûs* 14: 517–45.

1980b. 'The Problem of the Many', *Midwest Studies in Philosophy* 5: 411–68.

van Benthem, J. 1982. 'Later than Late: On the Logical Origin of the Temporal Order', *Pacific Philosophical Quarterly* 63: 193–203.

Van Cleve, J. 2008. 'The Moon and Sixpence: A Defense of Mereological Universalism', in T. Sider, J. Hawthorne and D. W. Zimmerman (eds.), *Contemporary Debates in Metaphysics*. Malden: Blackwell, pp. 321–40.

van Fraassen, B. C. 1966. 'Singular Terms, Truth-Value Gaps, and Free Logic', *The Journal of Philosophy* 63: 481–95.

   1970. 'Rejoinder: On a Kantian Conception of Language', in R. L. Martin (ed.), *The Paradox of the Liar*. New Haven: Yale University Press, pp. 59–66.

van Inwagen, P. 1990. *Material Beings*. Ithaca, NY: Cornell University Press.

van Rooij, R. 2011a. 'Implicit versus Explicit Comparatives', in P. Égré and N. Klinedinst (eds.), *Vagueness and Language Use*. Basingstoke: Palgrave Macmillan. pp. 51–72.

   2011b. 'Vagueness and Linguistics', in G. Ronzitti (ed.), *Vagueness: A Guide*. Dordrecht: Springer, pp. 123–70.

Varzi, A. 2005. 'Change, Temporal Parts, and the Argument from Vagueness', *Dialectica* 59: 485–98.

   2007a. 'Promiscuous Endurantism and Diachronic Vagueness', *American Philosophical Quarterly* 44: 181–9.

   2007b. 'Supervaluationism and Its Logic', *Mind* 116: 633–76.

Verheyen, S., De Deyne, S., Dry, M. J. and Storms, G. 2011. 'Uncovering Contrast Categories in Categorization with a Probabilistic Threshold Model', *Journal of Experimental Psychology: Learning, Memory, and Cognition* 37: 1515–31.

Verheyen, S., Dewil, S. and Égré, P. 2018. 'Subjectivity in Gradable Adjectives: The Case of Tall and Heavy', *Mind and Language* 33: 460–79.

Verheyen, S. and Égré, P. 2018. 'Typicality and Graded Membership in Dimensional Adjectives', *Cognitive Science* 42: 2550–86.

Verheyen, S., Hampton, J. A. and Storms, G. 2010. 'A Probabilistic Threshold Model: Analyzing Semantic Categorization Data with the Rasch Model', *Acta Psychologica* 135: 216–25.

Verheyen, S. and Storms, G. 2011. 'Towards a Categorization-Based Model of Similarity', in L. Carlson, C. Hölscher and T. F. Shipley (eds.), *Proceedings of the 33rd Annual Conference of the Cognitive Science Society*. Austin: Cognitive Science Society, pp. 614–9.

Volokh, E. 2003. 'The Mechanisms of the Slippery Slope', *Harvard Law Review* 116: 1026–137.

von Stechow, A. 1984. 'Comparing Semantic Theories of Comparison', *Journal of Semantics* 3: 1–77.

   2009. 'The Temporal Degree Adjectives *früh(er)/spät(er)* 'early(er)'/'late(r)' and the Semantics of the Positive', in A. Giannakidou and M. Rathert (eds.), *Quantification, Definiteness and Nominalization*. Oxford: Oxford University Press, pp. 214–33.

von Wright, G. H. 1963. *Norm and Action*. London: Routledge and Kegan Paul.

Wake, A. V. 2011. 'Spacetime and Mereology', *Erkenntnis* 74:17–35.

Wallace, M. 2014. 'The Argument from Vagueness for Modal Parts', *Dialectica* 68: 355–73.

Wansing, H. and Priest, G. 2015. 'External Curries', *Journal of Philosophical Logic* 44: 453–71.

Weatherson, B. 2004. 'True, Truer, Truest', *Philosophical Studies* 123: 47–70.

   2010. 'Vagueness as Indeterminacy', in R. Dietz and S. Moruzzi (eds.), *Cuts and Clouds: Essays on the Nature and Logic of Vagueness*. Oxford: Oxford University Press, pp. 77–90.

Weber, Z. 2010. 'A Paraconsistent Model of Vagueness', *Mind* 119: 1025–45.

Weber, Z. and Colyvan, M. 2010. 'A Topological Sorites', *The Journal of Philosophy* 107: 311–25.

Weber, Z., Ripley, D., Priest, G., Hyde, D. and Colyvan, M. 2014. 'Tolerating Gluts', *Mind* 123: 813–28.

Weir, A. 1996. 'Ultramaximalist Minimalism!', *Analysis* 56: 10–22.

    1998. 'Naïve Set Theory Is Innocent!', *Mind* 107: 763–98.

Wheeler, S. 1972. 'Attributives and Their Modifiers', *Noûs* 6: 310–34.

    1975. 'Reference and Vagueness', *Synthese* 30: 367–79.

    1979. 'On That Which Is Not', *Synthese* 41: 155–94.

    1983. 'Megarian Paradoxes as Eleatic Arguments', *American Philosophical Quarterly* 20: 287–95.

Williams, B. 1995. 'Which Slopes Are Slippery', in B. Williams, *Making Sense of Humanity and Other Philosophical Papers*. Cambridge: Cambridge University Press, pp. 213–23.

Williamson, T. 1990. *Identity and Discrimination*. Oxford: Blackwell.

    1992a. 'Inexact Knowledge', *Mind* 101: 217–42.

    1992b. 'Vagueness and Ignorance', *Proceedings of the Aristotelian Society Supplementary Volume* 62: 145–62.

    1994. *Vagueness*. London: Routledge.

    1995a. 'Definiteness and Knowability', *Southern Journal of Philosophy* 33: 171–92.

    1995b. 'Does Assertibility Satisfy the S4 Axiom?', *Crítica* 27: 3–22.

    1996a. 'Cognitive Homelessness', *The Journal of Philosophy* 93: 554–73.

    1996b. 'Putnam on the Sorites Paradox', *Philosophical Papers* 25: 47–56.

    1997a. 'Précis of Vagueness', *Philosophy and Phenomenological Research* 57: 921–8.

    1997b. 'Reply to Commentators', *Philosophy and Phenomenological Research* 57: 945–53.

    1997c. 'Imagination, Stipulation and Vagueness', *Philosophical Issues* 8: 215–28.

    1999. 'On the Structure of Higher-Order Vagueness', *Mind* 108: 127–43.

    2000. *Knowledge and Its Limits*. Oxford: Oxford University Press.

    2002. 'Soames on Vagueness', *Philosophy and Phenomenological Research* 65: 422–8.

    2007. *The Philosophy of Philosophy*. Oxford: Blackwell.

    2009. 'Reference, Inference, and the Semantics of Pejoratives', in J. Almog and P. Leonardi (eds.) 2009. *The Philosophy of David Kaplan*. Oxford: Oxford University Press, pp. 137–50.

Wilson, J. 2013. 'A Determinable-Based Account of Metaphysical Indeterminacy', *Inquiry* 56: 359–85.

Wittgenstein, L. 1953. *Philosophische Untersuchungen*. Translated into English by E. Anscombe. New York: John Wiley & Sons.

Wójcicki, R. 1988. *Theory of Logical Calculi*. Dordrecht: Reidel.

Wright, C. 1975. 'On the Coherence of Vague Predicates', *Synthese* 30: 325–65.

    1976. 'Language Mastery and the Sorites Paradox', in G. Evans and J. McDowell (eds.), *Truth and Meaning: Essays in Semantics*. Oxford: Oxford University Press, pp. 223–47.

    1987. 'Further Reflections on the Sorites Paradox', *Philosophical Topics* 15: 227–90.

    1992. *Truth and Objectivity*. Cambridge, MA: Harvard University Press.

    1995. 'The Epistemic Conception of Vagueness', *Southern Journal of Philosophy* 33: 133–59.

    2001. 'On Being in a Quandary: Relativism, Vagueness, Logical Revisionism', *Mind* 110: 45–98.

2003a. 'Vagueness: A Fifth Column Approach' in JC Beall (ed.), *Liars and Heaps: New Essays on Paradox*. Oxford: Oxford University Press, pp. 84–105.

2003b. 'Rosenkranz on Quandary, Vagueness and Intuitionism', *Mind* 112: 465–74.

2004. 'Intuition, Entitlement, and the Epistemology of Logical Laws', *Dialectica* 58: 155–75.

2007. ' "Wang's Paradox" ', in R. E. Auxier and L. E. Hahn (eds.), *The Philosophy of Michael Dummett*. Chicago and La Salle: Open Court Publishing Company, pp. 415–45.

2010. 'The Illusion of Higher-Order Vagueness', in R. Dietz and S. Moruzzi (eds.), *Cuts and Clouds: Essays on the Nature and Logic of Vagueness*. Oxford: Oxford University Press, pp. 523–40.

Yablo, S. 1989. 'Truth, Definite Truth and Paradox', *The Journal of Philosophy* 86: 539–41.

Zadeh, L. A. 1965. 'Fuzzy Sets', *Information and Control* 8: 338–53.

1975. 'Fuzzy Logic and Approximate Reasoning', *Synthese* 30: 407–28.

Zardini, E. 2006a. 'Higher-Order Vagueness and Paradox: The Glory and Misery of S4 Definiteness', *The Baltic International Yearbook of Cognition, Logic and Communication* 1: 203–20.

2006b. 'Squeezing and Stretching: How Vagueness Can Outrun Borderlineness', *Proceedings of the Aristotelian Society* 106: 419–26.

2008a. 'A Model of Tolerance', *Studia Logica* 90: 337–68.

2008b. 'Living on the Slippery Slope. The Nature, Sources and Logic of Vagueness'. PhD thesis, University of St Andrews.

2012a. 'Luminosity and Vagueness', *Dialectica* 66: 375–410.

2012b. 'Truth Preservation in Context and in Its Place', in C. Dutilh Novaes and O. Hjortland (eds.), *Insolubles and Consequences*. London: College Publications, pp. 249–71.

2013a. 'Higher-Order Sorites Paradox', *Journal of Philosophical Logic* 42: 25–48.

2013b. 'Luminosity and Determinacy', *Philosophical Studies* 165: 765–86.

2014a. 'Confirming the Less Likely, Discovering the Unknown. Dogmatisms: Surd and Doubly Surd, Natural, Flat and Doubly Flat', in D. Dodd and E. Zardini (eds.), *Scepticism and Perceptual Justification*. Oxford: Oxford University Press, pp. 33–70.

2014b. 'The General Missing from the Hierarchy', in F. Bacchini, S. Caputo and M. Dell'Utri (eds.), *New Frontiers in Truth*. Cambridge: Cambridge Scholars Publishing, pp. 176–200.

2015a. 'Breaking the Chains. Following-from and Transitivity', in C. Caret and O. Hjortland (eds.), *Foundations of Logical Consequence*. Oxford: Oxford University Press, pp. 221–75.

2015b. '∀ and ω', in A. Torza (ed.), *Quantifiers, Quantifiers, and Quantifiers: Themes in Logic, Metaphysics, and Language*. Dordrecht: Springer, pp. 489–526.

2017. '$K \nsubseteq E$', *Philosophy and Phenomenological Research* 94: 540–57.

2018a. 'Closed without Boundaries', forthcoming in *Synthese*.

2018b. 'First-Order Tolerant Logics', forthcoming in *The Review of Symbolic Logic*.

2018c. '*Seconde naïveté*', forthcoming in O. Bueno and A. Abasnezhad (eds.), *On the Sorites Paradox*. Dordrecht: Springer.

2018d. 'Against the World', ms.

2018e. 'Instability and Contraction', ms.

2018f. 'One, and Only One', ms.

2018g. 'Open Knowledge of One's Inexact Knowledge', ms.

2018h. 'Red and Orange', ms.

2018i. 'The Bearers of Logical Consequence', ms.

Index

abjunction, 52, 55, 172, 179
abortion, 229, 234
absolute adjective, 257–60
   maximum-standard, 257
   minimum-standard, 257, 259
abstraction
   from non-transitive relations, 171
   from use, 127
   levels of, 127, 193, 194
Academic Sceptics, 291–3
acceptable assignments, 82, 84–6
   and precisifications, 85
addition (logical principle), 179
additivity, 183
   super-additivity, 183
adjective
   absolute, *see* absolute adjective
   closed-scale, 258, 259
   comparative form of, 246–52, 254–8, 261
   gradable, 72, 73, 246–8, 251–3, 256–60, 262
   open-scale, 258, 259
   positive form of, 246–58, 260, 262
   relative, 257–60, 262
adjunction, 52, 55, 140, 179
   metadjunction, 179, 180, 185
admissible bivalent extension, *see* precisification
Ajdukiewicz, K., 177
Åkerman, J., 64, 66, 67, 69, 72
ambiguity, 5
analyticity, 87, 108, 109
   epistemic, 87
anti-luminosity argument, 103
Apollonius Cronus, 291
arbitrariness in the law, 233
Arcesilaus, 291–3
Aristotle, 190, 289, 291, 293, 296, 297
Armour-Garb, B., 149, 201, 202, 206
Arrow, K. J., 261
   Arrowian constraints, 261, 262
articulation (speech act), 191

Asenjo, F., 18, 180
Asgeirsson, H., 233
Asher, N., 58
attributive strategy (reply to the Sorites Paradox),
   207, 222
Aulus Gellius, 296

backward spread, *see* hysteresis, positive
Bald-Man Paradox, 289, 290, 294
Barnes, E., 214, 226, 227
Barnes, J., 296, 298
basic revisionary argument, 102, 105, 107
Beall, J. C., 60, 149, 166, 201, 202, 295
Beall, JC, 3
Běhounek, L., 153, 160, 166
belief functions, 183
Berry's Paradox, 189
better-than relation, 230, 235, 237, 238, 242
   all-things-considered, 238
biconditional, 140
   and tolerance, 135
   detachable added to *LP*, 140
   material, 138, 139
   non-detachable in *LP*, 139
   non-transitive in *LP*, 138
   strong-Kleene, 121
bivalence, 38, 52, 69, 74, 86, 95, 96, 98, 99, 102, 157,
   199, 202, 292, 298
Black, M., 18, 286
Blackburn, S., 265
Bobzien, S., 57, 296–8
Bogusławski, A., 255
Bonini, N., 283
borderline case, 4, 38, 41, 43, 83, 96–9, 102, 105, 106,
   109, 113, 114, 136, 198, 220, 229, 230, 284, 305
   borderline case of, *see* vagueness, higher-order
   contradictions about, 285
   definition in terms of $\mathbb{D}$, 54, 56, 57
   knowledge of, 35, 102–7, 185, 200
   liberalism about, 98, 106, 114, 116
   of moral predicates, 231